BEYOND THE ...

MEHRAN KAMRAVA

Editor

Beyond the Arab Spring

The Evolving Ruling Bargain in the Middle East

GEORGETOWN UNIVERSITY

School *of* Foreign Service *in* Qatar
Center for International and Regional Studies

HURST & COMPANY, LONDON

Published in Collaboration with
Georgetown University's
Center for International and Regional Studies,
School of Foreign Service in Qatar

First published in the United Kingdom in 2014 by
C. Hurst & Co. (Publishers) Ltd.,
41 Great Russell Street, London, WC1B 3PL

Printed in India

A Cataloguing-in-Publication data record for this book is available from the British Library.

ISBN: 9781849043472 *paperback*

www.hurstpublishers.com

This book is printed using paper from registered sustainable and managed sources.

CONTENTS

CONTENTS

ACKNOWLEDGMENTS

This book grew out of one of the research initiatives undertaken by the Center for International and Regional Studies at Georgetown University's School of Foreign Service in Qatar. In addition to the contributors to the volume, the group benefited from the insights and comments of a number of scholars and experts who took part in the research initiative at various stages. Grateful acknowledgment goes to Hatoon Al-Fassi, Mazhar Al-Zo'by, Zahra Babar, John Crist, Michael Driessen, Shahla Haeri, Jackie Kerr, Rami Khouri, Fred Lawson, Miriam Lowi, Mari Luomi, Suzi Mirgani, Gerd Nonneman, James Olsen, and Ahmad Sa'di. All provided invaluable feedback in discussions leading up to the project's crafting and on earlier drafts of the chapters. Dwaa Osman also read and commented extensively on many of the chapters, and Sana Jamal provided invaluable assistance with the editing process. My colleagues at the Center for International and Regional Studies, where the project was conceived and completed, were instrumental in helping create a most supportive and intellectually stimulating work environment. Their support and assistance with this volume, as with everything else I have written or edited since 2007, is most deeply appreciated. Grateful acknowledgment also goes to Qatar Foundation for its support of research and other scholarly endeavors.

THE CONTRIBUTORS

Ziad Abu-Rish is an assistant professor in the Department of History at Ohio University. He holds a PhD from the University of California Los Angeles (UCLA), and is a board member of the Arab Studies Institute. Abu-Rish also serves as a senior editor of the *Arab Studies Journal* and co-editor of *Jadaliyya ezine*.

Abdullah Al-Arian is assistant professor of history at Georgetown University's School of Foreign Service in Qatar. His research focuses on social movements and political Islam in the Middle East. He is the author of *Answering the Call: Popular Islamic Activism in Sadat's Egypt*.

Saïd Amir Arjomand is distinguished service professor of sociology and director of the Stony Brook Institute for Global Studies. He is the author of *The Shadow of God and the Hidden Imam: Religion, Political Organization and Societal Change in Shi'ite Iran from the Beginning to 1890*; *The Turban for the Crown: The Islamic Revolution in Iran*; and *After Khomeini: Iran under his Successors*. He is also the editor of several books, including *Constitutionalism and Political Reconstruction; Constitutional Politics in the Middle East*; *The Rule of Law, Islam and Constitutional Politics in Egypt and Iran* (edited with Nathan J. Brown); and *Social Theory and Regional Studies in the Global Age*.

Marie Duboc is assistant professor of Politics at the University of Tübingen in Germany. Her research interests focus on social movements in the Middle East. In 2012–2013, she served as a postdoctoral researcher at the National University of Singapore's Middle East Institute and was previously an academic visitor at St. Edmund Hall,

University of Oxford. She holds a PhD in Sociology from the School of Advanced Social Science Studies (EHESS) in France.

John Foran is the co-director of the International Institute for Climate Action Theory and professor of sociology at the University of California, Santa Barbara. His most recent book is *Taking Power: On the Origins of Third World Revolutions*. He is currently working on a book titled *Taking Power or (re)Making Power: Movements for Radical Social Change and Global Justice*, and is engaged in ethnographic research on climate justice movements. He has authored a number of articles and chapters, and edited volumes on twentieth-century revolutions, including Iran, and on the prospects for radical social change in the twenty-first century. His most recent paper is "From Critical Globalization Studies and Public Sociology to Global Crisis Studies and Global Justice Work: A Manifesto for Radical Social Change."

Bassam Haddad is director of the Middle East Studies Program and associate professor in the Department of Public and International Affairs at George Mason University, and is a visiting professor at Georgetown University. He is the author of *Business Networks in Syria: The Political Economy of Authoritarian Resilience* (Stanford University Press, 2011), and most recently co-editor of *Dawn of the Arab Uprising: End of an Old Order?* (Pluto Press, 2012). He is co-founder and editor of *Jadaliyya* ezine and is the executive director of the Arab Studies Institute, an umbrella for five organizations dealing with knowledge production on the Middle East.

Shadi Hamid is a fellow at the Project on U.S.-Islamic World Relations at the Brookings Institution's Saban Center for Middle East Policy, and the author of *Temptations of Power: Islamists and Illiberal Democracy in a New Middle East* (Oxford University Press, 2014). He served as director of research at the Brookings Doha Center until January 2014. Prior to joining Brookings, Hamid was director of research at the Project on Middle East Democracy (POMED) and a Hewlett Fellow at Stanford University's Center on Democracy, Development, and the Rule of Law. He is currently vice-chair of POMED, a member of the World Bank's MENA Advisory Panel, and a regular contributor to The Atlantic. Hamid received his B.S. and M.A. from Georgetown University and PhD in politics from Oxford University.

THE CONTRIBUTORS

Nader Hashemi is the director of the Center for Middle East Studies and an associate professor of Middle East and Islamic Politics at the Josef Korbel School of International Studies at the University of Denver. His intellectual and research interests lie at the intersection of comparative politics and political theory, in particular debates on religion and democracy, secularism and its discontents, Middle East and Islamic politics, democratic and human rights struggles in non-Western societies, and Islam–West relations. He is the author of *Islam, Secularism and Liberal Democracy: Toward a Democratic Theory for Muslim Societies* and co-editor of *The People Reloaded: The Green Movement and the Struggle for Iran's Future.*

Thomas Juneau is a senior analyst at the Canadian Department of National Defence, where he has worked since 2003. He is also assistant professor at the Graduate School of Public and International Affairs, University of Ottawa. He is the author of *Squandered Opportunity: Neoclassical realism and Iranian foreign policy* (Stanford) and first editor of *Iranian Foreign Policy since 2001: Alone in the World* (Routledge) and *L'Asie centrale et le Caucase: Une sécurité mondialisée* (Laval). He has published articles in Middle East Policy, Orbis, and International Studies Perspectives. The views expressed in his chapter are his own.

Mehran Kamrava is the director of the Center for International and Regional Studies at the Georgetown University School of Foreign Service in Qatar, and a professor at the same institution. In addition to a number of journal articles, he is the author of *Qatar: Small State, Big Politics*; *The Modern Middle East: A Political History Since the First World War*, 3rd edn; and *Iran's Intellectual Revolution*. His edited works include *The New Voices of Islam: Rethinking Politics and Modernity*; *The International Politics of the Persian Gulf*; *The Nuclear Question in the Middle East*; and *The Political Economy of the Persian Gulf*.

Bahgat Korany is a professor of international relations and political economy at the American University in Cairo (AUC) and director of the AUC Forum. He has been an elected member of Canada's Royal Society since 1994 and a visiting professor at various universities, from Paris to Oxford. In addition to around eighty-five book chapters/articles in specialized periodicals from *Revue Française de Sciences Politiques* to *World Politics*, some of which have been translated into Spanish, Italian,

Chinese, and Japanese, Korany has published twelve books in English or French. His first book, *Social Change, Charisma and International Behavior*, was awarded the Hauchman Prize in Switzerland. His *The Changing Middle East* (2010) has been noted by CNN as predicting the "Arab Spring" a year before it happened. He is on the editorial board of such periodicals as *International Studies Quarterly*, *International Political Science Review*, *El-Siassa El-Dawliyya*, *Mediterranean Politics*, and many others. He is currently the lead author of the tenth anniversary special volume of the UNDP's *Arab Human Development Report*.

Russell E. Lucas is an associate professor of Arabic studies and director of global studies in the Arts and Humanities at Michigan State University. His book, *Institutions and the Politics of Survival in Jordan: Domestic Responses to External Challenges, 1988–2001*, was published by SUNY Press. He has also published articles in a range of journals including: *Journal of Democracy*, *International Studies Quarterly*, *International Journal of Middle East Studies*, *Journal of Arabian Studies*, *Journal of Middle East Culture and Communication*, and the *Middle East Journal*. He is currently writing a new book on the politics of the Arab monarchies. He has previously taught at Florida International University and at the University of Oklahoma.

Quinn Mecham is an assistant professor of political science at Middlebury College. Mecham served as a Franklin Fellow at the State Department in 2009–10. He worked on the secretary of state's policy planning staff, with responsibility for the Gulf, political Islam, and global religious affairs. His current research focuses on Islamist political movements and Muslim political parties. Recent publications include an article in *Foreign Policy* magazine: "Erbakan's Unintended Legacy" (March 2011) and "Why Do Islamist Groups Become Transnational and Violent?" published by the Massachusetts Institute of Technology Center for International Studies Audit of the Conventional Wisdom in August 2006. Mecham graduated from Brigham Young University and received his master's and doctorate degrees from Stanford University.

Nadine Sika is an assistant professor of political science at the American University in Cairo (AUC), Egypt. Sika is the author of *Educational Reform in Egyptian Primary Schools Since the 1990s*, as well as a number of articles. She received a PhD in comparative politics from the University of Cairo. Before joining AUC, she was visiting scholar at the Political Science Institute of the University of Tübingen (Germany) and assistant professor of political science at the Future University (Egypt). She is currently consultant to the United Nations Development Programme (UNDP) and member of the board of directors of Partners in Development, an independent Egyptian think tank.

Dirk Vandewalle teaches in the Government Department and at the Amos Tuck School of Business at Dartmouth College. He is the former chair of Dartmouth's Asian and Middle Eastern Studies program. His research and teaching focus on the links between economic and political development in the Gulf states, North Africa, and Asia, and on development in oil states more generally. He is the editor of several books and volumes on Libya and North Africa, and is currently writing a manuscript on the economic emergence and prospects of the Gulf countries, based on research from a Fulbright Regional Research Award in the Gulf Cooperation Council countries. He has written numerous articles on economic development issues in the Arab world, and received, in addition to two regional Fulbright research awards, a Social Science Research Council Award for advanced research in Morocco and Yemen. He is on the editorial board of several scholarly publications, and lectures and consults widely in policy, business, and academic settings in the Middle East, Europe, and Asia. Vandewalle was political advisor to the UN Special Representative for Libya during the pre-assessment period in the summer of 2011, and is a senior political advisor to the Carter Center's electoral observation team in Libya.

Ella Wind is a graduate student in Middle East Studies at New York University, focusing on the political economy of Turkey and the Levant region. She is also a contributing co-editor for *Jadaliyya*'s Syria Page.

INTRODUCTION

Mehran Kamrava

The political upheaval that reverberated throughout the Arab world from December 2010 onwards caught many scholars of the Middle East off-guard. Until that point, much of the scholarship on Middle Eastern politics had concentrated on the durability of authoritarianism,[1] not-

[1] A small sample includes Eva Bellin, "The Robustness of Authoritarianism in the Middle East: Exceptionalism in Comparative Perspective," *Comparative Politics*, 36, 2 (Jan. 2004), pp. 139–57; Jason Brownlee, *Authoritarianism in the Age of Democratization*, Cambridge: Cambridge University Press, 2007; Stephen J. King, *The New Authoritarianism in the Middle East and North Africa*, Bloomington, IN: Indiana University Press, 2009; and Marsha Pripstein Posusney and Michele Penner Angrist (eds), *Authoritarianism in the Middle East: Regimes and Resistance*, Boulder, CO: Lynne Rienner, 2005. My own thoughts on the subject were equally pessimistic: "Despite the global resurgence of democracy in recent decades and the spread of the 'third wave' of democratization across South America and Eastern Europe, authoritarianism has shown remarkable resilience and staying power in the Middle East ... Given that in the Middle East the state is by far the more powerful and dominant partner in state–society relations, any meaningful moves toward a greater opening of the political process are likely to be initiated from within the state itself." Mehran Kamrava, *The Modern Middle East: A Political History since the First World War*, 2nd edn, Berkeley, CA: University of California Press, 2011, pp. 372–3.

withstanding what could be described as something of an "Arab Spring" in early 2005. In this latter period, which served as a dress rehearsal for the events that transpired in 2011, Iraqis went to the polls for the first time since the fall of Saddam, Syria withdrew from Lebanon after mass protests in downtown Beirut, Saudi Arabia staged municipal elections, and determined opposition by Egyptian activists forced Mubarak to give meaning and substance, albeit temporarily, to his promises of reforms.[2] Nevertheless, authoritarianism persisted unabated for another five years.

The final chapter of the Arab Spring has yet to be written. However, the unexpected nature of these Arab uprisings has provoked lively debate and fruitful scholarship around some of the existing assumptions regarding the region's domestic politics.[3] In recent decades, a robust scholarship has emerged on the durability of authoritarianism in the Middle East and the remarkable resilience of the region's political regimes. Much of this work is based on rigorous analysis of the patterns of socio-political behavior in the Middle East, both at the regional level of analysis and at that of individual states, and in particular on the carefully crafted "ruling bargains" between regimes and their citizens.

Both in the Middle East's monarchies and in the many presidential republics, a ruling bargain emerged between the governed and those governing that aimed to consolidate state–society relationships and maintain various forms of authoritarian rule. In broad terms, the implicit bargain underlying the nature of political rule in the region has required citizens to surrender their political and social rights to participatory government. They are expected to accept the legitimacy of the ruling regime, however grudgingly, and are rewarded with a variety of goods and services in return, most of them tangible but some also intangible, as well as socio-economic benefits. The scope of state munificence extended to the citizenry was dependent on the state's financial capacity, making the ruling bargain stronger in some states and weaker in others,

[2] Steven A. Cook, "Adrift on the Nile: The Limits of the Opposition in Egypt," Council on Foreign Relations, *The New Arab Revolt*, New York: Council on Foreign Relations, 2011, p. 57.

[3] See, for example, Jean-Pierre Filiu, *The Arab Revolution: Ten Lessons from the Democratic Uprising*, Oxford: Oxford University Press, 2011; Marc Lynch, *The Arab Uprising: The Unfinished Revolutions of the New Middle East*, New York: Public Affairs, 2012; and Roger Owen, *The Rise and Fall of Arab Presidents for Life*, Cambridge, MA: Harvard University Press, 2012.

or at least in relation to some citizens more than others. The elites judged to be crucial to the regime received substantially more than the average citizen, thereby introducing a distinct element into the ruling bargain that became part and parcel of the resentment directed towards local regimes.

Although much of the academic literature has been devoted to the durability of these ruling bargains, recent events indicate that inadequate attention has been paid to the potential causes for their erosion. The chapters in this volume probe some of the existing analytical assumptions in order to develop a new understanding of the drivers behind the historic change in the Middle East that began in late 2010 and early 2011.

The book is divided into two parts. The first part is designed to contextualize the Arab Spring, while the second focuses on individual case studies. Part 1 begins with a chapter that traces the rise and fall of ruling bargains in the Middle East and the growing primacy of only one of the elements of the ruling bargain, namely fear, as the main tool of governance across the Middle East and especially the Arab world, a process which began in the 1960s and the 1970s and lasted into the 2000s. The concept of a "ruling bargain," the chapter argues, has been employed in the study of Middle Eastern politics for a long period of time. These bargains can be defined in terms of the implicit, unspoken assumptions on which the general parameters of state–society relations were premised. According to these assumptions, states presented themselves as defenders of broadly defined, vaguely articulated, and changeable notions of "national interest"—in terms of providing security, economic opportunities, social goods, fulfillment of national aspirations, and so on and so forth—in return for general political quiescence on the part of social actors.

Different actors held different understandings and conceptions of the ruling bargain, some aspects of which were based on formal arrangements, and were at times even codified in national constitutions, some were based on informal arrangements and understandings. The bargains had several components, but fear and coercion were undoubtedly among the most important. As states could deliver on fewer and fewer of the promises and premises of their rule from the 1970s onwards, fear and repression became more and more pervasive. Various survival strategies were employed, ranging from heightened coercion to occasional concessions, resulting in the perpetuation of authoritarianism throughout the region. Attempts to co-opt, or at least to divide, opposition groups and activists were equally common. As Marsha Pripstein Posusney observed some time ago, "electoral engineering poses a formidable obstacle to democratization."[4] There are also always constituents who buy into the regime narrative, or are part of the patronage networks that have been deliberately created or have evolved over time, and are the beneficiaries of opportunities created by the state. Social actors seldom operate in a political vacuum in which the state is completely irrelevant to social welfare and the public good, however these terms are defined. In their ideal form, the ruling bargains that were originally crafted in the 1950s and the 1960s may have died some time ago. But their mutations remained in effect in one form or another across the Middle East, from Iran in the east to Algeria and Morocco in the west.

Once the element of fear was broken, it was only a matter of time before the ossified instruments of state coercion and the old methods of repression ceased to produce the desired results. It is at precisely these periods—when social actors feel empowered, and when the state's instruments of repression no longer inspire the fear and intimidation that they once did—that opportunities for revolutions emerge. Revolutions are rare historical occurrences in which social actors create or exploit institutional weaknesses in the state and capture political power. They are, therefore, essentially contests for political power. While this was true until relatively recently, John Foran argues that the revolutions that rocked the Arab world in 2010–11 are part of a new type of revolution—though they may be political in nature, and perhaps even in genesis, they are essentially movements motivated by popular notions of social justice, "new types of progressive experiments." In this sense, they should be viewed in the same mold as the May 1968 revolution in France and the Zapatista movement in Mexico in the 1990s: they are revolutions inspired more by a yearning for basic human dignity than by anything else. According to Foran, this helps explain the non-ideological character of the Arab revolutions, the slogans of which tell a much bigger story: "Employment is a right, you band of thieves!"

Foran's arguments highlight the growing sophistication of Middle Eastern societies over the four to five decades that preceded the Arab

[4] Marsha Pripstein Posusney, "The Middle East's Democratic Deficit in Comparative Perspective," in Posusney and Angrist, *Authoritarianism in the Middle East: Regimes and Resistance*, p. 9.

Spring. During this period, Middle Eastern youth had become increasingly educated and yet remained underemployed or unemployed while national wealth and opportunities were squandered by leaders more interested in office and power and worldly pleasure than concern for the greater good—heroes rose and fell in rapid succession, and the people looked on as their countries lagged behind the rest of the world in one development indicator after another. With the benefit of hindsight, it was only a matter of time before revolutions erupted across the region.

These revolutions were made possible, Nadine Sika argues in the next chapter, through the failure of the formal social and political institutions of the regimes in power and their gradual replacement with new, alternative institutions in the form of social movements that challenged the authority of the state. By focusing on the cases of Egypt, Tunisia, and Syria, Sika examines processes of regime formation through the employment of social and political institutions designed to control and manage the public sphere. After some initial successes, these institutions morphed into instruments of personal power, as in Egypt and Tunisia, and oligarchic or sectarian concentrations of power, as in Tunisia (and Bahrain). As state institutions were used to create greater levels of social exclusion, society increasingly became an arena for contestation. In each of the three cases Sika examines, the causes of social contestation were almost uniformly the same—the narrowing of political space at the hands of the state and a concomitant growth of social, economic, and political grievances. But the outcomes were different, depending on the state's willingness, and capacity, to use force and violence against its citizens. The importance Sika attaches to institutional variables is further confirmed in a number of subsequent chapters that also focus on specific case studies.

The volume then turns to a question of vital importance for the region's future: how are Islamists likely to fare as a result of the changes ushered in by the Arab Spring? On an electoral level, the Islamists have thus far achieved a moderate degree of success. According to Abdullah Al-Arian, they may even be able to play a constructive, central role in transforming the norms of governance that Brownlee views as obstacles to the success of any meaningful form of democracy. Groups such as the Muslim Brotherhood have historically served as significant social movement actors who have accumulated "a long record of democratic participation." As the Arab uprisings began to unfold, Islamist movements had to broaden their appeal and become "reform-minded organizations" in order to respond to a rapidly changing situation. As the travails of the Muslim Brotherhood in Egypt demonstrate, the fate of political Islam as a social movement remains far from settled. Al-Arian points to this "post-Islamism" as a critical period in determining whether the Muslim Brotherhood can transform its ideological and practical frames of reference into those supportive of accommodation, transparency, and tolerance.

Shadi Hamid applies a similar line of analysis to the development of political parties before and after the Arab Spring. Under the Middle East's autocratic regimes, the region's many "cardboard parties" meant little in terms of mass mobilization and political participation, despite their impressive membership rosters. Indeed, just to be on the safe side, the state instituted electoral laws meant to ensure that such parties remained weak and ineffectual. But the Arab Spring has once again placed parties at the forefront of popular mobilization and political activism. Most importantly, parties are finally functioning, at least in Tunisia, as important agents of conflict mediation and, therefore, moderation. The critical question, according to Hamid, is the nature of the issues and cleavages around which parties are beginning to coalesce. Economic cleavages are likely to be of secondary importance at best; individual opposition activists and the Muslim Brotherhood did not offer comprehensive economic programs that stood in contrast with those of the state, albeit with the exception of calling for an end to corruption and oligarchy. This leaves issues of identity and ideology. How these play out in the post-Arab Spring era, as galvanizing sources of ideological polarization, or as means of coalition-building and moderation, remains to be seen.

The transformation of social movements into political parties, and the role and interplay of parties with one another and with other political forces, are outlined and codified in national constitutions. Said Amir Arjomand draws our attention to regional processes of constitution-making. He begins by tracing the long history of constitutional politics in countries such as Iran and Egypt, paying particular attention to the state's incessant machinations with regard to its own legal framework in order to maintain a semblance of formal, constitutional legitimacy. In Egypt, this had the ironic effect of enabling regime opponents to use the law strategically in their efforts to undermine state authoritarianism. The

Egyptian judiciary was not necessarily politically activist, but "legal mobilization" in the country did provide legal pathways for professional groups and civic associations to chip away at the state's efforts to dominate the public sphere. When the state eventually fell in both Egypt and Tunisia, the negotiations between weakened state elites and empowered social actors primarily revolved around replacing the old constitutional framework with a new one. In Libya, where the rupture was more abrupt and bloody, efforts at crafting a new constitutional order were only able to begin once the Qaddafi state had been forcibly dismantled. As Dirk Vandewalle demonstrates in his chapter, the destruction and dismantling of all viable political institutions by Muammar Qaddafi had direct consequences for the way in which the country's revolution unfolded before degenerating into a civil war that eventually led to the fall of the 42-year-old dictatorship. The post-Qaddafi order had the benefit, or perhaps the handicap, of having to start from scratch. In Iran, meanwhile, legal mobilization was arrested after a slow start during the Khatami presidency, when the country's faltering steps toward democratization were stopped and reversed.

One of the questions arising out of the events of 2010–11 is whether the traditional conceptions of "revolutions" are in need of rethinking and reformulation. Are we witnessing the emergence of new revolutionary ideal types? What lessons can be drawn for the sociology of mass movements, the role of syndicate groups such as labor and unorganized or haphazardly organized protestors? And why have some uprisings succeeded and evolved into full-blown revolutions, whereas others morphed into civil wars, while still others were crushed and aborted or never started at all? These questions are addressed in Part 2 of the book, which focuses on individual case studies.

Part 2 begins with Nader Hashemi's analysis of Iran's 2009 Green Movement, which is not generally considered to be part of the Arab Spring. But the Green Movement did represent a popular, mass-based effort to reformulate the ruling bargain that had evolved under the Islamic Republic over the preceding thirty years. It arose out of the denouement of the reform movement that had climaxed in Khatami's presidency and the rise of the neo-conservatives in 2005 and the presidency of Mahmoud Ahmadinejad. The Green Movement represented a last-ditch attempt to democratize the system within the existing constitutional framework and to reverse its crisis of legitimacy. The state's brutal clampdown may have brought about the end of the movement, Hashemi claims, but it has also only deepened its own legitimacy crisis by making the office of the supreme leader, the institutional linchpin of the Iranian regime, devoid of meaningful popularity among the broader middle classes. With the official ideological narrative of the Islamic Republic a spent force, the domestic social and political preconditions for the appearance of democracy look promising. The same cannot be said for the international context within which Iranian politics takes shape, as the regime has effectively used the real threat posed to it by the United States to retain some public support. When, or indeed if, Iran can ever follow the path of the Arab Spring's success stories ultimately remains an open question.

Few anticipated the scale and scope of the street protests in Tehran and other Iranian cities that took place in the summer of 2009, largely because Iran had seldom tolerated such public shows of defiance in the past. In Egypt, however, the years before the country's 2011 uprising had seen progressively higher levels of political opposition, most of it organized, especially by labor. Marie Duboc's chapter examines one important, if less explored, aspect of Egypt's Tahrir revolution, namely worker activism and protest from 2004 onwards. The Egyptians who took to the streets in early 2011 did so within the context of a series of worker-led strikes, sit-ins, and protests—which Duboc describes as the "politics of visibility"—that took place across Egypt throughout the 2000s. As part of the ruling bargain, the Nasserist state had established a host of labor unions whose real function, it soon became apparent, was not so much to advance workers' rights as to control the workers' potential for militancy. Duboc outlines an important distinction between an officially ideal statist labor, which was incorporated into the regime's ruling bargain, and an expansive mobilized labor that more accurately reflected the country's economic maladies and political situation. As unions gradually lost their legitimacy, Egyptian workers frequently bypassed them and appropriated the unions' nationalist narratives in order to engage in collective action on their own. For such workers, the conditions of the factory floor reflected those of the nation at large, and, in the same vein, their actions and efforts at mobilization reflected those of the protestors in Tahrir Square.

It was precisely this history of protests and oppositional activities, both semi-organized and unorganized, that brought the residents of

Cairo into Tahrir Square in their droves in January 2011. Bahgat Korany's chapter offers a sociological analysis of the Tahrir demonstrators. Within a context of repeated labor strikes and industrial action—totaling 510 in 2010 alone—and the Kefaya ("enough") movement that started in 2004, Egyptian youth had been socialized into a culture of protest. When a window of opportunity presented itself for mass mobilization on a popular scale in the early weeks of 2011, the youth naturally converged in the iconic (and spacious) Tahrir Square. By this point most of the protestors had lost their faith in the efficacy of older opposition groupings and, now armed with the weapon of social media, they began to form their own organizations. As their numbers grew, Korany argues, three key components of "contentious politics" fell into place—resource mobilization, political opportunity structure, and frames—which made the expansive protests increasingly difficult to contain. The military, or the "deep state," the mosque, or "deep society," and the masses, or "a group of groups," began trying to outmaneuver each other in order to establish themselves as the revolution's victorious heirs. In the event, it was the Muslim Brotherhood that emerged on top, at least institutionally, but the manner of its rise mitigated the possibility that it would use its newly acquired instruments of power as a means to ensure the brutal elimination of its opponents and former colleagues. Revolutions, like Saturn, often devour their own children. As the turns and twists of the Egyptian revolution have so starkly demonstrated, the Arab Spring uprisings are no exception.

With the notable exception of Bahrain, the regimes rocked to their core by the Arab Spring have been republics, or, as the following chapter argues, republics in name. The region's monarchies appear to have weathered the storm largely on their own, or, in the Bahraini case, due to the support received from a fellow monarchy, Saudi Arabia. The region's monarchies are explored in three chapters, beginning with Ziad Abu-Rish's discussion of Jordan. Abu-Rish argues that while Jordan appears to be "forever on the brink," its specific history of state-formation has engendered institutional configurations and varied patterns of regime–society alliances and antagonisms that have so far impeded the possibility of a mass-based uprising against the state. Regional and international power relations have only served to strengthen the state and to reinforce the undesirability of engaging in contentious politics by those forces capable of doing so.

This reluctance to engage in contentious politics was underwritten by an authoritarian bargain based loosely on the state's provision of economic rewards, primarily in the form of employment and subsidies, its guarantee of political and military security, and its incorporation and calibrated relationship with diverse social groups such as East Bank tribes and West Bank petite bourgeoisie. When this ruling bargain began to break down in the late 1980s under its own economic weight, leading to scattered but frequent protests, the regime provided state-controlled means through which the public were able to express their frustration as part of its efforts to position itself as the vanguard of reform. Three years after the initial outbreak of the Arab Spring, these strategic adaptations appear to have yielded tangible results, at least from the regime's perspective. More importantly, through continued management of potential groups and spaces, the regime has been able to undermine the possibilities for cross-sectoral, oppositional alliances. Equally important is the bloody turn of the Syrian civil war next door, which has served as a strong disincentive for most Jordanians wishing to follow a similar path.

Russell Lucas continues the discussion of monarchies by focusing on the member states of the Gulf Cooperation Council (GCC), pointing to their resource wealth and regime flexibility as the primary cause of their relative stability. Their inordinate wealth, and relatively smaller populations, enabled the GCC's oil monarchies to maintain robust rentier bargains that sustained them even after the 2008 global financial meltdown. When some of the ripple effects of the Arab Spring finally reached the Arabian Peninsula's less well-resourced kingdoms, namely Saudi Arabia and Bahrain, the Saudis were quick to react, responding with a combination of targeted repression on the one hand—more indiscriminate in Bahrain and in Saudi Arabia's own Eastern Province—and lucrative financial incentives on the other. The GCC pledged $10 billion in development assistance to Bahrain and Oman, and the Saudi government pledged to invest as much as $130 billion into its domestic economy, which would lead to the creation of some 60,000 new jobs and the building of 500,000 new housing units. Lucas also credits the GCC states' adoption of the rhetoric of political liberalization, albeit more in style than in substance, as an impediment to the spread of the Arab Spring across the southern shores of the Persian Gulf.

Within the GCC the case of Bahrain merits separate analysis, and this is offered here by Quinn Mecham. Mecham argues that the small kingdom's ruling bargain had always been contested to some degree by a combination of structural features and strategic decisions by the governing elite. Compounding social and religious cleavages reduced the costs of political action, with continued rivalry between the Shi'a majority and the ruling Sunni minority having steadily increased the perceived political stakes. The regime's mixed strategy of concession and repression meanwhile accelerated popular expectations on the one hand and deepened social and political grievances on the other. And yet the monarchical regime has managed to preserve itself, at the cost of long-term stability, through a variety of repressive and other strategic means designed to maintain the strength of the state and to ensure that the opposition remains weak and fractured. The state has sought to achieve this goal by framing the political narrative as one of a demonized Shi'a opposition, a tool of Iran, thereby stoking the fears among Sunnis and liberals of the dominance of supposed Shi'a fundamentalists. The state has also outsourced its preservation to regional and international actors, namely the United States and Saudi Arabia. None of these efforts, Mecham argues, is likely to reverse the kingdom's deepening political crisis over the longer term. However, for the time being, so long as the state's instruments of repression remain intact, thanks largely to Saudi support, the prospects of real change in the country remain slim.

If Jordan is "forever on the brink," then Yemen is forever on the verge of implosion. Yet in much the same way as the country has managed to remain intact despite the seemingly irreconcilable centrifugal forces pulling it apart, the regime has also succeeded in weathering the events of the Arab Spring and surviving it with what has thus far has been only a change of elite personnel. In his chapter on Yemen, Thomas Juneau argues that the country's pre-2011 ruling bargain was largely a product of an intra-elite struggle for power. This bargain has essentially remained intact in the aftermath of the unrests of 2011–12 and the eventual departure of President Ali Abdullah Saleh from office after thirty-three years. Although the nature of the struggles may have shifted, politics in Yemen continues to be defined by intra-elite struggles. The uprisings which finally compelled the seemingly immovable Saleh out of office did, of course, open up some political space for the street opposition and civil society groups. But the election of Saleh's vice president, 'Abd Rabbu Mansour Hadi, to the presidency—in elections in which he was the only candidate—has changed neither the rules of the game nor the loosely knit factions that have constituted the country's political elite.

As Juneau's discussion of Yemen demonstrates, one of the keys to the survival of autocracies is their adaptability, a quality that both the Libyan and the Syrian regimes lacked due to their particular patterns of regime formation. In the Libyan case, Dirk Vandewalle traces the evolution of the ruling bargain that Colonel Qaddafi imposed on his country through the creation of extensive patronage networks which deflated pressures for political liberalization and enabled the regime to survive by relying on relatively small coalitions. But Libya's rentierism was of a comparatively weaker kind, with the money from the country's sizable oil resources frequently squandered through mismanagement and misadventure. Over time, those relying on state largesse had come to view their relationship with official institutions and policies as one of entitlements, thus making the state's decidedly one-sided ruling bargain especially tenuous and susceptible to collapse. When diffusion took the reverberations of the Tunisian and Egyptian revolutions to Benghazi and Tripoli, Qaddafi initially sought to wrest control of the uprisings by claiming that he was leading a new people's revolution. But few Libyans were now willing to buy into such theatrics. On a structural level the old tyrant had boxed himself in, given his systematic destruction of any viable institution which could have served as a source of political maneuverability. His only option was to fight, and that is precisely what he did until the bitter end. According to Vandewalle, the fact that the new stewards of Libya were able to start with a clean slate, free from the institutional legacies of a bygone era, is actually an asset. An entirely new ruling bargain can now be constructed, codified in a new constitution, and crafted through debates and negotiations.

The Syrian drama is being played out in a decidedly different context, nationally as well as regionally and internationally. Bassam Haddad and Ella Wind chronicle "the long and slow reversal" beginning in the mid-1980s of a carefully crafted "leveling egalitarianism" established by Hafiz Assad. Economic privatization meant the sale of a number of state assets to Assad cronies, resulting in the steady erosion of state support from many previously loyal groups. But the state's loss of popular support was not nearly sufficient to foster its collapse; nor was the opposition sufficiently united and cohesive to mount an effective and efficient challenge against the regime. The transformation of the Syrian uprising into a prolonged and devastating civil war was an inevitable product of the structural dynamics at work both within the state and within the groups opposing it.

The bloody turn of the Syrian uprising can also be explained by the regime's decision to meet the growing protests with determined repression rather than by attempts at co-option or by addressing some of the causes of popular grievance. In politics, violence often begets violence, and the brutality of the regime's response over time only strengthened the opposition's resolve to bring it down. Haddad and Wind point to two complicating factors that have prolonged the Syrian civil war. To begin with, the Syrian drama is being played out within a specific context in which an unusually large number of influential international actors are trying to shape and influence the course of the country's revolution. Equally important are the deep and multiple fractures within the opposition, which has thus far been unable to devise a coordinated, comprehensive plan for fighting the regime and outlining its vision of the post-Assad era.

Indeed, it remains to be seen whether the Middle East as a whole is on the brink of a new era. How will history ultimately judge the events of 2010/11? Will they resemble the European revolutions of 1848, ironically often called "Spring of Nations" or "Springtime of Peoples," whose fury left tens of thousands dead and brought chaos to the lives of countless others?[5] Or will they turn out like the revolutions of 1989, which dismantled communism and brought democracy to Eastern and Central Europe? Have we seen the last of the Arab Spring, or will the aborted revolution in Bahrain find new life from under the stifling repression of the state? Will the Jordanian state run out of options and be forced to accommodate demands for greater transparency and accountability? The revolutions of 2011 invariably started as non-ideological movements with simple goals of dignity and freedom. A year and a half earlier, the same motivations had brought millions of Iranians onto the streets to protest against the electoral coup within the state. But does the non-ideological genesis of these popular movements herald the dawn of a post-ideological Middle East, or are we likely to see the re-emergence of old ideologies adapted to new circumstances? We are, no doubt, witnessing historical changes. How lasting are their consequences, and what the shape of the things to come will be, are questions that only the future can answer.

[5] Mike Rappaport, *1848: Year of Revolution*, New York: Basic Books, 2009, p. 212.

PART 1

CONTEXTUALIZING THE ARAB SPRING

1

THE RISE AND FALL OF RULING BARGAINS IN THE MIDDLE EAST

Mehran Kamrava

The Arab Spring took place within a context in which the dominant "ruling bargain" that had sustained regional regimes from the 1950s onwards had begun to unravel. This ruling bargain is now being replaced by a new social contract that is redefining the sources of authority and legitimacy through a variety of devices (such as constitutions) and experiences and processes (mass protests, civil wars, and elections). This process also involves a redefinition of the roles, functions, and the structures of institutions (political parties and organizations, the armed forces, the executive) and personalities and personal actions and initiatives (agency). Across the Arab world and the Middle East, conceptions of "authority" and "political legitimacy" are being redefined and re-articulated. The central question in this regard centers on the new shape, voracity, and staying power of these new, emerging conceptions of authority.

This chapter examines the nature and evolution of ruling bargains across the Middle East, the political systems to which they gave rise, the steady unraveling of the bargains over time, and the structural consequences thereof for the systems concerned. It also examines the uprisings that engulfed much of the Middle East from December 2010 onwards. The chapter argues that implicit understandings emerged between state elites and social actors as the basis of regime legitimacy throughout the region, as a result of which a number of state services and functions were provided in return for general political acquiescence. These ruling bargains, or social pacts as they are sometimes called, were in reality imposed from the top by state elites rather than being mutually agreed upon and negotiated through a process of give-and-take between the state and social actors. As they were such, repression or the threat of repression was never far from the practice of politics, and the state remained fundamentally authoritarian. Nevertheless, bargains of various shapes came to underlie the legitimacy of one Middle Eastern state after another.

In the space of around two decades, these authoritarian ruling bargains began to unravel, and Middle Eastern states had to make various adjustments in order to retain their hold on power. Several developments began to unfold almost simultaneously. As states proved increasingly incapable of delivering on the promises and premises of the bargains they had crafted, they began to rely on ad hoc mixtures of controlled liberalization and reinvigorated authoritarianism to co-opt opponents, or, alternatively, to hold them at bay. Some allowed new parties to form; others banned old ones. All made promises of a democratic tomorrow. Meetings with amenable opponents were convened, national charters were drafted and signed, and new, supposedly free and fair, elections for long-pliant parliaments took place. Economic difficulties, meanwhile, coupled with the dictates of international investors and monetary agencies, especially the World Bank and the IMF, prompted many to liberalize their economies, albeit marginally, and to sell a limited number of state assets.

In doing all this, Middle Eastern authoritarianism proved itself adaptable and resilient, dynamic and persistent. However, despite the use of multiple survival strategies, including oscillating cycles or combinations of co-option and repression, fear gradually emerged as the main, elemental ingredient of the political formula, increasingly replacing whatever was left of the regime's political legitimacy. By the 1990s and the 2000s, little of the original ruling bargain remained. Its pillars, once sources of comfort and mass ebullition, were now comprised of fear, loathing, suspicion, and submission. All that was needed for this bargain to collapse—in fact for the whole basis of authoritarian rule to crumble—was for the grip of mass fear to be broken. When that happened, the Arab Spring followed.

The chapter traces the rise and fall of ruling bargains across the Middle East, the adaptability and resilience of dictatorships as the bargains they had imposed began to unravel, and how their dynamic adaptability prolonged their repressive tenure in office. The chapter then provides a summary of the uprisings that came to be known as the Arab Spring, before exploring how and why the Tunisian and Egyptian revolutions unfolded in the form of mass-based uprisings while the Libyan and Syrian rebellions took the form of civil wars. The chapter concludes with a discussion of what the central elements of the emerging sources of legitimacy—the evolving ruling bargain—are likely to be.

The Rise and Fall of Ruling Bargains

Most scholars of the Middle East have conceptualized ruling bargains in terms of corporatist arrangements in the national political economy whereby the state brings into its orbit, and politically pacifies, strategic social actors such as the civil service, entrepreneurs, and the broader middle classes. According to Steven Heydemann, these bargains "can be conceptualized not solely in terms of an institutionalized bargain among collective actors but also as encompassing a set of norms or shared expectations about the appropriate organization of a political economy in general." These norms revolve around which actors have legitimate claims to state resources, which institutional forms are accepted, and "what kinds of policy instruments state actors can legitimately deploy to achieve their aims."[1]

Along similar lines, Daniel Brumberg maintains that "to compensate for their subordination, popular groups obtained social benefits such as guaranteed public sector employment, food subsidies, and free higher education. This ruling bargain was given a philosophical gloss that celebrated the culturally 'authentic' traditions of class unity and coope-

[1] Steven Heydemann, "Social Pacts and the Persistence of Authoritarianism in the Middle East," in Oliver Schlumberger (ed.), *Debating Arab Authoritarianism: Dynamics and Durability in Nondemocratic Regimes*, Stanford, CA: Stanford University Press, 2007, p. 25.

ration."[2] Iliya Harik uses the label "patron state" to describe cases in which the state "is a business entrepreneur and a provider at one and the same time."[3] By using the economy primarily for political purposes, these patron states took on obligations they could not possibility meet, resulting in a failure of the quality and quantity of their services, an outcome perpetuated by a lack of funds and low productivity.[4]

The height of the ruling bargain was reached in the populist days of the 1950s and the 1960s, when states promised to ensure social justice, foster economic development, and guarantee national interests in return for the political acquiescence of the citizenry.[5] The Nasserist state in Egypt was emblematic of this pattern of political rule. Yet other states across the Middle East also struck ruling bargains with labor and the middle classes in which political parties were banned, while civil society organizations and trade unions came under government control in return for promises of state-provided employment, social and welfare services, free education and healthcare, and subsidies for food, housing, energy, and transportation.[6] These bargains were in no way unique to the Middle East. But the ideologies, institutions, and social conditions they involved were indeed unique to the region.[7]

Authoritarian ruling bargains rested on broad coalitions that embraced professionals, "national" capitalists, workers, and the military, who were subordinated to the state through clientelist, corporatist, and single-party mechanisms.[8] Far from becoming autonomous, states

[2] Daniel Brumberg, "Authoritarian Legacies and Reform Strategies in the Arab World," in Rex Brynen, Bahgat Korany, and Paul Noble (eds), *Political Liberalization and Democratization in the Arab World*, Boulder, CO: Lynne Rienner, 1995, p. 233.

[3] Iliya Harik, "Privatization: The Issue, the Prospects, and the Fears," in Iliya Harik and Denis J. Sullivan (eds), *Privatization and Liberalization in the Middle East*, Bloomington, IN: Indiana University Press, 1992, p. 2.

[4] Ibid. pp. 2–3.

[5] Saad Eddin Ibrahim, "Liberalization and Democratization in the Arab World: An Overview," in Brynen, Korany, and Noble, *Political Liberalization and Democratization in the Arab World*, p. 36.

[6] Dina Shehata, "Fall of the Pharaoh: How Hosni Mubarak's Reign Came to an End," in Council on Foreign Relations (CFR), *The New Arab Revolt*, New York: Council on Foreign Relations, 2011, pp. 138–9.

[7] Brumberg, "Authoritarian Legacies and Reform Strategies in the Arab World," p. 233.

[8] Ibid.

became dependent on their client social classes for their continued acquiescence to the ruling bargain. Practically any attempt by the state to renegotiate the bargain's terms by reducing its patronage ran the risk of provoking sharp reactions from those affected. This made it extremely difficult to introduce economic reforms.[9]

Nevertheless, beginning in the 1970s, the region's states began a messy, disorderly retreat from several socio-economic functions, leaving public spaces vacated and ready to be filled by religious extremists (as in Egypt and Algeria) or separatists (as in Sudan, Somalia, and Iraq).[10] Throughout the 1980s and the 1990s, Middle Eastern states sought to recalibrate the ruling bargains in ways that served their purposes, sometimes through liberalization, but more often by falling back on their default impulse of heightened repression. As the political bargains became discredited, the level of repression increased. The 1990s saw modest experiments with liberalization in one form or another across the region, with a political opening of sorts even taking place in Saudi Arabia, when King Fahd announced the convening of a national consultative council in 1992.[11] In Yemen, one observer went so far as to claim that "a democratic environment was flourishing."[12]

The emergence of a model of the patron state *par excellence*, based on particularly robust ruling bargains underwritten by massive state wealth, was particularly notable in the Arabian Peninsula among those countries that would later form the Gulf Cooperation Council (GCC). Throughout the Persian Gulf there emerged what Giacomo Luciani calls "the Gulf consensus," whereby the state plays a direct role in the emergence and continued growth of a nascent bourgeoisie. This has been achieved through a variety of state initiatives, such as the allocation of government contracts and procurements, and by creating an alliance between foreign investors and local partners.[13] Laurie Brand draws a distinction between a "rentier state," in which rent revenues accrue directly to the state, and a "rentier economy," in which rent revenues are smaller and

[9] Ibid. p. 234.
[10] Ibrahim, "Liberalization and Democratization in the Arab World," p. 37.
[11] Ibid. p. 47.
[12] Ibid. p. 49.
[13] Giacomo Luciani, "Linking Economic and Political Reform in the Middle East: The Role of the Bourgeoisie," in Schlumberger, *Debating Arab Authoritarianism*, p. 167.

come mostly from expatriate remittances or other sources, and in which the state has less of a role as a recipient and dispenser of rent income.[14] In rentier states, particularly of the kind found in the Persian Gulf, "the state is expected to provide a certain level of economic security, in exchange for which society grants state leaders considerable political autonomy," and "state–society relations seem predicated on the principle of 'no taxation, no representation.'"[15]

Corporatist arrangements rooted in national political economies were an important and integral part of ruling bargains across the Middle East, yet they were not the sum total of the implicit understandings that emerged between states and social actors across the region from the 1950s onwards. In addition to addressing the economic needs of the urban population, ruling bargains came to rest on another premise, namely state-crafted conceptions of national identity and national interest. In other words, the state presented itself as the primary defender of the national interest in the face of ever-present threats and hostilities—as the central pillar of nationalism—in a world where its deeds and actions were vital for the defense of the country and its interests.

For much of the 1960s, most social actors across the region bought into the nationalist narrative of the state—or "official nationalism"[16]—and viewed the many charismatic leaders of the time as would-be liberators and saviors from enemies near and far. Within the polarized international and regional environment of the 1950s and the 1960s, colorful, charismatic leaders assumed the role of spokesmen for regional aspirations and were largely popular both within their own countries and beyond. Populist nationalism swept across the region, and rhetoric and charisma combined to deepen the popularity of nationalist leaders from Nasser to Qaddafi and Bourguiba.

[14] Laurie A. Brand, "Economic and Political Liberalization in a Rentier Economy: The Case of the Hashemite Kingdom of Jordan," in Harik and Sullivan, *Privatization and Liberalization in the Middle East*, pp. 168–9.

[15] Rex Brynen, Bahgat Korany, and Paul Noble, "Introduction: Theoretical Perspectives on Arab Liberalization and Democratization," in Brynen, Korany, and Noble, *Political Liberalization and Democratization in the Arab World*, p. 15.

[16] For more on "official nationalism" as articulated by the state see Mehran Kamrava, *The Modern Middle East: A Political History since the First World War*, 2nd edn, Berkeley, CA: University of California Press, 2011, pp. 357–8.

But the defeat of 1967 shattered the myth of the state's official narrative, according to which it, and it alone, was the effective defender of the national interest. The state instead became exposed for its incompetence and impotence, with its capacity to articulate and defend the national interest increasingly questioned and, as time went by, challenged. By the mid-1970s few bought into the state's nationalist narrative. This disillusionment coincided with mounting economic difficulties across the region in the aftermath of the oil crisis of the late 1970s. Amid mounting economic difficulties, states scrambled to meet their obligations in order to sustain the ruling bargains on which they had come to rely. But there was little they could do to salvage what were fundamentally untenable economic arrangements underwritten by equally untenable ideological narratives. Mismanagement of the economy, after all, is an endemic feature of patron states, and the problems of state enterprises are all too often compounded by poor performance and inadequate management.[17] Before long, ruling bargains across the Middle East began to unravel.

According to Heydemann, ruling bargains "exhibit specific institutional configurations and ... such configurations vary in how they respond to changing economic conditions."[18] Despite persistent fiscal crises throughout the 1980s and 1990s, Middle Eastern states delayed much-needed structural adjustment programs—including reductions in subsidies or restructuring bloated bureaucracies—in order to avoid altering the entrenched ruling bargains, and instead sought new and additional means for generating rent revenues.[19] But by the 1980s and the 1990s it was no longer possible to delay at least some structural adjustment programs, and such programs often forced Middle Eastern states to scale back their provision of a number of welfare and social services. Religious welfare and charity organizations stepped in to fill the gap and to provide services left undelivered by the state's retreat, often with state

[17] Iliya Harik, "Privatization and Development in Tunisia," in Harik and Sullivan, *Privatization and Liberalization in the Middle East*, p. 230.

[18] Heydemann, "Social Pacts and the Persistence of Authoritarianism in the Middle East," p. 25. Giacomo Luciani, "Resources, Revenues, and Authoritarianism in the Arab World: Beyond the Rentier State?" in Brynen, Korany, and Noble, *Political Liberalization and Democratization in the Arab World*, p. 15.

[19] Brynen, Korany, and Noble, "Introduction," pp. 218–20.

encouragement, as was the case in Egypt.[20] Importantly, Islamic charity and social services did not grow solely through opposition to the state, but, as in Egypt, developed a symbiotic, mutually reinforcing relationship with it.[21]

This might have helped the regimes' survival strategy, but it did little to address structural economic problems. From 1990 to 2011, the year of the uprisings, the youth population aged fifteen to twenty-nine grew by 50 percent in Libya and Tunisia, 65 percent in Egypt, and 125 percent in Yemen. Youth unemployment, meanwhile, remained on average twice the global average, standing at 23 percent by 2009.[22] In 2010, for example, Syria's official unemployment rate was 8 percent, but independent estimates put the figure closer to 20 percent.[23] In the Arab world at large, by 2020, some 50 million jobs will be needed to absorb new entrants into the job market. Today, some 40 percent of new entrants into the job market in the Arab world cannot find jobs.[24] Unsurprisingly, poverty levels remain astoundingly high across the region. By early 2008, to take one example, some 40 percent of Egyptians were living on less than $2 a day.[25]

Statist policies driven by the imperative to supply urban markets with the latest in consumer durables, meanwhile, drove the domestic agricultural sector to ruin. Middle Eastern regimes relied on food subsidies to ensure political stability, fostering what one scholar has termed "food democracy." But food democracy only lasted as long as the costly subsidies were in place, and the region saw frequent "bread riots" throughout the 1980s in Algeria, Jordan, Morocco, and Egypt.[26] Small bread riots

[20] Daniela Pioppi, "Privatization of Social Services as a Regime Strategy: The Revival of Islamic Endowments (*Awqaf*) in Egypt," in Schlumberger, *Debating Arab Authoritarianism*, pp. 129–30.

[21] Ibid. p. 142.

[22] Jack A. Goldstone, "Understanding the Revolutions of 2011: Weakness and Resilience in Middle Eastern Autocracies," CFR, *The New Arab Revolt*, p. 336.

[23] Michael Broning, "The Sturdy House that Assad Built: Why Damascus is Not Cairo," CFR, *The New Arab Revolt*, p. 201.

[24] Jean-Pierre Filiu, *The Arab Revolution: Ten Lessons from the Democratic Uprising*, Oxford: Oxford University Press, 2011, p. 32.

[25] Annia Ciezadlo, "Let Them Eat Bread: How Food Subsidies Prevent (and Provoke) Revolutions in the Middle East," CFR, *The New Arab Revolt*, p. 232.

[26] Ibid. pp. 230–31.

also broke out in 2008 in Jordan, Morocco, Algeria, Lebanon, Syria, and Yemen.[27] But short of fundamentally redrawing what was left of the ruling bargain and implementing major economic restructuring, there was little the state could do to remedy its growing food crisis. By 2010, almost half of the world's top wheat importers were in the Middle East. The world's biggest wheat importer was Egypt, while others included Algeria (4th), Iraq (7th), Morocco (8th), Yemen (13th), Saudi Arabia (15th), Libya (16th), and Tunisia (17th).[28] By 2010, the Egyptian government was subsidizing bread to the tune of $3 billion a year.[29]

By the 1990s, little was left of the ruling bargain that Nasser had devised—state services were deteriorating, the state was incapable of delivering many of its assumed functions, and all Egyptians but a few of the wealthiest were suffering.[30] In instances where there has been a state-protected economic elite, as in Saudi Arabia, Iraq, Egypt, and Tunisia, they benefited from the privatization initiatives of the 1980s.[31] One consequence of this was to increase the amount of anger and resentment directed at the state and its cronies from the popular classes. Nevertheless, despite their best efforts, both Iraq and Saudi Arabia failed to foster anything remotely resembling a market economy.[32]

The Middle East instead saw an epidemic of crony capitalism starting in the late 1970s and the 1980s. The state often relied on capitalists to finance, or at least to oversee, many of its development projects and initiatives. Many of these capitalists, with intimate personal ties to the president and his family, were beneficiaries of the sale of state assets in uncompetitive bids at bargain prices.[33] The rise of state-tied crony capitalists had important structural consequences for Middle Eastern states. In most cases, the apex of the state came to be constituted by a small, interlocking elite of senior army officers, bureaucrats, and wealthy business oligarchs with a vested interest in protecting "both the regime and

[27] Ibid. p. 232.
[28] Ibid. p. 230.
[29] Ibid. p. 232.
[30] Shehata, "Fall of the Pharaoh," p. 139.
[31] Kiren Aziz Chaudhry, "Economic Liberalization in Oil-Exporting Countries: Iraq and Saudi Arabia," in Harik and Sullivan, *Privatization and Liberalization in the Middle East*, p. 147.
[32] Ibid. p. 163.
[33] Roger Owen, *The Rise and Fall of Arab Presidents for Life*, Cambridge, MA: Harvard University Press, 2012, p. 51.

themselves by limiting and controlling the impact of Western-inspired political and economic reform."[34]

Members of the president's family were often deeply involved in various business ventures. Sons and other relatives became "part of a single team dedicated to the promotion of mutual family interests."[35] In Syria, the president's cousin, Rami Makhlouf, was said to control as much as 60 percent of the country's economy.[36] In Egypt, the National Democratic Party—whose Deputy Secretary General was Gamal Mubarak, the president's son—became "the party of big business," with its top members including the likes of Ahmed Ezz, the steel magnate, and Taher Helmy, the president of the American Chamber of Commerce in Egypt.[37] The wealth of President Mubarak and his family was estimated at anywhere between $40 to $70 billion, and thirty-nine of Gamal Mubarak's associates are alleged to have made $1 billion each on average.[38] In Tunisia, the extensive network of close relatives who benefited from Ben Ali's commercial deals simply became known as "the Family."[39] The president himself was conservatively estimated to have amassed a fortune worth $8 billion.[40]

Thus it is hardly surprising that Arab politics became more personalized as the decades wore on, with the structures of political and economic power becoming increasingly dependent on the personal traits and personality of the leader and his relationships with his immediate family members and associates. At its highest levels, the system was reduced to intricate webs of political and business relationships between the president, his family members, and oligarchical business elites.[41] To

[34] Ibid. p. 2.
[35] Ibid. p. 44.
[36] Ibid. p. 52. Makhlouf's business empire included real estate, banking, a private airline, telecommunications, print and electronic media, and petrochemicals.
[37] Steven A. Cook, "Adrift on the Nile: The Limits of the Opposition in Egypt," CFR, *The New Arab Revolt*, p. 64.
[38] Goldstone, "Understanding the Revolutions of 2011," p. 335.
[39] Anderson, "Demystifying the Arab Spring," p. 322.
[40] When Ben Ali fled, Tunisian authorities confiscated 34 cars, 48 yachts, 117 companies and deeds to 233 properties belonging to the former president. Jenny Stevens, "Ousted Tunisian Leader Ben Ali's 34 Cars and 48 Yachts are Seized," *The Independent* (London), 4. Feb. 2012, p. 34.
[41] Owen, *The Rise and Fall of Arab Presidents for Life*, p. 6.

enhance their political longevity and ensure their continued tenure in office, presidents often surrounded themselves with men they felt they could trust, as well as an interlocking network of intelligence services, and, in most cases, a single government party. "Put simply," Roger Owen writes, "in such cases the people were subordinated to the state, the state to the party, and the party itself to the single ruler who was himself either responsible for its creation or who had become its master."[42]

Over time, the region saw the evolution of "security states" with highly uneven consequences for their citizens, allowing great freedoms and opportunities for enrichment to a few while closing off most life chances to others.[43] A pyramid-like structure emerged in which the president's office, at the apex, relied on a network of intelligence agencies, the police, senior members of the armed forces, and crony capitalists, followed by the main agencies of civilian administration—such as ministries and provincial governorships—and centers of ideological legitimation and control, the most important of which were universities, a tame judiciary, and an equally tame religious establishment.[44]

The predominant features of these states included a repressive and highly robust security apparatus that stifled dissent and spread fear across society; a cult of personality that placed the leader, and at times his family, above all else, representing the leader as indispensable to the nation's progress and well-being; and a token of republicanism as codified through *pro forma* elections with foregone conclusions.[45] And yet the region's regimes proved remarkably resilient. To compensate for their diminishing or non-existent legitimacy they often alternated between repressing and co-opting the opposition, and relied increasingly on elements of repression and fear to stay in power. By the late 1980s and the 1990s, little was left of the ruling bargain of the 1950s and the 1960s. But it would take over two decades until the Middle East's dictatorships were shaken to their very core.

Resilient Dictatorships

Adaptability was the key to the continued resilience of the region's authoritarian regimes. Middle Eastern authoritarianism is both persis-

[42] Ibid. p. 28.
[43] Ibid. p. 37.
[44] Ibid. p. 38.
[45] Ibid. p. 35.

tent and dynamic, with authoritarian regimes using limited openings to usher in what Stephen King called "new authoritarianism."[46] Middle Eastern authoritarianism proved itself to be an "adaptive, flexible style of rule."[47] Authoritarian states in the Middle East often exhibit what Heydemann has called "bounded adaptiveness," or "a capacity for adjustment and accommodation that is produced by the interaction of formal and informal modes of conflict resolution, bargaining, and coalition management."[48] Through bounded adaptiveness, Middle East regimes often rely both on formal and informal institutions and on multiple, and at times even competing, "rules of the game."[49] "Formal and informal modes of governance," in the context of social pacts, enable the systems to retain a degree of "adaptive capacity."[50]

This adaptability resulted from the interplay of three different but interrelated elements. These included a highly centralized, all-powerful executive, what Roger Owen has called a "monarchical presidency";[51] a closely intertwined and expansive network of intelligence agencies and police; and regular, though frequently *pro forma*, parliamentary and presidential elections. All three elements were used, sometimes simultaneously and sometimes separately and sequentially, as the state adapted its responses to emerging circumstances or crises.

While the region's monarchies proved adept at perpetuating their legitimacy, the Middle East's presidential systems found the same task to be particularly challenging. In all there was a deep contradiction: on the one hand centralizing power within a presidency intimately embedded within the armed forces or the police, while on the other hand relying on the legitimizing powers of the constitution and regularly held parliamentary elections.[52] They sought to demobilize the population politically while still trying to ensure a respectable voter turnout in the regime's

[46] Stephen J. King, *The New Authoritarianism in the Middle East and North Africa*, Bloomington, IN: Indiana University Press, 2009, pp. 4–5.

[47] Heydemann, "Social Pacts and the Persistence of Authoritarianism in the Middle East," p. 22.

[48] Ibid. p. 26.

[49] Ibid. p. 28.

[50] Ibid. p. 22.

[51] Owen, *The Rise and Fall of Arab Presidents for Life*, p. 5.

[52] Ibid. p. 3. For the regimes' fixation with constitutions, see Arjomand's chapter in this volume.

hollow elections, all the while promoting economic growth and development.[53] Yet across the board, the presidency remained paramount. In the late 1980s, to take one extreme example, Saddam Hussein is said to have remarked that "the law is anything I write on a scrap of paper."[54]

Presidents became increasingly convinced of "the myth of their own governing skills and so of their own role as guardians and promoters of their country's security and national progress."[55] As one observer of Tunisia noted, "Ben Ali's was a particularly insulting dictatorship" in which the state-run media and all its other agencies participated in creating a cult of personality. The president's portraits were everywhere, the media lauding his every initiative, "with Ben Ali the ever avuncular and enlightened ruler."[56]

To ensure a semblance of legal-rational legitimacy, presidential systems often engaged in elaborate constitutional engineering. The purpose of the constitutions was often to ensure that the president's power remained uncontested.[57] At the same time, they were meant to provide for a constitutionally sanctioned, smooth succession after the president's death in a manner that would cause the least amount of disruption to the ruling oligarchy.[58] In 1971, Anwar Sadat convened a diverse group of Egyptians—made-up of feminists, Islamic legal scholars, socialists, liberals, nationalists, and Christians—to draft a constitution. The resulting constitution promised a little to everyone, and a lot to the president.[59] Between 2005 and 2007 the parliament passed a series of constitutional amendments that were sold to the public as meaningful political reforms, but which in reality sharply curtailed the right to opposition activity and made running in elections by non-establishment actors extremely difficult.[60]

[53] Owen, *The Rise and Fall of Arab Presidents for Life*, p. 53.

[54] Ibid. p. 39.

[55] Ibid. pp. 8–9.

[56] Michel Penner Angrist, "Morning in Tunisia: The Frustrations of the Arab World Boil Over," CFR, *The New Arab Revolt*, p. 76.

[57] Owen, *The Rise and Fall of Arab Presidents for Life*, p. 54.

[58] Ibid. p. 5.

[59] Nathan J. Brown, "Egypt's Constitutional Ghosts: Deciding the Terms of Cairo's Democratic Transition," CFR, *The New Arab Revolt*, p. 126.

[60] Michele Dunne and Amr Hamzawy, "The Ups and Downs of Political Reform in Egypt," in Marina Ottaway and Julia Choucair-Vizoco (eds), *Beyond the Façade: Political Reform in the Arab World*, New York: Carnegie

But constitutional engineering can only go so far in protecting the presidency. A variety of praetorian institutions was employed to ensure the unassailability of the executive's near-absolute powers. As the primary institution from which presidents originally hailed, the military continued to serve as the "spine" of monarchical presidencies as diverse as Iraq, Syria, Egypt, Libya, and Algeria.[61] But in a number of Middle Eastern republics, the armed forces, while politically powerful, slowly pulled back from the political and administrative functions of the state and instead busied themselves more with economic and commercial ventures. This was particularly true of the Egyptian military during the Mubarak presidency, when the increasingly less ideological and more professionalized military involved itself in economic and business matters, acquiring its own economic interests.[62] In Algeria, President Bouteflika similarly oversaw a steady demilitarization of the state machinery in the 1990s, reinstating instead the executive presidency as the supreme arbiter of policy debates and conflicts of interests.[63] The Algerian military sought to push back against curbs on its powers, and was ultimately unsuccessful, having to contend with Bouteflika's reelection in 2004 and again in 2009. As the president's powers increased, so did his reliance on the police and intelligence agencies.[64]

The military's slow disengagement from politics paved the way for the state's reliance on the police and intelligence agencies in its efforts to root out opponents, stifle dissent, and instill fear among aspiring opposition figures. Military-based regimes steadily morphed into Mukhaberat or intelligence states. Before long, the number of people employed by the police and the security agencies in most of these states often exceeded the number of soldiers in the armed forces.[65] In Ben Ali's Tunisia, an estimated 10 percent of the population was sustained by

---

Endowment for International Peace, 2008, p. 26. For a list of the amendments passed during this time see ibid. pp. 41–2.

[61] Joshua Stacher, *Adaptable Autocrats: Regime Power in Egypt and Syria*, Stanford, CA: Stanford University Press, 2012, p. 5.

[62] Owen, *The Rise and Fall of Arab Presidents for Life*, p. 67.

[63] Hugh Roberts, "Demilitarizing Algeria," in Ottaway and Choucair-Vizoco, *Beyond the Façade*, p. 138.

[64] Ibid. p. 153.

[65] Owen, *The Rise and Fall of Arab Presidents for Life*, p. 46.

employment in the state's security services.[66] In Egypt, by the late 2000s the internal security service outnumbered the active military personnel by three to one and was estimated to be an astounding 1.5 million strong.[67] As Mukhaberat states "justified domestic repression in the name of national unity against an external enemy," the fact that they "diverted resources away from social priorities" mattered little to state elites and their Western allies.[68] Across the Maghreb and indeed throughout the rest of the Middle East, authoritarian regimes used the fight against Islamists to justify repressive policies.[69] So long as they succeeded in keeping the Islamist menace at bay and did not directly threaten Western interests, the West looked the other way, ignored their human rights violations, and gave them military, economic, and even political support.

For the monarchies, attempts to cultivate continued sources of legitimacy proved somewhat easier. The region's monarchies, more so than the Middle East's presidencies, have had to present themselves as outgrowths of a national tradition and to appeal to as wide a cross section of their peoples as possible. The task of the oil monarchies has been made easier largely due to the continued flow of petrodollars into the national economy. Oman, Jordan, and Morocco, the monarchies with little or no oil, have had to devise other means through which ruling bargains could be sustained. The case of Oman is particularly illustrative in this regard. Sultan Qaboos's legitimacy is built on his role as the central pillar of the country's state-building process, for which he relies on the powers of the state.[70] Along with attempts at co-opting traditional elites, the sultan has used employment opportunities, especially in the newly expansive health and education sectors, to replace the traditional legitimacy of the state based on *asabiyati* (paternalism) with patronage and clientelism. In the process, he has successfully merged traditional patrimonial practices—such as the co-option of merchants

[66] Ibid. p. 78.

[67] Stacher, *Adaptable Autocrats*, p. 7.

[68] Brynen, Korany, and Noble, "Introduction," p. 19.

[69] Azzedine Layachi, "Meanwhile in the Maghreb: Have Algeria and Morocco Avoided North Africa's Unrests?" CFR, *The New Arab Revolt*, p. 217.

[70] Marc Valerie, "State Building, Liberalization from Above, and Political Legitimacy in the Sultanate of Oman," in Schlumberger, *Debating Arab Authoritarianism*, p. 143.

and tribal elites, and his annual trips across the country—with the creation of a modern Omani national identity in order to solidify the legitimacy of his rule.[71]

With the exception of Iran's ill-fated Rastakhiz Party (1975–78), Middle Eastern monarchies have shown a natural aversion to mass-based political parties. But, elsewhere in the region, mass-based government parties designed to foster mass mobilization and to channel popular support for the state and its economic, social, and political programs became a regular feature of the presidential political systems. These parties were often closely tied to the office of the presidency. The preferred political structure for many regimes across the Middle East became the one-party state, which was seen as essential in fostering nation-building and providing much-needed political legitimacy for the authoritarian system.[72] In Tunisia, to take one example, the government party, the Constitutional Democratic Rally (RCD), claimed a membership of 2 million in a country with a total population of only 10 million.[73] In dictatorships, legislatures and official state parties frequently serve as "instruments of co-option" and enable dictators to make policy compromises and concessions.[74] They help with "controlled bargaining" and enable the dictator to "reconstitute his bargaining partner each time."[75] They help reduce political transaction costs and make the task of governing easier. State parties and pliant parliaments enable dictators to identify reliable bargaining partners, reveal information that may otherwise be unavailable or hard to come by, and help avoid popular mobilization.[76]

Stage-managed elections consequently became a regular feature of the Middle East's political landscape, especially from the 1970s onwards, even though they sometimes proved easier to manage than at other times. The precise timeline for controlled electoral politics differed in each country based on the specific political exigencies of the time and the needs of state actors. Throughout the 1970s, for example, Egypt and Jordan did not allow formal and informal opposition, whereas in the

[71] Ibid. p. 158.

[72] Owen, *The Rise and Fall of Arab Presidents for Life*, p. 18.

[73] Filiu, *The Arab Revolution*, p. 15.

[74] Jennifer Gandhi, *Political Institutions under Dictatorships*, Cambridge: Cambridge University Press, 2008, p. xviii.

[75] Ibid. p. 78.

[76] Ibid. p. 80.

1980s, Morocco started opening the political arena to loyal opposition groups.[77] In the 1980s Egypt witnessed what one observer called "patryism" and in the 1990s it saw a flourishing of civil society organizations. In the 1980s and 1990s Egypt saw the emergence of an "authoritarian opposition" that was "tightly controlled by the state and unable to engage for real competition for power."[78] Examples included the Free Social Constitutional Party and the Hizb al-Ghad (Tomorrow Party). Mubarak also permitted an opposition press to grow in the 1980s and an independent press to flourish in the 2000s.[79]

Similarly, under Saleh Yemen's system was "pluralized authoritarian," with "some space granted for alternative voices," albeit with "severe restrictions on the establishment of alternative institutionalized power centers that might threaten the elite."[80] Formal avenues of dissent helped bolster the appearance of regime legitimacy both domestically and internationally, and provided safety valves for pressures from below by offering avenues for the expression of opposition sentiments, however mild and sanitized.[81]

Parliamentary elections were not always as easy to manage, lending themselves to being under-managed, as was the case with the Egyptian parliamentary elections of 2005, or over-managed, as with the country's 2010 parliamentary elections.[82] In fact, it was the farcical nature of the 2010 elections which contributed directly to the spontaneous demonstrations that erupted in the following January and led to the fall of the Mubarak regime.[83] Unsurprisingly, the Egyptian regime's "reform discourse" failed to mask its essentially authoritarian nature and its determination to hang on to power at all costs.[84] Throughout the 1970s and

[77] Ellen Lust-Okar, "The Management of Opposition: Formal Structures of Contestation and Informal Political Manipulation in Egypt, Jordan, and Morocco," in Schlumberger, *Debating Arab Authoritarianism*, p. 40.

[78] Holger Albrecht, "Authoritarian Opposition and the Politics of Challenge in Egypt," in Schlumberger, *Debating Arab Authoritarianism*, p. 61.

[79] Brown, "Egypt's Constitutional Ghosts," p. 127.

[80] Sarah Phillips, "Yemen: The Centrality of the Process," in Ottaway and Choucair-Vizoco, *Beyond the Façade*, p. 233.

[81] Ibid.

[82] Owen, *The Rise and Fall of Arab Presidents for Life*, pp. 55–6.

[83] Ibid. p. 72.

[84] Albrecht, "Authoritarian Opposition and the Politics of Challenge in Egypt," p. 74.

the 1980s, despite considerable internal dissent, the Egyptian Muslim Brotherhood sought to find ways to accommodate the regime and to take part in parliamentary elections, but to no avail.[85] Similarly, in Tunisia in the 1980s, the Islamic Tendency Movement (MTI), the predecessor to the An-Nahda, accepted pluralism, and, by implication, the broad parameters of the ruling bargain as defined by the state.[86]

In Jordan, meanwhile, the unrest of the late 1980s ushered in a limited degree of political opening with the aim of gaining support for contentious economic policies rather than reforming monarchical autocracy. Through the December 1990 National Charter, the government gave the opposition a limited degree of elbow room in return for recognition of the legitimacy of the monarchy. Throughout the 2000s, however, mounting economic difficulties and growing political discontent led to an increased narrowing of political space.[87] By and large, Middle Eastern states were unwilling to embark on anything more than perfunctory elections with little or no substantive consequence for the state's composition or its functions. Yet the semblance of party politics nevertheless contributed to the legitimacy of the state and helped prolong the life of the incumbent regimes by at least a few years.[88]

In the Middle East, repressive authoritarianism and a vibrant civil society do not appear to be mutually exclusive.[89] In the 1970s, the Egyptian state combined brutal repression in Upper and Middle Egypt with "a cynical bargain with some devoted enemies of the secular idea."[90] In the 1990s, the state turned a blind eye toward the Islamist discourse so long as it did not directly challenge the state and its legitimacy.[91] But beginning in 2005, the Egyptian regime's authoritarian impulse kicked in with its suppression of the Kefaya ("enough") street movement that

[85] Gudrun Kramer, "Islam and Pluralism," in Brynen, Korany, and Noble, *Political Liberalization and Democratization in the Arab World*, p. 120.

[86] Ibid. p. 122.

[87] Julia Choucair-Vizoco, "Illusive Reform: Jordan's Stubborn Stability," in Ottaway and Choucair-Vizoco, *Beyond the Façade*, pp. 46, 50–1.

[88] Albrecht, "Authoritarian Opposition and the Politics of Challenge in Egypt," p. 61.

[89] Heydemann, "Social Pacts and the Persistence of Authoritarianism in the Middle East," p. 23.

[90] Fouad Ajami, "The Sorrows of Egypt: A Tale of Two Men," CFR, *The New Arab Revolt*, p. 7.

[91] Ibid. p. 8.

sought an end to Mubarak's rule.[92] Throughout the 2000s, amid relentless government efforts to politicize the judiciary, Egyptian judges struggled to maintain their institutional prerogatives and independence.[93]

The Moroccan monarchy, perhaps more than any other Middle Eastern state, took meaningful steps designed to co-opt oppositional elements into the state and to foster a loyal opposition in the process. In 1997, King Hassan implemented a reform known as "*alternance*," which brought opposition parties into the political establishment. The pace of reforms subsequently continued with Mohammed VI in the 2000s, significantly on the king's own initiative rather than being imposed on him from the outside. The monarchy launched a series of meaningful reforms improving human rights conditions, updating personal status laws, and denouncing corruption, all the while ensuring that the powers of the king remained unlimited.[94] In fact, the inclusion of the Islamist Party for Justice and Development has led to a win–win situation for both the state and the PJD, enhancing the legitimacy of the former and the electoral appeal of the latter.[95] In the process, Mohammed VI has become "the model of the authoritarian modernizer."[96] This prompted two scholars to comment in 2008 that "the change that has taken place in Morocco is real."[97]

Few of the Middle East's other monarchies followed suit, except, as already mentioned, for some cosmetic changes in Jordan. The Saudi monarchy, for example, underwent a significant consolidation of authoritarianism throughout the 1970s and the 1980s, and, faced with increased jihadi terrorism, it became downright repressive in the 1990s and the 2000s.[98] In Bahrain, the state retrenched and sought shelter in sectarian-

[92] Albrecht, "Authoritarian Opposition and the Politics of Challenge in Egypt," p. 70.

[93] Cook, "Adrift on the Nile," pp. 62–3.

[94] Marina Ottaway and Meredith Riley, "Morocco: Top–Down Reform without Democratic Transition," in Ottaway and Choucair-Vizoco, *Beyond the Façade*, p. 161.

[95] Eva Wegner, "Islamist Inclusion and Regime Persistence: The Moroccan Win-Win Situation," in Schlumberger, *Debating Arab Authoritarianism*, pp. 88–9.

[96] Julia Choucair-Vizoco, "Movement in Lieu of Change," in Ottaway and Choucair-Vizoco, *Beyond the Façade*, p. 262.

[97] Ottaway and Riley, "Morocco: Top–Down Reform without Democratic Transition," p. 169.

[98] Amr Hamzawy, "The Saudi Labyrinth: Is there a Political Opening?" in Ottaway and Choucair-Vizoco, *Beyond the Façade*, pp. 187–8.

ism throughout the 2000s as it continued to gerrymander electoral districts while embarking on a campaign involving the strategic naturalization of Sunnis from neighboring states. In 2006, the state refused to work with the Shi'a Al-Wefaq even after Al-Wefaq's decision to take part in parliamentary elections had resulted in the formation of a breakaway splinter group, Al Haq.[99] This cost the ruling family what little legitimacy it had left among the country's Shi'a population.[100]

Such was the state of Middle Eastern politics as the first decade of the twenty-first century was drawing to a close. Security states of various forms inundated the region, all maintaining a plethora of mechanisms for regime legitimation, including regular elections, occasional referendums, official or semi-official human rights organizations, and, invariably, a Ministry of Social Welfare, yet all fundamentally authoritarian and often, when needed, brutally repressive.[101] All were bereft of political, economic, or ideological legitimacy of any kind. They were ideologically bankrupt because they had watered down their own ideologies to such a degree that they invariably included little more than generic references to economic development and nationalism.[102] They were economically bankrupt and could hardly address many of the basic needs of their growing populations, never mind making good on the lofty promises they had made.[103] And, politically, there were four basic, reinforcing weaknesses: they could not adequately balance out their concern for stability with the need to open up the political process; they could not properly incorporate the young into their political and ideological projects; their primary domestic allies were crony capitalists with no social base who had become targets of popular anger; and they had limited capabilities to respond to emerging regional or domestic crises.[104] More

[99] Kristin Smith Diwan, "Bahrain's Shia Question: What the United States Gets Wrong About Sectarianism," CFR, *The New Arab Revolt*, p. 187.

[100] Ibid. p. 190.

[101] Owen, *The Rise and Fall of Arab Presidents for Life*, p. 39.

[102] Ibid.

[103] Jennifer Gandhi provides empirical evidence that dictatorships with even nominally democratic institutions experience better performance in terms of economic growth and output. Autonomy of the executive within the state apparatus, which prevailed in all but a handful of Middle Eastern states, dampens economic growth and development. See Gandhi, *Political Institutions under Dictatorships*, p. 160.

[104] Owen, *The Rise and Fall of Arab Presidents for Life*, pp. 174–5.

critically, the states themselves became stale and unresponsive and their leaders aged and frail. It was in this context that Roger Owen called the Middle East "a veritable kingdom of the old."[105]

By early 2010, the Middle Eastern regimes seemed to have weathered the storm and the wave of protests of the mid-2000s.[106] But this semblance of stability was only skin-deep. A collective political malaise gripped the larger Middle East. What Fouad Ajami wrote about Egypt in 1995 still held for the rest of the region: "Egyptians are not blind to what has befallen their country," he wrote. "They can see the booming lands in Asia, countries that were once poorer than Egypt, digging out of the poverty of the past. No way out has materialized for Egypt. The dreams of liberal reform, the hopes for revolution from above, the socialist bid of Nasser all withered away. The country drifts."[107] But the seeming stability of authoritarian regimes masked "deep structural changes in the public sphere" that had been underway for some time.[108] The regimes' old remedies no longer sufficed in beating down the public. As Marc Lynch observed, "Economic woes escalated, the middle class disappeared, the poor scrambled for survival, and youth found all doors closed to them. Sectarian and tribal conflicts broke out unpredictably. Labor strikes intensified and proliferated."[109] The Middle East was ripe for revolution. Regional states ruled through fear and little else. All that was needed was for the barrier of fear to be broken. And broken it was, late in 2010, in a small, nondescript town in Tunisia named Sidi Bouzid.

The Uprisings

The story of the 2011 Arab revolutions has been masterfully told by a number of scholars and does not need to be repeated here.[110] The following will simply highlight two developments related to the rise and

[105] Ibid. p. 172.
[106] Lynch, *The Arab Uprising*, p. 67.
[107] Ajami, "The Sorrows of Egypt," p. 15.
[108] Lynch, *The Arab Uprising*, p. 67.
[109] Ibid. p. 68.
[110] See, for example, Filiu, *The Arab Revolution*; James Gelvin, *The Arab Uprisings: What Everyone Needs to Know*, Oxford: Oxford University Press, 2012; Bahgat Korany and Rabab El-Mahdi (eds), *The Arab Spring in Egypt: Revolution and Beyond*, Cairo: American University of Cairo Press, 2012; and Lynch, *The Arab Uprising*.

fall of ruling bargains in the Middle East and the consequences for the way in which the uprisings unfolded. A first important contributing factor concerns the availability and spread of information across the Middle East. This had to do with the growth of educational opportunities across the region on the one hand, and the increasing accessibility of both traditional and new media to even the region's remotest corners on the other.

There is a direct link between higher levels of education and the likelihood of taking part in opposition activities and calling for political change, especially in adverse economic circumstances.[111] Beginning in the 1960s and 1970s, secondary school opportunities expanded significantly across the Middle East, whereas employment opportunities for high school graduates lagged seriously behind. Those countries that would later experience the Arab Spring saw particularly impressive rises in levels of education combined with chronically poor job prospects, especially for the relatively skilled.[112] The combination of highly skilled, urban middle classes with uncertain or precarious employment prospects proved lethal for regimes with little or no legitimacy.

This was reinforced by the dramatic rise in levels of media penetration throughout the Middle East, and the increasing availability of uncensored, and often unsettling, information. This phenomenon was magnified in the early 2000s, when Al Jazeera television's coverage of the Al Aqsa Intifada impressed upon the restless Arab masses the potency of "people power" and the efficacy of collective action and civil disobedience.[113] In the intervening years, Al Jazeera's importance as a source of information—and a potential mobilizer of public sentiments—had been complemented by the popularity and increased accessibility of the Internet. According to the 2011 *Annual Arab Public Opinion Survey*, in the five Arab countries surveyed, 15 percent of the respondents had acquired access to the Internet between the previous three to five years, 18 percent between the previous one to three years, and 27 percent in less than one year.[114] In 2011, no less than 20 percent of those surveyed

[111] Flipe R. Campante and Davin Chor, "Why Was the Arab World Poised for Revolution? Schooling, Economic Opportunities, and the Arab Spring," *Journal of Economic Perspectives*, 26, 2 (Spring 2012), pp. 167–8.

[112] Ibid. p. 174.

[113] Lynch, *The Arab Uprising*, p. 58.

[114] Shibley Telhami, *2011 Annual Arab Public Opinion Survey*, Baltimore, MD:

used the Internet as their primary source of international news, compared to 8 percent in 2009, with Al Jazeera remaining the dominant provider of international news among comparable broadcasters, though its viewership did decline from 58 percent in 2009 to 43 percent in 2011.[115] By the time the 2011 revolutions arrived in the Arab world, the information revolution had already engulfed the region for some time.

A second contributing factor is the response of the states affected to the emerging crisis. These responses have been structurally conditioned and constrained. Had the dictators involved been willing to give up power, agency might have played a role in determining the form and direction of the ensuing transitions. Across the board, however, in Tunisia, Egypt, Libya, Yemen, and Syria, autocrats fought to hang on, sometimes to the bitter end. The course of the events that followed was especially influenced by two interrelated institutional dynamics. First, as Joshua Stacher has argued, pre-existing levels of institutional centralization determined the types of transitions likely to occur. More specifically, centralized authority in Egypt resulted in a relatively swift transition whereas decentralized authority in Syria made the struggle for power protracted and bloody.[116]

In contrast to Egypt, whose executive branch had become increasingly centralized in the office of the presidency ever since the earliest days of Nasser's tenure in office, Assad had crafted a state containing multiple centers of authority, with Syrian elites scattered, and cooperating, across several institutions. This decentralization of power, which makes compromise and concessions difficult to achieve, prevents the elite from being adaptable.[117] Given the decentralized nature of decision-making and the ruling coalition, the preservation of elite cohesion made concessions risky and difficult, and mass defections were kept at a minimum, with Assad functioning more as a chief operation officer—of a terror factory—than a leader.[118]

University of Maryland, 2011, p. 56. The countries surveyed include Egypt, Jordan, Lebanon, Morocco, and the United Arab Emirates.

[115] Ibid. pp. 57–8.

[116] Stacher, *Adaptable Autocrats*, p. 4.

[117] Ibid. p. 23.

[118] Ibid. p. 17.

A second, related factor concerns the evolving patterns of civil–military relations in the different dictatorships. As we saw earlier, in a number of Middle Eastern countries the state had become increasingly demilitarized. This paved the way for the professionalization of the armed forces, the development of a strong *esprit de corps*, and the rise of corporate interests that were at times directly tied to commercial and business ventures. This was particularly the case in Egypt and, to a somewhat lesser degree, Tunisia. In these cases, when the military realized that the unfolding crisis could not be stopped and that continued alliance with the civilian leadership could harm its professional and corporate interests, it deliberately distanced itself from civilian dictators, making their demise inevitable. In both Egypt and Tunisia, the military's "aloof neutrality underscores that its role on the sidelines was intentional."[119] Tellingly, even as the edifice of the regime was crumbling, both the Egyptian and Tunisian military commands remained unified.[120] In fact, the Egyptian military saw itself as the guardian of the transition, seeing it as an opportunity to enhance its own political stature and economic fortunes in a post-Mubarak era.[121]

But not all regional militaries underwent a similar process of depoliticization and professionalization. In a number of countries, the armed forces remained firmly entrenched within the bowels of the state, their continued, intimate embeddedness guaranteed through a variety of ideological, familial, sectarian, or economic ties. In Libya, Syria, and Yemen, the president's relatives and family members retained powerful command positions within the military. In Syria, the military, the ruling elite, and the secret police are so intertwined that "it is now impossible to separate the Assad regime from the security establishment."[122] Assad also ensured that all combat units were commanded by Alawis and that none of their equipment was moved without his permission.[123] In Libya, one of Qaddafi's sons, Khamis, commanded his own special military unit known as the Khamis Brigade. In Yemen, the elite Republican Guards was led by Brigadier General Ahmed Ali Abdullah Saleh, the son

[119] Joshua Stacher, "Egypt's Democratic Mirage: How Cairo's Authoritarian Regime is Adapting to Preserve Itself," CFR, *The New Arab Revolt*, p. 100.
[120] Ibid. p. 99.
[121] Stacher, *Adaptable Autocrats*, p. 11.
[122] Broning, "The Sturdy House that Assad Built," p. 202.
[123] Owen, *The Rise and Fall of Arab Presidents for Life*, p. 45.

of President Ali Abdullah Saleh. Unsurprisingly, in all of these cases where the military's interests remained closely intertwined with those of state leaders, popular uprisings resulted in protracted, bloody civil wars.

Structural dynamics may have conditioned the responses of states to the unfolding crises, but leaders also did their share to ensure their fates were sealed. As the rebellions began to spread across cities and towns, for example, presidents, mocking the protestors, gave speeches that were "arrogant, patronizing, hypocritical, and just plain stupid."[124] Mubarak's promises of genuine reforms for the first time after nearly thirty years in office rang hollow, and his appointment of a vice president for the first time ever in his presidency did little to endear him to protesting Egyptians. Qaddafi's description of the protestors as "rats" and himself as a "revolutionary from the tent, from the desert" served only to encourage more Libyans to join the rebellion. And Bashar Assad's naming of the rebellious Syrians as treasonous lackeys of foreign powers, as paid agents of Israel, only encouraged more of his countrymen to join the movement to oust him.[125] In Bahrain, meanwhile, the regime's intransigence and its crackdown on peaceful protests resulted in a hardening of the demands of those gathering in the capital's iconic Pearl Square and a spread of the protests.[126] Before long, dismissive regimes realized they had nationwide protests and genuine threats on their hands.

Thus ensued mass-based revolutions that swept away regimes once thought unassailable. At their core these were spontaneous uprisings in their inception, initially leaderless and the product of little more than mass anger. The spark was the tragic self-immolation of a fruit vendor in Sidi Bouzid. From there, diffusion and demonstration effect took the local uprising to Tunis and other Tunisian cities, then to Cairo and other Egyptian cities, to Benghazi and Tripoli and other parts of Libya, and then to Deraa and elsewhere in Syria. Across the region, common themes emerged during the protests, with Fridays as days of rage throughout the Middle East. Protestors imitated tactics, such as the seizing and holding of public squares or the uploading of protest videos on YouTube. A powerful pan-Arabist outlook began to unite protestors

[124] Ibid. p. 176.
[125] For excerpts of speeches by Mubarak, Qaddafi, and Assad see CFR, *The New Arab Revolt*, pp. 408–13, 414–20, and 458–66 respectively.
[126] Diwan, "Bahrain's Shia Question," p. 190.

across national boundaries. "Protestors in Yemen or Morocco hung on every twist in Bahrain, while Syrians eyed the violence that met the Libyan challenge." They adopted identical slogans, and terms such as *baltagiya*, used in Egypt to refer to regime thugs, came into widespread use across the region.[127] What made these protests different was the success of the protestors, the backfiring of traditional repressive regime responses, and the framing of region-wide protests into "a single coherent regional narrative" on Al Jazeera and social media.[128]

In the same way that protestors appear to have drawn inspiration from one another in the earlier phase of the Arab Spring, in later periods fear appears to have become an increasingly important motivating factor. Early on, even Iraq, with the wounds of its civil war of the late 2000s still fresh, saw a "day of rage," 25 February 2011, when protests in Baghdad left more than twenty people dead.[129] The pervasiveness of protests across the country caught the state by surprise. The state has decided to dig in and to clamp down on protests, no doubt at the expense of long-term stability.[130] Similarly, in Algeria, where the memory of the bloody civil war of the 1990s still lingers on, a "rebellion by installments" of sorts occurred at around the same time.[131]

But the bloody turns of the Syrian uprising are also reminders to people in the rest of the region of the costs of rising up against entrenched dictatorships, of the devastating consequences of civil wars, and of the perils of having national unity, even if backed by a repressive regime, degenerate into sectarian conflict. What these painful lessons mean for Jordan, for example, remain to be seen. But, at least for now, they appear to have slowed the spread of revolutionary waves across national boundaries.

Looking Ahead

It is unclear where the Arab Spring goes from here. Marc Lynch warns that the lessons of the past are not particularly encouraging, with every

[127] Lynch, *The Arab Uprising*, p. 69.
[128] Ibid. p. 71.
[129] Raad Alkadiri, "Rage Comes to Baghdad: Will Iraq's Recent Protests Lead to Revolt?" CFR, *The New Arab Revolt*, p. 193.
[130] Ibid. p. 196.
[131] Owen, *The Rise and Fall of Arab Presidents for Life*, p. 177.

episode of mass mobilization and public euphoria designed to usher in a democratic era leading to a "reconsolidation of state authority, sometimes under new leaders and sometimes under surviving regimes." A "more repressive, stifling regional order" arising from a "deeper entrenchment of authoritarian regimes" may well be in the offing as a result of the 2011 uprisings.[132] Such might indeed turn out to be the case, but Middle Eastern history has seldom been kind to those who have been quick to draw long-term conclusions from immediate developments.

For now, these developments give us an indication of what the post-Arab Spring ruling bargain may look like, at least in Tunisia, Egypt, and Libya, the three countries in which the people's uprisings have led to changes in the political system. Four key, interrelated elements stand out. They include political Islam, nationalism, electoral legitimacy, and the delivery of economic goods and services. As the fateful events of the Arab Spring unfolded, each of these elements emerged as key organizing principles of the protests, as rallying cries of what the protestors wanted and what they expected. And, as we look beyond the Arab Spring, we see each of these elements play compelling roles in the new political orders emerging. How their interplay will take shape in the years to come, and where on the sliding scale from democracy to authoritarianism each polity will find itself, is a question too early to answer.

Islam as a force of political mobilization joined the Arab Spring relatively late in the game. From Benghazi to Alexandria, Tunis and Cairo to Tripoli, it was neither the force of Islam as personal faith nor its organizational power on the ground that brought out the throngs of protestors on to the streets. The protests, it must be remembered, started out as decidedly non-ideological affairs, motivated initially by little other than mass frustration and a simple yearning for change. Indeed, the Egyptian Muslim Brotherhood at first stood aside and did not endorse the protests outright. Slowly, however, as the demonstrations swelled in numbers and began to attract a much wider spectrum of people, and as the need for on-the-ground coordination and organization grew accordingly, the Muslim Brotherhood became one of the most visible drivers of the mass protests. In the heat of the revolution, Muslim Brotherhood supporters are estimated to have constituted about one-third of the protestors in Tahrir Square.[133] Most importantly, in Egypt,

[132] Lynch, *The Arab Uprising*, p. 65.
[133] Shehata, "Fall of the Pharaoh," p. 144.

the Brotherhood's organizational capabilities led directly to its ability to capture the office of the presidency in the first post-Mubarak presidential elections that followed.

Even in Tunisia and Libya, where Islamist forces did not participate in such an organized and overt manner to bring down the old orders, the uprisings did galvanize popular religious sentiments and expectations of Islam's role, in one form or another, in the new polity. As of this writing, none of the three countries under discussion have had their final constitutions drafted and ratified, and the shape of the post-revolutionary leaderships in Tunisia and Libya is yet to be determined. Nevertheless, a revived An-Nahda has become a significant political force in Tunisia. Whatever order emerges in any of these three countries, one cannot ignore the force and role of political Islam. The longer-term question remains how that political Islam will look, and how it will interact with the other elements of the ruling bargain.

Three of the other elements of the new ruling bargain were also present in the older bargain, but are now substantively different. The first includes nationalism. With the official nationalism of pre-revolutionary states long defunct, popular perceptions of state leaders as squanderers of national interests and resources deepened oppositional sentiments and aggravated political grievances. As these sentiments gave rise to mass protests, and as ordinary citizens defied government forces by pouring onto the streets in their hundreds of thousands, feelings of civic pride and of citizenship became increasingly more intense. The essence of the Arab Spring was as much nationalist as it was anti-establishment. And that sense of owning the political process, of having a vested interest in the welfare of the nation, is unlikely to recede anytime soon.

Closely related to nationalism is the importance of electoral legitimacy. From the outset, the Arab Spring was a profoundly anti-authoritarian phenomenon. And whatever ruling bargain emerges out of it cannot but contain institutional mechanisms that will enable the people to have their voices heard. The orders emerging out of the Arab uprisings will out of necessity have a strong element of electoral input attached to them. By itself, that does not necessarily make them democratic. The old orders, after all, also featured elections. But the assumption now is that elections matter and that they should no longer make a mockery of the people's wishes.

A final element in the creation of the new ruling bargains is the state's provision of economic goods and services. Employment opportunities and job security remain as ever-present of a concern today as they were prior to the events of 2011, as do prices of basic goods and general living standards. And the electorate, the newly empowered citizens, will continue to look to the state to create opportunities for their economic well-being. Given the legacies of economic underperformance that the emerging post-Arab Spring orders have inherited, the tasks ahead will undoubtedly be challenging. How they will go about solving their inherited economic problems is likely to be one of the most vexing issues of the coming years. Will old patronage and clientelistic networks re-emerge and be reconstituted, or will liberal market reforms become the order of the day? Or, as appears to be the case, will the oil monarchies of the Persian Gulf come to the rescue of the struggling economies of North Africa and the Levant?[134] Again, which option, or more likely which combinations of options, is likely to become dominant remains to be seen. What is certain is that the state's delivery of goods and services will continue to remain one if not the most significant aspect of the new ruling bargains taking shape.

Islam, elections, nationalism, and the economy have been resonant forces in the political history of the modern Middle East since the start of the twentieth century, and they are likely to continue shaping the region for years to come. The revolutions of 2011 fundamentally restructured domestic politics in some countries, prompted all others to rethink, or revise, or tighten up their own bases of rule, and redrew the strategic map of the whole region. The Arab Spring as it unfolded in 2011 may have come to an end, at least for now, but its repercussions will no doubt influence the shape of Middle East politics for years to come.

[134] Mehran Kamrava, "The Arab Spring and the Saudi-Led Counterrevolution," *Orbis*, 56, 1 (Winter 2012), pp. 96–104.

2

GLOBAL AFFINITIES

THE NEW CULTURES OF RESISTANCE BEHIND THE ARAB SPRING[1]

John Foran

If, one day, the people desire to live free, then fate must answer their call. Their night will then begin to fade, their chains will break and fall.

— Sung by a protestor in the 25 January demonstration in Tahrir Square[2]

"If Egypt could get rid of Mubarak, Wisconsin can get rid of Walker!" John Nichols, in *Uprising*, tells of a demonstrator in Madison who was

[1] I dedicate this essay to the memory of Anthony Shadid, truth-teller to power, story-teller extraordinaire, who died while trying to get the story of the Arab Spring. I also wish to thank Richard Widick, Mehran Kamrava, and the other participants in this project for their helpful comments.

[2] Quoted in Wael Ghonim, *Revolution 2.0: The Power of the People is Greater than the People in Power—A Memoir*, New York: Houghton Mifflin Harcourt, 2012, p. 188.

holding a sign with this slogan on a February night in 2011, the words written in Arabic. When Nichols asked the man how he had come to know Arabic, he replied, "I don't. I had it translated on Google last night." Nichols comments that when a middle-aged unionized American is sufficiently inspired by the Arab Spring to translate a slogan for his struggle in Wisconsin into Arabic, then something is going on. And something is indeed going on. Egyptian activist Maor Eletrebi sent a letter to Wisconsin, in which he wrote: "The beauty of Tahrir Square you can have everywhere, on any corner, in any city, or in your heart … Breathe deep, Wisconsin, because justice is in the air."[3]

Radical social change, in the sense of a deep transformation of a society, community, a region, or the whole world toward greater economic equality and political participation, and accomplished by the actions of a strong and diverse popular movement, is clearly in the air we now breathe. The signs are everywhere: the events of 2011 were of a world-historical order. And the Arab Spring—the overthrow of dictators by non-violent mass popular resistance in Tunisia and Egypt, by force of arms in Libya, with Syria in agony, and with the courageous stands of ordinary people in the streets of Bahrain, Yemen, and elsewhere—is the principal reason for this. Since 2011 we have also witnessed the *indignados'* revolt in Spain, student protests in Santiago and Quebec, street demonstrations and battles in England and Greece, movements around corruption in India and housing in Israel, striking miners in South Africa, Pussy Riot in Russia, wildcat strikes across China, and finally, the American Autumn of Occupy. It seems that 2011 was destined to pass into history as one of the most revolutionary ever, alongside 1789, 1848, 1905, 1917, 1968, 1979, 1989. This year may well be heralded in the future as prominent even by the standards set by these storied dates.

There is little doubt as to the significance of the Arab Spring—the overthrow of long-standing, seemingly secure tyrants and criminals is always to be welcomed, and the pace and scope of the events touched off by the Arab Spring is breath-taking indeed. The same can be said of the American Autumn: when demonstrators of such diversity also

[3] John Nichols told the story on Amy Goodman's *Democracy Now!* program on 15 Feb. 2012: http://www.democracynow.org/2012/2/15/on_1_year_anniversary_of_wisconsin, and cites Eletrebi in *Uprising: How Wisconsin Renewed the Politics of Protest, from Madison to Wall Street*, New York: Nation Books, 2012, p. 1.

being transformed in new directions. The "old" or classical cultures of revolution typically featured armed insurgents who directly engaged the state and its military, though they were aided in all cases by unarmed groups and organizations which provided crucial support activities. In Russia and China, and more loosely in Nicaragua and Cuba, socialist political parties existed alongside the revolutionary armies and gave direction to them. In Iran, the network of mosques and clerics provided the organizational base for the mass demonstrations and general strike that undermined the shah's government without taking up arms. A common thread across these cases is the hierarchical structure of the movements, with well-identified individuals at their head—Emiliano Zapata and Pancho Villa, Lenin and Trotsky, Mao Tse-tung, Fidel Castro and Che Guevara, Khomeini, and the Sandinista leadership of the Ortega brothers. The hierarchical nature of guerrilla militaries, socialist parties, and religious leadership meant that influential figures—always male, and often privileged in background—would lead in the name of the people.

These political cultures produced broad and powerful revolutionary movements, defeating highly militarized states with powerful external backers (usually, in fact, the United States). Once in power, however, they too often fragmented, as different groups had their own aims, and the common bond that had united them all proved fragile and difficult to sustain. This is not to say that the limitations of these revolutions can be laid entirely at the feet of the political cultures that made them—far from it. Of substantial weight in the outcomes of each were other factors that acted independently of political culture and human agency: external intervention and disadvantageous positions in the world economy chief among them. But the possibility remains that despite the strength and solidity of these revolutionary political cultures, so indispensable in overthrowing the states they opposed, they still possessed features—especially the combination of the leaderships' emphases on formal ideology over popular idiom, and the hierarchical nature of the organizations that came to power—which must be counted among the Achilles' heels of the disappointing and limited outcomes that followed.

In the twenty-first century, the nature of movements for what we might now call radical social change rather than revolution has itself changed, as activists, reformers, dreamers, and revolutionaries globally have pursued non-violent paths to a better world, intending to live and act as they would like that world to be. In other words, the ends of justice are no longer held to justify the means of violence; the means of non-violent resistance reflect and guarantee the ends that they seek.

To the century-old problem posed by Lenin, who is not a particular favorite of the movements under discussion—"What is to be done?"[6]—social movements in the last decade of the twentieth century and the first dozen years of the present one have been offering some strikingly new and interesting answers.

Two distinct and rather different paths to change have been pitted against each other by scholars and practiced by participants on the ground: the electoral path to state power being pursued by the elected left-of-center governments of the Latin American "Pink Tide," most radically in Venezuela and Bolivia; and the opposite route of turning one's back on state power, and instead carving out autonomous spaces both below it at the level of the community, as the Zapatistas are doing, or above it, as the global justice movement and Occupy have sought to do. The Arab Spring opens up a third new path, starting with massive non-violent direct action and following up with a protracted struggle for new democratic institutions. All of these paths can be distinguished from what came before, not least in the new political cultures that have attracted people to them.

Global Affinities

Precursors

It may be that the first harbinger of the new movements was the events of May 1968 in France. As in 2011, they seemed to come out of nowhere before growing with an unprecedented intensity and speed from small actions into a wave of revolt, involving occupations of schools and factories, demonstrations and direct action in the cobble-stoned streets of Paris, democratic, open debate with participation for everyone with something to say, and a massive general strike. The movement's tactics grew out of a vision of a different mode of everyday life, of a new community that would be personally liberating and empowering. It presaged a world of direct, participatory democracy, on as large a

[6] In *Anna Karenina*, Tolstoy's protagonist asks "What is to be done? What is to be done? What's the best way to act in this terrible situation?—that's what we must think about": see *The New York Times Magazine*, 23 Dec. 2012, p. 46.

scale as possible. In its best moments, "Many people, not only students, but old and young, men and women, intellectuals and workers, the specialized and the unskilled, spoke simply about what shape the world should take, what should they do and be, what life should be like."[7] Yet in the absence of common demands or goals, agreed upon by all involved, and without an organized political outlet, the forging of a political culture sufficiently strong and effective to hold together the disparate parts of the movement eluded them—by mid-June the movement had seemingly vanished into thin air as suddenly and surprisingly as it had appeared.

Or had it? Though the protests around the world in 1968 ended in defeats almost everywhere—perhaps most consequentially in France, Czechoslovakia, and Mexico—they created significant political and cultural legacies of protest which have been passed down in the form of new social movements today. As Cohn-Bendit told *Paris-Match*: "A different world is going to be made over"[8]—a remarkable prefiguring of the Global Justice Movement's famous slogan a generation later: "Another world is possible." And as Immanuel Wallerstein observed: "The spirit of 1968 flows through [the] Arab Spring and [the] Occupy Movement."[9]

Another twentieth-century precursor followed close on the students' heels when Chilean socialist Salvador Allende led the Popular Unity coalition to power with a slim plurality in the 1970 elections. By beginning to construct what his supporters called "the Chilean path to socialism" through legal, constitutional means and with massive popular enthusiasm and support, Allende departed sharply from the armed path to power of previous revolutions, and achieved a share of state power that had eluded the explosion in France. The political cultures of Chile's left and centrist social forces—perhaps two-thirds of the population—initially presented a lively, varied panorama of social justice-oriented, class-conscious, and articulate reformers and democratic revolutionaries. In the vise tightened by US economic and political destabilization,

[7] Mark Poster, *Existential Marxism in Postwar France: From Sartre to Althusser*, Princeton, NJ: Princeton University Press, 1975, p. 385.

[8] Quoted in Philippe Labro and the staff of *Edition Special*, *'This is Only a Beginning'*, New York: Funk & Wagnalls, 1969, p. 53.

[9] Immanuel Wallerstein, "The Contradictions of the Arab Spring," Al Jazeera, 14 Nov. 2011, http://www.aljazeera.com/indepth/opinion/2011/11/201111 11101711539134.html

Chilean society polarized politically. The democratic center and the democratic left lost confidence in each other and their capacity for unity. When the military seized power on 11 September 1973, the dictatorship that followed and the world's first neo-liberal economic model condemned Chileans to a reign of terror and loss. Chileans would restore their fragile democracy only fifteen years later, after numerous demonstrations, through a decisive repudiation of Pinochet at the polls.[10]

The Allende years represent a missed opportunity for the transformation of society through democratic means. At the time, many observers argued that revolutionary democratic paths to a better world were doomed by internal contradictions and powerful counter-revolutionary intervention, and the experiences of the Grenadian and Sandinista revolutions in the 1980s reinforced this view. Yet a quarter century later, the experiences of the Pink Tide governments in Latin America suggest that the Chilean path to socialism contains more positive lessons, with Venezuela, Bolivia, and Ecuador pursuing a "twenty-first-century socialism" that is democratic and original, reminding us that flexibility and imagination should temper historical analysis and political action itself.

A democratic socialism for the twenty-first century in Latin America

In the late 1990s, a democratic route to radical social change unfolded throughout much of Latin America, most vigorously in the Venezuela of Hugo Chávez, first elected in 1998, and in Bolivia under its indigenous president, Evo Morales, first elected in 2006. Chávez (now deceased) and his supporters have made gains in education, literacy, nutrition, and healthcare, with significant and growing popular participation among the poorer two-thirds of Venezuelan society, including residents of *barrios* and shanty towns, indigenous and Afro-Venezuelan people, women, and workers.

In both Bolivia and Venezuela there has been far less emphasis on an ideological appeal to socialism by the leaderships of these elected left-of-center governments, and in its place we find an upsurge in new, popular

[10] Among the best accounts of what happened in Chile are Jack Spence, "Class Mobilization and Conflict in Allende's Chile: A Review Essay," *Politics & Society*, 8, 2 (1978), pp. 131–64, Arturo Valenzuela, *The Breakdown of Democratic Regimes: Chile*, Baltimore, MD: Johns Hopkins University Press, 1979, and Marc Cooper, *Pinochet and Me*, London: Verso, 2001.

conceptions of social justice. When asked what he understood by "socialism," Morales replied: "To live in community and equality ... It is an economic model based on solidarity, reciprocity, community, and consensus. Because, for us, democracy is a consensus ... And beyond that, [it means] respecting Mother Earth, the Pacha Mama."[11]

Felipe Quispe, an Aymara indigenous leader who is critical of all politicians, including Morales, puts it in the following way: "The foreigners can stay as long as we get 90 percent of the power. If not, there will be war ... We will rewrite history with our own blood. There will be a new sun, and even the rocks and the trees will be happy."[12] Carlos Laime, a 33-year-old tailor, makes this connection: "I feel more Bolivian since an Aymara is in power. Now we can talk about majorities, and in [public] offices the people who are served are not only those wearing ties."[13]

In Morales's words, "if globalization does not admit difference and pluralism, it's a selective globalization, therefore it will be almost impossible to resolve environmental issues and save humanity ... So we're talking about a profound change in the economic models and systems."[14] Such a change will clearly draw on and require the embrace of new political cultures of opposition by a wide coalition of people, differently located but imbued with some common desires and dreams of deeply radical social change.

Despite their differences, the center-left governments of Brazil, Uruguay, Bolivia, Ecuador, El Salvador, Paraguay, Venezuela, Chile, and Argentina have all tapped into political cultures that differ markedly from the older revolutionary tradition, highlighting instead a democratic route to power and the effort to build a more participatory political system. The current of socialism is being reworked in new, more democratic directions in the post-Cold War era, and the depth of the

[11] Heintz Dieterich, "Communitarian Socialism, and the Regional Power Block," MRZine, http://mrzine.monthlyreview.org/dieterich070106.html

[12] Christian Parenti, "Bolivia's Battle of Wills," *The Nation* (4 July 2005), pp. 13–18, see p. 18.

[13] Juan Manrique, "Bolivia: Evo's Friends and Foes," *Latinamerica Press*, 14 (26 July 2006), pp. 8–9, see p. 8.

[14] Evo Morales, "Bolivian President Evo Morales on Indigenous Rights, Climate Change, Establishing Diplomatic Relations with Iran, Che Guevara's Legacy and More," Democracy Now! (26 Sep. 2007), http://www.democracynow.org/2007/9/26/bolivian_president_evo_morales_on_indigenous

democratic ideal is arguably proving a more solid barrier to external and internal intervention than in the more polarized era of the Allende experiment with this form of revolution in the 1970s. When looking at all of these cases together, we find a democratic route to power and the effort to build a more participatory political system on the parts of significant sectors of their populations.

"We Want a World in which Many World Fit": Re-Making the Nature of Power through Direct Action

Just before the emergence of the Pink Tide, the Zapatistas had opened the twenty-first century on 1 January 1994, the same evening that the Mexican and US governments were celebrating their NAFTA (North American Free Trade Agreement) deal. Behind masks of anonymity they rose to visibility and issued an invitation to join them that resonated powerfully with the first stirrings of the global justice movement, which heard the call that "Another World is Possible." Zapatismo is not an ideology, but a new way of making radical change, embracing the vision of changing the world without taking power, as the title of John Holloway's book so aptly puts it, and instead attempting to remake the nature of power altogether.[15]

The encounter of the Western revolutionary tradition with indigenous values and practice in Chiapas has shaped the nature of radical social change to this day. By turning their backs on established ideologies, and drawing instead on their own political idioms, indigenous communities provided core Zapatista principles such as *mandar obedeciendo*—"to rule, obeying"—arguing that leaders should serve the community and struggle for its issues, rather than the community existing to further the vision of the leadership. Another innovative Zapatista practice is suggested by the phrase *dar su palabra* (literally, "to have one's say"). The goal is to make decisions that benefit from the diverse insights of all present, thereby seeking solutions which have eluded them in the past. Such discussions can take much longer than formal debates followed by votes, but once decided they endow the group's choices with a broader legitimacy.

For Javier Elorriaga, the first coordinator of the Zapatista National Liberation Front (the above-ground political wing of the movement),

[15] John Holloway, *Change the World without Taking Power: The Meaning of Revolution Today*, London: Pluto Press, 2002.

"We have to do politics in a new way. You can't accept only what is possible because it will bring you into the hands of the system. This is a very difficult struggle. It is very, very difficult."[16] Or for the Zapatistas' charismatic spokesperson Subcomandante Marcos: "Zapatismo is not an ideology. It is not a bought and paid for doctrine. It is an intuition."[17] Part of this involves "walking at a slower pace" by acknowledging that change is a long and slow process, and something that will not be secured simply through the mere seizure of power or electoral victories. Indeed, the Zapatistas have said that they do not aspire to take state power in the traditional sense, but rather to create "a free and democratic space for political struggle."[18] They have inspired activism far beyond their own communities, drawing the emergent global justice movement to their 1996 "Intergalactic Encounter" against neo-liberalism.

The latter half of the 1990s witnessed the rise of a global justice movement, a "movement of movements" that achieved public visibility when a broad gathering of students, workers, and environmentalists joined in civil disobedience and direct action to shut down the meetings of the World Trade Organization in Seattle in November 1999. If we focus on the political cultures that animate the global justice movement, we can see some novel features, many of them paralleling the Zapatista rebellion. On the subjective side of experience and emotion, it is useful to point out that love—of life, of people, of justice—often provides the vital force that impels ordinary people into extraordinary acts. Love, as an expression of hope and optimism, provides a constructive counterpoint to those other powerful animating emotions, hatred and anger. To this can be added the subjective experience of hope, which offers people a positive vision of the future to counter feelings of hopelessness and despair. In the words of David Solnit, one of the organizers of the spectacular Seattle protests of 1999: "Hope is key. If our organizations,

[16] Quoted in Kara Zugman Dellacioppa, *This Bridge Called Zapatismo: Building Alternative Political Cultures in Los Angeles, Mexico City, and Beyond*, Lanham, MD: Lexington Books, 2009, p. 73.

[17] Interview in *Zapatista*, documentary film, Santa Barbara: Big Noise Films, 1998, www.bignoisefilms.com

[18] EZLN [Zapatista Army of National Liberation], "Second Declaration from the Lacandón Jungle: 'Today We Say: We Will Not Surrender!'" pp. 221–31 in Tom Hayden (ed.), *The Zapatista Reader*, New York: Thunder's Mouth Press and Nation Books, 2002, p. 226.

analysis, visions and strategies are lanterns, then hope is the fuel that makes them burn bright and attracts people to them."[19]

As with the Zapatistas, a sharp turn can be discerned here toward popular ways of speaking in preference to ideological texts. This rejection of ideology does not mean that these movements are "non-ideological" so much as that they are "anti-ideological," steeped in ideas and ideals even as they reject all "-isms." This vision entails radically different modes of struggle for an age of globalization where the location of the enemy is the increasingly interlocked institutions of global capitalism in the form of the WTO, the World Bank, transnational corporations, and Rich and Majority World states. They have mixed old and new modes of struggle: sit-ins, boycotts, strikes, and occupations of land or factories with civil disobedience, occupations of schools and public spaces, world gatherings such as the World Social Forum, web-based campaigns and networks of activists, the building of community-based institutions such as co-ops, people's kitchens, and clinics, and a hundred other forms of direct action aimed at undermining and transforming the system rather than reproducing it. In a no doubt conscious echo of the Zapatistas, Solnit writes: "The world cannot be changed for the better by taking power … Capturing positions of state power, either through elections or insurrection, misses the point that the aim of uprooting the system is to fundamentally change the relations of power at the root of our problems."[20] Occupy would emerge and learn from this movement.

Meanwhile, the US response to the September 11, 2001 attacks effected a large setback for projects of deep social change, militarizing the less overtly violent Clintonian course of globalization from above by a transnational elite and opening up a new and uncertain economic and geopolitical period. It also broke the growing momentum of the global justice movement with its "war on terrorism" discourse. It created horrifying facts on the ground in a shattered Iraq and Afghanistan that defy

[19] David Solnit, "The New Radicalism," interview with Rachel Neumann at AlterNet (2004), http://www.alternet.org/story/19308/the_new_radicalism

[20] This is a composite quote from Solnit, "The New Radicalism", and David Solnit, "Introduction: The New Radicalism—Uprooting the System and Building a Better World," pp. xi–xxiv, in David Solnit (ed.), *Globalize Liberation: How to Uproot the System and Build a Better World*, San Francisco: City Lights Books, 2004, p. xix.

restitution, and conjured up paralyzing new fears and amorphous threats in the United States where none existed before.[21] The cause of global justice was put on the defensive, forced to organize an anti-war movement, which in fact coordinated the largest anti-war demonstration ever on 15 February 2003, a month before the invasion of Iraq.[22] By 2005 or 2006, the Bush administration finally overplayed its hand, at home and abroad, stumbling in its prosecution of the war in Iraq, its response to Hurricane Katrina, the wire-tapping of its own citizens, its budget priorities and massive indebtedness, and its studied inaction on global warming and climate change, thereby giving renewed momentum to a movement that would eventually sow the seeds of Occupy.

The new political cultures and 2011

We arrive at last to the movements that shook the world in 2011. In January and March, long-entrenched dictators fell to popular uprisings in Tunis and Cairo, and newly elected political leaderships offered greater hope for positive social change than had existed in the region in decades. This came about through massive occupations of public space by broad-based social forces that resolutely resisted state repression with non-violent, ongoing, and creative direct action ("civil disobedience" seems too mild a term here). In both cases, and unlike elsewhere in the greater Arab Spring, the regimes they faced and the armies that supported them gave way to popular demands and stepped aside. The United States scrambled from stubborn disbelief and compromise maneuvers to withdrawing its support for the "democratic dictatorships" of Zayn al-Abidine Ben Ali and Hosni Mubarak, who then ceded power. After these clear targets were sent into exile or prison, the movements faced the structural obstacles of old regimes of the economic and (espe-

[21] The best account of this is still that of Anthony Shadid, *Night Draws Near: Iraq's People in the Shadow of America's War*, New York: Picador, 2006.

[22] In fact, "between January 3 and April 12, 2003, 36 million people across the globe took part in almost 3,000 protests against the Iraq war," according to French academic Dominique Reynié: Alex Callinicos, "Anti-War Protests do Make a Difference," *Socialist Worker*, 19 Mar. 2005, cited in Wikipedia, http://en.wikipedia.org/wiki/Protests_against_the_Iraq_War#March_20.2C_2003

cially in Egypt) military elites and quickly (in Tunisia) or slowly (in Egypt) pushed them into elections that cemented these non-violent political revolutions.[23]

It is possible to make sense of these revolutions in terms of the patterns of the great revolutions of world history, and the model of social revolutions put forward in *Taking Power*—namely, a political economy of dependent, neo-liberal capitalist development sharpened the grievances of populations living with high and rising levels of unemployment:

> Not only does [the] region stand out for the highest female unemployment rates in the world—a major feature of our underdevelopment—it also has the highest youth unemployment rates among men and women under the age of 25. The youth unemployment rate in what international organizations call the Middle East and North Africa (MENA) is about 24 percent, whereas it is no more than 12 percent in Sub-Saharan Africa and 15 percent in South Asia, even though they are quite a lot more impoverished and populated than our region. This is notwithstanding the fact that these figures are based on official statistics provided by states, and everyone knows that they are far below reality.[24]

When Ben Ali took power in 1987, unemployment in Tunisia was 5 percent; by 2010 it was more than 22 percent.[25] The official rates masked the true numbers, including the many with precarious work and those who had given up looking for work. The percentages of young people and women unemployed were also at record highs. Even as populations aged between fifteen and twenty-nine grew by 50 percent between 1990 and 2011 in Libya and 65 percent in Tunisia (to say nothing of Yemen's 125 percent), and in Tunisia, for example, 70 percent of the unemployed were under the age of thirty.[26] That the upris-

[23] A comprehensive take on the Arab Spring as a whole can be found in Kevin Anderson's two overviews, "Arab Revolutions at the Crossroads" (2 Apr. 2011), http://www.internationalmarxisthumanist.org/articles/arab-revolutions-crossroads-kevin-anderson, and "Year Two of the Arab Revolutions,", *Logos* (Spring–Summer 2012), http://logosjournal.com/2012/spring-summer_anderson/

[24] Gilbert Achar, "The Bouazizi Spark: The Beginning of a Long Revolutionary Process," 10 Jan. 2012, http://english.al-akhbar.com/content/bouazizi-spark-beginning-long-revolutionary-process

[25] Achar, "The Bouazizi Spark."

[26] Jack A. Goldstone, "Understanding the Revolutions of 2011: Weakness and Resilience in Middle Eastern Autocracies," in Council on Foreign Relations (CFR), *The New Arab Revolt*, New York: Council on Foreign Relations,

ings are entwined with the story of globalization is suggested by the fact that it was the generation of 2010 that made the revolts, not that of 1990 at the dawn of globalization's effects in the region.

The regimes that ruled both countries were classic cases of the type of dictatorship that has historically proven to be most vulnerable to revolutions: excluding the majority of the population from a meaningful vote, repressing dissidents ruthlessly, and personalistic in nature. In addition, rulers were often the richest families in the nation, at the apex of a group of cronies who manipulated and monopolized national economic opportunities—the Mubaraks are said to have amassed fortunes worth between $40 and $70 billion, and Ben Ali alone some $8 billion.[27] This meshing of the economic and political elite made the dictators in each case a clear target of popular wrath. We might think of the Middle Eastern variants of the personalist, exclusionary, repressive state as "presidential dictatorships" in Tunisia, Libya, Egypt, and Syria, and "monarchic dictatorships" in Jordan, Morocco, Bahrain, Saudi Arabia, and elsewhere in the Persian Gulf. With their façade of parliamentary politics, they were reminiscent of Mexico's long-lived "perfect dictatorship" under the PRI (Party of the Institutionalized Revolution) between the 1930s and 2000, only they were personalist as well, making them more vulnerable to popular discontent beyond the sham of the ballot box.[28]

The conjunctural elements of revolutionary outbreaks were also present by the end of 2010: the effects of a teetering global economy on already desperate populations fueled the economic downturns (again, a question of timing: 2010, not 2007 before the crisis). The interconnectedness of global crises meant that one could "read the world in a loaf of bread," as Christian Parenti put it: the hot summer of 2010

2011, pp. 329–43, see p. 336; Joel Beinin, "Working-Class Revolutions?" *The Nation*, 12 Sep. 2011, pp. 26–7.

[27] See Mehran Kamrava, Chapter 1 of this volume.

[28] Such states are good examples of what William Robinson calls "polyarchies," where a tight elite retains political power behind a façade of elections and constitutional rights, often, in both Latin America and the Middle East, propped up by the United States: William I. Robinson, *Promoting Polyarchy: Globalization, U.S. Intervention, and Hegemony*, Cambridge: Cambridge University Press, 1996.

devastated the Russian grain harvest, raising the cost of the people's staple later in the fall and bringing many to the point of rebellion.[29]

The international conjuncture was also critical to the movements' success. This is most obvious in the case of Libya, where NATO's intervention stopped Qaddafi's counter-offensive just short of Benghazi, then crippled his air force and the movement of heavy armor out of Tripoli. In the cases of Egypt and Tunisia, the timing of the revolutions owed much to favorable turns in the world system: the events in Tunis moved so swiftly that neither France nor the United States could react to them before Ben Ali was gone, while in Egypt, the United States wavered uncertainly in its support of Mubarak, and ultimately decided to cast him to the winds while trying to maintain its influence on the army, which wisely stood aside to protect its own interests and stay on the winning wide. In Syria and Bahrain, rebels enjoyed no equivalent geopolitical opening.

With regard to the political cultures of opposition that underlay the Arab Spring, as Mehran Kamrava notes in Chapter 1, the pillars of the ruling bargains, "once sources of comfort and mass ebullition, were now comprised of fear, loathing, suspicion, and submission." When crowds poured into the central squares of Tunis, Cairo, Tripoli, and Manama, they broke this fear, and perhaps long-structured or assumed patterns of deference more generally.

It is clear that the revolts of the Arab Spring were driven less by appeal to ideology than by tapping into popular idioms of everyday concern. These were concentrated in the slogans chanted by crowds, in the first instance against the dictatorships: in Egypt, "We won't leave until *he* leaves."[30] In Tunisia, "Bread, water, and no Ben Ali" adroitly capture the twinned economic and political demands of the movement.[31] In Tunis, "The tone of the protests was rather one of reappropriating patriotic language and symbols: Women and men lay in the streets to spell 'freedom' or 'stop the murders' with their bodies and worked together to tear down and burn the gigantic, Stalin-style portraits of Ben Ali on store-

[29] Christian Parenti, "Reading the World in a Loaf of Bread—Soaring Food Prices, Wild Weather, Upheaval, and a Planetful of Trouble," 19 July 2011, http://www.tomdispatch.com/archive/175419; see also James L. Gelvin, *The Arab Uprisings: What Everyone Needs to Know*, Oxford: Oxford University Press, 2012, pp. 21–3.

[30] Ashraf Khalil, *Liberation Square: Inside the Egyptian Revolution and the Rebirth of a Nation*, New York: St. Martin's, 2011, p. 5.

[31] Anderson, "Arab Revolutions at the Crossroads."

fronts and street corners."[32] And though the state responded with violence, the call in the crowds of Tahrir Square was typically for *salmeya* (staying peaceful).[33]

On top of these demands for an end to authoritarianism and a turn toward meaningful democracy were the economic and social demands. In Egypt, alongside the popular demand for "Dignity, Democracy, Social Justice" were calls for "Bread, Freedom, Social Justice," and the more direct, "We Want to Live! We Want to Eat!"[34] Graffiti in Sidi Bouzid, Tunisia, the cradle of the revolution, read "No to youth unemployment," and "No to Poverty."[35] It is no surprise that the uprising in Sidi Bouzid on 17 December 2010 heard the words "Employment is a right, you band of thieves!"—an echo of an earlier uprising of miners in 2008—or that the French Revolution's "Liberty, Equality, Fraternity" was transposed into "Work, Liberty, National Dignity."[36]

A coalition of young people and labor formed the backbone of the Arab Spring. Class and generation combined to create the nucleus of broad popular movements which provided both the numbers and the slogans that animated the political cultures in play. Students, including significant numbers of women, had engaged in anti-Mubarak demonstrations since the early 2000s. On the day the United States launched its invasion of Iraq, 20 March 2003, they and others were numerous enough to break the security force's cordon around Tahrir Square and hold it for several hours, with alternating cries of "Down with America!" and "Down with Mubarak!"[37]

In the summer of 2004, a movement of young leftists proclaiming its message in its name—Kefaya, Enough—emerged to challenge the official elevation of Mubarak's son Gamal as his eventual successor.[38]

[32] Nadia Marzouki, "Tunisia's Wall Has Fallen," MERIP (Middle East Research and Information Project) Reports, 19 Jan. 2011, http://www.merip.org/mero/mero011911

[33] Khalil, *Liberation Square*, p. 1.

[34] Beinin, "Working-Class Revolutions?" p. 25.

[35] Ellen Knickmeyer, "The Arab World's Youth Army," CFR, *The New Arab Revolt*, pp. 122–6, see p. 124.

[36] Achar, "The Bouazizi Spark."

[37] Khalil, *Liberation Square*, pp. 39–41.

[38] Ibid. pp. 43ff. It is interesting to note in this context that the Zapatistas' rallying cry had been "*Ya Basta!*" (Enough Already) and that the youth movement in Georgia that led the Rose Revolution in Nov. 2003 took the name

The online members and core activists of the April 6 movement, more than 70,000 in total, came out of Kefaya and used social media and organizational skills learned in Serbia and elsewhere to facilitate and coordinate actions in Egypt's eighteen days of revolt.[39] Young Egyptian activists of the April 6 movement had visited Serbia to learn the techniques of non-violent civil disobedience from the Otpor (Resistance!) youth movement that helped unseat Slobodan Milošević in October 2000 and was involved in training the Georgian and Ukrainian groups named above. Serbian youths, in turn, had read the works of US political theorist Gene Sharp, themselves steeped in the examples of Gandhi and Martin Luther King Jr.[40] They then set up the Center for Applied Nonviolent Action and Strategies (CANVAS) in Belgrade, which trained Mohammad Adel of April 6 in the summer of 2009.[41] April 6 took Otpor's distinctive clenched fist for their own logo, and carried it into Tahrir Square on their flags in the first days of the uprising.[42] And just after the events started on 25 January, a 26-page pamphlet, widely attributed to April 6, began to be distributed, titled "How to Protest Intelligently."[43]

Kmara! with the same meaning, while Ukraine's Orange Revolution's youth activists called themselves Pora (It's Time). See Tina Rosenberg, "Revolution U," CFR, *The New Arab Revolt*, pp. 127–42, see p. 132.

39 Ibid. p. 127.

40 Amazon's webpage asserts that "*From Dictatorship to Democracy* was a pamphlet, printed and distributed by Dr. Gene Sharp and based on his study, over a period of forty years, on non-violent methods of demonstration. Now in its fourth edition, it was originally handed out by the Albert Einstein Institution, and although never actively promoted, to date it has been translated into thirty-one languages. This astonishing book travelled as a photocopied pamphlet from Burma to Indonesia, Serbia and most recently Egypt, Tunisia and Syria, with dissent in China also reported. Surreptitiously handed out amongst youth uprisings the world over—how the 'how-to' guide came about and its role in the recent Arab uprisings is an extraordinary tale": http://www.amazon.com/Dictatorship-Democracy-Gene-Sharp/dp/1846688396/ref=sr_1_1?s=books&ie=UTF8&qid=1355440345&sr=1-1&keywords=Gene+Sharp. As we will see, April 6 compiled its own manual based on a range of sources and members' own experiences: Maryam Ishani, "The Hopeful Network," CFR, *The New Arab Revolt*, pp. 143–8, see p. 144.

41 Rosenberg, "Revolution U," pp. 127ff.

42 Ibid. p. 141.

43 Ibid.

When textile workers at the state-owned Misr Spinning and Weaving Company rose up against the police in Mahalla al-Kubra on 6 April 2008, they were riding a wave of labor actions that had been ongoing since 2004, and gave impetus to a new wave of labor actions in the run-up to 2011 that repudiated the state-controlled unions and forced economic issues such as a minimum wage onto the public stage.[44] Achar observes, "Nobody can ignore the fundamental role played by the Tunisian General Labor Union."[45]

Mahmoud al-Shaar, a leader at one of the occupied textile factories, said in 2011, "There is a spirit of optimism between all workers, in every sector. During the revolution, we were here from day one. But now it's reached the point where we look around and we recognize these other delegations from the days in Tahrir Square, people from totally different sectors: we know each other's faces, we shake each other's hands, we slap each other on the back."[46] One indication of the youth and class composition of the Tahrir demonstrators is provided by a medical volunteer: "Among the dead who fell during the recent demonstrations was found not a single well-known oppositionist, nor even a known activist. These are young people from disadvantaged neighborhoods, who put themselves on the front lines."[47] Nor were all participants from the middle and working classes: inhabitants of Cairo's slums, such as the garbage-pickers of Moqattam (mostly young men and children), also joined in.[48]

The originality of this approach to overthrowing dictators suggests that yet another path to radical social change has opened up in the twenty-first century: the sustained occupation of public space followed by the struggle for a more open democratic polity, a kind of third way between taking national power through elections and re-making power by wresting communities from neo-liberalism's clutches. The challenge now is to turn the political revolutions of the Arab Spring into social ones, and for the voices of workers, youth, and women to make themselves heard as they were when bringing down the dictatorships.

[44] Paul Mason, *Why It's Kicking Off Everywhere: The New Global Revolutions*, London: Verso, 2012, pp. 19–22; Khalil, *Liberation Square*, pp. 51ff.

[45] Achar, "The Bouazizi Spark."

[46] Quoted in Mason, *Why It's Kicking Off Everywhere*, pp. 22–3.

[47] Quoted in Cécile Hennion, "Au Caire, une foule de manifestants de tous horizons en quête de port-parole," *Le Monde*, 2 Feb. 2011, found in Anderson, "Arab Revolutions at the Crossroads."

[48] Mason, *Why It's Kicking Off Everywhere*, pp. 6–7.

Whether the political revolutions in Tunisia, Egypt, and Libya can be further pushed toward social transformation aimed at alleviating crushing poverty and redressing class inequality is an open question. What can be predicted is that their futures depend on the courageous engagement of the social movements and civil society organizations that forced the democratic openings and their ability to shape the direction and composition of the newly elected democratic leadership and parties (in Egypt this has proven extraordinarily difficult—effectively impossible). And this, in turn, depends on forging and sustaining the new political cultures—of democracy, reformist Islam, and popular sovereignty—that brought them victory in the first place. Experience, emotions, and idioms must find organizational expressions equal to this daunting task.

Occupy Everything

The second half of the year witnessed the rise of an equally improbable challenge at the heart of the system. Occupy Wall Street succeeded against all the historical and cultural odds to electrify ordinary Americans in the fall of 2011. It drew on some of the threads of resistance that we have traced since 1968: discussion-based decision-making, occupations of the commons, non- or post-ideological ways of speaking, affinity groups dedicated to addressing particular issues and sustaining the encampments—in sum, new yet not-so-new ways of doing politics. Its makers tapped the Arab Spring's techniques of struggle and the liberating public festivals of occupation in Spain, the street confrontations and creative actions in austerity-hammered Athens, and the temporary occupations by the English and Chilean student movements over the course of 2010.[49]

To these, the Occupy movement added its process of General Assembly and a brilliant discursive attack on the political and economic

[49] Among the best accounts to date are Mason, *Why It's Kicking Off Everywhere*, Noam Chomsky, *Occupy*, Brooklyn: Zuccotti Park Press, 2012, Astra Taylor et al. (eds), *Occupy! Scenes from Occupied America*, London: Verso, 2011, Sarah van Gelder and the staff of *YES! Magazine*, *This Changes Everything: Occupy Wall Street and the 99% Movement*, San Francisco: Berrett-Koehler Publishers, 2011, Lenny Flank (ed.), *Voices from the 99 Percent: An Oral History of the Occupy Wall Street Movement*, St Petersburg, FL: Red and Black Publishers, 2011, and Clare Solomon and Tania Palmieri (eds), *Springtime: The New Student Rebellions*, London: Verso, 2011.

elites, seen as "the 1 percent" responsible for the deteriorating lives of "the 99 percent." The process and the message resonated widely across the United States, spreading quickly from New York to other major metropolitan areas (Los Angeles, Boston, Oakland, Chicago, Detroit), smaller cities and towns, and educational institutions such as the University of California. An immense national discussion on the crisis was held, knocking the American political and economic establishments off balance for a time. By mid-autumn, there were occupations in motion across the globe. The system struck back in late fall with a police offensive coordinated by US mayors across the country, using strong-arm tactics to force Occupy to abandon most of its public spaces. The movement merged into many smaller, local forms in the course of 2012, with the occupiers discussing and acting on the ways to do this most effectively in the new conjuncture. Sociologist Keith Kahn-Harris has termed the movements of 2011 "the movement without a name," the expression of "A trend, a direction, an idea-virus, a meme, a source of energy that can be traced through a large number of spaces and projects. It is also a way of thinking and acting: an agility, an adaptability, a refusal to accept the world as it is, a refusal to get stuck into fixed patterns of thought."[50]

Problems and Prospects

The obvious political question is: can these new political cultures of opposition produce—or at least contribute to—some type of global transformation of the sort that is needed to deal with a world in crisis? These cases have shown their ability to move beyond ideology in favor of the strengths of popular idioms demanding social justice, and have shown us some of the advantages of horizontal networks over vertical hierarchies. But how to fashion large-scale popular spaces for democracy, and how to articulate the discourses that will bring together the broadest coalitions ever seen on to a global stage, constitute great challenges.

The left has achieved state power in an important set of Latin American countries: does it have the will, internal support, and global room for maneuver to redirect resources to the poorest sectors of society? The experience of Obama and the European center-left has shown

[50] Keith Kahn-Harris, "Naming the Movement," openDemocracy.net, 22 June 2011.

rather clearly the limited room for maneuver and the dimming prospects for significant reform, domestically or globally, through these parties. The Zapatistas have registered concrete gains on a local level: will they be able to generalize these accomplishments beyond Chiapas? The global justice movement has raised significant opposition to neo-liberal globalization. Can this movement, with all the others, reverse the tide of neo-liberal capitalism?

As the Zapatistas argue, and as the disappointing experience of Lula and the Workers Party in Brazil—watering down their radical program once in power—has shown, elections are not a magic solution to undoing fundamental structures of exploitation. This should be a continuing task for the post-Arab Spring decade that is underway. But neither is direct democracy a panacea, as the Zapatistas' containment in Chiapas and the dispersal of Occupy suggest. And yet the capacity to re-occupy public space is crucial for the long-term success of the Arab Spring, as the vigorous protests which culminated in the coup against President Mohammad Morsi in Egypt, and the flash uprisings in Turkey and Brazil, reminded us in the summer of 2013.

What, then, lies between direct action and elections? One idea is to combine electing "progressive" governments and forging social movements to push them from below and from the side to make good on their promises, and making links with other movements, nations, and organizations everywhere. In other words, rather than the dichotomous choice between seeking to change the world through elections and building a new society from the bottom up, the future of radical social change may well lie at the many possible intersections of deeply democratic social movements and equally diverse and committed political coalitions. The Pink Tide is already working near this intersection. Other struggles that point toward this include the long movement for radical reforms in Kerala, India; the experiences of the world's Green parties; the political movement that grew up in Iceland after the great crash of 2008; and the global climate justice movement.

In Kerala, for example, a series of elected, non-charismatic (in a positive sense) left-of-center governments over the past fifty years have raised the quality of life—whether measured in terms of nutrition, health, life span, access to food and shelter, and literacy education—to standards that are superior to elsewhere in India and would be the object of envy in most of the world. They have done this despite a lack of monetary resources and a low percapita GNP, and even with deep structural unemployment, because they have been pushed from below by strong, independent social movements in civil society, of workers, women, and lower castes. This synergetic relationship has succeeded in forging and maintaining relatively equitable, more participatory conditions of life for the more than 30 million people who live there, even in periods when the left has not been in power.[51]

The world's Green parties also embody the new political cultures of opposition, sometimes themselves operating to bridge the divide between those who seek to take state power and those who seek to transform the very nature of power. Though they are far from power in many places—notably in the United States and the UK—and have made truly invidious compromises when in government, as in Germany,[52] they also hint at the powerful combination of social movement dynamism from below and a new kind of party organization. Moreover, they are transnational in vision and organization in a way that other parties, including those on the left, are not.

Iceland is now involved in a hopeful political experiment, ever since the raucous banging of pots and pans in popular street protests in January 2009 forced the right-of-center government responsible for the precipitous collapse of Iceland's banks to yield power to a new governing coalition of socialists, democrats, greens, and the left, who were affirmed in power in a general election in April 2009. In the face of a horrific economic crisis, the creative actions of the Left–Green Movement and Social Democratic Alliance government, and the many networks that pressure and support them, have produced solutions such as the 2009 referendum in which 98 percent of the population rejected the previous government's agreement to repay the foreign debt of the failed banks, another indication of this new political culture. The fragility of the new situation was laid bare in the April 2013 elections, however, which returned the center-right to power.[53]

[51] Richard W. Franke and Barbara H. Chasin, *Kerala: Radical Reform as Development in an Indian State*, San Francisco: The Institute for Food and Development Policy, 1994, Patrick Heller, *The Labor of Development: Workers and the Transformation of Capitalism in Kerala, India*, Ithaca: Cornell University Press, 1999.

[52] Joachim Jachnow, "Green Trajectories," *New Left Review*, 81 (May/June 2013), pp. 95–117.

[53] Robert Wade and Silla Sigurgeirsdottir, "Lessons for Iceland," *New Left*

Two thousand eleven ended with the impact of Occupy on the UN climate negotiations when activists temporarily but very publicly "occupied" the main hallway to the negotiations in Durban, South Africa, in direct actions that were carried forward again at the end of 2012 in Doha, Qatar, and in 2013 with a massive walkout of civil society in Warsaw, Poland. The negotiations themselves produced the expected non-ambition and irresponsible delay, but a growing coalition of progressive countries inside the negotiations, young activists who raised their voices and built their own strong ties, and the global climate justice organizations that stood and sat with them in an occupation of the corridors worked together to deliver a different outcome than the triumphalist official one or the pessimistic verdict of some movement leaders.[54] The actions and communication processes established between the inside and the outside continue to work together for a fair and binding treaty to lower greenhouse gas emissions, perhaps the most pressing issue of our time.

Conclusion

The Arab Spring shares important characteristics with each of these new types of progressive experiments. In Tunisia and Egypt it achieved its first victories non-violently, while the Libyan and Syrian cases have involved the use of arms because their respective dictators irrationally thought they could stop the people from being heard. In the first three cases, and presumably in post-Assad Syria, democratic polities are in place. A crucial difference is that the winning political parties in these

---

Review, 65 (Sep.–Oct. 2010), pp. 5–29, Christophe Chataigne, "Iceland and the Saucepan Revolution," *Socialist Review*, Mar. 2009, http://www.socialistreview.org.uk/article.php?articlenumber=10735, Paul Krugman, "The Path Not Taken," *New York Times*, 27 Oct. 2011, http://www.nytimes.com/2011/10/28/opinion/krugman-the-path-not-taken.html, Rebecca Solnit, "News from Nowhere: Iceland's Polite Dystopia," *Harper's Magazine*, Oct. 2008, http://harpers.org/archive/2008/10/news-from-nowhere/, Andri Snaer Magnason, *Dreamland: A Self-Help Manual*, London: Citizen-Press, 2008.

[54] John Foran and Richard Widick, "Breaking the Stalemate on Climate Change: The Long Road from Durban," *Contexts: A Journal of the American Sociological Association*, 12, 2 (2013), pp. 34–9.

first elections did not always voice the sentiments or respond to the desires of the people who came out into every capital square, as the clashes between the Morsi government and a youthful section of Egyptian civil society showed in the course of 2012, inadvertently providing the opening for the tragic military takeover of July 2013. Clearly, it will take time for these open-ended revolutions to blossom and reach their full potential. Important to this process will be the articulation of powerful political cultures based on participatory (not formal, representative, elite-controlled) democracy and on economic alternatives challenging the neo-liberal capitalist globalization that created the conditions for their flowering in the first place.

Hamid Dabashi, the first great theorist of the Arab Spring, proposes that we consider the events as a new kind of revolution, as "open-ended revolutions":

> That ever-expanding public space and political participation are precisely what inform my idea of open-ended revolution, in which the distinction no longer exists between the French [Revolution's] (social) and American [Revolution's] (political) model, in Arendt's terms. But in fact the fusion of the two will have created a third model, closer to what Trotsky meant by "permanent revolution" (and that we hear in the Egyptian slogan *al-Thwarah al-Mustamarrah*), but this time in a more gradual, systematic, and grounded manner in which not just the working class but also women and students—that is, the two social formations that expand the economic into public space—will be integral to the revolutionary unfolding.[55]

It is entirely possible that the future of radical social change lies at the various intersections of deeply democratic social movements and equally diverse and committed political coalitions. The post-2011 democracies of Tunisia, Egypt, and Libya are young, and it will take time to fashion new parties that embrace the anti-authoritarianism, social-media facility, and radical promise of the occupants of squares named Tahrir, Mohammad Bouazizi, Pearl, Green (now Martyrs'), and elsewhere. If this happens, a new era may open in Middle East politics.

The people in each of these places—the most radical ones, the younger ones, the most savvy—rejected the ruling bargain altogether. They did not seek to renegotiate anybody's ruling bargain. And they succeeded. Or at least they have not failed. And, like their 2011 counterparts everywhere, they are not done yet.

[55] Dabashi, *The Arab Spring*, p. 247.

3

THE ARAB STATE AND SOCIAL CONTESTATION

Nadine Sika

Since the formation of the modern Arab state, Arab regimes have consistently tried to gain hegemony over both the political and the public spheres. Regional regimes were able to institutionalize their authoritarian rule through the creation of successful ruling bargains that lasted until the end of the first decade of the twenty-first century. Though the developmental paths of most Arab states were similar, the Arab uprisings have led to substantial differences in terms of the outcomes for the states concerned, and this merits further analysis. Why did Tunisia and Egypt encounter less violence during the apogee of their uprisings, for example, while Libya's leader was ousted through civil war and foreign intervention? Why is Syria undergoing a civil war? Why were the regimes in Bahrain and Yemen able to contain the uprisings, albeit to differing degrees, and what role did violence play in the outcomes for each of these countries?

This chapter argues that the divergent political outcomes in the post-uprisings era stem from the similarities and differences between regional countries in terms of the Arab state-formation process. By focusing on three countries, namely Egypt, Tunisia, and Syria, the chapter argues that the nature of the states concerned, and the extent to which the regimes were able to hegemonize both civil and political society, in addition to their use of state repression, played a decisive role in producing these different outcomes.

The chapter begins with an examination of the state-formation process of Arab states. It then goes on to analyze the economic liberalization projects initiated by Arab regimes from the 1990s onwards, and the impact these had on the different regimes' ruling bargains. Finally, the chapter turns to state–society relations in order to understand how large segments of the Arab population came to be excluded from the political process over the course of the past two decades, a factor which led to the subsequent rise of social movements that sought to challenge the authority of the state.

State Formation in the Arab World

Scholarly debates concerning the origins of Arab state formation are manifold. Some scholars attribute state formation in the region, especially the territorial boundaries of Arab states, to foreign interventionism, while others attribute state formation to the internal dynamics between rulers, tribes, and societies.[1] This distinction is particularly notable when looking at North African countries, albeit with the exception of Libya, whose state-formation process, though influenced by the colonial era, had already acquired functioning bureaucracies and centralized state systems prior to the colonial period. Hence, while the colonial era had a profound influence on these states, they had already developed a sense of statehood in the period prior to this. According to Nazih Ayoubi, in countries like Egypt and Tunisia, "the state comes forth out of an organic, internal process of social and cultural integration ... It emerges as a relatively autonomous entity that represents (and harmonizes) the entire society, not only the victorious bourgeoisie."[2] On the other hand, in the Levant, and especially in countries like Lebanon and Syria, where

[1] See, for example, Ilya Harik, "The Origins of the Arab State System" and Bahgat Korany, "Alien and Besieged Yet Here to Stay: The Contradictions of the Arab Territorial State," in Ghassan Salame (ed.), *The Foundations of the Arab State vol. 1*, London: Croom Helm, 1987.

[2] Nazih Ayubi, *Over-Stating the Arab State: Politics and Society in the Middle East*, London: I.B. Tauris, 1995, pp. 108–9.

the territorial state emerged as a Western construct, the "state is merely an arbiter among conflicting groups. It does not integrate or harmonize, but simply tries to neutralize classes, nationalities and ethnicities. This is done not in an 'organic' way that leads to the emergence of a 'nation,' but through the instruments of central rule such as the army and the bureaucracy. The state rules through pacifying the communities or balancing them (turning them) against each other."[3] The Arab states of the Persian Gulf, in contrast, can be viewed as "tribal states."[4] In these countries the state-formation process can largely be attributed to "political tribalism," where a contract emerged between merchant tribes who needed to protect their commercial activities and their trade both on land and sea. Khaldun al Naqib argues that this bargain was important for state-building, which secured the protection of trade by linking it with the tribal inlands, and subjugated the urban population to the authoritarian power of the tribal families.[5] The function of the state in this system is to "reproduce patriarchy, tribalism and ethnic domination in ways that are as compatible as possible with the preservation of an oil-exporting economy and the circulation of its revenues."[6]

These characteristics are also important when looking at the distinction between "regime" and "state." A "regime" represents both the formal and informal organization of political power and its relations with society at large—it determines who attains access to the thrust of political power and who is excluded. Regimes are normally less permanent structures than states.[7] A "state" is an authoritative set of institutions with sovereignty over a territory and the legitimate use of force.[8] The

[3] Ibid. p. 109.

[4] Bahgat Korany et al., *The Foreign Policies of Arab States: The Challenge of Change*, Boulder, CO: Westview Press, 1991, cited in Ayubi, *Over-Stating the Arab State*, p. 109.

[5] Khaldun Al Naqib, *Al-Mujtama wa al-Dawla fi al-Khalij wa al-Jazira al-Arabiyya* [Society and the State in the Gulf and the Arabian Peninsula], Beirut: CAUS, 1987, quoted in Ayubi, *Over-Stating the Arab State*, p. 126.

[6] Ayubi, *Over-Stating the Arab State*, p. 224.

[7] Robert Fishman, "Rethinking State and Regime: Southern Europe's Transition to Democracy," *World Politics*, 42, 3 (1990), pp. 422–40.

[8] This definition is primarily based on the Weberian definition of the state. For more analysis of the state see, for instance, Peter Evens, Dietrich Rueschemeyer, and Theda Skocpol (eds), *Bringing the State Back In*, Cambridge: Cambridge University Press, 1985.

idea of state authority is synonymous with legitimacy. The state has political legitimacy due to the fact that even those groups which oppose a given regime ultimately aspire to control the state and benefit from the legitimate use of force. While regimes may rise and fall within a certain state, states should consequently be more durable.

When looking at the past three decades in the Arab region, Egypt and Tunisia are cases where authoritarian regimes have unsuccessfully attempted to control state power. Two factors serve to explain this failure. First, due to the historical legacy of the independence of these states from colonial rule, regime efforts that aimed to control the state frequently gave rise to popular discontent. Second, and as a consequence of the first, citizens within these states failed to recognize the legitimacy and capabilities of the regimes involved, giving rise to a crisis of legitimacy.[9] However, this legitimacy crisis was confined to the "regimes" and not the "state." On the other hand, in Syria, Jordan, Libya, and the Gulf states, there is almost no distinction between the regime and the state. The rulers of these countries have managed to control both the coercive and non-coercive powers of the state in such a way so as to make the distinction between state and regime obsolete. Syria was able to do so through its extensive control over the coercive apparatus of the state and its use of sectarianism as a tool for governing. The Persian Gulf states have managed to do so through their dependence on both soft coercive measures and their redistributive roles within the economy through rents. In these states, when a crisis of legitimacy occurs, it is bound to affect the "state" itself and not merely the "regime," as in the North African cases.

State vs Regime

State expansion was pervasive in developing nations following the end of the colonial era. There were pressing needs to develop and maintain security and to establish control over the "nation state." Newly established and decolonized states also needed to attain economic prosperity and social welfare for their citizenry.[10] These needs were also present in

[9] See, for instance, Ghassan Salame, "'Strong' and 'Weak' States: A Qualified Return to the Muqaddimah," in Giacomo Luciani (ed.), *The Arab State*, Berkeley, CA: University of California Press, 1990, pp. 29–64.

[10] Roger Owen, *State, Power and Politics in the Making of the Modern Middle East*, 3rd edn, London: Routledge, 2004.

the Arab world. However, some factors were specific to the region, such as the need to create land reform programs in the 1950s, the need to expand the public sector, and the exodus of foreign officials and businessmen from Egypt and North Africa after the end of the colonial era.[11]

Egypt: The Development of a Strong Regime at the Expense of the State

The expansion of regime power in Egypt began with Nasser's ascent to power and gathered pace after the evacuation of British troops from the Suez Canal in 1955. The regime increased the strength of the police and the security forces, and enlarged the capacity of the armed forces. Economic reform was also introduced through land reform, the construction of the Aswan high dam, and development of the Helwan Iron and Steel Complex. Large-scale nationalization processes were also introduced which stimulated a state-led developmental process based on the nationalization of private enterprises from the 1960s onwards.[12] Nasser also introduced laws designed to further consolidate his popularity. He guaranteed state employment to all university and high school graduates, and introduced national insurance policies that facilitated the development of a new social contract.[13] He guaranteed economic rights to the working class and the peasantry.[14]

As far as the political process was concerned, the Revolutionary Command Council (RCC) was developed in 1952 as a mobilizational organization that worked as a leading political party. In 1956 the RCC was replaced by another type of mobilizational organization, the National Union, as the dominant political party, before this function was eventually assumed by the Arab Socialist Union (ASU) in 1962.[15]

[11] Ibid. p. 24.

[12] Ibid.

[13] Maye Kassem, *Egyptian Politics the Dynamics of Authoritarian Rule*, Boulder, CO: Lynne Rienner, 2004.

[14] Raymond Bush, *Economic Crisis and Politics of Reform in Egypt*, Boulder, CO: Westview Press, 1999; and Kassem, *Egyptian Politics*.

[15] Aley Eddin Hilal, *al-nizam al-siyassi al-misry: 1981–2010 bayn 'irth al-maady wa 'afaq al-mustaqbl* [The Egyptian Political System: 1981–2010—Between the Legacy of the Past and Future Aspirations], Cairo: Al-Dar al-Misriyya al-Libnaniyya, 2010 [Arabic].

Judges belonging to the Supreme Constitutional Court were coerced into joining the ASU, which ensured the loyalty of the three branches of government to the Nasserist project. Thus the regime retained political power and influence by developing a dominant political party system under which all opposition would be suppressed.[16] Nasser increased the regime's power, along with its ability to control national resources, by increasing the size of the bureaucracy. However, independent institutions were either co-opted or dissolved altogether by the Nasser regime.

Personalization of Power under Sadat and Mubarak

After coming to power in 1970, Sadat strengthened the executive office vis-à-vis all other institutions, including the military, in the 1971 constitution.[17] He liberalized the political system and legalized political parties. He established the National Democratic Party (NDP), a centrist party, and assumed its directorship. Members of the ASU left the party and joined the newly established NDP. The presidential office became the strongest institution in the state.

According to Joshua Stacher, "Mubarak inherited Sadat's engineered creation and doubled down by reinforcing the presidency's hierarchical command over the state's institutions. The bodies were hollowed out and existed to implement the presidential consensus in a top-down fashion."[18] These measures placed Egypt's social and political institutions in a weakened position for five decades, with the president retaining power over the executive, the legislature, and the judiciary. The president could also declare a state of emergency, was the commander-in-chief of the armed forces, proposed laws to the parliament, issued decrees, promulgated laws, and had the right to veto any laws proposed by the legislature. He nominated the prosecutor general, the president of the Court of Cassation, and the president of the Constitutional Court.[19] By centralizing all power in the presidential office, he increased the power of

[16] Enid Hill, *Mahkama! Studies in the Egyptian Legal System*, London: Ithaca Press, 1971.

[17] Joshua Stacher, *Adaptable Autocrats: Regime Power in Egypt and Syria*, Stanford: Stanford University Press, 2012.

[18] Ibid. p. 12.

[19] Nathalie Bernard-Maugiron, "The 2007 Constitutional Amendments in Egypt, and their Implications on the Balance of Power," *Arab Law Quarterly*, 22 (2008), pp. 397–417.

the regime, making it impossible to open the economy to the neo-liberal project without cronyism and nepotism.

As one of the leading protagonists of the neo-liberal economic project, the behind-the-scenes rise of Mubarak's son Gamal to power meant that it was impossible for businesses to flourish without having contacts with the presidential office or the president's associates. Thus the judiciary, the civil service, political parties, the rule of law, and Egypt's economic institutions were weakened while the relative importance of personal relationships increased. The most successful entrepreneurs were associated with members of the political elite, like Ahmad Ezz, who was initially a steel tycoon but later became the secretary of organizational affairs for the ruling National Democratic Party, and subsequently a parliamentarian. Cronyism and nepotism infested the ruling political party, with Mubarak occupying the highest office as the chairman of the NDP, followed by his son who was the party's deputy secretary general. Other party members were also associates of the Mubaraks. Not surprisingly, when both Mubaraks resigned from these positions on 5 February 2011, the party soon began to disintegrate and was dissolved the following April.

From the 1990s onwards, the size and capacity of the state security apparatus, especially of the police force, increased extensively in response to domestic terrorism, and later to the threat of international terrorism in the 2000s. The national budget allocated to the Interior Ministry increased substantially, and Mubarak hailed the police force for its role in reducing terrorist attacks. Egypt also received increased international support, especially from the United States, due to its close alignment with Washington in the so-called "war on terror."[20] At the same time, the country experienced an increase in human rights abuses. Samer Soliman argues that the growing influence of the police force through the 1990s was epitomized by the change in the Interior Ministry's motto from "The police in the service of the people" to "the police and the people: in the service of the law." Although this change in language was intended to place the public and the police on an equal footing, in practice the police consistently used force against civilians, especially

[20] See, for example, Eva Bellin, "Reconsidering the Robustness of Authoritarianism in the Middle East: Lessons from the Arab Spring," *Comparative Politics*, 44, 2 (2012), pp. 127–49.

during demonstrations, where large numbers of political and social activists were detained.[21] The regime and international actors turned a blind eye to unlawful detentions and other human rights abuses. In addition, the state security department in the Ministry of Interior gained expansive powers. However, according to Soliman, this department was important in securing the regime, not the state. Throughout the 2000s, the department consistently went after political activists and terrorists, while simultaneously refraining from detaining corrupt public officials who were tied to the regime apparatus. Though this contributed to the strengthening of the regime, it also undermined state capacity.[22]

The increasing power of the Interior Ministry and the police force came at the expense of the military and the Ministry of Defense. Moreover, the growing power of the capitalist class, which was associated with Gamal Mubarak, came at the expense of the military technocratic establishment, which had been at the heart of the regime's ruling apparatus during the 1980s and 1990s. Hence it is hardly surprising that the army refrained from using force against civilians when the Ministry of Interior was unable to suppress the uprising on 25 January 2011 due to the unprecedented numbers of mobilized individuals. The decision not to use force instantly enhanced the image of the Defense Ministry as the protector of the popular will. In the 1970s and the 1980s, when the military had intervened to suppress unrest in the streets, it had done so in order to preserve its own power within the regime. Two decades later, with the increasing marginalization of the military, the growing illegitimacy of the Mubarak regime, and his crony capitalist entourage, it did not take the military long to decide to turn against a regime that had favored the Interior Ministry and the state security department over the armed forces. Even though state capacity had been undermined by Mubarak, the military did not foresee the end of his regime as posing a threat to its power. On the contrary, removing an ailing autocrat, along with his crony capitalists, strengthened their position and the territoriality of the state.

After the ousting of Mubarak, and with the emergence of the first free and fairly fair elections, the Muslim Brotherhood's presidential contes-

[21] Samer Soliman, *The Autumn of Dictatorship: Fiscal Crisis and Political Change in Egypt under Mubarak*, Stanford: Stanford University Press, 2011, Kindle edn, location 1330.

[22] Ibid.

tant, Mohamed Morsi won the popular vote. Nevertheless, within six months, Morsi had sidelined the judiciary by giving himself extra judicial powers and had ratified a highly contested Islamist constitution. The constitution ensured that the army's interests were preserved by excluding parliamentary oversight over the army's budget, and it also contained provisions that enabled civilians to be tried in military tribunals.[23] Morsi issued a decree on 22 November 2012 which ordered the dismissal of Egypt's then Attorney General, Mahmud Abdel Meguid. In his place, he installed Talaat Abdallah, who was associated with the Brotherhood. He also moved towards a "Brotherhoodization" of Egyptian politics by forming a Brotherhood cabinet to hegemonize the political sphere. With rising public discontent against Brotherhood rule—and with Morsi threatening the interests of the military and the Egyptian state by implying that he would support *jihad* in Syria—the military directly intervened to oust Morsi from power following massive public demonstrations in June and early July 2013. The ruling bargain that has since emerged, as reflected in the 2014 constitution, does not appear to be more democratic than previous ruling bargains in Egypt as the constitution ultimately grants far more political power to the military than the president.

Tunisia: Strong Presidency, Weak Institutions

A national bureaucracy was established in Tunisia soon after decolonization. In 1956 the regime crafted a Constitution that gave the presidency paramount powers. As with the Egyptian presidency, the president held veto power over all laws enacted by the parliament and had the right to issue decrees, and to appoint all high-level military and civilian personnel.[24] In the 1960s, the Neo-Destour Party was used to ensure political and institutional stability, distribute patronage, and enhance cooperative networks among the elite.[25] After decolonization, the state bureaucracy seized all agricultural land that had previously been owned by the

[23] Joshua Stacher, "Why the Generals Back Morsi: The Invisible Hand in Egypt's Government," *Foreign Affairs*, http://www.foreignaffairs.com/articles/138623/joshua-stacher/why-the-generals-back-morsi

[24] Bahgat Korany, "The Maghrib," in Tareq Ismael and Jacqueline Ismael (eds), *Politics and Government in the Middle East and North Africa*, Miami: Florida International University Press, 1991, pp. 513–37.

[25] Lisa Anderson, "The State in the Middle East and North Africa," *Comparative Politics*, 20, 1 (1987), pp. 1–18.

French. This served to increase state power and capacity, especially in rural areas, and established an important industrial base through import-substitution policies.[26] Throughout his tenure as president, Habib Bourguiba personalized his authoritarian rule and weakened most other institutions. He developed his hegemony through the Neo-Destour party and through state nationalism.

After ousting Bourguiba through a peaceful coup d'état in 1987, Zine El Abidine Ben Ali was able to expand his presidential power under a façade of political reforms. One way in which he did this was to establish the Rally for Constitutional Democracy party, which was the ruling party, virtually merged with the state.[27] According to Sadiki, the Tunisian state:

> has not yet transcended the political syndrome of Bourguiba's "first republic": political singularity ... Under Bin Ali [*sic*], Tunisia gives the impression of having moved a long way from single party rule and exclusivity. Yet the country's latest two elections have done very little in terms of tilting the balance of power towards society or away from the ruling party.[28]

Ben Ali developed institutions that were tied directly to the presidential office and were highly personalistic. For instance, he used a "sovereignty fund" to create a parallel security apparatus, which was run from the presidential palace rather than the Interior Ministry.[29] As was the case in Egypt, the state security apparatus gained a great deal of power during the 1990s and the 2000s, aided by growing international concerns over terrorism. Ben Ali had extensive power and control over the party, the state institutions, and the security apparatus. According to Roger Owen, the number of police personnel totaled between 80,000 and 133,000 in a country with only 10 million people. The size of the secret services in the country also increased during Ben Ali's tenure, with almost 10 percent of the population being employed in the coercive apparatus of the regime.[30] Ben Ali was adept at using his personal con-

26 Owen, *State Power and Politics*, p. 26.
27 Larbi Sadiki, "Tunisia: Democracy by Non-Democratic Means," *British Journal of Middle Eastern Studies*, 29, 1 (2002), p. 63.
28 Ibid.
29 Christopher Alexander, "Back from the Democratic Brink: Authoritarianism and Civil Society in Tunisia," *Middle East Report* (Oct.–Dec. 1997), pp. 34–8.
30 Roger Owen, *The Rise and Fall of Arab Presidents for Life*, Cambridge, MA: Harvard University Press, 2012, Kindle edn.

nections and power over the police apparatus against opponents of his rule. When the founder of the Tunisia Free University published an online book that was critical of the Ben Ali family, for example, the Tunisian regime responded by closing the university.

As in Egypt and Syria, the regime also controlled the neo-liberal economy, which exhibited extensive levels of cronyism and nepotism based on the personal relationships between businessmen and the president. The process of privatization and liberalization led to the emergence of a wealthy class of Ben Ali's associates, who had direct personal links to Ben Ali.[31] This in turn created a system where state resources were used for the personal patronage system developed by Ben Ali. Public land was sold to crony capitalists, and licenses for public services and TV stations were given to Ben Ali's clients. These groups based their power on the contacts they held with the head of state, developing personalistic rule in the state apparatus.[32] The family of Ben Ali's wife became the country's most powerful business tycoons. Hence, the process of de-institutionalization and the control exerted over the executive branch by a small section of the elite led to a weakening of Tunisian state institutions and an increase in the power of the authoritarian regime.

The role of the Tunisian army in national politics had been subject to marginalization ever since the Bourguiba era, and this process only increased during Ben Ali's tenure in office. As a result, when public mobilization was at its apex in January 2011, the military did not intervene to kill civilians since the military command was already distinct from the ruling elite—the military consequently chose to abandon Ben Ali and to side with the public instead.[33]

Syria: Dynamics of Strong Institutions in a Weak State

In the Levant, state formation was a direct consequence of the artificial borders created out of the bargaining between Britain, France, and the

[31] Béatrice Hibou and John Hulsey, "Domination and Control in Tunisia: Economic Levers for the Exercise of Authoritarianism," *Review of African Political Economy*, 33 (2006), pp. 185–206.

[32] Owen, *The Rise and Fall of Arab Presidents*, location 1375 Kindle edn.

[33] See, for instance, Eva Bellin, "Reconsidering the Robustness of Authoritarianism in the Middle East."

Ottoman Empire.[34] Thus it is hardly surprising that the state-formation process in countries such as Syria and Lebanon share similar, if distinctive, features when compared to the North African states. After gaining independence in 1946, Syria lacked a political center and the structure and institutions of a state—it was not even clear where the geographic borders of the country lay.[35] The scope of state capacity increased as a result of the short union between Egypt and Syria in the United Arab Republic from 1958 to 1961, especially insofar as the police force, the armed forces, and the public sector were concerned. Land reform was also introduced. However, a large amount of land was not redistributed but remained under state control, thus providing the central government with an opportunity to deepen its power in rural areas by reducing the size and powers of the old landed elite and replacing it with a system of police, ministerial, and Baath party control.[36]

Central planning and state ownership of different segments of the economy prevailed until 1969. However, political uncertainty was the rule rather than the exception, with fifteen coups d'état between 1946 and 1970.[37] When he assumed the country's presidency in 1971, Hafez Assad promoted pan-Arabism through the Baath party as a way of coalescing the country's diverse identities into one "imagined community."[38] In so doing, Assad relied on a strengthened Baath party in order to stabilize the country. He freed the party from its populist ideology and expanded its social base. Assad also introduced limited economic liberalization measures while maintaining strong ties with the military and intelligence services.[39] He created a People's Assembly, whose members were appointed by Assad or by his advisors, who in turn were mainly drawn from the Baath party, the Arab Socialist Union, the Socialist Unionists Movement, and the Syrian Communist Party. It was this section of the elite that subsequently formed the Progressive National Front in 1971, which in turn crafted the country's constitution.

[34] Ayubi, *Over-Stating the Arab State*, p. 110.
[35] Stacher, *Adaptable Autocrats*, p. 49.
[36] Owen, *State Power and Politics*, p. 26.
[37] Stacher, *Adaptable Autocrats*, p. 49.
[38] See Stacher, *Adaptable Autocrats*, and Benedict Anderson, *Imagined Communities: Reflections on the Origin and Spread of Nationalism*, New York: Verso, 1983.
[39] Stacher, *Adaptable Autocrats*, p. 58.

The president was given extensive constitutional powers, including the authority to dissolve the Assembly and to assume its legislative functions,[40] and to nominate high court judges as well as provincial governors.[41] The Baath party remained an important pillar of the regime, with both Assad and the party depending on each another.[42] In a similar vein, Assad strengthened the power of the military and the security services, both of which became synonymous with political stability in the country. Nevertheless, Assad's close circle of trusted allies consisted mainly of fellow Alawites. A second circle was made-up of non-Alawite Baathist officers, mostly Sunnis, followed by a third circle comprising the officer corps.[43] Eva Bellin argues that due to the organization of the military along patrimonial lines, the military elite was directly linked to the regime. "The military elite [is] deeply invested in the regime's survival and perceives regime change as possibly ruinous. Under such conditions, the military leadership has significant reason to consider using lethal force against civilians in the name of defending regime survival."[44] Thus in 1982, troops following orders of Rifaat Assad, Hafez Assad's brother, massacred tens of thousands of civilians associated with the Muslim Brotherhood in Hama.[45]

Bashar Assad: The Path from Strong Institutions to Patrimonialism

When he succeeded his father in 2000, Bashar Assad maintained his grip on the authoritarian structure of the state, and retained his close contacts with the military and with the Baath party during the early years of his tenure. However, with time, Bashar Assad alienated the party cadres from power and patronage. As Bellin observes, "Much of the military elite is Alawi, whereas the majority of the rank and file as well as the general population of the country is Sunni."[46] During the

[40] Fred Lawson, "Syria," in Michelle Penner Angrist (ed.), *Politics and Society in the Contemporary Middle East*, Boulder, CO: Lynne Rienner, 2010, pp. 411–34.
[41] Ibid. p. 413.
[42] Stacher, *Adaptable Autocrats*, p. 58.
[43] Ibid. p. 90.
[44] Bellin, "Reconsidering the Robustness of Authoritarianism in the Middle East," p. 133.
[45] Ibid.
[46] Ibid.

Syrian uprising the Assad regime relied wholly on Alawites, fearing military defections by Sunnis.[47] These measures intensified sectarianism, precipitating more defections from the rank-and-file Sunnis, and increasing fears among Alawite and Christian citizens of political revenge in the post-Assad era.

Bashar Assad adopted a more liberal economic outlook than his father.[48] As a result, nepotism and corruption became widespread within the president's inner-circle of family and friends. Thus Assad's cousin Ramy Makhlouf emerged as the most powerful business tycoon in the country, while Makhlouf's brother, Hafez, served as the chief of intelligence in Damascus.[49] Similarly, Assad's brother, Maher, was commander of the Presidential Guard and a member of the Baath Party Central Committee, while his brother in-law, Assef Shawkat, was Deputy Minister of Defense.[50]

Due to the Assads' reliance on institutional power for support, Syrian state institutions appeared to be stronger than in Egypt, at least until the early 2000s. This was especially true with regard to the armed forces and the Baath party. But this did not prevent those within the inner circle from using other state institutions to their own personal advantage. Makhlouf, for instance, is said to have consistently manipulated the judicial system to his own advantage, and often allegedly used the intelligence services to blackmail his business rivals.[51] This served to increase patronage and corruption and channeled loyalties away from the Baath party in the direction of the Assad family. In the meantime, the peasant and worker unions, along with the party apparatus, were consistently marginalized and denied state funds, and were perceived as obstacles to economic reform.[52] These endeavors increased the personalization of the regime, unlike the earlier institutionalization of patronage to the Baath

[47] Ibid.

[48] Tarek Ismael and Jacqueline Ismael, *Government and Politics of the Contemporary Middle East: Continuity and Change*, London: Routledge, 2011.

[49] Anthony Shadid, "Syrian Elite to Fight Protests to 'the End,'" *New York Times*, 10 May 2011: www.nytimes.com/2011/05/11/world/middleeast/11makhlouf.html?_r=1&pagewanted=all

[50] Esther Pan, "Syria's Leaders," Council on Foreign Relations: http://www.cfr.org/syria/syrias-leaders, p. 9085.

[51] Ibid.

[52] Raymond Hinnebusch, "Syria: From 'Authoritarian Upgrading' to Revolution?" *International Affairs*, 88 (2012), pp. 95–113.

party during Hafez Assad's tenure. With the first waves of uprisings in Syria, the inner circle of the army consequently decided to crush the revolutionaries as they feared for their own survival, while some of the alienated rank and file defected.

The Crisis of Legitimacy and Authoritarianism

By the end of 2010, all Arab countries had what could be classified as authoritarian political systems. They all had limited political pluralism, with no guiding ideology, no intensive or extensive political mobilization, except at certain points within the political development process.[53] A leader or a small group of individuals exercised political power with ill-defined limits.[54] The idea of "limited pluralism" within authoritarian regimes has an important connotation in the Arab context. Arab regimes were determined to "institutionalize the political participation of the limited number of independent groups or institutions and even encourage their emergence without, however, leaving any doubt that the rulers ultimately define which groups they will allow to exist and under what conditions."[55] In this sense, opposition political parties were encouraged to exist. However, their primary purpose was a controlled opening of political space. Opposition and dominant political parties are an important tool for structuring and developing the political process and ensuring its effectiveness. They are able to expand civic participation, but they are also important in terms of political stability and development[56] in that they function in support of an authoritarian leader while at the same time marginalizing opposition forces in different areas. Ruling parties can settle differences in a power struggle and regulate competition between different elites. Therefore, loyal members of an elite become part of the dominant political party and consequently of the Cabinet, the military, or the police.[57] These parties assure the elites that

[53] Juan Linz, *Totalitarian and Authoritarian Regimes*, Boulder, CO: Lynne Rienner, 2000, p. 161.

[54] Ibid. p. 159.

[55] Ibid. p. 161.

[56] Samuel Huntington, *Political Order in Changing Societies*, New Haven: Yale University Press, 1968.

[57] Jay Ulfelder, "Contentious Collective Action and the Breakdown of Authoritarian Regimes," *International Political Science Review*, 23 (2009), pp. 311–34.

they will always have an opportunity to advance their political, social, and economic ambitions.

Apart from dominating the political sphere, Arab regimes have also dominated the public sphere. In authoritarian regimes, the ruling elite dominates the public sphere, including the media and civil society.[58] The result is an erosion of the public sphere: civil society's role in rationally assessing public policies diminishes where the public sphere loses its power to oversee the state.[59]

Co-opting Friends and Foes

Opposition political parties were tolerated in the three regimes discussed in this chapter. However, such parties were an integral part of the ruling regimes rather than a means for contesting political power. Some Arab scholars have gone so far as to define political parties as part of civil society rather than political society.[60] Thus rather than becoming venues for mobilizing citizens against the ruling elites, opposition political parties have demobilized citizens from political participation. Political parties were detached from the population at large; they had no mass following, especially in the cases of Tunisia and Egypt, where opposition political parties were tolerated to a greater extent than in Syria. After the mass uprisings in Egypt and Tunisia in 2011, many new political parties emerged, yet these new parties are still embroiled in elite conflicts and do not enjoy mass support. Islamist parties have proven to be more effective in mobilizing citizens to vote in their favor, and as the secular political parties in Egypt and Tunisia are engaged in power struggles among themselves, they have yet to provide political or economic alter-

[58] The public sphere, as defined by Jürgen Habermas, *The Structural Transformation of the Public Sphere: An Inquiry into a Category of Bourgois Society*, trans. Thomas Burger, Cambridge: MIT Press, 1991, is the free access realm between the family and the workplace, where citizens gather and organize to discuss the common good and public affairs.

[59] Sami Zubeida, "Capitalism, Democracy, the 'Public Sphere' and Globalization," in E. Kienle (ed.), *Politics from Above, Politics from Below: The Middle East in the Age of Economic Reform*, London: Saqi, 2003, pp. 21–32.

[60] See, for instance, Mustapha K. al-Sayyid, "The Concept of Civil Society and the Arab World," in Rex Brynen, Bahgat Korany and Paul Noble (eds), *Political Liberalization and Democratization in the Arab World: Theoretical Perspectives Volume 1*, Boulder, CO: Lynne Rienner, 1995.

natives to Islamist rule. For instance, in Egypt, when the Islamist president-elect hastened a referendum for an Islamist constitution, the secular opposition criticized the constitution and mobilized citizens to demonstrate against it, but they were unable to agree on another draft that would serve as an alternative. The Islamist parties, on the other hand, are more experienced and entrenched socially due to the work they have conducted in the field over many decades, which has enabled them to garner mass support by disseminating material goods to the poor before elections. They also have a substantial social presence, especially in mosques. By using the power of the pulpit, they are able to preach the importance of Islam as "*din wa dawla*" (that is Islam as inseperable from politics).

Civil society flourished in the Arab states from the 1990s onwards, with almost 130,000 organizations being created during this period. These organizations have been used by Arab regimes to control the public sphere. Arab governments, mainly in Egypt, Tunisia, Syria, and other middle- and low-income countries, have promoted civil society organizations with the aim of developing social services, rather than as a means for promoting the public's voice and fostering political accountability—civil society was simply used to fill the gap left by the government's inability to provide education, healthcare and other social services, especially in Egypt and Tunisia. At the same time, those civil society organizations that promote transparency or human rights were weakened by state harassment and restrictive laws.[61] Arab regimes also have a long history of intervening in trade unions in order to further control civil society. For instance, Baath members in Syria created and led civil society organizations that incorporated many leaders from trade unions, peasants, women, and the youth. Professional doctors, engineers, and lawyers' associations were often also controlled by the Baath.[62]

Social and cultural institutions were also subjected to state control. Two important cases included the Islamic institutions of al-Azhar in

[61] See, for instance, Clement Moore Henry and Robert Springborg, *Globalization and the Politics of Development in the Middle East*, 2nd edn, Cambridge: Cambridge University Press, 2010, and Amy Hawthorne, "Middle Eastern Democracy: Is Civil Society the Answer?" Carnegie Paper, 44, Mar. 2004: http://carnegieendowment.org /2004/03/01/middle-eastern-democracy-is-civil-society-answer/115

[62] Raymond Hinnebusch, "State and Civil Society in Syria," *The Middle East Journal*, 47, 2 (Spring 1993), pp. 243–57.

Egypt and Zaytuna in Tunisia. The first was used by the Egyptian regime to bolster the regime's legitimacy and power vis-à-vis Islamist movements. Nasser ensured that al-Azhar became part of the state by placing it under the jurisdiction of the Ministry of Endowments. The president nominated the grand shaykh of al-Azhar, who subsequently became beholden to the Egyptian president for his appointment.[63] Al Zaytouna was also marginalized due to the secularizing thrust of the presidencies of Bourguiba and Ben Ali. Under both rulers, Zaytuna morphed into a small institution of higher education, completely separated from the Zaytuna mosque and placed under the tight grip of the authoritarian state. Moreover, similarly to al-Azhar in Egypt, it was barred from playing any political role, even in the service of the authoritarian leader.[64]

Such state interference in social and cultural institutions, and the consequent hegemonic role over society, are important to note. The uprisings in both countries were secular in nature, and lacked any religious connotations. However, the political outcome of elections in both countries has brought political Islamists to power. In Egypt, Islamists have gained much more momentum than in Tunisia, especially through winning both legislative and executive power within the two years that followed the uprising. This can be attributed to the fact that the Egyptian regime tolerated the presence of the Muslim Brotherhood during the past two decades, while the Tunisian regime took a much harder line with Islamists. The Brotherhood were largely present in the public sphere, were tolerated in mosques, and were able to run for the legislature as independent candidates. As a consequence, they had personal and communal ties with Egyptian citizens. In Tunisia, on the other hand, the al-Nahda Islamist movement was not tolerated at all: its leader, Rashid al-Ghannoushi, was exiled, and only returned to the country after the January 2011 uprising against Ben Ali.

Social Exclusion and Contestation

The foregoing has shown how Arab authoritarian regimes have manipulated and controlled both state institutions and the public sphere. It is

63 Malika Zeghal, "Al Azhar and Radical Islam," *International Journal of Middle East Studies*, 31, 1 (2000), pp. 3–22.

64 Malika Zeghal, "Teaching Again at the Zaytuna Mosque in Tunisia," On Islam and Politics: http://onislamandpolitics.wordpress.com/tag/bourguiba/

clear that the three states in question have had their commonalities and differences in controlling both the political and public spheres. The common feature among these states was their co-optation of the public sphere, their control over the security and coercive apparatus of the state, and their exclusion of the majority of the population from the political process. From the 1970s onwards, each regime was seeking to ensure its grip on power by excluding the majority of the citizenry. Political and economic elites were co-opted and secluded from the rest of society, while citizens at large, especially the middle classes, were becoming more excluded from both the political and economic decision-making processes.

Social contestation has been the rule rather than the exception in the Arab world for the past century, especially during the colonization period. However, social contestation has gone through different waves, with the 1980s and the 1990s witnessing relatively few social protests and protest movements. But the beginning of the new millennium witnessed high levels of protests in the region. Income inequalities and social exclusion rose throughout the 2000s. With stagnant wages, the rising cost of living, and higher levels of education, citizens who had been marginalized for more than four decades demanded more political inclusion. Wealth inequality has been increasing, with wealth and assets becoming concentrated in the hands of a selected few. For instance, studies have shown that income inequality in the industrial sector in the Middle East and North Africa rose incrementally from the 1960s onwards. However, this increased dramatically between 1999 and 2002, with Egypt being an extreme case.[65]

Given increased population growth, social exclusion, the erosion of middle-class living standards, high unemployment levels, and large-scale corruption in the region, social activism and demonstrations had also increased substantially by the dawn of the new millennium. Syria, Lebanon, Bahrain, Yemen, Kuwait, Saudi Arabia, Palestine, Egypt, Morocco, Tunisia, and Jordan all witnessed street protests from different groups. In Algeria in 2002, the Berbers rallied for their right to uphold their language and cultural identity. In Yemen, Islamists and leftist opposition developed a joint organization against corruption and authoritarian rule. In Kuwait, demonstrations against electoral laws took place.

[65] Henry and Springborg, *Globalization and the Politics of Development.*

In Egypt, the Kefaya ("enough") movement, established in 2004, was the first of its kind to call for the end to the Mubarak regime. In Tunisia, under the auspices of an opposition group called the 18 October coalition, mass protests erupted in 2008, demanding better wages and working conditions for the employees of a major mining company.[66]

Most of the protests in Tunisia and Egypt were initially socio-economic rather than political in nature. The Egyptian workers' movement, as discussed in Marie Duboc's chapter in this volume, was especially successful in furthering its targeted demands precisely because it presented itself as largely disinterested in politics. It had no leader, it called for specific socio-economic rights and deliberately avoided challenging the existing authoritarian structure of the regime. By avoiding overt antagonism with the regime, it was able to negotiate and obtain many of their demands.[67] Arab governments often tolerated these types of protests and were able to bargain with the demonstrators. An important example of this tolerance is the demonstration of more than 27,000 workers in al-Mahala al-Kobra in 2006 to receive a two-month salary bonus, which had been promised by the prime minister. The government initially ignored the demonstrations, but this led to sit-ins and an expansion of the workers' demands to include wage increases and the establishment of a minimum wage. At this stage, the regime did not stop the demonstrators, but chose to negotiate with the workers. The factory's board of directors was dissolved and a new one was installed.[68] According to Hossam al-Hamalawy, these demonstrations were important due to the comparatively lenient reaction of the authorities—the abstention of the regime from using violence against laborers was essential in eliminating activists' fears elsewhere. The increasing media coverage of these demonstrations also heightened the possibility of disseminating the

[66] Marina Ottaway and Amr Hamzawy, "Protest Movements and Political Change in the Arab World," Carnegie Endowment for International Peace: Policy Outlook, 2011, http://carnegieendowment.org/files/ottaway-hamzawy_outlook_jan11_protestmovements.pdf

[67] Sameh Fawzy, "Demand Movements and Political Movements: A Comparative Critical Reading," in Dina Shehata, *'audat al-siyassa: al-harakat al-ihtijajiya fi misr* [The Return of Politics], Cairo: Al Ahram Center for Political and Strategic Studies, 2010.

[68] Rabab el-Mahdy, "The Workers of Mahala: The Emergence of a New Labor Movement," in Shehata, *'audat al-siyassa: al-harakat al-ihtijajiya fi misr.*

workers' victory to other areas within the country. Other workers and activists understood the importance of demonstrations and sit-ins for the attainment of socio-economic benefits.[69] These protests underscored the economic needs not only of the poor and the working class, but also of middle-class professionals.

In Bahrain, on the other hand, demonstrations and protests were mostly political in nature. Bahrain's "Right" movement, for instance, relentlessly called for reforms to the constitution, especially for the enhancement of citizenship rights.[70] Nevertheless, by 2007, with increasing unemployment levels, some demonstrations have been made by different groups like the "committee of the unemployed" and "the committee for subsidizing unemployed women graduates."[71]

The increasing tide of contentious politics became an important part of daily life in the Arab world. This taught activists new types of contention, new ways of framing their grievances, and more venues for citizens to encounter them through news media and social networking sites. Two years later, youth movements in Egypt were effective in combining both socio-economic and political demands, and, more importantly, in mobilizing people against authoritarian regimes.[72] For instance, the April 6 Movement in Egypt called for a general strike in 2008 in solidarity with al-Mahala workers. Different activists and bloggers demonstrated in downtown Cairo associating workers' rights with social justice and equal opportunity. These elements are at the heart of socio-economic demands, yet are essential for good governance and a democratic polity. Three years after the ousting of Mubarak and the beginning of the "democratization process" that started with Morsi's inauguration into power, contentious practices had not ceased to exist in Egypt. On the contrary, the number

[69] Hossam el-Hamalawy, "Revolt in Mahala," *International Socialist Review*, 59 (May–June 2008) online at: http://www.isreview.org/issues/59/rep-mahalla.shtml

[70] Heba Raouf, "al-harakaat al-ihtijajiyya fy al-bahrain: 'al-jadeed' fy harakat al-mujtama' al-siyassy fy al-bahrain" [Protest Movements in Bahrain: "The New" in the Political Movements in Bahrain], in Amr al-Shobaky (ed.), *al-harakaat al-ihtijajiyya fy al-watan al-'araby: misr, al-maghrib, lubnan, al-bahrain* [Protest Movements in the Arab World: Egypt, Morocco, Lebanon, Bahrain], Center for Arab Union Studies: Beirut, 2011, pp. 245–94.

[71] Ibid. p. 279.

[72] Ottaway and Hamzawy, "Protest Movements and Political Change in the Arab World."

of sit-ins and demonstrations actually increased. As discussed earlier they escalated two days after Morsi issued the 21 November decree, with activists calling for the "end of the Brotherhood regime." Demonstrations culminated six months later with the development of a new youth movement entitled Tamarrod ("Rebel"), backed by the military, whose petition to remove Morsi from power received almost 30 million signatories. Massive popular protests on 30 June then led to the military intervention that ousted Morsi from power on 3 July. This intervention in turn generated more tumult and violence on the street, culminating in the exclusion of the Brotherhood, which was now designated a "terrorist" organization, from the Egyptian political process.

Social contestation culminated in December 2010 with the unfolding of events in Tunisia's Sidi Bouzid that later caused Ben Ali to flee to Saudi Arabia. This incident was a catalyst for further social mobilization in a number of other Arab countries, from Egypt to Yemen, Libya, Syria, Jordan, Morocco, and Bahrain. In each case, the protestors learned from earlier experiences and combined their calls for socio-economic reform with political reform demands. The ineptness of subsequent Arab regimes in reacting to people's demands for reform, especially in Egypt, Libya, Yemen, and Syria, caused the demonstrations to become more politicized, with growing demands for the end of the different regimes.

While a number of years have now passed since the old Arab authoritarian regimes were ousted from power, demonstrations continue to play a role in the politics of the Middle East. Indeed, they have escalated in Egypt and Tunisia, leading to the ouster of the Islamists from power in Egypt and making their position vulnerable to popular mobilization in Tunisia. Though the Egyptian and Tunisian states have grown weaker since the Arab Spring, both countries have thus far avoided a civil war, unlike Syria.

Conclusion

Why did Tunisia and Egypt encounter less violence during the apogee of their uprisings, while Syria is experiencing more violence? In answering this question, the nature of state-building, the capacity of the authoritarian regime, and the extent to which the regimes in power historically used force against their citizens are undoubtedly the most decisive factors.

State-building processes and the capacity of authoritarian regimes differed in Egypt and Tunisia when compared to those of Syria. Egypt and Tunisia saw similar patterns in institutional development, state capacity building, regime power, the personalization of different institutions, and the rule of law. State hegemony over the public sphere was also similar in both countries, where the state used "soft" authoritarian measures in co-opting opposition forces and political dissent. This was juxtaposed with the development of a large state security apparatus, which was directly tied to the executive office. Both countries developed into "police states," where conventional political dissent was suppressed, with political protest movements and human rights activists consistently harassed and detained. However, such harassment did not extend to the majority of citizens. The way in which popular grievances were framed by protest movements proved decisive in the ousting of both Ben Ali and Mubarak. In Tunisia, Mohamed Bouazizi's dramatic suicide in Sidi Bouzid in response to the unfair treatment and humiliation he had received from the state security apparatus reverberated across the country. Different groups such as unemployed graduates, school teachers, and students who shared Bouazizi's grievances demonstrated in Sidi Bouzid. They "publicly proclaimed their rejection of political humiliation, their resentment over being the 'left behinds' of a development model that favors the northern parts of the country, their refusal of a political system where university graduates are excluded from public and economic life, and their anger at the growing imbalance in the job market ... For them, as for Bouazizi, the policeman and the Constitutional Democratic Rally (RCD) apparatchick embodied their experiences of political domination and corruption."[73] On 28 December 2010, unionists and lawyers in different parts of the country, especially in Safsa, called for solidarity demonstrations with the Sidi Bouzid movement, which by then had already featured calls for Ben Ali's resignation. When the regime faltered in responding to the demonstrations, the main frame changed to "the people demand the fall of the regime."

Egyptian activists, especially bloggers, used the ousting of Ben Ali on 14 January 2011 to call for demonstrations on 25 January, a symboli-

[73] Joel Beinin and Frédéric Vairel, "Afterword: Popular Uprisings in Tunisia and Egypt," in Joel Beinin and Frédéric Vairel (eds), *Social Movements, Mobilization, and Contestation in the Middle East and North Africa*, Stanford: Stanford University Press, 2012, p. 238.

cally charged date given that 25 January is a national holiday in Egypt commemorating the police force. From 14 to 25 January, many opposition websites boldly proclaimed that "Tomorrow Egypt will Follow Tunisia." Egyptians were thus prepared for mass demonstrations, which initially called for "food, freedom and human dignity." When the regime ignored these initial demands, the protestors soon followed the precedent of Tunisia—"The people demand the fall of the regime."

The regimes in both Egypt and Tunisia used violence against the protestors through the state security apparatus. The military, however, which had been increasingly marginalized by both presidents, decided to abstain from using violence against the protestors. Hence, in the case of Tunisia, the military decided not to intervene in the demonstrations. In Egypt, the military decided to side with the demonstrators after the "battle of the camels." At the same time, due to the increasing personalization of state institutions, the security apparatus and the police force proved weak and collapsed after the first wave of mass demonstrations in both countries.

Syria, on the other hand, had developed stronger and politically more independent institutions as a result of its fairly recent emergence as a nation state. The creation of stronger and more independent institutions led to more decentralization. The Syrian Baath party was consequently more powerful than the RCD and the NDP, and the military developed into a more powerful institution than, for instance, the Tunisian military. Nevertheless, the process of institutional development was accompanied by increased sectarianism, with the minority Alawite population possessing a disproportionate degree of power relative to the rest of the population. The regime also had a long history of using extra judicial measures and brutal repression in response to social discontent, especially from the Islamists—of the three case studies examined in this chapter, the Hama affair was undoubtedly the most brutal example of state repression by a regional regime.[74] As a result, beginning with the first wave of demonstrations, the military opted to side with the regime rather than the demonstrators. This strategy is not only designed to save the regime, but is also intended to save the army itself, given its close connection with the regime.

[74] The Hama affair refers to Rifaat Assad's 1982 massacre of tens of thousands of civilians associated with the Muslim Brotherhood in Hama.

Although the Arab uprisings share a number of similarities, this chapter has highlighted some of the differences between the public protests taking place in three distinct countries by focusing on the outcomes of the uprisings. Whether the processes of regime change and social contestation will lead to democratization or to an authoritarian transformation remains to be seen, especially in Egypt and Tunisia. While these issues are also relevant in the Syrian case, the situation is further compounded by the lack of clarity as to the exact nature of the Syrian state that will emerge in the aftermath of the Assad regime. Will the Syrian state disintegrate as a result of the increased sectarianism and violence, or will the state be able to survive? Though these questions are beyond the scope of this study, they will merit further analysis and research in the future.

4

ISLAMIST MOVEMENTS AND THE ARAB SPRING

Abdullah Al-Arian

In late 2010, the Egyptian regime of Hosni Mubarak held parliamentary elections that were reported to involve widespread voter intimidation, fraud, and vote rigging.[1] The country's leading opposition movement, the Muslim Brotherhood, saw its largest ever presence in Egypt's legislative body—eighty-eight members elected in 2005—dwindle to single digits. By the end of the year, due to the regime's constitutional amendments aimed at excluding the opposition, coupled with its effective consolidation of power through the latest round of parliamentary elections, the Muslim Brotherhood was said to have been "reduced to political nonexistence."[2] Yet barely two months later, as the tide of revolution was sweeping aside the decades-old authoritarian regimes across the Arab world, the Muslim Brotherhood and its regional offshoots rapidly emerged as the likely successors to the long-standing secular rulers. That

[1] Robert F. Worth and Mona El-Naggar, "Fraud Charges Mar Egypt Vote," *New York Times*, 28 Nov. 2010.

[2] Robert F. Worth and Mona El-Naggar, "First Round of Voting Ousts Islamists from Egypt's Parliament," *New York Times*, 30 Nov. 2010.

they were in this position largely as a result of their effective participation in the democratic process was not lost on most observers, even those traditionally critical of Islamist movements.[3]

Indeed, from Tunisia to Yemen, and even among those regimes that emerged from the wave of popular protests seemingly unscathed, the looming question concerns the role that Islamist movements are poised to play in the reformulation of the norms of regional governance. This process entails a transition from a system based on the tenuous arrangements between semi-authoritarian rulers and their subjects to one rooted in democratic legitimacy, independent institutions, and a redefined relationship between the state and its citizens. The future status of religious norms, and Islamic law or the *sharia* in particular, is central to this transition.

In order to address this question, the following pages chart the evolution of political Islam in the Arab world, beginning with its historical development as a significant social movement actor, while highlighting its various attempts at political engagement with the state. The decades of experience gained by groups such as the Muslim Brotherhood provide a rich pool of data from which conclusions can be drawn regarding the movement's posture in a post-authoritarian setting. Moreover, Islamist groups have a long record of democratic participation, albeit within a severely constrained political system, which provides some indication of this movement's goals and strategies in an open and democratic environment.

A secondary area of focus centers on the events of the Arab uprisings themselves and the conduct of the Islamist movements during this period. Though the weeks and months of protests that resulted in the ouster of long-standing regime heads in Tunisia, Libya, Egypt, and Yemen signify a watershed moment in the region's history, this period is perhaps equally notable for solidifying the transformation of Islamist groups—long considered to be revolutionary forces in Arab societies—into reform-minded organizations that had found some accommodation with the region's authoritarian regimes. Thus, with some notable exceptions, the role of Islamic politics in the crucial events of the Arab upris-

[3] Olivier Roy, "Islam: The Democracy Dilemma," in Robin Wright (ed.), *The Islamists Are Coming: Who They Really Are*, Washington, DC: Woodrow Wilson Center Press, 2012, pp. 13–20.

ings appears to have been largely muted, drowned out by a broader protest movement shaped by a non-ideological civic identity. Yet while they may not have played an initial leadership role, Islamic movements broadened the scope of their missions and adopted the popular refrain of "dignity, freedom, and social justice," around which millions of fellow citizens had united. Once these groups had employed their organizational strength and their capacity to mobilize supporters, the outcome of the popular revolts appeared to be far less uncertain.

Aside from their actions at the height of the protests to oust the regimes, the performance of Islamist movements in the transitional period that followed should be treated as a separate analytical category. The primary distinction between the two is, on the one hand, the pursuit of a common national objective around which all political factions were united, and the subsequent attempts to marshal support behind a particular political agenda, and indeed, to impose a distinct vision for the post-authoritarian order. This can be observed in Egypt, for instance, where, scarcely four weeks after Mubarak's removal, the Muslim Brotherhood found itself at odds with the country's other political forces over the very structure of the transitional period, preferring to hold legislative and presidential elections ahead of the task of rewriting the constitution.

It is the behavior of Islamist movements during the transitional period that provides the best insight into their vision for a post-authoritarian ruling order. It was during this critical historical moment that many such groups established official political parties for the first time, abandoned abstract slogans in favor of coherent political platforms, wrangled over the role of Islam in a revised constitution, and attempted to shape the powers and responsibilities of state institutions. The post-uprising period also witnessed the culmination of long-standing democratic participation (or attempts at it) by Islamist groups, and sealed the transition from broad social work to full-fledged political activism.

Finally, moving beyond the turbulence of the post-uprising settlement, it is useful to look ahead at the long-term trends developing out of the contributions of Islamist movements to the emerging governance structures across the Arab world. Specifically, the interpretations of the *sharia* (whether expansive or limited), the understanding of the nature of the civil state, and the shape of democratic participation will ultimately define future modes of governance. Moreover, just as the impact of Islamist movements on the state is subject to scrutiny, one can also examine the effects of governance on the movements themselves. The transformation from mass movement to political party will undoubtedly exacerbate the tension between these groups' quest for political power and their traditional social mission, while the need for greater pragmatism and compromise at the root of effective democratic governance will almost certainly challenge the ideological orientation of Islamic movements. The recent setbacks these movements have experienced following the resumption of state repression are certain to usher in an era in which the durability and utility of Islamist politics will undergo renewed scrutiny.

Reclaiming the Goals of the Faith

In attempting to explain the rise of the Islamic movement in Sudan during the early twentieth century, Abdelwahab El-Affendi posed the following question: "Why was it necessary to remind Muslims to abide by the faith they profess? Simple inertia should have dictated that Muslims should stick to their own lifestyles unless pressured to abandon them. We should not be asking why Muslims want to live as Muslims, but what reasons prevented them from doing so before."[4] The prevalent narrative among Islamist groups across the Arab world presents political Islam as the latest incarnation of the religious revivalist movements that erupted during the period of political and economic decline associated with the late Ottoman era and the rise of European colonialism. Shortly before he founded the Muslim Brotherhood in 1928, Hasan al-Banna identified an inherent conflict in the relationship between traditional Islamic norms and European colonial rule: "I believe that my people, because of the political stages through which they have passed, the social influences which have passed through them, and under the impact of western civilization … materialist philosophy, and foreign traditions, have departed from the goals of their faith."[5]

The movement he founded proceeded to address this concern, establishing a modern social organization with a strong missionary component. The Society of the Muslim Brothers promoted the reclamation of traditional Islamic values within a modern state setting. While it quickly

[4] Abdelwahab El-Affendi, *Turabi's Revolution: Islam and Power in Sudan*, London: Grey Seal, 1991, p. 1.

[5] Richard Mitchell, *The Society of the Muslim Brothers*, New York: Oxford University Press, 1969, p. 6.

spread across the Arabic-speaking parts of a fallen empire still reeling from the loss of the caliphate—the symbol of Islamic political and spiritual leadership for thirteen centuries—the movement nonetheless demonstrated an ability to adapt to local conditions. It successfully navigated the modern institutions that had developed in the individual Arab states, obtaining official government sanction, generating the funds and resources necessary to sustain its mission, and developing complex relationships with the various state organs that it was attempting to influence or replace.

With its universalistic Islamic message, the Muslim Brotherhood focused on recruiting members from all segments of society. Banna put forward a twofold strategy of reforming the individual through the internalization of Islamic norms and values in all aspects of one's life, which was to be followed by a broad-based public campaign for the rehabilitation of society's governing structures and institutions, a far more political goal. With a legion of highly motivated followers, a strong hierarchical structure suited for mass mobilization, and a powerful message that pledged self-empowerment and the reclamation of Islam's once ascendant place in society, the Muslim Brotherhood launched itself into the chaotic field of interwar Arab politics. Despite the fierce opposition of the state's colonial rulers and political elites, Islamic politics made inroads in Egypt, Syria, Sudan, Jordan, and Tunisia, among other countries.

In Egypt, Banna managed to gain some concessions regarding public morality laws from the Wafdist government. In Jordan, the Muslim Brotherhood established strong links with the monarchy as a bulwark against leftist movements, while in Syria, members of the Brotherhood were elected to a number of parliamentary seats in Damascus in the 1950s. In all Arab countries in which it maintained a prominent voice, the Islamist movement led the opposition to the colonization and division of historical Palestine, and became a critical player both in the war that erupted in 1948 and in trying to mitigate the refugee crisis that followed.

Whether on issues of domestic social policy or foreign affairs, forces of Islamic activism put forth a comprehensive vision of politics that centered on the application of religious principles, specifically those derived from the *sharia*, the Islamic legal tradition. However, by and large, successive governments attempted to subvert the role of religion in the state, preferring a secular model promoted externally by former colonial powers and internally through recently elevated institutions like the military or local monarchies supported by secular elites. The Muslim Brotherhood and its regional offshoots consequently faced official banishment and persecution in countries such as Egypt, Syria, Tunisia, and Libya, while being co-opted to the whims of the state in the cases of Jordan, Yemen, and Sudan.

Locating the Center

From its origins in the early part of the century through the 1960s, the modern Islamist movement was unable to gain a great deal of political experience. The primary *modus operandi* of Islamic groups, after all, was activism within society through popular religious, social, and charitable institutions rather than direct engagement in political participation. As Rachid al-Ghannouchi, the leader of Tunisia's al-Nahda movement characterized it, contrary to the historical Western fixation on liberating the state from religion, "in our context the problem is one of liberating religion from the state and preventing it from dominating religion, and keeping the latter in the societal realm."[6] It was only upon recognizing the pervasive role of the modern state in regulating the lives of citizens, including the freedom to live according to their interpretation of Islam, that Islamist groups saw political action as necessary for achieving their broader objectives.

In attempting to resolve this perceived conflict, the leaders of the Islamist movement failed to reconcile the tensions inherent in a project to reassert traditional religious values within the demands of a modern state system. Banna famously rejected the "partisanship" of adversarial, representative parliamentary politics on the grounds that it was un-Islamic. However, when the need arose to shift the Muslim Brotherhood's political tactics in the 1940s, Banna authorized members to run for parliament and even stood as a candidate himself in two separate elections. While this move did not signal a definitive shift in the trajectory of the Islamist movement, it nonetheless indicated that difficult

[6] Rachid al-Ghannouchi, "Secularism and the Relation between Religion and the State from the Perspective of al-Nahdha Party," Center for the Study of Islam and Democracy, Washington, DC, 2 Mar. 2012.

questions had yet to be answered about the nature of Islamic activism's relationship with the modern instruments of governance.

The ensuing decades were marked by the forced retreat of Islamism as secular Arab nationalism and conservative monarchies reigned supreme. It was not until the mid-1970s that these questions were revisited, coinciding with the re-emergence of the Muslim Brotherhood in Egypt and elsewhere, within a more crowded field of religious activism that included, among others, the Salafi, Sufi, Tablighi, and jihadi trends. Political Islam's engagement with the state, now rejuvenated by a new generation of cosmopolitan youth activists disenchanted by the failures of the Arab nationalist project, subsequently resumed on a large scale. In places such as Egypt, where conditions permitted, this engagement began with entry into leadership roles within the student unions of state colleges and universities, before expanding into professional bodies and eventually the parliament.

Though the Muslim Brotherhood remained officially outlawed, its leaders embraced the reformist path in the face of pressure from the militant fringe of the Islamic movement which was calling for violent revolutionary modes of opposing the Sadat regime. In denouncing this approach, Muslim Brotherhood leaders like Hasan al-Hudaybi and 'Umar al-Tilmisani affirmed the organization's commitment to fulfilling the movement's goals from within the state's existing institutions rather than by replacing them. Subsequent generations continued to develop the mainstream political ideology, with the result that, by the 1980s and 1990s, democratic participation had become part and parcel of Islamic activism from Algeria to Kuwait. By the mid-1990s, the moderate mainstream was further distinguished from competing trends with the rise of the *wasatiyyah* movement which proclaimed a centrist approach to Islamic politics that stressed the need to implement the spirit of the *sharia*, defined by the *maqasid*, or objectives, rather than the letter, expressed in the *ahkam*, or rulings. Building on the thought of intellectual luminaries such as Yusuf al-Qaradawi and Muhammad al-Ghazali, the *wasatiyyah* movement became a driving force behind the shift from militant activism toward greater political engagement, even yielding a political party in Egypt of the same name.[7]

[7] Raymond William Baker, *Islam Without Fear: Egypt and the New Islamists*, Cambridge, MA: Harvard University Press, 2003, pp. 20–22.

In the first decade of the twenty-first century, Islamic political movements appeared to have consolidated their gains, joining the ruling governments in Lebanon and Palestine while winning their largest ever share of parliamentary seats in semi-authoritarian systems such as Egypt, Jordan, and Kuwait. Even in closed political systems such as Tunisia, Libya, and Syria, exiled Islamist leaders began to conceive of a more pragmatic political course while charting their path to the future. Commentators observing this phenomenon began to speak of a "post-Islamist" transformation in Arab politics, in which traditional movements adopted the same language, strategies, and modes of contestation as non-religious political parties. According to Bayat, post-Islamism "represents an endeavor to fuse religiosity and rights, faith and freedom, Islam and liberty. It is an attempt to turn the underlying principles of Islamism on its head by emphasizing rights instead of duties, plurality in place of singular authoritative voice, historicity rather than fixed scripture, and the future instead of the past."[8] However, as soon as the Islamist movement had settled the most pressing questions regarding its goals and methods, it found itself at a critical historical juncture that would both challenge and affirm its reformist agenda and universalistic mission.

Freedom is the Solution

On the eve of the popular uprisings that began in Sidi Bouzid, Tunisia, in December 2010, the Islamist movement in the Arab world had undergone an extensive transformation—from being an organic societal force with the potential for revolutionary action against repressive secular regimes, the Islamist movement was now a reformist political actor that had adapted to the rules of the political game imposed by those same regimes and their patrons. The Muslim Brotherhood had all but abandoned its traditional refrain of "Islam is the solution" in favor of the far more universal "freedom is the solution."[9] But while these words may have dictated its electoral strategy in Egypt in 2005, when it sought to obtain a greater share of policy-making responsibilities under the

[8] Asef Bayat, *Making Islam Democratic: Social Movements and the Post-Islamist Turn*, Stanford: Stanford University Press, 2007, p. 11.

[9] Anthony Shadid, "Egypt's Path After Uprising Does Not Have to Follow Iran's," *New York Times*, 12 Feb. 2011.

Mubarak regime, they would subsequently take on an entirely new meaning during the height of the anti-regime protests in late January 2011.

From the outset of the Arab uprisings, much of the commentary in the Western press and academia stressed the spontaneous, unified, and non-ideological nature of the protests. In both explicit and implicit terms, this analysis attempted to demonstrate that Islamist movements—long thought to be the only viable alternative to secular dictatorships—had given way to a new phenomenon: the rise of a highly educated, cosmopolitan youth movement with a laudable commitment to non-violent protest, democratic reform, and personal freedoms. The pervasive use of social media, the flurry of images beamed from the public squares of Tunis, Cairo, and Sana'a, and the availability of English-speaking youth protestors to Western journalists greatly aided the construction of a narrative that supplanted political Islam's decades-long fixation on replacing secular regimes with a religious state. Instead, a new generation raised the banners of social justice and human dignity, overcoming the narrow ideological interests of competing social movements to offer a universal message to which all citizens could relate.

The events of the Arab uprisings did not emerge in a vacuum. The decade preceding the Arab Spring was rife with popular protests against government corruption and abuses across the region. Ad hoc coalitions were established, such as the Kefaya and April 6 movements in Egypt and the Joint Meeting Parties (JMP) in Yemen, which called for an end to the hereditary project of the regimes and for the creation of democratic institutions. The nature of popular opposition in parts of the Arab world had seemingly evolved to emphasize civic identity at the expense of religious and ethnic group affiliation.

This development was perhaps nowhere more evident than in the conduct of the youth movement within the Egyptian Muslim Brotherhood. Although the organization itself had made a conscious decision not to join in the protests scheduled for 25 January, young leaders such as Islam Lotfi and Muhammad 'Abbas, along with thousands of other Muslim Brotherhood members, were determined to participate in the marches to Tahrir Square. They believed that their identity as conscientious and proud Egyptian citizens trumped their membership in the Muslim Brotherhood and their obligation to observe the directives of its senior leadership.[10] However, these youth were

[10] Interview with Islam Lotfi.

equally as likely to stress that their decision to join the uprising did not emerge out of some newfound discovery of secular nationalism, but rather out of their belief in a cosmopolitan Islamism that views religious politics as a means to establish justice and social harmony.

As a natural outgrowth of the *wasatiyya* movement of the 1990s, this cosmopolitan Islamism offers a non-exclusivist vision that transcends the traditional view of religious activism as a distinct project operating in tension with broader social and political forces, from notions of the civil state to nationalism. As stated by 'Abd al-Mon'eim Abul Futuh, a former Muslim Brotherhood leader who left the group upon announcing his candidacy for president in April 2011, this vision is

> an extension of the broader Egyptian national project, internalizing in a modern way the greatness of the principles and values of Islam, in which all Egyptians take pride, whether Muslim or Christian. These values were developed by such figures as Rifa'a al-Tahtawi, Sa'ad Zaghloul, Muhammad Abduh, and Rashid Rida. As a political leader, Sa'ad Zaghloul was still the son of al-Azhar, and Tahtawi and others never abandoned the principles of Islamic civilization.[11]

In contrast to earlier modes of protest, in which sharp lines of identification were drawn, it was not uncommon during the Arab Spring to witness Islamist youth chanting religious and nationalist slogans in the same breath. Indeed, in a nod to their newfound comfort with state symbols, the political rallies of several major Islamist parties were strewn with Egyptian flags and frequently began with the playing of the national anthem—a far cry from the designation of such practices as a deviation from true Islam.

However, even as the redefinition of Islamist identity was developing among the younger generation of activists, the fact remains that, in virtually every case, the senior leadership of these movements opted not to lead the charge to overthrow dictatorial regimes. This decision was a product of several factors. The historical relationship between Islamist groups and the country's rulers was characterized by a legacy of conflict and severe repression that had nearly destroyed the movement's presence at every turn. Sheer survival instinct dictated that Islamist groups could ill afford to jeopardize their gains, however limited they may have been, by engaging in a revolutionary struggle.

[11] Interview with 'Abd al-Mon'eim Abul Futuh.

This historical experience of repression necessitated a strategic shift on the part of the leadership of these groups (which dated back to the 1970s), and as the relative political gains increased, this need only became stronger over time. Whether in Egypt, Jordan, or Yemen, the Muslim Brotherhood appeared to have more to lose by joining what was quickly becoming a zero-sum revolutionary moment. If this legacy were not enough, the Mubarak regime's security forces were sure to remind the Muslim Brotherhood of the risks involved, as it conducted wide-ranging sweeps to detain several members of the group's leadership, including Mohamed Morsi, during the initial stage of the protests.

However, in the cases of Tunisia and Libya, the long-term imprisonment and exile of the Islamist movement's senior leadership ensured that its capacity to mobilize followers and sympathizers would be extremely limited. Ghannouchi, who established al-Nahda in the mid-1980s, had been exiled from Tunisia for twenty-two years when he eventually returned from Europe after the fall of Ben Ali. As a result, the Tunisian protest movement did not claim to represent an Islamist agenda, but it also did not explicitly disavow what was a popular undercurrent that existed within Tunisian society in spite of the repressive political atmosphere. Reacting to the fact that Tunisia's revolution lacked a discernible ideological orientation, Ghannouchi claimed that: "No one can pretend that this revolution has been led by Islamists or communists or any other group for that matter. This is a popular revolution and all the trends in Tunisian political society are present on the scene. At the same time it is clear that the Islamists are the biggest political force in Tunisia."[12]

The situation in Libya on the eve of the uprising was even more complex, as the Islamist movement was divided between an exiled leadership that saw no possible accommodation with the regime and an internal movement that wavered between suffering long-term imprisonment and attempting to reach a negotiated settlement with the ruler's son, Saif al-Islam al-Qaddafi.[13] As the violent confrontation with Qaddafi's forces escalated during the early months of the popular uprising, the leaders of the Libyan Islamist movement attempted to hedge their bets, refusing

[12] "Tunisia: The Advent of Liberal Islamism—An Interview with Rashid Al-Ghannouchi," http://religion.info/english/interviews/article_516.shtml (last accessed 28 Aug. 2012).

[13] Omar Ashour, "Libyan Islamists Unpacked: Rise, Transformation, and Future," Doha: Brookings Doha Center, 2012, p. 3.

to endorse the uprising fully while simultaneously avoiding making any commitment to the regime's survival.

Another factor considered by the leadership of Islamist groups concerned the perception that their involvement would create among those Western countries whose response to the Arab uprisings could prove critical in terms of their ultimate success or failure. The fact that dictatorial regimes across the region had relied heavily on the support of the United States and its allies for decades was not lost on the protestors or movement leaders. Given the overt hostility expressed by Western policy-makers toward Islamist movements, particularly in the post-Cold War period, the Muslim Brotherhood's leadership believed that any vociferous endorsement for the anti-Mubarak protests would be interpreted as an attempt at an Islamic revolution in Egypt.[14] Members of the Brotherhood did not, after all, have to look too far back into history to witness a US response to an actual Islamic revolution, given the events which had occurred in Iran only three decades earlier. Similarly, in Libya, where foreign intervention would prove critical to the defeat of Qaddafi, Islamist leaders were mindful of creating the appearance that their movement was at the forefront of the revolution, something which would alarm their Western patrons and jeopardize the support of NATO. The same logic was also at play in the formation of the resistance to the Assad regime, as the Syrian Muslim Brotherhood's exiled leadership attempted to maintain a low profile to avoid giving the impression that the revolt in Syria was religious in nature. In a country with a recent political history of polarization and divisions along sectarian lines, the struggle against a minority Alawite regime could not be seen as being led by a religiously oriented Sunni movement.

Joining the Fray

As a result of these ideological and tactical considerations, Islamist movements remained peripheral to the initial stages of the uprisings. In Egypt, internal discussions within the Muslim Brotherhood's Guidance Bureau on 21 January yielded a decision not to engage in the planned protests as an organization, but also not to bar members from participat-

[14] Ernesto Londono and Leila Fadel, "Egypt's Muslim Brotherhood Faces Prospect of Democracy Amid Internal Discord," *Washington Post*, 21 Feb., 2011.

ing on an individual basis if they chose to do so. This decision was at least partly based on threats that had been delivered privately to the Muslim Brotherhood's leadership by state security officials, according to which any active participation in the protests by the organization would be met with a swift and brutal response.[15]

Yet in Tunisia as well as in Egypt, whose uprisings to overthrow the ruling families lasted only twenty-eight and eighteen days respectively, the lack of institutional backing from Islamist groups did not adversely impact the outcome. In both cases, the emphasis on popular protests in public spaces throughout the country and the relatively mild response from the state security agency (at least when compared with the more violent military response in other countries) ensured the success of the uprising despite the absence of a disciplined and hierarchical organization at the helm. If the goals of the protests continued to evolve throughout those weeks, so did the position of the leading Islamist movement. During particularly critical stages, when the outcome was far from certain, the Muslim Brotherhood's institutional support became critical to withstand the tide of state repression and significantly affect the outcome of the popular uprising.

Following the initial days of the uprising, the Guidance Bureau decided to place its organizational weight behind the protests, specifically by mobilizing its members and their families to rally to the support of those gathered in public places, to set up a field office for gathering real-time information on developments, and to occupy Tahrir Square and hold it against efforts by security forces to expel the protestors.[16] By the time the so-called "Battle of the Camel" took place on 2 February, the Muslim Brotherhood had gained a significant foothold within the ranks of the Egyptian protests and, indeed, its disciplined organizational capacity proved instrumental in withstanding the violent onslaught of state security forces and armed thugs as they attempted to disperse the crowds. This event was widely viewed as a turning point in the effort to overthrow Mubarak, who finally stepped down nine days later.[17]

[15] Interview with 'Usama Yasin, "Shahed 'Ala al-Thawra," Al Jazeera, 11 June 2011.

[16] Interview with 'Usama Yasin, "Shahed 'Ala al-Thawra," Al Jazeera, 20 Nov. 2011.

[17] Yasmine Fathi, "Egypt's Battle of the Camel: The Day the Tide Turned," *Al-Ahram English*, 2 Feb. 2012.

In Yemen, whose uprising was at a standstill months after protestors had first occupied the country's public squares, the Islah Party played a more complex role. On the one hand, it used its institutional networks to mobilize greater support for the protests, while it sought to leverage its power in the streets for a better position at the negotiating table on the other.[18] As Yemen's stillborn revolution moved to the political transition phase without successfully removing the regime's head, Islah leaders earned the ire of the revolutionaries for abandoning the protests in exchange for vastly limited political gains. Despite Islah's prominent role in cementing the presence of protestors in Change Square through the security, resources, and provisions it offered, it faced pressure from the revolutionary youth within its own ranks regarding its decision to reach a settlement with the regime.[19]

By contrast, events in Libya took a radically different turn. Following decades of repression and exile, and with the prospect of a civil war looming as the Qaddafi regime escalated its violent response to the peaceful protests, the Islamist movement emerged as a key actor in the ensuing conflict. Remnants of the Muslim Brotherhood as well as hard-line Salafis and jihadists were reorganized into rebel factions to fight Qaddafi's forces. One rebel commander in particular, Abdel Hakim Belhadj, earned a reputation as a fierce fighter who played a vital role in the battle for Tripoli that sent Qaddafi into hiding. Belhadj, who had formerly served as the head of the Libyan Islamic Fighting Group which had challenged the regime for a number of years until its defeat in the late 1990s, resurfaced as one of the main leaders of the Islamist movement in Libya following his release from prison just months prior to the outbreak of the anti-Qaddafi protests. His growing popularity during the height of the fighting in Libya appeared to indicate a high level of support for Islamist politics among many Libyans, though it had been absent from the Libyan political scene in any organized fashion for a number of decades. The fact that Qaddafi attempted to paint the anti-regime protests as an act of terrorism only further highlighted the role played by religiously motivated Libyans who sought to rid their country of Qaddafi's rule.

[18] Laurent Bonnefoy, "Yemen's Islamists and the Revolution," *Foreign Policy*, 9 Feb. 2012.

[19] Kareem Fahim, "Yemen's Opposition May Be Caught by its Own Double Game," *New York Times*, 2 Dec., 2011.

Islamist groups played a similar role in Syria, another country with a long history of violent confrontation between the regime and the Muslim Brotherhood. With most of the group's leadership in exile, it was left to individual members to organize themselves during the height of the protests and mobilize along with their fellow citizens. However, as an organization, the strength of the Islamist movement was severely limited within the country where it remained part of the oppositional Syrian National Council, which was made up of exiled leaders from various secular and religious factions. Though it did not retain the leadership of the council, the Muslim Brotherhood maintained a dominant voice nonetheless, in part due to its close relationship with Burhan Ghalioun, the council's first president. Leaders of the Muslim Brotherhood also provided extensive logistical support, with one figure reporting that "the Brotherhood does not just support with words. It might be money and it might be some tools and facilitation."[20] Exiled Muslim Brotherhood members used their networks in Lebanon, Turkey, and elsewhere to provide support for family members in Homs, Hama, and other major Syrian cities during the most pressing moments of the conflict. However, on an institutional level, Islamist groups remain considerably weaker than their counterparts in other Arab countries, their general popularity among Syria's more conservative population notwithstanding.

From Democracy to Islamism: The Political Transition

As the smoke settled in the aftermath of the revolutionary struggles in countries across the Arab world, the political settlement and the transition to democratic institutions featured more pronounced involvement of organized Islamist groups. In contrast to their conduct during the actual uprisings, in which they acted, at best, within a broad array of participating social actors, these groups moved quickly in an attempt to direct the outcome of this critical process. While important differences distinguish the nature of the political settlement in each local context, there are several parallel developments that can be observed across all of the cases.

From the moderate mainstream Islamist groups like the Muslim Brotherhood to the traditionally apolitical Salafis, and even former

[20] Nir Rosen, "Islamism and the Syrian Uprising," *Foreign Policy*, 8 Mar. 2012.

jihad-oriented organizations, the outward commitment to democracy as the basis for acquiring political legitimacy was a hallmark of the transition phase. But beyond token gestures and public platitudes, the Islamist movement demonstrated its propensity for democratic participation time and again, whether in helping to determine the rules of the game, and thereby stacking the chips in its favor, or through the effective and highly organized mobilization of its members and supporters during elections. Additionally, during the realignment of the centers of power across various state institutions throughout the transition period, Islamist movements were committed to negotiating a more influential position within the new arrangement, though their efforts in this regard were met with differing degrees of success. Finally, the immediate aftermath of the fall of one Arab dictator after another forced an abrupt internal shift in the resource allocation of Islamist groups, as many chose to establish parties for the first time, and as a result enhanced their political credentials, but only at the expense of their social mission.

When it became apparent that the Ben Ali regime was at an end, Tunisia's Islamists moved quickly to demonstrate that their long-standing support of democratic governance was not merely an empty promise made during the height of the country's authoritarian era. The movement's leading intellectual had long served as the spokesman for Islamic democracy throughout the Muslim world, and he was quick to assert al-Nahda's continued commitment to a free, open, and democratic political system, not as a convenient political tactic, but as a principle inherent in its "mainstream" interpretation of Islamic governance. Upon his triumphant return to Tunisia, Ghannouchi declared that:

> Democracy is crucial to dealing with and reconciling different and even conflicting interests in society. Islam has a strong democratic spirit inasmuch as it respects religious, social and political differences. Islam has never favored a monolithic state. Throughout their history Muslims have objected to the imposition of a single all-powerful interpretation of Islam. Any attempt to impose a single interpretation has always proven inherently unstable and temporary.[21]

The Egyptian Muslim Brotherhood similarly emphasized its long-standing commitment to democratic institutions as the basis for gover-

21 "Tunisia: The Advent of Liberal Islamism—An Interview with Rashid Al-Ghannouchi," http://religion.info/english/interviews/article_516.shtml (last accessed 28 Aug. 2012).

nance. On the eve of Mubarak's fall from power, Guidance Bureau official 'Esam al-'Erian asserted: "Moving forward, we envision the establishment of a democratic, civil state that draws on universal measures of freedom and justice, which are central Islamic values. We embrace democracy not as a foreign concept that must be reconciled with tradition, but as a set of principles and objectives that are inherently compatible with and reinforce Islamic tenets."[22]

The traditionally quietist Salafis proved to be particularly adept at effective political organization. After their initial condemnation of the anti-Mubarak protests, Salafi leaders also endorsed the transition to a democratic state, albeit being careful to distinguish between a "civil" and a "secular" state, the latter of which they categorically rejected. Nonetheless, al-Nour Party leader 'Emad 'Abdel Ghaffour also spoke in the language of democracy. When describing the future Egyptian state, he explained, "We mean one that is based on democracy, the power of law and human rights. We do not want a religious state, but we also do not want the nation to be unrelated to religion."[23] Not to be outdone, Egypt's jihadist leaders, who had historically operated outside of the political system, and thus stood in stark contrast to the Muslim Brotherhood's emphasis on social activism and political contestation, signaled a complete about-face. Following his release from prison for his role in the assassination of Anwar al-Sadat, 'Abboud al-Zomor of al-Gama'ah al-Islamiyyah stated his support for the democratic process. "The ballot boxes will decide who will win at the end of the day," he said. "There is no longer any need for me to use violence against those who gave us our freedom and allowed us to be part of political life."[24]

Libya's Belhadj also had to deflect past statements and associations related to his role in the armed resistance against the Qaddafi regime in the mid-1990s. In what was becoming a standard among Islamist groups in a new, open political environment, he espoused his support for a

[22] 'Esam al-'Erian, "What the Muslim Brothers Want," *New York Times*, 9 Feb. 2011.

[23] Sherif Tarek, "Q&A: Emad El-Din Abdel Ghafour, Chairman of the Salafist Al-Nour Party," http://www.jadaliyya.com/pages/index/3497/qanda_emad-el-din-abdel-ghafour-chairman-of-the-sa, 12 Dec. 2011 (last accessed 28 Aug. 2012).

[24] Neil MacFarquhar, "Religious Radicals' Turn to Democracy Alarms Egypt," *New York Times*, 1 Apr. 2011.

new Libya founded on the popular will. "We call and hope for a civil country that is ruled by the law which we were not allowed to enjoy under Gadhafi. The identity of the country will be left up to the people to choose."[25]

By contrast, in Yemen, which had yet to rid itself fully of the Saleh regime at the time of its political transition, the Islah Party's Mohammad Qahtan downplayed the role of Islamists, instead calling for unity among competing ideological trends within the opposition with the common goal of achieving a functioning democratic government: "We think that the need for the JMP in a post-Ali Abdullah Saleh Yemen is more pressing than ever. There is no doubt that—in light of the recent setbacks in Yemen—establishing a civil state and practicing democracy on a firm footing cannot be accomplished without a broad-based national coalition."[26] Islah Party activist and Nobel Peace Prize winner Tawakkul Karman expressed a more idealistic outlook in stating her vision for a new Yemen "based on the people's rights and on social contract between the governors and the governed through which the international values of human rights such as democracy, justice, equal citizenship, gender equality, freedom of speech, and press are respected."[27]

Syria's Islamist movement, the members of which were largely based in exile, wasted no time in pledging its support for a democratic transition. Even as the bloody insurgency against the Assad regime raged on during late 2011 and early 2012, prominent leaders within the Muslim Brotherhood put forward their vision for a post-authoritarian Syria. Farouk Tayfour, its deputy leader, touted the organization's legacy of participating in the elections of the 1950s and 1960s, at a time when even Christians were included in its party lists.[28] The former head of the

[25] Hadeel al-Shalchi and Maggie Michael, "Abdel Hakim Belhaj, Libya Rebel Commander, Plays Down Islamist Past," Associated Press, 2 Sep. 2011.

[26] "Democracy, Islam, and the 'New Yemen,'" al-Hayat interview with Mohammad Qahtan, republished in al-Monitor, 2 Feb. 2012, http://www.al-monitor.com/pulse/politics/2012/02/mohammad-qahtan-member-of-the-hi.html (last accessed 28 Aug. 2012).

[27] Nadia al-Sakkaf, "There is No Turning Back: Interview with Tawakkul Karman," The Daily Beast, 9 Oct. 2011, http://www.thedailybeast.com/articles/2011/10/09/tawakul-karman-interview-nobel-peace-prize-could-help-arab-spring.html (last accessed 28 Aug. 2012).

[28] Hazim al-Amine, "Leader of Syrian Muslim Brotherhood Discloses Secret

Muslim Brotherhood Ali al-Bayanouni echoed these sentiments for the future, writing, "All [opposition groups] would rally round a civil, plural state based on power sharing, free elections and a modern civil constitution in which all citizens—men and women—are equal. This is what the Syrians want, and what they are on course to achieve."[29]

Words to Deeds: Electoral Strategies and Movement Mobilization

The ambitious pledges of the Arab world's Islamist movements were immediately put to the test during the post-revolutionary transitions. As these groups had repeatedly declared their intention to act as merely one of many political actors within a pluralistic setting, they now faced the challenge of defining the limits of their participation in a rapidly evolving process. Due to their status as the sole organized political force representing a significant segment of society, Islamists were the only viable movement capable of determining the course of the transition, and they believed that they had the popular mandate to do so. What this process frequently entailed, however, was the establishment of institutional procedures and the delineation of road maps that appeared to privilege the nascent Islamist parties, effectively manipulating the odds in their favor. By the end of the transitional period, Islamist groups had largely cemented their role as the single most significant political actor emerging out of society. Yet along the way, they were frequently forced to reassess some of their most basic founding principles.

As a relatively homogenous society, Tunisia was able to avoid some of the more difficult moments that other Arab states faced during the post-revolutionary transition. Following Ben Ali's departure in January 2011, the country's political factions reached a consensus on a transitional process under a temporary government including of some officials of the previous regime while preparations were made for elections to the constituent assembly, which were scheduled to take place later that year. The military was relegated to the sidelines, and while protests occasionally

---

Offer from Iran," al-Hayat interview with Farouk Tayfour, republished in al-Monitor, 20 Jan. 2012, http://www.al-monitor.com/pulse/politics/2012/01/tayfour-to-al-hayat-iran-offered.html (last accessed 28 Aug. 2012).

[29] Ali al-Bayanouni, "Assad's Myth Needs Busting," *The Guardian*, 3 Aug. 2011.

erupted, even prompting major changes to the transitional government, the transition itself was relatively smooth.

Al-Nahda had maintained a decades-long presence within Tunisia's authoritarian political environment and was keenly aware of Tunisian society's more secular sensibilities, a fact reflected in its politically moderate tone during the electoral campaign. Moreover, its experience as a political party ensured that al-Nahda would not need to engage in the steep learning curve facing some ideologically driven social movements pressured to adopt pragmatic political platforms. Even as the Tunisian elections approached, Ghannouchi attempted to temper the expectations of its supporters, with al-Nahda making the strategic calculation not to dominate the incoming government or even to govern on an exclusively religious basis. "Islamists have to work with others," he said. "They should totally abandon the view that they can rule on their own. Furthermore, Islamists should relinquish the ambition to monopolize Islam and appear as the only voice of Islam."[30]

When the final votes were tallied in late October 2011, al-Nahda had won 41 percent of the votes, or 89 of the 217 seats in the transitional assembly. While it was not a clear majority, the figure far exceeded the gains of all other political parties. Through its extensive network of institutions and access to public spaces such as mosques, al-Nahda's mobilization efforts outweighed those of all competitors. The party chose to form a coalition government with several parties representing competing political trends. Representing al-Nahda in the post of prime minister was Hamadi Jebali, while the positions of president and parliamentary speaker were assumed by Moncef al-Marzouki and Mustafa Ben Ja'far, of the leftist Congress for the Republic Party and al-Takatol Party respectively.

When the coalition government set about the task of writing the nation's new constitution, it quickly faced a stumbling block on the question of Islam's role in the future Tunisian state. Whereas the former constitution stated that Islam was the state religion, some parliamentarians from al-Nahda put forward a proposal to establish *sharia* as the source of Tunisia's legislation, which led to an outcry from the secularist

[30] "Tunisia: The Advent of Liberal Islamism—An Interview with Rashid Al-Ghannouchi," http://religion.info/english/interviews/article_516.shtml (last accessed 28 Aug. 2012).

parties. The matter was eventually put to rest when al-Nahda's leadership refused to endorse the proposal, effectively killing it. Ghannouchi was particularly outspoken in his opposition to what would have amounted to no more than a symbolic gesture, in his view, rather than a measure with any enforceable mechanism. As it was a Muslim country, he argued, government representatives were sufficiently influenced by Islamic values, whether explicitly or otherwise, and therefore did not need a provision requiring legislation to adhere to Islamic law. This decision signaled a degree of political maturity on the part of al-Nahda that was rare among Islamist parties elsewhere.

The transition in Egypt played out in a dramatically different fashion from the events in Tunisia. When it soon became apparent that deeply entrenched state institutions, emboldened by remnants of the old regime and supported by powerful international actors, intended to retain significant political power and limit the effects of the Egyptian revolution, the political transition quickly became a contentious affair among social forces, led chiefly by the Islamists. In contrast to Tunisia, the transition was not overseen by a civilian government, but by the military leaders who made up the Supreme Council of the Armed Forces (SCAF).

In an effort to temper the expectations of the revolutionary youth who had led the way to Tahrir Square, SCAF tasked a committee of five constitutional law scholars, led by Tariq al-Bishri, a highly respected intellectual with Islamist leanings, to propose a road map for the transition. Also on the committee was Sobhi Saleh, another highly regarded scholar and member of the Muslim Brotherhood, though without a visible public profile. In appointing these figures, SCAF endeavored to gain the support of the only social force it believed could effectively challenge its control over the process and its eventual outcome. True to form, the Muslim Brotherhood placed its enthusiastic support behind the March 2011 referendum on the nature of the transition. In addition to calling for parliamentary and presidential elections ahead of rewriting the constitution, the document also suspended Egypt's current constitution and placed all legislative and executive powers in the hands of SCAF.

This proved to be the first major division within the ranks of the revolutionary forces, as liberals, leftists, and revolutionary youth vehemently opposed the proposed initiative due to their suspicions of the military's intentions and wariness of the Muslim Brotherhood's ability to dominate the impending political processes. For its part, the country's chief

Islamist movement perceived this period as a golden opportunity to make significant electoral gains at a time when there was no discernable opposition that was able to match its organizational capacity. In fact, its mobilization strengths were put on full display during the 19 March referendum, in which the proposals were passed overwhelmingly with 77 percent of the vote. Over 14 million Egyptians supported the initiative, including, to the surprise of many, the newly formed Salafi and jihadi parties, which saw in the referendum an opportunity to flex their own burgeoning political muscle. Fears that Egypt's transition could be marred by a secular–religious divide—with the military looking on—arose in the aftermath of the referendum.

That divide grew ever deeper over the course of the ensuing months. The revolutionary youth groups and many liberals objected to SCAF's increasingly authoritarian behavior, prompting renewed protests throughout the country. In several instances, these were met with a violent response from the security forces and armed thugs, along with waves of mass detentions and military tribunals. Meanwhile, the Muslim Brotherhood frequently attempted to hedge its bets, vocalizing its commitment to the aims of the revolution while withdrawing its actual support from events on the ground. Instead, having established the Freedom and Justice Party (FJP) as its formal political wing, it focused its energies on its electoral strategy and formulating its plan for governance. Unlike the days in which it stood with millions of Egyptians throughout the country's public squares, it also sought to avoid any outright confrontation with the state, instead cultivating a tenuous working relationship with SCAF in the hope that it would be granted the right to govern upon winning the elections.

By the time that parliamentary elections were held that fall, it was expected that no political force would be able to compete with the Muslim Brotherhood, which had spent decades preparing for the moment when it could take part in free and fair elections. In an attempt to level the playing field, liberal parties lobbied for a greater share of the seats to be determined by party lists rather than individual contests, which seemed to favor the better organized Islamist groups or the more well-known and better-financed *felool* (remnants of the old regime). In the end, two-thirds of the parliamentary seats were designated for party lists, with one-third going to individual candidate contests. In its response to the new electoral law, the FJP reversed its initial pledge to nominate candidates to only one-third of the seats, increasing that number to 40 percent, and eventually running in an unprecedented 80 percent of available seats.

When the dust settled following three phases of voting in late 2011 and early 2012, the massive mobilization efforts of the Muslim Brotherhood had clearly paid off. In the historic elections, in which more than 25 million Egyptian voters took part, the FJP received nearly 45 percent of the available seats in the People's Assembly. Perhaps even more surprising to observers was the fact that the Salafi bloc, politically an unknown quantity, received almost one-quarter of all votes, thereby giving the Islamist parties over 73 percent of the seats and effective control of parliament.

However, events in the period that followed revealed that an "Islamist bloc" was by no means a certainty. Fundamental differences existed in the visions of governance put forward by the Muslim Brotherhood and the Salafis, relating mostly to differing views on legislating moral codes for society, and the role *sharia* would play in a future constitution. Moreover, the Islamists had seemingly overplayed their hand. SCAF, which was determined to ensure that an Islamist bloc was not allowed to govern unchecked, refused to allow the new members to form a government, instantly transforming the just-elected body into a lame duck parliament. The consequences of this decision were twofold. In the short term it forced the Muslim Brotherhood, ironically, to rejoin the ranks of the revolutionaries and embark on protests against a transition that it had helped create. In the long term, however, the Guidance Bureau reassessed its political calculus, ultimately deciding to field a presidential candidate after a year of pledging that it would not do so. This blatant backpedaling, coupled with popular perceptions of a failed parliamentary experiment and a well-financed media campaign to discredit the organization, left the Muslim Brotherhood in a drastically weakened position.

The group's leadership also faced challenges from within. Several blocs of youth activists and even high-level officials broke ranks with the Muslim Brotherhood in the months leading up to the parliamentary elections, viewing the strict organizational hierarchy as stifling within the newly opened political environment. Several formed independent political parties with a moderate Islamist agenda. One leading figure, 'Abdel Mon'eim Abul Futuh, was expelled from the organization in the summer of 2011 due to his decision to run for the presidency at a time when doing so was expressly forbidden. But by the late spring of 2012, he faced the prospect of running against an FJP-nominated candidate in Mohamed Morsi.

The changing landscape of political Islam within post-revolutionary Egypt revealed the structural weaknesses within the Muslim Brotherhood. In the face of a repressive authoritarian system, commanding strict adherence and operating in secrecy were assets. In a free and open political environment, however, these features did not appeal to some followers, and the group's leadership did not adapt its modes of operation at a sufficiently quick pace. On matters of ideology, there was little separating the newly independent Islamists from their former organization. As Abul Futuh observed, "The Muslim Brotherhood is a school that every Islamic activist should go through. But eventually, one graduates from school."[31] In other words, while he and others believed in the intellectual roots of the organization, its guiding philosophy and social mission, they did not necessarily agree with every political calculation or strategic decision it made. At a time when pragmatism was bound to take precedence over principles, the budding political environment paved the way for the emergence of multiple views on the best course to pursue the mission of implementing Islamic principles in governance.

In time, the Muslim Brotherhood would have to contend with the growing diversity within the Islamist movement. At the height of the discontent against its political strategy, the FJP's candidate still managed to emerge as a finalist in the presidential race. But in order to convince a much larger share of the Egyptian populace to support Morsi's bid, the party would have to win over many of its political rivals, from expelled Muslim Brotherhood members and Salafis intent on charting an independent course to liberals and revolutionary activists. However, despite this seemingly monumental challenge, in the June 2012 second round run-off between Morsi and Ahmed Shafiq, a remnant of the Mubarak era running on a counter-revolutionary platform, the Muslim Brotherhood emerged triumphant with the slimmest of margins, receiving barely 51 percent of the vote.

The democratic election of an Islamist president was a watershed moment in the modern history of the Arab world. It threatened to undermine many long-held assumptions about the nature of political

[31] Interview with 'Abdel Mon'eim Abul Futuh.

power within these societies. Yet for his part, Morsi initially avoided confrontations with the existing centers of power, instead preferring to allow SCAF to retain its privileged status and to keep most state institutions in the hands of ministers from the previous government. His attempt to reinstate the dissolved parliament was met with a swift rejection from Egypt's highest court, and the Muslim Brotherhood saw its efforts to exert true political power frustrated yet again. In August 2012, as the situation further deteriorated, Morsi made use of a security crisis to dismiss leading military officials, including the head of SCAF and his deputy, from their posts. He proceeded to promote mid-level officials to senior positions, annulled the constitutional statement which served as the basis for SCAF's authority, and retained the powers of the presidency, effectively defusing the crisis and launching a new era in the post-revolutionary transition in Egypt. After emerging out of the early transitional period as the single most powerful political actor, the Muslim Brotherhood now faced the challenge of developing its vision for governance, beginning with the task of writing the country's new constitution, a process that further polarized Egyptian society in advance of its passage in December 2012.

The year that followed saw the achievements of Egypt's democratic transition reversed when the military forcibly removed Morsi from office on his first anniversary as president. In the shadow of the continued lack of security, economic stagnation, and an increasingly polarized political scene, liberal and leftist forces organized a grassroots campaign agitating for Morsi's overthrow, resulting in the 3 July military coup led by Minister of Defense Abdel Fattah al-Sisi. Those who opposed the measure as a betrayal of the revolution and an assault on the legitimacy of the democratic process were met with an unprecedented wave of violent repression. Following six weeks of continuous popular protests and sit-ins, the military unleashed the worst campaign of indiscriminate deadly force against civilians in Egypt's modern history, resulting in over 1,000 dead and many thousands more injured in August 2013.

In an instant, the Muslim Brotherhood found itself targeted for extermination, as the military's campaign to arrest its leaders, silence its media, destroy its institutions, seize its assets, and isolate its supporters became reminiscent of previous waves of total repression dating back to the Nasser era. As the military, along with the police and the intelligence services, began to reassert their control over Egyptian society, the purported gains of the 2011 uprising appeared to be very much in doubt.

Though less extreme in the drastic reversal of fortunes, Yemen's transition came under intense pressures from the previous regime and external forces vying for influence in the country. Following Saleh's departure after a stalemate that lasted for several months, the first major step in the transition was the election of Abed Rabbo Mansour Hadi, Saleh's vice-president, to succeed the ousted leader. Hadi ran unopposed, and the election was in fact a national referendum on the transitional process itself. Thus the process received overwhelming support from virtually all political factions in Yemen, including the leading Islamist party. Karman toned down her revolutionary rhetoric and endorsed Hadi's two-year interim presidency, "during which we will build Yemen," she said.[32]

Islah Party leaders expected to be included in a future government that incorporated the opposition. The party sought a period of transitional justice, coupled with a cleansing from state institutions of Saleh loyalists, to be followed by the process of writing the state constitution to guarantee political freedoms and democratic governance. This process stalled during the first year of Hadi's term in office. He faced frequent opposition to his attempts at removing powerful military figures from their positions and he rarely included oppositional leaders in his administration, some of whom took to resuming their public protests. In the meantime, Islah Party head Mohammad al-Yadomi continued to express his support for the transitional process, hopeful that by standing alongside Hadi and his powerful regional allies, the Islamists would eventually help shape the future Yemeni state.

In Libya, a country with no recent legacy of democratic elections or popular participation in government, the transition from the Qaddafi era would not be straightforward. Indeed, the process would be further complicated due to the country's competing ideological traditions and the looming presence of international forces, with pressures to achieve a pluralistic political system in a short period of time being exceedingly high. When the Transitional National Council (TNC), the body entrusted with overseeing the process of elections and writing the constitution, met at a victory celebration in October 2011, its leader Mustafa 'Abdel-Jalil announced the dawn of a new Libyan state based on Islamic principles. Though not an avowed Islamist, 'Abdel-Jalil

[32] "Nobel Laureate Lays Out Plans to Build Modern State," *Gulf News*, 20 Feb. 2012.

tapped into the perceived religious conservatism of Libyan society, declaring: "We are an Islamic country. We take the Islamic religion as the core of our new government. The constitution will be based on our Islamic religion."[33]

In the ensuing months, the now familiar divide between secular and religious forces appeared to have become fully realized. The interim prime minister of the TNC, Mahmoud Jibril, was openly critical of what he perceived as attempts by Islamists to hijack the revolution and manipulate its outcome in their favor. For their part, the newly founded Islamist political parties argued that they were adhering to the tenets of democracy. The Muslim Brotherhood, which had maintained a limited presence in Libya under Qaddafi, established the Justice and Construction Party (JCP) headed by Mohammad Sawan ahead of the elections in July 2012. The Nation Party, led by Ali Sallabi and also featuring Belhadj as a strong leader, offered an alternative Islamist vision free of the institutional constraints of the Muslim Brotherhood.

When the votes were counted, the Islamists had received a smaller share of seats in Libya than they had in neighboring countries, which appeared to stem the tide of Islamist gains in the post-revolutionary transitions across the Arab world.[34] While Jibril's coalition took twice as many seats as the JCP, it became readily apparent that this election was not a clear-cut defeat for the Islamists. Jibril faced internal pressures from former Muslim Brotherhood figures within his own coalition bloc, and went as far as to reassure voters of his Islamist credentials, declaring his support for *sharia* as the main source of legislation. Furthermore, the choice of Mohamed al-Magarief to serve as president of the General National Congress, the interim body tasked with governing Libya until the end of the transition period, was a nod to the Islamists. Though not a member of the Muslim Brotherhood, Magarief was widely viewed as identifying with its political views. His emergence as a consensus candidate to lead Libya's transition points to the fact that the country was not faced with the same deep ideological divisions that characterized other states. Even in the absence of a clear electoral victory, Islamist politics was poised to play a key role in the new Libya.

[33] Adam Nossiter and Kareem Fahim, "Revolution Won, Top Libyan Official Vows a New and More Pious State," *New York Times*, 23 Oct. 2011.

[34] David D. Kirkpatrick, "Election Results in Libya Break an Islamist Wave," *New York Times*, 8 July 2012.

Post-Islamism Redux

Prior to the wave of revolts that took the Arab world by storm in 2011, the prospect of an avowedly Islamist social movement reaching the height of political power in any state in the region appeared to be exceedingly dim. Some scholars had previously described the advent of "post-Islamism" as the defining characteristic of Arab societies in the authoritarian setting of the early twenty-first century. Others subsequently appropriated the term for a variety of purposes, from depicting the bankruptcy of militant groups to tracking the shift in political platforms and electoral strategies by popular social movements in a desperate attempt to remain a viable actor in an increasingly restrictive political context.

Even as the trajectory of Islamist movements in positions of authority skyrocketed in the aftermath of the Arab uprisings, seemingly rendering "post-Islamism" a premature fantasy, the term may yet have its uses. For Islamism, by its very definition, was a theoretical construct depicting the rise of a particular social movement functioning in tension with the existing order: the post-colonial, secular, nation state system that arose in the Middle East. But just as the supposed failure of that project is supposed to have yielded a post-Islamist world, so too will its potential success. As the aftermath of the Arab revolts has attempted to redefine the state on another basis, one that incorporates the spirit, if not the letter, of the Islamist mission, that mission's need to persist as a discernable social phenomenon will gradually decline, until it ceases to exist altogether. In that regard, Islamism is no different from all social movements that arise out of a particular historical moment only to recede once its aims have been achieved.

The experience of Turkey's Justice and Development Party (AKP) sheds some light on this possibility. After overcoming the considerable obstacles placed before it by virtue of its leadership's Islamist credentials, the AKP rose to become the leading political actor in Turkey in the first decade of the twenty-first century. By most accounts, during its time in power, the party reformed the country's political institutions, presided over consistent economic growth, and greatly enhanced Turkey's regional and international standing. However, in keeping with Turkey's strict constitutional ban on religious political parties, the AKP built its successful record without an explicitly Islamist platform.

Given the pressures faced by Islamist movements in the post-authoritarian setting of many Arab countries, it is no wonder that the "Turkish model" gained currency among the region's newly formed political parties, almost none of which feature Islam in their name. This approach promotes the notion that, insofar as Islamist movements existed on the margins of a political process that disavowed any religious influence, they were far more likely to frame their mission in religious terms, especially insofar as they claimed to represent a pious society against an impious ruler. With the political scene having been opened to the legitimate participation of Islamist groups, however, as they continue to represent the religious sensibilities of their fellow citizens, the need to define their mission in Islamic terms has since receded.

This transition has only just begun, but it can already be seen playing out in a number of challenges facing Islamist groups as they seek to redefine the nature of their systems of governance. On the issue of implementing the *sharia*, itself a fluid and adaptable legal system that does not easily lend itself to codification, a renewed emphasis on the *maqasid*, or objectives of the law, has begun to replace the long-standing fixation on applying the historical letter of the law. In Tunisia, Egypt, Libya, and elsewhere, this has meant that, in some ways, the political platforms of mainstream Islamist parties have become so generalized in some areas, whether on matters of the economy or foreign policy, as to become virtually indistinguishable from those of non-Islamist parties.

Moreover, a key lesson from the Turkish experience is that a political party will ultimately be judged by its performance once in power, not by its founding principles or guiding philosophy. While the move toward pragmatism accompanied the Muslim Brotherhood's foray into politics, this realization puts that transformation into a clearer perspective: its political leaders will be held accountable on the basis not of their personal religious devotion, but of their ability to conduct their public service faithfully and effectively. In Egypt, Morsi's government learned this lesson the hard way, and his subsequent expulsion from the presidency and the Muslim Brotherhood's renewed subjection to regime repression present a compelling challenge for the future of its political activism. In the hopes of avoiding a similar political crisis, Tunisia's Islamist movement withdrew from the leadership of the transition and ensured that it would still be a part of the political process even if it could no longer dictate its terms.

Islamist movements still face numerous challenges and contradictions that will only be addressed during the course of their experience in government. On the issue of citizenship rights, movement leaders have repeatedly expressed their support for national identity as the basis of a "civil state," but in practice it remains to be seen how legislating according to Islamic principles would avoid adversely affecting minority rights.

In terms of economic policy and social justice, the platforms put forward in the early stages of political contestation by Islamist parties lacked any imagination. They tended to vacillate between vague allusions to Islamic directives to tend to the needs of the most vulnerable segments of society and staunch commitments to the continuation of neo-liberal policies that were at the root of many of the socio-economic ills characteristic of the authoritarian era. Similarly, in the arena of foreign relations, platitudes about pan-Arab and pan-Islamic solidarity, such as the continued verbal commitment to the Palestinian struggle, were often outweighed by more narrow national interests that precluded actual policy changes. Pressures from global and regional powers such as the United States and Saudi Arabia offered new considerations to Islamist parties unaccustomed to dealing with uncomfortable geopolitical realities.

Despite the arduous trials that await Islamist movements as they attempt to negotiate their place in the nascent political order, the most prudent decision that these parties have made (whether freely or under pressure) is to avoid going it alone. In nearly every case, the Islamist movement exists within a broad national effort to determine the future structure of a state. In Libya and Yemen, Islamists are a junior partner in this endeavor, attempting to frame their participation within the context of the national interest rather than a narrow appeal to religious conviction. Before stepping down from the leadership role in Tunisia, al-Nahda was the senior partner working with other political forces to chart a path designed to ensure that individual rights are respected and that the state does not become an agent for legislating and enforcing piety. Even in the Egyptian case, the notable exception due to the Muslim Brotherhood's desire to dominate all aspects of the transition, the Morsi presidency began with promises of pragmatism and inclusion before finding itself in total isolation months later. Morsi drew his prime minister from the previous government and left several powerful ministries, including defense, foreign affairs, and finance, in the hands of officials unaffiliated with the Islamist movement. Instead, the FJP opted to develop its political credentials slowly, taking on several social services ministries such as housing, education, youth, and labor, in an effort to establish a track record of effective governance before tackling the larger challenges facing Egypt.

Internally, the Islamist movement faces its own challenges in attempting to temper its traditional ideology to the changing political realities, while also adapting its organizational structure to meet the needs of a democratic society. In Egypt, the Muslim Brotherhood experienced a significant number of defections because of its inability to respond adequately to the concerns of its vast following. The rise of Salafi groups in Libya and Tunisia, as well as Egypt, added yet another major player to the emerging landscape of post-revolutionary Islamist politics, forcing a recalculation of each group's religious credentials, or the questioning of whether such a metric will ultimately matter in the struggle for popular support for political power. In addition, the shift in resources toward the political sphere has adversely affected the social mission of Islamist groups in the period since the Arab uprisings began. While this may permanently transform the nature of Islamist organizations like the Muslim Brotherhood, it is likely to be viewed by its leadership as a positive step toward the realization of Banna's original vision which deems the ideal government to be the mirror image of a sufficiently Islamized society. In that scenario, the evolution of Islamist activism renders it practically undetectable within a state governed by its virtues.

5

POLITICAL PARTY DEVELOPMENT BEFORE AND AFTER THE ARAB SPRING

Shadi Hamid

Political parties have long struggled to gain traction in the Arab world due to a number of inhibiting factors, among them a potent mix of repression and government co-optation. But this is not to say that the region has lacked viable opposition forces. Islamist movements—most of which are branches or descendants of the Muslim Brotherhood—have over time consolidated their position as leading political actors in the region. Yet such movements are a far cry from traditional, Western-style parties. Most political parties, after all, do not double as states-within-states, with parallel networks of mosques, clinics, banks, businesses, daycare centers, and even Boy Scout troops. Islamist parties do. It was their long-term focus on education and social service provision—rather than on contesting elections—that ultimately helped propel Islamist movements, and later their associated parties, to political prominence.

Whether acting according to the traditional model of party competition (where winning elections is an end) or "alternative competitive" and "restricted competition" models[1] (where winning is a means), political parties generally seek to win elections and assume executive power. However, in the Arab world, parties were rarely given the opportunity to govern—or to even think about governing—at the local or national level. Citizens saw little utility in joining parties that would never be permitted a real stake in the political process. Only in one country, Morocco, was there a semblance of genuine multi-party competition. During 1998's "*alternance*," the Socialist Union of Populist Forces (USFP) led a left-of-center government, after winning a plurality in parliamentary elections.

Unlike Morocco, most Arab countries do not have a tradition of political party activity. On the eve of the 2011 uprising, most of Egypt's legal parties, for example, had memberships in the mere hundreds or thousands and were derided as "cardboard parties," or *ahzab cartoniya*. The liberal Wafd Party was something of an exception, as it could claim a storied tradition as one of Egypt's pro-independence parties during the country's short-lived "liberal era" of the 1930s and 1940s. During a brief political opening after Hosni Mubarak became president in 1981, the Wafd—which had reconstituted itself in the 1970s—seemed poised to regain some of its former prominence. But despite a solid showing in the 1984 elections, it subsequently descended into irrelevance, demonstrating the impossibility of developing healthy party politics in an authoritarian context.

Elsewhere in the region, the intellectual and ideological decline of the left has made it difficult for certain parties to re-emerge after repressive measures are lifted. In Jordan, the National Socialist Party of Sulayman al-Nabulsi briefly came to power in 1957 before an embattled King Hussein cracked down and curtailed the activities of political parties, eventually banning them altogether. When martial law was lifted, leftist and socialist parties tried to reconstitute themselves but failed to gain popular support and withered away.

In Communist South Yemen, the Yemen Socialist Party (YSP) was the longtime ruling party. After unification, it joined President Ali Abdullah

[1] This traditional model is best approximated by Anthony Downs's spatial model, first presented in *An Economic Theory of Democracy*, New York: Harper & Row, 1957. For alternative models, see Donald A. Wittman, "Parties as Utility Maximizers," *The American Political Science Review*, 67 (June 1973), p. 495.

Saleh's General People's Congress in a governing coalition. After the defeat of Southern forces in the 1994 civil war, the YSP was weakened considerably with leaders fleeing into exile and its organizational structures damaged. Just as importantly, though, the Saleh regime became increasingly authoritarian after the civil war, making it difficult for the YSP—and any other party besides the Brotherhood-affiliated Islah Party—to build significant support.[2]

In country after country, the growing tendency to resort to state repression—in Egypt, Jordan, Yemen, Algeria, and Tunisia—fatally weakened political party life in the 1990s. To the extent that citizens wished to become involved in politics, they tended to join civil society organizations, professional associations, and, as mentioned, religious movements. However, as inconsequential as they may have seemed, political parties still served a purpose under some semi-authoritarian regimes. Rather than eliminate dissent altogether, the ruling regimes hoped to manage and contain it. Political parties provided the illusion of freedom and pluralism. The totalitarian nature of Baathist Iraq and Syria had become quaint and outdated. The better, less costly way to subdue the opposition was to give it just enough room to breathe, but little more. Elections gave regimes a chance to "legitimize" their rule and employ the language of democracy for authoritarian ends. The whole enterprise was not particularly convincing, but nor was it entirely meaningless. Opposition parties used elections—and all their accompanying rules and procedures—to negotiate the boundaries of political contestation. As Nathan Brown writes, "Regimes and oppositions bargain continuously and without final resolution over who may run in elections, who will oversee balloting, how votes will be translated into seats, who may observe the electoral process [and] how campaigns will be conducted."[3]

Semi-authoritarian regimes also had political parties of their own, although these were almost exclusively vehicles for professional advancement, distribution of power to allies and friends, and the management of patron–client relationships. When the Tunisian and Egyptian revolutions occurred, the supposedly "mass" parties of the National Democratic

[2] For more on political parties in Yemen see Ahmed A. Hezam Al-Yemeni, *The Dynamic of Democratisation: Political Parties in Yemen*, Bonn: Friedrich Ebert Stiftung, 2003.

[3] Nathan J. Brown, *When Victory is Not an Option: Islamists Movements in Arab Politics*, Ithaca, NY: Cornell University Press, 2012, p. 26.

Party and the Constitutional Democratic Rally, each claiming membership in the millions, quickly crumbled. Some ruling parties, such as Yemen's General People's Congress (GPC), proved more resilient and survived the uprisings, albeit in a weakened state. Revolutions against ruling parties raise the question of what role, if any, those parties should be allowed to play during the transition, with Egypt, Libya, Tunisia, and Yemen opting for different approaches depending on the particular nature of the transition. As Ellen Lust notes, "Popular demands to ban or blacklist former regime allies are especially prevalent where elites have not defected from the old order to be at the forefront of reform."[4]

Importantly, the ongoing transitions in Tunisia, Libya, and Egypt (at least before the July 2013 military coup) have provided new spaces for the formation and development of political parties. With the fall of old regimes, parties were now, for the first time, allowed to win elections, thereby propelling them to a newfound prominence as the primary vehicle for political expression and representation. Past restrictions were lifted, allowing liberal and leftist parties their first real opportunity to reach new audiences, build party structures, and even play a role in government. Meanwhile, Islamist movements—the Egyptian and Libyan Muslim Brotherhoods and al-Nahda in Tunisia—established political parties that, while at least nominally independent, represent, to varying degrees, the interests of the parent movement.

Despite a flourishing of new parties in quantity if not in quality, those that found themselves in the halls of government in Egypt and Tunisia came under mounting criticism for their failure to address economic woes. Those in the opposition, meanwhile, too easily resorted to obstructionism while failing to provide coherent alternatives. Increased polarization in these countries raises the question: what makes a "loyal opposition?" Political parties themselves may decide that party politics is not the best avenue to challenge constitutional orders that they see as illegitimate. The resort to street protest and civil disobedience—as occurred in late 2012 over President Mohamed Morsi's moves against Egypt's judiciary and, later, with the 30 June 2013 mass protests—may

[4] Ellen Lust, "Voting for Change: The Pitfalls and Possibilities of First Elections in Arab Transitions," Brookings Doha Center—Stanford University Project on Arab Transitions, May 2012, http://www.brookings.edu/research/papers/2012/05/09-arab-democracies-lust, p. 2.

lead to a re-emergence of civil society and vibrant popular movements, but it is just as likely to arouse an anti-democratic populism and undermine the institutionalization of strong party systems.

The Development of Party Systems

Carles Boix defines a "party system" as "the national profile, in terms of number, size, and ideological preferences, of parties."[5] As the United States, Britain, France, and other early democracies developed in the eighteenth and nineteenth centuries, parties gradually cohered, adopting defined programs and exacting growing discipline from millions of members and supporters.

Party systems are products of a country's particular history. Over time, they become entrenched and self-sustaining. What happens at the start of the democratization process is not incidental, nor can it be easily reversed. This is what makes transitional periods particularly tense and polarizing. The stakes over a permanent constitution, separation of powers, and the role of religion in public life—in other words the very shape of institutions—are particularly high. And institutional frameworks are not easily changed. Referring to Brazil's transition, Frances Hagopian wrote that "individuals rise who are adept at the political game as it is played, and they use their positions to perpetuate modes of political interaction that favor them. In this way, political arrangements, once in place, condition future political behavior and possibilities."[6]

The electoral system, which Giovanni Sartori calls "the most specific manipulative instrument of politics," may be of even greater importance than constitutions.[7] Electoral laws can either encourage the development of political parties, or ensure that they remain weak and ineffectual. In the Middle East, Jordan is perhaps the most striking case. In the late 1980s and early 1990s, the country was experiencing what, for a time,

[5] Carles Boix, "The Emergence of Parties and Party Systems," in Carles Boix and Susan C. Stokes (eds), *The Oxford Handbook of Comparative Politics*, Oxford: Oxford University Press, 2006, p. 501.

[6] Frances Hagopian, "Democracy by Undemocratic Means? Elites, Political Pacts, and Regime Transition in Brazil," *Comparative Political Studies*, 23 (July 1990), p. 148.

[7] Giovanni Sartori, "Political Development and Political Engineering," *Public Policy*, 17 (1963), p. 273.

appeared to be a promising democratic "experiment." However, the move toward democracy was derailed with the advent of the now notorious "one-vote" electoral law, or *sawt al-wahid*, which was decreed in 1993 by King Hussein. The 1989 elections had been conducted under a plurality block voting system in which voters in a given district could cast a ballot for as many candidates as there were seats.[8] This benefited well-organized groups like the Brotherhood that could count on the commitment and discipline of their members. This dynamic would change dramatically under "one-vote." Now, in a district of six seats, each voter could cast a ballot for only one person rather than six. Single non-transferable vote (SNTV) is an increasingly rare electoral system, with only a handful of countries—including Afghanistan and Vanuatu—using it on the national level. As Democracy Reporting International notes: "A reason for the infrequent use of SNTV as an electoral system is that it is widely acknowledged to be specifically disadvantageous toward the development of political parties and because it tends to result in votes being cast for individual candidates or those who represent specific groups in a district rather than those who stand for political party platforms."[9]

In countries where ethnicity or tribal affiliation remains paramount, SNTV can prove even more damaging to party development. With only one vote, indigenous Jordanians were more likely to vote for a candidate from their tribe. As a result, "independents" dominated every subsequent parliament. In the 2007 parliamentary elections, political parties won less than 10 percent of the total seats. District size is another important variable. Where candidates can win a seat with only a few

[8] For example, if a district had six seats, Jordanians could vote for up to six candidates, which benefited groups like the Brotherhood. In turn, smaller leftist groups and Christian candidates sought alliances with the Brotherhood. Both sides benefited. A Brotherhood supporter could vote for the two Brotherhood candidates running in his or her district, vote for one Christian, one leftist, and still have one vote to spare. Similarly, a Christian, with a vote to spare, could vote for two Christian candidates as well as the two Brotherhood candidates. By being selective about which districts to contest and by forming alliances with a variety of individuals and groups, the Brotherhood could effectively guarantee the victory of nearly all its candidates.

[9] "Assessment of the Electoral Framework: The Hashemite Kingdom of Jordan," Democracy Reporting International and New Jordan Research Center, Berlin: Democracy Reporting International, 2007, pp. 16–17.

thousand votes, intimate personal connections and familial ties are the keys to electoral success.[10] Ideological or programmatic considerations become secondary to most voters, making it difficult for political parties to gain support.

Despite the experience of Jordan, Libya, under the guidance of the UN Support Mission in Libya (UNSMIL) and pro-democracy NGOs like the International Foundation for Electoral Systems (IFES), adopted SNTV to elect eighty out of the 200 seats for its General National Congress in 2012. The other 120 seats were reserved for independents. One of the rationales behind this was to prevent any one political party from dominating the elections, which would in turn prevent any one party from monopolizing the process of writing the permanent constitution. While Libya's electoral law is of course subject to amendment, there is, again, the matter of path dependence. Party systems are self-sustaining. Individuals and parties elected under a particular system are unlikely to use their power to propose an entirely different system. Interestingly enough, it is the Israeli model that may be most instructive here. Israel's pure form of proportional representation, enacted in 1948, was only expected to be a temporary arrangement. Once elected, a constituent assembly would then pass a permanent electoral law.[11] However, as Vernon Bogdanor notes, "this assumption overlooked [the fact that] those who thrive under a given electoral system come to have a vested interest in preserving it, fearing that any change might hurt them and help their opponents."[12] Despite efforts at reform, the electoral system of 1948 remains in place today. Yet for all its faults, the Israeli system did not necessarily impede party formation. Libya's system, on the other hand, does. The combination of SNTV and an institutional bias favoring independents, as well as the continued importance of tribal loyalties, does not bode well for the coherence or discipline of Libyan political parties.

[10] In the 2003 Jordanian elections, a majority of deputies won their seats with under 4,000 votes. See "Assessment of the Electoral Framework," p. 12.

[11] See Vernon Bogdanor, "Israel Debates Reform," *Journal of Democracy*, 4 (Jan. 1993), pp. 66–7.

[12] Ibid. p. 67.

The Historical Encounter with Hizbiyya

Each country has its own unique historical encounter with multi-partyism, or *hizbiyya*. It is this history that bears its weight on the present, albeit to varying degrees depending on the country in question. In the 1930s and 1940s, Egypt featured a deeply flawed but functioning parliamentary system. There were reasonably free elections, with power alternating between political parties. Yet the system was a far cry from democracy: Britain and its client monarchy routinely intervened in domestic politics. The period between 1944 and 1950 saw the rapid collapse of successive governments, eight in all.[13] As Joel Gordon recounts, "escalating political violence marked a period of increasing disillusion with parliamentary rule that encompassed all sectors of Egyptian society."[14] When revolution swept Egypt in 1952, it did away with the elements of the old regime, including the political parties. Not just in Egypt but across the region, avowedly nationalist leaders came to power, promising unity and purpose as part of a totalizing vision that brooked little dissent. What ensued was a massive, controlled project of social engineering, bankrolled by the largesse of the bureaucratic state. Unsurprisingly, political parties (except, of course, the one party) were seen as anathema.

Islamists, too, were suspicious of *hizbiyya*. As recently as the early 1980s, the Muslim Brotherhood was split on whether to formally take part in parliamentary politics. There was the legacy of founder Hassan al-Banna, who saw *hizbiyya* as a "device which has given legality to the appetites of the rulers and the tyrannies of authority."[15] He saw the various parties as elite structures beholden to special interests, which failed to give voice to the concerns of common Egyptians. Moreover, they were little more than pawns in the global chessboard, victims of Britain and the king's unending political machinations.[16] Similarly, Umar al-

[13] Joel Gordon, "The False Hopes of 1950: The Wafd's Last Hurrah and the Demise of the Old Order," *International Journal of Middle East Studies*, 21 (May 1989), p. 193.

[14] Ibid.

[15] Richard P. Mitchell, *The Society of the Muslim Brothers*, London: Oxford University Press, 1969, p. 261.

[16] Interestingly, however, Banna had better things to say about the American political system, which he saw as being bound by a national consensus and, therefore, united. The two parties competed during election season and

Tilmisani, general guide of the Brotherhood in the 1970s and 1980s, argued that political parties would "split public opinion into antagonistic factions."[17]

In Libya, political parties were banned, with only brief interruptions, from 1951 through to the end of Muammar Qaddafi's rule in 2011. Qaddafi, like Nasser before him, layered his opposition to partyism with ideological justifications. Among other things, he argued that political parties produced factionalism and division and were a "contemporary form of dictatorship."[18] Such views did not disappear overnight in Libya. In April 2012, after conducting nationwide focus groups, the National Democratic Institute (NDI) found that many Libyans still expressed "discomfort with political parties due to the legacy of Qaddafi's propaganda" and saw them as "untrustworthy, conniving, and motivated by secret agendas and possibly unduly influenced by foreign countries seeking to interfere in Libyan politics."[19] Qaddafi's legacy may help explain the lack of vocal opposition to an electoral law that disadvantaged political parties.

The Egyptian and Tunisian regimes, in contrast, allowed for some political party participation, however weak and circumscribed. At one time Egypt had relatively strong parties, such as the liberal Wafd, contesting elections—and winning them—in the 1930s and 1940s, as mentioned above. Even during the years of Mubarak and Ben Ali's repression, Egypt and to a lesser extent Tunisia had legal parties which ran candidates in elections and participated in parliament. After the uprisings in both countries, political parties did not have to start from a blank slate in terms of both popular perceptions and organizational structures. Two parties in Tunisia that would play an important role in the post-revolution period—the liberal Congress for the Republic (CPR) and the leftist Progressive Democratic Party (PDP)—had devel-

---

offered differing policy prescriptions. On issues of "sovereignty," however, they acted similarly. See Mitchell, *The Society of the Muslim Brothers*, p. 261.

17 Gilles Kepel, *Muslim Extremism in Egypt: The Prophet and Pharaoh*, Berkeley: University of California Press, 2003, p. 125.

18 "POMED Backgrounder: Previewing Libya's Elections," Project on Middle East Democracy, 5 July 2012, p. 9.

19 Megan Doherty, "Building a New Libya: Citizen Views on Libya's Electoral and Political Processes," May 2012, National Democratic Institute, p. 13.

oped some name recognition and political legitimacy as opposition parties under the Ben Ali regime (although the former was banned, while the latter chose to boycott successive parliamentary elections).

New Parties, Old Cleavages

History also matters in other ways. In their seminal study, *Party Systems and Voter Alignments* (1967), Seymour Lipset and Stein Rokkan argue that the process of state formation and modernization, along with fundamental shifts in economic structures—the Industrial Revolution and accompanying urbanization—gave rise to differences among citizens that provoked lasting cleavages.[20] The fact that economic cleavages are paramount in most Western democracies, then, is no accident, given the particular sequence of events in the modernization process. Meanwhile, it was in Catholic-majority countries that clericalism and anti-clericalism became a major dimension of conflict. On the other hand, where the Reformation succeeded in displacing the Catholic Church and its role in economic and political life, religious divides, while still relevant, tended to fade to the background.[21]

The economic dimension of conflict in Western Europe became institutionalized over time—or "frozen," in the terminology of Lipset and Rokkan—in the form of parties that self-defined according to economic concerns, in particular the distribution of capital and the state's role in economic production.[22] Yet it would be a mistake to think that party systems are historically determined. The literature on party alignment strongly suggests that "parties themselves ... are the main drivers behind party system change and stability."[23] As Nick Sitter puts it, "the parties have stolen the show."[24]

[20] Seymour Lipset and Stein Rokkan, *Party Systems and Voter Alignments: Cross-National Perspectives*, London: The Free Press, 1967.
[21] Boix, "The Emergence of Parties and Party Systems," pp. 502–3.
[22] For a useful discussion of the "freezing" and "thawing" of party cleavages, see Claude A. Bonilla et al., "Social or Political Cleavages? A Spatial Analysis of the Party System in Post-Authoritarian Chile," *Public Choice*, 146 (2011), pp. 9–21.
[23] Nick Sitter, "Cleavages, Party Strategy and Party System Change in Europe, East and West," *Perspectives on European Politics and Society*, 3, 3 (2002), p. 448.
[24] Ibid.

Parties decide which issues to prioritize in order to distinguish themselves from the competition. It is this process of parties interacting with the electorate and, of course, each other that gradually produces the party system. As Adam Przeworski and John Sprague note with regard to the rise of socialist parties in Western Europe: "Class is salient in any society, if, when, and only to the extent to which it is important to political parties which mobilize workers."[25] Again, party systems like electoral systems are unlikely to change dramatically, notwithstanding major internal or external shocks. Parties inject cleavages into politics. Those cleavages in turn become more salient, forcing other parties to respond to and address them in the public arena.

These considerations are important in situating the Egyptian and Tunisian experiences. Both countries feature underlying patterns of party stability, which are likely to hold, at least in some form, for the foreseeable future. The relevant historical episode, particularly for Egypt, can be tied to the events of 1967, when Arab countries were routed by Israel in the Six-Day War. Such a stark defeat provoked unprecedented soul-searching, leading many to conclude that the socialist experiment had failed. An emerging narrative—which would become the Islamist narrative—was that the Arab world had strayed from the teachings of Islam and that it needed to return to true Islamic principles. And so the Islamic revival began in earnest, spreading across the region, encouraged by the release of imprisoned Muslim Brotherhood leaders in the early 1970s. Gulf oil money provided an additional boost. Islam had yet to become the defining political issue, but it soon would.

The 1980s saw the Egyptian Brotherhood's foray into parliamentary politics. After being decimated by the Nasser regime, the group grew exponentially in the 1970s, reaching out to new audiences, gaining recruits, and rebuilding its organizational structures. When President Hosni Mubarak opened up Egyptian politics in the early 1980s and promised competitive elections, the Brotherhood entered the fray, despite its discomfort with party politics, and formed an alliance with the ostensibly secular Wafd Party. The Brotherhood's Salah Abu Ismail justified the decision on purely practical grounds: "They didn't allow us to form a party on the basis of *aqidah* (creed) … and closed the door of

[25] Adam Przeworski and John Sprague, *Paper Stones: A History of Electoral Socialism*, Chicago, IL: University of Chicago Press, 1986, pp. 10–11.

da'wa, so we are not able to raise our voices on the pulpit or through [our own] political party, so what is left for us except to work through an existing political party?"[26]

From the outset, Islamists lobbed accusations at the Wafd for not respecting Islamic law.[27] The Wafd certainly tried, revamping its electoral program to address the Brotherhood's concerns. In its original 1977 program, there was only one passing mention of *sharia* as the "original" (*aseel*) source of legislation. The 1984 program, in contrast, included an entire section devoted to the application of Islamic law, in which the Wafd stated its agreement that Islam is both *din wa dawla* (religion and state) and that *sharia* is the principal source of legislation.[28] The program also called for efforts to combat moral "deviation" in society, to purify the media of anything contradicting *sharia*, and to emphasize the media's role in actively guiding Egyptians toward a moral life.[29]

Its alliance with the Brotherhood was an important factor in pushing the party toward such a posture. But it was far from the only one. The Wafd was not operating in a vacuum. The political and religious context in the country was changing; Egyptians had become more religious and more concerned with applying Islamic law. The Wafd, in turn, needed to adapt to its environment and respond to the evolving preferences of an increasingly conservative electorate. Interestingly, much of the religious content of the 1984 program remained in the 1987 program, well after the alliance with the Brotherhood had come to an end.[30]

These developments would have far-reaching consequences for the evolution of Egypt's party system. At this point, the Brotherhood was acting like a "niche party," a term used by Bonnie Meguid to describe "single-issue" or limited agenda parties, whose raison d'être is to elevate an issue of importance that has been insufficiently addressed by mainstream parties. Niche parties, according to Meguid, "[adopt] positions only on a restricted set of issues ... [They] rely on the salience and

26 Hasanayn Tawfiq Ibrahim and Hoda Raghib Awad, *al-Ikhwan al-Muslimun wa al-Siyasa fi Misr* [The Political Role of the Muslim Brotherhood under Limited Political Pluralism in Egypt], Cairo: Markaz al-Mahrusa, 1996, p. 97.

27 Ibid. p. 137.

28 Ibid. p. 173.

29 Ibid.

30 Ibid. p. 176.

attractiveness of their *one* policy stance for voter support."[31] For the Brotherhood, the one overarching concern during this initial period of parliamentary participation was the role of Islam in public life. The group was much less like a traditional political party than a sort of "*sharia* lobby."

According to Meguid's niche party–mainstream framework of interaction (which she calls the "modified spatial theory"), mainstream parties (in 1980s Egypt, the ruling National Democratic Party and the Wafd would both qualify) have one of two choices when dealing with a newly introduced niche issue, in this case the application of *sharia*. They can opt for a "dismissive strategy" and treat it as insignificant, thus lowering its salience in the minds of voters. Conversely, the mainstream party can try to attract supporters of the niche issue by "acknowledging [its] legitimacy ... and [signaling] its prioritization of that policy dimension."[32] In this way, the introduction of a niche issue into the political arena does two things. First, it raises the issue's salience in the minds of voters and other opposition parties. Second, it provides incentives to the niche party to emphasize its distinctiveness on its niche issue, in order to ensure that voters still see it as the most credible proponent, despite mainstream party efforts at appropriation.

This framework helps provide a better understanding of the rightward shift in Egypt's political scene during the early transition phase (2011–13). More importantly, though, it explains the "freezing" of ideological and religious cleavages in Egypt and the broader Arab world. Islamists were helping to push Islam into the public discourse like never before. Liberal parties, some of which were trying to curry favor with religiously minded voters, were compelled to speak the language of religion. In a conservative country, many voters were susceptible to religious rhetoric. But it was the actions of groups and parties like the Brotherhood that capitalized on voters' receptiveness. The cleavages solidified, and they would continue to solidify in subsequent years.

[31] Bonnie M. Meguid, "Competition between Unequals: The Role of Mainstream Party Strategy in Niche Party Success," *American Political Science Review*, 99 (Aug. 2005), p. 348. See also Avital Livni, "When Niche Parties Go Mainstream: The Case of the Islamist AKP in Turkey," unpublished paper, Nov. 2008, pp. 1–3.

[32] Ibid. p. 350.

Party Systems in a Democratic Era

Egypt has had the distinction of being exceedingly polarized along "Islamist–secular" lines, but it is a matter of degree, not kind. Tunisia, informed by the tragic experience of the Algerian civil war—also fought along Islamist–secular lines—gravitated in a similar direction in the 1980s and early 1990s. It was then that al-Nahda, formerly the Movement of the Islamic Tendency (MTI), emerged as the main challenger to Zine al-Abidine Ben Ali's staunch secularist rule.[33] Despite widespread fraud, al-Nahda—which, like the Egyptian Brotherhood, was denied legal status as a political party—won 15 percent of the vote and as much as 30 percent in key cities in the 1989 elections. This was too much for Ben Ali, who soon launched a brutal crackdown on Islamists, sending as many as 10,000 to prison. Al-Nahda's leader Rachid Ghannouchi went into exile in London, where he was to remain for the next twenty years.

By defining themselves in opposition to the Islamists, secular autocrats played their own role in making Islamism, or the lack thereof, the defining political issue for a generation. This was often by design, helping rulers gain support from the international community—and many secularists at home—as the lesser of two evils. In addition, they could use the specter of Islamism to repress all opposition, including liberal and leftist political parties, which they did with marked enthusiasm. The religious dimension of conflict overlapped somewhat with the economic, although it was not always obvious where one ended and the other began. Regime allies in Egypt and Tunisia were not only opposed to Islamism; they were also using their close ties to the ruler to amass considerable wealth. The Mubarak and Ben Ali regimes both oversaw impressive annual GDP growth of 5 to 7 percent in their later years, benefiting a whole new breed of regime-dependent oligarchs. In 2008, the former head of the IMF, Dominique Strauss-Kahn, called the Tunisian economy an "example for emerging countries," while the World Bank named it a "top reformer" in regulatory reform.[34] Islamists

[33] For discussion of MTI's origins and rise, see Marion Boulby, "The Islamic Challenge: Tunisia since Independence," *Third World Quarterly*, 10 (Apr. 1988), pp. 590–614; and Emad Shahin, *Political Ascent: Contemporary Islamic Movements in North Africa*, Boulder, CO: Westview Press, 1997.

[34] *Doing Business 2009: Comparing Regulation in 181 Economies*, Washington, DC: World Bank & International Finance Corporation, 2008, p. 79.

and their backers were not necessarily poor, as the conventional wisdom had it, but they were shut out of business and investment opportunities. As repression worsened, their firms were closed and their assets seized. There was an economic elite, but, increasingly, also a counter-elite that felt unjustly excluded from sharing in economic gains.

By the time Egypt and Tunisia experienced their revolutions, the Islamist–secular divide was already well entrenched. Revolutions can introduce new patterns of identity and organization, and many hoped that democratic transitions would allow Arab polities to put the intense ideological polarization of the past behind them. And for a brief moment, it seemed like they might. In Tahrir Square, Muslim Brotherhood members, Salafis, liberals, and leftists found themselves on the same side, united in their desire to bring down a dictator. In the early days following Mubarak's fall, politicians and parties spoke of a new era that would transcend the old divisions. But, soon enough, Egypt fell back into its previous patterns, yet this time with a vengeance.

After the 2011 uprising, Egypt's economic situation deteriorated considerably. For most ordinary Egyptians, this was the abiding concern. The debate over *sharia*, on the other hand, seemed beside the point, having little effect on the daily challenges they faced. Yet in the media discourse and in election campaigns, the fundamental divide, as it had been since the early 1980s, was between Islamists and non-Islamists. Importantly, the proliferation of new parties created an atmosphere of "outbidding." The Brotherhood and its newly established Freedom and Justice Party no longer had a monopoly on the votes of the Islamist faithful. The emergence of Salafi parties—which won 28 percent of the vote and 25 percent of the seats in the 2011 parliamentary elections—led to a kind of "tea-party effect," dragging the political spectrum further to the right.[35] Egyptians, a large majority of whom are religiously observant, were naturally receptive to appeals based on religion. Yet it was Egypt's political elites and parties that aggressively pushed religion to the forefront of national debate. The advantages in doing so were obvious for the Islamists. But liberals as well as old regime elements—lacking a dis-

[35] For more on Salafi political participation after the revolution, see Stephane Lacroix, "Sheikhs and Politicians: Inside the New Egyptian Salafism," Brookings Doha Center, June 2012, http://www.brookings.edu/research/papers/2012/06/07-egyptian-salafism-lacroix

tinctive program or a clearly defined ideology—used the fear of religious rule to rally their base to the polls with varying degrees of success.

A related question is why the economy failed to emerge as an important cleavage in the early stages of the transition. Both Egypt and Tunisia seemed to be particularly ripe for economic, class-based appeals. Indeed, candidates routinely promised more jobs, better wages, and campaigns to root out poverty, corruption, and any number of other social ills. Yet it was hard to pinpoint significant differences between the circulating economic programs, which, with few exceptions, offered variations on the same theme: market-driven growth coupled with protections for the poor and social justice for all. Ironically, it was leftist rather than liberal parties that did the worst in the first parliamentary contests. To the extent that economics mattered in the elections, it was often in the form of old-fashioned patronage, such as when the Brotherhood launched the "*millioniyyat al-khayr*" initiative on the eve of parliamentary elections, providing 1.5 million kilos of meat to millions of Egyptians.[36]

The choices of the largest parties tend to set the contours of political debate, forcing competitors to react and respond. Islamist parties had never been known for focusing much attention on economic policy. To the extent they did, they promoted a surprisingly free market-oriented economic vision, something that was likely to play well with investors rather than ordinary voters. Meanwhile, because their economic platforms differed little from those of their Islamist counterparts, liberal and leftist parties found themselves constrained. And, in any case, their own economic vision, beyond the broad outlines, was similarly underdeveloped. Identity, on the other hand, was easy to argue. The lines seemed less ambiguous. One liberal candidate, who ran and lost in Egypt's 2011 elections, put it this way: "I did not run a political campaign; I was running a campaign that depended on me telling voters I'm not an atheist."[37]

Libya provides an interesting counterpoint to its neighbors. Unlike Egypt and Tunisia, Libya did not have anything resembling an existing political community. Qaddafi's rule was characterized by a purposeful,

36 Ikhwan Online, 25 Oct. 2011, http://www.ikhwanonline.com/new/Article.aspx?SecID=211&ArtID=93919

37 "The Beginnings of Transition: Politics and Polarization in Egypt and Tunisia," Brookings Doha Center, Apr. 2012, p. 2, http://www.brookings.edu/research/reports/2012/04/19-democratic-transitions

and ultimately brutal, effort to block the emergence of institutions. Even mildly autonomous institutions would weaken his grip on power. In a total autocratic order, this was not to be tolerated. There was no real judicial establishment, no political parties, no parliament, and no civil society. Just as there were no political parties, there was no "party system" nor any recognizable political cleavages.

After Qaddafi's fall, Libya's Islamists, well aware of their comparative advantage, tried to make religion an issue. Muslim Brotherhood leader Mohamed Sawan accused Mahmoud Jibril, former prime minister and leader of an alliance of liberal parties, of being a reincarnation of Qaddafi for not embracing Islam's role in public life.[38] Ali al-Sallabi, perhaps Libya's most prominent Islamist figure, called Jibril an "extreme secularist" who would take the country back toward "tyranny and dictatorship."[39] The strategy failed, partly because Islamists were attempting to create a cleavage that did not resonate in the Libyan context. Far from being a secularist, Qaddafi, for all of his anti-Islamist repression, was more than comfortable injecting his own idiosyncratic understanding of Islam into the public sphere. As George Joffe notes, Qaddafi "intended to express the original ideas put forward in [the] 1969 [revolution] in specifically Islamic form."[40] This included efforts at "Islamizing the economy" and "institut[ing] an austere morality based on Islam."[41] In Egypt and Tunisia, there was a "Westernized" secular elite that feared Islamists would threaten their very way of life. In Libya, "beer and bikini" voters did not exist, in part because there was neither beer nor bikinis.

The dozens of newly established parties that emerged in Libya reflected this conservative consensus. As George Grant of the *Libyan Herald* reported on the eve of the July 2012 elections: "It is very difficult to find a Libyan, either within the parties or on the street, who would describe himself as secularist, with an overwhelming majority insisting that Islam must play an important role in political life."[42] Even the most

[38] See Chapter 15, this volume.

[39] Patrick J. McDonnell, "Libyan Rebel Factions Showing Fissures," *Los Angeles Times*, http://www.denverpost.com/nationworld/ci_18888312

[40] George Joffe, "Islamic Opposition in Libya," *Third World Quarterly*, 10 (Apr. 1988), p. 622.

[41] Ibid.

[42] George Grant, "Elections Analysis: So Who Are They and What Do They

"liberal" party—Jibril's National Forces Alliance (NFA)—endorsed *sharia* as a principal source of legislation.[43] Other liberal parties followed suit with little hesitation. By appropriating Islam and, in effect, moving to the right, liberal parties were able to neutralize the Islamists' claim to religious authenticity. Unique among its Arab neighbors, the liberals of the NFA dominated the country's first elections, garnering thirty-nine out of eighty seats, while the Brotherhood's political arm, the Justice and Construction Party, won only seventeen seats.

However, it would be a mistake to assume that religion will not emerge as the primary cleavage in Libya. Nothing about the party system is "frozen." As the leader of the opposition, the Muslim Brotherhood is in a strong position to make Islam a much greater issue than it has been thus far. It is also unclear what alternative cleavages could develop, beyond allegiance to tribes and local notables. Underlying patterns of party stability matter. Libya has none, at least not yet. Cross-country comparisons with Egypt and Tunisia will offer opportunities for comparative inquiry into how and why particular party systems develop.

Are Strong Parties Good for the Arab World?

The architects of Libya's electoral law appear to have wanted a system that would forestall the domination of any one party. What it might do instead is constrain the development of strong, disciplined parties (the NFA was, itself, a party made up of more than forty smaller parties organized around tribal and regional allegiances). Some would argue that this is precisely the point. Similar concerns emerged in Egypt, where opponents of the Muslim Brotherhood warned against the monopolization of power by one party. The Brotherhood and its Freedom and Justice Party (FJP) won 37 percent and 52 percent of the vote in parliamentary and presidential elections, respectively, yet it formed a government in August 2012 that included only five FJP members out of more than thirty ministers. (Even after two limited Cabinet reshuffles in January and May 2013, less than a third of ministers hailed from the movement.)

Actually Stand For?" *Libya Herald*, 30 June 2012, http://www.libyaherald.com/?p=10156

[43] "Charter of the National Forces Alliance," p. 3, http://www.nff.ly/Eltahalof_Mesak.aspx

Due in part to higher levels of polarization, the notion of a technocratic government, presumably free of partisan allegiances, steadily gained favor in the Egyptian national debate.[44] President Morsi, in one of his first moves, appointed Hisham Qandil, a relatively unknown figure who had been a senior bureaucrat in the Ministry of Water Resources and Irrigation, to the position of prime minister. This push for technocratic governments reflects—as well as amplifies—the increasingly widespread view that political parties, despite (or perhaps because of) their popular mandate, cannot be trusted with something as serious as government. Perhaps more problematically, it makes it difficult for the electorate to hold political parties accountable for their performance in subsequent elections, since they are not fully implementing the partisan platform for which they were presumably elected. By depending on unelected technocrats, there is also the question of democratic legitimacy and the type of ruling bargain that will come into existence between leaders and their constituents. As Miguel Angel Centeno argues in his study of technocracy: "It seems that the very same characteristics that promote technocratic control also make it inimical to democratic rule. The empirical evidence certainly supports a pessimistic perspective."[45]

In the longer term, technocratic governments are likely to limit, or at least postpone, the emergence of economic or class-based cleavages, which, in turn, is likely to allow the religious dimension of conflict to remain dominant. The very premise of technocratic governments is that economic growth requires the implementation of ideologically neutral economic policies—a matter of doing what "works." Whatever the merits, this effectively removes economic policy from partisan debate. Opposition parties will, of course, criticize the governing party's stewardship of the economy, but more on the grounds of execution and performance than differing economic philosophies.

Another model is the coalition-building of Tunisia's transition period, which has put political parties at the forefront. While Tunisia's ideological cleavages are considerable, they had been mediated through a transitional process which was recognized as legitimate by most relevant

[44] See Sharif Elmusa, "Qandil and the Mystique of Technocratic Governments," *Egypt Independent*, 26 July 2012, http://www.egyptindependent.com/opinion/qandil-and-mystique-technocratic-governments

[45] Miguel Angel Centeno, "The New Leviathan: The Dynamics and Limits of Technocracy," *Theory and Society*, 22 (1993), p. 325.

actors. This, at least initially, depressed the desire for technocratic solutions. After the election of a constituent assembly in 2011, three parties—representing Islamists, liberals, and leftists—joined together in a coalition, known as the troika. Instead of selecting technocrats or unaffiliated figures, the parties divided cabinet ministries among themselves. But it did not last, with 2013 featuring mounting opposition calls for the removal of the government and the appointment of "independents." However, as Tunisia's transition has demonstrated, even if briefly, societal cleavages can be managed through a legitimate process that prioritizes accountability to the electorate. Yet after the uprisings, establishing—and maintaining—that legitimacy has proven the most difficult part.

6

REVOLUTION AND CONSTITUTION IN THE ARAB WORLD, 2011–12

Saïd Amir Arjomand

Written constitutions are compromises among heterogenous principles of order espoused by significant political forces at the time of their making.[1] Revolutions entail the rejection of the old regime and the construction of a new political order, with the constitutions made in the post-revolutionary period representing the new ruling bargains. Once finally made, they set the parameters of routine politics for the new regime. But this does not mean that constitutions are always implemented. On the contrary, constitutions are often honored in the breach. Yet their breach means breaking the rules, which impairs the legitimacy of the regime and gives ammunition to the opposition. Constitutions thus serve to frame the major issues for the politics of the future.

The establishment of a new political order purporting to embody the rule of God followed the Islamic Revolution of 1979 in Iran. The 1979

[1] S.A. Arjomand, "Constitutions and the Struggle for Political Order: A Study in the Modernization of Political Traditions," *Archives Européennes de Sociologie/European Journal of Sociology*, 33, 4 (1992), pp. 39–82.

Constitution of the Islamic Republic of Iran made Shi'ite Islam the cornerstone of constitutional reconstruction in a way that was far more substantive and far-reaching than the largely symbolic declaration of God's sovereignty in the 1956 Constitution of the Islamic Republic of Pakistan, the first state to be so designated in history. It is impossible to understand the constitutional placement of Islam after subsequent revolutions in the Muslim world without reference, positive or negative, to the historical watershed that is the entrenchment of Islam in Iran's constitution.

The Arab revolutions of 2011 had immediate success in Tunisia and Egypt, with much slower progress being made in Libya where regime change ultimately came about as a result of NATO military intervention. From the outset, all three cases were constitutional revolutions in their intent. The revolutions in Tunisia and Egypt were certainly seen that way by the revolutionaries themselves. Prominent among the slogans written on placards carried in Maidan al-Tahrir were "Constitution First!" and "No principles above the constitution." The lyrics chanted in the sit-ins held in a Tunisian kasbah early in the spring of 2011 went:

> Hey-Oh!
> Congratulations!
> A new constitutional Assembly!
> A new constitution![2]

The Libyan revolution also started as a constitutional revolution, being led by lawyers who represented massacred prisoners and who turned the Benghazi courthouse into the center of their provisional government, the National Transitional Council, chaired by a defecting Minister of Justice, Mustafa 'Abd al-Jalil. 'Abdul-Hafiz Ghogha, the leader of the lawyers' union, became its deputy head until his resignation in January 2012.

To understand the Arab revolutions of 2011 as constitutional revolutions, therefore, a historical and comparative perspective is needed that will highlight the important steps in modern Middle Eastern constitutional history, including the establishment of the Islamic Republic of Iran.

[2] Steve Coll, "The Casbah Coalition: Tunisia's Second Revolution," *The New Yorker*, 4 Apr. 2011, p. 40.

REVOLUTION AND CONSTITUTION

The Reception of Modern Constitutionalism in the Middle East and the Advent of Ideological Constitution-Making

The Tunisian constitution of 1861 was the oldest in the non-Western world, predating the 1876 Ottoman constitution and the 1889 Meiji constitution of Japan. One revealing feature of the constitution is the fact that it saw no incompatibility between Islam and the traditional monarchy it was seeking to rationalize. The movement for legal modernization and the codification of law for state-building in the Near East had begun by this time, reaching its culmination with the codification of Hanafi law in the Ottoman Empire in the mid-nineteenth century, and the semi-official codification in the posthumously published work of Muhammad Qadri Pasha (d.1886) in connection with the creation of the Egyptian national courts (*al-mahākim al-ahliyya*) in 1883. Qadri Pasha's codification followed Muhammad 'Abduh's reformist methodology for the translation of Islamic jurisprudence (*fiqh*) to positive law (*qānun*), which would culminate in the mid-twentieth century in 'Abd al-Razzaq al-Sanhuri's Civil Code of Egypt, Article 1 of which retained Islamic jurisprudence as a residual source of law in the absence of statutes.

Nineteenth-century Iran, by contrast, lacked both a comparable codification movement and a judicial reorganization. The constitutional government that followed the 1906 revolution inherited the dual judiciary system consisting of religious (*sharia*) and secular state courts. At the time, there was widespread discontent regarding the complete lack of organization in the state judiciary on the one hand, and the chaos created by the contradictory verdicts of the *sharia* courts in the absence of any judicial hierarchy and appeal system on the other. And there was broad consent, if not unanimity, that the remedy for this situation was to rationalize judicial procedure and to unify the judiciary as an organization. There was no suggestion of secularization, and indeed no Persian word for that concept.[3] On the contrary, the 1906 Iranian Constitutional Revolution was the first occasion in which a constitutional debate on Islam was generated. This debate in turn led to the creation of the committee of five religious

[3] Nevertheless, the fact that the reform was to be carried out by the constitutional government obviously implied state control over the unified judiciary of the future. The resulting predominance of the state law over the *sharia* has survived the Islamic Revolution of 1979, and the latter is valid in the Islamic Republic of Iran only as a residual category in the absence of statutory law.

jurists to assure compatibility between state legislation and Islamic law (*sharia*) in the 1907 Supplementary Fundamental Law.

The 1906 Iranian revolution was the first modern revolution in Asia, as well as the first to designate itself a constitutional revolution (*inqilāb-e mashrutiyyat*). It was followed by the Young Turks Revolution of 1908 which was similarly called the "second constitutional period" on account of its restoration of the Ottoman constitution. Meanwhile, in the period since its abortive constitution of 1861, Tunisia had become a French protectorate, where a Consultative Assembly set up in 1892 to represent the interests of French colonists was expanded in 1907 to include some Tunisian members before being replaced in 1922 by a Grand Council which included twenty-six elected Tunisian members. Like its predecessors, however, the Grand Council had little or no practical powers beyond discussing and approving the protectorate's budget. Tunisia's anti-French nationalist movement adopted the name Destour (constitution) and was led by the Destour (Constitution) Party, founded in 1920. However, the most significant popular mobilization was carried out by the Neo-Destour Party, which splintered from the Destour Party in 1934. In 1955–56, independence from France was negotiated by the Neo-Destour Party, whose leader, Habib Bourguiba, became president of independent Tunisia. The constitution of 1959, which was written by an elected constituent assembly, established a strongly presidential system. With Bourguiba as the head of both the state and the party, the lines between the two were blurred.[4] The party was renamed the Parti Socialiste Destourien by President Bourguiba in 1964, and Rassemblement Constitutionel Démocratique by his successor, President Ben Ali, in 1987—increasingly a misnomer for the single party of an authoritarian regime and the hub of a vast network of clientelism that comprised as much as one-fifth of the Tunisian population by 2010.

In comparative perspective, the 1979 Islamic Revolution in Iran can be considered the last of the great modern ideological revolutions, albeit one based on a novel Islamic ideology. In fact, it could even be said that Khomeini saw the 1979 revolution as the Counter (Constitutional) Revolution, one that sought to rectify what he considered the betrayal

[4] M. Penner Angrist, "The Expressions of Political Dissent in the Middle East: Turkish Democratization and Authoritarian Continuity in Tunisia," *Comparative Studies in Society and History*, 41, 4 (1999), pp. 748–52.

of the intellectuals in the Constitutional Revolution (1906–11).[5] Unsurprisingly, it produced the type of constitution I have called "ideological," a category to which the 1971 Egyptian constitution also belongs.[6] The Islamic ideology embodied in the 1979 constitution can, furthermore, be considered the basis for its revolutionary counter-constitutionalism, a term used here in the sense of an alternative constitutionalism, in the same way that the term "alternative modernity" is used.[7] In this sense, counter-constitutionalism is not anti-constitutionalism, but is instead the Shi'ite clericalist counterpart of modern constitutionalism. A theocratic government led by jurists was set up on the basis of an explicit clericalist ideology, namely Khomeini's revolutionary interpretation of the Shi'ite principle of the *velāyat-e faqih* as the divine mandate of the religious jurists to rule.[8] The 1979 Islamic Revolution in Iran could accordingly be characterized as Iran's Islamic counter-revolution, and thus a remarkable instance of revolutionary counter-constitutionalism.[9] As such, it offers a clear contrast to the so-called new consti-

[5] S.A. Arjomand, *After Khomeini: Iran under his Successors*, Oxford: Oxford University Press, 2009, Chapter 1.

[6] S.A. Arjomand, "Introduction," in S.A. Arjomand (ed.), *Constitutional Politics in the Middle East with Special Reference to Turkey, Iraq, Iran and Afghanistan*, Oxford and Portland: Hart Publishing, 2008, pp. 1–10.

[7] S.A. Arjomand, "Middle Eastern Constitutional and Ideological Revolutions and the Rise of Juristocracy," *Constellations*, 19, 2 (June 2012), p. 213.

[8] S.A. Arjomand, *The Turban for the Crown: The Islamic Revolution in Iran*, Oxford: Oxford University Press, 1988.

[9] Comparisons with other instances of indigenous counter-constitutionalism include the highly pertinent cases of Pakistan and Israel but should begin with Japan's constitutional reconstruction following the Meiji revolution from above. After an initial attempt in the 1890s by the modernizing bureaucrats to challenge the parliamentary reading of the Meiji Constitution with a doctrine of "transcendentalism," which invidiously contrasted the modernizing, developmental *telos* of the state with partisan parliamentary politics, there emerged a distinctly Japanese authoritarian theory of the family-state around the turn of the twentieth century. It was gradually transformed in contestation with liberal democracy and socialism in the era of mass politics, into a totalitarian ideology of Shintō ultranationalism, which became the official ideology of the Japanese nation state in 1937 and guided its entry into the Second World War as a holy war in the name of the emperor. (Japan's Asian empire was justified because the Japanese were the race that descended from gods and the emperor was the reincarnation of the sun god, Amatersu

tutionalism, where the constitutional courts developed their jurisprudence as a safeguard against fascist ideology in Germany and Italy, and against communist ideology in post-1989 Central Eurasia.[10] It also offers an interesting contrast to the emerging paradigm for ruling bargains in the post-2011 Arab world that can more accurately be described as Islamic constitutional democracy.

Iran from the Constitutional Revolution of 1906 to the Islamic Counter-Constitutionalism of 1979

Iran should also remain a critical point of reference for understanding the aftermath of the Arab Spring due to the predominance of Islamist parties in post-2011 Arab constitutional politics. Egypt and Iran shared the same model of centralized state-building and modernization. In both countries, state-building served to create, and was in turn helped by, an emergent modern legal profession; and in both countries this

---

Ōmikami.) This ideology was presented as an indigenous constitutional interpretation and was mainly the work of constitutional lawyers who were trained in Germany but came to consider the secularized Western civilization Japan's mortal enemy, and step by step, interpreted the 1889 Constitution of the Empire of Japan away from its German model, integrating it into Shintō cosmology and "Way of the Gods as Such." According to Kaheki Katsuhiko, the last in this line of constitutional interpreters, the "great life" was "the emperor and the masses united as one heart, same body. The state … was composed of the emperor and the masses (*okuchō*) who had abandoned their individual selves to serve the emperor" (cited in W. Skya, *Japan's Holy War: The Ideology of Radical Shintō Ultranationalism*, Durham, NC: Duke University Press, 2009, p. 198). Furthermore, its distinctive Shi'ite counter-constitutionalist ideology notwithstanding, the theocratic juristocracy or clerical monarchy of Iran shares a surprising characteristic with other regimes with constitutionalized ideologies, such as Turkey, where the Kemalist ideology remains entrenched: the organ of judicial review acts as the guardian of the ideological foundations of the regime rather than an instrument of protection of rights. See H. Shambayati, "The Guardian of the Regime: The Turkish Constitutional Court in Comparative Perspective," in Arjomand, *Constitutional Politics in the Middle East*, pp. 99–121.

[10] A. Stone Sweet, *Governing With Judges: Constitutional Politics in Europe*, New York: Oxford University Press, 2000.

modern legal profession had to contend with the traditional estate of clerical jurists, which had historically constituted an independent group and had carried out vital judicial functions. The relationship between the modern legal profession and the religious profession, or the old clerical estate, however varied enormously in the two countries. As compared to Egypt, the Iranian legal profession developed at a much later date and remained weak under the monarchy. Furthermore, unlike the Egyptian legal profession, which survived Nasser's infamous massacre of the judiciary in 1969, the Iranian judiciary was severely debilitated, if not completely destroyed, by the Islamic Revolution led by Khomeini and other religious jurists. The clerical estate or religious jurists thus played an important role in the construction of Iran's constitutional order and legal system even before the Iranian Revolution.

I have covered the history of legal modernization elsewhere,[11] and can only present my conclusions here. The transformation of Islamic jurisprudence (*fiqh*) into state law (*qānun*), or of Shiʿite law from "a jurists' law" to state law, or the law of the land, occurred in three stages. During the making of Iran's first constitution, 1906–7, the Shiʿite jurists had a significant impact as objectors to rather than drafters of the 1907 Supplement to the Fundamental Law. Legal reform in the subsequent four years was initiated by the new breed of modern law professors. Nevertheless, the religious jurists participated in drafting the laws on the organization of the judiciary and assured their conformity to Shiʿite jurisprudence despite a radical reform of the procedural law. In this first phase of Shiʿite constitutionalism, the *sharia*(*t*) appeared as a limitation to government and legislation. There was never a presumption that it should be the basis of the constitution itself. Islam was considered part of the larger issue of constitutional government, and was not seen as the basis for the constitution itself.

Modern lawyers also led the modernization of Iran's legal system under Reza Shah in the late 1920s and 1930s, but again, the Shiʿite jurists ultimately played the most prominent role in the creation of Iran's Civil Code. Given the *pro forma* character of the passing of the Civil

11 S.A. Arjomand, "The Shiʿite Jurists and Iran's Constitutional Order in the Twentieth Century," in S.A. Arjomand and N.J. Brown (eds), *The Rule of Law, Islam and Constitutional Politics in Egypt and Iran*, Albany, NY: State University of New York Press, 2013, pp. 15–56.

Code by the Majlis without any discussion, its enactment was only formally legislation. The work of codification was done in the drafting committees of the Ministry of Justice, and the active participation of the clerical jurists in codification was a very effective way of assuring the conformity of the most important corpus of Iranian law, the Civil Code, with the Shi'ite law. In fact, they performed more effectively to that end than could any committee of the five religious jurists envisioned by the dormant Article 2 of the Supplement to the Fundamental Law.

There was a major change in constitutional paradigms when ideological constitution-making, displaced in Europe by the new constitutionalism, became endemic in the Middle East before culminating in the 1979 Constitution of the Islamic Republic of Iran. In the earlier constitutional period, there had never been a presumption that Islam and the *sharia* should be the basis of the constitution itself. The idea of Islam as the basis for the constitution did not occur to the Iranian clerical jurists of the first four decades of the twentieth century. That idea was born at a later date in the ideological stage of Islamic constitutional history that began very slowly with the creation of Pakistan in 1947. With the importation of Islamic political ideologies into Iran during the Islamic Revolution of 1979, there was a radical shift from the idea of Islam as a limitation to that of Islam as the basis of the constitution and the state.

Khomeini's success in leading the 1979 Islamic Revolution on the basis of his theory of the Mandate of the Jurist (*vilāyat-e faqih*) turned Iran into a theocracy, or what I have called a clerical monarchy, its official designation as a republic notwithstanding.[12] Not surprisingly, this fundamental change went hand in hand with the clericalization of the judiciary and the severe debilitation of the already weak legal profession. Beyond that, however, there have been serious limitations to both the procedural and the substantive Islamicization of Iranian law. The one major instance of substantive Islamicization consisted in introducing the penal code of the *sharia*, which was historically in abeyance in Iran as in Egypt. The attempt to Islamicize the judicial procedure and the organization of the judiciary in the 1980s and 1990s—which sought to restore the informality of Kadi justice in the so-called "general courts" with no appellate hierarchy and no distinction between judge and prosecutor—was a failure, proving the wisdom of the earlier generation of clerical

[12] Arjomand, *After Khomeini*, pp. 187–91.

jurists who recognized the procedural inadequacy of Islamic law, and it was ultimately reversed in the 2000s. The decision to reverse the Islamicization of the organization of the Iranian judiciary in 2002, made by the former head of the judiciary, Ayatollah Mahmud Hashemi-Shahrudi, implied the same admission of the woeful inadequacy of Islamic procedural law that had motivated the judiciary reforms of the 1910s. What seems surprising, however, is that Shi'ite jurisprudence occupies a residual place in the legal order of the Islamic Republic of Iran, and can only be applied in the absence of statutory law.[13] This paradox is more apparent than real because the Shi'ite jurists of the earlier phases of legal modernization had already Islamicized much of modern Iranian law in substance, albeit without any ideological fanfare and without the theory of the Mandate of the Jurist. In short, the impact on Iranian law of the establishment of what Ran Hirschl alternately calls juristocracy and constitutional theocracy[14] has been somewhat minor compared to its major revolutionary impact on Iran's clerical monarchy.

The Rule of Law and Legal Mobilization

Tamir Moustafa highlights two interesting features of constitutional politics in Egypt that are distinctive and contrast with the major concerns of the current judicialization of politics and judicial activism elsewhere:[15] (1) the politics of resistance to authoritarian rule, using litigation strategically to challenge the government; and (2) Islamist politics of forcing the state to comply with its preemptive constitutionalization of the principles of the *sharia* as the main source of Egyptian law.[16]

[13] See S.A. Arjomand, "Shari'a and Constitution in Iran: A Historical Perspective," in A. Amanat and F. Griffel (eds), *Shari'a: Islamic Law in the Contemporary Context*, Stanford: Stanford University Press, 2007.

[14] R. Hirschl, *Constitutional Theocracy*, Cambridge, MA: Harvard University Press, 2010.

[15] T. Moustafa, *The Struggle for Constitutional Power: Law, Politics, and Economic Development in Egypt*, Cambridge: Cambridge University Press, 2007.

[16] Moustafa also covers the protection of private property and privatization by the SCC, but this was clearly a side show intended for catching up with the rest of the world. An interesting parallel can be found in the radical reinterpretation of Article 44 of the IRI Constitution by the clerically dominated Expediency Council in 2005 (see Arjomand, *After Khomeini*, p. 184). Here too, we have a side show and an attempt to follow a global trend,

Contrary to what is often claimed, Egypt's Supreme Constitutional Court (SCC) was not the creation of Sadat but resulted from the evolution of the Supreme Court in accordance with the constitution of 1971. Its growth had unintended consequences for the Egyptian president and the government. But while the court may have been renamed, in practice this simply meant that the Egyptian Supreme Court had acquired the power of judicial review. With due respect to Hirschl, the Islamists were in no way in the picture at the time.[17] While it is true that the famous or infamous declaration of the *sharia* as the source of Egyptian law in the amendment to Article 2 of the 1980 constitution was a preemptive measure in response to the rise of Islamic fundamentalism, it was a mere reinforcement of the original 1971 Article, with "a" being changed to "the." It should also be noted that the term has an external, non-Egyptian genealogy going back to the Kuwaiti constitution of 1938 and the Syrian constitution of 1950, where it was inserted by a member of the Syrian Muslim Brotherhood in the coalition government of the time.

Hans Kelsen argued that access to courts was also a political right as it enabled each citizen, formally speaking, to create a particular legal norm through a court verdict.[18] This insight is particularly important for understanding the phenomenon of the mobilization of law by elements of civil society in authoritarian and post-totalitarian regimes. The Egyptian judiciary is strong by Middle Eastern standards, having survived the onslaught of Nasserist ideology in the 1960s. Despite the dominance exerted over the legislature by the executive in the Egyptian authoritarian regime, this fairly robust and relatively autonomous judiciary, which includes a hierarchy of administrative courts headed by the Council of State, made access to courts a valuable political asset for the citizen, and thus facilitated legal mobilization from below. Recourse to

---

which has had the unintended consequence of rapidly expanding the economic empire of the Revolutionary Guards and making them a thorn in the flesh of the ruling clerical elite (Noah Arjomand, "The Economic Empire of Iran's Revolutionary Guards," senior thesis, Princeton University Woodrow Wilson School, 2010).

[17] R. Hirschl, "Constitutional Courts vs. Religious Fundamentalism: Three Middle Eastern Tales," *Texas Law Review*, 82 (2004), pp. 1831–2.

[18] H. Kelsen, *General Theory of Law and State*, trans. Anders Wedberg, Cambridge, MA: Harvard University Press, 1961[1949], pp. 87–90.

administrative courts, as well as the Supreme Constitutional Court, has been so frequent as to be characterized by Mona El-Ghobashy as "an alternative path to democratization."[19] This makes Egypt something of a paradigmatic case of "legal mobilization," one which is increasingly found in other authoritarian regimes such as China.[20] Egyptian judicial politics were not set in motion under Mubarak by the activism of the judges, whose outlook is surprisingly conservative,[21] but by judicial mobilization from below and the pressure of civic and professional associations, including the bar association or lawyers' syndicate. While the administrative courts provided a platform for legal activists to limit the sprawling power of the authoritarian state, a coalition of activists for constitutional reform set up the Political and Constitutional Reform Committee in 1999. The latter body brought together reformist Muslim Brothers, retired judges, lawyers, doctors, and old-guard Nasserists and Wafd nationalists in a sort of dress rehearsal for the events of 2011.[22] In April and May 2005, Egypt's authoritarian government made a forceful attempt to roll back the two-decade expansion of judicial power into politics, mainly through an assertive Supreme Constitutional Court which the president had begun to rein in by using his appointive power after its landmark 2000 decision requiring judicial supervision of elections. The imprisonment of the opposition's presidential candidate and the disciplining of two senior judges who had been publicly charged with electoral fraud provoked a major confrontation between the government and the judges, backed by the main opposition, the Muslim Brotherhood, and by massive demonstrations in the streets of Cairo in favor of judicial independence that were suppressed heavy-handedly. The Muslim Brotherhood, which included some prominent judges

[19] M. El-Ghobashy, "Taming the Leviathan: Constitutionalist Contention in Contemporary Egypt," Columbia University PhD Dissertation, 2006, p. 153.

[20] M.E. Gallagher, "Mobilizing the Law in China: 'Informed Disenchantment' and the Development of Legal Consciousness," *Law & Society Review*, 4, 4 (2006), pp. 783–816.

[21] M. Kamel Al-Sayyid, "Rule of Law, Ideology and Human Rights in Egyptian Courts," in Arjomand and Brown, *The Rule of Law*, pp. 211–32.

[22] M. El-Ghobashy, "Unsettling the Authorities: Constitutional Reform in Egypt," in J. Sowers and Chris Toebsing (eds), *The Journey to Tahrir: Revolution, Protest and Social Change in Egypt*, London and New York: Verso, 2012, p. 123.

among its members and won eighty-six seats in the People's Assembly in 2005 despite the arrest of over 800 Brothers before the elections and widespread electoral fraud, subsequently assumed the championship of constitutionalist contention. Members of the Brotherhood thus protested against the renewal of the state of emergency law at the end of April 2006 by wearing sashes emblazoned with "no to Emergency," making a spectacle of their internal elections as a "democratic celebration," and advocating constitutional reform.[23] In March 2007, President Mubarak struck back by rushing an immediate referendum through the People's Assembly on thirty-four illiberal constitutional amendments that not only replaced the state of emergency law in effect since 1981 by the constitutionally entrenched suspension of civil rights in terrorism cases (Article 79) but also removed the judicial oversight of elections, which was given to a state-appointed elections commission (Article 88).[24] The Muslim Brother parliamentarians wore sashes with "No to the Constitutional Coup!"

In contrast to the pattern of mobilization of law in Egypt, Iran's arrested legal mobilization was the result of the abortive attempt at democratization and reform from above under President Mohammad Khatami (1997–2005). Khatami sought to mobilize civil society through his program of the rule of law, thereby galvanizing Iranian society on an unprecedented scale in the closing years of the twentieth century. Women's rights activists, such as Mehrangiz Kar and Shahla Lahiji, are particularly noteworthy for their program providing legal education to women in order to increase their awareness of what limited rights they could realize through resort to courts, especially the special family courts. Although Khatami's efforts were frustrated by the ruling Islamic juristocracy and foiled by the supreme jurist and leader of the Islamic Republic of Iran, Ayatollah Khamenei, they greatly raised the hopes and expectations of Iranian middle-class women and youth. What was noted

23 S.H. Shehata, "Political *da'wa*: Understanding the Muslim Brotherhood's Participation in Semi-Authoritarian Elections," in Samer Shehata (ed.), *Islamist Politics in the Middle East: Movements and Change*, London: Routledge, 2012, pp. 129–30.

24 N. Bernard-Maugiron, "Legal Reforms in Egypt: the Rule of Law and Consolidation of State Authoritarianism," in Arjomand and Brown, *The Rule of Law*, pp. 179–210.

by one Chinese plaintiff could easily have been said by any number of his Iranian counterparts by 2005: "Our hopes are higher, so our disappointment is all the deeper."[25] It was this optimism that was ultimately dispelled by Khatami's failure to mobilize the rule of law, which no doubt fueled the massive and sustained popular protest against Ahmadinejad's electoral fraud in June 2009 that became known as the Green Movement.

With regard to Islam, it should be noted that in the closing decades of the twentieth century, the Supreme Constitutional Court of Egypt developed its own coherence theory centered on the placing of Islam in the constitutional order. The theory offers an interesting double contrast to those of the Constitutional Court of the EU civil law systems, most notably in Germany, and the coherence theory of Habermas, conceived in terms of the "co-originality" of democracy and rights, as well as Dworkin's theory for the United States that privileges rights over democratic governance. The Egyptian SCC firmly prevented decentralization of control and mutual reversals (*tahātur*) from resulting from the 1980 declaration of the principles of the *sharia* as the main source of legislation in the amendment to Article 2 of the constitution. To reduce the unpredictability of the law and to assure the stability of the judicial system, the Supreme Constitutional Court also considered this statement of the principle of Islamic normativity as being addressed to the legislature and not to judges, and placed it within the overall framework of the coherence of the entire corpus of constitutional and ordinary laws, thereby consolidating its own unique constitutional jurisprudence.[26] The distinctive mark of the Egyptian variant of the new constitutionalism was thus the accommodation between Islam and a remarkably illiberal inflection on human rights.[27]

The jurisprudence of the Iranian Guardian Council in the same period, by contrast, was stillborn. It has failed to generate any constitutional jurisprudence for the Islamic Republic of Iran because the coun-

[25] Quoted in Gallagher, "Mobilizing the Law in China," p. 813.

[26] B. Johansen, "The Relationship between the Constitution, the *Shari'a* and the *Fiqh*: The Jurisprudence of Egypt's Supreme Constitutional Court," *Zeitschrift für ausländisches öffentliches Recht und Völkerrecht*, 64 (2004), pp. 886–9.

[27] Al-Sayyid, "Rule of Law, Ideology and Human Rights in Egyptian Courts."

cil's unintended function as an agency of political control quickly eclipsed its intended function of *ex ante* judicial review of legislation.[28] The Shi'ite juristocracy of the Islamic Republic of Iran thus remained untouched by the post-1989 global wave of new constitutionalism that was to ebb on the North African shores of the Mediterranean in 2011.

Despite the prominence of the Muslim Brotherhood in Egypt and the Nahda in Tunisia, there is a clear and striking contrast between post-2011 Arab constitutionalism and the Shi'ite counter-constitutionalism of the Islamic Republic of Iran. Shi'ite juristocracy in Iran represents a special type of rule by laws, which is the opposite of the substantive rule of law in the new constitutionalism.[29] It legitimizes government by religious jurists through the state and its military and security apparatus with no judicialization of political contestation, which is the main feature of the new constitutionalism. There was no judicialization of politics because the jurisprudence of the Guardian Council was stillborn as it became the regime's instrument of political control and its gatekeeper by supervising elections and disqualifying challengers to the clerical jurists' right to govern. Furthermore, it is characterized by the intense politicization of the judiciary and the use of courts as instruments of repression. This politicization of the judiciary is in many ways the opposite of the judicialization of politics in the new constitutionalism.

The most important constitutional difference between the patterns of constitution-making in Iran and in the Arab world stems from the divergent goals of the Iranian and Arab revolutions: the establishment of Islamic government in Iran, as compared to a constitutional democratic order in Tunisia and Egypt. A recent survey conducted by Mansoor Moaddel found that 84 percent of Egyptians considered democracy and economic prosperity to be the primary goal of the Arab Spring.[30] The Islamic state, or more precisely "Islamic government" (*hukumat-e islāmi*), was the social and political myth behind Khomeini's

[28] Arjomand, "The Shi'ite Jurists and Iran's Constitutional Order."

[29] B.Z. Tamanaha, *On the Rule of Law: History, Politics, Theory*, Cambridge: Cambridge University Press, 2004.

[30] Project Syndicate: http://www.project-syndicate.org/commentary/moaddel5/English. The same survey showed 57 percent support for the enforcement of the *sharia* by the state, and other surveys show an even higher level of support for the implementation of its punishments against adultery and theft.

Islamic Revolution in Iran.[31] The slogan did not reappear in the Arab revolution in January or February 2011. The preamble to the 1979 Iranian constitution declared that it was based on Islamic ideology, which meant that Islam was the basis for the new political order. An Appendix accordingly supplied the Qur'anic and *hadith* citation on which the important articles of the constitution were allegedly based. There is no discussion of Islam as an ideology and no backing of the articles in any post-2011 constitutional documents in Tunisia, Egypt, or Libya. This major difference can be explained by the passing of the era of Islamic ideology.

The Islamist an-Nahda won 41 percent of the 217 seats in the Tunisian Constituent Assembly (and 80 percent of the quarter of seats reserved for women).[32] The interim Tunisian president and leader of the Congress for the Republic Party, Moncef Marzouki, donned a traditional cape,[33] and has also spoken against secularization and the sodomization of the Arabic language. The Muslim Brothers' Freedom and Justice Party and the Salafist al-Nour Party won 42 percent and 22 percent of the seats in the lower house of the Egyptian parliament respectively. Nevertheless, there is little evidence that these parties follow the Iranian constitutional paradigm regarding Islam. In fact, immediately after the departure of Mubarak, which coincided with the anniversary of the Islamic Revolution in Iran, the Muslim Brothers dissociated themselves from Iran's claim that the Arab revolution was even more Islamic than the Iranian model.

So what type of constitutional design do the Arab Islamist parties have in mind? The post-2011 Arab alternative, clearly influenced by the example of the ruling Justice and Development Party in Turkey, in contrast to Iran's Islamic regime, can be called Islamic constitutional democracy. As was the case with the Iranian Supplement to the Fundamental Law of 1907, the first constitutional document to discuss the limiting function of Islamic law in parliamentary government which re-emerged as the so-called "repugnancy clause" of the 1956 Constitution of Pakistan,[34] consid-

[31] Arjomand, *The Turban for the Crown*, pp. 99, 103–6.

[32] *The Economist*, 26 Nov. 2011, p. 58; 18 Feb. 2012, p. 50.

[33] *The Economist*, 14 Jan. 2012.

[34] The formula adopted in Pakistan and many other Muslim countries subsequently becoming independent followed the British colonial legal tradition, and asserted that no laws should be repugnant to the Sacred Law of *sharia*.

ered Islam and its Sacred Law as a limitation to the legislative power embodying national sovereignty. In this view, Islam is not considered an ideology, nor is the state viewed as an "ideological state" in the way that the Iranian constitution-makers of 1979 envisaged. None of the Arab Islamist parties in 2011, not even the Egyptian Salafist Nour Party, argued that the *sharia* should be the basis for the new constitution of an Islamic state. In their understanding, the *sharia* as one of the sources, or the source of law should be a limitation on legislation rather than the basis for the political regime.

The constitutional form taken by this limitation in Egypt and Libya, though somewhat parallel to that of the 1907 Iranian constitutional law, followed the formula of Article 2 of the Egyptian constitution as amended in 1980 to make the *sharia* the main source of legislation. The Egyptian Constitutional Declaration of 30 March and the Constitutional Principles of 14 August affirm the role of the *sharia* as the main source of legislation in the Egyptian "civil democratic state." Article 2 of 1980 was retained unchanged in the Egyptian constitution ratified by a referendum in December 2012. In his inaugural speech following the fall of Tripoli in August 2011, the head of the Libyan interim government, Mustafa Abdel Jalil, similarly declared the *sharia* to be the main source of legislation, a declaration which was confirmed by the Libyan interim constitution.[35] In February 2012, the National Transitional Council passed a law establishing a Dar al-Iftā' (center for issuing *fatwas*).[36] As we shall see, the Egyptian formulation was initially adopted by Nahda in Tunisia but was ultimately abandoned—and with it the substance of the constitutional limitation of legislation by the Sacred Law—in a historic compromise in March 2012.

Constitutional Politics and Negotiated Revolutions in Tunisia and Egypt

Gorbachev's announcement in 1989 that the Soviet army would not be used to restore order in Eastern Europe triggered the fall of one regime after another in Central and Eastern Europe, typically negotiated in

[35] *The Economist*, 27 Aug. 2011, p. 23.

[36] Law No. 15–2012. For this and other laws and constitutional documents of Libya, see the website of the Max Planck Institute for Comparative Public Law and International Law: http://www.mpil.de/ww/en/pub/research/details/know_transfer/constitutional_reform_in_arab_/libyen.cfm

round-table discussions with the opposition. The Central and Eastern European states were greatly weakened by the loss of coercive backing from the Soviet Union but did not collapse. Regime transformation was negotiated between weakened states and emboldened oppositions, a process that has been aptly described as "negotiated revolutions," as has the passing of the Apartheid regime in South Africa.[37] I have argued elsewhere that the European revolutions of 1848 were not only constitutional revolutions but also negotiated revolutions in that the old regimes survived, with the exception of France, while the old ruling bargains were altered through new constitutional settlements.[38] Similarly, the states were weakened but did not collapse in Tunisia and Egypt, and the experience of both countries in 2011 can thus be described as negotiated revolutions. It was only in Libya that the revolution was not negotiated with the old regime, with its success largely attributable to the NATO intervention.

There is a major difference between Tunisia and Egypt, however, regarding the role of the army and security forces in the constitutional negotiations that followed the revolution of 2011. In Tunisia, the army maintained its distance from the secret police. The army commander, General Rachid Ammar, refused to fire on the protestors on 9 January, neutralized the presidential guards who had bloodily suppressed the demonstrations in Kasserine, and sent former security officer Ben Ali packing on 14 January 2011, pledging that "the national army guarantees the revolution."[39] On 7 March 2011, the political police, the State Security Division, was abolished. In Egypt, by contrast, the army was slower and much more ambivalent with regard to the uprising, yet ultimately declared its "support for the legitimate demands of the people" a day before Mubarak was dispatched to Sharm al-Shaykh on 11 February 2011.[40] Although it did not, maybe could not prevent the sacking of

[37] See Mehran Kamrava, "Revolution Revisited: The Structuralist–Voluntarist Debate," *The Canadian Journal of Political Science/Revue Canadienne de Science Politique*, 32, 2 (1999), and George Lawson, *Negotiated revolutions: The Czech Republic, South Africa and Chile*, Aldershot: Ashgate, 2002.

[38] S.A. Arjomand (ed.), *The Arab Revolution of 2011 in Comparative Perspective*, Albany, NY: State University of New York Press (forthcoming).

[39] J.P. Filiu, *The Arab Revolution: Ten Lessons from the Democratic Uprising*, New York: Oxford University Press, 2011, pp. 62, 78–9.

[40] Ibid. p. 57.

security police offices in at least seven major cities, it has shown great reluctance to prosecute security officers, let alone dismantle their pervasive apparatus, the State Security Investigation Services, or Amn al-Dawla. Instead, the latter organization was merely renamed National Security (*amn watani*), while in July 2012 government-controlled media even celebrated the anniversary of its foundation.[41]

This major difference in the role of the armed forces in the two surviving states is crucial for understanding the constitutional settlements that resulted from the two Arab negotiated revolutions. In Tunisia, the second and last autocrat, Ben Ali, was overthrown on 14 January 2011, an event which triggered the current Arab revolution. The interim government of Tunisia sought to institutionalize the revolution immediately by setting up a Higher Commission for Political Reform, headed by a former judge of the Constitutional Court, Yadh Ben Achour, who was the son of the reformist former chief mufti of Tunisia. The commission was to be dissolved after the election for a constituent assembly, which was to write a new constitution and to devise interim structures for governing and form the new government. In March 2011, Ben Achour's commission was revamped to include the National Council for the Protection of the Revolution. This new body, the Higher Authority for Implementing the Objectives of the Revolution, Political Reform and Democratic Transition, was further expanded from 72 to 155 members, thus becoming more inclusive politically.[42]

The election was in fact held in October 2011 with a very high popular turnout and was generally applauded for its fairness and observance of democratic rules. The Islamist an-Nahda Party obtained 36 percent of the popular vote and became the predominant minority in the National Constituent Assembly which was inaugurated on 22 November 2011. The assembly elected Mustapha Ben Ja'far as its president, the leader of Ettakatol, the party which had come third in the elections. Ben Ja'far proposed a tripartite formula for the formation of a ruling coalition and division of power among its partners, which became the basis for an interim constitutional enactment or organic law on 10 December 2011. The Law on the Interim Organization of Public Powers defined

[41] *The New York Times*, 14 July 2012.

[42] J.P. Filiu, "The First Year of the Tunisian Revolution," in Arjomand, *The Arab Revolution of 2011 in Comparative Perspective.*

the constituent and legislative powers of the National Constituent Assembly under its president (Articles 4–8) and the division of executive power between the president of the republic and the prime minister, officially called the president of government. The president of the republic was to be elected by the National Constituent Assembly and could be dismissed by it, with his or her powers including the appointment of the mufti of the republic as the highest religious authority (Articles 10–11 and 13). The prime minister was to be chosen from among the members of the political party with the largest number of seats in the National Constituent Assembly and confirmed by the latter, with his or her powers including the proper execution of the laws (Articles 15–17). In an indication of the influence of the new constitutionalism of the global legal culture, the National Constituent Assembly was directed to enact another "organic law organizing transitional justice" (Article 24).[43]

It was in accordance with the "Three Presidents" terms of this constitutional law that a tripartite coalition government was formed and elected as president (of the republic) the leader of the second coalition partner, Congress for the Republic, Moncef Marzouki. The latter in turn appointed Hamadi Jebali as prime minister, who represented an-Nahda as the major coalition partner, while the Amir of an-Nahda, Rashid al-Ghannouchi, stayed out of government.

Early in February 2012, the an-Nahda published a draft constitutional proposal which included Islamic law as the main source of legislation in Article 10.[44] In reaction, the pressure by other political groups for the establishment of a "civic state" (*dawla madaniyya*) gathered momentum during the constitutional debates in March 2012.[45] On 25 March 2012, foregoing the Salafists' support and indeed provoking their open opposition,[46] an-Nahda irrevocably endorsed Article 1 of the 1959 constitution

[43] For the official Arabic and their French translations, see the website of the Max Planck Institute for Comparative Public Law and International Law/ Constitutional reform in Arab Countries: http://www.mpil.de/ww/en/pub/research/details/know_transfer/constitutional_reform_in_arab_/tunesien.cfm

[44] Ibid.

[45] As we shall see later, the term had been coined during the constitutional debates of the previous year in Egypt.

[46] On 11 and 12 June 2012, the Salafists targeted a courthouse, police stations, and trade union offices, clashing with the riot police in Tunis. The city was put under curfew (*The Economist*, 23 June 2012, p. 53).

which declares Tunisia an Arab and Muslim state but contains no reference to the *sharia* as a source of legislation.[47] Tunisia thus followed the "classic" pattern of constitutional reconstruction following a revolution through a constituent assembly. The three largest political parties in an-National Constituent Assembly hammered out the new ruling bargain without the interference of the armed forces. The new ruling bargain included a historic compromise by the main Islamist party, an-Nahda, with its coalition partners, according to which it would abandon its insistence on making Islamic law a constitutional limitation on legislation. This constitutional settlement could indeed be taken as the fulfillment of what one Nahda intellectual and disciple of Ghannouchi, his fellow exile in London, called the "charismatic, democratic system" that was needed to keep alive "the soul of our revolution."[48]

Constitution-making in Egypt's negotiated revolution followed a very different path. The writing of a new constitution was a priority in terms of political reconstruction following the Egyptian revolution of 25 January. The Supreme Council of the Armed Forces (SCAF), a pre-existing body that had forced Mubarak to leave after eighteen days of massive protests, quickly assumed control of the revolution. Not surprisingly, the reversal of Mubarak's 2007 constitutional amendments, as well as the authoritarian presidentialism of the 1971 constitution, was high on the agenda of those protesting in Maidan al-Tahrir in 2011. Within days of Mubarak's departure on 11 February, SCAF, a body comprised of eighteen generals, began the process of constitutional reconstruction with the appointment of a committee to draft constitutional amendments immediately. The committee included a Muslim Brotherhood politician, Sobhi Saleh, and Tareq el-Beshry, a prominent judge and former vice-president of Egypt's highest administrative court who was sympathetic to the Muslim Brotherhood. On 26 February the committee presented its short but significant constitutional amendments, which were approved by a national referendum on 19 March, restoring judicial supervision of elections and eliminating the suspension of human rights in terrorism cases. According to these amendments, the first parliament was to appoint a drafting commission of 100 members, who would not

[47] Filiu, "The First Year of the Tunisian Revolution"; *The Economist*, 31 Mar. 2012, p. 59.

[48] Anthony Shadid, "Arab Spring's Hope Rose from Deep Roots," *International Herald Tribune*, 18–19 Feb. 2012, p. 2.

necessarily be elected. Their selection was thus bound to be influenced by SCAF, which refused to relinquish power. The military junta, however, resisted abrogating the state of emergency law. It was only a year later, and in the face of massive demonstrations on the first anniversary of the revolution on 25 January 2012, that SCAF promised to ease the application of martial law, and even then it made an exception for cases of "thuggery" (*baltaga*). This opened a huge loophole, as SCAF added two articles to the criminal law which made thuggery a criminal offense for which hundreds or more were arrested in the following months.[49]

The transitional constitutional order established by SCAF supplemented the March 2011 referendum on constitutional principles with a number of decrees, including the "constitutional declaration," which was issued on 30 March and served as Egypt's governing document. It contained 63 articles, mostly from the 1971 constitution, as well as the 19 March amendments. This was followed by the declaration of a set of so-called supra-constitutional principles on 14 August 2011. The ostensible justification for these principles was that they amounted to a bill of rights, but in fact they also included the confirmation of the *sharia* as the main source of legislation in the Egyptian "civic democratic state."[50] The idea of the civic state (*dawla madaniyya*) was incidentally supplied by Al-Azhar. It resonated with the Muslim philosophers' notion of the virtuous city (*al-madina al-fadila*) and sounded more cognizant of the historic pattern of separation of religion from the state while avoiding the term secularism, which had been anathematized as a new form of idolatry by such Muslim Brother ideologues as Sayyid Qutb (d.1966). As we have seen, the notion quickly traveled to Tunisia. In Egypt itself, it immediately gained currency and was to become the basis for the implicit consensus that was reached a few months later in the spring of 2012.

Be that as it may, the implicit acquiescence of the Egyptian factions emboldened SCAF to add other constitutional principles on 1 November 2011 that gave it the right to supervise its own military budget as well as a strong hand in the writing of the new constitution.[51] The result was the

49 Y. El Rashidi, "Egypt: The Hidden Truth," *The New York Review of Books*, 59, 13 (16 Aug. 2012), pp. 24–6.

50 "Constitutional Principles," The Carnegie Endowment for Peace, accessed 4 Oct. 2011, http://egyptelections.carnegieendowment.org/2011/10/04/constitutional-principles

51 "The SCAF: An Overview of its Actions," accessed on The Carnegie

renewal of massive protests from 18 to 25 November. On 23 November, SCAF was forced to set a date for the presidential elections (promised in June 2012), and in December 2011 it was forced to retract the additional supra-constitutional principles and to recognize the parliament's exclusive right to draft the new constitution.[52] Meanwhile, after repeated delays, the elections for the lower house of parliament were completed in three stages between November 2011 and January 2012.

The state remained largely intact despite severe attacks on its security apparatus in Tunisia and in Egypt. In both countries the state has been able to impose a constitutional frame on the unfolding of the respective revolutions, while the far greater strength and predominance of the army in Egypt and a relatively strong judiciary make its constitutional revolution more constrained and in greater conformity with the Egyptian conservative tradition of the rule of law. This tradition comprises the legacy of authoritarian state-building in the form of rule by decree that the opposition has not succeeded in challenging.

The divergence from the pattern of negotiated transition in Tunisia became more marked in Egypt as SCAF showed its determination to steer Egypt's post-revolutionary constitutional development. SCAF was quite successful in eliciting the support of liberal parties and groups for its 14 August supra-constitutional principles by reminding them of the Islamist threat. However, massive protests exploded once again in the Maidan al-Tahrir reaction to SCAF's attempt to add to the supra-constitutional principles in November by making itself the guardian of "constitutional legitimacy." It was not at the negotiating table but from the streets of large and small cities that the opposition forced SCAF to back down. After the first round of elections on 28 November for the lower house of parliament, the National Assembly, had resulted in the overwhelming victory of the Muslim Brothers' Freedom and Justice Party and of the Nour Party of the Salafists, SCAF insisted on its continued authority to appoint and dismiss the government, and sought to reassert its constitutional role. On 7 December 2011, a SCAF member said it would oversee the formation of the constitutional-drafting com-

Endowment for Peace website, on 29 Jan. 2012: http://egyptelections.carnegieendowment.org/2012/01/05/the-scaf-an-overview-of-its-actions

52 *The New York Times*, 20 Nov. 2011 and 10 Dec. 2011.

mission because it did not believe the elected parliament would be adequately representative. Another SCAF member was forced to retract the statement within a couple of days, however. In-between, SCAF and the Muslim Brothers worked out a compromise that put the latter in control of parliament as a SCAF partner in government. By the end of January 2012, with the Islamist-dominated National Assembly in session, the Tahrir and other mass demonstrations in Egypt were turning against both SCAF and the Muslim Brothers for the first time.

The Muslim Brotherhood–SCAF cohabitation was riddled with tension. On the one hand, SCAF continued to issue decrees, some of which were of a constitutional order, without any serious challenge from the opposition. This can only be explained by the strong legitimacy of the state and the rule of law in Egypt. On the other hand, the Muslim Brothers in control of parliament reneged on the promise that they would avoid political domination and exclusivity. There was little interest in the elections for the upper house (*shurā*) in February 2012, with the turnout as low as 6.5 percent. The Islamists won again.[53] In March 2012, the Freedom and Justice Party used its parliamentary dominance to select the majority of the 100 members of the constitutional-drafting committee among Islamists and to make the party's secretary general and Speaker of the National Assembly, Muhammad Sa'd el-Katatny, its president. This provoked widespread protests from excluded groups and a crisis in Egyptian constitutional politics. The Writers' Union protested against this "majoritarian dictatorship," as did over a quarter of the non-Islamist members of the constitutional-drafting committee who refused to take their seats. SCAF took advantage of this attempt to monopolize constitution-making by turning to the judiciary—the other branch of the state which, far from being destroyed, had gained in legitimacy and therefore power due to the constitutionalist inspiration of the revolution. Thus began a three-way tug of war between the army, the newly elected parliament, and the judiciary.

Meanwhile, tension was mounting with the approach of the presidential elections that were scheduled to take place on 24 May. The Muslim Brotherhood, faced with the challenge posed by the candidacy of a charismatic Salafist preacher, Hazem Salah Aub Isma'il, on the one flank, and a defecting Muslim Brother, Abdel Moneim Abol Fotuh, on the

[53] *The Economist*, 10 Mar. 2012.

other, reneged on its promise of not fielding its own candidate and announced the candidacy of its deputy supreme leader, Khairat el-Shater, on 1 April. The courts were now fully dragged into the constitutional crisis. An administrative court issued an injunction suspending the constitutional-drafting assembly which was quickly dissolved by a higher administrative court. This meant that the president would be elected before the new constitution could be adopted, with the presidency inheriting vast powers from Mubarak's authoritarian regime. Although a new constitutional assembly was reconstituted in June 2012, it continued to be dominated by the Muslim Brotherhood.

By the time of the presidential elections, Egypt was in a constitutional crisis with SCAF in control of administration and police, the Muslim Brothers in control of parliament and the constitutional assembly, and the administrative courts and Supreme Constitutional Court as arbiters approached by all parties. SCAF successfully intensified its constitutional maneuvers, making behind-the-scenes deals with the Muslim Brothers and other oppositional groups alternately as it suited its purpose at hand.

Both in substance and procedurally, the hasty flow of constitutional law-decrees and contradictory statements throughout 2011 displayed a pattern closer to the mode of Europe's 1989 negotiated transition, than to the slower classic variant through a constituent assembly in Tunisia. The ad hoc and haphazard process of negotiated transition continued through the first four months of 2012, despite the opening of the National Assembly. Then, with the approach of the presidential elections, the divergence of the Egyptian from the Eastern European pattern of transition, too, became more marked by the intensified judicialization of constitutional politics in Egypt.

Real excitement in the presidential campaign began two days before the deadline for closing the list of candidates. Omar Suleiman, Mubarak's 74-year-old vice-president and head of General Intelligence Services for eighteen years who died later in 2012, pushed through his candidacy with the requisite 30,000 signatures, which he had miraculously collected from all provinces on his petition and with the support of at least one senior administrative court judge the day after the Islamist-dominated parliament passed a bill barring Mubarak high officials from running.[54]

[54] *The New York Times*, 13 Apr. 2012.

Meanwhile, an administrative court made a failed attempt to disqualify the Salafist candidate, Hazem Abu Isma'il. In the following week, the electoral commission disqualified Shater and Abu Isma'il as well as Suleiman, and referred the bill banning Mubarak high officials to the Supreme Constitutional Court. The Muslim Brotherhood put up a new lackluster candidate, Mohamed Morsi, who was a professor of engineering. At the same time, the opposition began legal action against the other SCAF candidate, Ahmad Shafiq, for his role in suppressing demonstrations while serving as prime minister.[55] Morsi and Shafiq won the first round of presidential elections with very narrow margins and less than half of the popular vote between the two of them.

On 1 June, just ahead of the presidential election, parliament finally revoked the state of emergency, fulfilling one of the most persistent demands of the Islamist parliamentarians. SCAF's reaction was not long in coming—it put the country back under martial law with its supplementary constitutional declaration in just over two weeks. On 14 June 2012, just two days before the runoff presidential elections, came the Supreme Constitutional Court's judicial coup, confirming the validity of Shafiq's candidacy on the day it heard the case and invalidating the election of a third of the members of parliament affiliated to political parties who had taken seats reserved for independents. Though the latter ruling was not unprecedented or unreasonable, its timing certainly was.[56] Once the elections took place with low turnout and very lukewarm demonstrations and the result of the runoff was known, the electoral commission refused to declare the winner, while SCAF, following up on the SSC judicial coup, unabashedly carried out its own constitutional coup. It issued a supplementary constitutional declaration, dissolving parliament and hand-picking 100 new members for the drafting commission, drastically reducing the power of the president while entrenching all military prerogatives and freezing SCAF in its present membership. Sa'd el-Katatny, Speaker of the National Assembly, declared that the military had no authority to dissolve parliament or to write a constitution, which would be done by the Islamist-dominated constitutional assembly.[57] Any doubt there may have been about the

[55] *The New York Times*, 5 June 2012.
[56] Nathan J. Brown, "Cairo's Judicial Coup," *Foreign Policy*, 14 June 2012.
[57] *The New York Times*, 18 June 2012.

coordination of the SCC and the SCAF coups was subsequently dispelled by the supplementary constitutional declaration which gave the SCC a binding veto on any constitutional provision on virtually any grounds.[58] Drawing on the state-centered Egyptian tradition of the rule of law, SCAF and its allies in the judiciary justified their constitutional coup with repeated appeals to the principles of legitimacy.

Rallies that were intended to place pressure on SCAF resumed in the Tahrir on 19 June and continued in the days that followed. Meanwhile, president-elect Mohammad Morsi was brought on board before he was declared president, turning the constitutional coup into a tacit tripartite deal. At the end of June, President Morsi swore the oath of office in front of his supporters in the Maidan al-Tahrir and again at the University of Cairo before doing so again at the official ceremony in the presence of SCAF before the chief justice of the Supreme Constitutional Court. He asserted his authority by convening parliament through an executive order on 8 July, cancelling the SCAF order which had dissolved it, but taking pains to state that this was not directed against the ruling of the SCC.[59] While the latter immediately confirmed its ruling, the National Assembly symbolically met on 11 July, but suspended parliament and proceeded to file an appeal with the Court of Cassation. Meanwhile, another legal action sought to void the election by the Islamist-dominated parliament of the constitutional-drafting commission. With such judicialization of constitutional politics, the head of the Judges' Club could not refrain from intervening in the constitutional crisis with a vitriolic attack on the Islamists.[60] Nevertheless, the constitutional assembly elected by the disbanded parliament soon began its work, dividing the drafting task among committees and vowing to finish the draft by October.

President Morsi was initially cautious in asserting his authority. He issued amnesties for 572 protestors on 20 July 2012, leaving many more to linger in detention. Four days later, he appointed Hisham Qandil as his prime minister, a technocrat who had served as water minister and

[58] N.J. Brown, "An Instant Analysis of Egypt's New Constitution," *The Arabist* (posted on the Carnegie Endowment website: http://carnegieendowment.org/2012/06/18/instant-analysis-of-egypt-s-new-constitution/bz0i).

[59] *The New York Times*, 9 July 2012.

[60] *The Economist*, 14 July 2012.

was not a member of the Muslim Brotherhood. A meaningful attempt to assert his authority only came later, on 12 August 2012, when Morsi took advantage of the military disgrace resulting from the killing of sixteen policemen by Islamic militants at a Sinai border station. In response, Morsi revoked the SCAF supplementary constitutional declaration and retired Field Marshal Tantawi, whom he had felt constrained to appoint defense minister, as well as the army chief of staff, General Sami Hafez Anan.[61] The chiefs of the intelligence service, the navy, and the air force were also sacked. Two days later, another prominent SCAF member who had commanded the Central Military Zone around Cairo announced his retirement.[62]

In short, the army's successful control of the Egyptian revolution for a year and a half perpetuated the legacy of Mubarak authoritarianism and enabled the constitutional manoeuvers of the surviving supreme military and judiciary organs of the old regime. This left a deep imprint on the process of this negotiated settlement, which became increasingly dominated by selective and non-inclusive consultation and ad hoc concessions to periodic protests rather than formal agreements with the opposition as a negotiation partner. Given this mode of restricted negotiated revolution, the legality of the discarded authoritarian regime increasingly channeled Egypt's post-2011 constitutional politics through the SCC and administrative courts, and thus shaped the character of the constitutional democracy emerging from Egypt's constitutional revolution.

The Final Making of Egypt's Constitution and its Definition of Islamic Law as a Constitutional Limitation

On 22 November 2012, President Morsi launched his own constitutional coup d'état with a "Constitutional Declaration," according to which his law-decrees and decisions and those of the threatened constitutional assembly would be immune from judicial review. He then instructed the constitutional assembly to ignore the boycotts and resignations of its opposition members and hammer out the draft constitution. This was done during a long session on 29 November that extended to the early hours of 30 November. President Morsi wasted no

[61] *The New York Times*, 12 Aug. 2012.
[62] *The Economist*, 18 Aug. 2012.

time and ordered a national referendum on the completed draft on 1 December. His coup amounted to a major confrontation with the Supreme Constitutional Court, and provoked a vigorous reaction on the part of the SCC and of the judiciary more generally, with judges going on strike in protest. The SCC, the General Assembly of the Cairo Appeals Court, and the Administrative Prosecution strongly objected to Morsi's constitutional declaration of 22 November, and the Judges' Club of the administrative courts only agreed to supervise the referendum on 10 December after the president partially rescinded his declaration and persuaded the Islamists to end their sit-in around the SSC building.[63] However, by that time disparate groups in the secular opposition had discovered that their voice had been much better heard in the Tahrir and other massive demonstrations than through the ballot box. Massive demonstrations comparable to those of the "Eighteen Days" that had toppled Mubarak took place nationwide, but this time they were directed against the Muslim Brothers and the elected president. The demonstrations turned violent, with several people killed in street fights, while the offices of the Muslim Brotherhood were ransacked in at least two dozen cities.[64] Particularly damaging was President Morsi's televised speech asserting that prosecutors had obtained confessions from hired thugs paid with black money to thwart the revolution. It turned out that it was the Muslim Brother thugs who had taken forty-nine captives and tried to extract confessions by beating them.[65] This was revealed by a judge investigating the case, a revelation that forced Morsi's public prosecutor to resign. The latter, however, retracted his resignation a week or so later when the situation had calmed down.[66]

Despite the resignation of some of his advisors, including the former judge and his vice-president, Mahmud Makki, President Morsi proceeded with the referendum even though he was forced to divide it into two stages because of the shortage of supervising judges. On 25 December 2012, the High Electoral Commission set up in accordance with the

[63] "Morsi's Constitutional Referendum: The State of Play," posted on the Carnegie Endowment for International Peace website on 8 Dec. 2012: http://egyptelections.carnegieendowment.org/2012/12/08/morsi%e2%80%99s-constitutional-referendum-the-state-of-play

[64] *The New York Times*, 9 Dec. 2012.

[65] *The New York Times*, 14 Dec. 2012.

[66] *The New York Times*, 21 Dec. 2012.

SCAF constitutional declaration of 30 March 2011 announced the ratification of the new constitution with the approval of 64 percent of the vote and a turnout of 33 percent of eligible voters. The constitution was then signed by President Morsi.

A shift in the composition of the revolutionary coalition against the regime had begun early in 2012 and was reflected in the demonstrations against the SCAF–Muslim Brotherhood cohabitation that was mentioned earlier. As SCAF's attempt to have its candidate, Ahmad Shafiq, elected president narrowly failed, president-elect Morsi suddenly found himself the inheritor of Mubarak's extensive presidential powers and the beneficiary of the Egyptian authoritarian tradition of the rule of law. It is thus unsurprising that he quickly stepped into SCAF shoes and began to issue constitutional law-decrees for which he claimed constitutional legitimacy.

Raucous but intermittent and inconclusive public debate in the constitutional assembly, marred by constant wrangling and repeated boycotts and threats of resignation by its non-Islamist members, contrasted with the quieter and much more effective bargaining behind closed doors among the state structures, notably the army, the judiciary, the bureaucracy and Al-Azhar, which were enjoying far greater autonomy than they had been accustomed to under Mubarak.[67] The abrupt closure of the inconclusive constitutional debate meant that the new constitution was in effect an extensively amended version of the constitution of 1971 which was used as its basis. Consequently, contrary to the revolution's cry against dictatorship and its vociferous demands for a parliamentary regime, the new Egypt retains a strongly presidential system and the office of prime minister will continue to be of relatively minor importance. The vested interests of the army were accommodated, partly explicitly in Articles 197–8, which carry over a National Security Council (with eight military members as compared to seven civilians, including the president) from the previous constitution (Article 197) and make the military judiciary an independent judiciary with competence for trying civilians in exceptional cases (Article 198), but mainly through "constitutional gaps"—that is, by omission to cover important

[67] Nathan J. Brown, "Egypt's State Constitutes Itself," posted on the Carnegie Endowment website on 19 Nov. 2012: http://egyptelections.carnegieendowment.org/2012/11/20/egypts-state-constitutes-itself

matters concerning defense and security services; and the same with interests of state bureaucracy. The accommodation of the vested interests of Al-Azhar (especially Articles 4 and 219) has rightly attracted considerable attention because it reveals a more traditional understanding of Islam that diverges considerably from that of the Muslim Brotherhood who dominated the constitutional assembly. I will discuss them separately below. Owing to the participation of the SCC in SCAF's last abortive coup and the firm opposition of prominent judges and the Judges' Club to President Morsi, the judiciary did not get as good a deal, but its vested interests were nevertheless represented through Vice-President Mahmud Makki and were reflected in the new constitution, even though the number of judges of the Supreme Constitutional Court was cut from the present nineteen to eleven, to be nominated by "judicial and other bodies" and appointed by the president (Article 176).[68]

Given the international spread of the formula in recent decades as well as the strength of the Islamist parties in the Egyptian parliament after 2011, the carry-over of the amended Article 2 of the old constitution was a foregone conclusion; and Article 2 of the 2012 constitution declares Islam the state religion and Arabic the official language, "and the principles of the Islamic *shari'a*, the main source of legislation." Article 219 then defines "the principles of the Islamic *shari'a* to include 'general proofs' [of the Islamic jurisprudence or *usul al-fiqh*] and its theoretical and practical jurisprudential rules, and its sources considered valid by the Sunni Rites/Schools of Law." The technical terminology of this Article belongs to the traditional Islamic jurisprudence of the *ulema*. It is consonant with the identification in Article 4 of "the senior *ulema* of Al-Azhar" (a reference to a council of forty Al-Azhar scholars recently set up by a controversial law) as the authoritative arbiters in matters concerning the Islamic *sharia*. As Brown and Lombardi point out, this traditional limitation to the legislative power of the state contrasts with the modernist Islamic jurisprudence of the Supreme Constitutional Court, whose opposition to the Muslim Brotherhood minimized its influence in the constitutional assembly, but also, and more surprisingly, with the reformist Islam of the dominant Muslim Brotherhood.[69] In

[68] For the official English translation of the Egyptian Constitution of 2012, see http://www.sis.gov.eg/newvr/theconistitution.pdf. I have, however, translated the critical articles I cite from the Arabic myself.

[69] Nathan J. Brown and Clark Lombardi, "Islam in Egypt's New Constitution,"

terms of Egyptian constitutional politics, this surprising fact can be explained by the inconclusiveness of public constitutional debate as against the closed door negotiations by the state institutions. There is, however, a more interesting comparative explanation as well. In her influential commentary on the draft constitution circulated in November 2012, the Egyptian lawyer and human rights activist Mona Zo-Al-Faqar criticized these Articles as establishing "the state based on the mandate of the jurist" (*dawla vilāyat al-faqih*) as against "the state of law" (*dawlat al-qānun*). There can be little doubt that the clerics of Al-Azhar were influenced by the Shi'ite ayatollahs of Iran in promoting the vested interest of their own clerical establishment. They thus established a Sunni variant of the constitutional authority of the jurists in the new Egyptian ruling bargain that is in sharp contrast to that of Tunisia in this respect. It is, however, more accurate to compare this Sunni constitutional limitation of legislation by Islamic law to that of Iran's old constitution of 1906–7, providing for a committee of five religious jurists with veto power over parliamentary legislation. It contrasts sharply with the counter-constitutionalist place of Islam in the 1979 Constitution of the Islamic Republic of Iran, owing to the latter's foundational clericalist Islamic ideology. Within a non-ideological frame, be it a Shi'ite one for Iran in 1907 or a Sunni one for Egypt in 2012, this limitation was and is compatible with constitutional democracy. This said, the desirability of such a limitation remains highly questionable—and certainly so from the viewpoint of women and religious minorities—and its practical consequences are unclear at this time.

Libya: Regime Change and Non-Negotiated Revolution

Libya offers a completely different pattern of revolution. Qaddafi refused to negotiate with the Benghazi rebels and would doubtless have suppressed them without NATO military intervention on 19 March 2011. His regime collapsed in August 2011 after nearly six months of intensive bombing by NATO air forces, and he himself was killed in October of that fateful year. The dismantling of state institutions had already taken

---

posted on the Carnegie Endowment website on 14 Dec. 2012: http://egypt-elections.carnegieendowment.org/2012/12/14/islam-in-egypts-new-constitution

place during Qaddafi's Jamahiriyya since the late 1970s and, to make matters worse, there had been no comparable prior tradition of the rule of law and constitutionalism in Libya. It is thus hardly surprising that no state, deep or shallow, survived the revolution.

The Tripoli Republic that was set up in November 1918 under the influence of Arab nationalists from Cairo was the first Arab republic in history. Yet it was subsequently dismantled due to internal divisions in 1923. Its effect beyond that date continued through the two Italian *Leggi Fondamentali* (Basic Laws) for Tripolitania and Cyrenaica, according to which eight Libyans were selected by Italian fascist rule and the parliament for a ten-man council which nominated officials for local administration.[70] Whatever impact such diminutive constitutional development may have had was, however, completely overwhelmed by the savage colonial war the Italians waged into the 1930s against the guerillas led by the shaykh of the Sanusi order of Cyrenaica—a war which devastated Libya and halved its population by most estimates. In short, as Lisa Anderson put it, the "efforts at state building—on the part of the Ottomans, the Sanusiyya, the Tripoli Republic, and even the Italians—to construct and maintain more elaborate administrations were all short-lived experiments that had ended in horrifying failure."[71]

After the Second World War, in preparation for the proclamation of independence on 24 December 1951, a National Constituent Assembly consisting of sixty men—twenty representatives from each of the three provinces—adopted a federal constitution for a constitutional monarchy under King Idris al-Sanusi. It divided power among the palace officials, the organs of federal government, and those of the provincial governments. The 1951 constitution was, however, amended in 1962 to abolish the provinces and end federalism.[72]

Libya's curious experience of "direct democracy" and revolutionary dictatorship under Qaddafi has variously been characterized as state

[70] L. Anderson, "The Tripoli Republic," in G. Joffe and K. McLahan (eds), *Social and Economic Development of Libya*, Wisbech: Menas Press, 1982, p. 52.

[71] L. Anderson, "Tribe and State: Libyan Anomalies," in P. Khoury and J. Kostiner (eds), *Tribe and State Formation in the Middle East*, Berkeley, CA: University of California Press, 1990, p. 294.

[72] K. Mezran, "Constitutionalism and Islam in Libya," in R. Grote and T.J. Röder (eds), *Constitutionalism in Islamic Countries: Between Upheaval and Continuity*, Oxford: Oxford University Press, 2012, pp. 521–5.

destruction and state avoidance.[73] Some three months after the Free Officers' revolution that brought Muammar al-Qaddafi to power, the Revolutionary Command Council issued the Constitutional Proclamation (*i'lān al-dustur*) of 11 December 1969. This was followed by the proclamation of the Authority of the People (*hukm al-sha'b*), affirming the Qur'an as the constitution of the Socialist People's Libyan Arab Jamahiriyya and establishing the General People's Congress as Libya's legislature. In between, however, Qaddafi announced a new Popular Revolution in April 1973, whose goals included eliminating "all forms of bourgeoisie and bureaucracy" and distributing arms to "the people who will point them at the chests of anyone who challenges the revolution."[74] Pursuant to that program, Qaddafi resigned from his official positions in December 1978 in order to act as the "Leader of the Revolution," and Revolutionary Committees were created for "maintaining the revolutionary ardor" in 1979, thus becoming the regime's watchdogs.[75] The real, albeit informal, power structure grew in the interstices of the popular and revolutionary branches of the Jamahiriyya, alongside the General People's Congress and what had survived of the old administrative structures by way of a formal structure of power.[76] Within the framework of this bifurcation of formal and informal politics, Qaddafi promoted a narrow circle of his political elite on the basis of ideological commitment, primordial, and personalistic ties.[77] During Qaddafi's rapprochement with the West and third unsuccessful attempt at liberalization from 2003 onward, the Ministry of Energy and other ministries were restored,[78] while the People's Security (*amn al-sha'b*) was strengthened for the war on terrorism (read the Islamic opposition).[79]

[73] L. Anderson, *The State and Social Transformation in Tunisia and Libya, 1830–1980*, Princeton, NJ: Princeton University Press, 1986. See further the chapter by Dirk Vandewalle in this volume.

[74] Quoted in Mezran, "Constitutionalism and Islam in Libya," p. 527.

[75] Ibid. pp. 528–31.

[76] H. Mattes, "Formal and Informal Authority in Libya since 1969," in D. Vandewalle (ed.), *Libya since 1969: Qadhafi's Revolution Revisited*, New York: Palgrave Macmillan, 2008.

[77] A.S.M. Obeidi, "Political Elites in Libya since 1969," in Vandewalle, *Libya since 1969*.

[78] Ibid. p. 108; Dirk Vandewalle, "From International Reconciliation to Civil War," being Chapter 9 in the revised edition of *Libya since 1969*, p. 224.

[79] A. Pargeter, "Qadhafi and Political Islam in Libya," in Vandewalle, *Libya since 1969*, p. 101.

Unlike Tunisia and Egypt, Libya thus had no historical experience of state-building. Furthermore, the power structure of the Jamahiriyya, as well as its armed forces and People's Security, failed to survive the revolution. Libya will consequently experience a different process from the negotiated revolutions elsewhere. It will most likely go through the stages of the revolutionary process found in the so-called great revolutions, for which I have proposed a sequence different from Brinton's anatomy model that generalized the pattern of the French Revolution of 1789.[80] That revolutionary process is brought to an end when the modern state manages to establish a monopoly over the legitimate use of violence. Given the extreme fragmentation of military power following the destruction of Qaddafi's patrimonial army, the power struggle among the militias that operate extensive protection and smuggling rings, the militias' control of cities, airports, and occasional attacks on the office of the prime minister and foreign diplomatic missions—including the killing of the American ambassador in Benghazi on 11 September 2012—this process will be a long and difficult one in Libya.[81] Popular demonstrations against militias following the murder of the American ambassador showed the extent of citizens' discontent with them, but the Libyan government's unsuccessful attempts to bring the militias under its control by integrating them into the army and police forces have so far done little to allay such discontent. On the contrary, the unruly Benghazi militiamen gunned down the police chief in November 2012, and kidnapped the chief police investigator of his murder in the early days of January 2013.

The current revolutionary power struggle is exacerbated by the resumption of the flow of oil revenue and struggle over its distribution among the three provinces before any appreciable institutionalization of centralized government. Citizens in Cyrenaica (Barqa), in particular, resent having been allocated only sixty seats in the new parliament (General National Congress), as compared to 100 for Tripolitania, while claiming to produce two-thirds of Libya's oil. Ethnic and tribal minority groups such as the Berbers (Amazigh), Tuareg, and Tabu are also restive as their constitutional demands for autonomy have not been addressed.[82]

[80] Arjomand, *After Khomeini*, pp. 14–15.

[81] "After Qaddafi," *Foreign Affairs*, 91, 6 (2012), p. 10.

[82] N. Pelham, "Is Libya Cracking up?" *The New York Review of Books*, 21 June 2012, pp. 66–9.

On the basis of that model of revolutionary process, a prolonged and violent power struggle among militias, as well as a political struggle between the provinces, especially Cyrenaica and its capital Benghazi, over the appropriation of oil rent, is likely to take place before the Libyan revolution is brought to an end through the concentration of military force in a centralized state. There are, however, other processes and indications at work in the opposite direction. Revolutions are also integrative processes in that they incorporate previously excluded elements of the population into political society. The Free Officers' revolution of 1969 and Qaddafi's Jamahiriyya already constituted an integrative revolution by bringing the tribes originating in the Sahara into the political community and the semi-nomadic families who had migrated to the coastal areas into the top echelons of decision-making.[83] Against most predictions, the 7 July 2012 national elections went well and without significant clashes in an electrifying atmosphere,[84] and can indeed be considered a revolutionary festival celebrating Libyans' much-deepened integrative revolution. The election day was Libya's revolutionary feast, a nationwide public celebration as the ritual antidote to the widespread sense of cynicism, atomization, and apathy caused by the chasm between the previous regime's formal structure and the reality of its informal politics.[85]

The constitutional developments since the success of the revolution can be summarized as follows. On 10 August the National Transitional Council (NTC) made public the Interim Constitutional Declaration it had passed a week earlier, and its president, Mustafa Abd al-Jalil, affirmed its declaration of the *sharia* as the main source of legislation. The Interim Constitutional Declaration was amended in March 2012, however, extending the timeframe for drafting the constitution and clarifying the composition of the drafting assembly with sixty members—twenty from each of the three provinces. The amendments of 5 July 2012, which were passed by the NTC on the eve of the first national elections, were somewhat more significant in that they deprived the National Congress of the power to appoint the assembly to draft the constitution, which was to be elected later and separately (according to criteria to be established by the

[83] Mattes, "Formal and Informal Authority in Libya," p. 70.
[84] See the chapter by Dirk Vandewalle in this volume.
[85] D. Vandewalle, "Libya's Revolution in Perspective," in Vandewalle, *Libya since 1969*.

National Congress), and further entrenched Islam as the main source of legislation.[86] The most consequential legislation of the transitional government in practical terms, however, was the electoral laws passed from February 2012 onwards with the advice of international consultants. These laws appeared to be mindful of lessons drawn from Iraq, where proportional representation had facilitated the dominance of a single, better-organized party, as well as the Islamist electoral victories in Egypt and Tunisia. Only eighty of the 200 seats in the National Congress were given to the parties on the basis of proportional representation, with the remaining 120 seats going to independents on the basis of a single non-transferable vote system. The law is thus strongly biased against the development of political parties.[87]

Given the extreme fragmentation of the power structure in the Qaddafi regime, Libyan society was deeply depoliticized. A plethora of political parties sprang into being in the months after August 2011, but none of these was particularly well organized and none could be taken to represent Libyan national unity. For the majority of representatives who occupied the independent seats, the latter would be better represented by a single individual instead, with Dr Mohammad al-Mugharief, the foremost opponent of Qaddafi, being such a personality. On 8 August 2012, the Transitional National Council formally transferred its powers to the new National Congress. On the following day, it elected Mugharief its president despite the fact that his party, the National Party, had not done nearly as well as Mahmud Jibril's National Alliance coalition or even the Muslim Brothers' Party for Justice and Construction. The choice of a prime minister proved to be a more drawn-out affair, and after the failure of the first attempt 'Ali Zidan was elected in mid-October. However, it was not until 14 November 2012 that the first elected government of Libya was sworn in.

Conclusion

Considering constitutions as the formalization of the political reconstruction and the establishment of new ruling bargains for regimes following

[86] For the texts, see the website of the Max Planck Institute for Comparative Public Law and International Law/Constitutional reform in Arab Countries: http://www.mpil.de/ww/en/pub/research/details/know_transfer/constitutional_reform_in_arab_/libyen.cfm

[87] See the chapter by Shadi Hamid in this volume.

revolutions, this chapter has surveyed the three evolving ruling bargains that followed the success of the Arab revolution of 2011 in Tunisia, Egypt, and Libya. The chapter's comparisons centered on four types of variations: variation in the traditions of the rule of law; variations in the character of the old states and the power structures sustaining them; variation in the extent of negotiated change versus variations forced by revolutionary violence; and variation in the constitutional placement of Islam. A distinction was made between negotiated revolutions, where the old state persists and negotiates a new ruling bargain with the opposition, and revolutions in which the state is destroyed and the revolutionary power struggle among competing groups determines the outcome of the revolutionary process. Tunisia and Egypt fall into the first category, while Libya belongs to the second.

The absence of a tradition of rule of law and a strong legal culture in Libya as compared to its long history in Tunisia and Egypt makes the outcome of the Arab revolution of 2011 largely dependent on the revolutionary power struggle. Even if the argument that democracy is easier to build on a *tabula rasa* is correct, the Libyan democratic leaders will still need to concentrate the legitimate use of violence in a state they are building and remain in control of it—something that has not happened so far. Secondly, this chapter contrasted Qaddafi's state destruction and emasculation of the professional army with the building of strong bureaucratic states and professional armies in Tunisia and Egypt, on the one hand, and important differences between the Tunisian and Egyptian state structures, on the other. Two sets of differences stood out as the most salient. In Tunisia the army remained aloof from revolutionary and constitutional politics in Tunisia, whereas in Egypt the army quickly gained control of the revolution and became the major arbiter of its constitutional politics. Perhaps an equally important difference between Tunisia and Egypt has been the far greater extent of the judicialization of constitutional politics in the latter country due to a stronger judiciary in Egypt and its involvement in two decades of legal mobilization against the excesses of Mubarak's authoritarianism. Thirdly, the chapter sought to explain the very different itineraries of negotiated revolution in Tunisia and Egypt in terms of the first two sources of variation.

Finally, the chapter compared the constitutional placement of Islam in Iran after its Islamic revolution in the 1979 Constitution of the Islamic Republic of Iran with that in Egypt's Islamist constitution of

2012 and in the Tunisian and Libyan constitutional documents. The Iranian constitution was based on a clericalist Islamic ideology that made Islam the basis of the new political order and its constitution. It thus represented Shi'ite counter-constitutionalism in the heyday of Islamic political ideologies. With the passing of the age of ideology in the Middle East, Islam has been proposed by the Arab Islamist parties as a limitation on the legislative power of the "civic state" and in sharp contrast to the Iranian counter-constitutionalist premise that it should be the basis of the constitution of an Islamic ideological state.

The Arab revolutions of 2011 had not come to a standstill in the three countries under consideration when this chapter went to press. The events that followed, however, can be taken as a confirmation of our comparative analysis as the differences between the three have only been accentuated further. Libya has descended deeper into anarchy as the revolutionary power struggle continues with no centralization of coercive power and no constitutional settlement in sight. In Egypt, the alliance of the armed forces and the SCC against the Muslim Brotherhood government of President Morsi culminated in the counter-revolution of 3 July 2013, which abrogated the Islamist constitution of 2012 after just half a year. The counter-revolution quickly claimed constitutional legitimacy by having its new constitution ratified by a national referendum in January 2014. The new constitution retains the principles of the *sharia* as the main source of law but reverts the jurisdiction over determination of repugnancy to the SCC. Last but not least, the Tunisian National Constituent Assembly has completed the slow process of consensus based constitution-building by finally adopting a new constitution on 26 January 2014, with 200 of its 216 members in favor. The new constitution sealed the historic compromise of March 2012 and omitted all references to the *sharia*, creating a distinctive Tunisian model for constitutional democracy in the Muslim world.

PART 2

CASE STUDIES

7

RENEGOTIATING IRAN'S POST-REVOLUTIONARY SOCIAL CONTRACT

THE GREEN MOVEMENT AND THE STRUGGLE FOR DEMOCRACY IN THE ISLAMIC REPUBLIC

Nader Hashemi

The 2011 pro-democracy uprisings in North Africa and the Middle East have been widely viewed as an exclusively Arab affair. However, future historians looking back on this period might challenge this claim by including Iran in the picture. For it was in the summer of 2009, after a stolen presidential election, that similar protests against authoritarian rule erupted, prefiguring the Arab Spring. This event gave birth to Iran's Green Movement (Jonbesh-e sabz), with characteristics that bear a distinct resemblance to the revolts of the Arab Spring.

In both the Arab and Iranian contexts the uprisings were unexpected and unprecedented. They were largely leaderless with the initial organizational work carried out by small groups in urban centers using social media. A Middle Eastern "youth bulge" was at the core of these protests. A new generation of highly educated and globalized young people, frustrated by bleak economic prospects and angry at their repressive political contexts, had now come of age and were newly assertive.

Moreover, the protestors on the Arab and Iranian street were non-ideological in terms of their political preferences. Some of the protestors were secular, others were religious, and many inhabited an undefined space in between. In terms of a *modus operandi*, the overwhelming majority of the participants were committed to non-violent political change (with Libya being the sole exception). More broadly, these protestors were united by their shared demand for democracy, dignity, and social justice. It is perhaps due to these similarities that historian Nikki Keddie writes that the "Green Movement of 2009 may be considered part of the 2009–2011 [Middle Eastern] revolutionary wave, but its influence on Arab movements cannot be assumed."[1]

This is not to say that the rise of Iran's Green Movement in 2009 directly inspired or had an immediate diffusion effect on the 2011 Arab Spring. Evidence of a link is sparse. However, when Wael Ghonim, a key organizer of the Egyptian protests, was asked why he wore a green wristband like the supporters of the Green Movement, he replied: "That was just a coincidence, but I'm happy you ... made the connection!" He then went on to state, "I would tell Iranians to learn from the Egyptians, *as we have learned from you* ... that at the end of the day with the power of people, we can do whatever we want to do."[2] In reflecting on this connection Keddie has suggested that the general effect of Iranian pro-democracy politics on the Arab world is at best indirect, "showing that the masses of people of varying views could be mobilized even against a strong autocratic government and in suggesting means of mobilization."[3]

[1] Nikki Keddie, "Arab and Iranian Revolts 1979–2011: Influence or Similar Causes?" *International Journal of Middle East Studies*, 44 (Feb. 2012), p. 151.

[2] Emphasis added. See, for example, "Egyptian Activist's Message to Iranians: Learn from Egyptians and We Learned from You," International Campaign for Human Rights in Iran (10 Feb. 2011). http://www.iranhumanrights.org/2011/02/wael-ghonim-on-iran/ (accessed 20 June 2012). For more on this topic see Charles Kurzman, "The Arab Spring: Ideals of the Iranian Green Movement, Methods of the Iranian Revolution," *International Journal of Middle East Studies*, 44 (Feb. 2012), pp. 162–5.

[3] Nikki Keddie, "Arab and Iranian Revolts 1979–2011: Influence or Similar Causes?" p. 151.

In comparing democratic struggles in Iran and the Arab world, an important common denominator uniting both cases is the crisis of legitimacy facing authoritarian regimes across the region.[4] In this context it should be noted that the social conditions that bolster authoritarianism and impede democratization vary from country to country. The nature and character of authoritarian rule and the internal crisis of legitimacy facing political regimes are different.[5] Each country has its own internal story and, notwithstanding the broad structural similarities in terms of economic and political grievances that have produced these revolts, the more we focus our analytical lens the more we see that democratic forces confront different obstacles in each country, related to class and minority cleavages, the strength of the military and state institutions, and the unity and coherence of opposition forces.

Having recently completed a comparison between the uprisings in Iran and the Arab world in 2009 and 2011,[6] in this chapter I turn to an exploration of the crisis of legitimacy facing the Iranian Islamic Republic after the 2009 presidential elections. The chapter argues that the emergence of the Green Movement in 2009 was the second attempt of the reformist movement to renegotiate Iran's post-revolutionary social contract through democratic means. The Iranian social contract was formed in the immediate aftermath of the 1979 Revolution and was embodied in the Constitution of the Islamic Republic of Iran which was confirmed in a referendum in the same year. For the first thirty years of the Iranian Islamic Republic's existence, this political arrangement remained largely intact and enjoyed broad support within Iran. But it has now unraveled. The electoral crisis in June 2009 is a key turning point in Iranian politics—Iran today faces what Jürgen Habermas has called a "legitimation crisis."

[4] Thirty-three years ago Michael Hudson wrote about this topic in his influential study *Arab Politics: The Search for Legitimacy*, New Haven, CT: Yale University Press, 1979.

[5] Eva Bellin, "Reconsidering the Robustness of Authoritarianism in the Middle East: Lessons from the Arab Spring," *Comparative Politics*, 44 (Jan. 2012), pp. 127–49.

[6] Nader Hashemi and Mahmoud Sadri, "The Arab Spring and Iran's Green Movement: A Comparison," in Brian Calfano and Emile Sahliyeh (eds), *After the Spring: Looking Ahead to the New Seasons of Political Change and Stasis in the Middle East*, Lanham, MD: Lexington/Roman and Littlefield, forthcoming.

According to Habermas, as individuals become increasingly disillusioned with the political status quo, the state is faced with the possibility of a mass withdrawal of loyalty and support. The core organizing principles of a society that previously existed now serve to prevent the resolution of political problems that are critical for its continued existence, thus leading to a "legitimation crisis."[7]

The chapter begins with an examination of Iran's 1979 Revolution and the social contract that emerged as result of this political upheaval. This section also contains a brief discussion of social contract theory and its links to political legitimacy. The chapter then turns to an analysis of how and why Iran's post-revolutionary social contract began to unravel and how it led to both the rise and fall of the reformist movement in the late 1990s and its second iteration in the form of the Green Movement in 2009. The similarities and differences between these two movements will be examined. Finally, the chapter examines the Green Movement itself. What are its political origins, key characteristics, strategies for democratization, strengths and weaknesses, and what obstacles does it face in terms of democratizing Iran? The chapter concludes with a commentary on the challenges and the future political trajectory of the Green Movement.

Social Contract Theory and Political Legitimacy

In its broadest sense, the concept of a social contract refers to a voluntary agreement made among people in order to form an organized society. The moral and political obligations that members of this society owe to one another and to their government are a byproduct of this agreement. In short, social contract theory helps explain the origins of political community and the normative relationship among its members, including the rights and responsibilities that go with membership and citizenship.

One of the first references in political philosophy to a social contract appears in the early Platonic dialogue between Socrates and Crito. Socrates argues that he is morally obligated to remain in prison and accept his death sentence because of an unwritten social contract he has implicitly endorsed and benefited from by virtue of his citizenship in

[7] Jürgen Habermas, *Legitimation Crisis*, trans. Thomas McCarthy, Boston: Beacon Press, 1975. I thank Danny Postel for this reference.

Athens. A less favorable treatment of a social contract appears in Plato's *Republic*, Book II, when Glaucon discusses the nature of justice.[8]

The first modern theory of a social contract is attributed to Thomas Hobbes. Self-interested yet rational individuals, Hobbes argues, fleeing the chaos and uncertainty of the state of nature, agree to establish a new society where they exchange their natural rights and unlimited freedom in the state of nature for the security, stability, and predictability of civil society. One person or an assembly is then established as the sovereign authority (the Leviathan) to enforce the social contract and ensure compliance with the laws.[9]

Building on this rough outline, John Locke and Jean-Jacques Rousseau developed more democratic readings of a social contract, where the moral basis of legitimate political authority and the origins of community are rooted in the "consent of the governed" (Locke) or the "general will" of the populace (Rousseau). In the twentieth century, social contract theory was revived through the influential work of John Rawls and David Gauthier.[10]

In *The Legitimation of Power*, David Beetham explores the underpinnings of a modern social contract that is rooted in different forms of consent. At the outset he acknowledges that consent is conceptually confusing, and its relationship to political legitimacy doubly so. Elections, he argues, "are not the only form of action that can demonstrate consent or confer legitimacy on the powerful, or that there are not other types of action which, failing to meet the liberal criteria for voluntary agreement, may not have or have had a legitimating force within

[8] Plato, *The Last Days of Socrates*, ed. Christopher Rowe, New York: Penguin, 2010, see Crito, pp. 51c–53a; Plato, *The Republic*, 2nd edn, trans. Desmond Lee, New York: Penguin, 2003, pp. 357b–358a.

[9] Thomas Hobbes, *Leviathan*, ed. Richard Tuck, Cambridge: Cambridge University Press, 1996.

[10] John Locke, *Two Treatises on Government*, ed. Peter Laslett, Cambridge: Cambridge University Press, 1988; Jean-Jacques Rousseau, *On the Social Contract*, trans. David Cress, Indianapolis: Hackett Publishing, 1987; John Rawls, *Theory of Justice: Original Edition*, Cambridge, MA: Harvard University Press, 2005, and *Political Liberalism*, 2nd edn, New York: Columbia University Press, 2005; David Gauthier, *Morals by Agreement*, New York: Oxford University Press, 1987.

the conventions of different social systems."[11] There are three forms of action, he suggests, which can imply consent and confer legitimacy on an established or new social order: swearing an oath of allegiance, taking part in consultations or negotiations with the powerful, and finally, publicly acclaiming a popular leader or cause at a political rally.

On this latter form of implied consent Beetham observes that there is "no denying that demonstrations of popular support and mass mobilization confer a distinctive legitimacy in the age of popular sovereignty; and that a party or movement that can harness the enthusiasm and commitment of a mass following thereby enhances the prestige and authority of those who lead it." This form of consent through mass mobilization, in the context of a revolution, especially on a continuous and ongoing basis in its aftermath, "confers enormous moral authority on a new regime."[12]

At the end of his book Beetham entertains a short discussion on political legitimacy in the Islamic world. He notes that the emergence of Islamist movements at the end of the twentieth century challenges the long-standing presupposition in the Western social sciences that political legitimacy can only be grounded on a secular basis.[13] The 1979 Islamic Revolution in Iran was one of the key events to have raised this issue politically, intellectually, and academically. It has now resurfaced in the aftermath of the 2011 Arab Spring and the subsequent victory of Islamist parties in elections in Tunisia and Egypt, thereby giving this topic a pressing new relevance.[14]

Iran's 1979 Ruling Bargain

The 1979 Iranian Revolution has been described as "one of the epic events of postwar history" and "as significant and as unprecedented in

[11] David Beetham, *The Legitimation of Power*, Atlantic Highlands, NJ: Humanities Press International, 1991, p. 92.

[12] Ibid. p. 94.

[13] Ibid. pp. 191–204.

[14] Examining why political legitimacy in many Muslim societies has emerged in the late twentieth century with a particular religious underpinning is beyond the scope of this chapter. I briefly examine this topic in Nader Hashemi, "The Multiple Histories of Secularism: Muslim Societies in Comparative Perspective," *Journal of Philosophy and Social Criticism*, 36 (2010), pp. 325–38.

world history as the French revolution of 1789 and the Russian revolution of 1917."[15] It was a genuinely popular revolution in which at least 10 percent or more of Iran's citizens participated in street protests and general strikes. By comparison, the French Revolution relied on the participation of approximately 2 percent of the population, while less than 1 percent participated in overturning Soviet communism.[16] The tidal wave of popular opposition that swept Iran's US-backed monarchy from power reverberated throughout the world and is today considered the touchstone event marking the rise of Islamic fundamentalism in international affairs.

The 1979 Revolution also marked a key historical juncture in Iranian political development. It established a path dependency that has deeply shaped Iran's political trajectory for the past thirty-five years, and will likely do so for the foreseeable future. On the ruins of the Pahlavi monarchy a new social contract emerged. This social contract was developed and constructed in the immediate aftermath of the revolution and was a reflection of Iran's modern historical experience, especially since 1953 when the desecularization of Iranian politics began.[17] The key events that embodied this new social contract were two national referendums in 1979. According to official results, and based on massive voter turnouts, on 30–1 March 1979, 98.2 percent voted in favor of establishing an "Islamic Republic," and on 2–3 December 1979, 99.5 percent voted in favor of the new constitution which divided sovereignty between the people and the clerics, with the latter having special privileges and a unique role in leading the new regime that was not subject to direct democratic accountability or checks and balances.[18]

[15] Fred Halliday, *Islam and the Myth of Confrontation: Religion and Politics in the Middle East*, London: I.B. Tauris, 1996, p. 42 and Said Amir Arjomand, *The Turban for the Crown: The Islamic Revolution in Iran*, New York: Oxford University Press, 1988, p. 3.

[16] Charles Kurzman, *The Unthinkable Revolution in Iran*, Cambridge, MA: Harvard University Press, 2004, p. viii.

[17] Ali Mirsepassi, *Intellectual Discourse and the Politics of Modernization: Negotiating Modernity in Iran*, Cambridge: Cambridge University Press, 2000, pp. 65–95; Arjomand, *Turban for the Crown*; and Nikki Keddie, *Modern Iran: Roots and Results of Revolution*, updated edn, New Haven: Yale University Press, 2006, Ervand Abrahamian, *A History of Modern Iran*, Cambridge: Cambridge University Press, 2008.

[18] Asghar Schirazi, *The Constitution of Iran: Politics and the State in the Islamic*

Numerous criticisms have been raised about the accuracy of these figures, and especially the fairness of the political process that led up to the votes.[19] The writing of the 1979 constitution is particularly noteworthy for the strong-arm tactics of the Islamist supporters of Ayatollah Khomeini who manipulated the constitution-writing process to guarantee clerical supremacy.[20] Notwithstanding this fact, there was clearly a huge turnout for these votes, and Ayatollah Khomeini was undoubtedly a popular and highly charismatic figure. Even if the clock could be turned back in order to guarantee a completely balanced and transparent constitutional-writing process, Khomeini's popularity and his sophisticated network of support, in contrast to the divisions and disagreements among the nationalist, socialist, and secular opposition groups, ensured that his vision of a future Iran won out over competing visions in the post-revolutionary power struggle. The populist politics of Khomeini and his disciples, and their ability to engage in mass mobilization, thus imbued the Iranian Republic with a significant degree of political legitimacy, lending it a distinct staying power that has lasted for most of the past thirty-five years.[21]

Furthermore, there is broad agreement that until 2009 the Iranian Islamic Republic organized regular presidential and parliamentary elections that were, on balance, basically "fair but not free." Candidates for public office had to be screened for an ideological commitment to the Iranian Republic (as interpreted by the Guardian Council), but once they passed this test and elections were held the announced results generally reflected the preference of the voters.[22] These elections, which took

Republic, trans. John O'Kane, New York: I.B. Tauris, 1997, pp. 27, 52. Schirazi does an excellent job in examining the political environment and debate in Iran at this time, especially the hidden agenda of supporters of Khomeini for a clerical-dominated state.

19 Mohammad Maleki, "Lessons from the Past for Elections," Roozonline, 26 Nov. 2011, http://www.roozonline.com/persian/opinion/opinion-article/archive/2011/november/26/article/-31c3a941bf.html (accessed 15 Aug. 2012).

20 Schirazi, *The Constitution of Iran*, pp. 27–57; Shaul Bakhash, *The Reign of the Ayatollahs: Iran and the Islamic Revolution*, revised edn, New York: Basic Books, 1990, pp. 71–91; Mohsen Milani, *The Making of Iran's Islamic Constitution*, 2nd edn, Boulder, CO: Westview Press, 1994, pp. 154–62.

21 Ervand Abrahamian, *Khomeinism: Essays on the Islamic Republic*, Berkeley: University of California Press, 1988, pp. 13–38.

22 The first sign of vote tampering coincides with the rise of the reform move-

place over a thirty-year period, generally involved a high voter turnout that compares quite favorably with elections elsewhere, not only by regional standards but also on a global level. In the 2009 presidential election, for example, the officially announced figure of 85 percent voter participation is widely accepted.

These facts suggest that Iran's post-revolutionary social contract retained a strong degree of internal legitimacy among the majority of Iranians. Though there were certainly robust criticisms and increasing complaints about clerical hegemony and corruption, the act of consistent voting in large numbers over a long period of time is an unambiguous measure of consent that highlights the legitimacy and staying power of Iran's post-revolutionary social experiment, notwithstanding its authoritarian and repressive nature. The year 2009, however, was a turning point in Iranian history. According to General Mohammad Ali Jafari, the senior commander of the Islamic Republican Guards Corps, the rise of the Green Movement in the aftermath of a stolen election posed a greater threat to regime stability and political order than Saddam Hussein's 1980 invasion of Iran and the subsequent eight-year Iran–Iraq War (1980–88).[23]

---

ment. In the 2000 parliamentary elections, former President Hashemi-Rafsanjani was headed for a humiliating defeat. The Guardian Council delayed releasing the results of the vote and repeatedly declared huge blocks of vote invalid in order to grant Rafsanjani one of the thirty seats allotted to the district of Tehran. See Geneive Abdo, "Iranians Cry Foul as Hardliner Rafsanjani Scrapes Home in Poll," *The Observer*, 27 Feb., 2000. Mehdi Karoubi issued a similar protest after the 2005 presidential election. For background see Nader Hashemi, "The Rowhani Challenge: Electoral Authoritarianism inside the Islamic Republic," *Cairo Review of Global Affairs* (Summer 2013), pp. 27–39.

[23] Scott Peterson, *Let the Swords Encircle Me: Iran—A Journey Behind the Headlines*, New York: Simon and Schuster, 2010, p. 549. After the crushing of the protests and the arrest of the Green Movement leaders, a senior clerical official acknowledged that a key reason why there could not be a public trial was because of the popularity of the movement within Iranian society, including among senior clerics. See, "Those Who Are Quiet About The Sedition Are No Different Than Those Who Support It," Farsnews, 1 Jan. 2012. http://www.farsnews.com/newstext.php?nn=13901011000514 (accessed 20 June 2012). For analysis of political trends in Iran after the 2009 electoral coup see Mehran Kamrava, "The 2009 President Elections and Iran's Changing Political Landscape," *Orbis*, 54 (Summer 2010), pp. 400–12.

The Origins of the Green Movement

The genesis of the Green Movement is inextricably linked to the 2009 presidential campaign of Iran's former prime minister Mir Hossein Mousavi. As the leading reformist candidate in these elections, Mousavi chose the color green to represent his political campaign because of its traditional association (in Muslim societies) with Islam.[24]

Adopting the color green was also a strategic decision that shielded Mousavi from criticism by hardline groups that his campaign was not authentically indigenous. A further reason for choosing green was to deny supporters of Mahmoud Ahmadinejad a monopoly on the use and interpretation of Islamic terms and symbols. Finally, from an international perspective, green is associated with the politics of environmental consciousness and indirectly with non-violence and movements for peace and social justice, thus giving his political campaign and the subsequent Green Movement a global appeal.

The Green Movement is a byproduct of the rise and fall of the reform movement in the Islamic Republic of Iran,[25] with which it is philosophically, intellectually, and politically linked. This movement broadly coincided with the two-term presidency of Muhammad Khatami (1997–2005) and reached its zenith in terms of political influence in August 2000. The movement's efforts to reform and democratize Iranian politics from within the framework of the existing constitution can be understood as an attempt to renegotiate Iran's post-revolutionary social contract. The specific strategy of the reform movement was famously described by one of the movement's leading strategists, Saeed Hajjarian,

[24] Muhammad Sahimi, "The Green Path of Hope," in Nader Hashemi and Danny Postel (eds), *The People Reloaded: The Green Movement and the Struggle for Iran's Future*, New York: Melville House, 2011, p. 126. A young supporter of Mousavi in Mashhad, Ruhollah Shahsavari, first suggested the use of this color in the early phase of Mousavi's presidential campaign. In an interview on the topic he noted that they "got the idea from other countries notably the US … [we] were impressed that pacifists defeated warmongers in the US and decided we should do the same in Iran by portraying Moussavi as a pacifist through a colour" (Najmeh Bozorgmehr, "Moussavi Rides a Green Wave," *Financial Times*, 12 June 2009).

[25] Ali Ansari, *Iran, Islam and Democracy: The Politics of Managing Change*, 2nd edn, London: Chatham House, 2006, pp. 176–229 and Mehran Kamrava, *Iran's Intellectual Revolution*, Cambridge: Cambridge University Press, 2007, pp. 120–72.

as "*feshar az payeen, chaneh zani az bala*" (pressure from below, haggling at the top).[26] The basic idea was that by strengthening civil society and engaging in mass mobilization (leading to electoral victories), the reformists could gradually democratize Iran by changing its moral context and political culture. The hardliners would be shamed in the court of public opinion, leading to their neutralization and thus the gradual democratization of Iran.

The Islamic Republic of Iran experienced an "Iran Spring" moment in the late 1990s. The reform movement that emerged with the landslide presidential victory of Muhammad Khatami in 1997 electrified the country. After an initial period of success, where reformist candidates won a series of electoral victories at the municipal, parliamentary, and presidential levels, the wave of reform was brought to an end, albeit gradually, by a hardline clerical counteroffensive.[27] While it is beyond the scope of this chapter to provide a retrospective review of this story, the strategy that the reformists adopted contained an in-built bias that favored the regime's hardliner and conservative forces.

President Khatami had repeatedly stated that democratizing the Iranian Islamic Republic could only take place "*dar chahar choob-e qanun*" (within the framework of the law). But what if the law itself was the fundamental problem? In the event of a conflict between popular and clerical sovereignty, Iran's constitution left little room for doubt that the latter was always supreme.[28] Iran's ruling oligarchy was happy to play by these rules because the law was on their side. It favored their interests and enabled them to assert control over the judicial system with ruthless efficiency. This inbuilt legal bias allowed them to shut down all the leading reformist publications, jail prominent journalists and intellectuals, and ban prominent reformist candidates from public office. When such measures were insufficient, political assassinations were used to silence demands for democracy.

[26] Saeed Hajjarian, interview with *Rah-e No*, 23 May 1998. For more on Saeed Hajjarian's political thought see his *Jomhuriyyat: Afsoon-zadat az ghodrat* [Republicanism: The De-Mystification of Power], Tehran: Tarh-e No, 2000, and Saeed Hajjarian, "Dowlat-e Polisi, Dowlat-e Padegani" [The Police State, the Garrison State], *Aftab* (Nov.–Dec. 2002), pp. 4–7.

[27] Said Amir Arjomand, *After Khomeini: Iran under its Successors*, New York: Oxford University Press, 2009, pp. 90–111.

[28] A. William Samii, "Dissent and Iranian Elections: Reasons and Implications," *Middle East Journal*, 58 (Summer 2004), pp. 403–23.

The rise of Mahmoud Ahmadinejad and Iran's "neo-conservatives" in 2005 officially marked the reform movement's denouement. A period of soul searching and reflection began on what went wrong, the lessons learned, and the way in which supporters of reform could move forward.[29] In 2009, the reformists attempted a comeback. A second attempt was launched to try to rewrite the Iranian social contract by capturing Iran's presidency, as had been done in 1997 and 2001. The reformists' core demands remained the same: full implementation of the constitution with an emphasis on people's rights, greater democracy, respect for basic freedoms, support for civil society associations, and a less confrontational foreign policy.

The Deeper Roots of the Green Movement

The deeper roots of the Green Movement can be traced to the intra-Islamist conflict that first surfaced in the mid-1980s. After Ayatollah Khomeini and his loyalists in the Islamic Republic Party had consolidated their political power, an ideological split emerged between right- and left-wing Islamists. Three core issues became a source of conflict: the nature of the economic system, Iran's foreign policy orientation, and socio-cultural issues. The different philosophical positions on these issues gradually led to an acrimonious debate. It was not long before different readings of religion would also emerge as a source of conflict, pitting a relatively dynamic and malleable understanding of Islam against a static and inflexible interpretation vis-à-vis modern-day socio-political problems.[30] Equally important were the different emphases put on interpreting the constitution—whereas the left-wing factions would

[29] Abbas Abdi, "Sarnavesht-e Matoom: Tahleel-e Jameah Shenakhti Sevom-e Tir" [Manifest Destiny: A Sociological Analysis of the Third of Tir], 25 Jan. 2007, http://www.ayande.ir/new/Sar%20neveshte%20mahtoom.pdf (accessed 22 Mar. 2010); Saeed Hajjarian, "Zendeh Bad Eslahat" [Long Live Reform], *Ayeen* (2005), pp. 11–17; Akbar Ganji, "Manifest-e Jomhurikhaee" [A Republican Manifesto], (2002); Kazem Alamdari, *Chera Eslahat Shekast Khord* [Why Did the Reforms Fail?] Woodland Hills, CA: Sayeh Publishing Corporation, 2008.

[30] Mehran Kamrava, *Iran's Intellectual Revolution*, Cambridge: Cambridge University Press, 2007, Chapters 4 and 5.

emphasize its republican aspects, the right-wing factions would highlight its religious dimensions.[31]

The left wing, known as the Islamic Left (*chap-e eslami*), comprised laymen and mid-ranking clerics.[32] During the 1980s, their politics mirrored those of other left-wing nationalist parties in the developing world in terms of their strong anti-imperialist stance, a belief in the export of revolution, and support for national liberation struggles in the global South.[33] Ideologically, this faction bears a close resemblance to other political Islamist groups within the Sunni Muslim world during the same period, particularly in their anti-American militancy. The students who seized the US embassy in Tehran in 1979, for example, came almost exclusively from this faction. Their original point of conflict with their conservative allies was over economic policy. Members of the Islamic Left were strong advocates of a centralized economy, a redistributive state, and egalitarian social programs. The backbone of this faction was composed of groups such as the Majma-e ruhaniyun-e mobarez (Combatant Clerics Society), and the Sazman-e mojahedeen enqelab-e Islami (Organization of the Mojahedeen of the Islamic Revolution), and the student-led Daftar-e tahkim-e vahdat (Office for the Consolidation of Unity). Their key journals were *Salam*, *Asr-e ma*, and *Rah-e No*. Most of the key leaders of the Green Movement in Iran today can be traced back to this political Islamist orientation.

The Islamic Left underwent a gradual intellectual transformation in the direction of democracy, moderation, and liberalism in the aftermath of Khomeini's death in 1989. In reflecting on this period, Alireza Alavi-Tabaar, a prominent Green Movement and reformist intellectual, identifies several events that led to this transformation: the end of the Iraq–Iran War and the withering away of revolutionary fervor, the banning of Islamic Left candidates from the fourth parliamentary elections, the creation of new intellectual journals such as *Kiyan*, and the fractious

[31] For a longer discussion see Mehdi Moslem, *Factional Politics in Post-Khomeini Iran*, Syracuse: Syracuse University Press, 2002, pp. 37–49.

[32] Wilfred Buchta, *Who Rules Iran? The Structure of Power in the Islamic Republic*, Washington, DC: Washington Institute for Near East Policy and the Konrad Adenauer Stiftung, 2000, pp. 78–120.

[33] In doing so they drew inspiration from an important plank in Ayatollah Khomeini's political platform. For background see Abrahamian, *Khomeinism: Essays on the Islamic Republic*, pp. 13–38.

religious debates related to the removal of Ayatollah Montazeri as a successor to Khomeini.[34]

Simultaneously, however, the Islamic Left faction, which formed the core of the reform movement in the late 1990s, remained loyal to the ideals of the 1979 Revolution and the political thought of Ayatollah Khomeini. They tried to reconcile their newfound commitment to toleration and political pluralism by elevating Khomeini's populist and democratic ideas while ignoring his illiberal and authoritarian political convictions. Although explicit loyalty to the founder of the Iranian Islamic Republic was a strategic necessity and a precondition for participation in the country's politics, in retrospect it can argued that many senior reformist leaders and intellectuals suffered from delusions about the nature of Khomeini's political project and the willingness of Iranian hardliners to share political power and accept the outcome of democratic elections.

A subtle but qualitative shift took place among some of the leaders of the reform movement in the period between 2005 and 2009. The key difference was that this time these individuals were ready to challenge and oppose the edicts of Iran's supreme leader in public rather than simply acquiescing to his demands. The following anecdote exemplifies this shift.

The month of August 2000 marked a critical turning point in the reformist–conservative struggle in Iran. At this time, the reform movement was in its prime, winning one election after another by wide margins. Hope for democratic change was in the air as reformers captured all of the most important democratically contested institutions of the state in quick succession, to the shock and dismay of their conservative rivals.

The first item on the legislative agenda of the reform-dominated sixth parliament (2000–4) was to overturn an illiberal press law passed in the final days of the outgoing hardline-controlled parliament. The print media in Iran had flourished during President Khatami's first term and quickly became a leading bastion of support for pro-democracy activists. Courageous journalists and editors were breaking political taboos

[34] Ali Mirsepassi, *Democracy in Modern Iran: Islam, Culture and Political Change*, New York: New York University Press, 2010, pp. 125–47; Moslem, *Factional Politics in Post-Khomeini Iran*, pp. 111–27; Farhang Rajaee, *Islamism and Modernism: The Changing Discourse in Iran*, Austin, TX: University of Texas Press, 2007, pp. 193–236.

by transcending the narrow ideological confines of Iran's post-revolutionary elite consensus. A new public sphere was created through which Iranian society was in full-scale debate—to the annoyance of the ruling clerical establishment—about the relationship between tradition and modernity, religion and democracy, and the moral basis of legitimate political authority.

As the parliamentary debate on the press law began, with the eyes of the nation watching the proceedings, the Speaker suddenly intervened to halt deliberations. He announced that he had just received an important summons from the office of the Supreme Leader, Ali Khamenei, demanding that the existing (illiberal) press law not be revised and that all debate on this topic cease immediately. Khamenei's letter—which angry MPs forced the Speaker to read into the parliamentary record—specifically warned: "Should the enemies of Islam, the revolution and the Islamic system take over or infiltrate the press, a great danger would threaten the security, unity and the faith of the people ... The current [press] law ... has been able to prevent the appearance of this great calamity, and [therefore], its amendment and similar actions that have been anticipated by the parliamentary committee are not legitimate and not in the interest of the country and the system."[35]

Scuffles and fistfights broke out among rival members of parliament. Several deputies walked out in protest as chaos enveloped the parliamentary chamber. The Speaker tried to restore calm by reminding everyone that the supreme leader's actions were legally permissible: "Our constitution has the elements of the absolute rule of the supreme clerical leader [*velayat-e motlagh-e faghhih*] and you all know this and approve of this. We are all duty-bound to abide by it."[36]

The Speaker at the time was Mehdi Karoubi, a 2009 reformist presidential candidate and now a leader of the Green Movement. His open defiance of and resistance to Khamenei today, in contrast to his deference a decade ago, are worth noting. They suggest that, in the new iteration of the reform movement in Iran, the senior leadership is openly willing to disobey the explicit wishes of the leaders of the Iranian Islamic Republic. How far they will take their defiance remains to be seen, however, given that the senior leadership of the Green Movement is under house arrest and all contact with the outside world has been severed.

[35] Voice of the Islamic Republic of Iran (Tehran). Radio 1, 6 Aug. 2000.
[36] Ibid.

The Green Movement: Key Characteristics

The Green Movement is currently in a state of abeyance. While the movement has experienced extensive repression due to severe state-sanctioned violence, it still exists and popular support remains strong, as revealed after the 2013 election where, according to one report, "images of Moussavi were more prominent even than those of the newly elected Rowhani."[37] Muhammad Sahimi, an astute observer of Iran, captured it well when he likened the movement, quoting a Persian proverb, to a "raging fire under a heap of ash," one "with the potential to come to the surface again at any moment."[38]

The Green Movement is a large umbrella organization with different layers of support across Iranian society. Diverse political views also exist under this broad umbrella. There are radical and moderate wings within the movement, a secular and religious divide, as well as a generation gap among its supporters. When it first emerged it was best described by Hamid Dabashi as a "civil rights movement."[39]

The core of the movement's support resides within Iran's sizable middle class, which, according to some estimates, constitutes 50 percent of the population. Young people, about two-thirds of Iran's population, are drawn to the Green Movement, as is most of Iran's intellectual class, along with university students, artists, filmmakers, lawyers, women's rights groups, and dissident clerics.

[37] Tehran Bureau correspondent, "Iranians Express Cautious Optimism after Hassan Rowhani's Victory," Tehran Bureau blog, 18 June 2013, http://www.guardian.co.uk/world/2013/jun/18/iranians-optimism-hassan-Rowhani-victory. Also see, Robert Mackey, "Iran's President-Elect Confronted with Plea Detained Opposition Leader's Freedom," *New York Times*, 17 June 2013, http://thelede.blogs.nytimes.com/2013/06/17/irans-president-elect-confronted-with-plea-for-detained-opposition-leaders-freedom/?ref=middleeast

[38] Muhammad Sahimi, "The Green Movement at One Year," Tehran Bureau, 8 June 2010, http://www.pbs.org/wgbh/pages/frontline/tehranbureau/2010/06/the-green-movement-at-one-year.html (accessed 4 Dec. 2012).

[39] Hamid Dabashi, "Iran's Green Movement as a Civil Rights Movement," in Nader Hashemi and Danny Postel (eds), *The People Reloaded: The Green Movement and the Struggle for Iran's Future*, New York: Melville House, 2011, pp. 22–5 and Hamid Dabashi, "Iran's Greens and the American Civil Rights Movement: An Interview with Cornel West," in Hashemi and Postel, *The People Reloaded*, pp. 284–8.

The rank and file of the movement's supporters, particularly young people, is both more radical and more secular than the leadership of the organization, which is politically conservative and cautious. This is partly due to the fact that the leaders of the Green Movement, Mir Hossein Mousavi, Mehdi Karoubi, and Mohammad Khatami, were formerly senior stalwarts of the Islamic Republic. They served as prime minister, speaker of the parliament, and president respectively. Most of the youth supporters of the Green Movement, by contrast, were born after the 1979 Revolution, and their frame of reference and political experience have thus been qualitatively different from those of their leaders, who were politicized and shaped by their experience under the secular authoritarianism of the Pahlavi monarchy.

Three Phases of the Green Movement

The Green Movement has gone through several phases of development. It is still an organization in its infancy and will likely undergo further transformations as it begins a long and arduous struggle for the future of Iran. To date, three distinct periods are discernible.

The first phase of the Green Movement lasted from June 2009 until February 2010. During this initial phase, the movement's strategy relied on street demonstrations against the June 2009 electoral results. One of the most popular slogans at this time was "Where is my vote?" suggesting that its key demands in this early period were modest, with a focus on the results of the recent election. As an official permit to organize their own demonstrations was repeatedly denied, the Green Movement instead encouraged its supporters to come onto the streets on officially sanctioned days of public protest.

After the establishment of the Islamic Republic of Iran, several dates during the calendar year were designated days of public protest on which citizens were encouraged to come onto the streets. Some of these prominent holidays are: "Jerusalem Day," the last Friday of Ramadan, a day of solidarity with Palestinians; "Students Day," 7 December, which coincides with the anniversary of the deaths of three students who were killed in 1953 when protesting against Richard Nixon's visit to Iran; and Ashura, the tenth day of the Islamic calendar month of Muharram, a day of street festivals and mourning that marks the death of Hussein, the grandson of the Prophet Muhammad and a revered figure in Shi'a Islam.

On each of these days, Green Movement supporters came onto the streets in order to subvert state-organized political rallies. They did this rather effectively by joining the crowds, but distinguished themselves with separate slogans rooted in the recent stolen election and the human rights crackdown that followed. Images of Green protestors were then recorded and posted on YouTube for the world to see. The strategy proved effective because it was extremely difficult for the Iranian regime to prevent this from happening—cancelling Jerusalem Day or Ashura was simply out of the question.

December 2009 was particularly bloody in Iran. Not only were protests against the stolen election continuing six months after the event, but the death of Grand Ayatollah Hossein Ali Montazeri brought more people on to the streets. Montazeri was one of the most senior religious figures in Shi'a Islam, a leader of the 1979 Islamic Revolution, and the one-time designated successor to Ayatollah Khomeini. Prior to his death he was widely regarded as the conscience of the Green Movement due to his lifelong struggle against human rights abuses and political despotism under both the Shah and the Islamic Republic of Iran.[40] His funeral attracted hundreds of thousands of people, and the fact that his death coincided with Ashura led to more street clashes and arrests, causing a general panic to set in among Iran's ruling oligarchy.

Unable to suppress the protests, the regime upped the ante with mass arrests, a new campaign of targeted assassinations, and public calls for executions by senior regime officials.[41] The big fear was that with the anniversary of the 1979 Revolution approaching in February—a day when massive rallies would normally take place across Iran and to which the foreign press would be invited—there was potential for the occasion to be transformed into another embarrassing episode for the Iranian regime, where the Green Movement would again subvert a state-sanctioned holiday. State repression and a massive influx of regime supporters who were bussed into the capital appeared to work. However, opposition protests ultimately failed to materialize, partly due to a lack of organization. In the wake of this, the Green Movement entered its second phase of development.

[40] Nader Hashemi, "A Life Animated by Conscience, Not Power," CNN.com, 22 Dec. 2009; Payam Akhavan, "Ayatollah Montazeri's Brave Struggle for Justice," in Hashemi and Postel, *The People Reloaded*, pp. 148–50.

[41] Hashemi and Postel, *The People Reloaded*, pp. xi–xxiii.

The Green Movement's second phase was characterized by reflection and reformulation. It lasted from February 2010 to the dawn of the Arab Spring in January 2011. Due to regime repression, street demonstrations were no longer viable in this period. The leaders of the Green Movement realized that a campaign of civil disobedience would take a long time to bear fruit, and they consequently set aside time to develop a series of ideas and a political platform aimed at democratizing Iran over the long term. Via a series of interviews, essays, and official statements, the basic principles, political vision, and reformist agenda of the movement were announced to the world.

From its inception, the Green Movement was faced with the challenge of defining itself. What did it really stand for, what strategy was it adopting, and what were its ultimate goals? As its senior leadership had occupied important positions of power after the revolution, where did it stand in relation to the Islamic Republic of Iran, the Iranian constitution itself, and the ideas of Ayatollah Khomeini? The answers to these questions were provided in the most important document to emerge during this period: the official Charter of the Green Movement.[42] This charter, which was officially released on the first anniversary of the Green Movement, 15 June 2010, has since been updated and revised twice. The following excerpts identify precisely what the movement stands for and its *modus operandi*:

- Based on its commitment to basic principles and fundamental human, religious, moral and national values, the Green Movement considers itself to be a purifier and reformer of the course taken in the Islamic Republic after the Revolution. Therefore, it will focus its efforts within the framework of the Constitution [of the Islamic Republic of Iran] and [ensure] respect for the people's votes and opinions.
- According to Green activists, the people of Iran want [to be part of] a proud, honorable and developed country. The Green Movement supports pluralism and opposes all attempts to monopolize it. Therefore, we do not tolerate animosity or maliciousness [directed] at any social group.
- The Green Movement insists on the continued presence of a compassionate religion characterized by forgiveness, spirituality, morality,

[42] The full text appears in Hashemi and Postel, *The People Reloaded*, pp. 332–44.

and the appreciation of human dignity. Furthermore, it points out that emphasizing the ethical and compassionate aspects of Islam and the Islamic Republic is the only way to strengthen religious values. The fundamental principles of the Green Movement should take into account [our] national–religious legacy and desire for development and progress; they should steer clear of coercing people into an ideology, sect or clique; they should oppose the use of religion as a political instrument and protect the independence of religious institutions and clergymen from the state to preserve the prominent position of religion; and, finally, they should maintain the continuous and important role of religion in our society.

- Human Rights are given by God and hence no ruler, government, parliament, or other power can take them away or interfere with protecting them. Realizing protection of these rights requires respect for fundamental principles such as equality, tolerance, dialogue, peace, and peaceful problem solving. These fundamental principles can be upheld if we start to free the independent press, stop censorship, obtain free access to information, strengthen civil society, respect citizens' privacy, enable NGOs to act freely, and reform laws and regulations to eliminate any type of discrimination in society.
- The Green Movement is a social movement that is committed to non-violence. It is committed to working within the constitutional framework. It believes that people are the primary victims of any type of violence and so it depends on dialogue and peaceful resistance to advance its agenda. Non-violent resistance is a value that cannot be compromised by this movement.
- Implementing the constitution with no negligence is the main fundamental strategy of the Green Movement. This movement believes that overcoming the crises that we are facing today and pursuing the development and progress of our nation can only be possible through returning to the law and enforcing its implementation on all institutions, and punishing those who do not abide by it in whatever position they may hold.
- The national laws, including the constitution, are not eternal and unchangeable documents. Every nation has the right to reform its current laws, in the quest for correcting its general direction. However, note that changing the constitution is only valid when it is put forth through a process of negotiation and dialogue in the society, with the

participation of all groups and factions among the people, avoiding any dogmatism, exclusiveness, and bullying.
- Expanding civil society and strengthening the public sphere are the main principles of the Green Movement. This movement believes that in order to safeguard our national interests, achieve the goals of the Islamic Revolution, and reduce the unpleasant effects of the recent crisis, representatives of various schools of thought and political groups should engage in negotiations and dialogue. In this regard, we welcome any invitation to transparent negotiations and discourse aiming at defending the rights of the people and solving social conflicts.

The third phase of the Green Movement coincided with start of the Arab Spring in early 2011. With the ouster of Zine El Abidine Ben Ali, and with Hosni Mubarak's regime teetering on the verge of collapse, Mir Hossein Mousavi issued a statement which claimed that the Middle East is

> on the verge of great events that can impact the fate of this region, the world and the peoples of the region. Undoubtedly, what is taking place aims to contest an oppressive system which has kept the destiny of many nations in the region in its claws, and without a doubt, in order to find the starting point of the protests in Tunis, Sana'a, Cairo, Alexandria and Suez, one must look into the protests in Tehran on June 15, 18 and 20 which were in the millions. Days on which people came to the streets with the "Where is my vote?" slogan and peacefully sought their lost rights.[43]

Inspired by these regional protests for democracy, the Green Movement called for a public rally in solidarity with Tunisia and Egypt. This marked a subtle but new strategy for the movement in that they were no longer calling their supporters into the street on officially prescribed days of public protest. Instead, they were choosing their own time and date to assert their democratic demands.

This was also a smart move from a public relations perspective. The Iranian regime was celebrating the Arab Spring, albeit with an ideological spin, by claiming that these revolutions were "Islamic Awakenings" inspired by the legacy of Ayatollah Khomeini and the 1979 Islamic Revolution in Iran. Denying a group of Iranians a permit to support an

[43] "Mir Hossein: Today's Pharaohs Heed the Demands of the People When it is too Late," Kalame, 29 Jan. 2011, http://www.kaleme.com/1389/11/09/klm-45443/?theme=fast (accessed 20 Aug. 2012).

event that the Iranian regime was loudly applauding proved to be a political embarrassment. In open defiance of the regime, the Green Movement called for a demonstration on 14 February 2011.

News reports and YouTube videos suggest that tens of thousands of people participated in this event. Rallies took place in different parts of Iran's major cities and a massive crackdown and wave of arrests soon followed.[44] The Iranian regime was deeply embarrassed and shocked by this turn of events, largely because it had been claiming since June 2009 that the Green Movement was a foreign-inspired plot with no public support, which the regime had successfully crushed. The best indication of the paranoia and deep embarrassment felt by the Iranian regime was evident on the floor of Iran's hardline-controlled parliament. The following day, over 100 members of parliament acted out a medieval-style mob scene as they gathered around the podium of the Speaker and began to chant in unison for the hanging of the leaders of the Green Movement.[45]

Soon afterwards, Mir Hussein Mousavi and Mehdi Karoubi were kidnapped along with their wives. Their whereabouts were unknown for weeks. It was later revealed that they had been placed under house arrest and all contact with the outside world had been severed.

What is revealing about the incarceration of the Green Movement's leaders is that their arrest was never officially announced by the public prosecutor. According to the official line of the Iranian regime, these men are quietly residing in their homes. The primary reason for such duplicity is that a public announcement of the arrest and trial of respected political leaders of the opposition could create a social disruption that might weaken the regime's base of support, thus affecting regime stability. On several occasions senior Iranian officials have publicly acknowledged this point.[46]

[44] Amnesty International Report, "'We Are Ordered to Crush You': Expanding Repression of Dissent in Iran," Mar. 2012, http://www.amnesty.org/en/library/asset/MDE13/002/2012/en/2b228705-dfba-4408-a04b-8ab887988881/mde130022012en.pdf (accessed 1 Dec. 2012).

[45] See YouTube clip, http://www.youtube.com/watch?v=4KaXuXJBjfM (accessed 20 Aug. 2012).

[46] "The Representative of the Supreme Leader to Revolutionary Guards: We Cannot Bring Mousavi and Karoubi to Trial because they have Support," 2 Jan. 2012, BBC Persian Service, http://www.bbc.co.uk/persian/iran/2012/01/120101_l17_sepah_saeidi_mousavi_karoubi.shtml (accessed 2 Dec. 2012).

In September 2011, Mir Hossein Mousavi privately revealed to his family that his kidnapping, incarceration, and current situation were very similar to Gabriel García Márquez's novel, *News of a Kidnapping* (1996). The book recounts the kidnapping, imprisonment, and eventual release of a handful of prominent figures in Colombia in the early 1990s by the Medellín Cartel, operated by Pablo Escobar. When this news became public in Iran, Márquez's book, which had been translated into Persian, sold out within a few days.[47] This vignette reveals two important things about Iran: first, the continuing popularity of the Green Movement; and second, the cultural sophistication of Iranian society, where the writings of a Latin American novelist can be used to interpret and understand Middle East politics.

The final key development to have taken place during the Green Movement's third phase is the appointment of official representatives abroad to speak on behalf of the leadership. The arrest of the movement's senior leadership, coupled with severe internal repression, forced the remaining leadership to move abroad. Ardeshir Amir Arjomand is Mousavi's official spokesperson, currently residing in France, and Mojtaba Vahedi is the official representative of Mehdi Karoubi, who is currently residing in the United States. Together they have formed the "Coordination Council for the Green Path of Hope", which seeks to represent the movement while its leaders are under arrest. To date, they have given a series of media interviews and lectures seeking to mobilize the Iranian expatriate community in support of democracy in Iran.[48] They also repeatedly issue communiques, press releases, and statements on contemporary Iranian affairs, including calls for Iranians to observe silent forms of protest on key anniversaries.

[47] Saeed Kamali Deghan, "Gabriel García Márquez Book Inspires Iran's Opposition Movement," *The Guardian*, 20 Sep. 2011.

[48] See the remarks by Ardeshir Amir Arjomand at MIT in June 2011: "Iran Document: Opposition Advisor Arjomand. 'The Goals, Networks, and Methods of the Green Movement.'" Available at: http://www.enduringamerica.com/home/2011/6/19/iran-document-opposition-advisor-arjomand-the-goals-networks.html (accessed 1 Dec. 2011). In 2012 Mojtaba Vahedi resigned as spokesperson for Mehdi Karroubi citing irreconcilable differences over the nature of the Islamic Republic and how democracy should be pursued. For details see Mohammad Reza Yazdanpanah, "Exclusive Interview with Mojtaba Vahedi after Resignation," Roozonline, 23 July 2012.

The Strategy of the Green Movement

As the Green Movement Charter makes clear, the movement is reformist rather than revolutionary. There are many reasons for this, but arguably the most salient factor is that the experience of a violent and disruptive revolution in 1979 has left Iranians, especially the middle class, with little appetite for another political convulsion. The age of radicalism is over and only those programs and political agendas that are moderate, reformist, and non-violent have mass appeal. This might, however, change in the future as Iran's crisis of legitimacy, spurred by a collapsing economy, deepens.

Furthermore, there is a very thin line in contemporary Iranian politics between reform and revolution. If, for example, only one of the key demands of the Green Movement were to be met, such as freedom for political parties and the press, or freedom for political prisoners, the implementation of any one of these reforms could lead to a huge internal crisis for the regime that might affect regime stability. In a very real sense the Green Movement's demand for "reform", rooted in the full implementation of the Iranian constitution, can thus be interpreted as a revolutionary act on its own. It is also strategically wise to insist on reform as opposed to revolution, as it makes it far more difficult for Iran's clerical oligarchy to tarnish the reputation of the Green Movement. After all, how can calling for the rule of law and the implementation of the constitution (which Iran's rulers swear by) be an act of treason?

With regard to this point, Mohammad Ayatollahi Tabaar has accurately described the political strategy of the Green Movement as one of exploiting the "Grey Zones" in Iranian society through a policy of patience and endurance.[49] These "grey areas" are comprised of influential sectors of Iranian society made up of socially and politically conservative religious associations and traditional factions. While they do not currently support the Green Movement, and are philosophically closer to the worldview of Iran's clerical establishment, they are also upset with the policies that Mahmoud Ahmadinejad implemented. The hope is that by proceeding deliberately, but cautiously, these influential groups

[49] Mohammad Ayatollahi Tabaar, "Laying Low But Not Gone: Iran's Green Movement and the Grey Strategy of Patience," in Hashemi and Postel, *The People Reloaded*, pp. 277–80.

can perhaps be wooed over to the Green Movement or at least be rendered politically irrelevant. Tabaar observes that this strategy:

> rests on the ability of the Green Movement to broaden its appeal into those conservative "Grey Zones." The Movement has already created an unprecedented gap within the conservative establishment. Capitalizing on impeccable revolutionary resumes that date back to the consolidating years of the Islamic Republic, the leaders of the Green Movement have striven to push the fault-line as deep as possible into the conservative camp so that when the next crisis hits, they can draw deeper into society for support.[50]

The 2013 presidential election that brought Hassan Rowhani to power was widely celebrated by democratic forces within Iran. Rowhani was repeatedly asked throughout the presidential campaign about the ongoing house arrests of the Green Movement leaders and whether he would seek their release upon becoming president. He replied in the affirmative on every occasion. At this moment it remains unclear how Rowhani's presidency, which echoes many of the most prominent themes of the Green Movement, will affect the movement itself.[51] What is clear, however, is that the legacy of the Green Movement continues to haunt Iranian politics. This was clearly on display during the parliamentary confirmation hearings for Rowhani's Cabinet, where the debate was focused on the relationship the proposed Cabinet ministers had with the Green Movement.[52]

Two Ideological Weapons: Islamic Authenticity and Anti-Imperialism

The above strategy of patience and endurance that the Green Movement adopted is related to two critical themes that have served to bolster authoritarianism in Iran. These themes are obstacles that Iranian democrats have to overcome, thus necessitating a cautious strategy for democratization.

[50] Ibid. p. 278.

[51] See interview with Saeed Hajjarian where he suggests strong support for the new Iranian president. "Detailed Interview with Saeed Hajjarian and Tasnim News," Tasnim News Agency, 11 Aug. 2013.

[52] "The Shadow of the 2009 Protests Hover over First Day of Assessing Rowhani's Proposed Cabinet Ministers," BBC Persian Service, 12 Aug. 2013. For analysis see Farideh Farhi, "Iran's Telling Ministerial Confirmation Hearings," Lobe Log: Foreign Policy, 16 Aug. 2013, http://www.lobelog.com/irans-telling-ministerial-confirmation-hearings/

In the case of Iran, its authoritarian regime has a genuine and authentic base of support that is deep, but not very wide. A significant section of the population, approximately 20 percent, is deeply loyal to the regime due to a combination of ideological conviction and material interests that are tied to the preservation of the political status quo.[53] In this latter sense Iran is no different from any other authoritarian regime. Millions of people are on the government payroll, working in various government-affiliated jobs. The bureaucracy and the vast security and intelligence apparatus collectively benefit from the extensive patronage system, bolstered by oil sales, for their economic livelihood. With respect to ideological conviction, however—and this is where Iran is qualitatively different from many Arab regimes—the Islamic Republic relies on two powerful ideological weapons that shape Muslim identity today, which it cynically manipulates to generate support and to immunize itself from criticism: Islamic authenticity and anti-imperialism.

In the ideological narrative of Iran's clerical oligarchy, the Islamic Republic of Iran is portrayed as the embodiment of Islamic purity and authenticity. High-level regime officials, drawing on the political theology of Ayatollah Khomeini, repeatedly claim that the existence of the Iranian Islamic Republic is the closest approximation to Qur'anic ethics and the teachings of the Prophet Muhammad and the Shi'a Imams. Should it collapse, according to this narrative, the very existence of Islam on earth would be placed into jeopardy. Thus loyalty and acquiescence are generated by manipulating the religious identity of Iranians, who are given a stark choice: it is either us or foreign domination and atheism.

After the 2009 electoral coup, for example, the Iranian regime repeatedly sought to manipulate the theme of Islamic authenticity to shore up its sagging legitimacy. In the words of a leading clerical hardliner, Ayatollah Mesbah Yazdi, the people of Iran were told that obeying Mahmoud Ahmadinejad was the equivalent of obeying God. "The rule of the just jurisprudent is one of the main pillars of [Iran's] Islamic establishment which no other Islamic state or nation possesses." Yazdi added: "The just jurisprudent is the representative of the hidden [Shi'a] Imam [Mahdi] but the president is chosen by the people … [When] the

[53] Determining the exact degree of loyal regime support is impossible in the absence of a free and fair election. This figure is an estimate based on the last time fair elections were held in Iran (1997 presidential election and the 2000 parliamentary elections) where no one disputed the results.

President is endorsed by the Leadership [of the Islamic Republic] he becomes the Leader's agent." Therefore, when "the president receives the Leader's approval, subservience to him becomes subservience to God."[54] In a later formulation Mesbah Yazdi was even more blunt: "Disobeying the Supreme Leader is apostasy."[55]

As the office of the supreme leader and its current occupant, Ali Khamenei, have come under increasing scrutiny, particularly after the 2009 crackdown on the Green Movement, the Iranian regime has responded by trying to frighten and guilt the Iranian religious masses into submission. In 2011, for example, in a Friday prayer sermon that was broadcast on state television and radio, Hojatoleslam Kazem Sadighi relayed a story where one of the Cabinet ministers allegedly told him of the extreme devotion and obedience the senior ministers of the government have toward the Supreme Leader: their admiration, respect, and religious zeal are so absolute that "if his Excellency [Supreme Leader] decrees the divorce of the president's wife, the president's wife will become *haram* [religiously forbidden] for him and the president will no longer be able to touch her."[56]

More recently, Ali Saeedi, the representative of the supreme leader in the Islamic Revolutionary Guard Corps, quoted Khomeini as saying that the "'same authority that the Shia Imams had in leading society, also applies to a qualified Islamic jurist [today] and likewise the same obedience applies.' In other words, to the same extent that obedience to the Shi'a Imams is obligatory [on Shi'a Muslims], obedience to the leadership [of Iran] is also required and there is no difference between the two."[57]

While many people in Iran scoff at these claims, particularly the urban middle class and the educated segments of society, a substantial

[54] "Ayatollah Mesbah: Obeying the President is Obeying God," Farda News, 12 Aug. 2009, http://www.fardanews.com/fa/pages/?cid=88589 (accessed 18 June 2012).

[55] Saeed Kamali Dehghan, "Ahmadinejad Allies Charged with Sorcery," *The Guardian*, 5 May 2011.

[56] Hojatoleslam Kazem Sadighi, Friday Prayer Sermon, 6 May 2011, available on YouTube at: http://www.youtube.com/watch?v=MWmMSIXaNs8&feature=player_embedded#!, accessed 21 Aug. 2012.

[57] "Obedience to the Leader is Obligatory: A Religious Government without a (Clerical) Leader is Unrecognizable," Farsnews, 10 June 2012, http://www.farsnews.com/newstext.php?nn=13910319000372 (accessed 18 June 2012).

group remains that is influenced by this kind of rhetoric. This segment of society, still sizable in number and deeply religious, live in the poor and rural parts of Iran without access to alternative sources of information; they are particularly vulnerable to this manipulation of their religious identity. This policy of constantly invoking the theme of Islamic authenticity partially immunizes the Iranian regime against criticism, allowing it to retain a level of support among the population, and, if needed, this theme can be invoked to generate mass mobilization in defense of the regime.[58] The fact that it is only a minority of the nation that will heed such a call is compensated by the fact that they will be heavily armed and ideologically motivated.

Secondly, there is the powerful theme of anti-imperialism. The Iranian Islamic Republic uses this concept with equal utility to bolster its support base and to shield itself from criticism, mostly domestically, but also regionally and internationally. This theme has arguably been more effective than the manipulation of religion for reasons of state.

In Iran's official ideological narrative, the regime portrays itself as the vanguard state opposing Western imperialism and defending the rights of the oppressed Muslim masses. The plight of the Palestinians features prominently in this description, which also includes solidarity and support for those Muslims who are struggling against Western-backed dictatorships. Thus, in the context of the Arab Spring, Iran has been celebrating the revolutions and popular struggles in Tunisia, Egypt, Bahrain, and Yemen, while maintaining a relative silence when it comes to the uprisings in Syria and Libya.[59]

The theme of anti-imperialism has a deep resonance within Iran due to its troubled relationship with the West over the past 200 years.[60] The

[58] On a related note the Iranian regime goes to considerable length to censor and silence alternative interpretations of Islam. It has established a Special Clerical Court that seeks to silence dissenting interpretations of Islam. The case of Grand Ayatollah Hossein Ali Montazeri is a perfect illustration of this point.

[59] Similarly, the Iranian regime has little to say about the plight of Muslims in Chechnya or the Uyghur Muslims in China as the reasons of state and the national interest take precedence over ideology.

[60] For background see Ervand Abrahamian, *A History of Modern Iran*, Cambridge: Cambridge University Press, 2008, and Nikki Keddie, *Modern Iran: Roots and Results of Revolution*, updated edn, New Haven, CT: Yale University Press, 2006.

long history of external intervention, subversion, occupation, and manipulation of Iranian affairs, culminating in the 1953 CIA coup d'état and the strong Western support for the Pahlavi dictatorship, has deeply affected Iranian political culture and has led to paranoia and conspiracy theories. Even the late Shah of Iran claimed that his overthrow was the result of a Western conspiracy.[61]

The Islamic Republic has similarly invoked this foreign intrigue to generate nationalist support for itself. Iran broke away from an alliance with the United States and since the 1979 Revolution its policies have frequently clashed with those of the West and its regional allies, resulting in conflict, sanctions, and the threat of war. As a result, the Iranian regime feels entitled to spin a David and Goliath narrative around the theme of anti-imperialism. The current dispute over Iran's nuclear program is a case in point.

The Iranian regime has been able to present the argument over Iran's nuclear program as the culmination of a dispute over Iran's energy independence that started with the nationalization of the oil industry by Mohammad Mossadegh. The claim of the regime is that the West is once again bullying the people of Iran by dictating how Iranians can develop their internal energy needs. The double standards of the West are pointed out, whereby Israel, Pakistan, and India—none of them signatories to the Non-Proliferation Treaty—are allowed to possess nuclear weapons, while Iran—a signatory of the treaty whose nuclear program is under regular international inspection—is criticized, sanctioned, and threatened. It is for these reasons that Iran's nuclear program enjoys broad popular support. Most Iranians, regardless of their ideological orientation, view the nuclear question and the ensuing conflict with the West through the prism of Iranian nationalism.

In light of the above discussion of Islamic authenticity and anti-imperialism, it is illustrative to compare and contrast Iran with Egypt and Tunisia. Neither Ben Ali nor Mubarak could invoke the theme of Islamic authenticity to bolster their rule. Both men had very weak religious credentials and both were products of their respective military and security institutions rather than the religious seminaries. Moreover, their

[61] Mohammad Reza Shah Pahlavi, *Answer to History*, New York: Stein and Day Publisher, 1982. Also see Abrahamian, *Khomeinisim: Essays on the Islamic Republic*, pp. 111–31.

regimes were ideologically rooted in various interpretations of secular Arab nationalism. They oversaw a set of authoritarian modernization policies that undermined their religious credentials in the eyes of their populations, despite the fact that both men claimed to be practicing Muslims while their countries' constitutions specifically designated Islam as the official state religion.

Similarly, with respect to anti-imperialism, Ben Ali and Mubarak were unable to invoke this powerful Muslim identity theme in order to bolster their credentials. In contrast to the Islamic Republic of Iran, both men and the regimes they presided over were strong allies of the West. Their foreign policies were closely coordinated with Washington, and the broad perception among opposition groups was that they were very much part of the imperialist camp. This fact did not help Ben Ali and Mubarak during the Arab Spring; indeed, if anything, it further impugned their credibility and legitimacy, thus contributing to their demise.

Conclusion

Upon his return from exile, Ayatollah Khomeini delivered a famous speech at Tehran's main cemetery, Behesht-e Zahra, in February 1979:

> The destiny of each generation must be in its own hands. For example, we were not alive at the beginning of the Qajar period [1785–1924]. Let us suppose that the Qajar dynasty were founded in accordance with a referendum, and that the people had voted unanimously for Agha Muhammad Khan Qajar [1742–97] to become their ruler, to be followed by other Qajar monarchs. By the time we came into the world, Ahmad Shah [1898–1930] was ruling and none of us had ever seen Agha Muhammad Khan. If our ancestors had voted in favor of the foundation of the Qajar dynasty, would they have had any right to determine that Ahmad Shah should rule over us? The destiny of each generation is in its own hands. The nation as it existed one hundred ... years ago had the right to determine its own destiny, but it did not have the right to impose any particular ruler on us.[62]

These words have been dug up and recirculated in Iran among supporters of the reform and Green Movement. In their attempt to rewrite Iran's post-revolutionary social contract, the ideas of the Iranian Islamic

[62] Ruhollah Khomeini, "Address at Bihist-i Zahra," in *Islam and Revolution: Writings and Declarations of Imam Khomeini*, trans. and annotated Hamid Algar, Berkeley, CA: Mizan Press, 1981, p. 255.

Republic's founder have been invoked to make their case. Yet while doing so helps win a propaganda war with Iran's clerical establishment, it does little to affect the overall balance of power in the country. As we have learned from recent events in the Arab world, struggles for democracy require considerable organization, mass mobilization, sacrifice, and, most of all, an opportune moment.

The prospects for democracy in Iran look promising over the long term. All the key social science indicators that are typically used to assess the preconditions for democracy exist in the Iranian case.[63] The crisis of legitimacy facing Iran has significantly contributed to this development. Today, the model of governance that the Green Movement and its supporters aspire to is similar, but not identical, to other liberal democratic societies in the West. Important battles have been won that bode well for an eventual democratic transition, specifically the development of a consensus among Iranian democrats on the need for a separation between religion and state.[64] But huge challenges remain, the most notable of which include reaching out to the urban poor and those in rural areas of the country, and addressing their economic needs.

Regionally, the social conditions for democracy have qualitatively changed for the better over the past year. Not only are foreign troops withdrawing from Iran's borders, in Iraq and Afghanistan, making it more difficult for the Iranian regime to exploit this fact to block democratization, but the democratic revolutions in the Arab world have already had a contagion effect on Iranian politics. As a result of the Arab Spring, a new global spotlight is now being directed toward the region that exposes and scrutinizes the policies of authoritarian regimes while simultaneously giving voice to democratic opposition movements. This is a deeply worrisome development for Iran's clerical leaders, for it puts them in the awkward position of publicly supporting pro-democracy protests in the Arab world, while simultaneously cracking down on identical protests in their own backyard (and in Syria).

Internationally, however, the political conditions for democracy have not been good. The policies of the United States and its allies toward

[63] Michael McFaul, "Chinese Dream, Persian Realities," *Journal of Democracy*, 16 (Oct. 2005), pp. 74–82.

[64] Julie Poucher Harbin, "Kadivar: Secularization of the Islamic Republic Unstoppable," Duke Today, 18 Apr. 2012, http://today.duke.edu/2012/04/kadivartalk (accessed 21 Aug. 2012).

Iran, rooted in economic sanctions, threats, and the possibility of a military strike on Iran's nuclear program, have inadvertently strengthened the Iranian regime while weakening the middle class and making the work of pro-democracy forces more difficult. This must change. Given the very troubled history of the relationship between Iran and the West, which stretches back 200 years, and in which the 1953 CIA coup was a seminal moment, the struggle for democracy in Iran is strongly dependent on a suitable international context. Otherwise, the Iranian regime will be able to continue to manipulate public opinion by exploiting fears of another great power intervention or assault on Iran's territorial sovereignty and its national dignity.

Reflecting on the rise of the Green Movement, its successes, its shortcomings, and the challenges that lie ahead, Ray Takyeh has presciently noted:

> The achievements of the Green movement are impressive: It has fractured the state, won the intellectual argument regarding the future of Iran, and attracted a large segment of the public. But it is important to stress that there is no guarantee that the Greens will succeed the theocratic autocrats. Although the Islamic Republic is heading relentlessly yet uneasily to history's junkyard, the future of Iran is still a subject of contention and struggle … The series of decisions that the United States and its allies make today will help condition the contours of power in tomorrow's Iran.[65]

[65] Ray Takyeh, "The Struggle for a New Iran," *New York Times*, 27 Dec. 2010.

8

CHALLENGING THE TRADE UNION, RECLAIMING THE NATION

THE POLITICS OF LABOR PROTEST IN EGYPT, 2006–11

Marie Duboc

The unprecedented mobilizations that ended Hosni Mubarak's presidency in February 2011 involved a broad range of Egyptians with shared economic and political grievances against his rule. The protests took place against a background of increasing mobilization over the previous ten years, fueled by a steady degradation of Egyptians' living conditions. Between 2004 and 2010, over 2 million workers had voiced their grievances through labor strikes, sit-ins, and other forms of protest against the erosion of wages, rising inflation, and precarious employment. In 2001–2003, demonstrations were organized by residents against water cuts or poor housing, as well as sit-ins staged in front of the parliament or the prime minister's Cabinet in 2010 to voice Egyptians' grievances publicly.[1]

[1] In addition to labor protests, demonstrations were organized by Cairo-

This chapter focuses on the upsurge of labor action in Egypt that began in 2006. It analyzes the nature and demands of these protests, and examines what the notion of a "ruling bargain" has entailed for the Egyptian labor movement and how this arrangement has been questioned. The previous Egyptian regime had lost its legitimacy long before Mubarak was ousted in 2011, as shown by the upsurge of collective action as well as by the rise of frustration among Egyptians. While the erosion of legitimacy is not sufficient to explain social movements and mobilization, analyzing the processes whereby the different perceptions, norms, and practices that laid the foundation of the ruling power began to shift provides a heuristic for understanding the political scope of protests and the conditions under which they can take place.

The notion of a social contract, which defines state–society relations, has shown the formidable "adaptive capacity of authoritarian regimes in the Middle East" that have relied on a "national–socialist populist pact" to ensure the quiescence of populations in exchange for financial and welfare concessions.[2] In Egypt, labor is emblematic of such a ruling bargain or "corporatist bargain" that has institutionalized different social groups into the political system and defined their relationship to the state.[3] For labor this process has taken place through the Egyptian Trade Union Federation (ETUF), the state-controlled union grouping that the Nasserist regime created in 1957 to organize labor's interests by co-opting labor activists into state projects in exchange for social and welfare benefits such as job security for public service workers.[4]

---

based intellectual elites organized demonstrations in support of the second Palestinian Intifada and against the US-led invasion in Iraq. They led to the formation of Kefaya, a group denouncing President Hosni Mubarak's repressive regime and his attempts to designate his son, Gamal, as successor.

2 Steve Heydemann, "Social Pacts and the Persistence of Authoritarianism in the Middle East," in Oliver Schlumberger (ed.), *Debating Arab Authoritarianism: Dynamics and Durability in Nondemocratic Regimes*, Stanford, CA: Stanford University Press, 2007, p. 22.

3 Eva Bellin, "Contingent Democrats: Industrialists, Labor, and Democratization in Late-Developing Countries," *World Politics*, 52, 2 (2000), pp. 175–205.

4 Joel Beinin and Zachary Lockman, *Workers on the Nile: Nationalism, Communism, Islam and the Egyptian Working Class, 1882–1954*, new edn, Princeton, NJ: Princeton University Press, 1992, pp. 444, 446.

Corporatism has been the prevailing strategy for controlling and co-opting organized labor.[5] But labor protests over the past decade speak of a widening gap between workers and the trade union organization that claims to represent them. Prior to Mubarak's ouster, all but one of the labor strikes was organized without the involvement of the ETUF. In other words, the wave of labor protests prior to 2011 demonstrated the tension between statist labor and mobilized labor on the ground. It is important to make this distinction in order to correct an assumption present in the literature on Egyptian corporatism, which has primarily understood labor through the lens of "organized labor," thus overlooking the underlying transformations that took place among the rank and file beyond the framework of the state-organized trade union structure.[6]

Labor protests in Egypt show that while the ruling bargain relied on corporatist governance mechanisms that shaped the nature of labor strikes by channeling grievances within the existing system of rule rather than against it, the ETUF was no longer able to sustain its role as a buffer designed to "permit the maintenance of the system."[7] And far from it becoming an organization that benefited from increased autonomy from the state, the leadership of the ETUF remained the arm of the ruling regime.

The limits of a corporatist bargain

Egyptian labor has been organized through a corporatist ruling bargain that has defined state–society relations since the 1950s. Philippe

[5] Robert Bianchi, "The Corporatization of the Egyptian Labor Movement," *Middle East Journal*, 40, 3 (Summer 1986), pp. 429–44.

[6] Bellin, "Contingent Democrats"; Bianchi, "The Corporatization of the Egyptian Labor Movement"; Agnieszka Paczyńska, *State, Labor, and the Transition to a Market Economy: Egypt, Poland, Mexico, and the Czech Republic*, University Park, PA: Pennsylvania State University Press, 2009. In her study of workers' responses to privatization during the 1990s Nicola Pratt makes a distinction between workers' formal initiatives (those involving the trade union) and informal ones such as strikes. In the 1990s the tensions between the ETUF and workers were considered as illustrating the fragmentation of the ETUF because some local union committees supported strikers. Nicola C. Pratt, "Legacy of the Corporatist State: Explaining Workers Responses," Working Paper, University of Durham, 1998.

[7] Heydemann, "Social Pacts and the Persistence of Authoritarianism in the Middle East," p. 36.

C. Schmitter has defined corporatism "as a system of interest representation in which the constituent units are organized into a limited number of singular, compulsory, noncompetitive, hierarchically ordered and functionally differentiated categories, recognized or licensed (if not created) by the state and granted a deliberate representational monopoly within their respective categories in exchange for observing certain controls on their selection of leaders and articulation of demands and supports."[8] One characteristic of this delegated representation system is its reliance on "powerful mechanisms of inclusion."[9]

Three elements underpin this relationship. First, the incorporation of labor into the political system took place through the state-controlled trade union federation. The ETUF, which was founded in January 1957, was designed to control the labor movement rather than represent workers' interests, in exchange for a number of economic and social benefits. The Free Officers' regime that took power in 1952 prevented the formation of an independent labor and trade union movement, but in December 1952 and April 1953 a series of laws was adopted that granted significant material gains to workers: free transport and medical care, restriction of dismissals, and an increased number of paid leave days. These measures, and particularly those which provided job security, helped the Nasserist regime secure the support of many workers and union leaders.[10] According to Joel Beinin and Zachary Lockman, in 1957 a majority of the labor movement's leaders accepted the creation of a trade union federation that would promote the interests of the regime by controlling workers' militancy in exchange for personal gains—positions within the new federation—and social benefits such as job security for public service workers.[11] In instances when labor activists were divided on what positions to adopt vis-à-vis the Free Officers

[8] Philippe C. Schmitter, "Still the Century of Corporatism?" *The Review of Politics*, 36, 1 (1974), p. 93.

[9] Béatrice Hibou, *The Force of Obedience: The Political Economy of Repression in Tunisia*, trans. Andrew Brown, 1st edn, Cambridge: Polity Press, 2011, p. xiv.

[10] Moreover, the Trade Union Act passed in 1953 eased union membership conditions, including for farmers, and limited to a single authorization the government's oversight for the creation of unions. However, in practice the text put in place a trade union structure that impeded trade union pluralism. See Bianchi, "The Corporatization of the Egyptian Labor Movement," p. 431.

[11] Beinin and Lockman, *Workers on the Nile*, pp. 444, 446.

and the Nasserist regime, the default consensus was to support a patriotic regime that promoted workers' economic interests.

These economic and political rewards have been seen as "aristocratic privileges" inhibiting the political role that labor could play by encouraging trade union leaders to maintain a "cozy relationship with the state" in order to ensure that their interests remain protected.[12] Labor, of course, was not the only beneficiary of these policies, which laid the foundations of a model of Arab socialism or state capitalism. Nationalizations and distributive measures such as free education, food subsidies, healthcare, guaranteed jobs for university graduates, and agrarian reform were all part of the social and welfare policies underpinning a state-building project aimed at creating support for emerging regimes without necessarily involving developmental objectives.[13]

In Egypt, the underlying consequence of this corporatist ruling bargain was to organize labor through the sole framework of a state-organized trade union structure and to blend trade unionism and labor as if they represented the same organic interests. The trade union Law 35 of 1976 legalizes and protects the ETUF monopoly on trade unionism by prohibiting the formation of other trade unions. While strikes became legal as a result of the Labor Law passed in 2003, the same legislation also mandated that all industrial actions had to be approved by the ETUF executive committee. This occurred only once, in 2009, when a strike was held at the Tanta Flax Company, which had been privatized in 2005.

The ETUF should not be seen as a uniform organization that has always been submissive to the state's policies. Its leadership, for example, was largely opposed to the privatization policies of the 1980s, and as a result was given greater prerogatives in decision-making processes.[14] The

[12] Bellin, "Contingent Democrats."

[13] Massoud Karshenas and Valentine M. Moghadam, "Introduction," In Massoud Karshenas and Valentine M. Moghadam (eds), *Social Policy in the Middle East: Economic, Political, and Gender Dynamics*, Basingstoke: Palgrave Macmillan, 2006, p. 4.

[14] The 1980s were marked by tensions both within the ETUF and between the union and the state caused by the adoption of economic reform policies: Marsha Pripstein Posusney, *Labor and the State in Egypt*, New York: Columbia University Press, 1997; Bianchi, "The Corporatization of the Egyptian Labor Movement."

close relationship between the ETUF and the state continued unabated, however. In fact, far from weakening the regime's ability to control organized labor or to "expand the political space that labor institutions enjoy" as argued by Paczyńska,[15] limited state concessions extended the means of co-optation. The ETUF remained largely unaccountable to its members and its strategy focused mainly on direct negotiations with government officials.[16] Workers in the workplace therefore adopted a different strategy by going on strike despite the hostility of their trade union representatives. This process started in the 1980s in a context of economic reform and then intensified from the early 2000s onwards.[17] It resulted from a split between statist labor, whose existence relied on a "cozy relationship with the state," and mobilized labor, whose interests were no longer represented by the trade union. This distinction is an important one to make in order to provide a nuanced account of the limitations of the ruling bargain. Statist labor continued to benefit from corporatist policies by retaining its positions of power, and it has in turn remained hostile to any attempts from workers to voice their grievances through labor actions. But by doing so, the ETUF lost much of its power and influence among Egyptian workers.

Secondly, corporatist policies gave rise to a number of expectations from labor in terms of economic and social benefits. The notion of "moral economy" captures these reciprocal expectations. In her work on workers' protests from the 1960s to the early 1990s, Marsha Pripstein Posusney argues that workers' protests "reflect the existence of a moral economy of protest."[18] But in describing the expectations resulting from the contractual agreement that defined the state–labor relationship, she argues that labor protests aim to preserve the status quo rather than to question it. E.P. Thompson formulated the notion of "moral economy" in his analysis of the social and political contexts underlying food riots

[15] Paczyńska, *State, Labor, and the Transition to a Market Economy*, p. 30.

[16] Mubarak's regime ensured that the leadership of the ETUF would remain co-opted by preserving its positions of power within the ruling party and curbing any dissident unionists. See John Waterbury, *Exposed to Innumerable Delusions: Public Enterprise and State Power in Egypt, India, Mexico, and Turkey*, Cambridge: Cambridge University Press, 1993, p. 242.

[17] Omar El Shafei, *Workers, Trade Unions and the State in Egypt, 1984–1989*, Cairo: American University in Cairo Press, 1995; Posusney, *Labor and the State in Egypt*.

[18] Posusney, *Labor and the State in Egypt*, p. 89.

in England during the eighteenth century. He argued that these protests were not irrational actions driven by purely material interests but involved feelings of injustice as the ruling elites were not fulfilling their responsibilities towards citizens.[19] In other words, by focusing on protesters whose rights were violated, Thompson argued that riots had to be repositioned in a "moral" context of expectations and reciprocity between the ruling regime and the protestors. For Posusney, the moral economy of labor strikes for Egyptian workers in the 1990s consisted in maintaining the political status quo in order to preserve their economic entitlements. But such an analysis creates a dichotomy between economic and political demands and overlooks the dynamics of labor protests. Organizing a strike and calling for the state to protect workers' wages do not mean acceptance of the ruling regime. This is what Béatrice Hibou has argued when using the notion of moral economy to analyze how the Tunisian uprisings responded to the "political economy of domination" in Tunisia, which involved a pact based on "powerful mechanisms of inclusion."[20]

Until 2011, the labor protests in Egypt called on the state and its representatives to solve strikers' demands but refrained from overtly calling for the overthrow of Mubarak's regime. This corroborates the idea that the ruling bargain had successfully "permitted the maintenance of the system"[21] by acknowledging the state's power or by containing dissent in "support of the state."[22] Workers in some factories carried pictures of Hosni Mubarak during strikes, not to attack him but to call on the president to solve their grievances. This was the case during the strike held at the Indorama company in Shibin al-Kawm in March 2009.[23] Workers organized a strike with the unexpected support of their trade union committee[24] in order to ask for the disbursement of an annual bonus that the

[19] E.P. Thompson, "The Moral Economy of the English Crowd in the Eighteenth Century," *Past and Present*, 50, 1 (1971), pp. 76–136.

[20] Béatrice Hibou, *The Force of Obedience: The Political Economy of Repression in Tunisia*, trans. Andrew Brown, 1st edn, Cambridge: Polity Press, 2011.

[21] Ibid.

[22] William Zartman, "Opposition as Support of the State," in Adeed Dawisha and William Zartman (eds), *Beyond Coercion: Durability of the Arab State*, London and New York: Croom Helm, 1988, pp. 61–87.

[23] Author's observation.

[24] In Feb. 2007, when a strike was held in Shibin after the privatization of the

management of the company had not paid to workers. The strikers called on the government, and as a last resort the president, to pressure the company management to pay the bonus. Strikers carried pictures of Mubarak and posters displaying the following slogan: "Hosni, son of Munufiyya [the region where the company is located and where Mubarak's family is from] rescue the workers of Shibin."

However, this acknowledgement of power was largely rhetorical. As one of the workers stated: "We don't support Mubarak but as the saying goes 'if a dog owes you something, call him Sir to get what you want from him.'"[25] This event reflects the complex dynamics of the state–society relations that have shaped the protests, while it also highlights the inability of a simplistic dichotomy between "material and political demands" to capture this. Strikes, which here can be described as contained forms of contestation under authoritarianism, had to reflect a strong need for the state despite its arbitrary, repressive, and humiliating policies. This is where the notion of a social pact proved to be a powerful instrument of rule because it enshrined the idea that only the ruling regime, and ultimately the president, could solve workers' grievances. It does not follow, however, that workers believed in this idea, especially since economic reforms have gradually eroded the social contract. During the strikes workers made sure to "act as if" they were convinced by the state's propaganda, which never ceased to present the ruling regime as the champion of workers' interests.[26] Challenging this narrative would have undermined the strikers' opportunities to win concessions, and would have increased the risk of repression.

Lastly, in the political system that emerged after 1952, state–society relations were not solely based on economic and social expectations, as the overarching framework of the ruling bargain was also defined in nationalist terms. Workers were one of the groups that contributed to the nation's economic and political independence. The state, in turn, had the responsibility to protect the homeland (*waṭṭan*); in exchange for workers' labor, it gave them financial and social rewards (*muqābil*). The

---

company, the members of the trade union committee claimed that the strike was illegitimate.

[25] Interview with a worker, Shibin al-Kawm, 11 Mar. 2009.

[26] Lisa Wedeen, *Ambiguities of Domination: Politics, Rhetoric, and Symbols in Contemporary Syria*, Chicago: University of Chicago Press, 1999.

legitimation of power was also based on the idea that the state and the homeland formed a single entity because the political system (*niẓām*) had the responsibility to protect the interests of the *waṭṭan*. Under Mubarak, many Egyptians felt that this nationalist contract had been broken and that the state undermined rather than promoted the nation's interests.[27] This view was a response not only to economic policies but also to the state's political decisions and its inaction on issues such as the plight of the Palestinians and the corruption and impunity of economic and political elites. Privatization policies, the growing power of foreign companies, and other economic and social structural problems meant that workers felt they no longer received a *muqābil*. The failure of the state to solve social issues, and the steady replacement of the welfare state by the security state, should not overshadow the incapacity of the state to address national concerns, a situation which discredits *misr al-ḥukūma*, that is, Egypt as represented by the state.[28]

In the 1980s and 1990s, workers' demands were mostly articulated through factory occupations and sit-ins rather than strikes, in order to ensure that workflow and production process were not disrupted. This form of protest was seen as demonstrating the workers' commitment to the national economic project. However, beginning in the early 2000s workers organized sit-ins inside the factories' premises in addition to taking part in work stoppages, thereby challenging restrictions on the right to strike. This also demonstrated that the nationalist contract was not working.[29] The organization of strikes contributed to a sense of collective responsibility and legitimized labor action as a struggle to reclaim the nation at the local level. In this sense, for many Egyptians the fall of Mubarak in 2011 meant that they had succeeded in fully reclaiming the nation.

[27] On this issue see Galal Amin, *Egypt in the Era of Hosni Mubarak, 1981–2010*, Cairo and New York: The American University in Cairo Press, 2011.

[28] *Misr al-waṭṭan* is part of the symbolic realm, it refers to nationalism as an ideology being reproduced by a hegemonic discourse and everyday practices. By contrast, *misr al-ḥukūma* embodies the materiality of power, the feeling of frustration and disillusion that the political regime has fueled among Egyptians.

[29] Mustafa Basiuni and Omar Sa'id, *Rayat al-idrab fi Sama' Misr: 2007, Haraka 'Ummaliyya Jadida*, Cairo: Markaz al-dirasat al-ishtirakiyya, 2007.

A further indication of Egyptian labor's "tactical innovations"[30] and radicalization of its repertoires of contention was the organization of sit-ins and demonstrations in front of government offices, especially the parliament and the office of the prime minister. As discussed below, by using public spaces to voice their grievances publicly rather than keeping them confined to the workplace, these strikes carved "spaces of visibility," which in turn helped undermine the foundations of the regime's corporatist ruling bargain. However, these tactical innovations should not be understood merely as direct confrontational strategies against the ruling elites. Rather, they displayed a strong need for the state and its institutions to take action, in order to be tolerated by the regime. This is similar to what happened in the Shibin factory when strikers carried pictures of Mubarak to win concessions, despite confessing that they despised the president. However, these protests were aimed at neutralizing the framework of political deinstitutionalization imposed by the state to contain discontent—namely the ETUF, the restrictions on the right to strike and protest, and on freedom of association.

Strikes and the "Politics of Visibility"

Between 2004 and 2010, over 2 million workers voiced their grievances through strikes, sit-ins, and other forms of protest against the poor living conditions caused by the erosion of wages, rising inflation, and precarious employment. These protests, which were the largest wave of labor action since the 1950s, involved public and private sector factory workers, bakery shop workers, civil servants, teachers, tax collectors, medical doctors, transportation workers, and garbage collectors. Sit-ins were also staged in front of the parliament or the prime minister's Cabinet in 2010 to voice Egyptians' grievances publicly.

There was a turning point in the number of labor protests in 2004, with a rise from 86 in 2003 to 266 the following year. However, beginning in 2007 labor mobilization intensified, with no less than 614 protests organized in 2007 as compared to only 222 in 2006.[31] In December

[30] Doug McAdam, "Tactical Innovation and the Pace of Insurgency," *American Sociological Review*, 48, 6 (Dec. 1983), pp. 735–54.

[31] Markaz al-ard li-huquq al-insan [Land Center for Human Rights], *Silsilat al-huquq al-iqtisadiyya wa-lijtima'iyya*, 34 (July 2004); 35 (Feb. 2005); 39 (Aug. 2005); 42 (Jan. 2006); 49 (July 2006); 54 (Feb. 2007); 56 (July 2007);

2006, in the Nile Delta city of Mahalla al-Kubra, workers in the Egypt Spinning and Weaving Company—the largest textile company in Egypt, employing some 22,000 employees—went on strike for the first time in twelve years to demand disbursement of an annual bonus that they had not received.[32] Workers were granted their bonus after a three-day strike and occupation of the factory, during which workers' representatives negotiated with company management and government officials from the ministries of investment and labor. The private press that emerged at the beginning of the 2000s widely covered the Mahalla strike and its successful outcome.[33] Labor protests spilled over to other textile factories and to companies operating in different sectors, such as cement companies and railway transport companies. In September 2007 workers at the Mahalla factory went on strike again and demanded the implementation of the financial plan that had been negotiated during the December 2006 strike.

The private sector had also participated in this wave of strikes. In October 2004, workers at the Ghazl Qaliub textile company, a branch of Esco, organized a strike following the company's privatization.[34] Production was stopped at the Asmant Tora cement factory in January 2005 due to the uncertainty of the workforce's status after its sale to a private investor.[35] In February 2007, workers in Ghazl Shibin, a spin-

---

58 (Feb. 2008); 65 (Mar. 2009); 78 (Feb. 2010); 84 (Aug. 2010); 88 (Jan. 2011). www.lchr-eg.org. These numbers are based on reports by the Land Center, a Cairo-based non-governmental organization focusing on workers and farmers' rights. Founded in 1996, the Land Center publishes a yearly report of labor protests taking place in the public and private sectors by using press articles.

[32] Founded in 1927 in the city of Mahalla al-Kubra by the banker Tala'at Harb, the Egypt Spinning and Weaving Company is a public company with a history of labor militancy dating back to the 1930s and 1940s. During the 1970s and 1980s workers organized a number of protests. When company employees went on strike on Dec. 2006, however, it had not experienced labor action since 1994.

[33] On the media coverage of labor strikes see Marie Duboc, "Journalisme et Militantisme: Les Formes D'engagement dans La Couverture Médiatique des Grèves Ouvrières en Égypte," in Marc Lavergne (ed.), *2009–2010, En Marche Vers Tahrir*, Cairo: Cedej, 2012.

[34] Husam 'Abd al-Hamid and Shaymaa Abu al-Layl, *al-'Arabi*, 24 Oct. 2004.

[35] Husam 'Abd al-Hamid and Shaymaa Abu al-Layl, *al-'Arabi*, 9 Jan. 2005.

ning company located in the Nile Delta region, went on strike for a week to ask for the payment of bonuses that they were supposed to receive before the privatization of the company. They resumed industrial action two years later when the management refused to pay annual bonuses equivalent to 228 days of salary due to the company's losses caused by the global financial crisis.

Labor protests took place in a context of rising inflation and the implementation by Prime Minister Ahmad Nazif's government (July 2004–January 2011) of a privatization program that also included the restructuring of public sector companies. Attempts to reform and privatize the public sector date back to the early 1990s as part of the "open door" (*infitah*) neo-liberal turn introduced in 1974 by President Sadat, Nasser's successor.[36] However, 2004 marked a turning point in the intensification of economic reforms: between 2005 and 2009 the state's total revenues from privatization were nearly eight times higher than they had been in the period from 2000 to 2004. The objective of these policies was not to transform the economic structures but to represent the private interests of the ruling elite without being held accountable.[37] In other words, the welfare state disappeared but the state continues to play a key economic role. Not surprisingly, economic reforms over the decades in Egypt fostered more corruption and brought about greater restriction on freedom of association. New labor legislation was also passed in 2003 to legalize short-term employment contracts and to lift the restrictions on

[36] Law 203 of 1991 organized the management and restructuring of 314 public enterprises eligible for privatization through holding companies. However, the economy remained dominated by the government's activities and by public spending which actually increased throughout the 1980s. See Khalid Ikram, *The Egyptian Economy, 1952–2000: Performance, Policies, and Issues*, New York: Routledge, 2009, p. 48; Waterbury, *Exposed to Innumerable Delusions*, p. 242.

[37] Eberhard Kienle, *A Grand Delusion: Democracy and Economic Reform in Egypt*, London and New York: I.B. Tauris, 2001; Olivier Dabène, Vincent Geisser, and Gilles Massardier, "Introduction: La Démocratisation Contre La Démocratie," in Olivier Dabène, Vincent Geisser, and Gilles Massardier (eds), *Autoritarismes Démocratiques Et Démocraties Autoritaires Au XXIème Siècle*, Paris: La Découverte, 2008, pp. 7–26; Ulrich Wurzel, "Limits to Economic Reform in an Authoritarian State," in Laura Guazzone and Daniela Pioppi (eds), *The Arab State and Neo-Liberal Globalization: The Restructuring of State Power in the Middle East*, Reading: Ithaca Press, 2009, pp. 97–124.

dismissing employees.[38] Many Egyptians had also been concerned about the degradation of their purchasing power, with the average inflation rate rising from 2.9 percent in 2000–3 to 16.5 percent in 2004.[39] In 2008 inflation peaked at 18 percent when global food prices soared.[40] Over half a million Egyptians protested in the workplace in 2008, which, along with the intensification of collective action in the streets to denounce the skyrocketing increase of food and commodity prices, made it a year of unprecedented mobilization in Egypt.

These actions provide a heuristic for understanding shifting forms of political participation that were increasingly based on the "politics of visibility" (that is relying on overt protests to voice grievances). As shown by the upsurge of demonstrations, factory occupations, and strikes or sit-ins organized in front of the parliament, protests became a highly visible form of performance. This shift, whereby overt protest became a widespread form of action across Egypt, is critical in understanding how Egyptians took to the streets in early 2011. The process had been building up over for over a decade.

By shifting the focus of research from the state and its elites to the "people," studies of urban and rural subalterns in the global South have contributed to the broadening of the definition of political participation.[41] Much of this emphasis has been placed on "everyday forms of resistance" (that is ordinary behavior and tactics that marginal and poor people resort to in order to respond to domination). They have shown that these behaviors lead to non-collective, unplanned direct action. These actions may take multiple forms depending on people's circumstances: tax-dodging,

[38] Unified labor law 12 of 2003.

[39] Capmas, "Inflation Rate Consumer Price Indices 1993–2010," *Egypt in Figures 2011*.

[40] Ibid.

[41] Vinayak Chaturvedi, *Mapping Subaltern Studies and the Postcolonial*, London: Verso, 2000; Asef Bayat, "Globalization and the Politics of the Informals in the Global South," in Ananya Roy and Nezar AlSayyad (eds), *Urban Informality: Transnational Perspectives from the Middle East, Latin America, and South Asia*, Transnational Perspectives on Space and Place, Lanham, MD: Lexington Books, 2003; Diane Singerman, *Avenues of Participation: Family, Politics, and Networks in Urban Quarters of Cairo*, Princeton, NJ: Princeton University Press, 1995; James C. Scott and Benedict J. Kerkvliet (eds), *Everyday Forms of Peasant Resistance in South-East Asia*, London: Frank Cass, 1986.

electrical meter tapping, informal housing, and so on. These actions typically took place quietly, and therefore went unnoticed.

One of the underlying assumptions that characterizes this literature, namely the idea that individuals resorting to these forms of resistance are marginal, live an informal life, and are excluded from official economic and political structures, deserves greater attention. Indeed, the very reason why people design coping strategies is economic hardship and the failure of economic and political institutions to respond to their needs. They exhibit the decline of the social contract in the daily lives of Egyptians. However, by reading too much into marginality and exclusion, such analyses could fall into the trap of essentialism, describing these strategies as the only channels of mobility open to the marginalized, and, therefore, as the only forms of political participation and expression available to them.

Another assumption that should be questioned is the idea that economic and political exclusion has merely led individuals to resort to hidden, quiet, and token forms of political participation. Diane Singerman argues: "Within this [authoritarian] environment, men and women use informal political institutions, beyond the supervision and control of the state, to pursue their collective interests. Remaining invisible then, is essential to building a limited degree of political autonomy."[42] By focusing on the siege of Imbaba in 1992 in Egypt, she shows that informality provokes more visible and organized social and political movements, but only in exceptional circumstances.[43]

Asef Bayat makes a similar argument: "The repressive policy of the state renders individual, quiet, and hidden mobilization a more viable strategy than open, collective protest ... Under such conditions, collective and open direct action takes place only at exceptional conjunctures."[44] For Bayat, the "political street" brings together different forms of political action: "the quiet encroachment of the ordinary" and the demonstrations of workers or students. While these actions have in common the use of the public space and the expression of collective

[42] Diane Singerman, "The Politics of Informality in Egypt: Networks, Family, the Economy and Islamists," Mac Arthur Consortium Working Paper Series, Minneapolis: University of Minnesota, 2007, p. 1.

[43] Ibid. p. 17.

[44] Asef Bayat, *Street Politics: Poor People's Movements in Iran*, New York: Columbia University Press, 1997, p. 21.

sentiments, they remain distinct as a result of the actors' different institutional capital.[45]

My contention is that workers have become deinstitutionalized both as a result of the erosion of their economic and social status and owing to the lack of a trade union organization representing their interests. The demise of trade unionism resulting from the informalization of labor and the downsizing of the public sector has not undermined class-based movements. Nor have individualistic strategies prevailed with workers supposedly characterized as being "more loyal to their bosses than to fellow workers."[46] Rather, they have been extending their grievances collectively and publicly and have been followed in this process by informal workers and unemployed graduates or housewives protesting against the shortage of water, gas, or housing.

The split between overt and hidden mobilization should be nuanced to take into account changes in the political culture of protest. Egyptian factory workers are not only integrated into the formal labor market, sometimes as civil servants when employed by public companies, but they also engage in strikes and demonstrations, carry banners, write leaflets, and conduct interviews with the media to voice their grievances about wages and bonuses. The economic hardships they face involve the same daily struggles as shopkeepers, taxi drivers, and workers in the informal economy, and the same concerns about finding the resources to pay for medical expenses or private lessons for their children. For instance, factory workers, like state employees and the vast majority of the Egyptian population, are compelled to take on second jobs in addition to their work in the factory. Likewise, they may have bank accounts, but they do not take loans from banks, preferring to rely on a cooperative lending system organized with their neighbors to avoid paying interest. In other words, while they are part of the formal economy and engage in collective, public protests against their working conditions, they also devise informal tactics to improve their living conditions.

Factory workers have experienced the "destabilization of the stable," a phenomenon according to which the "growth of precariousness now reaches into previously stable zones of employment."[47] While the

[45] Asef Bayat, *Life as Politics: How Ordinary People Change the Middle East*, Stanford, CA: Stanford University Press, 2010, p. 212.

[46] Ibid. p. 215.

[47] Robert Castel, *From Manual Workers to Wage Laborers: Transformation of*

boundaries between stable and unstable employment are becoming blurred, the differences are still considered significant, because more stable employment continues to provide advantages such as retirement pensions and health insurance. More broadly, the fear of economic and social insecurity is widespread and noticeable in everyday life. Thus there is a need to go beyond the idea that there is a split between integrated economic actors whose political actions are public, and marginal ones whose political actions are concealed. While these destabilized groups constitute a minority in relation to the vast majority of Egyptians working in the informal economy, the process of casualization has challenged the idea that their "aristocratic status" would encourage them to maintain the status quo.

The culture of overt protest that has been shaping political participation over the past decade in Egypt and elsewhere in the Middle East provides empirical evidence of these changes. They exhibit the demise of the "mechanisms of inclusion" that have been at the center of state–society relations. The following section illustrates this point by focusing on workers' initiatives to challenge the trade union structure. While steps to ask for the resignation of the local trade union committees have not constituted a widespread process, these initiatives are nonetheless part of a repertoire that has questioned the legitimacy of the trade union. Indeed, owing to the restrictions on the freedom of organization and expression, the very act of going on strike takes place against the trade union structure.

Challenging the Status Quo through the Trade Union

Beginning in the 1980s, workers' initiatives to withdraw confidence from the local trade union committees were the first indications of cracks in the trade union system.[48] If the union, although imposed by force, made sense in a corporatist system, how can it impose its legitimacy in a capitalist economy when it has no autonomy from the ruling

---

the Social Question, trans. Richard Boyd, New Brunswick, NJ: Transaction Publishers, 2003, p. 387.

[48] For an account of labor protests in the 1980s and 1990s see Posusney, *Labor and the State in Egypt*; El Shafei, *Workers, Trade Unions and the State in Egypt, 1984–1989*.

regime and its economic policies?[49] This has been the challenge faced by the leadership of the ETUF since the 1980s. Beginning in 2007, the ETUF's situation became increasingly untenable.

The wave of strikes that has swept Egypt since 2006–7 must be seen within the context of the 2006 trade union elections, which in many factories fueled of against company management and showed that workers had no genuine representatives even among the trade union committees.[50] Although fraud had been a feature of union elections, in 2006 it was reported to have been uncharacteristically high.[51] It clearly demonstrated the gap between statist and mobilized labor and the failure of a strategy that some labor activists had followed for many years. This strategy consisted in using the ETUF and the structures of power as the framework to advance workers' claims with the aim of reforming trade union representation from within rather than opposing it.

In 2006 the purpose of the fraud appears to have been twofold. On the one hand it was aimed at purging the local committees of their most militant members, while on the other hand it was designed to keep in check the influence of the Muslim Brotherhood.[52] A consequence of the elections was to widen the gap between the ETUF and the rank and file and to undermine the already crumbling notion of a corporatist pact protecting workers' interests.

On 7 December 2006, a few weeks after the announcement of the trade union election results, the Egypt Spinning and Weaving Company in Mahalla went on strike to ask for the payment of a bonus that had been announced by the prime minister at the time, Ahmad Nazif.

[49] Another factor that further undermined the ETUF's legitimacy was the fact that it represented only a small proportion of Egypt's labor force: at its peak, the ETUF represented 4,500,000 workers out of a labor force of 24 million. This figure does not include the informal sector.

[50] Françoise Clément, "Élections Ouvrières: Entre Fraude et Chasse aux «Frères Masqués»," in Enrique Klaus and Chaymaa Hassabo (eds), *Chroniques 2006*, Cairo: Cedej, 2007, pp. 59–86.

[51] Dar al-khadamat al-niqabiyya wa-l-'umaliyya, *Waqai' Ma Jara, Al-intikhabat Al-niqabyyia Dawra 2006–2011* [What Really Happened: The Trade Union Elections in 2006], Cairo: Markaz al-mahrusa li-l-nashr wa-l-ma'lumat, 2006.

[52] In the fall of 2005 the Muslim Brothers had made an unexpected breakthrough in the legislative elections by winning 20 percent of the seats of the national assembly.

In Mahalla and in other factories, the fraud during the 2006 trade union elections had exacerbated workers' distrust of the union system by exposing its collusion with the management against workers' demands. Fraud contributed to closing of the meager channels of expression and representation that were open to factory workers until that point. As a result, it encouraged ousted candidates to resort to other forms of organization in order to advance workers' demands. In Mahalla, most of the leading organizers of strikes ran as candidates in the 2006 union election.

By relying on the support they had built ahead of the vote, these candidates were able to mobilize their fellow workers during the strikes. To run in the trade union committee elections, a candidate has to rely on a broad network of support developed within the factory over time. A strike leader in Mahalla who claimed to have been a victim of electoral fraud in 2006 explained that he reached his colleagues through a wide range of activities, including helping them gain access to medical services in the company hospital or intervening in family conflicts on their behalf.[53] The capacity of a candidate to provide practical support to his colleagues and thereby to win their trust was considered crucial to running in the local union committee. Another candidate explained that he and other candidates had representatives (*mandūbīn*) across the factory in various departments, to help them keep abreast of ongoing issues.[54]

By itself, fraud cannot account for the resurgence of strikes beginning in 2007. However, the combination of fraud with the non-payment of bonuses triggered mobilization at a time when defeated candidates were able to mobilize support inside the factory. In the majority of workplaces where strikes were organized, the trade union was a target of workers' protests. In some factories it led to initiatives asking for the dismissal of their trade union committee and for the organization of free elections.[55] This was the case in January 2007 at the Misr Spinning and

[53] Interview with a worker, Alexandria, 23 Oct. 2009.

[54] Interview with a worker, Mahalla al-Kubra, 30 June 2009.

[55] The struggle for meaningful representation did not necessarily translate into organized action beyond the scope of the strike. While overt protests and the politics of visibility were widespread across Egypt, there were conflicts between workers in different workplaces regarding the strategy to follow. For some workers' leaders the priority was to first secure financial concessions before taking steps to form an independent union.

Weaving plant in Mahalla al-Kubra where 13,000 workers signed a petition, asking for the dismissal of their trade union committee. During the strike, the local union committee and the leadership of the textile union claimed that workers' demands were illegitimate. None of their members had participated in the organization of the strike. Thus the petition not only aimed to challenge the local trade union representatives but also defied the leadership of the ETUF, the organization that had been controlling rather than supporting workers' activism since 1957. Similar initiatives took place in other plants during 2007, particularly in the spinning company Indorama, located in Shibin al-Kawm.

The most successful initiative starts with tax collectors. In December 2008, the real estate tax collectors formed the first union independent from the ETUF, called the Real Estate Tax Authority Union (RETA), with the aim of stripping the ETUF of its legitimacy and opening the way for an independent labor movement in Egypt. Led by Kamal Abu Eita, a Nasserist labor activist, the RETA was formed one year after 55,000 real estate tax collectors had organized a strike that resulted in a 325 percent salary increase.[56] The tax collectors' strike was significant because of its scale and because it successfully put an end to the ETUF's monopoly over trade union representation.

On 30 January 2011, the formation of the Egyptian Federation for Independent Unions (EFITU) was announced in Tahrir Square during the demonstrations that called for the overthrow of Mubarak. The formation of the EFITU was a joint initiative including the RETA, the healthcare professionals', the teachers' and the retirees' unions, all of which had been established in 2010. While these newly formed independent unions had faced limited organizational capacity, and in some cases internal divisions, the formation of the EFITU in the first days of the Egyptian uprising clearly meant that regime change had to involve reforms of the trade union legislation in order to ensure pluralism and freedom of organization. This was not a new demand. In 2009–10 several labor activists, including lawyers, members of parliament, and NGOs had started a campaign to draft new trade union legislation and pass it in parliament before the end of the 2010 legislative session. The draft was completed but the initiative was aborted by the regime.

[56] Kamal Abu Eita was an elected member of the local committee of the General Union of Bank, Insurance and Finance Employees in Giza during the 1990s and 2000s. But like in Mahalla he was not re-elected in 2006.

Autonomous Strikes? Leadership and Political Parties

One aspect of collective action that deserves greater attention is the idea that protestors' action is independent from political groups. This narrative is widespread among workers who participated in strikes. It carries the legacy of corporatism that has dominated labor organization since the 1950s with the aim to "depoliticize" the labor movement. To discredit labor strikes, the Mubarak regime regularly accused strikers of advancing the agenda of political opposition groups—namely the Muslim Brothers—instead of representing workers' demands. Political parties and groups have played marginal roles in the strikes as they do not have much of a presence in the factories. While the Muslim Brothers had members in local trade union committees and among workers, they were not generally involved in the organization of strikes due to fear of repression. Local and national leaders of the Muslim Brotherhood allowed their members to participate in strikes in their individual capacity but the organization as a whole did not use labor action for mobilizational purposes.

Within this context, the insistence of workers to present themselves as independent from political groups exhibited their concern to legitimize their demands in order to be able to secure financial concessions from the company management or from the state. While there is no labor quiescence, there is a reluctance to be seen as a political opponent by being associated with an opposition group. So the tacit rules of the game, of the bargain, were shifting from quiescence to contained forms of protests that called for the state or sometimes the nation (when demonstrating in front the parliament) to intervene. Political parties are largely distrusted by workers, but they were still regarded by older strike leaders as structures that forge political experience and knowledge. In Mahalla, from the 1970s to the 1990s, leftist political parties had members among the workers' leaders: members of the Nasserist party, the Tagammu' or the Communist Party were involved in the organization of strikes. Increasingly, workers, including the most militant, defined themselves as "natural leaders" (*qiyadat tabi'iyyn*) to indicate their distance from formal political parties. As one labor activist put it:

> Strike leaders used to be members of political parties but now they are created during the strikes. They are called "natural" leaders (*taba'iyyin*) because they

come from the ranks of the workers and the workers gather around them, spontaneously ...[57]

For another worker who participated in the strikes in the 1980s and 1990s, being a "natural leader" stood for a lack of political and organizational experience:

Natural workers emerged during the first strike [December 2006]. They had no role, they were not members of a political party. There was even a member of the National Democratic Party (NDP) with us. They are leaders who just pop up from the rank of workers, who are not educated (*muthaqqaf*) or members of a party ... I went to the Baath school [lived in Iraq for three years]. Here in Egypt I was a member of Tagammu' but I left it because it became an instrument of the regime. So I joined the Communist Party. I was educated politically.[58]

According to these workers, what defined a labor leader was his political experience, and "political training" was gained gradually by participating in industrial action. This learning process did not exist in a context dominated by the decline and demobilization of political parties beginning in the mid-1990s. However, "natural leaders" were not totally cut off from political parties. Their activism differed from practices that prevailed in the 1980s. It was more intermittent and loose as they sought to free themselves from the organizational constraints of discredited political parties. In the eyes of their older colleagues, they were seen as inexperienced and coming "out of nowhere." But older workers also began to distance themselves from political organizations from the late 1990s onwards. The fact that a number of strike leaders in Mahalla had participated in the trade union elections of 2006 adds a degree of nuance to the idea that their involvement in the strikes was merely spontaneous. By participating in the trade union elections campaigns, as mentioned earlier, they built visibility within the plant. An important part of their activities also involved gathering information on the labor legislation in order to better understand the legal rules on which they could base their demands.

Their loose connection to parties sometimes blurred any attempts to give them a political label. In Mahalla, two strike leaders explained to me with amusement that their colleagues and even the intelligence services considered them to be either communists or members of the

[57] Interview with a worker, Mahalla, 21 June 2009.
[58] Interview with a worker, Mahalla, 3 Oct. 2009.

Muslim Brotherhood. All of the strike leaders would fail to fit this description—one of the workers involved in the organization of strikes in Mahalla, for example, was an active member of the ruling National Democratic Party. However, because of the lack of alternatives and given the country's repressive politics, activist workers struggled to identify other avenues that young workers could follow in order to gain political experience. After more than three decades of a façade of multipartyism, political groups had been prevented from gaining any real power and independence. The fall of Mubarak has put an end to the restrictions on the formation of political parties, but much remains to be done for these groups to gain the confidence of Egyptians beyond the ballot box, particularly in the factories.

The tension and defiance between political parties and workers was manifest in the spring of 2008 when workers at the Miṣr li-l-ghazl wa-l-nasīj plant in Mahalla announced that they would go on strike on 6 April in order to secure a pay raise and an increase in several allowances. Some political parties and opposition groups announced their solidarity with Mahalla workers by trying to organize a general strike. Their demands included the implementation of a minimum wage but were more generally aimed at confronting the Mubarak regime's policies. Ahead of the strike date, the head of the ETUF summoned seven workers' leaders to a meeting in Cairo to intimidate them into calling off the strike. Five of them agreed to cancel the strike in exchange for a higher food allowance, while two refused to back down. High repression and the deployment of security forces throughout the city of Mahalla also intimidated the majority of workers from going on strike on 6 April. Elsewhere the call for a national strike was not heeded. Nevertheless, riots did take place in the city of Mahalla on 6 and 7 April, and two young men were killed and hundreds were wounded in the clashes that ensued between protesting workers and the police. Three workers from Miṣr li-l-ghazl wa-l-nasīj were arrested and several faced arbitrary transfers or pay cuts to intimidate them from taking part in future protests. Although the call for a general strike focused on broader concerns about food prices and wages, it ultimately stemmed from labor grievances at the Mahalla factory.

Following the unrest, workers at the Mahalla company were often harassed by the security forces and were intimidated from taking part in further industrial action. Internal divisions between labor leaders also prevented a reemergence of worker activism in the short run. The 6 April events show the boundaries that contentious action could not cross under Mubarak. The corporatist bargain, along with heavy-handed repression, could still work to contain workers' action. In exchange for some concessions, such as an increase in the food allowance, some workers' leaders rejected the idea of the strike escalating into a larger movement linked to opposition groups. They later justified their decision to back down in terms of this pact, explaining that as long as the government consented to make financial concessions workers should not go on strike. This was the message sent by government representatives immediately after the clashes. On 8 April a ministerial delegation, comprised of the prime minister, the minister of manpower, and the investment minister, visited the Egypt Spinning and Weaving factory in Mahalla. The prime minister announced that 400 million £LE would be invested in the companies to improve their equipment facilities. The minister of manpower also had good news to announce to workers. They were to receive a bonus amounting to a month's salary. Through these measures the regime was indicating that it "cared" for the workers and that they had more to win by avoiding a confrontational stance with the regime. With a combination of repression and concessions, described by one worker arrested on 6 April as "bribes" to silence workers, the regime successfully aborted all attempts to organize a strike in Mahalla until 2011.[59]

The call for protest on 25 January 2011 was in many ways reminiscent of April 2008. The 2011 protests turned out to be a successful attempt at overcoming the obstacles that the earlier campaign had faced. Not surprisingly, the slogan that was chanted across Egypt in January and February 2011—"bread, dignity, and social justice"—captured the issues that Egyptians had raised during a decade of collective action. However, the calls for civil disobedience and mobilization against the ruling regime in 2011 were not framed as part of a labor struggle alone—or of a specific group. The context had certainly changed in light of Ben Ali's fall from power in Tunisia. Taking to the streets en masse against the regime now had a pointedly political meaning, one that shifted from fear to hope as radicalization was perceived as a more palpable and accessible alternative.[60] While the EFITU was formed in the

[59] Interview with a worker, Mahalla al-Kubra, 29 July 2009.

[60] On revolutionary action being perceived as a "thinkable alternative" by social movement actors see Charles Kurzman, *The Unthinkable Revolution in Iran*, Cambridge, MA: Harvard University Press, 2004.

first days of the revolution by labor activists, most Egyptian workers participated in the demonstrations as individuals. The factories were not the epicenter of the uprising, but they did become an integral part of the protest movement against the ruling regime, first through workers' individual participation in demonstrations, and then when they went on strike starting on 4 February. The expansion of protests across Egypt made it possible to advance both material demands and the fall of the regime. On 11 February the Supreme Council of the Armed Forces (SCAF) deposed Mubarak and assumed power. Strikes did not stop in factories as workers continued to advance demands for better working conditions. In Mahalla strikers also asked for the resignation of the CEO of the Egypt Spinning and Weaving Holding Company, whose management style had been criticized by workers for years. During 2011 around 900,000 Egyptians participated in over 1,400 labor actions.

There was continuity between the anti-labor policies SCAF implemented and those of Mubarak's presidency, despite initiatives from the interim minister of manpower and migration to recognize freedom of organization and to dissolve the ETUF's board of directors. SCAF blocked draft trade union legislation approved by the Cabinet in August 2011 that would have granted workers the right to form independent unions. Apart from its former head, much of the ETUF pre-revolutionary leadership was reinstated by SCAF.

Labor actions did not stop after the election of Mohamed Morsi in June 2012, thereby showing that political and economic demands were not distinct. Rather, the strikes indicated that regime change had to address socio-economic issues. However, during Morsi's presidency, policies attacking freedom of organization and workers' representation continued unabated. The constitution adopted in December 2012 permitted the dissolution of unions by judicial order (Article 52) while decree 97 of 25 November 2012, which amended the trade unions law, aimed at ensuring the control of the Muslim Brotherhood over the ETUF through the appointment of its members in the board of the organization.[61]

Although the fall of Mubarak has marked a new conjuncture in Egyptian politics, it has only partially affected the context of labor mobilization. Since 2011 the constraints that labor activists have faced

[61] Joel Beinin, "Workers, Trade Unions and Egypt's Political Future," *Middle East Research and Information Project*, Jan. 2013.

have been modified but not lifted, while the issues at stake remain the same. The overthrow of Morsi by the military in July 2013 has led to the co-optation of labor activists. It is reminiscent of the processes that took place in the 1950s. In July 2013 Kamal Abu Eita, head of the EFITU, was appointed minister of manpower in the transitional government led by al-Biblawy. The EFITU has been divided over the entry of Eita into the government. However, the EFITU and the other two independent federations formed since 2011 have heeded General Sisi's call to join protests on 26 July in support of the military's rule. Meanwhile a steelworkers' strike in Suez was broken up by the police and the military in August for allegedly being organized by the Brotherhood. Despite Abu Eita's promises to speed up the adoption of new trade union legislation, the future of independent trade unions remains uncertain as repression against workers' protests has not stopped. However, workers are likely to continue to organize strikes to voice their grievances.

Conclusion

Labor–state relations in Egypt have been shaped by a corporatist bargain between the ruling regime and organized labor. Institutionally, labor interests were incorporated into the political system through the ETUF, the state-controlled trade union federation whose primary purpose was to ensure the quiescence of workers in exchange for social benefits. While the ETUF should not be seen as a monolithic organization, it served as a state instrument to curb labor militancy rather than an organization representing labor interests. Labor protests took place beginning in the early 2000s without the support of the ETUF, highlighting the tensions between statist labor and mobilized labor. By focusing on the upsurge of labor protests since 2006, this chapter demonstrates that the ruling bargain in Egypt was not challenged by statist labor (since the ETUF remained loyal to the ruling regime), but by mobilized workers who became deinstitutionalized because of both the erosion of their economic and social status and the lack of a trade union organization representing their interests.

The wave of strikes that swept Egypt toward the end of the 2000s must be seen in relation to the 2006 trade union elections, which were marred by fraud and purges of local workers' committees. By organizing strikes without the support of the ETUF, workers challenged the channels of political participation imposed by the state to contain corporatist demands. This arrangement was further contested in 2007 when a number of factory workers asked for the resignation of their local trade union committees and for free trade union elections. The formation of an independent trade union by the tax collectors was the most successful attempt to challenge one of the pillars of the regime. However, due to organizational constraints and repression most strikes could not directly confront the ruling regime and had to be seen as "autonomous" from political groups.

The spread of strikes, sit-ins, and demonstrations over the past decade provides a heuristic for understanding shifting forms of political participation that contested sites of power in the last decade of the Mubarak regime. The need for grievances to be publicly articulated is part of the "politics of visibility," the process whereby overt protest becomes a form of action widespread among Egyptians and across Egypt to voice grievances. This process is rooted in the failure of the state to solve social issues and the decline of the welfare state in favor of the security state. It has two additional characteristics that a new ruling bargain will need to address: the failure of the state to address nationalist concerns—in Egypt and regionally, especially in relation to Palestine—and the broader process of deinstitutionalization from the political system as Egyptians are no longer willing to give up their political voice.

9

A MICROCOSM OF THE ARAB SPRING

SOCIOLOGY OF TAHRIR SQUARE

Bahgat Korany

This book's subtitle, "The Evolving Ruling Bargain," evokes two traits of the Arab Spring: (a) a multiplicity of groups/participants; and (b) processual dynamics. This chapter focuses on these two aspects of the Arab Spring.[1] Al-Midan, also known as Tahrir Square (Liberation Square), is used in the chapter as a microcosm for an analysis of the build-up to, and the events of, the eighteen-day mass protests—between 25 January and 11 February 2011—which culminated in the ousting of President Hosni Mubarak.

[1] Part of the analysis of this chapter, especially the analytical framework, is based on my recent book (with Rabab el-Mahdi and other colleagues) *The Arab Spring in Egypt: Revolution and Beyond*, Cairo: American University in Cairo Press, 2012. The footnotes indicate my debt. However, the analysis has been updated with fieldwork in Tahrir and its environs, as well as informal discussions with regular Tahrir participants, shopkeepers, the proverbial taxi-drivers, and also some policemen. The closest analogy to the chapter's methodology is that of the anthropologist's "participant observation."

Tahrir Square was not just the locus of the mass uprising that brought the Mubarak regime down, it also remained the central public space for political expression long after Mubarak's fall. More than two years after the Mubarak regime fell, Tahrir continued to be the center of national and international media attention. During numerous sit-ins and protests, Egyptians denounced the referendum scheduled for 15 December 2012 on the draft constitution proposed by the Muslim Brotherhood-dominated Constituent Assembly. According to the protestors, in both content and process the constitutional draft did not represent the legitimate social contract or the desired outcome of the political bargaining they had been working for since Mubarak's fall in February 2011. Liberals, leftists, the majority of Egyptian women and youth, and representatives of the Egyptian Church had boycotted the Assembly and returned to Midan Tahrir in November and December 2012. Tahrir thus confirmed its credentials as the public space par excellence of contentious politics in search of the "right" bargaining formula for political rule, as shown during the uprisings against President Mubarak's regime.

Though less well documented, the mass protests of 2011 were preceded by a number of other protests, especially by the labor movement, which included more than 510 strikes and sit-ins in 2010 alone.[2] Why did the Al-Midan protests of 2011 prove successful and lead to the demise of the regime? Was it a function of the middle-class youth that sparked them? Was it the massive use of new social media tools that young protestors proved highly adept at using? Was it the aggravation of social ills, such as corruption or increasing poverty (as Kamrava's chapter indicates, around 40 percent of Egypt's 84 million people live below $2 a day)? Or did their success simply reflect the erosion of an authoritarian regime that had become overly complacent, thus becoming provocative and insulting? The gross fraud of the 2010 parliamentary elections is surely an indicator of regime excesses. Dignity, after all, was a main component of the slogans chanted in Tahrir Square.

All of the above certainly played a part. But why did police brutality fail to work in this situation when it had so often proven effective in suppressing protests in the past? What impact did Bouzizi's self-immolation and Ben Ali's speedy flight from Tunisia on 17 January 2011 have on Egypt's "Arab Spring?"

[2] See Marie Duboc's chapter in this volume.

This chapter begins by briefly situating Al-Midan in Egypt's modern social history, emphasizing its efficacy for mass protest as the meeting place of nine main arteries. It was Al-Midan's geographical location in Cairo that helped the protestors overpower police forces and consequently compelled them to flee as early as the evening of 27 January 2011. The following section outlines the chapter's analytical framework, namely a form of contentious politics that has been adapted to fit the focus of the chapter and is used to inform the analysis of data. A final section focuses on what the chapter identifies as the three *M*s: the military, the mosque, and the (liberal–leftist) masses.

Group diversity notwithstanding, the chapter argues that the Al-Midan protests were initially led by the youth. The first half of the chapter is consequently devoted to the specific context of youth organizations: their political socialization into mass protests through organizations such as Kefaya and the National Coalition for Change led by Mohamed ElBaradei. The emphasis here is on the impact this process of political socialization had on the protestors. However, disillusionment subsequently pushed the youth to take matters into their own hands and to establish their own organizations, such as Harakat Shabab 6 abril (April 6 Youth Movement), and Kollena Khaled Sa'eed (We are all Khalid Sa'eed).[3] Analysis of the actions of these organizations suggests that there is an under-researched generational divide among the protestors. The chapter then goes on to investigate the impact of new techniques of mobilization and framing, especially social media, in what has sometimes been dubbed the "republic of Facebook."

When Revolution Brings World Fame to Places

Places, like dates, can become iconic. The Bastille is perhaps the most well known in modern times. The storming of this prison not only ushered in the age of modern revolutions, but also embodied the new world of "*Liberté, egalité, fraternité.*"

[3] Khalid Sa'eed (1982–2010) was arrested by the police in Alexandria and was beaten to death. Photos of his mangled corpse were leaked and went viral on the Internet. The April 6 Youth Movement was established in 2008 by a group of activists in support of workers in the city of El-Mahalla El-Kubra who had chosen 6 April as a date for going on strike.

Each city seems to have its own square: New York's Time Square, London's Trafalgar Square, Madrid's Puerta del Sol, or Beijing's Tiananmen Square.[4] But only a few reach global fame, as Midan Tahrir has done relatively recently. Yet Midan Tahrir in fact has a long association with mass protest in Egypt, one that stretches back many decades. On 25 January 1952, for example, protests also erupted in Al-Midan when British occupation forces in the Suez Canal attacked unarmed Egyptian police forces and massacred dozens of officers. These mass protests led to some downtown areas being set on fire, including the iconic landmark Shepherd's Hotel. Though Tahrir Square is thus engraved in the memory of Egyptians, the 2011 mass protests made it a global symbol of revolt, inspiring other forms of contention such as "Occupy Wall Street." Foreign visitors often ask for hotels near Al-Midan, or to be accompanied there on a tour. US Secretary of State Hillary Clinton and Guido Westerwelle, Germany's foreign minister, made a point of being photographed there soon after the revolution. Such is its fame, Al-Midan is almost Egypt's fourth pyramid.

Tahrir is not in fact a square but is round in shape, a *midan*. It is an arena, a huge public space, with nine entry points that facilitated the arrival of the masses from different corners of the city and beyond. Thus it is both the openness and geographical location of the square that enabled Al-Midan to be politically and socially central to the Egyptian uprising.

In the history of Cairo's urban planning, Tahrir Square was associated with a certain conception of twentieth-century modernity, as Khedive Ismail's mimicry of Europe—Cairo becoming a Paris on the Nile. Tahrir thus emerged as a counterpart to old Islamic districts such as Al-Azhar

[4] For more on Tahrir Square, see *Cairo Districts* [in Arabic]. Squares can also be reflections of other types of revolution. For instance, Times Square is iconic in a different sense. It was named so after the *New York Times* moved in 1904 to mid-town Manhattan on one of the world's busiest intersections, that of Broadway and 7th Avenue. Times Square witnessed the first electronic advertisement, is frequented by about 39 million tourists annually, and is the place to gather to celebrate traditions from the World Series to presidential elections. New York's Mayor Giuliani (1994–2002) chose Times Square to administer the oath of office to his successor, Michael Bloomberg, as part of the 2001–2 New Year celebrations with 500,000 revellers attending. Joe Mckendry, *One Times Square: A Century of Change at the Crossroads of the World*, Jeffrey, NH: David R. Godine, 2012.

and Khan Khalili. The old name of Tahrir—Ismailiya—was actually associated with Khedive Ismail. It was President Gamal Abdel-Nasser and the Free Officers of the new republican regime, claiming to have brought liberty to Egypt, who changed the square's name to Tahrir.

Due to the square's openness and central location, it became the site for the headquarters of different institutions ranging from the Arab League to Egypt's Foreign Ministry and the Egyptian Museum, with the British and American embassies located nearby. With the passage of time, the Omar Makram Mosque and five-star hotels such as the Hilton and the Intercontinental were also built nearby. It is no wonder, then, that Tahrir Square became a popular mass meeting place. During the eighteen days from 25 January to 11 February, Tahrir symbolized the recovery of political public space, becoming almost a liberated mini-state.

Since January 2011, Al-Midan has continued to serve as a source of symbolic and practical significance for the revolution. Beyond its association with the early days of public mobilization and protest, and well after the revolution's eventual victory, Al-Midan is also becoming a symbol of political legitimization. In 2011, for example, the first post-revolution prime minister, Essam Sharaf, was chosen by the "people of Al-Midan"; he accordingly chose to be sworn in at a ceremony in Al-Midan. In June 2012, following his success in the presidential elections, Mohamed Morsi, Egypt's first civilian president, gave his "oath to the people" in Al-Midan prior to swearing the oath of office before the Supreme Constitutional Court. As the mass protests of December 2012 against the draft constitution confirm, Tahrir continues to be an iconic microcosm of the rise and evolving fortunes of the Arab Spring in Egypt and beyond.

Contentious Politics and Group Dynamics

The focus on Al-Midan as the locus of the protests logically invites the choice of "contentious politics" as the most relevant paradigm to decode and understand the situation on the ground. Contentious politics refers to "a phase of heightened conflict across the social system … A combination of organized and unorganized participation and sequences of intensified … information flow and interaction between challenges and authorities."[5] The contentious politics paradigm is useful in the present

[5] Sydney Tarrow, *Power in Movement: Social Movements and Contentious*

context given the intensity and density of the 2011 protests, something which has served to distinguish the "Arab Spring" in Egypt and elsewhere in the region from previous uprisings.

For the purposes of this chapter, it is important to emphasize three pillars of an analytical framework for examining "contentious politics": (a) resource mobilization; (b) political opportunity structure; and (c) frames.

Resource mobilization denotes collective action as the essence of contentious politics.[6] For instance, in January 2011, when Mubarak's government cut off cell phone and Internet facilities, many parents had no choice but to rush to the streets to get news about their sons and daughters. They then witnessed instances of police brutality first hand. Provoked and shocked by this brutality, they spontaneously pulled together for self-defense and the defense of their young. As a result, improvised food chains were initiated, sleeping tents with blankets were brought to Al-Midan, and doctors established emergency clinics. Indeed, the cutting off of communication channels was transformed from a constraint into an opportunity. This example leads to a second conceptual pillar of the contentious politics approach.

Political Opportunity Structure (POS) emphasizes the process itself: why people participate and why their numbers increase in contention. POS is thus a "consistent—but not necessarily formal, permanent or natural—dimension of the political struggle."[7] Consequently, POS is useful in accounting for the evolution of the contention, and for its chances of success or failure.

As mentioned in the example above, the cutting off of communication channels and the ensuing police brutality provoked ordinary people's sentiments so much that their numbers in the streets increased rather

---

Politics, Cambridge: Cambridge University Press, 1998, p. 142. For a wider application by a pioneer of the contentious politics school see Charles Tilly et al., *The Rebellious Century, 1830–1930*, Cambridge, MA: Harvard University Press, 1975.

[6] Though Mancur Olson has pioneered neo-liberal approaches to the collectivity dimension, the current "contentious politics" approach is different and opposes the market-based reasoning of Olson's. Thus contrary to the "free rider" aspect, the present contentious politics approach emphasizes the pooling of political, financial, and cultural resources.

[7] Tarrow, *Power in Movement*, p. 19.

than decreased. As the volume of protestors increased, the police force became overpowered to the point of collapse. The eventual evacuation of the police from the streets indicates an increase in the POS. Another increase in POS arose due to divisions within the political elite. Indeed, an argument took place between Mubarak and his Minister of Interior, Habib Al-Adly, when Mubarak had to ask the armed forces to quell the demonstrations shortly after the police had left, but the army refused to fire on the people. Contrary to the orders given, photos taken in the streets of Cairo, Alexandria, and other cities show scenes of camaraderie between the armed forces and the protestors.

POS thus acts like an open door that protestors realize they can pass through, or, alternatively, a door they realize they are strong enough to push open. POS therefore plays a double role. It is a process factor that accounts for the chances of the protest's success. Equally important, POS addresses the problem of agency versus structure, and acts like a bridge between the two to emphasize the impact of agency—the protestors—in influencing the contention's political results. POS reveals the organic interaction between agency and structure.

This organic interaction could be seen in the street as a result of information provided by both the old and the new media. Satellite stations such as Al Jazeera and Al-Arabiyya are now bolstered by social media sites such as Facebook or Twitter. When the photos of massive protests and camaraderie between armed forces and demonstrators were widely diffused, the media—both old and new—participated in increasing the strength of POS. It has to be noted, however, that the media did not cause the contention; but they certainly fueled it. Communication action is essential to collective action. For people in the localities away from the action, in cities and villages—as well as sympathizers abroad—communication action creates a vivid picture of events and validates the existence of a common cause and a joint frame of action. This brings us to the third pillar of the contentious politics approach: framing.

Frames help people define their interactions in a similar way, thereby coming together (that is to achieve a frame of ideological or cultural alignment). Frames create this cultural and/or ideological glue by offering people "interpretative schemes … to make sense of events." This common perception of events creates a collective, shared feeling that transforms a mass of protestors into a unified and coordinated group.[8]

[8] Ibid.

The paradigm of contentious politics has more often been used in the context of European and US politics than in explaining politics in the Middle East. However, it has implicitly informed some more recent analyses, and it has even been promoted by some as an explicit framework for understanding events in the Middle East.[9] Tahrir Square certainly highlights the applicability of the paradigm's concepts with regard to mobilization and POS. Moreover, since new media have been amply used and have become a characteristic of the Arab Spring, the paradigm's third pillar, framing, is also relevant in accounting for the predominance of new media in Egypt's revolution.

The epistemology underlying the paradigm, and its applicability to contexts beyond the region, raise clear questions regarding the supposed "exceptionalism" of the Middle East.[10] However, certain features specific to the protests in Al-Midan need to be introduced in order to explain the Egyptian uprising. The predominant conceptualization of contentious politics is based on a dichotomy between protestors and the authorities. Though this was initially true of Al-Midan, the events in Tahrir reflected a much more complex situation where there were multiple groups within each camp. The main groups are referred to in this chapter as the three *M*s: the military, comprising both the army and the nineteen-member Supreme Council of the Armed Forces (SCAF); the mosque, a designation of the various currents of Islamists; and thirdly, the masses, a residual category comprised mainly of the liberal–leftist youth and feminist groups. The three *M*s are used here as a shorthand designation for the principal groups containing sub-groups within each *M*, all of which were present in Tahrir.

Organizations such as the April 6 Youth Movement, Kollena Khaled Sa'eed (named after the blogger who was tortured and beaten to death by the police in Alexandria, that is, Egypt's Bouzizi), Kefaya, and ElBaradei's Coalition for Change initiated the mobilization of protestors in the streets on 25 January. They were then joined by other youth groups and formal and non-formal members of different organizations. Established political parties of the opposition declined to join. Even the

[9] Notably the works of Assef Bayat. For example, Asef Bayat, *Life as Politics: How Ordinary People Change the Middle East*, Stanford, CA: Stanford University Press, 2010.

[10] Bahgat Korany, *The Changing Middle East: A New Look at Regional Dynamics*, Cairo: American University in Cairo Press, 2010, pp. 7–42.

Muslim Brotherhood, the most organized and feared opponents of the regime, adopted a wait-and-see attitude. On 25 January, the Brotherhood reaffirmed its opposition to the regime but declined to participate as an organization. However, some of its younger members disobeyed and joined their peers in Tahrir. Group diversity also existed within the third *M*, the liberal–leftist masses. By definition, the latter are an agglomerate of diverse groups with a range of ideological differences. They found themselves united in the aim of ousting the existing Mubarak regime, even if some of the feminist groups had approved of the regime's gender policies. Diversity similarly existed within the first *M*, the military. The regime's most central pillar finally dissented and joined the opposition.[11] Indeed, the military's assertion of political independence reflected fragmentation within the highest circles of the political pyramid. It was not simply a matter of top commanders jumping ship.

Thus although the contentious politics paradigm is relevant and useful in decoding Tahrir's microcosm, it has to be supplemented with a recognition of "group diversity." Without this, any explanation of the events in Tahrir will be far too simplistic.

If Egypt is not to be analyzed as a monolithic society, neither should its microcosm, Tahrir Square. Though Al-Midan might appear as a predominantly Cairene representation, in the process of the January revolution it became a national one. In addition to the middle-class youth who initiated the revolution, many young Egyptians poured in from Cairo's slums, to be joined by people from the countryside (the opposite of the Tunisian pattern). As a result, Al-Midan became a national melting pot, with even young, unveiled women moving freely in a city infamous for sexual harassment. In addition to this mix of people from across the country, as well as different genders and social classes, one of the most notable features of Al-Midan in its early phase was the sheer number of young people present in the square. This reflects the demographics of Egypt and the region as a whole, where people under thirty years of age constitute almost two-thirds of the population. Thus although the Al-Midan microcosm was a national phenomenon—comprising the rich and the poor, males and females, and urban and rural citizens alike—the predominant feature of the initial phase of the protests was the vast number of young people who gathered in Tahrir.

[11] This is substantiated by photos of the military in Tahrir mingling with the protestors, including some photos of protestors on tanks with "army brothers."

In fact, when parents and the older generation joined the protests, they tended to play a supporting role to the youthful initiators by providing medical supplies, food and drinks, and blankets. The older generation did not initiate the protests in Tahrir Square, and they even hesitated before joining them. Their physical participation came by coincidence, due mainly to a miscalculation on the part of the authorities in cutting off access to cell phones and the Internet. As explained above, this move backfired as parents had no alternative but to go on to the streets, and join the youth in greater numbers to overpower the police forces. Unintentionally, then, the authorities' increased the protestors' POS and added credibility to the youthful revolt. In a society where advanced age still symbolized wisdom and maturity, the older generation's participation provided legitimacy to youthful enthusiasm. This participation broadened the base and added to the multi-group diversity of Al-Midan, a diversity that would increase with the passage of time.

Mapping the Different Groups

The Military

The military is used here to refer to the governing regime, both as a formerly unified force and later as a fragmented entity in the face of the Tahrir Square protests.

Mubarak was the fourth military president to have assumed power since Egypt became a republic in 1953.[12] His regime became increasingly obsessed with maintaining security—it could even be described as a "securocracy"—and was accordingly very dependent on the secret police. Though the army profited from $1.3 billion per annum in aid from the United States, the Ministry of the Interior's budget continually grew from the 1990s onwards at a much faster rate than that of the army. This became an element of concern and a source of jealousy for the armed

[12] For a recent overview and fieldwork research by two experts on the subject see Yezid Sayegh, *Above the State: The Officers' Republic in Egypt*, Washington, DC, and Beirut: Carnegie Endowment, Aug. 2012; and Hazem Kandil, "Back on the Horse? The Military between Two Revolutions," in Bahgat Korany and Rabab El-Mahdi (eds), *The Arab Spring in Egypt: Revolution and Beyond*, Cairo: American University in Cairo Press, 2012.

forces. The secret police even seemed to control the state bureaucracy, as it had the final say in the nominations of ministers, top media personnel, and even the deans and heads of university departments.

Yet surprisingly, the demonstrators were able to overpower this repressive structure in less than three days. On 28 January, the minister of interior was rebuked by Mubarak and told to stay at home. As police forces were deserting their posts and fleeing, the army was asked to go on to the streets. The collapse of the police was the first open rift at the top, but regime fragmentation continued. The newly appointed secretary general of the governing National Democratic Party (NDP), Hossam Badrawi, was not allowed to start his job and ultimately had to resign. Even when Mubarak was pressured to appoint a vice president after twenty-nine years of refusing to do so, he chose his confidant, the all-powerful head of intelligence, Omar Suleiman. But Suleiman's appointment was resisted, and the fact that he was the victim of an assassination attempt before his appointment could be made public indicates that the attempt on his life came from the regime's inner circle. In fact, the taciturn Suleiman is on record as linking this assassination attempt with Gamal Mubarak and his associates who believed that his appointment would endanger plans for Gamal to succeed his father in the presidency.[13] Fragmentation and group multiplicity within the regime came to the fore with the quasi-defection of the army, the most important base of the regime's material power. This defection did not start with the army formally taking power after Mubarak's official departure on 11 February. The army's independent role had already started on 28 January, when troops went on to the streets to replace the fleeing police. Some soldiers in fact joined the protestors in reciting the slogan "People and Army are One." Though somewhat unnoticed, the second meeting of the Supreme Military Council was held in early February without Mubarak's presence—contrary to the first meeting a few days earlier—although he was technically still its supreme head.

Once formally in power after 11 February, the military, through the Supreme Council of the Armed Forces (SCAF), emphasized that it was on the side of the revolution. A content analysis of 140 SCAF documents—from official statements to press/website releases—revealed the

[13] Gehad El-Khazen's account of his meeting with Omar Suleiman in his column, *El-Hayat*, 8 Aug. 2012.

military's emphasis on its role as "protector of the revolution" and "shield of the homeland."[14] Willingly or unwillingly, it was the military that arrested and put on trial their former governing partners and their boss: from Mubarak to the two speakers of the People's Assembly and El-shoura Council (upper house), as well as several ministers and Mubarak's two sons. After 25 January, SCAF—the dissenting part of the old regime—almost became the new regime and in the process became the most important base for this evolving political process. But the developments of 2012–13 show that the battle for political control between military and mosque has yet to come to an end.[15]

The Mosque

If the military and the police represent the "deep state" (even after retirement, high-ranking officers from the army and the police continued to serve as governors and heads of civilian state bureaucracies), Islamist organizations represent "deep society." When the Muslim Brotherhood, for instance, was pushed underground for most of its eighty-four years of existence—officially dubbed "*al-mahzoura*" or extra-legal—the organization's socio-political roots remained strong.

The Islamists were able to achieve this in a number of ways. First, the widespread diffusion of its social units at the grass roots level—clinics, educational tutoring, informal banking—constituted a huge social capital for mass backing of different shades of Islamists, especially in the rural areas.[16] Secondly, "the mosque" held face-to-face meetings, poten-

[14] Fatma Abdel-Fattah, "This is How SCAF Talked," *El-Masry El-Youm*, 15 Aug. 2012, pp. 15–17.

[15] On 12 Aug. 2012, however, another important episode in political control took place: the sacking of the old military guard. The newly elected president had begun a few days earlier by firing the all-powerful head of intelligence. He followed suit by appointing a new minister of defense, a new chief of staff, and new heads of the navy, air force, and army. Amid speculation that the Islamist president was proceeding with the Muslim Brotherhood's project to Islamize the country, the military deposed President Morsi in July 2013, dissolved his Cabinet, and installed an interim administration pending new elections. The Muslim Brotherhood was subsequently banned amid what many considered a military coup. In Jan. 2014, a new constitution was approved in a popular referendum.

[16] For early fieldwork tracing this grassroots aspect in one important sec-

tially five times a day, in addition to a weekly general assembly during Friday noon prayers. Even in developed countries such political coordination and institutionalization are rarely present. As a result, the Muslim Brotherhood was among the best placed in terms of its political organization to mobilize and protest, and, eventually, to take over the reins of government. But divisions existed even here.

Soon after the January revolution the Brotherhood discovered it was not the only organization talking in the name of Islam. While the Sufi groups were still reluctant to play an explicit political role, Salafi or ultra-conservative groups were active and enthusiastic to compete in the elections, and despite their relatively recent political mobilization, they were able to win around 25 percent of the seats in the first post-January parliament. The Salafis also presented a very popular presidential candidate who was barred at the last minute from competing in the presidential election campaign. They continue to be strong among many mosque imams with the impact of their sermons being evident in the streets, especially in the countryside.

By 28 January, the tide was already turning against the regime. This coincided with the Brotherhood's decision to join the demonstrations. However, the regime reacted to the Brotherhood's decision by arresting its key leaders, including a handful of Executive Committee members. But the Brotherhood was not deterred. Its four statements between 29 January and 1 February show an escalation in terms of the type of rhetoric used, with the last statement calling on Mubarak to step down.

In the background, however, Islamists continued to be fragmented and their top leadership was becoming divided. The Brotherhood itself had already realized, on the eve of 25 January, that dissidents existed within its own membership. When it declined to go to Tahrir as a political organization on 25 January, it soon realized that many of its young members were not willing to comply. It consequently had to leave participation open to individual choice, and many of its young members flooded Tahrir Square to join their peers from other groups and organi-

---

tor where the state is deficient, see Janine Clark, "Democratisation and Social Islam: A Case Study of the Islamic Health Clinics in Cairo," in Rex Brynen, Bahgat Korany, and Paul Noble (eds), *Political Liberalization and Democratization in the Arab World*, Boulder, CO: Lynne Rienner, 1995, vol. 1, pp. 167–86.

zations, unifying their cause. The Brotherhood constantly changed its position until 28 January, thereby reflecting the different currents within its ranks.[17]

For their part, on 30 January the Salafis condemned the "destruction of public property," which signified their unease about aspects of the protests. The Sufi orders as well as the official Islamic establishment remained silent. Following Mubarak's second speech on 1 February, Al-Azhar's grand sheikh and Egypt's grand mufti both hailed Mubarak's announcement that he would not stand for a new mandate in September 2011.

In all these Islamic arenas, a generational divide seemed to exist to varying degrees. Some Sufi sheikhs, Al-Azhar's young scholars, and young Brotherhood members joined protestors in Tahrir Square. Young Islamic activists, even members of the Brotherhood, criticized the top leadership who had agreed to participate in a dialogue with the newly appointed Vice President Omar Suleiman. The pressure worked and the Brotherhood withdrew after the first round of talks. With the passage of time and the increasing retreat of the regime, various Islamist groups closed ranks. Thus the official religious establishment remained silent and refrained from public support, whereas others suggested a road map for the post-Mubarak era.

The (Liberal–Leftist) Masses

As the liberal–leftist masses manifested a great deal of multiplicity and diversity, it is harder to delineate this category than the other groups discussed above. It is indeed a group of groups.

A convenient distinction, however, can be drawn between labor groups and other groups. Labor is more institutionalized and more easily identifiable.[18] Its groups feel that pioneered the process long before

[17] Ibrahim El-Houdaiby, "Islamism in and after Egypt's Revolution," in Bahgat Korany and Rabab El-Mahdi (eds), *The Arab Spring in Egypt: Revolution and Beyond*, Cairo and New York: American University in Cairo Press, 2012; and for a comparative approach of the official religious discourse, both Islamic and Christian, see Nadine Sika, "Dynamics of a Stagnant Religious Discourse and the Rise of New Secular Movements in Egypt," in Korany and El-Mahdi, *The Arab Spring in Egypt*.

[18] For specific focus on the workers' role leading to the Tahrir protests, see Dina Bishara, "The Power of Workers in Egypt's 2011 Uprising," in Korany and El-Mahdi, *The Arab Spring in Egypt*.

anyone else. According to some estimates, during the four-year period between 2006 and 2009, more than 2 million workers engaged in more than 2,100 strikes, sit-ins, and other forms of protest.[19] Content analysis of workers' demands shows that they tended to be rather sectorial and much more focused on immediate material issues such as wages, working hours, and working conditions. However, these demonstrations and protests established the principle of public contentious politics and showed the means and effectiveness of mobilization tactics. Moreover, in their confrontation with the police, workers demonstrated that the fear of authority was declining in Egypt. In this sense, their protests served to lay the foundations for what would follow, while their seemingly sectorial demands constituted a prelude to the centrality of social justice demands that characterized the later Tahrir slogans.[20]

Youth Groups and their Political Socialization Organizations

The extent of group multiplicity and diversity was at its highest within the youth component of the masses gathered in the square. At first glance such diversity seems counter-intuitive. Tahrir is commonly perceived as a reflection of a unified youth front. Indeed, the youth pioneered the protests and displayed the expected unity emanating from peer-group feelings and a common mindset. This togetherness came from shared problems, a shared worldview, and shared behavioral reactions. Generally, youth are accepted as a unit of analysis not only in the Middle East, but around the world.[21]

This youth commonality notwithstanding, multiple youth groups existed and were even institutionalized before 25 January. Despite fever-

[19] For a convenient recent introduction and fieldwork research, see Joel Beinen and Hossam el-Hamalawy, "Strikes in Egypt Spread from Center of Gravity," Middle East Report online, 9 May 2007; Joel Beinin, "The Egyptian Workers Movement in 2007," Cairo, Chroniques du CEDEJ (Centre d'Études et de Documentations économiques, juridiqes et sociales), 2007, http://www.cedej-eg.org/spip.php?rubrique35

[20] For more details about labor mobilization in Egypt, see Marie Duboc's chapter in this volume.

[21] Amani Kandil, "Youth in the Arab World," Annual Report of the Arab Organisation for Civil Society Organisations, Cairo 2007 [in Arabic]; World Bank, *A Generation in Waiting*, New York: World Bank, 2008; and for an overview Dina Shehata, "Youth Movements and the 25 January Revolution," pp. 105–124, in Korany and El-Mahdi, *The Arab Spring in Egypt*.

ish efforts at coordination in Tahrir Square, multiplicity persisted and was even accentuated after Mubarak's departure. In fact, many analysts attribute the difficulties of the post-February transition as well as some successes of the "counter-revolution" to the fragmentation and division of the youth groups. When SCAF launched one of its "national dialogues" in the autumn of 2011, it announced that as many as 153 youth groups had agreed to participate. These groups did not encompass all the existing youth groups, as many and some of the best-known declined to participate. The main point here is that in the post-January era, many organizations were established, many of which existed in name only. Therefore the emphasis here is on those organizations which conducted their protests both in public and before they actually came en masse to Tahrir Square.

Many members of these youth organizations received their initial political socialization and public training from emerging mass protest organizations rather than established political parties. Kefaya is a prime example of this.[22]

Kefaya ("Enough", or Egyptian Movement for Change) was a true pioneer and catalyst of street protests. Kefaya worked outside the main opposition political parties and did not have any explicit institutional link with established civil society organizations. Its formal origins can be traced to the street protests against the 2003 US invasion of Iraq, and against Egypt's initial tacit approval of the invasion. Kefaya's main contention, however, was the regime's domestic practices of corruption and nepotism, and especially the ever contentious issue of the presidential succession, with Gamal Mubarak being groomed to succeed his father. Such opposition formally came into existence in August 2004, when around 300 signatories called for political reform, which entailed instituting direct presidential elections among competing candidates. These signatories included mainly middle-class intellectuals, journalists, university professors, and other professionals. Their 12 December protest was a "first," making it historically significant. Between 500 and 1,000 activists stood on the steps of Cairo's High Court, surrounded by an almost equal number of anti-riot police and secret service elements. To avoid violent confrontation, when they were outnumbered at this early

[22] Manar El-Shorbagy, "Kefaya," in Dina Shehata (ed.), *Return of Politics*, Cairo: Al-Ahram Center for Political and Strategic Studies, 2010 [in Arabic].

stage, the activists remained silent with the word "*kefaya*" written on tape covering their lips.

Kefaya's members attacked the government for its gravely deficient social welfare policies, the lack of job creation, the deteriorating quality of education, and widespread corruption. Journalist Abdel-Halim Kandil, the spokesman for the movement until the beginning of 2007, stated: "Our movement targets Egyptians. We want them to put away their fears and demand their political and economic rights."[23]

It is this domestic focus, this call for the end of fear, and the explicit public politicization of the middle class that justify identifying Kefaya as a truly pioneering movement. Kandil was kidnapped, beaten up, and thrown half-naked with broken spectacles into the desert outskirts of Cairo. But this intimidation did not prevent him from writing two books, with his second title, which featured a quasi-disfigured Mubarak face on the cover, prophetically announcing *The End of the Mubarak Regime*. Thus Kefaya's criticisms of the regime were not only explicit and political in nature, but even went so far as to target the head of the regime. In retrospect, its rhetoric can consequently be seen as a precursor to the youth shouts in Tahrir Square in January: "*Yaskot yaskot hukm Mubarak*!" (Down, down with Mubarak!).

Kefaya was also a precursor to the Tahrir Square mass youth protests in two other respects. First, it acted outside the main established political parties, which are mistrusted by the youth and regarded as part of the outdated established system. Apart from coordination and collaboration with some human rights activists, Kefaya kept its distance from many civil society organizations which were perceived as being too close to the regime or else beholden to foreign donors. Kefaya even kept its distance from other mass-based opposition movements such as the Muslim Brotherhood. Kefaya's distancing from established structures made it more attractive to young people. Second, not only was Kefaya secular, it also continually sought to emphasize its "non-ideological" character. It acted as a national front organization, bringing in all shades of Egyptians: Muslims, Copts, liberals, leftists, and many human rights activists, including those lobbying for women's rights. Kefaya's orientation inspired other branch organizations such as "Journalists for Change,"

[23] Farhad Khosrokhavar, *The New Arab Revolutions that Shook the World*, Boulder, CO: Paradigm Publishers, 2012, p. 44.

"Doctors for Change," and even "Youth for Change." In 2005, Misr Digital became Kefaya's online source of information, emphasizing the impact of new media that would become Tahrir's trademark. Google's executive, Wael Ghoneim, and his proficiency with this new media, after all, were the basis for Kollena Khalid S'eed, a pillar of Tahrir.

At the time, Kefaya did not gain the success it merited because it was narrow in terms of mobilization. It was mainly an urban phenomenon, geographically limited even further to certain parts of downtown Cairo, and it tended to remain so throughout its existence. Moreover, it was not only recruited from the middle class, but also led by middle-aged men. The young within its ranks were marginalized. But Kefaya was also hindered by the prevailing political situation. Certain characteristics of the Egyptian political milieu, and the prevalence of feelings of fear and a belief that protest was futile, worked against its efforts at mass mobilization. Bouzizi's self-immolation and Ben Ali's hasty flight from Tunisia had yet to take place, and thus the favorable political context needed for Tahrir's protests and for helping mass mobilization by youth organizations had still to be created. Three of these youth organizations deserve special attention.

The National Coalition for Change/ElBaradei

In composition and ideological orientation, this group falls somewhere in-between Kefaya and the overtly youth organizations such as April 6 Youth Movement and Kollena Khalid Sa'eed. The National Coalition for Change is identified with Mohammed ElBaradei (b.1942)—a former diplomat, former head of the International Atomic Energy Agency, and Nobel Prize winner. These impressive credentials functioned as valuable assets (and also liabilities) in his leadership of mass protests on the eve of the Tahrir protests.

Even before retiring in December 2009 from his highly visible international post, ElBaradei went on record to criticize the Egyptian regime, insisting on the necessity of drastic political reform. He suggested reducing the mandate for the presidency, the necessity of multiple candidates, and complete transparency in the election process. Prior to his making these criticisms, Mubarak had received and honored ElBaradei with the highest Egyptian award following his 2005 Nobel Prize. But the regime's tone toward him changed when he began to criticize it. An orchestrated media campaign was carried out via the government press, which included a campaign against his family (e.g. the diffusion of carefully chosen pictures of his daughter in a swimsuit amid wine glasses). But this strategy backfired. If anything, the regime's volte face toward ElBaradei confirmed its hypocrisy and obsession with eliminating any potential rival to Gamal Mubarak's succession. Indeed, this governmental persecution only increased ElBaradei's popularity—contrary to the established opposition parties, he now appeared to be the honest "outsider" and a credible political alternative.

When ElBaradei returned to Egypt on 19 February 2010, the scene at Cairo airport was reminiscent of a national celebration, worthy of a national hero. Though the numbers of the welcoming crowd were relatively small, about 2,000 people in total, those who were present had courageously overcome police barriers and harassment. The crowd, headed by a few political activists, included a large number of young people, especially from governorates outside Cairo, who raised Egyptian flags and banners of support for ElBaradei's calls for political reform. The scene appeared to be an all-national protest movement in support of immediate political change, a movement keen and happy to find its national leader.

ElBaradei, bolstered by this enthusiastic support, met with different currents of the political spectrum. They all reiterated the need for immediate constitutional change and the abolition of the thirty-year state of emergency law as a prelude to general political reform. Like Kefaya, ElBaradei acted outside the established political parties. He ignored and was ignored by official media. But such official neglect did not have a negative effect on his political visibility. On the contrary, he was interviewed extensively in a range of private media outlets, including newspapers and TV talk shows aired at peak hours. Moreover, Facebook and various online forums used by young activists added to his visibility among the youth.[24] Many of these activists subsequently joined his campaign. *The Times*' correspondent, Ashraf Khalil, documents this youth involvement and enthusiasm:

[24] Wael Ghoneim, *Revolution 2.0*, Cairo: Dar El-Shorouk, 2012. (I am using the Arabic edition to respect the intention of the author—the admin of the site Kollena Khaled Sa'eed—who insisted on using colloquial Arabic to avoid "elitism." But an English edition was published at the same time.)

> In the summer of 2010, I accompanied a group of El-Baradei volunteers gathering signatures in Hadayek Helwan, a middle class Cairo suburb … The evening was a clear window not only into the power of El-Baradei's appeal … The volunteers, led by volunteer Maha El Gamal were a diverse bunch—Moslems and Christians, veiled women alongside fashionable ladies in tight jeans with bejewelled belt buckles. They worked their way up the street, approaching passers-by, local fruit sellers and store owners, even calling up to residents looking down from their balconies.
>
> El-Baradei's seven-point list of petition demands amounted to sweeping domestic reform and would have required the re-writing of three separate articles of the constitution. It included the establishment of international polling station monitoring and the removal of legal obstacles designed to prevent an independent presidential candidacy.
>
> But it was the first demand—the immediate repeal of the emergency laws—that struck the strongest chord with ordinary citizens, and El-Baradei's volunteers knew that was their strongest card to play.[25]

ElBaradei's initial success was due not only to his courage and sincerity but also to his immunity from the fear that had prevented many Egyptians from opposing the regime. As a well-known international civil servant and Nobel Prize winner, he knew that the regime would hesitate before hurting him. "I had a sort of immunity so I could speak a little louder," he told Khalil in the summer of 2010.[26]

But ElBaradei's immunity from fear or police torture was not enough to guarantee the sort of success that would subsequently ensue in Tahrir Square. Though an important figure, ElBaradei was never part of the local protest movement and even appeared to stay deliberately outside it. Despite being a potential presidential candidate, ElBaradei placed too much emphasis on his international schedule and ultimately spent more time outside Egypt in 2009–10 than he did within the country. One of his senior deputies, fellow political scientist Hassan Nafaa, repeated to me how frustrating, dysfunctional, and even demoralizing ElBaradei's absence was. Nafaa, like many others, was sad to abandon the project, despite his absolute commitment to the cause. These repeated absences meant that ElBaradei was often seen as distant from the masses. Ashraf Khalil's remarks are revealing in this regard:

[25] Ashraf Khalil, *Liberation Square*, Cairo and New York: AUC Press, 2012, p. 108.
[26] Ibid. p. 110.

a pivotal moment [in understanding this handicap] came on June 25th 2010 when he attended—amid great hype—the protest in Alexandria in memory of Khalid Sa'eed. Anger was running high, especially in Alexandria, and ordinary apolitical citizens were starting to uncharacteristically take to the streets. El-Baradei's planned attendance had stoked expectations that this would be the real start of his street-level campaign against the Mubarak regime.

Instead he lasted less than ten minutes in public, waving to the crowd and giving a short interview to CNN before departing. The disappointment among spectators was palpable …

Six months later, I interviewed El-Baradei for more than an hour at his home in a posh gated community near the pyramids. He struck me as a sincere, intelligent man who clearly understood the depths of Egypt's problems and was upset about all the right things …

I could not help but ask him about that day in Alexandria. When I put forth the theory that he just didn't seem comfortable being the centre of attention in large crowds, the normally self-assured and verbose El-Baradei actually stammered a bit, seemingly lost for words. His wife, Aida, who was sitting with us, chimed in reassuringly, "Don't worry, you will get better at it".

In recalling that demonstration, El-Baradei made a comment that speaks volumes about his life experience. He remembered emerging from the downtown Alexandria mosque after noon prayers and surveying the three-thousand strong crowd, surrounded as usual by a massive deployment of black-clad riot police.

"It was the first time I've seen all this Central Security. It was like a war zone. It was an amazing scene to me to realise how repressive and how much of a police state we have become", he told me. I was shocked; the fact that he had never seen a Central Security deployment basically meant that he had never attended a single demonstration in Egypt.[27]

ElBaradei's young supporters, newly disillusioned, were again left to themselves. "It was a disaster," explained Maha El-Gamal—the long-time activist working with ElBaradei. She added: "El-Baradei surrounded himself with amateurs and opportunists who were never on the same page with each other."[28]

Young protestors had no choice but to depend on themselves in order to establish their own organizations. Two of these have been central in El-Tahrir: Harakat Shabab 6 Abril (April 6 Youth Movement) and Kollena Khaled Sa'eed.

[27] Ibid. pp. 112–14.
[28] Ibid. p. 111.

Harakat Shabab 6 Abril

The creation of the April 6 Youth Movement coincided with the mass labor protests of 6 April 2008. These took place in El-Mehalla Al-Kobra, an industrial textile town located in the middle of the Delta. In that year labor unrest had intensified in response to police repression, with protestors also demanding higher wages to counterbalance rising food prices.[29] The Harakat's founders were all young men and women, with Ahmed Maher, Asmaa Mahfouz, and Israa Abdel-Fattah, who later became very active in Tahrir Square, subsequently becoming household names. By 2009, the movement could count on connections with about 70,000 young and educated sympathizers.

As some of its members had visited Serbia in order to see how non-violent means had toppled Slobodan Milošević, they tended to promote similar tactics in Egypt. But such a *silmeyia* (non-violent) approach did not prevent police attacks and repression. On 6 April 2009, the Harakat was attacked, its websites hacked, and many of its members arrested. Though their demonstrations failed to rally more than a few hundred people, the movement learned how to organize a convergence of protestors to a central point from numerous street directions. This was a technique that finally overpowered police forces around Tahrir Square during the January revolution and forced them to flee. Harakat members also learned how to mitigate the effects of tear gas by covering their faces with handkerchiefs soaked in vinegar and how to make rudimentary armor for use against the riot police. These tactics were to prove vital in the success of Tahrir Square.[30] National and international networking was also a characteristic of these youth movements, as seen with the Kollena Khaled Sa'eed movement.

Kollena Khaled Sa'eed

Sa'eed was a 28-year-old who was arrested and publicly beaten to death by police in Alexandria in June 2010. Contrary to police claims that he

[29] Beinen and Hamalawy, *Strikes in Egypt*. Hamalawy—the well-known blogger—was himself a frequent visitor to El-Mahalla, long before the 2008 strikes, and continued to visit afterwards.

[30] Parents, shopkeepers, some residents, and many passers-by were very active in offering the needed supplies.

had choked to death on drugs, photos that his brother had taken, which were later circulated on the Internet, showed his mutilated, beaten body lying in the morgue. Like Tunisia's Bouzizi, who triggered the long-suppressed resistance against Ben Ali, Khaled Sa'eed became a symbol of police brutality and the callous state in Egypt. Mass protest movements usually need a spark to ignite them, and Sa'eed's torture and mutilation—much like Bouzizi's self-immolation—provided this spark. A correspondent for *The Times* witnessed how ElBaradei's supporters used the Khaled Sa'eed case to incite people to mobilize and rise up:

> Mehitab Jellani, a young veiled woman and long-time political activist, kept a copy in her purse of Khaled Sa'eed's iconic autopsy, pulling it out to remind the undecided about the casual daily police brutality that had become commonplace under the emergency laws.[31]

Wael Ghoneim, Google's Middle East executive and the secret administrator of Kollena Khaled Sa'eed, starts his book on the organization with a description of his kidnapping on the streets of downtown Cairo just a few days before the January revolution erupted in Tahrir Square. He recounts how the illuminated downtown streets suddenly became shrouded in darkness when he was pushed into a car, handcuffed, and blindfolded. One of the two security policemen holding him pushed his head down to his knees so that nobody outside could see what was happening, in contrast to the public beating of Khaled Sa'eed. But once Ghoneim arrived at the secret police headquarters, the beating started in earnest amid a mixture of sadistic police laughter and insults.[32] In contrast to the torture of Khaled Sa'eed, Ghoneim was blindfolded and did not know where the flood of kicks and slaps would come from. Ghoneim appropriately titles his first chapter "The Republic of Fear."

The title of Ghoneim's autobiography and documentation of the Kollena Khaled Sa'eed site is also revealing: "The Power of the People is Greater than the People in Power." His life history and personal testament amply confirm this title.[33] The website and its administration are

[31] Khalil, *Liberation Square*, p. 109.

[32] More horrible torture details were also confirmed to me by another peaceful activist that was a former student. Long after his street arrest/prison experience, he remained so traumatized that he found it difficult to continue to talk about his experience, even tête-à-tête.

[33] *Time Magazine* put Ghoneim in first place on its 2011 list of the world's 100 most influential people. Arabian Business ranked him second on its list

an embodiment of the mobilizing impact of social media on the road to Tahrir.[34] The call for the 25 January event was diffused through the website and its network.

Though social media did not make the revolution, they certainly fueled it. They also substantiated the third pillar of the contentious politics paradigm: framing. Instant messaging activated a community of frustration that acted as a collective force in the streets. The impact of social media continued and was self-generating when Ghoneim remained in solitary confinement for eleven days. Moreover, if Google had not publicized the cry "Where is Ghoneim?" at a global level he may well have become another Khaled Sa'eed. Social media assets were directed toward the service of one whom the youth had thought and hoped to be Egypt's savior: ElBaradei. Although ElBaradei was extremely appreciative of having the social media asset with its 150,000 visitors, Ghoneim, as we saw above, became disappointed and dropped out. The death of Khaled Sa'eed, however, brought him back to political activism through the effective use of social media.

The establishment of the Kollena Khaled Sa'eed site came as an immediate reaction to Ghoneim's traumatic experience of seeing the disfigured face of a young man like himself publicly beaten to death. In fact, his wife caught him crying feverishly in his home office and had to calm him down. However, what Ghoneim needed to reduce his suffering was to take some positive action, and to awaken others from their passivity. The site was then designed as a call for action against this widespread and extreme police brutality. It is written in colloquial Arabic to avoid any elitist rhetoric and to reach as many people as possible. The reaction was certainly impressive: 300 subscribers in the first two minutes, 3,000 in the first hour, then 100,000 about a week later

---

of the world's 500 most influential Arabs. He continued to enjoy audience-packed rooms in book-signing ceremonies. When Caroline Kennedy presented him with the JFK Profile in Courage Award in May 2012, she stated that he was receiving it in the name of the Egyptian people.

[34] In the case of Ghoneim, and even before becoming an ME Google Executive, social media had shaped his life as that of his generation, politically, professionally, and even personally. Ghoneim talks about how he dated his future wife, Ilka Johannson, an American Muslim, through the Internet. Ghoneim, *Revolution 2.0*, pp. 27–8.

before settling at 250,000 frequent visitors.[35] The language used is vehement, rebellious, lively, and highly provocative, with reference to folk songs in order to energize mass feelings of protest and translate them into action. The site was also connected to other website pages such as El-Naggar's of the ElBaradei campaign, and to well-established bloggers such as the award-winner Wael Abbas. With such networking, this site substantiates the idea of social media as a revolutionary alternative to the established press and TV media. As the Kollena Khaled Sa'eed group repeatedly insisted: Egypt should not be the same as it was before this young man's death. Indeed, change was taking place.

Analysis of the site before January 2011 reveals the flow of suggestions on how to carry out this change. Ideas focused on means of protest and the practice of street politics. They proposed to start mobilizing in Alexandria and to spread shortly thereafter to Cairo and other Egyptian cities. Reuters estimated that one of the protests in Alexandria involved 8,000 participants.[36]

Part of the mobilization strategy was to shame the regime with regard to some of its actions, such as the excessive and crude fraud evident in the 2010 parliamentary elections, which was orchestrated by a close Gamal Mubarak confidant, businessman Ahmed Ezz. In the outcome of these elections, the governing NDP "won" 90 percent of the seats. The site repeated street jokes and commented sarcastically on Ezz's three self-congratulatory *Al-Ahram* articles hailing the popularity of the NDP. A special file, titled "Black Day of Egypt's Elections," included numerous photos that documented the widespread fraud. The strategy made clear that this election fraud was part and parcel of continuous regime failings.

A few days before 25 January, the site published what it sarcastically described as regime "achievements," one of which was the number of suicides in the previous four years, 12,000 in total, with 5,000 suicides in 2009 alone. There were more than 100,000 attempted suicides per year, which is five times higher than the 2005 rate. More than two-thirds of these suicides were by people less than twenty-five years of age. The site's source of data was no less than the government's Central Body for Statistics, as reported by the equally governmental *Al-Ahram* newspaper.[37]

[35] Ibid. p. 135.
[36] Ibid. p. 97.
[37] Ibid. p. 181.

Mobilization efforts intensified in preparation for 25 January. The site published a six-page reminder of the government's "achievements."[38] These included youth unemployment, systemic corruption at the highest levels, widespread poverty, increasing levels of child anemia, and growing rates of national depression. The site specified four demands to be immediately met in order to cope with the disastrous situation, such as abolishing the state of emergency laws and limiting the presidential mandate. It concluded by specifying meeting points for mass protests: four in Cairo, two in Alexandria, two in Ismailia, as well as others in Mahalla El-Kubra, Tanta, and Souhag. There were suggestions for slogans, including two inspired by the Tunisian revolution. Also included in the site's publication were practical guidelines for demonstrator protection and maximum effectiveness.[39]

And eventually the 25 January demonstration took place. After a long day and night in Tahrir Square, the site administrator wrote: "January 25th is not the end of the regime but the beginning of its end."[40] Social media were vital, not only in mobilizing people for that day in Tahrir Square, but also in saving Ghoneim from Khaled Sa'eed's fate. When he was released on 7 February, he was received by no less a figure than the minister of the interior. He was accompanied home by the newly appointed secretary general of the NDP, Dr Hossam Badrawi. When negotiating his appearance on one of the most popular talk shows, "The 10 p.m.," he imposed his conditions: to speak uninterrupted, and to receive a fee of 1 million Egyptian pounds that were to be given in his name to the families of the 25 January martyrs. Both conditions were immediately accepted.[41] During the program, the vision of Ghoneim collapsing into tears when discussing the martyrs before storming out of the studio served to further highlight the callous nature of the outgoing regime. Its end was in sight, as Mubarak finally stepped down three days later, on 11 February.

Conclusion

Tahrir Square has become an iconic symbol of the "Arab Spring," depicting the peak of contentious politics and inspiring other movements in

[38] Ibid. pp. 189–94.
[39] Ibid. p. 188.
[40] Ibid. p. 200.
[41] This refers to a talk-show with well-known anchor woman Mona El-Shazly.

Libya, Syria, and Wall Street. In terms of Middle Eastern politics and society, Tahrir primarily reflected the by-passing of the established opposition politics represented by the traditional political parties, and even many civil society organizations. Tahrir brought in new political actors that are here to stay, indicating the rising complexity of the "evolving ruling bargain."

Though active and inspiring as a unified "national front," these new political actors have not rallied around a consensual program of action or an identifiable leadership. In this sense they are at the opposite extreme of Egypt's "1952 revolution," which was initially a military coup, reflecting the military's mindset of extreme discipline and hierarchy. In contrasting the 1952 and 2011 episodes, the assets and liabilities of extreme vertical versus horizontal organization are clearly visible.

The new actors in 2011 are proud of the horizontal organization of their movements, the spontaneity of their action, and the absence of a clear leader. In an interview with the influential US TV program "60 Minutes," the system administrator of Kollena Khaled Sa'eed told Harry Smith:

> Our revolution is like Wikipedia, okay? Everyone is contributing content, you don't know the names of the people contributing the content. This is exactly what happened. Revolution 2.0 in Egypt was exactly the same. Everyone contributing small pieces, bits and pieces. We drew this whole picture of a revolution. And no-one is the hero in that picture.[42]

This statement describes the movement's horizontal organization and reflects the faith that its members have in it. As a result, the middle-class youth and the social media that fueled the 25 January revolution are now joined in Tahrir by other groups, from soccer fans known as Ultras to Egypt's slum dwellers, pedlars, and even some thugs. Tahrir thus retains its iconic nature as a reflection of evolving state–society relations and the bargain for political control. It embodies Egypt's multiple competing legitimacies and mirrors transition challenges.

These competing legitimacies and transition challenges underline the present complexity of the "evolving ruling bargain." This complexity is

[42] Stated in an interview on "60-Minutes," http://techpresident.com/blog/entry/ghoneim-ourrevolution-wikipedia (accessed 8 July 2012). He repeats the same idea, reiterating his strong faith in horizontal organization. Ghoneim, *Revolution 2.0*, p. 165.

not only defined by the presence of multiple new actors, but also by the learning of new roles by old actors. Whereas youth and their organizations have to be familiar with the evolving "rules of the game," Islamists face their own political learning curve. As parliamentarians, as ministers, and even as the president of the republic, they have to adapt to a change in political status from opposition and underground action to the practice of (accountable) government—whether alone or in partnership with other political groups. With the military's overthrow of Morsi and the banning of the Muslim Brotherhood in 2013, competing legitimacies are likely to continue to undermine the coherence of the Egyptian polity.

Consequently, Tahrir continues to be iconic in the post-Arab Spring era, mirroring this complex bargaining process as an arena for political war. For one group, the Tahrir of 25 January has been "won." Its characteristic mass protests succeeded not only in ousting the head of the *ancien régime* and putting him and members of his regime on trial, but also in electing the first civilian president. Accordingly, revolutionary legitimacy has reached its destination and should cede its place to an institutional legitimacy with the new presidency, the drafting of a new constitution, and the election of a new parliament. Not at all, retort a second group of those who insist that the revolution is incomplete (hijacked?) and needs to continue.

The acuteness of contention demonstrates the ups and downs of the evolving ruling bargain. Contestation of both the process and outcome of the Constituent Assembly is the last—but not final—instance in this respect. In this sense, though the new president took his presidential oath in Tahrir Square, Al-Midan's significance is not due to its reflection of formal and institutional politics. It is much more a mirror of informal politics, a reflection of the evolving ruling bargain. In this sense, Al-Midan incarnates not only the sociology of the Arab Spring and its initiation but also its evolution. This is why Tahrir is still alive and kicking more than two years after the start of the revolution, a symbol of competing legitimacies that mirror the challenges of transition, democratic or otherwise.[43]

[43] For a relevant and most recent analysis of some of these challenges, see Rex Brynen, Pete Moore, Basel Salloukh, and Marie Joelle Zahar, *After the Arab Spring*, Boulder, CO, and London: Lynne Rienner (forthcoming), and Bahgat Korany, "Egypt and Beyond: The Arab Spring, the New Pan-Arabism and the Challenges of Transition." Korany and El-Mahdi, *The Arab Spring in Egypt*, pp. 273–94.

10

PROTESTS, REGIME STABILITY, AND STATE FORMATION IN JORDAN[1]

Ziad Abu-Rish

In the period since the eruption of mass mobilizations across the Arab world in 2011, scholars, analysts, and activists have invested significant resources into narrating and analyzing the processes and dynamics that

[1] I would like to express my appreciation to Tania El Khoury for her encouragement to compile and elaborate on what had hitherto been a disparate set of arguments I had been making about different aspects of the history and contemporary politics of Jordan. A great deal of gratitude is also directed at Sherene Seikaly and Hesham Sallam for their generous time and productive feedback on earlier drafts of this chapter. I have also benefited immensely from conversations with Tariq Tell, who was kind enough to be forthcoming with the insights and experiences associated with his own research and activism in Jordan. Some components of this chapter were previously presented at George Mason University's Middle East Studies Program, the American University of Beirut's Issam Fares Institute for Public Policy and International Diplomacy, and Georgetown University's Center for Regional and International Studies in Qatar. I am grateful for these invitations to present and for the feedback of those in attendance. Other parts of this chapter were previously published on Jadaliyya as part of a series of articles I had written as the protest dynamics unfolded.

made up the Arab uprisings.[2] A concomitant exercise has involved developing a comparative framework for conceptualizing these uprisings in order to account for the varied trajectories of protest movements and regime strategies in the different Arab states.[3] In the case of Jordan the analysis has—for the most part—been less than inspiring, either repeating clichéd notions about Jordanian politics or hedging bets by asserting that Jordan is "forever on the brink" of revolt.[4] The discussion that follows seeks to improve on these approaches by offering an alternative understanding of the persistence of the political status quo in Jordan.[5] In short, what some analysts have referred to over the past twenty years as the "reform game" is ongoing in the Hashemite Kingdom of Jordan, with little indication (thus far) of a rebellion against the conventional rules of Jordanian politics. More specifically, significant socio-political formations that hold the capacity for anti-regime collective action continue to be invested in the status quo, either as active supporters of the regime, or as an opposition that nevertheless does not question the legitimacy of the underlying political framework—even if only for strategic reasons. While these dynamics are by no means fixed or permanent, the opportunities for changing them, without significant shifts in institutional–strategic realities, remain limited.

[2] See, for example, Hamid Dabashi, *The Arab Spring: The End of Postcolonialism*, New York: Zed Books, 2012.

[3] For one of the earliest as well as more systematic and sophisticated attempts at this, see James L. Gelvin, *The Arab Uprisings: What Everyone Needs to Know*, Oxford: Oxford University Press, 2012.

[4] For an example of the "forever on the brink" argument, see Marc Lynch, "Jordan, Forever on the Brink," *Foreign Policy*, http://lynch.foreignpolicy.com/posts/2012/05/07/jordan_forever_at_the_brink (accessed 1 Dec. 2012).

[5] In doing so, I draw on some of the more critical scholarship on the history and contemporary politics of state formation, regime security, and popular mobilizations in Jordan. These include, but are not limited to, Betty Anderson, *Nationalist Voices in Jordan: The Street and the State*, Austin, TX: University of Texas, 2005; Joseph Massad, *Colonial Effects: The Making of National Identity in Jordan*, New York: Columbia University Press, 2001; Pete W. Moore, *Doing Business in the Middle East: Politics and Economic Crisis in Jordan and Kuwait*, Cambridge: Cambridge University Press, 2009; Eugene L. Rogan, *Frontiers of the State in the Late Ottoman Empire: Transjordan, 1850–1921*, Cambridge: Cambridge University Press, 2002; Tariq Tell, *The Social and Economic Origins of Monarchy in Jordan*, New York: Palgrave Macmillan, 2013.

The acts of protest—marches, strikes, and sit-ins—that took place in Jordan between January 2011 and January 2013 have differed from those in Bahrain, Egypt, Libya, Syria, Tunisia, and Yemen. Authoritarian systems of rule govern all these countries, including Jordan. They offer little in the way of transparency, accountability, and civil liberties. They feature increasingly exclusionary economic policies that erode the ability of the average citizen to meet their basic needs.[6] However, the number of citizens that took to the streets in Jordan was relatively small in comparison to the massive turnout elsewhere. What set Jordan even further apart was the nature of the protestors' demands, which centered on calls for changes in the regime-sponsored governments and for a variety of political and economic reforms. In other words, these mobilizations were never about regime change, even if some anti-regime sentiments were expressed in them. A significant portion of the population may in fact share these sentiments. It is also true that many of the popular mobilizations that shook Bahrain, Egypt, and Tunisia began with a call for reform and moved to demanding the fall of the regime. What, then, has constrained cross-sectoral mass mobilization in Jordan? And what factors have tempered the anti-regime orientation of the so-far limited mobilizations that occurred in the country?

This chapter seeks to locate these dynamics in a genealogy of state formation in Jordan. By attending to the subtle specificities and the history of this process, this approach transcends the simplistic—but compelling and all too salient—urge to identify Jordanians as adhering to "pro-regime popular values," or to characterize the regime as ostensibly "benevolent" and non-coercive.[7] At first glance Jordan's trajectory of state formation

[6] For a general (if somewhat problematic) overview of these dynamics, see, United Nations Development Program, *The Arab Human Development Report 2004: Toward Freedom in the Arab World*, New York: United Nations Publications, 2004; United Nations Development Program, *The Arab Human Development Report 2009: Challenges to Human Security in the Arab Countries*, New York: United Nations Publications, 2009. For a more in-depth analysis of these dynamics, see Oliver Schlumberger (ed.), *Debating Authoritarianism: Dynamics and Durability in Non-Democratic Regimes*, Stanford: Stanford University Press, 2008; Joel Beinin, *Workers and Peasants in the Modern Middle East*, Cambridge: Cambridge University Press, 2001, pp. 114–69. It bears noting that since 2011 the term "governed" needs to be qualified in the particular cases of Libya and Syria.

[7] Such reasoning has been an integral part of the regime's (and its allies') inter-

mirrors that of other Arab authoritarian states. However, the divergences between the cases of Tunisia, Egypt, Libya, and Syria highlight the importance of historical–institutional and historical–strategic differences.[8] This chapter consequently approaches the history of state formation from these two levels of analysis—institutional and strategic—in order to shed light on the present possibilities for political mobilization.

The chapter begins by tracing the history of Jordanian state formation, the relevant political, economic, social, and institutional developments, and the patterns of alliances and conflicts they engendered. It then identifies the major socio-political forces that are capable of mass collective action, highlighting their strategic interests vis-à-vis the question of regime change. Finally, the chapter explores the potential for an alternative socio-political force to emerge. Institutional and strategic relations—themselves a function of the particular history of state formation in Jordan—impinge directly on the possibilities of mobilization. On the one hand, they produce important disincentives to the desirability of anti-regime mobilization for those forces capable of organized mass-based contentious politics. On the other hand, they impose considerable constraints on the capacity for mass-based contentious politics for those individuals and potential groups that are interested in anti-regime mobilizations.

---

national public relations campaign since the accession of King Abdullah II to the Hashemite throne in 1999, but in particular after January 2011 and the emergence of protests movements across the Arab world. The appearance of the king on the 25 Sep. 2012 episode of Jon Stewart's *The Daily Show* was perhaps the most explicit rendering of such a simplistic (even if strategically motivated) line of reasoning. For details of the king's appearance on the show and a critical analysis thereof, see Kifah and Jennifer, "Jon Stewart's Theater of the Absurd," Jadaliyya, http://www.jadaliyya.com/pages/index/7646/jon-stewarts-theater-of-the-absurd (accessed 1 Dec. 2012).

[8] For a comparative examination of the Syrian case, see Bassam Haddad, *Business Networks in Syria: The Political Economy of Authoritarian Resilience*, Stanford: Stanford University Press, 2012, pp. xiii–xiv; Bassam Haddad, "Syria, the Arab Uprisings, and the Political Economy of Authoritarian Resilience," *Interface Journal*, 4, 1 (2010), pp. 113–30; Bassam Haddad, "Syria's Stalemate: The Limits of Regime Resilience," *Middle East Policy*, 19, 1 (Spring 2012), pp. 85–95; Bassam Haddad, "Why Syria is Not Next … So Far," in Bassam Haddad, Rosie Bsheer, and Ziad Abu-Rish (eds), *The Dawn of the Arab Uprisings: End of An Old Order?* London: Pluto Press, 2012.

The Importance of History

In considering the varied manifestations of the Arab uprisings, I argue that the differences in protest dynamics, regime strategies, and political–economic outcomes revolve around three important factors. While these three factors alone do not explain everything about protest movements and regime responses in Jordan since 2011, it is impossible to understand contemporary Jordanian politics without them. First, there are the particular state-building legacies of each country and the institutional configurations it produced. Also important is the history of regime–society relations, as well as the varied alliances and antagonisms it engendered. Finally, there is the strategic importance of a given regime to both regional and international power relations. Together, these three factors—explained in greater detail below—provide a framework for understanding the politics of the uprisings in Jordan.

The British Empire established Jordan as one of the many successor states to the Ottoman Empire after the latter's defeat and dismemberment at the end of the First World War.[9] Originally declared the Emirate of Transjordan in 1921 and governed by a British mandate, it was granted independence in 1946 and renamed the Hashemite Kingdom of Jordan in 1949. On a broad level, the trajectory of state formation in Jordan was similar to that in many Arab and other postcolonial late developing states. Like elsewhere, authoritarian rule emerged as a particular state-building strategy to consolidate both the regime and the state in the face of domestic instability and external threat.[10] This strategy was underpinned by the establishment of a corporatist system of interest representation, which incorporated the major social, economic, and political groups that made up Jordanian society.[11] Even in the absence of an offi-

[9] On the defeat and dismemberment of the Ottoman Empire at the end of the First World War and the establishment of successor states, see James L. Gelvin, *The Modern Middle East: A History*, Oxford: Oxford University Press, 2008, pp. 180–205. On the specific case of the territorial and political establishment of what would become known as the Hashemite Kingdom of Jordan, see Anderson, *Nationalist Voices*, pp. 33–60; Tell, *The Social and Economic Origins*, pp. 42–71.

[10] For comparative analyses of authoritarian rule as a strategy of state formation, see Juan J. Linz, *Totalitarian and Authoritarian Regimes*, Boulder, CO: Lynne Rienner Publishers, 2000, pp. 159–261; Jill Crystal, "Authoritarianism and its Adversaries in the Arab World," *World Politics*, 46 (1994), pp. 262–89.

[11] For a comparative discussion of corporatist systems of interest representa-

cial ruling party, authoritarian rule in Jordan, similar to that in other Arab states, was premised on a ruling coalition with the regime (the monarchy in the case of Jordan) as the major partner and select sectors of society as the junior partners.[12] Such coalitions were typically forged around a political economy that featured a state-led economic development program, the particular institutions and policies of which reflected the nature of regime alliances and regime capacities.[13] While most Arab countries followed a similar trajectory, the institutional and strategic differences across them loomed large.[14] In fact, it is in these very differences that one can begin to appreciate the divergent manifestations of the Arab uprisings across the region in general and in Jordan in particular.

In the specific case of Jordan, during the initial period of state formation the country's demography was segmented in a particular form. The Hashemite family transplanted itself into Jordan primarily from the Hijaz, with the assistance of the British, and as part of a complex array of political and military calculations that need not be elaborated here.[15]

---

tion in authoritarian states throughout the Middle East, see Nazih N. Ayubi, *Over-Stating the Arab State: Politics and Society in the Middle East*, New York: I.B. Tauris, 1995, pp. 209–21; Alan Richards and John Waterbury, *A Political Economy of the Middle East*, 2nd edn, Boulder, CO: Westview Press, 1998, pp. 314–21. For a specific discussion of the corporatist representation of civil society organizations in Jordan during the 1990s, see Quintan Wiktorwicz, "Civil Society as Social Control: State Power in Jordan," *Comparative Politics*, 33 (2000), pp. 43–61.

12. For a discussion of the ways in which monarchical families serve the equivalent function of ruling parties in monarchical authoritarian settings, see Lisa Anderson, "Absolutism and the Resilience of Monarchy in the Middle East," *Political Science Quarterly*, 106 (1991), pp. 1–15.

13. For a general discussion of this dynamic, see Beinin, *Workers and Peasants*, pp. 114–41. For a discussion of the Syrian case, see Haddad, *Business Networks in Syria*, pp. 36–83. For a discussion of the Jordanian case, see Moore, *Doing Business in the Middle East*, pp. 57–80; Tell, *The Social and Economic Origins*, pp. 73–129.

14. See Haddad, "Why Syria is Not Next … So Far."

15. See Anderson, *Nationalist Voices*, pp. 36–42; Massad, *Colonial Effects*, pp. 18–25; Panayiotis J. Vatikiotis, *Politics and The Military in Jordan: A Study of The Arab Legion, 1921–1957*, London: Frank Cass and Co., 1967, pp. 37–45; Tariq Tell, "Guns, Gold, and Grain: War and Food Supply in the Making of Transjordan," in Steven Heydemann (ed.), *War, Institutions, and*

Competing local rural tribal leaderships, as well as a network of Levantine bureaucrats and merchants that had moved to the East Bank as part of late Ottoman administrative developments, economic transformations, and population movements, made up the elite of the population within the new borders.[16] Upon the declaration of the Emirate of Transjordan in 1921, Prince Abdullah bin Hussein faced the twin challenges of: (1) instantiating the new state into the everyday lives of its citizens, and (2) securing Hashemite rule within the state.[17] Abdullah I and his retinue were initially more successful in meeting the former challenge. For various reasons, the initial bureaucratic and institutional composition of the regime—its supporting state officials in particular—was made up of this Levantine elite, which deprived Abdullah I of a domestic social base.[18] In fact, the regime faced a number of rebellions, uprisings, and protests in its first ten years. It ultimately disciplined coercively most of the tribal formations within the new state during the 1920s, and subsequently incorporated them into the institutional base of the regime beginning in the 1930s.[19]

With the aim of establishing a local social base for itself—a political necessity for any regime—the Hashemite regime eventually consolidated a ruling coalition composed of key tribal formations that made up the social landscape of the nascent state. This coalition was rooted in a system of "military Keynesianism" made up of the transportation and communication infrastructure of the armed forces, the incomes and expenditures of its enlisted men, and its demand for basic and consumption goods.[20]

Social Change in the Middle East, Berkeley: University of California Press, 2000, pp. 33–58; Tell, *The Social and Economic Origins*, pp. 41–71.

[16] On these processes and the concomitant (re)formation of a local elite, see Rogan, *Frontiers of the State*; Tell, *The Social and Economic Origins*, pp. 27–54.

[17] For the dynamics of these challenges during Abdullah I's first decade of rule, see Tell, *The Social and Economic Origins*, pp. 55–71.

[18] On the initial bureaucratic and institutional composition of the regime and the question of identity, see Adnan Abu-Odeh, *Jordanians, Palestinians & the Hashemite Kingdom in the Middle East Peace Process*, Washington, DC: United States Institute for Peace, 1999, pp. 19–22; Anderson, *Nationalist Voices*, pp. 42–4; Tell, *The Social and Economic Origins*, pp. 59–82.

[19] See Anderson, *Nationalist Voices*, pp. 44–59; Massad, *Colonial Effects*, pp. 11–12; Tell, *The Social and Economic Origins*, pp. 67–77.

[20] A related conceptualization of the Hashemite ruling coalition in Jordan can

The ruling coalition was further consolidated and broadened through the radical reorganization of the land tenure and taxation systems.[21] Combined, this "Hashemite compact" brought together the majority of the agro-pastoralist population of the Jordanian rural areas along with an urban-based network of merchants and bureaucrats.[22] The ruling coalition thus found initial institutional expression in the armed forces and the tax system, which incorporated the junior partners of the regime through various forms of employment and protectionism. As part of the broader phenomenon of postcolonial state-led economic development and authoritarian state formation, such incorporation was eventually expanded through the enlargement of the armed forces, the establishment of security services, a bloated civil service, and import-substitution industrialization.[23]

There are four important elements within the above trajectory that directly impinge on the regime, its policies, and the societal dynamics they engendered. The first is the dependence of the Hashemite regime,

---

be found in Anne Mariel Peters and Pete W. Moore, "Beyond Boom and Bust: External Rents, Durable Authoritarianism, and Institutional Adaptation in the Hashemite Kingdom of Jordan," *Studies in Comparative International Development*, 44 (2009), pp. 256–85. Therein, Peters and Moore refer to this coalition as a "tribal–merchant coalition," which they primarily ground in the institution of the armed forces. However, Tariq Tell's deployment of Michael Mann's term "military Keynesianism," his detailing of the pillars of such "military Keynesianism" in Jordan, and his problematizing of the way in which "tribe" is used in the literature on state formation in Jordan seemed to better capture the nature of the coalition and its institutional manifestations. See Tell, *The Social and Economic Origins*, pp. 28–33, pp. 73–4. For more on various readings of the nature of this coalition, see Abla Mohammed Amawi, "State and Class in Jordan: A Study of State Autonomy," PhD Dissertation, Georgetown University, 1992; Anderson, *Nationalist Voices*, pp. 61–83; Massad, *Colonial Effects*, pp. 100–10; Moore, *Doing Business in the Middle East*, pp. 58–80, pp. 101–17; Tell, "Guns, Gold, and Grain"; Vatikiotis, *Politics and the Military*, pp. 75–96.

21. Tell, *The Social and Economic Origins*, pp. 95–112.
22. The term "Hashemite compact" is borrowed from Tariq Tell. See, in particular, Tell, *The Social and Economic Origins*, pp. 12–14, pp. 111–12.
23. On the armed forces and security services, see Tell, *The Social and Economic Origins*, pp. 119–23. On the civil service and import-substitution industrialization, see Moore, *Doing Business in the Middle East*, pp. 101–19; Peters and Moore, "Beyond Boom and Bust," pp. 267–74.

from the moment of its inception, on external rents made up of military supplies, budgetary and development assistance, and preferential trade agreements. Such rent accrual is the function of both the inability of the regime to maintain its distributive commitments without such rents, and the strategic importance of the regime/state to broader regional and international political, economic, and military arrangements.[24] Initially, the British Empire was the primary supplier of such rents.[25] However, from the 1950s onwards it was US aid and sponsorship in the Bretton Woods institutions (the World Bank and International Monetary Fund) and various UN agencies that emerged as the primary source of such rents.[26] This

[24] On the dependence of the regime on such rents for maintaining its distributive commitments throughout various phases of state building, see Peters and Moore, "Beyond Boom and Bust." For a brief reflection on the role of rents in sustaining the Hashemite regime, the stakes of such rents, and the shift from British to US sponsorship of external rent flows to the regime, see Tell, *The Social and Economic Origins*, pp. 119–23. For a specific exploration of rent accrual through alliances with various Arab regimes, see Laurie Brand, *Jordan's Inter-Arab Relations: The Political Economy of Alliance Making*, New York: Columbia University Press, 1995.

[25] On the strategic importance of the Hashemite regime and the territory it ruled over to the British Empire at the time of the former's establishment, see, for example, Abu-Odeh, *Jordanians, Palestinians*, pp. 17–18; Anderson, *Nationalist Voices*, pp. 35–6; Tell, *The Social and Economic Origins*, pp. 55–71. Beyond the political and military logics that undergirded the creation of Jordan's territorial space and British dependence on Abdullah I to "rule" over it, there is an ongoing legacy of close alliance and coordination with whichever power butters the Hashemites' bread. The 1941 Transjordanian intervention in Iraq to assist the British in crushing an anti-colonial revolt is one example of this dynamic under British patronage. Another is Abdullah I's navigation of the Jordanian–Zionist alliance in the context of his territorial ambitions vis-à-vis Palestine and possibly Syria. On the political and military logics that undergirded the creation of Jordan's territorial space and dependence on Abdullah to rule it, see Tell, *The Social and Economic Origins*, pp. 59–66. On the 1941 Transjordanian intervention in Iraq, see Tell, *The Social and Economic Origins*, pp. 108–9. On the early history of Jordanian–Zionist collusion, see Avi Shlaim, *Collusion Across the Jordan, King Abdullah, the Zionist Movement, and the Partition of Palestine*, Oxford: Clarendon Press, 1987; Tell, *The Social and Economic Origins*, pp. 80–82, 96–7, and 113–18.

[26] Thus, similar to Abdullah I's importance to the British was his grandson Hussein's capacity to cater to US interests. For the importance of the Hashemite regime to the United States during the 1950s, 60s, and 70s, see Abraham Ben-Zvi, *The Origins of the American–Israeli Alliance: The Jordan*

reflected the fact that the imperial mantle in the Middle East informally passed from the United Kingdom to the United States in the 1950s as a result of complex political, economic, and military factors.[27] These rent flows have given Jordan one of the oldest and most substantive records of foreign aid. This external aid was crucial to the longevity of the above-mentioned modes of socio-political incorporation, and it continues to be so today.

A second important element is the territorial and demographic expansion of the Jordanian state in the wake of the 1948 *Nakba* and the attendant Arab–Israeli war. The Jordanian state emerged from the war with the West Bank and East Jerusalem under its control, formally annexing them in 1950 and not officially ceding its claim to the territories until 1988.[28] The state would again experience a territorial and demographic transformation in 1967, this time a contraction—as Israel invaded and subsequently occupied the West Bank and East Jerusalem, along with the Gaza Strip, the Sinai Peninsula, and the Golan Heights.[29] Despite this contraction, the dynamics of the 1948–67 period bequeathed important legacies to the broader history of state formation in Jordan.[30] The wars themselves

---

Factor, New York: Brill, 2007; Stephen S. Kaplan, "United States Aid and Regime Maintenance in Jordan, 1957–1973," *Public Policy* (Spring 1972), pp. 189–217.

27 On the Hashemite regime's maneuvering through this transfer, see, for example, Douglas Little, "A Puppet in Search of A Puppeteer? The United States, King Hussein and Jordan, 1953–1970," *The International History Review* (Aug. 1995), pp. 522–8; Tell, *The Social and Economic Origins*, pp. 118–20.

28 For an analysis of the actual performance of the Arab Legion (the Jordanian army) in the 1948 Arab–Israeli war, see Eugene Rogan, "Jordan and 1948: The Persistence of an Official History," in Eugene L. Rogan and Avi Shlaim (eds), *The War for Palestine*, Cambridge: Cambridge University Press, 2001, pp. 104–24. For an analysis of the nature of Jordanian rule throughout the West Bank and East Jerusalem, see Kimberly Katz, *Jordanian Jerusalem: Holy Places and National Spaces*, Gainesville: University Press of Florida, 2005; Massad, *Colonial Effects*, pp. 222–75; Tell, *The Social and Economic Origins*, pp. 115–24.

29 On the 1967 Arab–Israeli war, see Wm. Roger Louis and Avi Shlaim (eds), *The 1967 Arab–Israeli War: Origins and Consequences*, Cambridge: Cambridge University Press, 2012.

30 See, for example, the chapter entitled "The Nation as an Elastic Entity: The Expansion and Contraction of Jordan," in Massad, *Colonial Effects*, pp. 222–75.

introduced a refugee population into Jordan, which in 1948 alone almost doubled the population within the original borders of the Jordanian state. Consequently, this population, combined with that of the West Bank and East Jerusalem (which in 1948 roughly equaled that of the population of Jordan), dramatically altered the demographic composition of the population over which the Hashemite regime ruled. Within the context of this demographic and territorial transformation, the Hashemite regime was faced with several strategic decisions, whereby it deepened its alliance with the East Bank population, both expanding its base within and playing it off against the newly enfranchised population. Furthermore, weary of the full political–economic incorporation of this new "foreign" population, regime preferences and their concomitant policies established lasting power dynamics between Trans-Jordanians (those of East Bank origin) and Palestinian–Jordanians (those of West Bank origin), which were and remain in the former's political favor but the latter's demographic favor. Palestinian–Jordanians were differentially incorporated in both the civil service and armed forces—and in large part excluded from the officer corps and upper echelons of the armed forces. Furthermore, in selecting its private sector partners for recruitment into the nascent public sector industrial elite of the ISI era, the regime opted for the inclusion of members of the Trans-Jordanian community while suppressing the participation of Palestinian capital.[31] Additionally, those Palestinian refugees requiring educational, health, and social services assistance in light of their dispossession and displacement were to seek it from the United Nations Reliefs and Works Agency (UNRWA), the organization set up in 1950 to address Palestinian refugee needs in Jordan, Lebanon, Syria, the West Bank, and the Gaza Strip.[32] Furthermore, modification to the laws regulating both parliamentary life and political party affiliation—between independence (1946) and the imposition of martial law (beginning in 1957 and culminating in 1967)—enabled the regime to engage in several experiments in the authoritarian management of formal political competition—a theme that would reemerge with the resumption of parliamentary life in 1989.[33]

[31] Peters and Moore, "Beyond Boom and Bust," pp. 267–8.

[32] Ibid. pp. 269–72. See also Yusef A. Sayigh, "Economic Implications of UNRWA Operations in Jordan, Syria, and Lebanon," MA Thesis, American University of Beirut, 1952.

[33] See Anderson, *Nationalist Voices*, pp. 117–206; Tell, *The Social and Economic*

The third element was the repertoire of coercion and violence developed by the regime in its policies vis-à-vis domestic opposition. The regime has a long history of brutally suppressing local dissent. As discussed above, the initial state-formation period featured the suppression (sometimes with the assistance of British Royal Air Force bombing campaigns) of various rebellions, uprisings, and protests. This would again resume during the 1950s and 1960s, culminating in 1970 with the brutal attack on, and subsequent expulsion of, the Palestinian guerilla movements and many of their civilian supporters.[34] This historical moment solidified the split between Trans-Jordanians and Palestinian–Jordanians. It also demonstrated both the regime's willingness to resort to outright civil war and the support that its major allies (the United States and the United Kingdom) would provide towards such ends. The entire trajectory of state formation relied on the deployment of violence. "Complacency" was not merely "bought off." It was produced through a variety of institutional and security practices, ranging from the bureau-

---

Origins, pp. 119–24. On the regime's strategies for managing electoral contestation since 1989, see various sections dealing with Jordan in Ellen Lust-Okar, *Structuring Conflict in the Arab World: Incumbents, Opponents, and Institutions*, Cambridge: Cambridge University Press, 2005. For a discussion of the managing of electoral contestation in the 2010 and 2013 parliamentary elections, see, respectively, Ziad Abu-Rish, "Jordan, Liberalism, and the Question of Boycott," Jadaliyya, http://www.jadaliyya.com/pages/index/295/jordan-liberalism-and-the-question-of-boycott (accessed 1 Dec. 2012); Ziad Abu-Rish, "Romancing the Throne: The New York Times and The Endorsement of Authoritarianism in Jordan," Jadaliyya, http://www.jadaliyya.com/pages/index/9949/romancing-the-throne_the-new-york-times-and-the-en (accessed 1 Mar. 2013).

[34] On the domestic oppositional politics of the 1950s and 1960s, see Anderson, *Nationalist Voices*; Tell, *The Social and Economic Origins*, pp. 113–29. On the 1970 civil war, or what is otherwise referred to as Black September, see Frances S. Hasso, *Resistance, Repression, and Gender Politics in Occupied Palestine and Jordan*, Syracuse: Syracuse University Press, 2005, pp. 29–39; Massad, *Colonial Effects*, pp. 236–49; Yezid Sayigh, *Armed Struggle and the Search for State: The Palestinian National Movement, 1949–1993*, Oxford: Oxford University Press, 2000, pp. 143–318. Also important, even if uncharacteristically and problematically sympathetic to the regime itself, is Tell, *The Social and Economic Origins*, pp. 125–9. For a journalistic account, see John K. Cooley, *Green March, Black September: The Story of the Palestinian Arabs*, London: Frank Cass, 1973.

cratization of associational and political life to the surveillance, infiltration, arrest, torture, deportation, and co-optation of individuals and groups that were potential sources of anti-regime mobilization.

A final element within the trajectory of state formation is the fact that the Hashemite monarchy in Jordan is the only regime, with the exception of the Al Saud monarchy in Saudi Arabia, that has been able to maintain its rule since the demise of the Ottoman Empire and the establishment of its successor states. This is despite the wave of successive challenges it experienced throughout the twentieth century. Beginning with the tribal revolts of the 1920s and 1930s through the oppositional mobilizations of the 1950s and 1960s, the monarchy built up and then sustained a deeply institutionalized loyalty among key social groups. The 1970–71 confrontation with Palestinian guerilla movements equally struck at the core of Hashemite rule. Yet, as with the riots of the late 1980s and early 1990s, the regime was able to overcome such challenges by virtue of cohesive—even if disgruntled—armed forces and security services, which when coupled with its other institutional linkages throughout society, reflected a core of regime supporters (even if that core was itself segmented by various interests and strategic calculations vis-à-vis the regime). The 2011–12 protest waves, as "unprecedented" or "unexpected" as they were, failed to dislodge the monarchy from the conduits of power. While fully exploring the implications of such a legacy of political survival is beyond the scope of this chapter, it is worth stressing that such a capacity to survive consecutive challenges reflects dynamics that cannot merely be attributed to coercive force or great power backing alone. This is not to say that the Hashemite regime—whose formation is coeval with that of the Jordanian state—is impervious to crisis, challenge, or collapse. It is, however, to say that such longevity needs to be taken seriously.

By 1989, the Hashemite regime had ruled for over sixty years and was in firm control of both the polity and the economy, even if problematically so. A bloated bureaucracy, overgrown military, and basic subsidies allowed the Hashemite regime to forge institutional linkages and a popular social base. Again, the key socio-political forces were an East Bank set of tribal formations—themselves hierarchically incorporated into the ruling coalition through employment in the civil service and armed forces—and a network of East Bank merchant families. Palestinian–Jordanian capital was suppressed as private capital in favor of the public sector and the political–economic imperatives the latter served. This is not to render invisible the refugee camp-based Palestinians as a potential socio-political force. However, their complete political disenfranchisement, combined with the near total security grip in place since 1970, has relegated those communities—at least insofar as collective mass action is concerned—to political insignificance. Through various practices of co-optation, repression, and divide-and-rule, the regime has been able to exploit the Trans-Jordanian/Palestinian–Jordanian communal division at the popular level to prevent national mobilization. All the while, various formal and informal financial and marital ties further consolidated the ruling coalition, which pivoted primarily on the alliances captured by the term "Hashemite compact."[35]

Jordan's state-formation trajectory from 1921 to 1989 serves as a microcosm for the more general phenomenon of the authoritarian bargain in the Arab world. Regimes disciplined their populations and provided them with their economic needs in return for the latter's complacency regarding the absence of political freedoms as well as public accountability and transparency. Those remaining segments of the population that dissented were met with continuous state violence.

Post-1989: Restructuring the Economy and Reconfiguring Political Participation

In 1989, the fiscal crisis that symbolized the failure of Jordan's economic development model forced the regime to embark on a series of economic reforms.[36] These primarily involved the liberalization and privatization of the economy, as well as various cuts to state-provided social safety nets. These measures, which were implemented throughout the 1990s and 2000s, would unravel the state-led economy that the regime had constructed in the period since 1921. On the one hand, this shift in economic policy was an attempt to attract local and foreign private capital that had hitherto been excluded but which the regime now needed. On the other hand, the emerging economic policies were simultaneously designed to meet the conditions established by the World Bank (WB) and International Monterey Fund (IMF) for the disburse-

[35] See section in this chapter entitled "The Importance of History."
[36] See Moore, *Doing Business in the Middle East*, pp. 145–73.

ment of various loans to Jordan. However, such economic policy changes posed a threat to the nature of the ruling coalition that had long buttressed Hashemite rule.

The regime was forced into a strategic dilemma: it had to incorporate the business sector into its ruling coalition while not alienating preexisting junior partners whose economic interests could conflict with the logic of austerity, privatization, and liberalization. Given the divergent policy preferences of the business community from those of the masses of people incorporated through the Hashemite compact, this need for economic reconfiguration posed a problem. If the Egyptian regime, for example, was able to do this by jettisoning labor and the peasantry and bringing in the business community wholesale, the stakes were altogether different in Jordan.[37] Tribal formations were not an economic class of citizens, but a social group that cut across classes, represented historical allies of the regime, and formed the backbone of the armed forces and civil service. Consequently, there appeared to be a divergence of economic interests among the reconfigured ruling coalition—namely between the existing junior partners (that is, the regime's historic popular social base) and the new junior partners (the hitherto unincorporated business community).

Most accounts of liberalization and privatization assume static economic practices. However, a more critical account of economic restructuring in Jordan sheds light on how the regime mitigated the process of wholesale replacement of one junior coalition partner with another.[38] For starters, and as pointed out by Anne Mariel Peters and Pete W. Moore, it is important to note that economic policy shifts in Jordan primarily centered on the privatization of state-owned enterprises and lands, the floating of the Jordanian dinar, opening up the domestic market to foreign imports, instituting Valued Added Tax (VAT), and

[37] On the political incorporation of the business community in Egypt, see Eberhard Kienle, *A Grand Delusion: Democracy and Economic Reform in Egypt*, New York: I.B. Tauris, 2001; Marsha Pripstein Posusney, *Labor and the State in Egypt: Workers, Unions, and Economic Restructuring*, New York: Columbia University Press, 1997; Samer Soliman, *The Autumn of Dictatorship: Fiscal Crisis and Political Change in Egypt under Mubarak*, Stanford: Stanford University Press, 2011.

[38] My own account of economic restructuring in Jordan in this section draws heavily from Moore, *Doing Business*; Peters and Moore, "Beyond Boom and Bust."

eliminating food subsidies.[39] These practices, combined with rising global food prices, have had important negative consequences for average Jordanians in that their purchasing power has decreased while rates of both unemployment and poverty have increased.

However, social polarization in and of itself is not a sufficient cause of rebellion—in the sense of mobilizing to overthrow the regime. If it were, the manifestation of uprisings across the Arab world should have corresponded to economic indices; which it did not. Furthermore, it is important to recall that the strategy of economic restructuring in Jordan has differentially affected the population, taking into account the difference between those that pose a threat of collective action and those that do not. As Peters and Moore have highlighted, this has been accomplished in several ways. First, public employment and the associated welfare benefits have not been cut in any drastic way:

> between 1989 and 2001, expenditures on wages and salaries consistently accounted for around [45] percent of the [state] budget, and from 2001 to 2005, employee compensation grew by [6] percent. Military expenditures lingered between [26] and [28] percent of total expenditures, even though external threats to Jordan have ebbed.[40]

This is in large part a function of the budget support offered by foreign aid and privatization proceeds. Second, the regime mitigated against threats of mass layoffs to former public sector employees in privatized industries. This was accomplished in one of two ways. On the one hand, there was recourse to the 1999 privatization law which gives "the government" a veto option vis-à-vis decisions made by the newly formed boards of directors in public–private ventures.[41] On the other hand, the government in other cases stipulated a time period within which privatized enterprises could not engage in layoffs.[42] Third, privatization has been uncompetitive in nature, such that it has offered business families allied with the regime the opportunity to either purchase

[39] Peters and Moore, "Beyond Boom and Bust," pp. 274–8.

[40] Ibid. pp. 276–7. See also Anne Marie Baylouny, "Militarizing Welfare: Neoliberalism and Jordanian Policy," *Middle East Journal*, 62 (2008), pp. 277–303.

[41] Peters and Moore, "Beyond Boom and Bust," p. 277.

[42] Ibid. See also Hamed El-Said, "The Political Economy of Reform in Jordan: Breaking Resistance to Reform?" in George Joffé (ed.), *Jordan in Transition*, London: Hurst, 2002, pp. 254–77.

public enterprises and lands themselves or, alternatively, serve as middlemen for foreign—mainly Gulf—investors.[43]

If these three strategies have offered solutions to regime political survival in the face of privatization, there are other strategies that have done the same in the face of liberalization.[44] First, loyal merchant-industrialists have been the primary beneficiaries of regional and bilateral trade agreements that offer duty-free export for select products.[45] Second, the regime has restricted local participation in regime-backed megaprojects to select individuals, families, and businesses long allied with the regime.[46] Third, government procurement of local goods and services is non-competitive—even in the face of privatization—and thus geared toward the benefit of local merchant-industrialists allied with the regime.[47]

The combination of these strategies has sheltered important segments of the regime's already-incorporated social base from the broader consequences of economic liberalization and privatization, even if differentially so. They have failed, however, to shield social groups that are not fully allied to the regime. These include tribal groups that were much less incorporated through public employment, or the vast majority of Palestinian–Jordanians. Nevertheless, the fact that certain social groups allied with the regime have been (relatively) able to weather the economic restructuring should not obscure the fact that the overall economic development model since 1989 has largely failed to provide

[43] Peters and Moore, "Beyond Boom and Bust," p. 277.

[44] Again, the work of Peters and Moore is quite illustrative. See Peters and Moore, "Beyond Boom and Bust," pp. 277–8. For a regionally comparative analysis of such dynamics, see Stephen King, "Sustaining Authoritarianism in the Middle East and North Africa," *Political Science Quarterly*, 122 (2007), pp. 433–59.

[45] Peters and Moore, "Beyond Boom and Bust," pp. 277–8. See also Pete Moore and Andrew Schrank, "Commerce and Conflict: US Effort to Counter Terror with Trade May Backfire," *Middle East Politics*, 10, 3 (2003), pp. 295–315; Marwan Kardoosh and Michelle Leanne Burgis, "A Story of Qualified Success? Qualifying Industrial Zones, Economic Policy-Making & Governance in Jordan," Jordan Center for Public Policy Research and Dialogue, 2006.

[46] Peters and Moore, "Beyond Boom and Bust," p. 278. See also Anne Mariel Peters, "Special Relationships, Dollars, and Development: US Aid and Institutions in Egypt, Jordan, South Korea, and Taiwan," PhD Dissertation, University of Virginia, 2009.

[47] Peters and Moore, "Beyond Boom and Bust," p. 278.

adequate employment, income, and purchasing power to the vast majority of the population. The regime's strategies cushioned—rather than eliminated—the effects of these failures. This development model has been premised on securing local and foreign investment within a market-oriented climate. It has emphasized investment in non-productive sectors (such as tourism and commerce) and enterprises that offer little real added value to the economy. At the same time, it provides quick and large returns to those select Jordanians with privileged access to such investment arrangements. In addition, a misplaced faith in the alleged trickle-down effects of the market (that is when the market economy grows, everybody benefits) has in turn resulted in an exclusive concern with macroeconomic growth rates as the defining indices of the economy's productivity and vitality.

In parallel with economic restructuring, the Hashemite regime has embarked since the late 1980s on a project of reconfiguring political participation in media publication, associational life, and parliamentary elections. This multifaceted political project reflects the breaking down of the authoritarian bargain, but not of authoritarianism itself. It is an attempt to provide controlled outlets for political pressures arising from economic restructuring. The literature on "political reform" is quite extensive and thus does not necessitate a full elaboration here.[48] However, a few points are worth enumerating. Political reconfiguration in Jordan has followed a similar trajectory to that in other Arab authoritarian states. The monarchy (or ruling party) has set itself up as the vanguard of reform in the country: it claims to plot the course of reform and manage its dangers. The dynamics of top-down regime-managed political reform have offered several controlled outlets for public frustration. These include organized demonstrations, new media forums, and parliamentary elections. However, they have simultaneously maintained the concentrated and unaccountable nature of power in both the polity and

[48] For two of the more critical accounts on "political reform," see Daniel Brumberg, "Authoritarian Legacies and Reform Strategies in The Arab World," in Rex Brynen, Bahgat Korany, and Paul Noble (eds), *Political Liberalization & Democratization in the Arab World: Volume 1, Theoretical Perspectives*, Boulder, CO: Lynne Rienner Publishers, 1995, pp. 229–60; Steven Heydemann, "Upgrading Authoritarianism in The Arab World," Analysis Paper Number 13, Washington, DC: The Saban Center for Middle East Policy at the Brookings Institute, 2005.

the economy. This has been accomplished through processes of policy formulation and implementation that are shielded from public scrutiny, or—when policies are pursued through formal and public institutional channels—through backdoor mediation and diverse coercive strategies.

Jordan's Uprising and the Terrain of Existing Socio-Political Forces

Protests began to erupt across the Arab world in January and February 2011, and Jordan was no exception. On Friday, 14 January 2011, protests of varying sizes were held across Jordan as part of a call for a "Jordanian Day of Anger."[49] Some activists organized Friday protests for nine consecutive weeks. Additionally, a diverse array of state employees organized a strong series of public sector strikes and sit-ins.[50] Finally, others brought into being a diverse array of campaigns, initiatives, and contentious actions in the following months. All three sets of activities were widespread yet largely uncoordinated. The specific demands varied, and included both economic and political ones. However, as mentioned above, the demands were ultimately reformist in nature. They echoed grievances that opposition political parties, non-governmental organizations, and human rights groups had publicized prior to 2011. These grievances were articulated in reformist calls, leaving the primacy of the monarchy and its prerogatives to command the heights of both the polity and the economy unchallenged. Furthermore, the number of people who participated in these activities was relatively small, with the largest protest not exceeding 7,000 demonstrators.

Thus despite repeated public criticisms of corruption, the state of the economy, and flawed mechanisms for political participation and accountability, the "reform game" is still in play in Jordan. Perhaps most representative of this fact is that by the summer of 2011 there were very few manifestations of contentious politics around the country.[51] More

[49] See Ziad Abu-Rish, "Jordan's Day of Anger," Jadaliyya, http://www.jadaliyya.com/pages/index/460/jordans-day-of-anger (accessed 1 Dec. 2012).

[50] See Fida Adely, "The Emergence of a New Labor Movement in Jordan," *Middle East Report*, 264 (Fall 2012).

[51] The intention here is not to limit the scope of what constitutes political praxis worthy of attention and analysis to a narrow definition of "contentious politics." Rather, it is to highlight a relatively quick return by opposition forces to a dependence on the formal political game, which channels interests and mobilizations through regime-managed rules and limits.

to the point, the thrust of explicitly cross-sectoral mobilizations had dissipated. What remained was much more diffuse and isolated in nature, taking the form of a combination of disparate public sector employee strikes, university campus violence, and confrontations between security forces and either tribal or Islamist groups. However, rather than representing a Jordanian uprising, these acts are better viewed as the traces of Jordan's authoritarian system of rule and the always present tensions therein. In other words, the repertoire and legacies these acts generate are integral to an uprising should one occur, but they do not in and of themselves constitute an uprising against or a rejection of the "reform game." The only potential exception to this was the spontaneous taking to the streets that occurred in November 2012.[52] However, even this development was structured by the dynamics discussed in this chapter: a lack of desirability for anti-regime mobilization among those forces capable of organized mass-based contentious politics, and constraints on the capacity for mass-based contentious politics for those individuals and potential groups that are interested in anti-regime mobilization—a point elaborated upon below.

What has become painfully evident about politics in Jordan is that groups with the capacity for mass-based collective action continue to be invested in the status quo. For some, this investment is positive in that they are the primary beneficiaries of the status quo. For others, the investment is negative in that they are not confident of faring better—or even similarly—in any potential "day after" scenario. This incentive structure is an outcome of the particular state-formation trajectory in Jordan, particularly as it relates to the internal socio-political demographics, political and economic institutional legacies, and the country's strategic position. The remainder of this section aims to outline some of the workings of this incentive structure. It should be clear that such a structural approach is not meant to rule out the possibility of mass-based anti-regime collective action. Rather, it is intended to highlight the constraints and dilemmas that animate any attempts at such collective action.

All the major socio-political forces are in favor of reforming rather than overthrowing the regime. This is primarily manifested in the infor-

[52] See Ziad Abu-Rish, "Getting Past the Brink: Protests and the Possibilities of Change in Jordan," Jadaliyya, http://www.jadaliyya.com/pages/index/8375/getting-past-the-brink_protests-and-the-possibilit (accessed 1 Dec. 2012).

mal consensus—recognized by King Abdullah II himself to a certain extent—among most potential and actual opposition forces for some form of monarchy. It thus seems more apt to describe the ongoing struggle in the Jordanian political field as one over the nature of that constitutional monarchy rather than over its existence. On the one hand, regime loyalists envision the persistence of a political system in which the Hashemite dynasty as a whole participates in and dominates the ruling coalition. On the other hand, reformists of varying types would see such prerogatives restricted to the king alone and thus open up space for increased participation in the political system. What exactly such restrictions on the king, and concomitant increased participation by individuals outside the monarchic circle, would look like is itself subject to conflicting visions. Nevertheless, it should be clear that such visions do not challenge the supremacy of the monarchy. This is not to deny a much more ambiguous attitude on the part of both loyalists and oppositionists, whether Trans-Jordanian or Palestinian–Jordanian, towards King Abdullah II himself. However, a distinction between the attitudes towards the monarchy versus attitudes towards a particular member of the ruling family is important, as it speaks to broader strategic calculations among the various socio-political forces. The remainder of this section will highlight some of these strategic calculations, and how the regime has either taken direct advantage of them or at the very least been buttressed by them.

Since the early 1990s, the most significant nationally organized opposition force in the Jordanian political field is the Jordanian Muslim Brotherhood and its political wing (its electoral vehicle) the Islamic Action Front (IAF). It is the only political party with a mass following, albeit one that is limited to particular parts of Amman, al-Zarqa, and Irbid—the three largest urban centers in the kingdom. There are certainly a host of other political parties, including Islamist, pan-Arab, leftist, communist, and centrist movements. However, these parties range from representing a marginally small (even if genuine) following of supporters to representing the personal following of select regime figures and tribal members. Most of the literature on opposition parties views them as antagonistic to the ruling system. However, what has become quite obvious throughout the regional uprisings—and for some of the more nuanced analysts, since before the uprisings—are the ways in which opposition parties are themselves central components of the ruling system.

Many observers view the IAF as the most antagonistic political party vis-à-vis the regime. However, a more critical appraisal would appreciate its investment in the ruling system, which is a function of its privileged position as the opposition party. The IAF has restricted its activities to the formal political game—itself set up as limited and ineffective political competition through elections—rather than contentious politics. This was the case even during the nine weeks of Friday protests where the IAF (and the Muslim Brotherhood more generally) wavered back and forth before fully committing to participation in the protests.[53] While it was sufficiently emboldened by the regional uprisings to call openly for an elected prime minister, the IAF has consistently been a supporter of the ruling system as a whole rather than an outspoken critic. Most exemplary of this was the IAF's repeated condemnation of any and all anti-regime rhetoric and mobilizations during 2011 and 2012. Such a reformist strategy on the part of the IAF can be attributed to several factors. First, the organization itself has historical ties to the Royal Court and the intelligence services. This is in some senses a function of the effective penetration and co-optation of all formal opposition groups. However, it is also a function of the particular history of the regime's collusion with the Muslim Brotherhood (and other Islamist forces) against the secular and leftist opposition the regime faced in the second half of the twentieth century. Second, and representative of the constraining nature of the existing political game, there are too many

[53] This of course is not too dissimilar to what transpired with the Egyptian Muslim Brotherhood (MB) in the initial period of the eighteen-day uprising that toppled Hosni Mubarak. However, that mobilization was rapidly transformed into one that explicitly called for regime change. It was only after the MB youth broke ranks with the leadership, and the cost of maintaining a reformist posture vis-à-vis the regime outweighed the benefits, that the Egyptian MB joined the protests and subsequently "played a central role in holding the frontlines of the protests, 'along with the rest of the political movements that took part in it.'" See Jadaliyya and Ahram Online, "Freedom and Justice Party," Jadaliyya, http://www.jadaliyya.com/pages/index/3154/freedom-and-justice-party (accessed 1 Dec. 2012). For a more long-term analysis of the MB's relationship to the Egyptian regime, and a more thorough discussion of its calculations during the 2011 Egyptian uprisings, see Wael Eskandar, "Brothers and Officers: A History of Pacts," Jadaliyya, http://www.jadaliyya.com/pages/index/9765/brothers-and-officers_a-history-of-pacts (accessed 1 Mar. 2013).

questions as to whether the IAF would be a significant political force should political participation be dramatically expanded, in terms of both the rules of the electoral system and the spectrum of legitimate political parties. Comparatively speaking, while the 2011 parliamentary and 2012 presidential elections in post-Mubarak Egypt showcased the electoral capacities of the Muslim Brotherhood there, they also highlighted the tenuous (and contested) nature of such a performance.[54] The IAF, to complete the comparison, does not have a similar set of strategic resources—such as a rural electoral base. Also of note—and not unlike its Egyptian counterpart—is the IAF's almost non-existent economic program, rendering it more a legitimating force for the regime's economic policies than a center of critical opposition. More importantly, the Jordanian Muslim Brotherhood and IAF face a potential existential threat should they mobilize for the fall of the regime without making any meaningful alliance with the coercive institutions—or segments therein—that would actively prevent a crackdown on the organization. This represents a serious dilemma for the Muslim Brotherhood even if—for whatever reason—it chose to mobilize against the regime. The issue to watch for, therefore, is how radicalized will such groups become with respect to their own demands. They are most likely not going to put themselves out ahead of everyday people or protestors. That course of action would risk them being detached from popular will (which they themselves are trying to gauge) and thus not only isolate themselves, but make themselves susceptible to a regime crackdown. The IAF is thus dependent on some sort of alliance with its long-time adversaries (that is the organized Trans-Jordanian socio-political forces) for a meaningful opportunity to even consider such anti-regime mobilization.[55]

If the IAF represents the majority of the organized urban Palestinian–Jordanian "opposition," then the National Committee of Retired Servicemen (NRSC) which was formed prior to the uprisings, and the

[54] See Hesham Sallam, "Post-Elections Egypt: Revolution or Pact?" Jadaliyya, http://www.jadaliyya.com/pages/index/4314/post-elections-egypt_revolution-or-pact (accessed 1 Dec. 2012); Hesham Sallam, "Morsi Past the Point of No Return," Jadaliyya, http://www.jadaliyya.com/pages/index/8881/morsi-past-the-point-of-no-return (accessed 1 Mar. 2013).

[55] Again, this is not unlike its Egyptian counterpart and its relationship to the Supreme Council of the Armed Forces (SCAF). See Eskandar, "Brothers and Officers."

local coordinating committees, which sprang up during 2011 but began to unravel in late 2012 and early 2013, represent the most formalized vehicles for Trans-Jordanians of both the capital and the hinterland. Much of the existing analysis on the NRSC has focused on its anti-Palestinian–Jordanian rhetoric and demands. However, its primary mobilizations have centered on protecting the privileges of the current and former members of the traditional armed forces, safeguarding the institutional channels through which their relatives and the broader Trans-Jordanian community have been incorporated into the regime, and fighting high-level corruption. Thus the idea—advanced by some who decontextualize the NRSC's mobilizations—that the monarchy is losing the loyalty of the armed forces seems very much off the mark (at least under the present circumstances), since it is the monarchy itself that guarantees the privileges of this particular constituency in the face of a Palestinian–Jordanian demographic majority.[56] This is to say nothing of the coup-proofing the regime has been hard at work on for several decades.

For the NRSC, these problems are not endemic to the regime but specific to King Abdullah II's rule. Since ascending the throne in 1999, Abdullah II has sought to reconfigure the armed forces. Two contexts are particularly relevant in this regard. The first is an attempt made to shore up an independent base in the regime's coercive apparatus so as to buffer against any would-be dissenters or detractors, given the sudden succession change before King Hussein's death. The second is the newly emerging international–regional security arrangements, most notably the global war on terror. The three pillars of this program to reconfigure the armed forces are: (1) the creation of the Gendarmerie Force (*darak*) as a new coercive force separate from both the military and police; (2) a dramatic expansion of the Special Forces (*Quwwat al-Khassah*), which Abdullah II was head of prior to his ascension; and (3) a radical substitution of the core members of the Royal Guard (*al-Haras al-Malaki*). The combination of these policies has resulted in a significant shift in the flow of privileges—whether financial or in-kind—accruing to the standing army and its leadership. New equipment, advanced training, and various forms of

[56] For an example of such decontexualization, see Assad David, "The Revolt of Jordan's Military Veterans," *Foreign Policy*, http://mideast.foreignpolicy.com/articles/2010/06/15/the_revolt_of_jordans_military_veterans (accessed 1 Dec. 2012).

patronage are now flowing to these new institutional bases of support. Furthermore, the NRSC views the economic reconfigurations that have been underway with great suspicion, seeing them as derived more from high-level corruption rather than from genuine economic policy-making. This view is primarily a function of the encroachments on the existing distributive arrangements that economic restructuring has produced. However, such a view has also been colored by the fact that Palestinian–Jordanian capital—suppressed until 1989—was a primary beneficiary of the investment opportunities opened up by privatization and liberalization. It was these investment opportunities that were tied to several of the high-profile cases where public sector employment opportunities were undermined or state expenditures were squandered. The political demands of the NRSC crystallized around a call for a return to the 1952 constitution, though they were not the exclusive advocates of this demand. Again, such demands represent calls for reforming the regime rather than overthrowing it, and reflect concerns with Abdullah II in particular rather than the monarchy as a whole. It is worth noting that much of the justification for a return to the 1952 constitution among NRSC members has to do with the liabilities—for their own interests—of not having a Cabinet selected by the parliament. Primary among these is the lack of transparency and oversight to address corruption and the potential transfer/sharing of the king's prerogatives to/with relatives—most notably Queen Rania. However, such concern about the rule of Abdullah II is not equivalent to calling for regime change. Most importantly, the historical animosity between the social backbone of the armed forces and the Palestinian–Jordanian populations raises significant concern around the potential unseating of the regime, or even the unmanaged expansion of electoral participation. Thus whatever the current grievances of the NRSC may be, they are first and foremost going to guard against the further opening up of the civil service and the armed forces to the Palestinian–Jordanian population, which would raise both ideological and economic concerns.

For their part, the local coordinating committees primarily represent Trans-Jordanians from the economically isolated regions of the south and northeast.[57] Their demands have centered on the lack of opportuni-

[57] See Ziad Abu-Rish, "Jordan's Current Political Opposition Movements and the Need for Further Research: An Interview with Tariq Tell (Part 2),"

ties for the growing ranks of that particular demographic. In many ways, the antecedents of the local coordinating committees can be found in the 1989 austerity riots. At that time—as Tariq Tell has aptly noted—the "uprising in the south" represented a shift in the nature of regime–society confrontation, from regions of mixed populations to those of the historical socio-political bases of regime support.[58] These protests highlight regional fissures that have also taken on an economic dimension due to the neglect of these areas in Jordan's economic development strategy (urban and service-based) as well as its aid flows (urban and camps-based). However, they are best read as communicative action vis-à-vis the regime for better treatment rather than an outright rejection of the regime. The lopsided parliamentary representation of these regions since 1989 was partially geared towards substituting development and subsidies with electoral offices and their concomitant patronage networks. However, privatization and liberalization since 1989 have entailed a dramatic reduction in the rent-producing nature of these patronage networks, especially when one takes into account demographic expansion. Despite these grievances, the core of the local coordinating committees understand far too well that an overthrow of the regime would result in far fewer opportunities given that their constituents' privileges in the armed forces, civil service, and electoral politics would be severely threatened.

Analysts of the Middle East have long taken for granted the existence of an urban-based, primarily Palestinian–Jordanian opposition in the Hashemite Kingdom (even if they have also mistaken their parliamentary opposition for an anti-regime opposition). However, the emergence of an alliance between the NRSC and the local coordinating committees that were at the forefront of the majority of protests in 2011 and 2012 has caused many such analysts to claim that the pillars of the regime are crumbling, and thus its fall impending.[59] This belief was further entrenched when the IAF allied itself with the NRSC and the local

---

Jadaliyya, http://www.jadaliyya.com/pages/index/7007/jordans-current-political-opposition-movements-and (accessed 1 Dec. 2012).

[58] Ibid.

[59] For the most explicit articulation of this argument, see Marc Lynch, "Jordan, Forever on the Brink," *Foreign Policy*, http://lynch.foreignpolicy.com/posts/2012/05/07/jordan_forever_at_the_brink (accessed 1 Dec. 2012).

coordinating committees to bring about the fall of Samir al-Rifa'i's Cabinet in early 2011. Such analysis is premature, especially since it ignores the historical, institutional, and strategic factors that shape the political options of both the NRSC and local coordinating committees. Institutionalized privileges as well as the uncertain outcome of overturning the regime severely constrain the political options of the NRSC and the local coordinating committees. However problematic the current status quo is for them, they stand to lose much more without the regime in the absence of certain (currently non-existent) guarantees. Such a calculation is made even more relevant in light of the failed peace process and the concomitant lack of any serious Palestinian repatriation to the territories of historic Palestine. Furthermore, it must be noted that within the existing competition between tribes, the regime has since its inception emerged as a mediator of sorts, envisioned at times as preventing tribal competition from turning into destabilizing violent confrontation. Irrespective of the validity of this imagery, it plays an important role in the calculation of various tribal formations. On the one hand, dominant and privileged tribes are concerned about their standing under a radically different political economic system. On the other hand, less powerful tribes are dependent on the regime to maintain their share of the economic and political pie—no matter how small—given the alternative risk of being completely crowded out. It is unclear for all tribal formations what the pie, or their share of it, would look like under a different configuration of power.

It bears (re)emphasizing that the Hashemite regime is one of several lynchpins in the network of alliances among dominant Arab states (primarily rooted in the Gulf) as well as between the Arab state system and international powers (primarily the United States, but other countries as well). This strategic importance is what facilitates the accrual of rents to the Jordanian regime. As discussed above, the prevailing economic model in Jordan provides little in the way of purchasing power, employment, and income-generation. The plethora of direct aid in the form of budget support, and foreign-funded projects—whether they be from the Gulf states, the United States, or international institutions—has created rent flows that have helped smooth out some, even if not all, of the potential political challenges to the regime. This rent flow has effectively produced two strategic effects. First, it has created an understanding among local populations that inclusion and exclusion in these flows are largely related to the regime's strategic calculations in privileging those loyal sectors of society. Secondly, it has also created an understanding that these projects are a function of the regime's "good" international standing and that alternative power centers might not be as effective in delivering such rent flows.

Could mass mobilization reach the level at which the IAF, the NCRS, or other bases of regime support or accomodationist groups can no longer play the reform game? Can the situation reach a point where elite opposition groups can no longer afford to remain silent on the question of the downfall of the regime? Yes. However, reaching that point involves its own set of conditions.

Assessing the Potential for Mass Cross-Sectoral Anti-Regime Mobilization

The previous section described the institutional and strategic factors that deter existing socio-political forces from mobilizing against the regime. It is thus worth discussing the potential for an alternative socio-political force to emerge, one that would not be bound by the aforementioned institutional relations or strategic calculations. This is a pivotal issue, as other cases (such as Tunisia, Egypt, and Syria) have shown. Unless ordinary people turn out en masse and definitively demand its fall, formal political groups and collective social groups will not publicly call for its fall (if they do at all) on their own. However, such an emergence of alternative political formations depends on the rapid development of (institutional) capacities to mobilize people, as well as the level of polarization vis-à-vis the regime (that is, strategic calculations). Thus the initial turnout of people across the country is a necessary, but not sufficient, step towards mass-based anti-regime mobilizations. The possibility for such a potential formation certainly exists in the abstract. However, the probability thus far is quite low. Several factors undergird such an assessment.

Foremost among these factors is the fact that the regime has been quite adept at managing potential groups and spaces where such cross-sectoral alliances are likely to be formed. This has been a function of both violence and space. While the types of confrontation between protestors and the regime that characterized the mobilizations in Bahrain, Egypt, Libya, Syria, Tunisia, and Yemen were nowhere to be seen in Jordan, the regime's strategy was not void of coercive measures. The nature of protestors' demands and the numbers of those mobilized were manageable independent of violent dispersal, especially in light of extra-coercive strategies. However, three particular instances—beyond the general fact of continuing authoritarian rule—reminded the population of the potential/reality of violence and other forms of coercive action without radicalizing existing or would-be protestors. The first took place during one of the weekly Friday protests (18 February 2011), when plain-clothed assailants attacked demonstrators with sticks, stones, and makeshift whips.[60] Despite the usual police and gendarmerie presence, not one of the assailants was apprehended during the attack. While the government publicly denounced the assailants, discussion of an official inquiry and prosecution of those responsible eventually faded without any semblance of accountability. The second instance was during the 24–5 March 2011 sit-in at the Gamal Abdul Nasser Roundabout (more commonly referred to as Duwwar al-Dakhiliyya, due to its proximity to the Ministry of Interior), when "loyalist counter-protestors" first attacked the protestors, before the gendarmerie violently dispersed them.[61] Here too, the regime denounced vigilante acts, but did little in the way of holding the plain-clothed assailants or the gendarmerie accountable for their actions, despite over 100 reported injuries and one confirmed death. It is one thing to hold weekly demonstrations with generic calls for reform, but quite another to hold an indefinite sit-in, articulate specific demands, and do so in a space offering a Tahrir Square-like feel with respect to its public visibility and potential numerical increase. This incident, perhaps more than that of 18 February 2011, echoed loud and clear throughout the Jordanian news media and blogosphere, and effectively ended much of the contentious politics that did not come under the umbrella of one of the major existing socio-political

[60] See Joel Greenberg, "Jordan Protesters Attacked by Government Supporters in Amman," *Washington Post*, 18 Feb. 2011, http://www.washingtonpost.com/wp-dyn/content/article/2011/02/18/AR2011021804081.html (accessed 1 Dec. 2012); Ranya Kadri and Isabel Kershner, "Violence Erupts at Jordan Protest," *New York Times*, 18 Feb. 2011, http://www.nytimes.com/2011/02/19/world/middleeast/19jordan.html?_r=0 (accessed 1 Dec. 2012).

[61] See "Jordan's March 24 Youth Sit-in Violently Dispersed," Jadaliyya, http://www.jadaliyya.com/pages/index/1012/jordans-march-24-youth-sit-in-violently-dispersed- (accessed 1 Dec. 2012); "One Killed as Jordan Police Disperse Clash," Reuters, 25 Mar. 2011, http://www.reuters.com/article/2011/03/25/us-jordan-protests-idUSTRE72O4FC20110325 (accessed 1 Dec. 2012).

forces discussed above. Finally, there was the reintroduction of the requirement for all male citizens between the ages of eighteen and thirty-four to update their military service deferment status. This followed a long period where such requirements, in the aftermath of the 1994 peace accords between Jordan and Israel (and the concomitant downscaling of military recruitment in Jordan), had been unofficially canceled. By doing so, the regime demonstrated its willingness to engage in control tactics that a majority of the affected citizens possibly found too costly a price for participating in or supporting reform-oriented public agitation.

In addition, the uprising in Libya marked an important turning point in the discourse of opposition and protest activists in Jordan. This was because the ensuing civil war and the subsequent North Atlantic Treaty Organization (NATO) intervention dissuaded some existing—as well as some potential—allies in Jordanian society from participating in the protests. After initial optimism at the potential of mass-based uprisings to bring about change as occurred in Tunisia and Egypt, the subsequently emerging argument was that uprisings do not always result in a smooth transition and the result could instead seem too high a cost for regime change. However, the Syrian uprising has hit closer to home for many Jordanians watching developments in the neighboring country. The discourse of sectarianism, civil strife, and even civil war has deepened concerns for many Jordanians. Rightly or wrongly, many view the existing competition between tribal groups as well as the Trans-Jordanian/Palestinian–Jordanian divide as potential seeds for a bitter and violent confrontation should a zero-sum game develop among existing socio-political forces (including the regime). Indeed, such seeds are ever present in the simplest of attempts at organizing within Jordanian society, as evidenced by many dissolved dialogue groups and mobilization meetings.

Finally, and independent of domestic considerations, there is a clear understanding by all concerned groups that the Jordanian regime is tightly woven into regional and international networks of power relations. In the case of Jordan, this is particularly so as a function of the new Arab cold war as well as the country's proximity to Israel. There is little doubt, following the case of Bahrain, as to the lengths to which external powers allied with the Hashemite regime will go to in order to prop up the regime in the face of a mass-based movement to overthrow it.

Yet notwithstanding the above, spontaneous taking to the streets can still occur. This was amply demonstrated on Tuesday, 13 November

2012, when protestors took to the streets across several cities in Jordan. The immediate spark for the protests was the government's announcement that it would cut fuel subsidies as a means of addressing its budget deficit and securing a $2 billion loan from the IMF. Such cuts were poised to generate price increases of 50 percent for cooking gas, 33 percent for heating gas, and 14 percent for low-octane car gasoline.

Specific figures have been difficult to ascertain, but estimates for the Amman protests in November 2012 averaged between 2,000 and 3,000 people, while those in Salt and other urban centers outside the capital numbered several hundred to a little over a thousand each. In addition, public transportation workers blocked several roads in downtown Amman. The initial reaction of riot police and gendarmerie to the protests was a general strategy of containment without engagement. However, as protests grew that day, various clashes ensued around the country. During the early hours of the morning of Wednesday, 14 November, security forces violently dispersed protestors from the Duwwar al-Dakhiliyya area near the Ministry of Interior, the main site of protests in Amman in this period. As the second day of protests came to a close, security forces were preventing the reassembly of protestors in the area. Security forces also used water cannon and tear gas against protestors in Salt, Tafila, M'an, Irbid, and Dheban. After four days of such unrest, there was one confirmed death among protestors, and (still) unconfirmed reports said that in some areas, protestors had burned tires, thrown rocks, and attempted to set fire to government buildings. Despite repeated calls to reassemble at different locations in Amman and elsewhere, the protests eventually ended—but not without the arrest of over 100 protestors in Amman and elsewhere.

In the first official response to those particular protests, and in a direct challenge to protestors, Prime Minister Abdullah al-Nsour asserted in an Al Arabiyya interview that "it is impossible to backtrack" on the decision to cut fuel subsidies, claiming that the alternative to such cuts would be worse. He went on to claim that "seventy-three percent of the population would not feel one *fils* [equivalent to one one-thousandth of a Jordanian dinar] of an extra cost" in their daily lives because of other forms of financial support the government is allegedly set to offer. Beyond claiming that there would be "*da'm*" [support] for the "poor and middle class," Nsrour failed to provide any details or explain how it made any fiscal sense to eliminate fuel subsidies if those cuts were going to be offset "by an amount that is greater than the increase in prices." Even so, the boldness and firmness he exuded in the interview spoke to a particular confidence on the regime's part of its ability to implement such a policy while at the same time surviving the consequences.

One of the dynamics that journalists and analysts were quick to highlight in November 2012 was the way in which the slogans chanted during the protests directly addressed and criticized the king:

Ya bitsallih al-hin, ya bi-tilhaq al-Abidine (Either fix it now, or follow [Zein] [al-] Abdine [Ben Ali]).

Haza al-Urdun urdunna wa-al-khayin yab'id 'anna (This Jordan is our Jordan, and the traitor should get away from us).

Hurriyye, hurriyye, mish makarim malakiyye (Freedom, freedom, not royal handouts).

Hurriyye min Allah, ghasban 'annak Abdullah (Freedom from God, against your will oh Abdullah).

Al-sha'b yurid isqat al-nizam (The people want the fall of the regime).

Yasqut, yasqut hukm al-az'ar (Down, down with the rule of the scoundrel).

The demands of the protestors were unequivocal in their condemnation of the recent decision to cut fuel subsidies, as well as the dismal state of the economy, and the lack of political accountability and transparency. However, many observers misread the presence within demonstrations and online discussions of calls for the fall of the regime as representing the majority of forces mobilized at the time, or those that could potentially become mobilized in the future. The fact was that, at the same protest, some chants called for the king to take corrective action, while others called for his downfall. While grievances against existing policies are widely shared, the positions held by protestors towards the king, monarchy, and/or the regime are much less coherent.

The official statements of both the Teachers' Union and the IAF, to take two examples from the November 2012 protests, are highly instructive in this regard. The Teachers' Union, which itself was formed amid the mobilizations of 2011, called for a general strike in protest against the announced cuts in fuel subsidies. However, when pressed by an Al Jazeera reporter to comment on slogans calling for the fall of the regime, the spokesman of the union declared that the union was "for reform" in Jordan and not for the fall of the regime. Furthermore, the IAF had issued a statement calling on the king to revoke the decision to cut fuel subsidies and to form a national salvation government. The fact that the Teachers' Union and IAF continued to invoke the king as the final arbitrator of policy and Cabinet selections should caution those who believed that either group had thrown its weight behind calls for the fall of the regime. While the position of other political, professional, and labor groups was never fully articulated before the protests completely ended, it is fair to say that their positions, however uneven across the spectrum, had not departed from a long-standing reformist posture.

None of the above is to claim that a mass uprising against the regime is impossible in Jordan. Rather, it is simply to caution against assuming that such mobilizations are inevitable and will naturally flow from existing grievances. Simply put, the possibility of such mobilizations depends on the ability of a range of actors to overcome dilemmas of collective action and strategic rationale, which have been structured in particular ways as a result of the trajectory of state formation in Jordan. As of this writing, the Hashemite regime recently mobilized society (and its supporters therein) for a new round of parliamentary elections that the king hailed as the hallmark of his (now) serious approach to reform. With the exception of discussions with regard to minor changes in the rules and regulations governing the elections, news headlines and analyst commentary on the January 2013 elections could easily have been confused for those during the build up to the November 2010 parliamentary elections.[62] Furthermore, the confidence of the regime and its appointed government(s) in being able to outlast any potential protest was further demonstrated by the previous government's passing of an Internet censorship law, and the government's most recent passing of increases in both electricity prices and cellphone usage taxes.

Conclusion

Since early 2011, any social or political unrest in a given Arab state is often viewed as a precursor to an impending uprising that will ultimately overthrow the ruling regime. This has been particularly notable

[62] See Ziad Abu-Rish, "Jordan, Liberalism, and The Question of Boycott," Jadaliyya, http://www.jadaliyya.com/pages/index/295/jordan-liberalism-and-the-question-of-boycott (accessed 1 Dec. 2012).

in the case of Jordan. The above discussion was not intended to narrate a series of events that make up the socio-political developments in Jordan between January 2011 and January 2013. Rather, the purpose was to highlight the fact that mass-based cross-sectoral anti-regime protests, irrespective of the country, face particular collective action dilemmas. Different demographic realities, institutional legacies, and strategic calculations variously animate such dilemmas, which tend to be inherent in all acts of collective action. Many have argued that history is the product of the interaction between structures and contingencies. It is hoped that the above discussion sheds light on some of the structures that mitigate against mass-based anti-regime collective action. Barring a contingency that would undermine or reconfigure such structural factors, it would be presumptuous to expect an uprising similar to that in Tunisia, Egypt, or even Syria. The above discussion sought to outline the trajectory of state formation in Jordan as well as the institutional and strategic dynamics it produced vis-à-vis formal political groups and potential alternative political formations. The conduct of such groups toward the regime will ultimately be colored by the short- and long-term strategic calculations within the said historical context and contemporary legacies. These calculations center on the perceived and real likelihood of a violent regime crackdown, self-assessments of how each group would fare in the potential day-after scenarios, the imagined and/or real fears surrounding a potential Islamist victory, or even the potential for some form of widespread civil strife. Also important are perceptions about powerful external actors, such as the Gulf monarchies, the United States, and Israel, particularly in the ways in which they might come to the aid of the regime.

In the final analysis, three potential scenarios are likely in Jordan. The first is that the regime game will continue to be in play, offering little in the way of structural transformation, but enough restructuring to allow for the dissipation of pressure. This, for now, seems the most likely scenario, based on what has been discussed thus far and barring a contingency that would radicalize regime–opposition dynamics. The second scenario is the sacrificing of the king by the monarchy/regime. Such a scenario would not be unprecedented in Jordan or other monarchies/regimes. It is worth noting that the bulk of publicized critiques of the monarchy have specifically targeted King Abdullah II rather than the Hashemites as a whole. However, and as discussed above, King Abdullah

II himself has long taken precautions against such moves on the part of other elements within the monarchy/regime. Finally, there is the scenario in which the monarchy/regime in its entirety is toppled. This would be the most difficult task to accomplish, though it would represent the deepest levels of transformation (without really indicating what would come in its place).

Which of these three possibilities is more likely to occur depends on the level of polarization, and the rationale of calculation by various groups of how they would fare in the status quo as opposed to any number of potential day-after scenarios. Facile explanations of "enough is enough" or "the regime has run out of cards" ignore this fact. There has always been criticism, dislike, even hatred for the regime. The fact that the current situation has emboldened some to voice such sentiments publicly should not be lost on us. But neither should the fact that such sentiments, however much they are shared by the rest of the population, do not necessarily or uniformly translate into broad-based mobilization or widespread demands for the fall of the regime. In other words, the possible outcomes depend largely on the circumstances in place, which in turn structure differently the rationale of various collective social actors that make up the Jordanian political field.

There are those that assert the existence of a fourth possibility, that what is happening might lead to a new status quo in which King Abdullah II (or the monarchy as a whole) could continue to rule, but in a manner that is much more constrained and on a route toward greater checks on his power and more parity in his relationships with parliament. This, in effect, is another way of claiming that the reform game is a viable option for meaningful transformation. Yet beyond the dismal empirical record of more than twenty years of "reform" in Jordan and across the region, there are the socio-political facts that regimes do not willingly give up power and that formal politics offer limited avenues for structural transformation when sought from below. One need only consider the dilemma Egyptian activists faced in the aftermath of the fall of Hosni Mubarak when faced with the choice between electoral participation and contentious politics—or even the more difficult choice when faced with the presidency of Mohammad Morsi and the broader context of a Muslim Brotherhood pact with the Supreme Council of the Armed Forces. It would be naïve to think that the current state of polarization and mobilization in Jordan (as they stand today) is enough to force the hand of the regime into meaningful change. Again, protests could erupt and escalate, while their demands could become more radicalized. But that is currently not the case, and the above discussion sought to explain why it is not necessarily inevitable.

In conclusion, it should be stressed that the above does not represent a normative judgment on the desire of those wishing for the fall of the regime in Jordan. Rather, it represents an analytical caution against the claim that Jordan is "forever on the brink." As the vast majority of Jordanians continue to struggle to meet their needs and realize their aspirations, one should note that getting to "the brink" will depend on a number of factors. These include the ability of alternative forms of political mobilization to take hold, the ability to expand such mobilizations to incorporate important social and political forces, the radicalization of the demands in the resultant coalition, and the ability to sustain such a mobilization whereby the alternative to meaningful change becomes too costly for the regime (and its allies) in the long run rather than the short-term. Such abilities are not simply a function of will alone, but are informed by a series of institutional, strategic, and resource constraints. While such constraints are not impossible to overcome, and might be completely undone as a consequence of some unexpected contingent event, they are nevertheless significant and currently determinant.

11

THE PERSIAN GULF MONARCHIES AND THE ARAB SPRING

Russell E. Lucas

Has the Arab Spring caused a major change in the way that the six Arab monarchies of the Gulf Cooperation Council (GCC) are governed? The public perception of the Persian Gulf monarchies as belonging to an isolated desert oasis has now been superseded by the hyper-globalized skyline of Dubai. Yet on a political level, the GCC states continue to be viewed as being ruled by long-standing autocrats. However, recent scholarship on the GCC states has uncovered slow but increasingly meaningful steps towards political reform.

The explosion of protests in the Arab world, labeled the Arab Spring, has not left the Gulf monarchies untouched. It would be a gross overstatement to speak of the GCC states as having been affected by the Arab Spring as a unified bloc. As with the whole of the Middle East, in the Gulf monarchies there has been a variety of popular and government reactions to the events that started in North Africa in 2010. Protests in the GCC run from the quiet on the streets of Doha to the simmering insurgency of nearby Manama. Yet, unlike their North African counterparts, no regime in the GCC has fallen.

This chapter argues that the ruling bargain in each of the GCC countries—Bahrain, Kuwait, Oman, Qatar, Saudi Arabia, and the United Arab Emirates—has evolved but not radically changed since 2011. After describing how events in the GCC have proceeded since the Arab Spring, the chapter analyzes why the GCC seems to stand out in terms of the number and severity of protests compared to the rest of the Arab world, even though the challenges facing the GCC states are not fundamentally different from those facing all Arab states.

The following section notes that, just as the degree and severity of protests have varied in each of the GCC countries, reactions by their monarchs have also differed—and not always in ways directly in proportion to the nature of the protests. Nevertheless, the policies of the GCC monarchies share some similarities that amount to an evolution of the ruling bargain in the Gulf. Economic stimulus packages were used to quell the initial wave of protests in all of the Gulf monarchies. In most GCC states, political concessions have also been granted that provide for a limited degree of political liberalization—if not now, then in the future. However, the most notable change in the ruling bargain in the Gulf has been the increased use of repression by state authorities against oppositional groups and individuals. Censorship, imprisonment, and even torture have become much more commonplace in the GCC during the Arab Spring. Finally, the GCC states have used the framework of regional dynamics to link domestic disputes to larger geopolitical forces in the "securitization" of sectarian identities as a cover for their imposition of greater repression.

The chapter concludes by discussing how citizens in the various GCC states view the evolution of their countries' ruling bargains. While there is growing dissatisfaction with the monarchies of the GCC, popular discontent has thus far been contained. This situation stems from the fact that Gulf citizens are not facing the existential economic deprivations that exist in other Arab states. And across the GCC, neo-liberal economic policies have not made middle-class citizens as downwardly mobile as they were in states such as Egypt, Tunisia, or Morocco. The economic safety net from petroleum wealth has kept the floor from falling out under Gulf citizens. This classic rentier trade-off of economic wellbeing in return for political quiescence still seems to hold in the Gulf. Economic stimulus and the securitization of sectarian identities brought Gulf regimes some political breathing space. Gulf leaders state that they had always promised "leadership" rather than democracy—unlike the phony democracy provided for in Mubarak's or Ben Ali's elections. But the rentier bargain in the Gulf is nevertheless beginning to fray. Marginalized groups in the Gulf are sustaining political activity because of new technologies and greater international interest in Arab activism. The increased use of repression—while effective in the short term—has served to unmask forms of coercive activity which previously had little presence, let alone visibility, in countries such as Kuwait or the Emirates. Repression will likely serve to further undercut the rentier bargain and draw attention to the lack of economic and political equality between the rulers and the ruled in the GCC.

The GCC since the Tunisian Revolution

There was a far greater variety in the series of events in the Gulf Arab Spring than in either the Maghreb or the Mashreq. While each Arab state had its own pre-existing conditions that helped to channel the outburst of youth protests in 2011, it is only in certain countries of the Gulf that the streets remained completely quiet.

In terms of domestic politics, Qatar seems to have been almost completely unaffected by the Arab Spring. Public protests against the regime, or even specific government policies, have been conspicuously absent. The expression of dissent online has also been muted when compared to the rest of the Arab world. Qatar's small population in conjunction with the state's rapidly rising gas and oil revenues has allowed the ruling al-Thani family to deepen the pre-existing rentier bargain. Nevertheless, Amir Hamad promised to hold parliamentary elections in late 2013,[1] despite negligible public demands for parliamentary life (the regime has been promising to hold these elections since 2003). In contrast to Qatar's domestic quiet, Amir Hamad's foreign policy during the Arab Spring has been frantic. As "the mouse that roared,"[2] Qatar has emerged as a leading

[1] Justin Gengler, "Qatar's Ambivalent Democratization," Foreign Policy Middle East Channel, 1 Nov. 2011, http://mideast.foreignpolicy.com/posts/2011/11/01/qataris_lesson_in_revolution

[2] Robert Fisk, "Arab League's 'Roar' at Syria Shows how Tiny Qatar is Starting to Flex its Muscle," *The Independent*, 14 Nov. 2011, http://www.independent.co.uk/news/world/middle-east/robert-fisk-arab-leagues-roar-at-syria-shows-how-tiny-qatar-is-starting-to-flex-its-muscle-6261944.html

actor in the recent transitions of other Arab states. Qatar's foreign activity rests on the twin pillars of the Al Jazeera satellite television network and the amir's personal diplomacy. Al Jazeera's coverage has been identified as crucial in the "scaling-up" of protests in Tunisia and Egypt and in the contagion of the protest meme across the Arab world in early 2011.[3] Qatar supported the armed opposition against the incumbent regimes in Libya and later in Syria. The amir has also led calls in the Arab League for regime change in the two countries, thereby helping to open the door for NATO intervention in Libya. Yet Qatar has been accused of not only supporting the end of dictatorship in other countries, but also playing favorites in supporting the rise of Islamist groups in the transitions of other Arab states.[4] Nevertheless, it has been noted that Al Jazeera remains remarkably (if not unsurprisingly) quiet about politics inside Qatar. It is doubtful that Qatar will see many significant changes as Amir Hamad passes power to his son, Tamim.

Like Qatar, the UAE has not experienced significant public protests during the Arab Spring, the small segment of political activists that utilized petitions and social media to express their grievances being quickly repressed. Abu Dhabi's role within the federation also seems to be consolidating in the wake of Dubai's decline after the 2008 financial crash. This process has been reinforced by Abu Dhabi's political decisions domestically and externally with regard to the demands arising from the Arab Spring.

Those who have expressed dissent in the Emirates have called for greater reforms of the federal structure rather than revolution. Political activists have especially called for greater suffrage in the elections to the Federal National Council (FNC), the UAE's legislative body, and for the FNC to be given greater parliamentary powers. As a nod to some of these demands, the total number of those eligible to vote for half of the seats in the forty-member chamber in the September 2011 FNC elections (the remainder are appointed by the Federal Executive) was increased to around 129,000. Nevertheless, only 28 percent of eligible

[3] Jon B. Alterman, "The Revolution Will Not Be Tweeted," *The Washington Quarterly*, 34 (2011), pp. 103–16.

[4] Guido Steinberg, "Qatar and the Arab Spring," *Stiftung Wissenschaft und Politik Comments*, 7 (2012), http://www.swp-berlin.org/en/publications/swp-comments-en/swp-aktuelle-details/article/qatar_and_the_arab_spring.html

voters participated. Petitions, online and traditional, that called for limiting the executive branch's power have stemmed from two main, but generally small, groups: "liberals" and "Islamists." The former group saw some of its activists, the "UAE 5," jailed in September 2011, but they were later pardoned. However, one, Ahmad Abd al-Khaleq, was eventually deported to Thailand. In the summer of 2012 a larger roundup took place of members of the al-Islah association (a group styled along the lines of the Muslim Brotherhood), with over a dozen arrests.[5] The continued harassment of even reformist demands has demonstrated the sensitivity of UAE leaders to even the mildest dissent. However, the number of political activists in the Emirates remains small, and the groups involved are ideologically divided in the face of a citizen population that feels uneasy about their minority status among large numbers of expatriate non-citizens—especially in Dubai and Abu Dhabi. This sensitivity—especially on the part of Abu Dhabi's leaders—extended to the Emirate's contribution of military forces to the GCC's Peninsula Shield forces in Bahrain in March 2011 (see below).

While Qatar and the UAE have experienced little by way of protest, Saudi Arabia and Oman have both faced occasional protests. In both countries, protestors have failed to build diverse alliances among groups to push for regime change beyond a specific constituency. Instead, the Saudi and Omani regimes have maintained the initiative in promoting economic stimulus more than political reforms. Repression also increased steadily in both countries after the initial wave of protests in February/March 2011 had subsided. However, in both Saudi Arabia and Oman, notable protests reemerged in the summer of 2012.

Protests in Saudi Arabia, while frequent, have not become widespread or sufficiently significant to force the regime to make substantial political changes. The "day of rage" planned for 11 March 2011 in Riyadh—which activists had intended to spur Tahrir Square-like demonstrations—failed to achieve a critical mass due to heavy-handed police blockades. Since then, the Saudi capital has witnessed only minor protests. Most protests in Saudi Arabia have instead taken place in the Eastern Province—home to most of the kingdom's Shi'a minority. While

[5] Angelia Shaw, "Detentions of Activists are Reported in U.A.E.," *New York Times*, 18 July 2012, http://www.nytimes.com/2012/07/19/world/middleeast/detentions-of-activists-are-reported-in-uae.html

grievances in the Eastern Province long predate the events of 2011, the protests of Saudi Shi'ites have crested twice since the Arab Spring: first in the spring of 2011 and then in the summer of 2012. The killing of supporters of the Nimr Baqir al-Nimr in July 2012 in Qatif following the Shi'a shaykh's arrest reignited regular protests in the region. The demands of Eastern Province protesters for the greater economic, social, and political inclusion of Shi'ites have not linked significantly into the demands of groups in other regions—especially in the capital. However, protests do seem to be occurring more frequently in Saudi Arabia—in March 2012, for example, King Khalid University students protested against poor campus services, leading to the death of a student and the injuring of dozens of others.[6]

The sectarian focus of Eastern Province protestors has served to hinder the protest movement in Saudi Arabia from broadening its popular appeal. In order to ensure that these protests do not spread to other sectors of the country the regime has tried to pre-empt economic and political demands while isolating protestors by framing these protests as sectarian in order to dismiss them. Most notably the Saudi government undertook a significant economic stimulus initiative in February and March 2011, with the total package estimated to be worth up to $130 billion. Key elements of the plans called for raising the minimum wage, building half a million new housing units, and creating up to 60,000 new jobs in the Ministry of the Interior.[7] Moreover, the municipal elections which had been delayed since 2009 were held in September 2011, although the solely male electorate was only able to choose half of the members for each of the councils while the remainder was appointed by the government. In April, a number of women attempted to register as electors, but their applications were rejected. Nevertheless, on the eve of the elections King Abdullah announced that women would be allowed to run and vote in the 2015 elections and to be appointed to the Shura Council.[8] Protests demanding that women be allowed to drive also per-

[6] "Saudi Arabia's Female Students Stage Cleaning Protest," *The Guardian*, 11 Mar. 2012, http://www.guardian.co.uk/world/2012/mar/11/saudi-arabia-female-students-protest

[7] Steffan Hertog, "The Costs of Counter-Revolution in the GCC," *Foreign Policy Middle East Channel*, 31 May 2011, http://mideast.foreignpolicy.com/posts/2011/05/31/the_costs_of_counter_revolution_in_the_gcc

[8] Neil MacFarquhar, "Saudi Monarch Grants Women Right to Vote," *New York*

colated through the summer of 2011. By addressing some of the economic issues spurring discontent in Saudi Arabia, coupled with its limited political reforms, the Saudi regime has partly nullified the demands of protestors. When protests are held, they are repressed; activists are regularly jailed and are often labeled as foreign-inspired provocateurs.

Oman witnessed significant protests in 2011 but they were not as sustained as those in Saudi Arabia. Like Saudi Arabia's, Oman's protests tended to emerge from a specific aggrieved sector—in the sultanate's case, the labor movement. The previous quiescence of Omani activists made the outburst of protests in Muscat—and more violently in Sohar—in February 2011 all the more surprising. While government responses generally dampened the public protests, dissent has also moved online. As in most of the other GCC states, the Omani government's early reactions focused on economic stimulus. The government raised the minimum wage by a third and pledged to create 50,000 jobs. The GCC also offered financial assistance to Oman (and Bahrain) in the form of a "Marshall Plan" to help pay for the economic concessions. The sultan even sacked a number of controversial ministers, thereby responding to many of the protesters who supported the sultan while opposing the Cabinet and its policies. The sultan also promised new powers and elections for the legislative assembly.[9] While parliamentary elections were held in October 2011, the parliament has only begun to test these new powers.

Government policy changes appeased some activists, and eventually the remaining protestors in Sohar were eventually forcibly removed by the army. Yet labor unrest, such as the Fahoud oil workers' strike in late May and early June 2012, has continued in Oman.[10] Repression against

Times, 25 Sep. 2011, http://www.nytimes.com/2011/09/26/world/middleeast/women-to-vote-in-saudi-arabia-king-says.html

[9] Sunil K. Vaidya, "Protesters in Oman Happy with Qaboos' Decision to Give Council of Oman Powers," *Gulf News*, 13 Mar. 2011, http://gulfnews.com/news/gulf/oman/protesters-in-oman-happy-with-qaboos-decision-to-give-council-of-oman-powers-1.776309; Ra'id Zuhair Al-Jamali, "Oman, Kind of Not Quiet?" Foreign Policy Middle East Channel, 7 Nov. 2011, http://mideast.foreignpolicy.com/posts/2011/11/07/kind_of_not_quiet

[10] Fahad al-Mukrahsi, "Protestors Demand Release of Activists in Oman," *Times of Oman*, 2 June 2012, http://www.timesofoman.com/echoice.aspx?detail=5763; "Rights Group Urges Oman to Drop Cases Against Activists Facing Jail for Questioning Ruler," *Washington Post*, 21 July 2012, http://

activists has also continued. However, in comparison with Saudi Arabia—where violence increased as the protestors' demands grew more radical—the demands of Omani labor activists have generally remained parochial. Yet not all activists have been satisfied with the limited changes that the sultan has made, which has led some to turn to online activism and commentary to express their grievances. Thus, like in the UAE, prosecutions of activists and bloggers increased in 2012 with laws against *lése-majesté* being amended and more frequently enforced.

Protests in Kuwait were seemingly slow to start. However, they have since become frequent with protestors increasingly demanding a fundamental reorganization of constitutional powers; protestors have thus called for the transformation of the regime rather than its downfall. These protests have led to the sacking of the prime minister—a member of the ruling Al Sabah family. These developments follow from the increasing tension between the National Assembly and the Al Sabah as well as factionalism within the ruling family itself: both of which predate the Arab Spring. The use of public protests, however, has been magnified by regional events. Nevertheless, the protests in Kuwait continue to be concerned with the recalibration of the balance of power between existing institutions rather than seeking a revolution of the entire political order.

Amir Sabah's announcement of an economic grant worth 1,000 dinars to every citizen in January 2011 placed Kuwait at the forefront of the GCC in terms of using economic stimulus to head off public protests, even if Kuwait's "Bidoon," as stateless former Bedouin, failed to receive the grant.[11] However, the grant did not prevent protests from emerging in the summer of 2011 over the alleged corruption of Prime Minister Shaykh Nasser al-Mohammed. Both the government and the National Assembly used parliamentary maneuvers to stem the crisis through the fall, as both parliamentarians and Cabinet members were also implicated in corrupt dealings. The protests escalated until a group of opposition

---

www.washingtonpost.com/world/middle_east/rights-group-urges-oman-to-drop-cases-against-activists-facing-jail-for-questioning-ruler/2012/07/21/gJQAZm2UzW_story.html

[11] Human Rights Watch, "Prisoners of the Past: Kuwaiti Bidun and the Burden of Statelessness," New York: Human Rights Watch, 2011, http://www.hrw.org/reports/2011/06/13/prisoners-past-0

leaders and protesters stormed the parliament during a demonstration on 16 November. Shaykh Nasser then resigned as prime minister and the amir dissolved the National Assembly and called for new elections. Thus for the first time in Kuwait's history a premier had been forced to step down due to popular pressure. Shaykh Jabir al-Mubarak, the Defense Minister, was subsequently appointed in his place, thereby keeping the job within the Jabir branch of the Al Sabah family.

While opposition candidates from Islamist and tribal backgrounds did well in the February 2012 parliamentary elections, the liberal opposition candidates performed poorly. In June, after vetoing a constitutional amendment in May that would have made the *sharia* the only source of legislation in the country, the amir suspended the National Assembly for a month in order to prevent the Interior Minister, Shaykh Ahmad, from being questioned.[12] A week later, Kuwait's Constitutional Court nullified the February 2012 elections on a technicality and reinstated the previously elected parliament. The amir appointed a reshuffled Cabinet under Shaykh Jabir, before calling the reinstated National Assembly that had been elected in 2009 back into session. However, due to a boycott by the deputies it never held a quorum, and the amir dissolved it again in October.

There was a marked deterioration in relations between the supporters of the ruling family and the multifaceted opposition in Kuwait during the fall of 2012. In September, the Constitutional Court failed to issue a ruling that would have supported the Al Sabah in abrogating the election law which had been rewritten in 2006 in response to popular demands for greater representation in the National Assembly.[13] The amir, undeterred by large protests in front of the court demanding that the electoral law be upheld, issued an emergency decree amending the law in the absence of parliament—keeping the five electoral districts but limiting voters to one vote (instead of four) in order to "preserve

[12] "Kuwait: Islamic Law Proposal Blocked," *New York Times*, 18 May 2012, www.nytimes.com/2012/05/18/world/middleeast/kuwait-islamic-law-proposal-blocked.html; "Kuwait's Ruler Suspends Parliament for a Month," *The National*, 19 June 2012, http://www.thenational.ae/news/world/middle-east/kuwaits-ruler-suspends-parliament-for-a-month

[13] Elizabeth Dickinson, "Kuwait Rejects Election Law Change," *The National*, 26 Sep. 2012, http://www.thenational.ae/news/world/middle-east/kuwait-rejects-election-law-change

national unity," a move which was interpreted as being designed to reduce the opposition presence in parliament.[14] These decrees resulted in the largest protests in Kuwait's history on 15 and 21 October, with violence often being used to quell these displays of public discontent.[15] The opposition vowed to boycott the December elections.

The demands of the opposition currently center on the creation of a "constitutional monarchy," in which the Cabinet is appointed by the parliament and will thus represent the "will of the voters," and on the legalization of political parties.[16] However, despite the relatively modest nature of these demands—with the various opposition groups seeking to reform the constitutional order rather than overthrowing the regime—they have nevertheless resulted in the arrest of a number of former MPs.[17] One reason for the regime's response is the fact that the reforms, however limited they may appear, would fundamentally alter the balance of power between the Al Sabah and other social groups in Kuwait. Judicial authorities have also entered the Kuwaiti political fray by dissolving the assembly elected in February 2012 and then again by dissolving the December 2012 assembly. While the July 2013 elections tempered the situation, it has not been resolved. Whether this impasse

[14] "Police Use Tear Gas and Stun Grenades at Kuwait Vote Protest," *The National*, 22 Oct. 2012, www.thenational.ae/news/world/middle-east/police-use-tear-gas-and-stun-grenades-at-kuwait-vote-protest

[15] "Kuwait Police Fire Tear Gas at Protesters," Al Jazeera, 21 Oct. 2012, http://www.aljazeera.com/news/middleeast/2012/10/20121021632723537.html; Fahed Al-Sumait, "A Boiling Kettle: Kuwait's Escalating Political Crisis," Jadaliyya, 26 Oct. 2012, http://www.jadaliyya.com/pages/index/8057/a-boiling-kettle_kuwaits-escalating-political-cris

[16] "Opposition Announces 'Declaration for Nation,'" *Kuwait Times*, 17 July 2012, http://news.kuwaittimes.net/2012/07/16/opposition-announces-declaration-for-nation/; "Oppn [*sic*] Demands Constitutional Reforms, Parliamentary Govt—Thousands Protest Court Ruling that Scrapped Feb Polls," *Kuwait Times*, 26 July 2012, http://news.kuwaittimes.net/2012/06/26/oppn-demands-constitutional-reforms-parliamentary-govt-thousands-protest-court-ruling-that-scrapped-feb-polls/

[17] "Kuwait Cracks Down on Opposition as Crisis Deepens," *The National*, 20 Oct. 2012, http://www.thenational.ae/news/world/middle-east/kuwait-cracks-down-on-opposition-as-crisis-deepens; "Kuwait Goes After Opposition Leader," *Al-Akhbar English*, 30 Oct. 2012, http://english.al-akhbar.com/content/kuwait-goes-after-opposition-leader

over the constitutional division of power in Kuwait will fade or serve to further exacerbate the existing tensions remains to be seen.

Bahrain is alone among the GCC states in having witnessed sustained popular protests that have sought the downfall of the existing regime.[18] The roots of Bahrain's domestic instability can be traced to long before the Arab Spring, while the regime's framing of the conflict in sectarian terms—Sunni regime versus Shi'ite opposition—also has a long history in the kingdom (regardless of its accuracy).[19] Protestors in Bahrain have been subjected to severe use of force from the kingdom's security forces, backed up by GCC Peninsula Shield units. Yet on the eve of the Arab Spring tension in Bahrain seemed to be on the decline due to the king's attempts to foster a degree of political liberalization and participation. The largest opposition group, al-Wifaq, had agreed to run in parliamentary elections in 2006 and 2010 after boycotting them in 2002.

Following the developments in Tunisia and Egypt, a number of Bahrainis assembled at Manama's Pearl Roundabout on 14 February 2011, with protestors initially demanding greater governmental transparency and accountability. On 17 February, security forces forcibly cleared the site, leaving four dead. The protesters then returned after the security forces had left, leading to massive protests on 22 February. With a further escalation of the violence used by the security forces, the protestors' demands expanded from seeking good governance to demanding the sacking of the long-serving prime minister, Shaykh Khalifa bin Salman, who is also the king's uncle, and ultimately to calls for the downfall of the monarchical regime. Crown Prince Salman responded by trying to start negotiations with the various opposition groups. However, as his position was undermined by the security services, who were more loyal to the prime minister and hard-line members of the regime, his terms were rejected. The opposition had initially framed its demands in terms of national unity, yet with greater repression, the opposition began to use more sectarian, Shi'ite language. According to some analysts, this use of sectarian rhetoric can be seen as responding to the way the regime has consistently framed the protests—in which the

[18] See Chapter 12, this volume, for a detailed discussion of Bahrain.

[19] Fred Lawson, "Repertoires of Contention in Contemporary Bahrain," in Quintan Wiktorowicz (ed.), *Islamic Activism a Social Movement Theory Approach*, Bloomington: University of Indiana Press, 2004, pp. 89–111.

Shi'ite protestors are portrayed as being supported by Iran (and thus as foreign and illegitimate)—as well as the counter-mobilization of hard-line Sunni Bahrainis.

Military forces under the banner of the GCC's Peninsula Shield forces—with representation from all six states, although the largest contribution has come from Saudi Arabia and Abu Dhabi—entered Bahrain on 14 March 2011, thereby freeing Bahraini military and security forces to suppress the protests. Although protestors were removed from the Pearl Roundabout a few days later, the protests still continued. Sporadic protests, met with continued repression, subsequently spread across the country.

In responding to the protests, the regime has tried to chart a course between a Syrian- or Libyan-style scorched-earth crackdown and significant regime-transforming reforms. On the one hand, Bahrain went further than any incumbent regime in offering an investigation into the events of the spring of 2011, in the form of the Bahrain Independent Commission of Inquiry (BICI).[20] Under the leadership of Mahmoud Cherif Bassiouni, a law professor and previously a UN war crimes investigator, the report details the events of the protests and the government's response. It found that torture and indiscriminate force were commonly used but that "there is no doubt that what occurred in February/March, and subsequently, was the result of an escalating process in which both the Government and the opposition have their share of responsibility in allowing events to unfold as they did."[21] This conclusion was not sufficient for the protestors, but it went too far for regime hard-liners. Moreover, the commission did not investigate the political causes and decisions that led to the protests and the regime's response, and the report's recommendations have not been implemented consistently. Thus while the government claimed that progress had been made on many fronts, the Project on Middle East Democracy found that only three of the twenty-six recommendations had been fully implemented one year after the report had been released.[22] The publication of the report in

[20] Bahrain Independent Commission of Inquiry, http://www.bici.org.bh/

[21] Mahmoud Cherif Bassiouni et al., "Report of the Bahrain Independent Commission of Inquiry," Manama, BICI, 2011, p. 416.

[22] Kareem Fahim, "Bahrain Government Defends Changes," *The New York Times*, 22 Nov. 2012, http://www.nytimes.com/2012/11/22/world/middleeast/bahrain-government-defends-changes.html; Project on Middle East

November 2011 consequently did little to stem what has become an incipient insurgency: by June 2012, Human Rights Watch attributed at least forty deaths and over 1,600 arrests to the government crackdown.[23]

The regime's response to the protests has been further complicated by intra-elite conflict, notably the long-running tug-of-war for power within the royal family between King Hamad and his son Salman, and the king's uncle, Prime Minister Khalifa, and hard-line relatives within the security establishments. The king and the crown prince have sought to use political liberalization as a means to undermine rivals within the family and to reinforce the family's legitimacy without surrendering power to the public. In addition, Bahrain's Sunnis, who have now mobilized in opposition to the Shi'ite majority, are also making demands on the Al Khalifa in exchange for their continued support.[24]

Why Were Protests Muted?

Is there a difference between the monarchies of the GCC and other Arab states in terms of the effects of the Arab Spring? Why, with the exception of Bahrain, have popular protests in these six states been muted relative to the major transformations of their republican neighbors?

The challenges facing the GCC monarchies are not fundamentally different from those facing the other Arab states. The economic grievances and political demands of an educated and growing youth population are different in their degree in the GCC—but they do not significantly differ in terms of substance. One important factor in explaining the generally peaceful nature of events in the GCC states could be the fact that the protests were not initially on as large a scale as they were in North Africa, which gave the countries concerned more time to pursue reactive policies—reforms in the eyes of some, counterrevolution in the

---

Democracy, "One Year Later: Assessing the Implementation of the BICI Report," Nov. 2012, http://pomed.org/wordpress/wp-content/uploads/2012/11/POMED_BahrainReport_web-FINAL.pdf

[23] Human Rights Watch, "Bahrain," World Report 2012, http://www.hrw.org/world-report-2012/world-report-2012-bahrain

[24] Justin Gengler, "Bahrain's Sunni Awakening," Middle East Report Online, 17 Jan. 2012, http://www.merip.org/mero/mero011712; Jane Kinninmont, "Bahrain: Beyond the Impasse," June 2012 http://www.chathamhouse.org/publications/papers/view/183983

eyes of others. These initial conditions and the respective regime responses should be viewed in light of the economic endowments of the GCC and the flexible institutional arrangements of monarchism, while the different outcomes that the protests produced can be attributed to the differences between the GCC states themselves.

How can the variation between the various Arab states in terms of the degree and severity of protests be explained? The first distinction that needs to be made is with regard to periodization. In doing so, a distinction also needs to be made between structural conditions (that is those that were in place prior to January 2011) and later policy reactions. This is not to say that conditions in the different Arab states were static before this point. However, when the protests quickly spread from Tunisia to the rest of the Arab world in the first quarter of 2011, each of the states concerned responded in slightly different ways.

One source of instability that the GCC and other Arab states share is the proportion of the youth in relation to the rest of the population. All of the Arab states have experienced a substantial rise in the number of youth, and while this section of the population has benefited from improvements in health and education, there is a lack of economic opportunities for young people and a limited number of avenues through which they are able to express themselves politically. Moreover, the fact that this has coincided with a period of technological progress in electronic communications and social media has given the youth opportunities to engage in forms of communication that are beyond centralized state control (at least until the security agencies become aware of them). However, while the youth and social media have played an important part in the Arab Spring, it is impossible to understand the latter event without taking account of the economic and political contexts of the Arab world.

Economic issues have been one of the key motivations for the protests. Issues of economic inequality, uneven growth, corruption, crony-capitalism, and unemployment—especially among the youth—have all been expressed throughout the protests. Yet while economic grievances were common to all of the protests in the Arab world, the wide variation in the region's different economic systems means that this factor, in and of itself, is unable to serve as the sole explanation for the Arab Spring and the variation it has produced in terms of political outcomes. Thus on the one hand, the lack of protests in Qatar and the UAE can largely be explained by the small size of their populations and each country's respective rentier wealth, with the rentier bargain in these states remaining intact despite the 2008 financial crisis. In addition, the presence of an imported working class—and often a private sector middle class as well—meant that economic grievances were less of an issue in these states, particularly as the grievances of the guest workers can simply be ignored. Rentier states with less extreme levels of wealth—Saudi Arabia, Oman, and Kuwait—have experienced more protests, with Bahrain, the poorest of the Gulf states, experiencing the most protests of all.[25] However, the economic standing of the average Bahraini is still much higher than that of an average citizen in Jordan or Morocco, countries where protests have been less widespread. It should also be noted that rentier wealth failed to guarantee stability in Libya. Thus while wealth *per se* cannot explain the variation in protests between the GCC and the other Arab states, it does help to explain the variation within the GCC in terms of the severity of protests. Another grievance, corruption, was widely seen as a target of protests. Recent neo-liberal economic reforms that often seemed to benefit only the well-connected and failed to spread growth to the majority were hardly restricted to those countries with more numerous protests. Finally, unemployment, especially among the young, motivates many protests. Nevertheless, each of these factors, while present in the GCC states, is mitigated relative to non-petroleum-producing Arab states.

Within the GCC, the concentration of inequality and unemployment in certain sectors helps explain why the protests took on a geographic or sectarian character. It is notable that tales of poverty emerged "even in Saudi Arabia" during 2011.[26] Unemployment, and especially youth unemployment, is an important issue for many Saudis. However, the perception of the Shi'ites in the Eastern Province that the region's share

[25] Ala'a Shehabi, "Bahrain's Flashy Crony Capitalism Cannot Last," *The Guardian*, 20 May 2012, http://www.guardian.co.uk/commentisfree/2012/may/20/bahrain-flashy-crony-capitalism

[26] Robert Mackey, "Saudi Video Blogger Reportedly Detained for Showing Poverty in Riyadh," *The Lede: The New York Times*, 19 Oct. 2011, http://thelede.blogs.nytimes.com/2011/10/19/saudi-video-blogger-reportedly-detained-for-showing-poverty-in-riyadh/; Badr al-Ibrahim, "Why Are Saudis Killing Themselves?" *Al Akhbar*, 26 Apr. 2012, http://english.al-akhbar.com/content/why-are-saudis-killing-themselves

of national wealth is lower—despite it being the home of the country's oil industry—has served to reinforce social divisions. Similar grievances are felt among Kuwait's Bidoon or Bahrain's Shi'ites.

In Tunisia and Egypt, political activists were able to harness economic grievances in order to create mass protests. If the activists had framed their protests purely in political terms, it is unlikely that they would have been able to harness the power of the masses in bringing about the downfall of Ben Ali and Mubarak.[27] Yet while the Bahraini protestors sought to present their demands in similar terms, the response of the government, and the fact that the core groups of protestors were Shi'ite, allowed sectarian framing to take hold, thereby limiting the popular appeal of the protests. In contrast, Oman's economic issues have allowed the protestors to maintain their momentum; however, the tendency of Omani protestors to restrict their demands solely to the economic rather than the political sphere has meant that this has not had the same effect as in Egypt.

The lack of political freedom and democracy in the Arab world has been identified as the third major component in the region's recent uprisings. The lack of responsiveness of Arab governments to their citizen's concerns—especially in relation to the growing economic difficulties of unemployment and inequality—fed into the perception of corruption surrounding most Arab regimes. However, while no regime in the region could be classed as democratic in the period before the Arab Spring, scholars frequently noted that the Arab monarchies generally offered a greater degree of political liberalization than the Arab republics.[28] Yet political liberalization in the Gulf monarchies did not ultimately offer any real potential to change the behavior of incumbent

[27] Alterman, "The Revolution Will Not Be Tweeted."

[28] It should, however, be noted that across both regime types there was a large degree of variation in political liberalization—the UAE and Saudi Arabia allowed for almost no liberalization, while some political liberalization had taken place in Egypt and Algeria. Rex Brynen et al., "Trends, Trajectories or Interesting Possibilities? Conclusion: Liberalization, Democratization, and Arab Experiences," in Rex Brynen, Bahgat Korany, and Paul Noble (eds), *Political Liberalization and Democratization in the Arab World, Volume 1*, Boulder, CO: Lynne Rienner Publishers, 1995, p. 276; Daniel Brumberg, "The Trap of Liberalized Autocracy," *Journal of Democracy*, 13 (2002), pp. 56–68; Russell E. Lucas, "Monarchical Authoritarianism: Survival and Political Liberalization in a Middle Eastern Regime Type," *International Journal of Middle East Studies*, 35 (2004), pp. 103–19.

elites—let alone to change the elites themselves. Moreover, the perception that the liberal aspects of these regimes were being reversed also contributed to the outbreak of protests.

All GCC states had implemented some degree of political liberalization in the years leading up to the Arab Spring—dramatically in the case of Kuwait and gradually in the case of Saudi Arabia. In Kuwait, the National Assembly had earned the power to interpellate, or "grill," Cabinet ministers. As this procedure developed, it began to lead to the regular resignation of ministers. It also led to parliament being dissolved and early elections being held, with no parliament finishing its full term since 2003. However, while the National Assembly's power has grown at the expense of the Cabinet, this has come at the cost of political stability. In other countries, less powerful parliaments had been introduced, as in Oman, or reintroduced, as in the case of Bahrain. The Emirates had begun to allow voting for the Federal National Council, albeit with a very narrow electorate. Saudi Arabia even formed the appointed advisory Shura Council, which was allowed to suggest legislation. Qatar had promised parliamentary elections after holding municipal elections even in the absence of any prominent demands for them.[29]

These reforms were important in shaping the demands of protestors in the GCC countries during the Arab Spring. In Kuwait, protestors eventually forced the prime minister to resign, for the first time, when opposition MPs demanded that they be able to question him in parliament. Early in Bahrain's protests demands were made for increasing the power of the Chamber of Representatives and limiting the power of the Consultative Council—an issue that had prompted the opposition's decision to boycott the 2002 election. These reforms also proved to be important in shaping the way the GCC states responded to the protests in that they provided a framework for GCC leaders to address the protestors' demands.

Reshaping the Ruling Bargain in the GCC

A key element in the reactions of the GCC regimes to the Arab Spring has involved economic stimulus and subsidy packages to address or to

[29] Anoushiravan Ehteshami and Steven Wright (eds), *Reform in the Middle East Oil Monarchies*, Reading: Ithaca Press, 2007; Joshua Teitelbaum (ed.), *Political Liberalization in the Persian Gulf*, London: C Hurst & Co., 2009.

preempt protests based on economic grievances. Since 2011 all GCC states have implemented some form of economic assistance to their citizens, including: increases in public sector wages, increased minimum wages in the private sector, additional consumer subsides, job creation packages in the public sector—often in the security services—additional housing allowances and building proposals, and increased pension payouts. The increase or introduction of new welfare programs fits into the long-established rentier state pattern in the Gulf. However, these rentier payouts came after a decade and a half of economic reforms that were designed to reduce the role of the public sector in providing support for GCC citizens. In the 1990s and 2000s economic reforms aimed to increase the role of the private sector and to encourage foreign investment.[30] While the financial crash of 2008 slowed the process of globalization in the Gulf, the concurrent rise in oil prices meant that the budgets of the GCC states were not as badly affected as would otherwise have been the case.

However, not all of the GGC states were in a position to launch large-scale stimulus packages, with both Oman and Bahrain needing fiscal backing from the other GCC members in what was described as a "Marshall Plan." And even in those countries that could afford to do so, such packages did not always produce the desired results. The steering of economic benefits to select groups of citizens, for example, often exacerbated the issue of citizenship—this is especially the case in Kuwait, where the tendency for Kuwaiti parliamentarians to dispense state benefits to their own constituents has come at the expense of Kuwait's Bidoon. Similarly, the initial wave of economic concessions in early 2011 did not end the demands for benefits from GCC citizens. In Oman, protests and strikes continued in which workers demanded increased pay or improved working conditions.

Yet, on the whole, the economic stimulus packages of 2011 generally reduced the severity of the protests in the GCC states, at least in the short term. However, a number of questions have been raised about the long-term sustainability of these economic concessions.[31] First, the stimulus packages often served to reinforce rather than to reform the

[30] David Held and Kristian Ulrichsen (eds), *The Transformation of the Gulf: Politics, Economics and the Global Order*, New York: Routledge, 2011.

[31] Hertog, "The Costs of Counter-Revolution in the GCC."

underlying rentier political–economic relationship between the state and its citizens. The economic benefits were distributed according to the existing logic of patrimonial beneficence, which reinforced many of the more political demands emerging in the GCC with regard to greater transparency and representation. Second, many of the jobs that the GCC states aimed to create were in the public sector, and the packages adopted hence appeared to run contrary to the need for private sector growth which had informed the previous decade's economic diversification policies. While Dubai's model of growth had been tarnished by the 2008 financial crash, the post-2011 public sector binge will likely create further problems for center–periphery disparities within the GCC states—Riyadh versus the Eastern Province, Abu Dhabi versus the poorer Emirates, and so on. Finally, greater public expenditure will likely necessitate an unsustainable appetite either for greater petroleum rents or for future deficits to be incurred. Saudi Arabia, for example, is estimated to need the price of a barrel of oil to rise above $300 by 2030 in order to finance its budget—and this need will only become more pressing as the country's own consumption of oil increases.[32]

The political reforms adopted by the GCC states in the post-2011 environment, to the extent such reforms have been implemented at all, are similarly flawed. Thus unlike Morocco, none of the GCC states has implemented significant constitutional reforms. Indeed, it is only in Oman where major concessions appear to have been made in allowing political institutions to have a greater public input and public voice. And even here, questions remain about the role of these advisory institutions in the context of the sultan's undiluted political power, with a public that is now increasingly politically aware.[33] In Bahrain and Kuwait, the political concessions that the regimes have made were not sufficient for the protestors, which has led to significant political crises in the two countries. Kuwait's political battles have generally been fought within normal institutional bounds of elections, interpellation,

[32] F. Gregory Gause, "Saudi Arabia in the New Middle East," Council on Foreign Relations Special Report Dec. 2011, p. 12, http://www.cfr.org/saudi-arabia/saudi-arabia-new-middle-east/p26663; Jim Krane, "The End of the Saudi Oil Reserve Margin," *Wall Street Journal*, 3 Apr. 2012, http://online.wsj.com/article/SB10001424052702303816504577319571732227492.html?mod=googlenews_wsj

[33] Al-Jamali, "Oman, Kind of Not Quiet?"

and now the courts, but public protests have also become a regular mode of contention. However, in Bahrain, the role of repression has led to political disputes and the marginalization of "normal" institutions in favor of more violent modes of contention.

An important factor in explaining the paucity of political reforms in the GCC states is the nature of the GCC monarchies themselves. Generationally, the elderly monarchs of the Gulf are far removed from the youth generation that led the street protests—King Hamad of Bahrain and Shaykh Mohammed Al Maktoum of Dubai are both in their sixties. However, even if these leaders understand the needs of their youth, they are constrained by intra-family disputes over power and resources. This seems to have played into Amir Hamad's decision to hand Qatar's leadership to his 33-year-old son, Tamim. King Abdullah's concerns over the succession have only increased as two of Saudi Arabia's crown princes have passed away. Family disputes in Bahrain and Kuwait have caused reforms to be undermined.[34] In some cases, dissenting members of the ruling family have even fueled the disputes. In Bahrain, the crown prince's plan for dialogue was quickly sidelined not only due to escalating demands from the opposition, but also because his rivals in Al Kahlifa let loose the batons of the security forces.

Aside from economic stimulus packages and some modest political reforms, the most common reaction of the GCC states to the protestors has been to repress demonstrations and to silence critical voices. While the level of violence that the GCC states have inflicted upon protestors does not come close to that used by the Libyan and Syrian regimes—only in Bahrain (and to a lesser extent Saudi Arabia) have protestors been targeted and killed, and even there the number of deaths has not entered into triple digits—the number of individuals arrested and imprisoned for political activities has sharply increased across the GCC. As dissent within previous bounds had often been tolerated in the past, as in the case of Kuwait, or compliance gained through familial or tribal intercessions, as in the case of the UAE, this is a relatively new and worrying development. Another new development in terms of state censorship and repression concerns the policy of the GCC states towards the Internet

[34] F. Gregory Gause, III, "Why Reform in the Gulf Monarchies Is a Family Feud," Foreign Policy Middle East Channel, 4 Mar. 2011, http://mideast.foreignpolicy.com/posts/2011/03/04/why_reform_in_the_gulf_monarchies_is_a_family_feud

and social media during the Arab Spring. Previously, the GCC states had simply filtered and prevented access to certain websites that the regimes deemed unacceptable or immoral. However, since early 2011 there have been a growing number of incidents where individuals have been arrested for web posts or tweets that are overly critical of authorities, with the cases of Ahmed Abd al-Khaleq in the UAE and Hamza Kashgari in Saudi Arabia attracting a great deal of international attention.[35] While these arrests and censorship target a full spectrum of dissent, different groups or sectors seem to have been targeted in each of the GCC states—whereas members of the Muslim Brotherhood-affiliated al-Islah movement in the UAE have been suppressed, in Oman the regime appears to have deliberately targeted labor-affiliated protestors.

However, the leaders of any given regime cannot take their ability to repress protesters for granted. Public protests can become so overwhelming that the security forces will lack the capability to control massive crowds. The throngs of protestors in Tunisia and Egypt highlight this limitation. Of all the GCC states, it is only Bahrain that has experienced such crowds—on 25 February about a fifth of the capital's population participated in the protests based in the Pearl Roundabout.[36] The October 2012 protests in Kuwait also threatened to bring overwhelming numbers of protestors on to the streets, although they ultimately failed to do so. Not only must regimes be capable of using repression, but they must be willing to do so as well in order to prevent crowds from swelling to an unmanageable size. In Egypt, the military commanders chose not to support the police in dispersing peaceful protesters. The divisions between the military and security forces in Libya and Syria demonstrate

[35] Al-Khaleq was arrested in the UAE for insulting the government; although he was pardoned, he was later expelled from the country. See Rori Donaghy, "In the UAE, the Future for those who Continue to Speak out Looks Bleak," *The Guardian*, 18 July 2012, http://www.theguardian.com/commentisfree/2012/jul/18/uae-emirates-battle. Kashgari was jailed for tweeting messages deemed insulting to the Prophet Muhammad in 2011. He was released two years later. See J. David Goodman, "In Morocco and Saudi Arabia, Limits Seen to Speech on Social Media," *The Lede: The New York Times*, 9 Feb. 2012, http://thelede.blogs.nytimes.com/2012/02/09/in-morocco-and-saudi-arabia-limits-seen-to-speech-on-social-media/?_php=true&_type=blogs&_r=0

[36] Michael Slackman and Nadim Audi, "Protesters in Bahrain Demand More Changes," *New York Times*, 25 Feb. 2011, http://www.nytimes.com/2011/02/26/world/middleeast/26bahrain.html

the limited willingness of certain institutions to use excessive force. In other words, the "successful military repression of the uprising turned on the question of will."[37] In the GCC states, the military and security forces are under the control of the regime (and not vice versa, as in Egypt). Moreover, the leadership of the coercive apparatus is tied to the regime through many reinforcing ties of family and tribe, while the rank and file often has tribal and regional characteristics that keep it separate from the protesting public. The fact that significant levels of state violence have not been used in the GCC outside of Bahrain and Saudi Arabia means that the will and the capacity of coercive forces to repress popular protests have not truly been tested in the GCC as a whole.

In the two instances where this has been tested, there has also been an increasing "securitization"[38] of sectarian identities. In public discourse, and especially that emanating from Saudi Arabia, the protests in the GCC states are represented as reflecting Shi'ite sectarian demands and as being inspired and led by the Iranian regime. The blame attributed to Iran for the protests in Bahrain and the Eastern Province fits into a larger pattern presenting Iran as a threat—exporting its revolution, its nuclear program, its new influence in Iraq, and so on. However, although it is likely that Iran will continue to be used as a scapegoat by these respective regimes, the accusations leveled at Tehran assume both an intent and a capability that the regime currently lacks.

The GCC states, with Saudi Arabia at the forefront, have sought to use the Iranian threat as a means to justify their foreign and domestic policies. The securitization of sectarianism has allowed the GCC to gain US (and European) silence, and even begrudging support, for the crackdown in Bahrain and now the Eastern Province. Moreover, the GCC regimes' linking of the various themes—of domestic unrest, Iran's nuclear program, Hezbollah, and the Syrian rebellion—has enabled the GCC to support long-standing foreign policy alignments (against Iran, Syria, and Libya) through their support for foreign protest movements while denying the freedom of their own citizens to protest at home. As a result, the GCC states have been able to characterize dissent as unpatriotic, thereby dividing the different aggrieved sectors from one another.

[37] Eva Bellin, "Reconsidering the Robustness of Authoritarianism in the Middle East," *Comparative Politics*, 44 (Jan. 2012), p. 131.

[38] Barry Buzan, Ole Waever, and Jaap De Wilde, *Security: A New Framework for Analysis*, Boulder, CO: Lynne Rienner, 1997.

The GCC, nevertheless, should not be considered as an entirely cohesive foreign policy collective. Serious diplomatic and economic reservations with regard to the Iran policy emanate from Oman and some of the Emirates. This variance was clearly visible with Saudi King Abdullah's proposal for the GCC to turn into a Gulf Union as a response to foreign and domestic threats. Whereas Bahrain responded positively, Kuwait demurred while Oman rejected the idea outright.[39]

Thus the reactions of the GCC monarchies to the protests also have regional and geopolitical dimensions. While the GCC states are often seen as leading a counter-revolution, this view neglects important variations in terms of the reactions of individual GCC states both domestically and internationally. Most notably, the rise of Qatar as a regional actor that "punches above its weight" has created a new dynamic between Qatar and the Gulf's traditional Arab heavyweight, Saudi Arabia. In some instances, there has been a degree of congruence between the policy interests of Saudi Arabia and Qatar and this has led to a revitalized role for the Arab League, as was the case in the League's support for the Libyan revolution or the broader GCC effort to support the Syrian rebellion. In others, however, as during the January/February revolution in Egypt, Al Jazeera seemingly sided with the revolutionaries while Saudi Arabia grew discontented, if not frightened, by the downfall of Mubarak. Moreover, Qatar's support of the Muslim Brotherhood organizations, both diplomatically and via Al Jazeera's coverage, stands in contrast to the UAE's crackdown on the organization.

The use of the GCC as a foreign policy tool first emerged with the May 2011 opening of membership bids by Jordan and Morocco. While it seems that this desire to expand the institution's membership has now faded, Jordan and Morocco have benefited from the GCC's financial assistance and the GCC from increasing openness to their workers—especially as employees in the security sectors. The financial beneficence of the GCC has not been restricted to other monarchies, however. Qatar,

[39] Ghazanfar Ali Khan, "GCC Leaders Back Call for Union of Gulf States," *Arab News*, 21 Dec. 2011, http://www.arabnews.com/node/401615; David Roberts, "Gulf Disunion," Foreign Policy Middle East Channel, 2 May 2012, http://mideast.foreignpolicy.com/posts/2012/05/02/gulf_disunion; "Oman's Foreign Minister Says There is No Gulf Union," *Gulf News*, 6 June 2012, http://gulfnews.com/news/gulf/oman/oman-s-foreign-minister-says-there-is-no-gulf-union-1.1032092

for instance, supported Egypt's Muslim Brotherhood-led government by recapitalizing the Egyptian Central Bank.[40] Yet not all GCC initiatives have been successful. The GCC attempts at management of the crisis in Yemen—while arranging for the soft landing of outgoing president Ali Abdullah Saleh—were generally secondary in influencing the outcome of events in Yemen as compared to local events on the ground.

Perceptions of the Evolving Ruling Bargain in the Gulf

The fact that the citizens of the six members of the GCC do not face the same dire economic conditions as in Egypt or Tunisia has conditioned their perception of events in the Arab Spring. The old ruling bargain in the Gulf—with the exception of Kuwait—did not include a significant element of political participation being granted in return for economic security. In most Middle Eastern and North African states, in contrast, the reconfiguration of the ruling bargain during the 1990s and 2000s led to a degree of political liberalization being granted in return for neo-liberal economic reforms (see Chapter 1, this volume). In the words of Jamal Khashoggi:

> In the Gulf, a monarchy's covenant is between a population and a royal family. The population was never promised the right to vote or even to name ministers. Although the bond is unfair, it was always thus, never built on "fraud and deceit" as in those republics where people were falsely promised the right to choose their ruler.[41]

In North Africa, it was the combination of economic malaise and illiberal political policies that ultimately led to the successful mass protests of 2011. It is hardly surprising, therefore, that the two GCC states where the largest protests have emerged are Kuwait and Bahrain. In the former, the perception that liberal political policies were being rolled back led citizens to the streets, whereas both economic marginalization and political inequality have fueled the protests in the latter.

[40] "Egypt Expects First Qatar Payment This Week," *Al Akbar*, 13 Aug. 2012, http://english.al-akhbar.com/content/egypt-expects-first-qatar-payment-week

[41] Jamal Khashoggi, "The Saudi King Never Promised Democracy," *The New York Times: Room for Debate*, 29 Aug. 2012, http://www.nytimes.com/roomfordebate/2012/08/28/the-staying-power-of-arab-monarchies/the-saudi-king-never-promised-democracy

There is a limited amount of data available from polls in the region due to the fact that such polls rarely take place and, when they do, they frequently fail to address politically "sensitive" topics. However, those surveys which have taken place indicate that, while democracy may be an ideal to strive for, GCC citizens prefer the "security" of the status quo over potentially destabilizing democratic reforms.[42] In one survey in Qatar, for example, those polled overwhelmingly agreed (or strongly agreed) that democracy is a preferable form of government (78 percent in 2011); but they also expressed very strong support for deference to government decisions even if they disagreed with them (74 percent in 2011).[43] Moreover, economic issues generally outrank concerns for political participation as both public and individual interests—a finding that applies in a variety of Middle Eastern and North African countries as well as the Gulf.

A further explanation for the strength of the Gulf monarchies in the face of popular protests concerns the more tribal nature of their populations.[44] However, though this factor is frequently cited in the literature, the use of tribalism as a policy of divide and rule has come back to haunt the Gulf monarchs. Thus while competing tribal groups may undercut one another with demands for patronage, they may also begin to coalesce into a "tribal bloc," as has happened in Kuwait, where "tribes are now the largest bloc in the opposition."[45] Consequently, explanations of Gulf citizen attitudes that focus solely on the primordial nature of their societies take an ahistorical view of how tribal identities can both support and undercut the rule of Gulf monarchs.[46]

[42] Gengler, "Qatar's Ambivalent Democratization"; Justin Gengler et al., "Civil Society and Democratization in the Arab Gulf," Foreign Policy Middle East Channel, 25 July 2011, http://mideast.foreignpolicy.com/posts/2011/07/25/civil_society_and_democratization_in_the_arab_gulf

[43] SESRI, "Omnibus Survey: A Survey of Life in Qatar 2011," Doha: Social & Economic Survey Research Institute, 2011, http://www.qu.edu.qa/sesri/documents/Projects/Projects_formatted/Omnibus_2011_summary.pdf

[44] Anthony Billingsley, *Political Succession in the Arab World: Constitutions, Family Loyalties and Islam*, New York: Routledge, 2010; Victor Menaldo, "The Middle East and North Africa's Resilient Monarchs," *Journal of Politics*, 74, 3 (July 2012), pp. 707–22.

[45] Gwenn Okruhlik, "The Identity Politics of Kuwait's Election," Foreign Policy Middle East Channel, 8 Feb. 2012, http://mideast.foreignpolicy.com/posts/2012/02/08/the_identity_politics_of_kuwait_s_election

[46] Sultan Al-Qassemi, "Tribalism in the Arabian Peninsula: It is a Family Affair,"

As a result of the economic stimulus packages and the reaffirming of the rentier bargain, most citizens in the GCC have generally continued to accept the political status quo. The same does not apply, however, to non-citizen residents of the GCC states. While expatriate and "guest" workers have remained generally quiescent during the Arab Spring, vocal protests have emerged from marginalized groups like Kuwait's Bidoon, non-citizen Bedouin residents of the state. It is precisely these marginalized groups—the Bidoon in Kuwait, the Shi'ites in Bahrain and Saudi Arabia, workers in Oman, and Emiratis from the poorer Emirates—that have instigated the Arab Spring protests in the GCC.

Many of these groups' grievances predate the Arab Spring but found new life (or attention) because of it. As such, protests from marginalized groups have called attention to the issue of economic performance in the evolving ruling bargain in the Gulf. If economic wellbeing—which has also been defined in more and more expansive terms over the past generation—does not continue to rise then groups that become marginalized will feel that the ruling bargain is not being upheld, which often turns the question to non-economic matters such as representation. This process moved very quickly in Bahrain because of the regime's failure to address earlier grievances. In Kuwait the process has moved into a discussion about representation and the balance of constitutional power between the legislature and the executive, both of which are issues that predate the events of the Arab Spring. While the protests in Oman and Saudi Arabia have not spread from the more marginalized sections of society, looming succession issues may also encourage the broader population into asking questions about greater political influence as well as economic benefits.

The increasing role of repression in the evolving ruling bargain in the Gulf currently has some degree of support. As the protestors continue to be seen as marginal—Islamists in the UAE, Shi'ites in Saudi Arabia, Internet activists across the Gulf—the repression directed against them has failed to inspire sympathy from the broader public.[47] However, in

---

Jadaliyya, 1 Feb. 2012, http://www.jadaliyya.com/pages/index/4198/tribalism-in-the-arabian-peninsula_its-a-family-af

[47] Sultan Sooud Al Qassemi, "A Liberal Emirati's Rant," Felix Arabia, 10 Aug. 2012, http://sultanalqassemi.blogspot.com/2012/08/a-liberal-emiratis-rant.html

those instances where state repression and violence have been less selective, as in Bahrain and Kuwait, the protests have escalated. In other words, for most citizens of the Gulf, repression has not reached a tipping-point whereby it acts as an incentive to reject the ruling bargain.

Yet while the strategy of repression has proven effective in suppressing the Gulf protests, albeit to varying degrees, the securitization of sectarian identities has only yielded modest dividends, and has occasionally produced unanticipated, and unwelcome, consequences. In Bahrain, for instance, the hidden role of Iran in the Shi'ite cause is an article of faith for the monarchy's supporters, but this kind of anti-Shi'ite discourse has also emboldened the Sunni opposition to make demands of its own. Likewise in Saudi Arabia, the shifting of blame for protests in the Eastern Province onto Iran also has support in some hardline Wahhabi circles.

However, it seems that the attention to regional events—in Libya and then Syria—has reinforced the image of both *fitna* and GCC initiatives in supporting the opposition, especially against Iranian schemes. The public in the GCC may be following the lead of their governments in seeing Iran as a threat—in Qatar, for example, only 17 percent of those polled in 2010 viewed Iran as a threat, whereas the respective figure in 2011 was 57 percent.[48] However, the more important actor in securitizing the Iranian threat has been Washington—which has generally followed the GCC's lead. However, these foreign policy "victories" do not address the lingering issues at home within the GCC states—these will continue to grow as petroleum resources begin to fade, putting further pressure on regional rulers to find a ruling bargain based on something other than rentier assumptions.

Conclusion

A variety of events unfolded in the GCC states during the Arab Spring, with the scale of the protests in each of the six states concerned varying significantly. Whereas the streets of Qatar and the UAE remained relatively peaceful, Bahrain seems unable to escape a vicious cycle of protest and repression, and both Saudi Arabia and Oman have also faced opposition from significant sectors of aggrieved groups. Kuwait's political dynamics—or dysfunctions—have only been magnified due to the protests over the Kuwaiti constitution.

[48] Gengler, "Qatar's Ambivalent Democratization."

The protests in the GCC have consequently been less widespread and sustained than those in other Arab states. The reasons for this relative quiet can be traced to preexisting factors and the policies that the Gulf monarchies used to respond to the Arab Spring. The monarchies were better positioned than many Arab countries because petroleum rents had allowed for improvements in living standards and welfare benefits, even though there continue to be significant disparities in terms of individual wealth. Moreover, while modest in scope, the political reforms of the first decade of the twenty-first century in many of the GCC countries had avoided the perception of political stagnation, despite there being few fundamental changes in the nature of each of the GCC regimes. Thus when faced with the outbreak of protests in 2011, the GCC regimes usually had the fiscal ability to address economic grievances—at least in the short term. The structure of the respective regimes also allowed them a freer hand to use military and security forces as a tool of repression when necessary without the fear of a coup (as in Egypt) or a divided regime (as in Libya). While the level of repression used in the GCC states—including Bahrain—remains modest in comparison with Syria, imprisonment and censorship have become much more frequent in the region when compared to the period before the Arab Spring. Finally, the securitization of sectarianism has allowed the GCC to use geopolitical alignments, and particularly the US fear of Iran, to their advantage in avoiding external pressure for reform.

The Gulf monarchies are not immune from the forces demanding social and political change in the region. Yet the social contract in the GCC has not been fundamentally rewritten as a result of the Arab Spring—in fact, the leaders of the GCC countries generally seem to have followed an old script. However, it remains an open question whether the structural and institutional factors that allowed the Gulf monarchies more time to respond and more tools to use in making reforms to ride the wave of the Arab revolts will be able to serve as the basis for their longevity in the future.

12

BAHRAIN'S FRACTURED RULING BARGAIN

POLITICAL MOBILIZATION, REGIME RESPONSES, AND THE NEW SECTARIANISM

Quinn Mecham

Bahrain's "ruling bargain," like most of those in the Arab world, was neither negotiated nor agreed upon by key stakeholders or major social groups. It was instead an arrangement imposed by the ruling family, and inconsistently acceded to by relevant social stakeholders, including economic, family, and religious groups. In the context of the Arab uprisings of 2011 and 2012, Bahrain's tenuous and controversial ruling bargain came under intense pressure and rapidly evolved into a high-stakes political standoff, punctuated by periods of both unilateral political decision-making and multilateral demonstrations of force. This period of mass mobilization built on existing tensions and grievances within the previous social order, yet it also relied on many common assumptions about the accepted roles of both ruling and opposition political actors in the way that these tensions worked toward resolution. What distinguishes the events of 2011–12 from previous political negotiations, however, was the intensity of the popular mobilization, the state's reliance on violent repression, and the increasing shift from economic and political grievances to sectarian religious conflict.

This chapter argues that although Bahrain's ruling authorities remained in power during a period in which other Arab leaders were less fortunate, both the remarkable levels of popular mobilization and the sectarian framing of the conflict in 2011–12 dramatically altered the character of the underlying ruling bargain in Bahrain. Although this ruling bargain has always been contested to some degree, it underwent a seismic shift in the context of broader regional mobilization. There are several reasons for this.

First, the kingdom's history of social and religious cleavages primed Bahrain for mass mobilization against the existing regime. As Bahrainis observed the "successful" protest movements in Tunisia and Egypt, protest coordination became easier and the coordination costs of collective action decreased. The considerable shared history of social grievances and contentious politics in Bahrain only required a convergence of the mass expectations about what others would do in order to lower individual coordination costs. This led to dramatic levels of popular mobilization, including the highest per capita levels of popular protest in the Arab world. Second, experiments with political reform in the previous decade had created an institutional and ideational framework through which popular demands against the ruling elite could be framed, while failing to allow for the effective communication and resolution of grievances through state institutions. This created unmet expectations for political dialogue that would lead some to reject the ruling bargain outright. Third, the regime employed a strategy that involved both concession and repression, which simultaneously accelerated popular expectations and amplified social and political grievances. Strategic inconsistencies within the ruling elite failed to create popular confidence that the normal rules of Bahraini politics were still applicable. Finally, Bahrain's small size and its strategic position between rival Sunni and Shi'a power centers further stimulated mass political participation and increased the perceived political stakes of what would otherwise be considered a local conflict.

The chapter begins by discussing the unique Bahraini context and identity cleavages that have long been prominent within society and which established the foundation for Bahraini nationalism as well as group conflict. The chapter then highlights the country's foundational "ruling bargain," as well as historical patterns of Bahraini sectarianism. Next, the chapter turns to Bahrain's experiments with political reform, and particularly the quasi-democratic experiments under King Hamad from 1999 to 2010. The chapter subsequently examines the characteristics, causes, and effects of mass popular mobilization beginning in 2011, as well as the effects of the Bahraini regime's responses to this unprecedented challenge to the monarchical system. The chapter concludes by assessing the possibilities for mending the ruptured ruling bargain, as well as the options facing both the regime and its opposition as that ruling bargain is renegotiated (in part, through force) in the context of new pressures and heightened regional tensions.

National, Religious, and Class Identity in Bahrain

Despite its small size, Bahraini society is socially diverse. Among its 1.2 million inhabitants, approximately 50 percent are not Bahraini citizens, but are foreigners resident in Bahrain who are employed in a wide range of positions throughout the economy. The largest subgroup of resident foreigners is made up of Indian nationals, but other expatriates from South Asia, East Asia, the Middle East, Europe, and beyond contribute diversity to the country's economy and society. Despite these expatriates' clear economic and social relevance to the country's future, most of the political challenge regarding Bahrain's ruling bargain has come from within the Bahraini national community.

However, the Bahraini national community is itself very diverse, with individual identities emerging from a complex mixture of Bahraini nationalism, ethnic or family origins, religious tradition, and economic class. Despite the fact that the national population is overwhelmingly Arab and Muslim, both religious and ethnic identities within these broader categories matter in understanding social status and political preferences. Given Bahrain's small size (300 square miles), and high population density (the fourth highest of any country in the world), different identity groups have regular opportunities to observe one another and often interact, either collaboratively or under conditions of social conflict. Bahrain's small size and historical isolation as an island have also proven advantageous in the development of a unique Bahraini national identity, which has retained its prominence despite other existing identity cleavages. As the expatriate population has grown over the years, Bahraini nationals have had increasing opportunities to identify with one another vis-à-vis non-nationals. It is during periods of political tension or economic strain that divisions within Bahraini national identity appear most stark.

The most striking and well-known identity cleavage is between the majority Shi'a and minority Sunni communities. Despite Shi'ism's minority status within the broader Muslim world, the Shi'a make up the dominant religious community in Bahrain and are estimated to make up around 70 percent of the national population.[1] This Shi'a demographic dominance is particularly significant because the ruling family comes from the minority Sunni population, giving Bahrain some similarities to Iraq, in which a Shi'a majority was historically ruled by a Sunni minority regime. In the Bahraini national mythology, the current Sunni ruling family conquered the island and its inhabitants, with Bahrain's historical founder Ahmed (died *c.*1795) known as *al-fateh* ("the conqueror"), a claim that is not lost on many Shi'a who believe that the reference makes them "the conquered."[2]

Sunni Muslims compose about 30 percent of the national population, although both Sunni and Shi'a communities have their own internal divisions based primarily on historical national origin. In the Sunni community, identity divisions exist between Sunni families originally from central Arabia (Najdis), from Kuwait (including the ruling al-Khalifa family), or from Persia (known locally as the Huwala). Divisions also exist along lines of family origin within the Shi'a community, the most notable being the distinction between Arab Shi'a and Persian Shi'a. The Shi'a of Persian origin, in particular, have long faced social discrimination in Bahraini society and traditionally established themselves in particular urban districts of Bahrain (including the capital Manama), remaining rather segregated from other groups.[3]

[1] J.E. Peterson, "The Nature of Succession in the Gulf," *Middle East Journal*, 55, 4 (2001), pp. 580–601.

[2] This national mythology of the progenitor of the ruling al-Khalifa family is enshrined in the largest mosque in Bahrain, Masjid al-fateh (Al-Fateh Grand Mosque), which primarily serves the Sunni community.

[3] Fred H. Lawson, *Bahrain: The Modernization of Autocracy*, Boulder, CO: Westview Press, 1989, p. 10.

Sect and national origin have also corresponded reasonably well to social class, compounding the divisive effects of these identity markers. In contrast to some of the other Persian Gulf states, Bahrain retained a sizable indigenous working class, as well as an agricultural class, into the twentieth century. The indigenous working class is predominantly urban and has played an important role in the industrial centers of Manama and Muharraq in the north, and is dominantly but not exclusively Shi'a. Sunnis in the industrial center of Muharraq have historically been less affluent than Sunnis in other parts of Bahrain, and have had few ties to tribal families allied with the ruling al-Khalifa.[4] This has led to collective action around economic grievances in both religious communities, with social mobilization at times bridging the Sunni–Shi'a divide.

In addition to sect and class, family affiliation is a dominant identity marker, as it is in other parts of the Persian Gulf. Family status within Bahrain's historical mythology, and as an indicator of access to political favors or economic resources, has political meaning and provides leverage in the social marketplace. Generational identity matters as well, both within families and across Bahraini society more broadly. With half of the Bahraini population under thirty years old, youth as an identity group have experienced shared grievances (including increasing unemployment) and are generally less likely to acquiesce to the traditional Bahraini ruling bargain than older generations.

As a country in which individuals have a large number of potentially relevant identity markers, including sect, class, nation, family, and generation, political mobilization in Bahrain is more multifaceted and complex than in many other small monarchical systems.

Bahrain's Historic Ruling Bargain

As it is a state scarcely over forty years old (Bahrain became independent in 1971), which has been ruled by only two monarchs, much of contemporary Bahraini politics is shaped by patterns of social development prior to independence and during the country's early years. As in other small Gulf states, an early ruling bargain was struck between the present royal family and the merchant class, which controlled much of Bahrain's economy prior to the exploitation of petroleum resources. The al-Khalifa

[4] Ibid. p. 13.

family gave the predominantly Sunni merchant class relatively free reign over commercial affairs, including the development of commercial monopolies, in exchange for recognition of the family's political leadership. Over time, the al-Khalifa developed a network of Sunni tribes that supported them, and these tribes were rewarded with considerable autonomy and economic benefits.[5]

The claims of the al-Khalifa to political authority were reinforced by the British Empire, which saw in the family a useful ally in pursuing its strategic and naval interests in the Persian Gulf.[6] However, the British also brought challenges to the family, as Bahrain's position as a trading crossroads led the empire to import non-Arab labor into the country, chiefly from the British domains in India. Bahrain's status as a commercial trading center within the empire proved a threat to the island's local identity, and the al-Khalifa family reinforced its position by defending the indigenous merchant community against outsiders and simultaneously framing a Bahraini identity in opposition to external interests.

Likewise, the exploitation of petroleum provided the ruling family with independent resources to expand administrative control over the island, reinforcing the family's leverage over the merchant class as petroleum revenues increased. The crisis environment during the Second World War proved a timely catalyst for the expansion of the ruling family's administrative control, and by the end of the war the family's administrative "state" as an institution had expanded to be the dominant partner in what was originally a social "contract" in which the merchant class played a more equal part.[7]

One of the ways in which the al-Khalifa made themselves valuable to social groups outside of the royal family was as a broker, both across Bahrain's diverse and sometimes segregated communities, and between indigenous Bahrainis and British agents. Divisions between the Sunni community, as well as between the Sunni and Shi'a communities, occasionally required mediation, which the royal family could provide with

[5] James Olney, "Transnational Merchants in the Nineteenth-Century Gulf: The Case of the Safar Family," in Madawi Al-Rasheed (ed.), *Transnational Connections and the Arab Gulf*, New York: Routledge, 2005, pp. 71–2.

[6] Nelida Fuccaro, "Persians and the Space in the City in Bahrain 1869–1937," in Al-Rasheed, *Transnational Connections*, p. 41.

[7] Lawson, *Bahrain*, pp. 48–53.

at least a mixed degree of success. The al-Khalifa also began to use their status as allies of the British Empire to represent the interests of the Bahraini economic elite under the conditions of British hegemony. This allowed them to pivot between acting on behalf of British and local interests, with both groups recognizing the royal family's central role in bringing stability to the existing Bahraini order. The historical role of the Bahraini monarchy thus demonstrated some similarities to that of the Jordanian monarchy, which provided brokerage between British and local interests, and later between East Bank Jordanian and Palestinian interests. After a series of local political challenges to British imperial (and, by extension, al-Khalifa) rule in the 1950s, the al-Khalifa conceded a measure of autonomy over economic activities to the merchant class in exchange for acknowledgment of their authority to preside over the most important parts of the central bureaucracy.[8]

When the British formally withdrew from the Persian Gulf in the early 1970s, conditions emerged that would facilitate Bahraini independence, and therefore a renegotiation of the country's ruling bargain. After consideration and rejection of several options for participation in a regional federation, Bahrain became an independent country in August 1971, with Sheikh 'Isa bin Sulman al-Khalifa continuing in his place as ruling amir (since 1961)—now also the head of an independent state with the ability to redefine the rules of the political order.

A few months after independence, Sheikh 'Isa proposed the adoption of a Bahraini constitution, which would be drafted by a constitutional assembly. The creation of a popular assembly was envisioned to be a forum for consultation (following the Islamic concept of *shura*) rather than a legislative body with powers that could effectively limit the monarchy.[9] Founding national elections took place at the end of 1972, which led to a constitutional assembly composed of twenty-two elected and twenty appointed (including Cabinet ministers) members. This assembly articulated a constitution that went into effect the subsequent year, with elections for the new National Assembly taking place in 1973. The pre-independence ruling bargain thus acquired a veneer of constitutional legitimacy and provided limited opportunities for popular participation by giving voice to participants desiring to shape the future outcome of that bargain.

[8] Ibid. pp. 68–9.
[9] Ibid. pp. 87–9.

The National Assembly was composed of both elected and appointed members, and could be dissolved at any time by the amir, which would lead to new elections. The assembly had the right to advise, but not to propose its own legislation, which would be done by the appointed Cabinet. This experiment in electoral participation was supported by many educated professionals, nationalists, tradesmen, working-class Shi'a, and some leftists, though the influential commercial elite remained aloof and did not participate. Although it was designed as a means to build popular support for the amir and serve only as a consultative body, the new assembly soon began to discuss controversial issues, including those of labor and internal security, which implicitly challenged the amir and his brother, Prime Minister Khalifa bin Salman al-Khalifa. It quickly became apparent that the ruling family did not substantively intend to alter their dominant role in the ruling bargain, and after less than two years, when the assembly chose not to ratify the state security decree, the amir dissolved the National Assembly indefinitely and gave the appointed Cabinet full legislative powers.[10] This sent a clear signal that central issues of importance to the ruling family were not open to renegotiation.

However, the founding 1973 elections provided some insight into the most important stakeholders in Bahrain's potential ruling bargain. The ruling family and the commercial elite are two key stakeholders who did not actively compete in the elections, but who nevertheless remain particularly consequential. Of the electoral participants, three main blocs came to the forefront in the 1973 elections: a labor bloc, a Shi'a religious bloc, and a less structured bloc of independents with generally pro-market economic leanings. The first held grievances against the regime regarding Bahrain's high levels of economic inequality, while the second bloc held grievances against it regarding discrimination against the Shi'a community. Both of these groups had meaningful ideological perspectives that challenged the ruling family's vision for Bahrain. The third group of pro-market independents was less ideological and more personalistic in their politics, though members had individual interests in achieving a greater degree of autonomy from the state, much like the commercial elite.[11]

[10] Ibid. p. 91.

[11] Human Rights Watch, *Routine Abuse, Routine Denial: Civil Rights and the Political Crisis in Bahrain*, New York: Human Rights Watch, 1997, pp. 17–19; also Lawson, *Bahrain*, pp. 90–91.

One of the political lessons of the 1973–75 National Assembly period was that despite its unifying national rhetoric, the ruling family's political and economic interests did not mirror the interests of a large portion of Bahrain's population. The implication of this was that the ruling family would need to protect its interests from political challengers by leveraging its two key advantages, control over the distribution of economic resources and use of the security establishment.

Although Bahrain's commercial elite maintained a significant degree of autonomy over the course of the twentieth century, something which led them to accede to political dominance by the al-Khalifa, the ruling family also controlled large economic resources, which increased with the rise of petroleum production in the 1960s and 1970s. Though Bahrain has less petroleum than its Gulf neighbors, it maintained a consistent supply of energy resources by reducing and stabilizing petrochemical production over time. It also strategically diversified its economy away from oil production and toward refining, offshore banking, transportation, and heavy industry (such as aluminum and iron processing). Bahrain's comparatively free market economic system facilitated substantial economic growth, and also moderate government budgetary growth, even as petroleum reserves have remained the backbone of the government budget. An estimated 85–90 percent of the government budget comes from petroleum revenues, although only about 25 percent of GDP comes from petroleum.[12] The government has also received budgetary support from regional allies, including Saudi Arabia, the UAE, and Kuwait. This has maintained Bahrain's status as a rentier state, and allowed the ruling family to control substantial patronage resources that it can distribute at will, in terms of both government benefits and access to economic opportunities. This has also led to the extensive accumulation of private wealth by those well connected to the royal family and its dominantly Sunni allies.[13]

The Bahraini government has also come to depend on its security services to maintain its ruling bargain. Like other Gulf countries, Bahrain has had a policy of voluntary military service, although the

[12] Personal interview with Mansoor al-Jamri, Sep. 2012.

[13] Sahar F. Aziz and Abdullah Musalem, "Citizens, Not Subjects: Debunking the Sectarian Narrative of Bahrain's Pro-Democracy Movement," Institute for Social Policy and Understanding, 14 July 2011, pp. 10–11.

limited military is well funded, equipped, and trained by larger allies. Bahrain's tiny size and its precarious position between long-standing rivals Iran and Saudi Arabia have meant that it has cultivated powerful military allies, including the United States (which currently stations its Fifth Naval Fleet in Bahrain) and Saudi Arabia (which has provided extensive training and support for Bahraini national defense).[14]

Most relevant to the maintenance of the domestic ruling bargain, however, is the role of the police forces, which played a substantial role in the early years of independence in maintaining the dominance of the ruling family and suppressing dissidents. From the 1970s, the national police force demonstrated its willingness to enforce the dominance of the monarchical regime through repression, although Bahrain has sought to avoid both the image and the reality of a police state. That changed substantively for periods in the 1990s, when arbitrary arrests appeared to target the Shi'a community disproportionately, political protests were violently suppressed, and some detainees were subjected to torture by security services. The imposition of emergency law during protests in the 1990s demonstrated that the government was willing to use substantial force to suppress dissent, at the same time as it sought other non-violent methods to resolve challenges from the political opposition.[15]

Bahrain's historic ruling bargain has thus been one in which substantial economic privileges and autonomy have been provided to relevant allied (largely Sunni) groups, and the government attempts to provide political stability and economic growth in exchange for popular deference to the al-Khalifa family, while meaningful leftist and religious (largely Shi'a) challengers exist but are usually contained by a mixture of economic concessions and repression. These challengers demonstrated their potential to disrupt the system during the 1990s through a series of protests that took on sectarian overtones, and this provided the context for new, more enduring attempts at political reform

[14] Hamad Bin Isa Al-Khalifa, *First Light: Modern Bahrain and its Heritage*, London: Kegan Paul, 1994, pp. 83–4.

[15] Staci Strobl, "From Colonial Policing to Community Policing in Bahrain: The Historical Persistence of Sectarianism," *International Journal of Comparative and Applied Criminal Justice*, 35, 1 (Jan. 2011), pp. 26–8; also Aziz and Musalem, "Citizens, Not Subjects," pp. 8–9.

after the death of Sheikh 'Isa and the accession of his son, Sheikh Hamad, in 1999.

Sectarianism and Political Reform under King Hamad

Sectarian riots have occurred throughout much of Bahrain's history, including the pre-independence period. Under British rule, British security services were supplemented by Sunni police forces, establishing a pattern of Sunni dominance over internal security that continues to the present day.[16] Systematic discrimination against the majority Shi'a community has led to numerous outbreaks of violence in Shi'a areas dating back at least as far as the 1950s. A state of emergency was declared in 1953, leading to numerous detentions of (primarily Shi'a) Bahrainis without trial. The state security law of 1975 again articulated the legal right to detain dissidents without trial. The perceived threat of Shi'a opposition to the Bahraini regime increased after the 1979 Iranian Revolution, leading to large-scale arrests of Shi'a citizens accused of planning militant activities. Again in the mid-1990s, Shi'a protests against discrimination led to thousands of arrests and sustained detentions without trial, as well as numerous cases of police brutality and torture against Sunni protestors.[17]

This political contention occurred across the sectarian divide both because the security services represented the ruling Sunni minority against primarily Shi'a dissidents, and because the Shi'a had substantial grievances stemming from the discrimination they had received from the government. These practices of discrimination are well documented and include unfavorable treatment in the areas of employment, travel, housing, and political opportunities, among others.[18] The Shi'a have fewer job opportunities and are rarely brought into senior positions in the state bureaucracy or large, Sunni-led commercial enterprises. This pattern of discrimination intensified in the wake of the 2011 uprisings. In the period between 14 February 2011 and 15 August 2012, for example, only around 14 percent of all government appointments went

[16] Strobl, "From Colonial Policing to Community Policing in Bahrain," pp. 25–6.
[17] Ibid. p. 27.
[18] Falah Al-Mdaires, "Shiism and Political Protest in Bahrain," *Domes*, 11, 1 (2002), p. 20.

to Shi'a, despite their demographic majority.[19] Likewise, Bahraini citizens of Persian ancestry may be denied full citizenship rights and passports, despite their families having lived in Bahrain for several generations. Under Bahrain's government-subsidized housing regime, Shi'a may have to wait for housing for long periods, while even naturalized Sunni immigrants who work in the police force are given housing almost immediately. The government has granted full citizenship to many thousands of Sunni immigrants in an attempt to reduce the Sunni demographic disadvantage in Bahraini society.[20] The potential militant political threat from Bahraini Shi'a has often been highlighted by the Bahraini regime to justify its unequal treatment of this population, with most scholarly observers agreeing that the regime deliberately exaggerates the potential revolutionary threat of the Bahraini Shi'a in order to justify its discriminatory practices.[21]

When Sheikh Hamad acceded to the throne after the death of his father, Sheikh 'Isa, in 1999, the underlying sectarian and economic tensions within Bahraini society were well established. One of the new ruler's largest challenges upon taking power was to chart a course that would defuse these social and political tensions while maintaining economic growth in the face of dwindling petroleum reserves. While seeking to attract greater foreign investment in an open market economy, Hamad also embarked upon a number of political reforms that were designed to increase popular support for the Bahraini regime and maintain the ruling family's control.

In comparison to his father, Hamad has been open to a degree of political reform, although in the more than thirteen years of his rule he has also demonstrated an unwillingness to engage in any fundamental alteration of the political structure of the Bahraini system. When juxtaposed against Bahrain's Gulf neighbors, the country projected an image during the early years of Hamad's rule of a progressive political system that was willing to experiment with a measure of reform within a monarchical framework. Hamad's signature political reforms were codi-

[19] Personal interview with Jalil Khalil, Sep. 2012.

[20] Aziz and Musalem, "Citizens, Not Subjects," p. 16.

[21] Laurence Louer, "Houses Divided: The Splintering of Bahrain's Political Camps," Carnegie Endowment for International Peace, 2012; also Strobl, "From Colonial Policing to Community Policing in Bahrain" and Aziz and Musalem, "Citizens, Not Subjects."

fied in the National Action Charter, which was overwhelmingly passed by popular referendum in February 2001, and under which he was formally designated king (rather than amir) of Bahrain.

These constitutional reforms removed the stringent state security laws, and the charter created a new National Assembly, outlining plans to reinstate popular elections beginning in 2002. A bicameral parliament was established, creating a forty-member National Assembly elected by popular vote and an appointed Shura Council (upper house) selected by government appointment. The upper house possesses veto rights over legislation coming from the lower house. These reforms were initially quite popular, and the National Action Charter portrayed the upper house as an advisory rather than legislative body. However, some opposition groups saw the institutionalization of the upper house as a political guarantee for the monarchy, and believed that the constitutional reforms failed to address the core problem of equitable political representation.[22] Disillusionment with the National Charter came quite quickly as some groups began to see the charter as paving the way for the king to take additional powers above and beyond what he had historically possessed, along with the new title.[23]

Despite the fact that major religious opposition parties boycotted the inaugural 2002 polls in protest against the veto powers given to an unelected upper house, subsequent polls were held in 2006 and 2010 in which most major opposition parties participated. Some opposition parties participated beginning in 2006 in part because of productive talks with the regime, and a sense that they could do more for their agenda inside the system rather than outside.[24] Women were given the right to vote, and the first woman was appointed to a Cabinet post in 2004. In the 2006 and 2010 elections, it became clear that opposition and religious parties would dominate the lower house, the largest party being the Shi'a al-Wefaq party, which took seventeen of forty seats in 2006, and eighteen of forty seats in the 2010 elections. The largest other parties that took seats in the National Assembly are Sunni religious parties, including Al-Asalah and Al-Menbar, which together took thirteen of the forty seats

[22] Neil Quilliam, "Political Reform in Bahrain: The Turning Tide," in Anoushiravan Ehteshami and Steven Wright (eds), *Reform in the Middle East Oil Monarchies*, Ithaca, NY: Ithaca Press, 2008, pp. 81–3.

[23] Personal interview with Jalil Khalil, Sep. 2012.

[24] Ibid.

in the 2006 elections, although their share of seats declined in 2010. As in the 1973 elections, electoral results in the last decade demonstrated that there was a large popular undercurrent of dissatisfaction with the ruling regime, but that much of this opposition was willing to work within the institutional framework created by King Hamad.

That new institutional framework did in fact reinforce the king's own power, effectively giving the monarch veto power over legislation as well as the right to appoint and dismiss ministers. A context of continued international investment in Bahrain and concomitant economic growth provided the king with some breathing room in managing social discontent, but the ruling family still relied on extensive monarchical privilege to deal with the opposition. The king's role in making final political decisions remained clear, and the vast majority of land in Bahrain still technically belongs to the al-Khalifa family, symbolizing the monarch's all-reaching authority.[25] Although the government legalized political demonstrations in 2002, when opposition groups used a petition to challenge the powers of the Shura Council, protestors continued to be arrested for participating in illegal activities.[26]

Frustration with the slow pace of political change, particularly among Shi'a activists, led to increasing protest mobilization by the mid-2000s, and the regime sought to strengthen its internal security capacity as a result. Neighboring Saudi Arabia became increasingly concerned over Bahraini Shi'a political activism and advised the king to take a tough line against the Shi'a opposition.[27] A general agreement between the main participatory Shi'a opposition bloc (al-Wefaq) and the government in 2006 muted some of the social protest, led to some economic reforms that benefited Shi'a populations, and reinforced the Bahraini welfare state. Nevertheless, the initial promise of King Hamad's reforms remained unfulfilled for many Bahrainis, who came to recognize that fundamental changes in the power balance between the monarchy and its people were not forthcoming.

It is important to recognize, however, that divisions within the Bahraini royal family exist regarding how much power should ultimately be devolved to the National Assembly, and what popular freedoms should be protected. In the original 1972 elections, internal divisions

25 Aziz and Musalem, "Citizens, Not Subjects," pp. 11–12.
26 Quilliam, "Political Reform in Bahrain," pp. 85–7.
27 Ibid. pp. 90, 98.

over the political reforms led to extensive internal discussion about the role of electoral politics. "Tribalists" in the royal family opposed the need to institutionalize nominally participatory government, while others in the family argued that popular concessions short of devolving substantive power were politically useful.[28] As the short-lived parliamentary experiment in the 1970s illustrates, that debate remained unresolved even after the elections were held, and divisions among royal powerbrokers created the political climate that led to the parliament's subsequent closure.

In the contemporary period, King Hamad has been seen as a moderate in the royal family on issues of popular political participation, while his father's brother, Prime Minister Khalifa, is considered more of a royalist despite his role leading the National Assembly. Because Sheikh Khalifa has served as prime minister since Bahraini independence and is a generation senior to the current king, his interests in preserving royal prerogatives and his status in family decision-making processes remain high. Khalifa has strong relationships with the traditional merchant families in the private sector and is a traditional pillar in the Bahraini ruling bargain. The royal court minister, Khalid bin Ahmed, as well as the head of the army, Khalifa bin Ahmed, are likewise known as strict conservatives when it comes to preserving the royal prerogatives of the regime.[29] On the other hand, the most politically liberal of senior royals is the current Crown Prince, Salman bin Hamad al Khalifa. Prince Salman has a Western education and has articulated a preference for greater openness in the political system. These divisions in political preferences among the royal family came to play a role in regime responses to the mass popular mobilization of 2011. Under conditions of duress, however, the traditional tribal norms of the Bahraini and other Gulf royal families also have a tendency to bring ruling families together to reinforce their interests against outside threats.[30]

[28] Emile Nakhleh, *Bahrain: Political Development in a Modernizing Society*, New York: Lexington Books, 2011, p. 149.

[29] They are also considered part of the *khawalid* group within the royal family, which was largely out of power during the previous period of Sheikh Isa's rule.

[30] Aziz and Musalem, "Citizens, Not Subjects," p. 26.

The Political Challenge of the 2011–12 Bahraini Uprising

The recent period of mass Bahraini political mobilization, which began on 14 February 2011, occurred in the context of other uprisings throughout the Arab world, most notably in Tunisia, Egypt, Yemen, and Libya. Thus, its timing and cause should be at least partially attributable to a major demonstration effect coming from other parts of the Arab world. However, the context of sectarian grievances, a history of political protest, and the mixed success of political reform in the previous decade all helped to set the stage for the drama of the Bahraini uprising. Each of these factors contributed to both its outbreak and its sustained activity. The scale of the uprising, the regime's mixed response, and the fragmentation of the political opposition have all altered the underlying ruling bargain between regime and society, a bargain that was already evolving and being tested by political actors on all sides during the previous decade.

By the end of 2010, many of the enduring social grievances of the Bahraini majority had not yet found effective political avenues for resolution, a fact that had become increasingly apparent the longer King Hamad's decade-long political experiment had to unfold. The October 2010 elections were controversial, with some prominent groups deciding to boycott them and with numerous arrests of opposition figures prior to the elections. The electoral success rate of opposition parties at both the 2006 and 2010 elections was clear, but the opposition's success in changing the realities on the ground after elections took place was not. As Smith Diwan notes, "the outbreak of the Arab revolutions … came at a critical point in the evolution of Bahrain's opposition politics. By providing a model of regime change through mass protest, the Tunisian and Egyptian examples reinforced the Bahraini opposition's drift away from formal politics back into the street."[31]

A general cause of the mass mobilization was thus unresolved popular grievances in the context of disappointment with the ability of formal political institutions and processes to resolve them. While the potential for mass mobilization existed prior to the start of the February 2011 uprising, the individual costs of popular coordination around those griev-

[31] Kristin Smith Diwan, "Bahrain's Shia Question: What the United States Gets Wrong about Sectarianism," *Foreign Affairs* (2 Mar. 2011), http://www.foreignaffairs.com/articles/67555/kristin-smith-diwan/bahrains-shia-question

ances declined rapidly: first because of controversial regime actions during the October elections, and second with the advent of mass protest in Tunisia and Egypt. As individual interest centered on the dramatic events in North Africa, and as the expectation that these protests would lead to change increased (President Mubarak of Egypt was deposed on 11 February), the coordination costs for Bahraini activists and opposition groups to engage the public in street protest went down dramatically.

The February uprising took the form of large-scale demonstrations centered on Manama's symbolic Pearl Square, with a Bahraini nationalist orientation. These protests were explicitly peaceful in orientation, non-sectarian, and articulated goals of political reform well short of removing the monarchy. The protestors' general demands included "more transparency in governance and allocation of state resources, an end to corruption, greater participation in electoral politics, legalization of political parties, and a transition to constitutional monarchy."[32] Over the coming months, the protests maintained many of these characteristics, but violent clashes increased, the conflict became more sectarian in how it was understood (and framed by the government), and a sub-set of protestors began to call for the removal of the Bahraini monarchy. As the character and demands of the protests changed, the government and protestors became increasingly polarized, leading to both general and targeted repression that dampened but did not extinguish the uprising. The opposition also began to fragment over how to frame and press popular demands, and divisions within the opposition increased over time.

The first major day of protest, a "Day of Rage," occurred on 14 February, a date chosen by activists because it was the tenth anniversary of the popular referendum on King Hamad's National Action Charter. The protest, which drew thousands of participants, highlighted how little Hamad's reforms had done to increase social, political, and economic equality. Although most protestors were Shi'a, Sunni youth and activists also participated, demonstrating that the grievances were not confined to Shi'a. Protestors were met with repression, and a number of participants sustained injuries, for one leading subsequently to death. The popularity of the protest and the regime's repressive response prompted the largest Shi'a opposition group, al-Wefaq, to move from the sidelines and declare its solidarity with the protestors. Protests continued in subsequent days, and other injuries and fatalities occurred.

[32] Aziz and Musalem, "Citizens, Not Subjects," p. 19.

On the fourth day of protests, security services launched a night raid on protestors camped out on Pearl Square, which resulted in several more deaths, hundreds of injuries, and numerous detentions. The speed and brutality of the raid, including the targeting of medics who were attending to the wounded, helped to shape anger toward the regime, and even triggered verbal attacks on the monarchy. Al-Wefaq's elected members of parliament all submitted their resignations in response to the regime's actions, leaving the National Assembly discredited and bereft of its largest bloc. Protests continued over the coming days, culminating in a mass popular rally on 22 February in support of those killed or injured in the previous protests. A remarkable percentage of Bahrainis participated in the rally, with up to 25 percent of Bahraini adults participating in some form, and as many as 150,000 people gathered together at the Pearl Roundabout. This level of mobilization, enabled by Bahrain's small geographic size, reinforced the government's belief that it had lost political control over the situation. Both the opposition and the regime were entering new territory in which Bahrain's social contract may have to be renegotiated, and through demonstrations of force rather than through amiable collaboration.

The regime responded to this new sense of threat by tapping its natural supporters, who held a large counter-demonstration in support of the government on 2 March. King Hamad also released political prisoners and dismissed some Cabinet ministers in concessions to the opposition. However, as provocative protests continued, with some protestors now calling for the removal of the prime minister and even the king, the monarchy moved to a dominantly repressive strategy by the middle of March. In consultation with allies in the Gulf Cooperation Council (GCC), Bahrain brought in 1,000 troops and armor from Saudi Arabia and 500 police from the UAE in a show of force that constrained the subsequent potential for large-scale protest. A state of emergency was declared and troops cleared protestors from Pearl Square, pulling down the pearl statue there that had come to symbolize the protest movement. Security forces became active in pre-empting any further mass protests throughout the spring of 2011, detaining and beating many activists. By May 2011 the protest situation had stabilized, and the strategies of both the government and opposition began to evolve into a mixture of smaller protests, repression, and governmental concessions.

Sectarian tensions evolved rapidly in this series of confrontations between the ruling regime and the opposition. Although the initial protests explicitly avoided using references that could frame the conflict as a sectarian one, some structural characteristics of the conflict increased its sectarian nature, as did the government's public framing of the popular challenge that it faced.

A key structural reason for increasing sectarianism is the overwhelmingly Sunni composition of the Bahraini security forces. The military is exclusively Sunni, and has strongly supported the regime throughout the confrontation. Likewise, the Bahraini police forces include large numbers of naturalized Sunni, who despite being foreign-born, receive greater state benefits than most native Shi'a, a long-held grievance of the latter.[33] The regime's strategy of naturalizing non-Bahraini Sunni is a point of contention for Shi'a opposition groups, and sectarian clashes broke out in early March 2011 between Shi'a youth and some naturalized Sunni.[34] The sectarian amplification effect of the composition of security forces was further reinforced after Sunni troops and police from Saudi Arabia and the UAE arrived, the Saudis being well known for particularly harsh discrimination against their own Shi'a population.[35]

Saudi–Iranian rivalry has also played a role in framing the conflict as a sectarian one. Although the early protestors avoided references to broader Shi'a identity[36] and revolutionary Iran, and wanted "nothing more than for Tehran to stay out of the sectarian dispute unfolding in the tiny kingdom,"[37] the regional rivalry between the two powers over Bahrain has led some participants to understand Bahrain's conflict within this larger context. Iran has vocalized support for the Bahraini Shi'a, while Saudi Arabia has condemned the protests, portraying Shi'a protestors as tools of the Iranian regime.[38]

33 Yasser M. El-Shimy, "The Arab Spring Gathers Clouds: Why the Revolts for Change Have Stalled," *Insight Turkey*, 13, 4 (2011), pp. 52–3.

34 Bahrain Independent Commission of Inquiry, "Report of the Bahrain Independent Commission of Inquiry," 2011, p. 117, http://www.bici.org.bh/BICIreportEN.pdf

35 Nakhleh, *Bahrain*, p. 144.

36 S. Mabon, "The Battle for Bahrain: Iranian–Saudi Rivalry," *Middle East Policy*, 19 (2012), p. 89.

37 Genieve Abdo and Jasim Husain Ali. "Misunderstanding Bahrain's Shia Protestors," Al Jazeera, 3 Apr. 2011. http://www.aljazeera.com/indepth/opinion/2011/03/2011329827429887l2.html

38 Jane Kinninmont, "Anger Management," *The World Today* (2011), p. 7.

In addition to established regional rivalries that situate the conflict as a Sunni–Shi'a religious conflict with security implications, the Bahraini regime itself has sought to portray the popular mobilization as an Iranian-inspired threat to Sunni hegemony in the region. Though many politically active Bahrainis recognize that the regime's portrayal is a self-serving interpretation, and that the shared grievances against the regime are both real and cross-sectarian, the regime's vocal warning of a Shi'a threat has taken on some characteristics of a self-fulfilling narrative as the conflict has evolved.

Over time the regime's preferred narrative to explain the uprising has divided the Sunni and Shi'a opposition, and made it more difficult for ordinary Sunni citizens to participate in protests dominated by al-Wefaq without being perceived as siding with "the enemy." Economically disadvantaged Sunnis originally supported the protests (as well as Shi'a from all economic backgrounds), but this Sunni support became much more tepid after the first few months of the uprising.[39] Subsequently, even Sunnis who have long held grievances against the ruling family began to go quiet out of fear of being seen as siding with Shi'a and losing status within their own sectarian community.[40] In May 2011 there was widespread vandalism of Shi'a holy sites, including more than forty mosques, shrines, and cemeteries, with some of the Shi'a sites being destroyed on government orders.[41] Several thousand people, the greater number of them Shi'a, lost their jobs in the spring of 2011 for alleged participation in the protests, and many did not return to their previous positions despite subsequent governmental pledges to restore them. A Sunni sectarian movement known as the National Unity Gathering called for a boycott of Shi'a businesses in Madinat Hamad as a result of the protests, creating further distance between Bahrainis with different sectarian identities. Aggressive Sunni mobilization against the perceived Shi'a threat continued to build, and led to sporadic Sunni–Shi'a clashes throughout 2011.[42] In some Shi'a-dominated towns and villages, proto-militias began to develop and Shi'a-dominated riots occurred in many

[39] Justin Gengler, "Bahrain's Sunni Awakening," *Middle East Research and Information Project*, 17 Jan. 2012.

[40] Personal interview with Sunni respondent, Sep. 2012.

[41] Caryle Murphy, "Bahrain Campaign to Humiliate Shiites Goes Beyond Politics," *The Christian Science Monitor*, 7 June 2011.

[42] Gengler, "Bahrain's Sunni Awakening."

areas around the capital. The demonization of the Shi'a population among security forces facilitated the systematic detention and torture of many Shi'a protestors, journalists, and even medical personnel, while reinforcing Shi'a perceptions of Sunnis as unjust and creating widespread anger against the police.

One effect of the sectarian framing of the conflict has been a decisive split in the original protest coalition, with Shi'a groups losing many of their original Sunni allies; this has facilitated the regime staying in power in the short run, but has led to a longer-term rupture in the ruling bargain that will be very difficult to mend. A systematic reinforcing of the sectarian divide over the course of 2011 prevented the Bahraini opposition from building the coalition necessary to force the regime to capitulate, as eventually occurred in Tunisia and Egypt. Even among Shi'a groups, the opposition has fragmented over whether the ruling family has forever discredited itself through its support for violent repression, or whether there should be an ongoing role for the al-Khalifa in governance. The degree of fragmentation across the opposition has made a negotiated solution increasingly difficult to achieve and has enabled the regime to maintain power under conditions of a tense stalemate.[43] Despite continued popular pressure, divisions in the opposition allowed the regime to avoid any clear moves toward a negotiated resolution.

Since the spring of 2011, mass Bahraini political mobilization has continued to occur, but generally under more restrictive conditions and with less coherent objectives than in the early months of protest. During this period the regime made a number of limited concessions, in parallel with extensive repression by the security services. One of the most notable concessions was the king's decision to set up the Bahrain Independent Commission of Inquiry (BICI), led by prominent independent human rights attorney Cherif Bassiouni, to look into alleged abuses by the security forces during the events of February and March 2011. An offer of regime–opposition dialogue made by the crown prince in March 2011 was rejected by the main opposition groups, and the regime-sponsored National Dialogue announced in July 2011 was boycotted by al-Wefaq, which credibly argued that the dialogue had no credible mechanism for discussion and included far too little representation from the Shi'a majority.

[43] Louer, "Houses Divided."

A major opposition rally was held in June 2011, but an active security presence limited the success of other planned protests throughout the summer and through the autumn. In September, by-elections were held for the assembly seats earlier vacated by al-Wefaq, with very low turnout (17 percent). Controversial trials of medical professionals accused of anti-regime activity continued into the autumn, leading to the sentencing of twenty individuals in September, and then a retreat from the sentences in the wake of international condemnation.

In October 2011, five opposition groups, including al-Wefaq, issued what came to be known as the Manama letter,[44] which reiterated the opposition's call for substantial political reform, broadcast the opposition's intent to continue protest in the absence of reform, and also indicated the groups' willingness to enter into a more substantive dialogue with the regime. In November, the BICI (Bassiouni) report was released, highlighting wide-ranging abuses and torture by the Bahraini security services earlier in the year, although the extent of accountability of senior regime leaders was not explicitly specified.[45] By the end of 2011, the emergency law was lifted and Saudi troops withdrew from Bahrain. This triggered renewed protests that continued into 2012 and 2013.

During the first half of 2012, the regime continued to announce plans for some concessions, including a plan for more integration of Shi'a into the police force, as well as the potential for further constitutional changes such as the right of the National Assembly to question ministers and approve (though not select) Cabinet ministers. These conciliatory gestures were made in parallel with continued repression in Shi'a areas, with further detentions and violent clashes. Opposition protests became much more vigorous in the first half of 2012, with a large portion of the Bahraini population (between 100,000 and 200,000 people) participating in a protest called by the prominent Shi'a cleric Isa Qassim on 9 March. Subsequent large-scale protests also occurred in April (in anticipation of the Bahrain Grand Prix), in May (in protest against potential union plans between Bahrain and Saudi Arabia), and in June. By July 2012, faced with a renewed cycle of mass mobilization, the government moved once again to ban opposition marches. This was followed by a number of attempted protests and new clashes between

[44] Bahrain Justice and Development Movement, Manama Document (13 Oct. 2011). http://www.bahrainjdm.org/2011/10/13/manama-document-english/

[45] Bahrain Independent Commission of Inquiry Report.

protestors and security forces. Since that time, protests have continued and the government has moved aggressively to detain and jail popular opposition figures.

The Regime's Mixed Strategy

One of the most interesting factors in the eighteenth-month period from February 2011 to July 2012 is the clear attempt by the regime to play what might be described as a mixed, or alternating, strategy to contain the challenge of mass popular mobilization. The regime systematically repressed the opposition throughout this period (muzzling the media, making widespread arrests, preventing protests, and using violence against political activists), but it also made a number of limited concessions (release of political prisoners, establishment of an independent inquiry, and calls for dialogue) that indicated the government's desire to return to some form of ruling bargain based on popular consent rather than repression.

Alternating strategies of both concession and repression may arise because of uncertainty about which strategy will most effectively quell protest. Offering concessions may reduce anger and increase satisfaction with the regime, but concessions may also signal regime weakness and lead to further demands that rulers may be unwilling to meet. Using repression, on the other hand, has the potential to reduce protest and quell popular demands through the use of fear, but it is also likely to increase the level of anger toward the regime, which could further fuel protest and accelerate demands on the government if levels of popular anger outpace fear of further repression. For regime leaders whose principal objective is to stay in power, it may be difficult to choose which strategy is most likely to succeed in meeting their objectives over time. One option in the face of uncertainty is to experiment with both limited concessions and repression and observe their effect in levels of popular mobilization before formulating future strategies. This appears to be the strategy used by the government in the case of Bahrain. The Bahraini regime used a strategy of both repression and concession, although acts of repression outpaced substantive political concessions over time.

An alternating regime strategy of repression and concession may also result in cases where there is a division in the strategic preferences among prominent figures in the regime. In these cases, the "hard-liners" are more likely to see a strategy of repression meeting their long-term objectives and will worry about concessions becoming a slippery slope to ever increasing popular demands. "Soft-liners," on the other hand, are more likely to worry about the unsustainable nature of repression and the long-term negative effects on the relationship between state and society after a period of violent repression. In the case of Bahrain, divisions between members of the ruling family appear to support different preferred strategies, with Crown Prince Salman at the forefront in calling for dialogue and demonstrating willingness to strike a deal with the opposition, while other established members of the ruling family, such as the prime minister, the royal court minister, and the minister of defense, are quick to condemn protestors and resort to national security arguments in favor of repression.

While a mixed strategy of concession and repression may be chosen either out of uncertainty or because of different preferences among the ruling elite, it is not necessarily more likely to succeed in maintaining the regime's power than either dominantly repressive or conciliatory strategies. The main liability of such a strategy is that it has the potential to backfire on rulers by creating the anger that comes from repression, while simultaneously causing the opposition to believe that change is possible and that protest can trigger that change. In this case, the governing regime experiences the liabilities of both a repressive strategy and a conciliatory strategy, while failing to maintain control over popular mobilization.

In evaluating the government's strategy in the case of Bahrain, it is useful to compare patterns of concession and repression with several other Arab governments that encountered mass popular mobilization at the same time. Figure 1 compares regime responses to mass protest in the four countries of Bahrain, Egypt, Syria, and Yemen over the course of 2011. The lines represent the average score on concession and repression by month (as coded from major public regime actions) across these four countries. Positive numbers represent periods in which the number and/or degree of conciliatory regime actions is greater than repressive regime actions. Negative numbers represent periods in which repressive actions are greater in number and/or degree.[46]

[46] Coding guidelines for the data used in Figure 1 are as follows:

Repression Scale

1 No loss of life; mobilization of security forces; verbal condemnation of protests by leader

Note that regime actions in Bahrain during 2011 are on balance repressive (mean score =–1), but that there is considerable fluctuation from month to month, which leads to a sense of regime inconsistency and amplifies the perception of the regime playing a mixed strategy in response to protest. After some early conciliatory signals, the regime's response became highly repressive, leading to the death and injury of many protestors. Over the summer of 2011, conciliatory moves were again signaled to the opposition (including the formation of the Bahrain Independent Commission of Inquiry), which raised hopes that the regime would work to renegotiate the now fractured ruling bargain. As the year continued, however, political repression increased and members of the government who preferred a more conciliatory strategy were increasingly marginalized. The regime responses in both Yemen and Syria were considerably more repressive than in Bahrain overall, and generally became more repressive as 2011 progressed.[47] In the Egyptian case, the regime pursued a moderately conciliatory path in the wake of Mubarak's ouster in February 2011, but became more consistently repressive during the second half of the year.

This disproportionately repressive but alternating regime strategy in Bahrain had two principal effects on the Bahraini opposition. First, it led to a major rupture between the government and opposition forces,

2 No loss of life; confrontation between security forces/demonstrators
3 Loss of life <10; mass-arrest campaign
4 Loss of life 11–100; use of armed forces against opposition; foreign military intervention on behalf of government
5 Loss of life 100+; part of sustained repression by state against anti-government forces

Concession Scale

1 Verbal promise; mention of future reform or change
2 Tangible steps toward reform; monetary concession; controlled foreign monitoring
3 Low- to mid-level administration reshuffle; low- to mid-level resignation; holding of referendum; mass pardon for political prisoners
4 Senior-level resignation/ouster; holding of unscheduled elections; major constitutional reforms
5 Leader concedes power

[47] President Saleh's agreement to step down in Nov. 2011 represents one major concession at the end of the year in the case of Yemen.

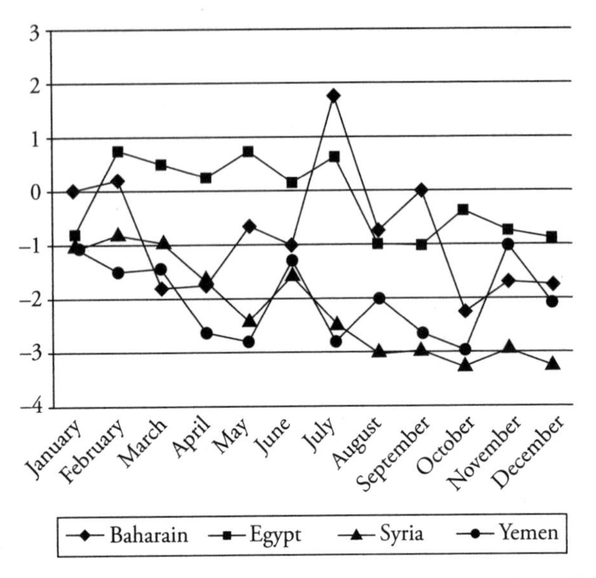

Figure 1. Average Concession/Repression Score by Month and Country: Bahrain, Egypt, Syria, and Yemen

one which is qualitatively different from the previous conflicts between the regime and its opponents. Second, it has divided the opposition between those who benefit the most from regime concessions (primarily the Sunni opposition) and those who suffer the worst from regime repression (the major Shi'a opposition groups).

The Bahraini opposition has a long history of challenging the regime, including through protest and violence, but those episodes of protest and violence have never been severe or sustained enough to prevent the largest sections of the opposition[48] from collaborating with the regime on political issues or from participating (subsequent to the 2002 elections) in the limited openings created by the al-Khalifa. After February 2011, however, the rupture between the government and opposition deepened, primarily because of the new levels of targeted violence inflicted on political activists and because the opposition realized its enormous potential to mobilize Bahraini citizens on behalf of its cause.

[48] Which by 2001 was dominantly represented by the Shia Islamist al-Wefaq party.

This mobilization was fueled by popular anger and was most successful when protests were called to mourn political "martyrs"; participants also observed that mass mobilization could lead the regime to make a number of conciliatory gestures, and that it therefore had the potential for political efficacy. This means that the opposition developed less intrinsic interest in playing by the king's rules under conditions of a severe breach of trust. It also recognized that it could wield substantial informal political power outside the boundaries of the regime's self-defined political rules, fueled by the anger that resulted from governmental repression.

Secondly, the events of 2011–12 polarized elements within the opposition, making cross-sect collaboration more difficult and dividing the opposition with regard to the extent of its political demands. Regime violence has disproportionately and purposefully targeted Shi'a dissidents, fomenting distrust between Sunni and Shi'a despite their initial collaboration in pushing for political reform. The Saudi "invasion" of 2011 and the regime's branding of Shi'a dissidents as Iranian-inspired security threats have poisoned the atmosphere and have made it difficult to craft a broad social coalition that can agree on the specific demands that it can make of the regime. Those who have been the targets of violence have pushed to escalate pressure on the regime, while those who have seen potential individual benefits from proposed concessions are less willing to take a confrontational stand. This has meant that, while the potential for political mobilization remains high, it is difficult for political activists to find the common ground that would successfully enable them to renegotiate the ruling bargain in Bahrain.

Alternate Paths Forward in Bahrain's Ruling Bargain

The Bahraini monarchy has so far survived the remarkable popular challenge against the prevailing ruling bargain. But it has done so by making short-term decisions (to repress and divide the opposition) that will make it very difficult to sustain the traditional ruling bargain over the longer term. By increasing popular levels of both anger and fear, the regime's response to the uprising has deepened the social divisions within Bahrain, making the long-standing Bahraini social and political challenges more severe than they have ever been before. The use of repression has also backed the king into a corner, from where he cannot now turn to a dominantly conciliatory strategy and still preserve the ruling family's perceived interests. Because the events beginning in 2011 greatly hardened popular feelings against the monarchy, truly opening up the political system would inevitably put severe and unwelcome demands on the monarchical system.

Despite this, the king appears not to have abandoned the hope of pacifying his restive population through some degree of political reform. The king and many members of the government have continued to talk as if Bahrain has an open and free political system, and market the country both domestically and internationally as one with a progressive political system. This has led to many instances in which governmental leaders and the opposition appeared to be talking right past each other—officials highlight political opportunities and reforms, while the opposition highlights continued police brutality and political detentions. The reality is that security services have continued to target dissidents, and the most provocative activists have been handed severe prison sentences or even stripped of their citizenship, even as the monarchy tries to imagine a new set of political rules that will allow it to maintain its power with popular consent.[49] The solution space for this outcome has severely narrowed, however, and it will be increasingly difficult to find a coalition in the ruling family that will be willing to risk any substantive political changes in such a climate of fear and mistrust.

The less costly, but also less constructive, solution that the ruling family has pursued is a sustained narrative strategy for framing the actions of both the regime and its opposition. The Bahraini government has aggressively sought to control the political narrative in three ways: by restricting local flows of information, by hiring elite public relations firms to craft the regime's international image, and by demonizing the Shi'a opposition. Independent journalists have been restricted and the government has used its ample resources to put the official narrative front and center using numerous Facebook and Twitter accounts to enhance the image of its public support. At least a dozen public relations firms have been utilized by the regime to compete with the media activities of human rights activists and opposition leaders.[50] Bahraini state

[49] Toby Jones, "We Know What Happened in Bahrain: Now What?" Carnegie Endowment for International Peace, 1 Dec. 2011.

[50] Nada Al-Wadi, "The War of the Words: Bahrain's Struggle over Local Coverage," Carnegie Endowment for International Peace, 3 May 2012,

television practically ignored the first anniversary of the uprising, focusing instead on the beneficence of the royal family and the anniversary of the constitutional reforms, a predictable move that inevitably reinforced the lack of trust between the government and a knowledgeable population that has had extraordinary participation rates in the popular protests. The government's continued framing of the uprising as a vehicle for the extension of Iranian influence in the country likewise discredits the regime in the eyes of many Bahrainis who can distinguish between local grievances and international intrigues within a small country where news travels quickly within social networks.

What the government has done successfully is to create mutual suspicion across opposition actors by building on Sunni fears of Shi'a dominance, and by playing liberal activists off against conservative religious activists.[51] Using the bicameral parliament, the Bahraini monarchy countered the popular Islamic religious parties that dominate the assembly with a mixture of liberals and loyalist appointees in the Shura Council. The royal family has thus reinforced its image as a critical social arbiter that can preserve the interests of more liberal and/or Sunni elites against the possibility of a religious Shi'a deluge if the political floodgates were to open fully. Maintaining a divided opposition may help the monarchy to survive in the short term, although it fails to resolve any of the fundamental social grievances that drive opposition to the regime. For many, the current government has simply gone too far in its human rights abuses to ever reclaim the previous levels of citizen loyalty without enacting fundamental changes in the way the political system operates.[52] This makes sustained pressure on the Bahraini regime likely over time despite a fragmented opposition.

Another way that the Bahraini regime has sought to preserve itself is by outsourcing its preservation to regional or international actors with a large stake in Bahraini politics. Saudi Arabia is the most obvious

http://carnegieendowment.org/sada/index.cfm?fa=show&article=48037&solr_hilite=Bahrain

51 A tactic increasingly common among monarchs in the Arab world. See Hillel Frisch, "Why Monarchies Persist: Balancing Between Internal and External Vulnerability." *Review of International Studies* (1 Sep. 2010), p. 184. Also see Jennifer Gandhi and Adam Przeworski, "Authoritarian Institutions and the Survival of Autocrats," *Comparative Political Studies* (Nov. 2007).

52 Personal interview with Khalil al-Marzooq, Sep. 2012.

example of a regional actor that is unwilling to let the Sunni al-Khalifa regime fall victim to a Shi'a majority through either revolution or reform. For Saudi Arabia, the Bahraini regime must be preserved in order to prevent political pressure and Shi'a-led protest from spilling over into its own system. Talk of political unification between Bahrain and Saudi Arabia in 2012 reflected the two countries' common interest in maintaining the al-Khalifa's dominance, although such a proposal was widely opposed throughout Bahrain, where many fear the possibility of the country's independence being compromised by Saudi interests. In addition, other Gulf monarchies remain wary of political change in Bahrain because of Bahrain's similarities to their own systems and fear that change in Bahrain would complicate their own domestic politics. Despite the US interest in human rights in Bahrain, and its widely appreciated public condemnation of attacks on Shi'a religious sites, the United States also remains wary of political change because of its extensive military investment in the country and traditional alliance with King Hamad on a range of regional issues.[53]

Although real political reform that effectively incorporates all major stakeholders in Bahrain may be the best way to create social stability in the long term, it will require either newly courageous leadership from the monarchy or sustained popular pressure over time to realize this possibility. Substantive political reform at present will inevitably risk the royal family's political and economic position; as a result, stakeholders within the family are likely to work aggressively to preserve the existing system, even if it is rebranded and reintroduced to the public with cosmetic changes. An increasingly tough line on the opposition in the second half of 2012 and into 2013 illustrated that real political reform remains a long way from the minds of regime leaders.

This resistance could potentially be overcome in the face of a deepening political crisis, in which the risks to the monarchy of failing to change are ultimately greater than the risks of leading that change. Increased pressure on the regime is only likely, however, in the event that sectarian divisions within the opposition can be bridged, or alternatively, in the worst case scenario, if sectarian violence dramatically increases. At present, the opposition remains determined to continue its campaign of public pressure, but is divided on strategy. Explicitly sectarian violence

53 Nakhleh, *Bahrain*, pp. 96–7.

remains sporadic. This means that the government and opposition remain in a stalemate in which neither has the power to bridge the rupture in the traditional ruling bargain, although both sides have an interest in renegotiating a political deal that will return the country to political stability.

Ultimately, a path forward in Bahrain will require difficult political compromises if it is to be jointly created through the actions of domestic stakeholders. If this does not happen through domestic political leadership, it is likely that international stakeholders will be necessary to define the terms of a political resolution. These terms are dependent to a large degree on the position of Saudi Arabia, but could be mediated by a broader coalition of countries across the GCC, and could include a productive role for the United States or the United Kingdom. If the terms of a resolution are defined by stakeholders from the neighboring region, it is likely that they will buttress the Bahraini monarchy against its domestic challenges, enabling that monarchy to preserve itself and its privileges, even in the face of a failed ruling bargain that will detract from the country's long-run success.

At present there remains only limited space for bargaining between the ruling family and the country's largest opposition groups, in which a political agreement much like the one that emerged at the time of Bahrain's independence might be possible. Patience with the possibilities of such a resolution has worn thin among many segments of society, however, and polarization has continued to harden stakeholders on both sides. To the extent that the monarchy itself can make the tough decisions necessary to expand its base of social support across sectarian and economic communities, it will be more likely to create the conditions under which a meaningful ruling bargain can be sustained over time, and Bahrain's independence and remarkable social diversity can be preserved. The longer the political stalemate remains, however, it becomes less likely that Bahrain will maintain a self-enforcing ruling bargain, leading to sustained social instability or increasing dependence on Saudi Arabia for the regime's preservation.

13

YEMEN AND THE ARAB SPRING

Thomas Juneau

"Nothing was going to change until Saleh was gone, but now that he's gone, nothing very much has changed."[1]

In November 2011, after months of street protests and growing violence, Ali Abdullah Saleh, Yemen's president of thirty-three years, agreed to resign and transfer power to his vice-president. At the time, some observers anticipated that the Arab Spring would prove to be the spark that pushed Yemen toward state collapse, a prediction that many had been making for years. For other, the popular uprisings that were sweeping the region would provide Yemen with a golden opportunity to escape the spiral of state fragility and to move towards state-building and democratization. Instead of overhauling state–society relations, however,

[1] Alan Duncan, Minister of State for International Development for the United Kingdom, "DFID Minister of State Alan Duncan on Yemen," Chatham House, 14 Mar. 2012, www.chathamhouse.org/audio-resource/182549 (accessed 11 July 2012).

the Yemeni version of the Arab Spring is leading to more of the same: a perennially unstable country where elite factions dominate the political landscape and constantly struggle for the spoils of power.

In order to discuss the evolution of the ruling bargain in Yemen in the wake of the Arab Spring, this chapter starts by providing some background on the country. It will explain, in particular, how the pre-2011 ruling bargain was largely the product of an intra-elite struggle for power. It will also propose an overview of the uprising that led to the resignation of Saleh. The chapter then argues that despite the important changes brought by events since 2011, the ruling bargain in Yemen has not fundamentally changed: politics are still largely about an intra-elite struggle for power, even though the nature of this struggle has shifted. The chapter concludes by proposing key indicators to monitor the evolution of the situation.

Yemen: On the Verge of Failure

The Republic of Yemen was born in 1990 as a result of the unification of the Yemen Arab Republic (commonly known as North Yemen) and the People's Democratic Republic of Yemen (or South Yemen, which had been independent since the British departure in 1967). Unification was a difficult process which left many problems unresolved. Lingering tensions burst into the open in 1994 in a brief civil war during which forces loyal to the north trounced southern separatists. The unification agreement had promised a multiparty system allowing free elections and the development of civil society. In practice, however, unified Yemen witnessed the gradual centralization of power in the hands of its president, Ali Abdullah Saleh, who had ruled North Yemen since 1978 and then took the reins of unified Yemen.[2]

Yemen has long been labeled a prime candidate for state failure due to the convergence of the multiple economic and political challenges it faces. Yemen is the poorest country in the Arab world—it suffers from high unemployment, weak government capacity, decaying infrastructure, a very limited manufacturing base, high illiteracy, and massive corruption. Most critically, the country is running out of oil and water.

[2] For an overview of Yemen's history, see Paul Dresch, *A History of Modern Yemen*, Cambridge: Cambridge University Press, 2000.

Never a major producer, Yemen relies on its oil exports for the majority of government revenue. Yet production in 2010 had declined by more than a third from its peak in the middle of the 2000s. As a result, exports could run out before 2020. Even worse, the country's water reserves are fast declining; by some accounts, Sana'a could be the world's first capital city to run out of water within five to ten years.

The country is also wracked by a number of conflicts. In the capital Sana'a, prior to 2011, tension had been mounting for years between Saleh and his allies on one side and a number of other senior regime figures on the other. In the north, an insurgency by a group known as the Houthis has led to six successive rounds of fighting since 2004.[3] In the south, many are dissatisfied with unity; for some, the answer is federalism, but for many others, it is separation. Finally, Al-Qa'eda in the Arabian Peninsula (AQAP), the local franchise of the global terrorist network which has been described by American officials as the main threat to the US homeland, has steadily increased its presence in the country, especially in the southeast.[4]

The Ruling Bargain in Yemen before 2011

Politics in Yemen prior to the Arab Spring was essentially the product of an intra-elite struggle for power in which the Yemeni people had little say. At the center of this system of elite competition was the country's president and most powerful man, Ali Abdullah Saleh. Originally a tank commander, Saleh rose through the ranks of the military to seize the presidency after the assassination of his predecessor in 1978. A skilful manipulator and political operator, he built a complex system of relationships through which he managed the country's affairs. He did so largely by integrating military, tribal, clerical, and business leaders into an elaborate and flexible system of patronage.

Despite the inclusiveness of this system, Saleh increasingly stacked the senior ranks of the military and security services with family members

[3] The Houthis, like around 35 percent of Yemen's population, are Zaydis, a branch of Shi'a Islam. The other 65 percent of Yemenis are mostly Shafi'i Sunnis.

[4] On Yemen's multiple challenges, see Thomas Juneau, "Yemen: Prospects for State Failure—Implications and Remedies," *Middle East Policy*, 17 (2010), pp. 134–52.

and kinsmen. His son Ahmad Ali, in particular, became the commander of the Republican Guards, the country's best trained and equipped unit. In recent years, the country was also rife with rumors that Saleh was attempting to position his son to succeed him. A Saleh half-brother was commander of the air force, a relatively capable force with some functioning fighter aircraft and helicopters. Three of Saleh's nephews also held key positions in the security bureaucracy: 'Ammar was the deputy head (but *de facto* leader) of the powerful National Security Bureau while Yahya commanded the Central Security Forces, a US-trained and equipped counter-terrorism unit, and Tariq commanded the Third Brigade, an elite unit based around Sana'a which played a key role in regime protection.

Saleh's networks extended throughout all sectors of society. In the civil service, key positions, especially those controlling access to funds, were in the hands of loyalists. The former president was a master at manipulating tribal politics, constantly shifting and calibrating alliances to maintain a delicate balance of power among fiercely independent tribes. In the private sector, Saleh also ensured that trade in strategic goods was controlled by sympathetic businessmen. The General People's Congress (GPC), established in 1982 as a quasi-party regrouping a wide array of factions, was one of the main vehicles for his ambition. The GPC has no unifying ideology other than to ensure the consolidation and perpetuation of Saleh's power. Reflecting this purpose, its membership ranges from Arab secular nationalists to Islamists and from tribal chiefs to urban intellectuals, and spans the spectrum from left to right.

Arguably the second most powerful man in Yemen was Major-General Ali Muhsin, the commander of the First Armored Division and of the northwest military region and a kinsman of the president. For decades, Ali Muhsin was a close ally to Saleh; he helped him reach the presidency and, as his right-hand in the military, was responsible for many of the regime's most sensitive campaigns and initiatives. He had close ties, for example, to Salafi and jihadi militias, with which the Saleh regime held ambiguous ties for years. However, tensions between Saleh and Ali Muhsin rose in recent years, in particular around the growing power of Ahmad Ali.

Until 2011 the formal opposition to Saleh was mostly an opposition in name only. Its leaders had been co-opted by the president and had become incorporated into the system's patronage networks. The formal opposition's main vehicle emerged as the Joint Meeting Parties (JMP), a coalition of six parties formed in 2002 and led by Islah and the Yemeni Socialist Party (YSP).[5] The key feature of the JMP, which is crucial for understanding the events that followed the onset of the popular uprising in 2011, is the fact that its leaders were deeply embedded in the system that Saleh built. They benefited from the status quo; they were neither democrats nor reformists. Despite growing friction with Saleh and the GPC starting in the late 1990s, JMP leaders did not seek to have Saleh removed before 2011; tensions were mostly due to efforts by Saleh to reduce their share of power.

Islah was formed in 1990 as a coalition regrouping the Yemeni branch of the Muslim Brotherhood, northern tribal elements, and businessmen.[6] From the beginning, it was dominated by its Islamist core and by the al-Ahmar family. Its leading founder was Abdullah bin Hussein al-Ahmar, the paramount sheikh of the Hashid tribal confederation, the country's most powerful. For many years al-Ahmar was the speaker of parliament and the main tribal power-broker in Yemen. He was also the third member of the country's ruling triumvirate along with Saleh and Ali Muhsin. His alliance with Saleh ensured that the Hashid broadly supported the president.

Islah is the only party other than the GPC with appeal throughout the country and a broad grassroots network. From 1994 to 1997, it was a member of coalition governments with the GPC, solidifying its entrenchment in the system. In 1994, it sided with Saleh against the south in the brief civil war that pitted southern separatists against the regime in Sana'a. After the GPC won enough seats to govern alone in the 1997 parliamentary elections, Islah formally left government but Abdullah al-Ahmar and most of the party's leaders remained Saleh allies. Some of Islah's members, however, especially among its grassroots, increasingly bristled at the alliance with Saleh. Thus tensions gradually rose throughout the 2000s.

[5] See Michaelle Browers, "Origins and Architects of Yemen's Joint Meeting Parties," *International Journal of Middle East Studies*, 39 (2007), pp. 565–86.

[6] Jillian Schwedler, "The Islah Party in Yemen: Political Opportunities and Coalition Building in a Transnational Polity," in Quintan Wiktorowicz (ed.), *Islamic Activism: A Social Movement Theory Approach*, Bloomington: Indiana University Press, 2004, pp. 205–28; and April Longley Alley, "The High Water Mark of Islamist Politics? The Case of Yemen," *Middle East Journal*, 61 (2007), pp. 240–60.

The YSP, the second largest party in the JMP, is the descendant of the ruling party of the former South Yemen. As a result, it generally adheres to a leftist and secularist ideology. Even though it is the junior partner to Islah, it still benefits from strong support in the south. The JMP also includes smaller parties, including the Union of Popular Forces, al-Haqq, and the Nasserist Popular Unionist Party. All three, however, have struggled to make their voices heard within the coalition given Islah's predominance.

Over the decades Saleh painstakingly built a complex and largely informal web of patronage reaching deep into the military and security services, tribal networks, clerical and Islamist circles, and the bureaucracy, which allowed him to govern through a mixture of bargaining, co-optation, and coercion.[7] Saleh offered inducements such as government posts, access to or control over smuggling networks (sometimes with an understanding that the security services would turn a blind eye), direct payment, and various other privileges and benefits. In exchange, he expected acceptance of and deference to the status quo. Moves to challenge this status quo would be met by negotiation, increased payoffs, or intimidation and violence. Decisions were made through negotiation; Saleh would make deals with power-brokers, buying them off when possible but using violence when necessary. This flexibility provided members of the elite with a say in the management of the country's affairs and access to the spoils of power. This is a crucial feature of the ruling bargain in Yemen: the members of the elite who split from Saleh in the wake of the popular uprising that started in 2011 still maintained a vested interest in the perpetuation of the old order.

Saleh understood that one of his most valuable assets to maintain his position at the center of this constellation of networks was to keep the system permanently off balance. By manufacturing and manipulating crises, he systematically portrayed himself as the one indispensable figure that could ensure stability. The outcome was a personalized system centered on the president, with influence stemming partly from proximity to Saleh and his close allies and from integration into patronage net-

[7] For more on Saleh's management style, see April Longley Alley, "The Rules of the Game: Unpacking Patronage Politics in Yemen," *Middle East Journal*, 64 (2010), pp. 385–409; and Sarah Philips, *Yemen and the Politics of Permanent Crisis*, London: International Institute for Strategic Studies, 2011.

works. The Yemeni state, as a result, was built on brittle formal institutions, while channels for the expression of the popular will were weak. Elections, for example, were largely pre-arranged affairs partly driven by negotiation among the elite before and after the vote.

This political order was heavily contested, sometimes violently, by a number of actors who were kept outside of the system. Two key dissatisfied actors, in particular, are the Houthis and the Southern Movement. Both resent the monopolization of power in Sana'a and are frustrated by the lack of economic development in their respective areas. To these grievances is added a mixture of local and religious factors: the Houthis seek to protect their Zaydi identity and are angered by the activities of Salafis in the Sa'ada area, while southerners seeking autonomy or independence claim that their separate identity is incompatible with rule by tribally minded northerners.

This delicate equilibrium was under growing strain even before the onset of the Arab Spring, especially as a result of three sets of pressures: efforts by Saleh to concentrate power in his hands and those of his inner circle, the steady shrinking of the country's economic pie, and growing tensions in the north and south.

Efforts by Saleh to concentrate power in his hands and those of his immediate allies were causing growing resentment among other members of the elite, with his attempts to position his son Ahmad Ali as his successor causing the most frustration. The Republican Guards commanded by Ahmad Ali, in particular, were receiving the best equipment as well as elite training from the United States. Much of the political and military empowerment of Ahmad Ali was done at the expense of Ali Muhsin. Relations between Ali Muhsin and the Saleh clan, as a result, gradually deteriorated over the years. In fact, a popular interpretation held that the Houthi wars between 2004 and 2010 were at least in part a by-product of this rivalry. According to this view, the six rounds of fighting were the result either of attempts by Saleh and his son to weaken Ali Muhsin, or of efforts by Ali Muhsin to bolster his position.[8]

Another event that widened the gap within the elite was the death in 2007 of Abdullah al-Ahmar, who had managed to keep the leadership of the delicate Islah coalition generally allied to Saleh. His responsibili-

[8] International Crisis Group, "Yemen: Defusing the Saada Time Bomb," *Middle East Report No. 86* (27 May 2009), p. 15.

ties were divided among his sons. Hamid, one of the richest men in Yemen, took over the business side, while Sadiq replaced his father as paramount sheikh of the Hashid and Himyar became deputy speaker of parliament. Tensions between some of the al-Ahmar brothers and Saleh became increasingly deep and public after the patriarch's death. A key turning point came in August 2009 when Hamid gave an interview to Al Jazeera in which he severely criticized Saleh, especially for his corruption, and called on him to resign.[9]

Second, the economic pie available for the elite to share has been shrinking, with the growing awareness that this shrinking will accelerate. Before 2011, oil exports—never high even at their peak around 2005—amounted to about 90 percent of the country's total exports and provided 75 percent of central government revenues. Yemen's oil reserves are diminishing, however, and the country's export capacity could disappear before the end of the decade.[10] With looming oil and water crises, the prospects for economic development in Yemen are bleak. More specifically, a shrinking national budget implies fewer funds for the elite to divide among themselves, which in turn leads to intensifying competition for access to increasingly scarce resources.

Third, growing tensions in the south and north were also putting the ruling bargain under strain. After unification in 1990, Saleh attempted, with some success, to co-opt and integrate the southern elite.[11] Popular resentment against northern control of the south's politics and economy, however, has been rising over the years. At the same time, a growing number of leading figures from the former South Yemen either distanced themselves from Sana'a or were marginalized within the regime. Protests, led by the Hirak, an umbrella movement for a variety of southern factions, became especially strong after 2007, with a growing number of southerners calling for autonomy or independence and a minority willing to use violence to achieve its ends.[12] Among the elite and the

[9] For the video and a transcript of the interview (in Arabic), see http://www.aljazeera.net/programs/pages/23ae76c1–9b9a-4fca-8f5d-0a4d0fa2510d (accessed 11 June 2012).

[10] On Yemen's economic problems, see Charles Schmitz, "Crisis in the Yemeni Economy: A Troubled Transition to Post-Hydrocarbon Growth," Middle East Institute, Dec. 2011.

[11] See Noel Brehony, *Yemen Divided: The Story of a Failed State in Southern Arabia*, London: I.B. Tauris, 2011.

[12] Stephen Day, "The Political Challenge of Yemen's Southern Movement,"

general population of the south, some seek outright separation, while others seek federalism, devolution of power, and an end to the northern domination of the south. In the middle, some southern leaders have put forward a proposal that would see the establishment of a federal system with significant regional devolution of power, followed after five years by a Sudan-style referendum on separation.

In addition to tension in the south, northern Yemen has seen six rounds of fighting since 2004 between government forces and their tribal and Salafi allies against the Houthis. The latter, who are named after the family that leads their movement, harbor a number of grievances arising from economic inequality and a perceived denial of their identity by the central government.[13] By 2010, about 300,000 people had been internally displaced by the fighting, while the Houthis progressively gained control of swaths of territory in and around Sa'ada governorate.

Yemen's ruling bargain, in sum, was under growing strain by the end of 2010 not because of societal claims on the state, but due to the growing fractures within the elite and in the delicate equilibrium managed by Saleh. It is in this tense context that the Arab Spring, after sweeping through Egypt and Tunisia, reached Yemen. These protests acted as a catalyst for a definitive break among the elite—but not for the establishment of a fundamentally new ruling bargain.

The Arab Spring in Yemen

The Arab Spring started timidly in Yemen. Even after Tunisian President Zine el-Abidine Ben Ali was forced to flee on 14 January 2011, demonstrations in Sana'a remained scattered. They gained momentum in February, when the resignation of Hosni Mubarak in Egypt persuaded thousands of Yemenis to pour into the streets of major cities. Initially, the protests were dominated by a loose coalition of youth, NGOs, and democracy activists, while Islah and other members of the formal oppo-

---

in Christopher Boucek and Marina Ottaway (eds), *Yemen on the Brink*, Washington, DC: Carnegie Endowment for International Peace, 2010, pp. 61–74.

[13] Lucas Winter, "Conflict in Yemen: Simple People, Complicated Circumstances," *Middle East Policy*, 18 (2011), pp. 102–20.

sition kept their distance. Gradually, however, the JMP overcame its reluctance to challenge the system from which it benefited and called on its members to take to the streets.[14] From the outset, street protesters were suspicious of the organized political parties, which they viewed as little different from Saleh.

The situation dramatically changed on 18 March when government-affiliated snipers shot and killed over fifty demonstrators and injured dozens more. Not only did this inflame important segments of popular opinion against Saleh, more importantly it also led to a wave of defections. Within days, dozens of MPs, diplomats, tribal leaders, and military officers announced that they were withdrawing their support for the president. Of note were the defections of Major-General Ali Muhsin, members of the al-Ahmar family, and much of the leadership of the JMP. Unlike many of the street protestors who called outright for Saleh's departure, however, Islah and the JMP still proposed a negotiated transition. This led to an awkward dynamic: Hamid al-Ahmar financed the street protests while Ali Muhsin's troops protected them from further repression by troops loyal to Saleh.

The situation remained tense throughout 2011. Violence ebbed and flowed, with occasional bouts of fighting in Sana'a and elsewhere. In early June, Saleh was critically injured and a number of senior regime figures killed or maimed by a bomb attack on a mosque inside the presidential compound.[15] The president then traveled to Saudi Arabia to receive medical treatment. The country's politics were somewhat frozen over the summer. Saleh's son Ahmad Ali moved into the presidential palace, clearly signaling that the clan intended to hold on to power. Saleh returned to Yemen in September in a highly volatile climate. In October and November, with armed militias and rival military units facing each other in Sana'a and elsewhere, it became clear that neither side was strong enough to defeat the other. The country seemed to be moving towards a prolonged and violent stalemate and appeared closer to collapse than ever before.[16]

[14] On the early days of the street protests, see International Crisis Group, "Popular Protest in North Africa and the Middle East (II): Yemen between Reform and Revolution," Middle East/North Africa Report No. 102 (10 Mar. 2011).

[15] It remains unclear who was responsible for the attack.

[16] For an overview of the main events surrounding the Arab Spring in Yemen,

Starting in April 2011, the Gulf Cooperation Council (GCC), led by Saudi Arabia and backed by the United States and the EU, had sought to push forward a deal easing Saleh out of power and proposing a framework for a transition.[17] The deal was negotiated among traditional power-brokers in Sana'a—Saleh, Ali Muhsin, the al-Ahmar brothers, and the JMP—and excluded the Houthis, the Hirak, and the street protestors, which only served to confirm their long-standing distrust of the organized opposition. Saleh agreed to the deal on three occasions throughout the year, but reneged on his promise each time.[18] He finally signed in Riyadh in November.[19] The agreement called for Saleh's gradual phasing from formal power in exchange for immunity for him and his main allies. Saleh was also allowed to keep his role as head of the GPC. Power was to be gradually transferred to his long-serving vice-president, 'Abd Rabbu Mansour Hadi, who was viewed at the time as a lightweight with no power base of his own. Hadi was a compromise choice, acceptable to every faction because he was perceived as unthreatening.[20] As per the deal, elections were held in February 2012, with only Hadi on the ballot. A national unity government was formed, with the GPC and JMP sharing Cabinet seats evenly. The agreement also estab-

---

see Khaled Fattah, "Yemen: A Social Intifada in a Republic of Sheikhs," *Middle East Policy*, 18 (2011), pp. 79–85; and Ibrahim Sharqieh, "Yemen: The Search for Stability and Development," in Kenneth Pollack et al. (eds), *The Arab Awakening: America and the Transformation of the Middle East*, Washington, DC: Brookings Institution Press, 2011, pp. 221–9.

[17] The GCC regroups the six petro-monarchies of the southern shore of the Persian Gulf: Bahrain, Kuwait, Oman, Qatar, Saudi Arabia, and the United Arab Emirates.

[18] This has been a recurring tactic on Saleh's part: in past years, he often pledged that he would resign or that he would not be a candidate in future elections, only to hold on to power. See Gregory D. Johnsen, "Salih's Road to Reelection," *Middle East Report* (13 Jan. 2006).

[19] "Yemen's Saleh Agrees to Transfer Power," Al Jazeera English (24 Nov. 2011).

[20] Tom Finn, "Filling Saleh's Shoes," ForeignPolicy.com (21 Mar. 2012), http://www.foreignpolicy.com/articles/2012/03/21/filling_salehs_shoes?page=full (accessed 24 Mar. 2012). For a biography of Hadi, see "*Ma'reb brys yanshar as-syra adh-dhatiyya li-ra'ys al-muntazhir 'Abd ar-Rahman Mansour Hadi*" [Ma'reb Press Publishes an Autobiography of Acting President Abd Rahman Mansour Hadi], Ma'reb Press, 16 Feb. 2012, http://www.marebpress.net/news_details.php?sid=40645 (accessed 24 June 2012).

lished a framework for a national dialogue, constitutional revisions, reforms in the military and security apparatus, and presidential elections in 2014.[21]

The evolving ruling bargain in Yemen: more of the same

The 2011 protests acted as a catalyst that caused this long-brewing elite struggle to take an explosive turn. In a context where tension was running high, the formal opposition seized the opportunity offered by the uprising to attempt to remove Saleh and his allies from power. The GCC deal, in this context, punted major problems down the river without actually solving them; it reshuffled the framework in which elite competition occurs but did not overhaul the rules of the game. The fragile equilibrium that barely kept the country together until 2011 has not been fundamentally transformed: the ruling bargain in Yemen is still essentially about an intra-elite struggle for power. That said, some of its features have changed, and are still evolving.

One of the defining features of the old order has certainly changed. In the past, the political order had come to be increasingly built around the persona of President Saleh; in the game of elite competition, he was *primus inter pares*. One of the driving purposes of politics in the country was indeed the perpetuation and strengthening of Saleh's position as the center of gravity of the ruling bargain. This has changed.[22] Saleh is not *primus inter pares* anymore: the former president and his allies are now fighting it out with their rivals on more equal terms.

Indeed, the balance of forces within the elite has changed: the Saleh clan has been weakened while its adversaries have been strengthened. Saleh, in particular, has lost the presidency, while the JMP has gained access to half the Cabinet seats. Hadi has in fact done more to undermine Saleh's position than many had expected, surprising observers by assertively seeking to establish control over the military and security services.[23] The new president fired or reshuffled many Saleh allies includ-

[21] Laura Kasinof, "Yemen Gets New Leader as Struggle Ends Calmly," *The New York Times*, 24 Feb. 2012.

[22] I thank Gerd Nonneman for suggesting this point.

[23] Hadi's actions have angered Saleh and his clan, who resent the fact that, as they perceive it, they are being unjustly targeted while the authority of Ali Muhsin and his allies is left untouched. See "*Hadi yathar mu'asasat al-yaman:*

ing, in his first sixty days, four civilian governors and more than twenty senior military commanders close to Saleh.[24] Most strikingly, Hadi disbanded the Republican Guards and sent Ahmad Ali Saleh off to the United Arab Emirates as ambassador, and dismissed Saleh's three nephews from their dominant positions in the security services and the military.[25] Saleh's powerful half-brother Mohammed Saleh, the commander of the air force, was also shuffled to a position with symbolic but no real influence. He initially refused to step down, even having his men seize Sana'a International Airport in protest. Under pressure, including from the UN envoy in Yemen, he relented.[26] Yet other powerful Saleh allies and family members still remain in place throughout the military, the security services, and the bureaucracy. His patronage network also remains strong, through the GPC and its tribal allies, while the GPC retains a strong parliamentary majority until the next elections.

Despite these setbacks, Saleh has no intention of leaving the scene. Both he and his allies are holding on to their remaining levers of power and are resisting efforts to further marginalize them.[27] From the former president's perspective, the uprising is primarily the result of a plot by his rivals, especially Ali Muhsin and the al-Ahmar family, to remove him from power and take control of the state for themselves. Saleh remains the head of the GPC, which is stacked with his loyalists, many of whom believe that the marginalization of the former president would also lead to their own partial or complete marginalization. The GPC was built as

---

Qaa'imat min rumuuz al-fasaad, yasta'id ar-ra'ys bil-inaaba li-tarhylihim min manaasabihim ua Salih yatahaddath 'an tajaauuz lisilaahyaatihi" [Hadi Cleanses the Foundations of Yemeni Politics: List of Symbols of Corruption, Acting President Prepares to Remove them from their Positions while Salih Discusses his Abuse of his Authority], Ma'reb Press, 23 Dec. 2011, www.marebpress.net/news_details.php?lang=arabic&sid=38987 (accessed 25 May 2012).

[24] "President Sacks Ex-Regime Loyalists," Al Jazeera English, 6 Apr. 2012.

[25] Sasha Gordon, "A New Wave of Military Restructuring Decrees in Yemen," *Critical Threats* (11 Apr. 2013), http://www.criticalthreats.org/yemen/gordon-new-wave-military-restructuring-decrees-yemen-april-11–2012 (accessed 13 Aug. 2013).

[26] Khaled Al Hammadi, "Saleh's Death Grip Pulls Yemen's Army into Enemy Camps," *The National* (20 Apr. 2012).

[27] Bernard Haykel, "Yemen after Saleh," Majalla (30 Mar. 2012), http://www.majalla.com/eng/2012/03/article55230344 (accessed 2 Apr. 2012).

a patronage machine that allowed Saleh to maintain his grip on the country. Many elements of this network remain intact, which gives Saleh significant levers to continue shaping political developments. The country is rife with rumors, moreover, that Ahmad Ali will be the GPC's presidential candidate in 2014.[28]

Another feature of the evolving ruling bargain in Yemen has been the clear break between the formal opposition and Saleh. In the past, despite growing tension and ambiguity, their relationship was one of mutual necessity and dependence. Since March 2011, former Saleh allies such as Ali Muhsin and the al-Ahmar family have pursued twin objectives: to ensure the perpetuation of the old order, but to remove Saleh and his allies from its head. This is a crucial distinction: should the system be completely overhauled, they would lose their political and economic privileges, an outcome they want to avoid. Under President Hadi, they have been quietly but actively seeking the marginalization of Saleh and his allies.[29] At the same time, they have been engaged in a scramble for the greatest possible access to the spoils of the system. Many JMP leaders, for example, are taking advantage of their presence in Cabinet by seeking to wrest control over appointments in the bureaucracy from GPC officials, whether prestigious positions (ambassadorships) or potentially lucrative ones (governorships).[30]

The Arab Spring in Yemen has also seen the emergence of a new actor on the country's political landscape. The street opposition consists of a loose coalition of disenchanted youth, lower and middle urban classes, and civil society movements. A number of tribesmen, frustrated with their sheikhs whom they accuse of having become corrupt and detached from local realities, also joined the street. They initially led the uprising, but their movement was gradually hijacked by the formal opposition. Islah, in particular, took control of, or at least came to exert strong influence over, many of the committees managing the daily affairs of the protests.[31] Because of its diversity, the street opposition's intentions are

[28] Tom Finn, "Voting Saleh Out," ForeignPolicy.com (22 Feb. 2012), http://mideast.foreignpolicy.com/posts/2012/02/22/voting_saleh_out (accessed 26 Feb. 2012).

[29] International Crisis Group, "Yemen: Enduring Conflicts, Threatened Transition," Middle East Report No. 125 (3 July 2012), p. 22.

[30] Ibid. p. 18.

[31] Letta Tayler, "Yemen's Hijacked Revolution," ForeignAffairs.com (26 Sep. 2011),

unclear. Broadly, its leaders seek democratization, an end to corruption and violence, and the removal and indictment of the leaders of the current system—not only Saleh and his allies, but also some JMP leaders and Ali Muhsin, of whom they remain highly suspicious.[32] Hence, there is a crucial difference between the street and what used to be the formal opposition: while both seek the departure of Saleh and his allies, the former wants a complete overhaul and ultimately the democratization of Yemeni politics, unlike the latter.

The street opposition has had influence over the unfolding of the Arab Spring in Yemen in the sense that its protests catalyzed important changes in the country's political order. It has still not emerged, however, as a full-fledged actor with an actual say in the game of politics as in Egypt or Tunisia, where opposition groups reached positions of power. Because it remains disorganized and fragmented, the street opposition has not been able to insert itself into a system that is unwilling to grant it influence. It is largely for this reason that most of its groups rejected the GCC deal and the transition process, accusing the likes of Ali Muhsin and the al-Ahmar family of seeking to perpetuate the old order.

In addition, those actors who were not part of the system before the uprising mostly remain outside. The Houthis and the Hirak, in particular, rejected the GCC deal and boycotted the February 2012 elections. For both groups, the transition agreement only perpetuates the domination of Yemeni politics by northern, Sana'a-based elites, the very system they have opposed for years. Like civil society movements, they resent the immunity granted to Saleh and his allies. This bodes ill for future stability: their grievances have been left unaddressed and are unlikely to be tackled by the central government as long as the old order remains in place. This is not to argue that the door is completely closed. There have, in fact, been conflicting signals as to whether they are willing to engage the nascent political process. The Houthis opposed the transition agreement and rejected calls to lay down their arms,[33] but they have been

http://www.foreignaffairs.com/articles/68298/letta-tayler/yemens-hijacked-revolution (accessed 29 Sep. 2011).

[32] On the street opposition, see Stacey Philbrick Yadav, "Opposition to Yemen's Opposition," ForeignPolicy.com (14 July 2011), http://mideast.foreignpolicy.com/posts/2011/07/14/opposition_to_yemen_s_opposition (accessed 12 June 2012).

[33] Khaled Fattah, "Yemen's Sectarian Spring," Sada (11 May 2012), http://carn-

active participants in the national dialogue launched in March 2013, along with some moderate southern leaders.

External actors, finally, have played an essential role in shaping these changes to the ruling bargain in Yemen. A primary US and Saudi interest in Yemen is stability. More specifically, Riyadh and Washington hope to contain instability actually or potentially radiating out of Yemen and, in the longer term, to prevent state failure. For both the United States and Saudi Arabia, this primarily translates as supporting and cooperating with Yemeni actors in the fight against AQAP. Saudi Arabia is also concerned with the impact of the Houthi conflict, smuggling, and possible refugee flows. It is in this context that, increasingly anxious at the prospect of prolonged instability in Yemen, Riyadh and Washington pushed throughout 2011 for the adoption and implementation of the GCC deal. By doing so, the United States and Saudi Arabia helped to prevent the emergence of more fundamental changes to the ruling bargain in Yemen: assessing that the risk of state collapse was growing, they supported an agreement that broadly perpetuates the old order. Ultimately, both are willing to support the faction or coalition of factions that will best ensure stability. Since assuming power in February 2012, President Hadi's willingness to mount an aggressive campaign against AQAP as well as his apparent acceptance of US drone strikes have thus been key in attracting US and Saudi support. Nonetheless, Washington and Riyadh are waiting to see how events develop. Both recognize that they have a limited ability to shape outcomes on the ground and are allowing the elite struggle to unfold; in the meantime, they are hedging their bets by keeping open lines of communication with various factions.

The presidential election—or "selection"—that led to Hadi's uncontested elevation to the presidency in February 2012 best illustrates how politics in Yemen remain controlled by the same elite. The former vice-president was the only candidate, and he was chosen solely as the result of the Saudi-brokered, US-backed compromise between Saleh and his rivals.[34] In this context, the election was not an opportunity for the people to have a say, but merely one phase among many for the elite to

---

egieendowment.org/2012/05/11/yemen-s-sectarian-spring/attg (accessed 27 May 2012).

[34] Tom Finn, "Abd Rabbu Mansour Hadi Who?" *The Guardian*, 20 Feb. 2012.

arbitrate their ongoing conflicts. Actors outside of the system—civil society, the Houthis, or the Hirak—were not consulted at any step in the process.

Looking Ahead

Yemen thus begins the post-Saleh era facing a highly uncertain transition period. Despite the intensity of street protests since 2011, elite factions have succeeded in closing off access to networks of power to new actors, some from civil society and some dissatisfied traditional ones from the north and south. Elite factions are still jockeying for position in structures similar to those of the pre-Arab Spring era; they are seeking to defend the status quo while simultaneously attempting to constrain the influence of rival factions. Despite mounting pressures from within and below, it is therefore difficult to be optimistic about the likelihood of a more inclusive ruling bargain emerging in Yemen, one that would see the integration of civil society and dissatisfied groups into the structures of power. The situation is likely to remain as unpredictable and volatile as it was before 2011: as long as the old political order is perpetuated, Yemen will not be able to tackle the myriad social, economic, political, and security challenges it faces. There is, as a result, a strong possibility of protracted instability in Yemen, with violence ebbing and flowing along with the intensity of elite struggles.[35]

The most important variable shaping the future of Yemeni politics is the status of the Saleh clan. Hadi has surprised observers with his willingness to take on the former president and his allies. The new president, as mentioned above, has ordered shuffles in senior ranks of the security services, the military, and the bureaucracy, with many Saleh allies, including his son, half-brother, and nephews, losing their positions. Yet even though Hadi has been more assertive than many had anticipated, he is unlikely to be strong enough to remove the remaining pillars of the Saleh clan and the leaders of what used to be the formal opposition such as Ali Muhsin. On the one hand, as long as Saleh remains powerful, necessary reforms will not be adopted and imple-

[35] On the assessment that the most likely future scenarios for Yemen all imply prolonged instability, see Thomas Juneau, "Yemen and the Arab Spring: Elite Struggles, State Collapse and Regional Security," *Orbis*, 57 (2013), pp. 408–23.

mented. On the other hand, there is a strong likelihood that if threatened with complete marginalization, the Saleh clan would act as a spoiler. This could prove highly destabilizing.

Indeed, despite Hadi's efforts, important elements of Saleh's patronage networks remain in place. Saleh himself remains influential as head of the GPC. The former president also maintains allies in the military and the security services and the bureaucracy, and through his tribal networks. He is also reported to be developing ties to some southern leaders and the Houthis. Hadi's reforms have been unable to remove all of Saleh's allies. The country's electoral authorities, for example, were mostly appointed by Saleh. As part of the military's restructuring, in addition, Hadi created a Chancellery of the Supreme Commander of the Armed Forces, a six-person committee directly advising the president—yet it has at least three members with ties to Saleh.[36] Similarly, many units from the disbanded Republican Guard have mutinied, indicating the Saleh clan's ongoing ability to spoil developments.[37] Overall, the future of the clan's influence is unclear; it is certainly on the wane, but it is very unlikely to disappear altogether.

The internal cohesion of what used to be the formal opposition is another key indicator to watch. It is a loose and heterogenous coalition of diverse and often contradictory interests and mutually suspicious personalities. In particular, the sustainability of the ties that have bound Ali Muhsin to Islah and the al-Ahmar family since March 2011, as well as the level of unity within Islah and, more broadly, within the JMP, is questionable.[38] Some cracks, in fact, have begun appearing, with smaller parties within the JMP feeling marginalized by the more powerful Islah. The selection process for the preparatory committee for the national dialogue, for example, was monopolized by the GPC and Islah and

[36] Gordon, "A New Wave of Military Restructuring Decrees in Yemen."

[37] Sasha Gordon, "Mutiny in the Yemeni Military," *Critical Threats* (10 July 2013), http://www.criticalthreats.org/yemen/gordon-mutiny-yemeni-military-july-10–2013 (accessed 13 Aug. 2013).

[38] Hadi's military restructuring decrees have also targeted Ali Muhsin, formally disbanding the First Armored Division and naming him a presidential advisor on military affairs. Ali Muhsin nonetheless remains very influential within the military, maintaining extensive ties with units formerly under his command. He also continues to receive financial support from Saudi Arabia. Bernard Haykal, "Yemen's Domestic and Regional Politics," Norwegian Peacebuilding Resource Centre Policy Brief (May 2013), p. 2.

excluded other actors, either from the JMP or from the country as a whole.[39] Islah itself, moreover, has come under some strain since 2011, especially as a result of a growing rift between its old guard and younger grassroots members. While the former seek to perpetuate the old order, some in the latter, such as Nobel Peace Prize laureate Tawakkul Karman, seek more fundamental change.[40] As long as Saleh remains in Yemen and continues to seek to play a role, it is likely that the glue that holds those actors together will remain strong. However, if or when the Saleh clan's power further decreases, this glue could weaken.

The evolution of the *de facto* alliance between the JMP, Ali Muhsin, and the street opposition in 2011 will also be crucial to the future of the ruling bargain in Yemen. The relationship has been an awkward one from its beginning. The street opposition benefited from, and recognized the necessity of, protection from Ali Muhsin's troops and money from Hamid al-Ahmar. At the same time, both sides recognize the fundamental incompatibility of their respective goals: the JMP and Ali Muhsin seek the perpetuation of the old order but without Saleh at its head, while the street opposition seeks the democratization of the system. The former, as a result, elicits much suspicion among the various civil society movements that took to the streets in 2011. Should the JMP, especially its dominant component Islah, eventually succeed in marginalizing the Saleh clan, growing tension with the street would be likely to ensue.

A key unknown concerns Hadi's intentions. Does he view himself as a transitional figure or is he seeking to develop a power base of his own in order to position himself as the country's new strongman? One interpretation argues that Hadi may very well have the ambition to compete in the 2014 presidential election. If this is his objective, his initial efforts at weakening the Saleh clan probably aim to establish a closer balance between Saleh and what used to be the formal opposition. He could then seek to attract support from both sides by presenting himself as the inevitable candidate. Supporting this hypothesis are reports that he has been replacing Saleh allies in the security services and the bureaucracy

[39] International Crisis Group, "Yemen: Enduring Conflicts, Threatened Transition," p. 23.

[40] Stacey Phibrick Yadav, "Tawakkul Karman as Cause and Effect," Middle East Research and Information Project (21 Oct. 2011).

by loyalists who, like him, hail from Abyan Province.[41] Should this scenario come about, the pre-Arab Spring ruling bargain would be perpetuated: Yemeni politics would be led by Hadi but would be defined by the competition between his faction and remnants from the old order led by Saleh, Ali Muhsin, and the al-Ahmar family. A more optimistic reading suggests that Hadi, keenly aware of the weakness of his position, realizes that without a power-base of his own, his survival is a constant challenge and his ability to push through reforms is non-existent. According to this second view, Hadi seeks to weaken Saleh, the first obstacle to reforming the system, as well as Ali Muhsin and the al-Ahmar family. Only then would he be in a strong enough position to launch deeper reforms. If this is his intention, he faces tremendous obstacles given the massive advantages in terms of resources that both the Saleh clan and the Ali Muhsin–JMP alliance possess.

A crucial development in this regard will be the National Dialogue, the third pillar of the GCC transition agreement after Saleh's removal and the election of Hadi. Will it take into consideration the full spectrum of Yemeni actors, including the Hirak, the Houthis, and civil society, or will it evolve into a venue for the traditional elite to perpetuate their dominance of the country's politics? Will the dialogue be empowered, or will it simply evolve into a talking shop providing an opportunity for various groups to be heard but not to gain influence? In May 2012, after some hesitation and already late in terms of the transition agreement's timeline, Hadi established a preparatory committee charged with reaching out to stakeholders and setting the ground for the dialogue. In a positive development, the Houthis participated in the committee's work, though they insisted that this did not mean they recognized the GCC deal.[42] As a result, two out of the twenty-five members of the committee were Houthi representatives. Some southern factions also agreed to participate in the Dialogue, though hard-liners, especially those allied with Ali Salim al-Baydh, a former leader of South Yemen and vice-president of unified Yemen until the 1994 civil war, rejected any involvement.

[41] Laura Kasinof, "For Yemen's New President, a Battle for Control and a Tug of War with the Past," *The New York Times*, 13 June 2012.

[42] Mohammed Ghobari and Mohammed Mukhashaf, "Northern Rebels Agree to Join Talks on Yemen's Future," Reuters, 5 June 2012.

The National Dialogue, tasked with laying the groundwork for a new constitution and a presidential election in 2014, was finally launched in March 2013. It included nine working groups, discussing the northern and southern issues, state-building, national issues, governance, military and security issues, special entities, rights and freedom, and development. At the time of writing in August 2013, the first plenary session had been completed, and some of the working groups had tabled their preliminary reports which were scheduled to be debated in the second plenary. At its midway point, the National Dialogue had exceeded most expectations: the simple fact that it had been launched and had proceeded largely peacefully was considered a success. The active participation of the Houthis and many civil society actors, including youth and women, provided further encouraging signs. Some of the committee reports submitted in June also detailed constructive recommendations for the way ahead. But such early promises were due to the frozen state of Yemeni politics in the wake of the GCC agreement, not to concrete reforms to the country's ruling bargain. As a former member of the GPC mused to a journalist, the Dialogue and the transition deal can be likened to "prescribing a sedative for someone with a serious illness."[43] While some Dialogue committees had made progress, for example, others were paralyzed, including the crucial transitional justice and northern ones.[44]

Indeed, it is unlikely that whatever outcome emerges from the Dialogue will be able to satisfy the complex demands of the many dissatisfied groups or succeed in reconciling the divergent interests of the competing factions in Sana'a. There are many reasons for this pessimism. In addition to the constant efforts by the old elite to defend their privileges, numerous challenges will vastly complicate the Dialogue and future efforts to promote reform. Pressures from below in favor of a new ruling bargain will continue. The precedent of street mobilization has been set; even though the informal opposition remains fragmented, since 2011 there has been an unprecedented level of political awareness. In fact, popular expectations for improvements in the country's economic, social, and political situation have risen to such an extent that it

[43] Adam Baron, "A Day in Sanaa Reveals the State of Yemen's National Dialogue," *The National* (15 June 2013).

[44] Farea Al-Muslimi, "Fighting Paralysis in Yemen's Dialogue," *Daily Star*, 1 July 2013.

is unlikely that any transition administration will be able to meet them. It is in this context that there has been much talk of a "parallel revolution," of mounting anti-corruption protests and labor strikes targeting regime officials. Some protests, such as those at the national airline, Yemenia Airways, have led to the dismissal of former regime officials, whereas mutinies, for example within the air force, added to the pressure on Saleh allies.[45] Even though the impact of ongoing labor protests has so far been limited, it does represent an additional variable in an already combustible mix.

Underlying this uncertainty are the tremendous and mounting economic and security challenges facing the country. Pressures which dogged Saleh's Yemen and led to repeated predictions of state failure have not disappeared; if anything, they are stronger than they were before 2011. Transitional authorities and whichever regime emerges from the National Dialogue and the 2014 elections—assuming they occur—may be overwhelmed, even if they have the best of intentions, by the depth and breadth of these problems. Economic decline, in particular, has accelerated since 2011. The economy contracted by 10 percent in 2011 and by around 1 percent in 2012, increasing already high levels of poverty and unemployment.[46] In 2012, the UN consequently estimated that 10 million Yemenis, out of a population of about 24 million, were food insecure and that 5 million required emergency aid.[47]

[45] Sasha Gordon, "The Parallel Revolution in Yemen," *Critical Threats* (6 Mar. 2012), www.criticalthreats.org/yemen/gordon-parallel-revolution-march-6–2012 (accessed 17 Mar. 2012). The long-standing director of Yemenia, Abdul Khaleq al-Qadhi, Saleh's son-in-law, was suspended and eventually replaced. See "*Tabaadul silmy li-sulta daman thaura al-mu'asasaat; Majlis idaara al-khutuut al-jauiyya al-yamaniyya yaqir bil-ijmaa'a taklyf al-kaabitan al-'aluaany ra'ys limajlis al-idaara ua al-Qadhy yad'am juhuud at-taghyyr*" [Peaceful Power Transfer in the Revolution of the Institutions; Board of Directors for Yemenia Airways Decides Unanimously to Appoint Captain al Alwani President of the Board and al Qadhi Supports the Change Efforts], Ma'reb Press, 8 Jan. 2012, www.marebpress.net/news_details.php?lang=arabic&sid=39473 (accessed 27 May 2012).

[46] Martin Dokoupil and Tom Finn, "Yemen Donors Running Out of Time to Stem Crisis," Reuters, 8 June 2012.

[47] Office for the Coordination of Humanitarian Affairs, "Food Insecurity Doubled in Two Years," *Humanitarian Bulletin—Yemen*, 2 (5 Apr. 2012).

In addition, even though the transition from Saleh to Hadi was surprisingly smooth, the threat of large-scale violence remains. Intra-elite struggles could slide back into armed confrontation. Violence, in particular, could escalate between pro- and anti-Saleh forces should the former president engage in provocative actions to retain his influence. Strife in Sana'a, moreover, has led the government's already tenuous grip on the country to slip further; swaths of rural areas are now even farther from state control. The Houthis, in particular, have consolidated their influence over vast areas of north Yemen, taking advantage of the retreat of government forces throughout 2011. In early 2012 they controlled all of Sa'ada governorate and significant portions of the neighboring governorates of 'Amran, Hajja and Jawf. The conflict, moreover, has taken a sectarian overtone as violent clashes have increased in frequency and intensity between the Houthis and Salafi militias.[48] Perhaps most critically, the refusal of most Hirak factions to participate in the Dialogue bodes ill for the resolution of the southern issue.

Yet as long as the current political order is perpetuated in Sana'a—with whichever faction at its head—the central government is unlikely to accept the massive reforms demanded by the Houthis and the Southern Movement, especially with regard to decentralization and democratization. Indeed, all the main actors from the old order—Saleh and the GPC, Islah, Ali Muhsin, and the al-Ahmar brothers—are opposed to major changes and support a strongly centralized state. As long as the old ruling bargain is not fundamentally overhauled, there is therefore a structural tension that is difficult to resolve between the center and dissatisfied groups on the periphery. Key actors throughout the country continue to accumulate weapons, further illustrating how the potential for more violence in Sana'a, the south, and the north remains high.[49]

Finally, adding to these already complex dynamics, AQAP and its insurgent arm, Ansar al-Shari'a (AS, meaning partisans of Islamic law) took advantage of the security vacuum created in 2011 to seize swaths

[48] Fattah, "Yemen's Sectarian Spring."

[49] "Report to the Security Council by the UN Special Envoy to Yemen," 11 June 2013, http://www.securitycouncilreport.org/atf/cf/%7B65BFCF9B-6D27–4E9C-8CD3-CF6E4FF96FF9%7D/s_pv_6976.pdf(accessed 13 Aug. 2013), p. 3.

of territory in southeastern Yemen. In early 2012, AS further expanded the territory under its control and even started to provide basic services in some towns. Starting in April 2012, however, President Hadi, with US support and in coordination with local militias, seized much of it back.[50] In fact, Hadi has surprised observers with his willingness to confront AQAP and AS. Nevertheless, AQAP and AS remain strong in and around Abyan, with a pool of hundreds of well-trained fighters and a network of relationships among local tribes. AQAP has shown that it possessed both the will and the capability to launch attacks against local, regional, and international interests in the past. Future attacks are therefore likely, as are continued clashes with the central government, adding another variable to the combustible mix of Yemeni politics.

The ruling bargain in Yemen prior to the onset of the Arab Spring was the product of a complex struggle among a loosely knit group of elite factions. The popular uprising that began in early 2011 acted as a catalyst that has modified the balance of forces among the regime's main factions and forced a change in some of the rules of the game. Nonetheless, the ruling bargain itself has not fundamentally changed: politics in Yemen are still defined by a struggle among the same old elites. Dissatisfied groups such as the Houthis and the Southern Movement remain on the periphery, while civil society movements, despite unprecedented mobilization, have not been able to insert themselves into networks of power in Sana'a. Yemen, as a result, will likely witness ongoing elite struggles for control over a weakening state, high popular frustrations because of unfulfilled aspirations, the constant threat of violence in the south and north, an al-Qaeda insurgency, and a continually deteriorating economy.

[50] Casey Coombs, "The Ansar al-Shari'a Insurgency in Southern Yemen: The View from the Ground," Jamestown Foundation, 9 May 2012.

14

THE FRAGMENTED STATE OF THE SYRIAN OPPOSITION

Bassam Haddad and Ella Wind

This chapter examines the state of the Syrian opposition. It argues that the opposition's current fragmentation can be attributed to the strategies that the regime has employed and to certain structural factors within the Syrian political landscape. The regime's role in contributing to the opposition's fragmentation is rooted in a divisive pattern of state–society relations from the 1960s onwards, a pattern which passed through several stages in the period prior to 2011. After the eruption of the Syrian uprising in March 2011, the cracks within the internal and external opposition became evident and the rift between the internal and external dimensions of the opposition also grew considerably. But the regime's strategies over the past few decades do not constitute the sole variable in explaining the schisms within the oppositional landscape: shortly after the uprising began, the opposition was also infiltrated by external actors who further exacerbated the existing rifts and actively segmented off those parts that served the interests of sponsor countries.

It is difficult to disentangle causality when attempting to attribute reasons for the fragmentation of an opposition over a long period of time. Thus, when discussing the state of the opposition before the uprising, this chapter focuses on the role of the regime strategies and behavior that undermined collective action and contributed to the creation of a narrow and contradictory incentive structure for social mobilization. It begins by examining the Assad regime's historical alliance-making policies that sought to create a system of "leveling egalitarianism" by linking various interest groups to the regime. The subsequent reversal of the redistributive economic system, which created an uneven playing field and led to the emergence of opposition groups prior to the 2011 uprisings, is then outlined. The chapter then goes on to map the structural factors in the political landscape that impede the unification of Syria's opposition, and apply it to the opposition's trajectory since 2011.

The Syrian regime: how did it do it?

The Syrian regime was able to rule for more than forty years through a combination of coercion, alliance-making, and accommodation. These tools are used by all regimes, especially authoritarian ones, but not all such attempts succeed in derailing collective action even during times of crisis and brutal violence against civilians. Fear is not a sufficient explanatory variable in this regard, nor is the claim that the regime has broad support. In order to explain its longevity, a brief examination is needed of the alliance-making strategies used by the regime following Hafez al-Assad's launch of the "Corrective Movement" in 1970. It was in this latter period that the regime deposed the more leftist wing of the Baath party and its remnants, embarked on a multi-pronged strategy of power consolidation, and violently put down any threatening opposition.

Institutionally, the Syrian regime forged a set of state–society relations that buttressed its rule by fragmenting society on the one hand, while forging binding relations with key social groups on the other. When the Baath first captured power in 1963, the regime presented itself as the representative of the exploited against the social and political forces that dominated Syria's polity, locally and regionally. It championed the cause of labor, and created a coalition that embraced various populist forces including labor, the peasantry, the syndicates, and, naturally, the army. All organized opposition was outlawed and only those forces that were not actively hostile were allowed to join the Progressive National Front, a coalition of purportedly independent parties that stood alongside the leading Baath party. The regime also sought to expand its support in the countryside by creating party branches, youth groups, and a nationwide network of peasant associations.

The social standing and religious practices of the minorities were protected—sometimes by force of arms—as was the case for Syria's Christians. Other religious minorities were elevated from a disadvantaged and exploited position, as was the case for the Alawis, while the Druze, the Ismailis, and the Shi'a were also privileged in relation to their former standing under an urban Sunni-dominated polity. This produced a system of sectarian egalitarianism which came at the expense of formerly dominant groups.

This institutional and relational strategy proved successful because it rested on the regime's distributive policies and political commitment to those social and religious groups whose interests had been ignored or neglected for decades, under both colonial and liberal rule. It is noteworthy that the former dominant class of urban Sunni notables did not include the majority of largely impoverished Sunnis in the countryside, the outskirts of various cities, and the conservative districts of metropolitan cities. This new formula did not lead to freedom and prosperity for all. However, it leveled the playing field across most sectors of society, precluding the rise of the state bourgeoisie, its small but powerful set of conservative business allies, and pockets of the old bourgeoisie that remained relatively faithful to the new Baathist reign after 1970.

Thus President Hafez al-Assad successfully created what can be called a "leveling egalitarianism," where most social sectors were partially represented, partially repressed, and partially provided for by a distributive state that purported to serve all Syrians and to defend their interests locally and regionally. This image of the Syrian state contrasted sharply with the reality of a state that pandered to the interests of elites domestically and was a pawn of greater powers regionally and internationally. The outcome, whether intended or otherwise, was to bind the interests of various groups—or majorities within them—to the state in general, and the regime in particular, irrespective of whether these groups viewed the regime as legitimate.

The Long and Slow Reversal

This pattern of alliance-making (a form of bargaining), accommodation, and divisiveness constitutes the background to the political landscape that has emerged in Syria since March 2011. The net result has been a dramatic reduction in the potential of marginalized or excluded groups to engage in collective action. The efforts made to bring opposition groups together, even covertly, were also riddled with collective action problems. It was not that discontent was in short supply, but that many Syrians feared losing what they had for the sake of taking great risks that could ultimately fail to produce any meaningful change. High stakes were consequently involved in any confrontation with the regime, with the Muslim Brotherhood being the sole group to confront it in the period between the late 1970s and 2011. From this period onwards the regime sought to manage the system of leveling egalitarianism, yet a shift in alliances and socio-economic policies beginning in the mid-1980s gradually shattered both the veneer and the reality of egalitarianism.

In the mid-1980s the regime started "bringing business back in" through the back door, a move which came at the expense of a substantial segment of the regime's natural supporters, namely labor, the urban poor, and most of agrarian society. The newly ascendant business class, and the "embourgeoisified" state elite, to use Raymond Hinnebusch's term, emerged as the new upper class along with the neo-liberal policies and capitalist lifestyles that would became a staple of Syrian social life in the 2000s.[1] The final blow to the state's redistributive commitments came in 2005 with the inauguration of the "Social Market Economy," an odd mixture of market and state-centered economic strategies. Thus the last element that had made up the redistributive Syrian economic system (state subsidies for gas and food) began to diminish in the lead-up to the spring of 2011. The economic situation facing the regime's natural supporters was further compounded by an unprecedented drought that struck the Syrian countryside in 2003 and devastated various forms of agriculture along with the families and businesses that relied on an abundance of water. The government's wasteful management of these resources and a lack of investments, which were instead used for inner-city development schemes, exacerbated the problem. Within half a decade, more than a million Syrians were displaced as internal migration pushed rural inhabitants to the towns and metropolitan cities.

[1] Raymond Hinnebusch, *Authoritarian Power and State Formation in Ba'thist Syria*, Boulder, CO: Westview, 1990, p. 154.

Directly before the uprising, the opposition was composed of a number of rather stagnant and small groups which had declined from positions of greater influence. The four most influential opposition movements in Syria predating the 2011 uprising were the Muslim Brotherhood (MB), the National Democratic Assembly (NDA), the Damascus Declaration (DD), and the various oppositional communist movements and parties. At the beginning of the uprising in March 2011, all of these oppositional factions were in total disarray and incapable of organizing any sort of serious challenge to the regime.

The Muslim Brotherhood

The Brotherhood, which draws significant support from Syria's Sunni Arab majority, constitutes the largest opposition group in Syria. It was driven into exile in the early 1980s after a failed uprising. Its sectarian character has made many secular Syrians and religious minorities wary, but the group has tried to quell such fears over the past decade by calling for democracy and religious tolerance.[2]

At the beginning of the 2011 protests, the Brotherhood cautiously held back from participation. It only issued its first official statement in support of the uprising at the end of April 2011, when it called openly for the downfall of the Assad regime. Since then, the Muslim Brotherhood has played an influential role in the uprising, not least through the Facebook page (titled "The Syrian Revolution 2011") of MB member Fida' ad-Din as-Sayyid, which has served as one of the main sources for news, rumors, and coordination around the Syrian uprising.[3] The Brotherhood helped co-found the Syrian National Council and originally accounted for around a quarter of the council's composition. Critics contend that this share exceeds the movement's actual size in the revolution, thanks to the numerous groups it formed in exile and its experience in political organization.[4]

[2] Aron Lund, "Divided They Stand: An Overview of Syria's Political Opposition Factions," Uppsala: Foundation for European Progressive Studies, Olof Palme International Center, 2012, p. 10.

[3] "Admin of the Syrian Revolution 2011 Facebook Page," YouTube, uploaded 23 Apr. 2011, http://www.youtube.com/watch?feature=player_embedded&v=QrqPAIIdFtk

[4] "The Muslim Brotherhood in Syria," Carnegie Middle East Center, http://carnegie-mec.org/publications/?fa=48370 (accessed 22 Jan. 2013).

Communist movements and parties

In recent decades Syria's communist groups have splintered into several factions, some forming a tacitly allowed "loyal opposition," while others have adopted a more hardline stance toward the regime. The National Committee for the Unity of Syrian Communists (NCUSC), also known as the Party of the Popular Will or Qassioun, is the largest communist "loyal opposition" group. It is led by Qadri Jameel, who enjoys the support of a small but active base of loyal followers, and holds close ties with both the regime and the Russian government. The party does not advocate the overthrow of the regime, and instead calls for national dialogue, political reform, and a government of national unity.[5] The second largest communist group within the loyal opposition is the Syrian Social Nationalist Party (al-Intifada) or SSNPI, a secular, social-nationalist party, led by Ali Haidar. Though unlicensed, the party is tolerated by the Assad regime.[6] Finally, the most stringently anti-regime communist party is the Syrian Democratic People's Party (SDPP), originally known as the Syrian Communist Party (Political Bureau). It is part of the National Democratic Assembly (NDA) and the Damascus Declaration bloc within the Syrian National Council (SNC). One of its members, George Sabra, has frequently been proposed as a potential candidate for president of the SNC. The party rejects dialogue with the regime and calls for arming the opposition and for external military intervention. The SDPP is renowned for its hardline stance against the regime and its historic alliances with Islamist groups.[7] Other communist opposition parties include the Workers' Revolutionary Arab Party and the Syrian Communist Party.[8]

[5] Official Qassyoun Party Website, http://www.kassioun.org/ (accessed 22 Jan. 2013); "The National Committee for the Unity of Syrian Communists (The Party of the Popular Will)," Carnegie Middle East Center, http://carnegie-mec.org/publications/?fa=48566 (accessed 22 Jan. 2013).

[6] "The Syrian Social Nationalist Party (al-Intifada)," Carnegie Middle East Center, http://carnegie-mec.org/publications/?fa=48565 (accessed 22 Jan. 2013).

[7] "The Syrian Democratic People's Party," Carnegie Middle East Center, http://carnegie-mec.org/publications/?fa=48357 (accessed 22 Jan. 2013).

[8] "The Arab Revolutionary Workers' Party," Carnegie Middle East Center, http://carnegie-mec.org/publications/?fa=48359 (accessed 22 Jan. 2013); "The Communist Labor Party," Carnegie Middle East Center, http://carn-

National Democratic Assembly

The NDA (*al-tajammou al-watani al-dimouqrati*) was formed from a coalition of Arab nationalist and leftist parties in the late 1970s and was quickly repressed under the Hafez Al-Assad regime. It served as the primary umbrella organization for the secular opposition until the creation of new opposition groups during the "Damascus Spring," following Bashar al-Assad's assumption of power. The NDA is made up of six parties, and, although it remains weak, it constitutes the most important bloc of traditional opposition groups inside Syria due to its contacts and long experience of opposition.[9]

The Damascus Declaration

In 2005, a joint statement called the "Damascus Declaration" (*i'lan dimashq*) (DD) was released by numerous opposition groups demanding a gradual and peaceful transition to a multi-party democracy. The initiative was spurred on by popular discontent over Syria's involvement in Lebanon and its conflict with the United States over Iraq and Palestine.

The group included the NDA and MB, Kurdish and Assyrian parties, and a number of prominent independent dissidents. Naturally, such a broad grouping quickly faced problems regarding internal cohesion—in particular, it was unable to reconcile the wishes of the MB with secular and leftist groups. The group soon began to fracture, with the MB splitting off into the Saudi-backed National Salvation Front (NSF), while arrests of its senior figures, and disagreements among its leaders, paralyzed the remaining factions. By the beginning of the 2011 uprising, the DD represented little more than an unimpressive opposition in exile composed of the socialist Syrian Democratic People's Party, the Islamist Movement for Justice and Development, and some Kurdish and Assyrian groups.[10]

---

egie-mec.org/publications/?fa=48362 (accessed 22 Jan. 2013); Tariq Ismael and Jacqueline Ismael, *The Communist Movement in Syria and Lebanon*, Gainesville, FL: University Press of Florida, 1998.

[9] Aron Lund, "Divided They Stand," Olof Palme International Center: 2012, p. 11.

[10] Ibid. pp. 11–12; http://carnegie-mec.org/publications/?fa=48514

The labor groups and migrants that had been disenfranchised as a result of Syrian policy formed a social force to be reckoned with, yet they remained largely unorganized and were divided along the same lines as the groups discussed above. Nonetheless, these marginalized groups, who had once been among the principal beneficiaries of the regime, formed a large proportion of the front line in the protest against the regime in the spring of 2011.

As of 2011, the Syrian opposition consequently remained fragmented and was largely confined to the less metropolitan areas and the smaller cities and towns. By the time the uprising reached the two biggest metropolitan cities, Damascus and Aleppo, the internal and external state of the civilian opposition was overshadowed by militancy. The historical patterns of interest formation across various segments of Syrian society helped to slow down the formation of a unified opposition and, among some groups, created a proclivity to extremism as the only way to challenge Syria's brutal dictatorship.

Structural Factors within the Syrian Political Landscape

The historical and structural factors that animated the rise and development of the opposition in Syria continue to set the stage for divisions within society. Four factors are particularly important in order to understand the fragmentation of the opposition and the obstacles it has faced before and during the 2011 uprising: the geography of Syria's cities, the heterogeneity of society, the media landscape, and the regional and international context of the uprising. While these factors are not all-encompassing, they consistently feature as impediments to the unification of the Syrian opposition.

Space and Geography

Syria's geographic situation and relations with regional powers have contributed to the fragmentation of the opposition in the period since 2011. Almost all of Syria's cities lie along its borders, with a huge swath of mostly depopulated desert in the middle. These cities often have historical, social, and commercial ties with hinterlands across national borders: Homs and Northern Lebanon, Aleppo and the south Turkish countryside, Deraa and the Houran farming plateau which extends into northwest Jordan, and Deir Ezzor with western Iraq.

The relatively porous borders on each side of Syria (with the exception of the Israeli-occupied Golan Heights) have allowed various opposition groups in different cities to obtain supplies, weapons, and logistical support independently of one another. Although national coordination is a pressing ideological and political need, such groups thus have little incentive to unite for economic or logistical reasons.

The large size of Syria's most important cities (Damascus and Aleppo), and the heavy security presence in these areas, have also made mass mobilization difficult and have pushed protests into the suburbs surrounding these cities. In Damascus itself, the hilly landscape and the large areas separating the capital city's different neighborhoods have likewise served as important obstacles impeding mass mobilization.

Heterogeneity of Society

Syrian society is one of the most diverse in the Arab world. Approximately 70 percent of the country is Sunni Muslim, with large minorities of Alawites and various Christian denominations, as well as a small percentage of Shi'a and other Muslim denominations. Syria is also ethnically and linguistically diverse, with a significant Kurdish population in the northeast, a small but influential Armenian community, and a variety of other small ethnic groups concentrated in specific regions around the country. The myriad of tribes in Syria, especially in the south of the country, further adds to this social heterogeneity. It is notable that the uprising began in the city of Deraa' in the Houran plains after the regime arrested, tortured, and killed children from some of the city's prominent and influential tribes.[11]

At the outbreak of the uprising, the regime was quick to raise the specter of sectarianism by warning that Syria's diverse society would face destruction should more people support the uprising. In particular, the regime emphasized the threat that the uprising could pose to the Alawite and Christian minorities, and frequently framed it as an Islamic war against the secular Baathist government. These attempts to exacerbate social divisions in Syria proved to be a significant challenge for the

[11] Haian Dukhan, "Tribes and Tribalism in the Syrian Revolution," Open Democracy, 2012, http://www.opendemocracy.net/haian-dukhan/tribes-and-tribalism-in-syrian-revolution

opposition. Moreover, while certain sects and ethnic groups were able and willing to form alliances with particular countries (for example pious Sunnis with Gulf donors), other groups did not want to cooperate with opposition organizations that were heavily allied with other particular countries (such as the Syrian Kurds with Turkey).

One of the less frequently discussed obstacles to the formation of a united opposition that would be able to negotiate plans for a future regime change is the opposition's inability to incorporate the Kurds. With the Syrian army busy in other parts of the country, Kurdish groups have taken over security in much of the northeast region near the Turkish and Iraqi borders. Various Kurdish groups have sometimes coordinated with different opposition groups, but the overall relationship has been characterized by a degree of mistrust. Increasingly, pictures from the Kurdish region of Syria have shown the Kurdish flag hoisted alone without the green, white, and black flag associated with the greater Syrian uprising, and there has been growing talk of an autonomous or even independent Kurdish region, with little comment from the Arab opposition.[12]

Regional and International Context

One of the factors that serve to distinguish the Syrian uprising from the uprisings that have taken place elsewhere is its importance at a regional level. The Syrian uprising quickly became more than merely a national uprising. It now involves, encompasses, and engages a number of conflicts and issues of wide-ranging regional and international significance: the Syrian case engages the Arab–Israeli conflict; the question of resistance to imperialism generally; the question of Hezbollah; the power struggle between Iran, Syria, and Hezbollah on the one hand and Saudi Arabia, Qatar, and the GCC countries on the other; the tension between Sunnis and Shi'as (nearly always instrumentally exacerbated by political actors); and, most recently, the question of regional Islamism due to the Syrian uprising's Islamist dimension.

[12] "Map of 'Syrian Kurdistan' Releases Cautiously Marked Borders," Al-Arabiya, 2012, http://english.alarabiya.net/articles/2012/12/31/258016.html; Ben Gittelson, "Syria's Kurds Look to Iraqi Minority for Support," *The New York Times*, 31 Jan. 2013, http://www.nytimes.com/2013/01/31/world/middleeast/31iht-m31-kurds.html?_r=0

The Syrian conflict also differs from the uprisings of the broader Arab Spring due to the degree of attention and intervention it has received from international actors, including the United States, some of the European countries, Russia, and China. Most of these actors are primarily interested in the implications any eventual outcome will have for their interests in the region and beyond, much more than in what actually happens in Syria.

In sum, regional and international factors, with a wide range of powerful actors intervening and interacting in various ways, have played a significant role in complicating the dynamics of the Syrian uprising. Their behavior is often a function of a combination of self-interest, anticipated outcomes, and the position of their allies.[13]

Media Landscape

Unlike other countries in the region, such as Egypt for example, Syria lacked any sort of internal dynamic media environment, with activists and citizen journalists building up most of the internal media infrastructure in the period since the uprising began. The authorities' complete monopolization of the traditional public sphere and political spaces drove Syrians to the Internet in an attempt to reclaim their political agency.[14] Yet while the Internet allowed for a more open arena of contestation in one sense, it also facilitated the production of media based on dubious sources, with unverifiable claims being made on both sides of the conflict. In many ways a media blackout consequently continued within Syria, but with a propaganda war of doctored and real images, video footage, and statements from both regime supporters and the opposition that served to bring about even more confusion. On top of this, the facility and low cost of creating and growing an expansive media outreach campaign with the rise of social media meant that the opposition elements had little need to coordinate their message or method of outreach.

The same legal restrictions with regard to domestic media also applied to the international media, and these restrictions only became more pronounced once the uprising began. Faced with the need to find voices

[13] A lengthier treatment of such regional and international factors is discussed by this author in a forthcoming article in the *London Review of Books*.

[14] Hamzeh Al-Moustafa, *Al-Majal Al-Iftirady lel-Thawra Al-Soureyya* [The Syrian Revolution's Virtual Realm], Doha: ACRPS, 2012.

from inside, as the crisis rapidly escalated, international outlets conducted interviews over Skype or by phone with "activists" whom they had not met and whose identities, locations, and positions were unverified. While journalists have since been able to establish contacts inside the country, they still tend to privilege certain voices over others.

Lastly, there has been a great deal of controversy around the role of popular media outlets based in the Gulf and their coverage of the conflict. The media coverage of any state-owned media outlet reflects the position of the state at least to some degree, even in a large-scale, international news network like Al Jazeera. Several Arab commentators have claimed that Al Jazeera's biased coverage of the events in Syria has destroyed the network's credibility.[15] Accusations of biased coverage have also been made against other Gulf networks. Meanwhile, the popular Lebanese newspaper *al-Akhbar*, which is politically sympathetic to Hezbollah and the Palestinian resistance axis, has come under fire for publishing "pro-Assad propaganda."[16] Attempts have even been made to form new media outlets with the aim of providing alternative coverage on Syria, such as the Lebanese satellite station al-Mayadeen, which is headed by a former Al Jazeera talk show host and has been accused of being a propaganda platform for Iran and Hezbollah.[17]

Trajectory of the Opposition

It is difficult to appreciate the current state of affairs in Syria without recourse to the different opposition groups and the ways in which these have developed over time. The following consequently provides a survey of the key events that highlight the difficulties the opposition has faced in undertaking collective action since 2011. This survey demonstrates

[15] Sultan Qassemi, "Breaking the Arab News," *Foreign Policy* (2012) http://www.foreignpolicy.com/articles/2012/08/02/breaking_the_arab_news?wp_login_redirect=0

[16] Max Blumenthal, "A Farewell to al Akhbar and Assad's Apologists," Al-Akhbar English, 20 June 2012, http://english.al-akhbar.com/node/8674

[17] "Anti 'Al Jazeera' Channel Al Mayadeen goes on Air," France 24, http://www.france24.com/en/20120612-al-mayadeen-new-anti-al-jazeera-channel-media-lebanon-syria; https://now.mmedia.me/lb/en/reportsfeatures/al_mayadeen_political_pandering_or_objective_media2, http://www.asharq-e.com/news.asp?section=5&id=29984

the ways in which the factors enumerated above have contributed to the fragmentation of the opposition in specific periods.

Given Syria's long history of imprisoning dissidents and the almost total government control over the media, there were barely any independent organizations, or anything approaching civil society, when the uprising began. Alternative political parties were already crippled, outdated, and disconnected from ordinary Syrians.[18] The first political organizing that sprung up in the wake of the uprising came in the form of the "*tansiqiya*" (coordinating committees), with several other important groups developing in the spring and summer of 2011 that would subsequently form the main factions of the opposition.

Tansiqiya

The first appearances of *tansiqiya* in early 2011 came from neighborhood gatherings in locations across the country where representatives of active anti-regime groups met in order to get to know each other better and to build trust. They were partly inspired by similar networks in Tunisia, Egypt, and elsewhere in the Arab world.[19] Over time, these gatherings developed into organized structures.[20] They grew into a web of commissions, councils, and unions that continually sought more widespread coordination among themselves. Many of the larger committees participated in the planning and coordination of protests.[21]

However, rather than participating, the *tansiqiya* primarily covered the protests with the aim of relaying information to Arab and international media outlets. Rafif Jouejati, spokeswoman for the opposition Local Coordination Committees of Syria (LCCS), explained some of the techniques that the *tansiqiya* used to relay reliable information from areas foreign journalists were unable to enter and when the regime began denouncing activist videos as fakes. One such technique was to ensure

[18] Asi Abu Najm, "Syria's Coordination Committees: A Brief History," Al-Akhbar, 2011 http://english.al-akhbar.com/content/syria%E2%80%99s-coordination-committees-brief-history

[19] Lund, "Divided They Stand."

[20] Anthony Shadid, "Coalitions of Factions from the Streets Fuels a New Opposition in Syria," *The New York Times*, 30 June 2011.

[21] See the website of the Local Coordination Committee of Syria, www.lcc-syria.org

that the people narrating the videos would say the name of the city and the time photographs were taken, while the videos themselves would feature recognizable landmarks. "We realized we had to counter every argument. You want to try to find newspapers with current date. You want to prove it happened on that date."[22] Due to the English skills and technical knowledge required for such a task, *tansiqiya* have a high proportion of educated young people within their ranks.[23]

As these committees spread across Syria they experienced brutal repression, but they also developed larger umbrella groups, such as the Local Coordinating Committees of Syria or Syrian Revolution General Commission (SRGC), which have members from most cities and many smaller towns across Syria. Some *tansiqiya* act as intermediaries between the political sphere and activists on the ground, while others were formed to play a more explicitly political role.[24] They vary in size, geographical spread, and degree of affiliation with one another. Hozan Ibrahim, an LCCS spokesperson, describes the relations between the various *tansiqiya*: "Some groups are local, others are countrywide. The differences are in geographic location and sometimes in the reading of events and reactions to it. Anyway, you can't join them all in these terrible circumstances, but … we are connected and coordinating on many levels."

However, aside from their opposition to the regime, these groups had only loose ideological ties and there was little logistical coordination between them, with coordination frequently achieved more easily from outside the borders than within. As the *tansiqiya* are based inside the country, this clearly demonstrates the way that geographic factors have inhibited the opposition's ability for collective action. Each individual coordinating committee obtained funding from or had media connections with a few groups from a vast array of organizations based in different locations around the world. This meant that while each individual committee could successfully disseminate news from inside to some groups outside, there was little immediate need to build a larger organization based on a real ideological consensus, which could spearhead and

[22] Joe Sterling, "For Syrian Activists, YouTube is a Sword and a Shield," CNN, 14 Mar. 2012, http://articles.cnn.com/2012-03-14/middleeast/world_meast_syria-youtube-uprising_1_local-coordination-committees-syrian-uprising-cell-phones/2?_s=PM:MIDDLEEAST

[23] Najm, "Syria's Coordination Committees."

[24] Ibid.

advocate political initiatives. The short-term survival of any individual committee was not dependent on other *tansiqiya* inside Syria. Disagreements over the means of revolt could be ignored, and dialogue on such issues between these internal groups lacked a sense of urgency.

As a result, there was a need for a large, pan-opposition umbrella group which could lead the future transition. A series of conferences were held throughout 2011 with the aim of unifying the Syrian opposition. Yet while the conferences were successful at bringing the various groups together, they also produced competing steering committees and umbrella groups. By the fall of 2011, it became clear that the Syrian opposition had become divided between two dominant groups: the Syrian National Council (SNC) and the National Coordination Bureau (NCB).[25]

National Coordination Bureau for Democratic Change

The NCB's origins can be traced to April 2011, when a group of activists within the secular Arab opposition established a working group dedicated to political unification to run parallel to the other unification conferences. The principal goal of this working group was to unify the leftist–nationalist flank of the Syrian opposition into a coalition that would be able to rival the hardline exiles of the then-emerging "Istanbul Group" (later to become the Syrian National Council).[26] These dissidents were united in their suspicion of Western military intervention, believing that it could only lead to sectarian warfare and a loss of national independence in the long term. The NCB consequently hoped to prevent the creation of a pro-intervention government in exile that would encourage a NATO intervention along the lines of what was happening in Libya.

The National Coordination Bureau for the Forces of Democratic Change, which this group of dissidents eventually established at the end

[25] Randa Slim, "Meet Syria's Opposition," Foreign Policy Middle East Channel, 14 May 2012, http://mideastafrica.foreignpolicy.com/posts/2011/11/02/meet_syrias_opposition#sthash.kGwAWwtj.dpbs

[26] According to working group member Hazem al-Nahar, their goal was "to stop the flow of irresponsible and maverick statements and initiatives, stem the tide of conferences and pronouncements by the Syrian opposition in exile, and simultaneously persuade Syrians at home that there was a political organization capable of managing a post-regime transitional period."

of June, failed to live up to expectations. At its founding, the group claimed to comprise fourteen political parties, including the bulk of the leftist–nationalist National Democratic Assembly, the Marxist Left Assembly, a few Kurdish parties, and some recently created groups and independent dissidents. However, the large and influential Muslim Brotherhood, the Damascus Declaration, and most Kurdish parties refrained from joining. The lack of support from Sunni Islamists has severely limited any opportunity the NCB may have had of reaching out to a broader section of society.[27]

Nevertheless, the secular NCB has a stronger record of minority participation than the SNC.[28] A number of high-profile Alawite activists participated in its founding. While they do not represent the large body of opinion within minority communities, they contribute a great deal to the NCB's message of anti-sectarianism and communal tolerance.

Syrian National Council

At the same time as the working group that would establish the NCB was meeting, the diaspora community was heavily involved in conferences held outside of Syria in Turkey, Belgium, and Qatar. The MB and DD focused most of their energy on these conferences, which they felt were more conducive to their own ideologies. Independent dissidents who were part of this congress circuit soon formed a working alliance. The Islamist National Action Group for Syria, the Democratic Coordination Meeting (composed of independent academics), and the Independent Islamic Current (a non-MB Islamic group) joined with other, smaller opposition networks to form the "Istanbul Group."

In August, this group declared its intention to form the "Syrian National Council," whose first congress would be held in September.[29] Representatives of the MB and DD attended, and were reported to be on board with the council. However, both groups appeared to be wavering, having just returned from the failed Doha talks sponsored by supporters of the rival NCB.

27 "Guide to the Syrian Opposition," BBC News, 17 Oct. 2012, http://www.bbc.co.uk/news/mobile/world-middle-east-15798218
28 Slim, "Meet Syria's Opposition."
29 "Syrian Activists Form a 'National' Council," CNN, 23 Aug. 2011, http://articles.cnn.com/2011–08–23/world/syria.un.resolution_1_syrian-opposition-top-syrian-officials-syrian-observatory?_s=PM:WORLD

A second unification meeting was therefore convened in Istanbul a few weeks later, which established the SNC in its present form. The participants included: the former Istanbul Group, the MB, the DD; some *tansiqiya* networks including the LCC, the SRGC, and the HCRS; some Kurdish groups; the Assyrian Christian ADO; and some independents. Most of the attendees agreed to join the SNC, which was expanded and given a new leadership structure. The SNC's early September declaration established a quota whereby 60 percent of its members would be drawn from inside Syria and 40 percent from those in exile. In reality, however, nearly all of its members, and especially those on its Executive Board, appeared to be Syrians in exile, although the SNC asserts that it has additional committee members based inside Syria who must remain anonymous.[30]

Free Syrian Army

The formation of the Free Syrian Army (FSA) was announced on 29 July 2011, roughly five months into the uprising, through a statement presented by seven defecting military officers in a YouTube video. The statement, read by the FSA Commander Colonel Riyad al-As'ad, called on all officers and men of the army to defect immediately and join the FSA. He went on to say that the Syrian army had come to represent "gangs that protect the regime" and that all security forces involved in killing civilians and besieging cities would now be considered legitimate targets.[31]

The militarization of the opposition began sometime before this event, however. It came as a response to the regime's gradual escalation of the situation to a zero-sum game by allowing the security services to use crude and repressive tactics in order to roll back the protest movement. These included a compartmentalization of territory by creating a network of checkpoints; stimulating sectarianism in order to strengthen communal divisions; and using scare tactics to create a pervasive climate of fear. In many ways these methods largely backfired, with the opposition continuing the use of song, wit, and peaceful demonstrations to counter the regime. At the same time, armed opposition groups gradually organized

[30] "Structure of the SNC," Syrian National Council Official Website, http://www.syriancouncil.org/en/structure/structure.html (accessed 12 July 2012).
[31] "Announcement of the Formation of the Free Syrian Army," YouTube, 2011, http://www.youtube.com/watch?feature=player_embedded&v=SZcCbIPM37w

themselves to protect areas in which peaceful protest movements could proceed. These small anti-regime neighborhood vigilantes soon found themselves joined by a steady stream of army defectors.[32]

As these opposition groups grew in number and confidence, they increasingly went on the offensive, weeding out informants, tracking snipers, attacking checkpoints, and ambushing busloads of loyalist troops. Tit-for-tat killings ebbed and flowed but progressively became a daily pattern.[33] Elements within both the security services and the opposition started to engage in criminal activities, including kidnapping for ransom as well as carjacking. However, these violent and criminal elements appeared to be relatively isolated. During this period, the FSA's and other armed groups' behavior was, for the most part, "constrained by the need to safeguard civilians, defend the aforementioned culture of dissent and assist in the overarching, legitimate goal of toppling the regime by demonstrating its lack of support on the streets."[34] For this reason, most of this aggressive militarization went unreported by the media, and was only revealed well after these processes had been put in place. While the opposition eagerly underscored the role of defectors, the regime maintained that "armed groups" were responsible for the violence. Both views are almost certainly true.[35]

Riad al-As'ad has stated that the FSA has no political goals except the removal of the current Syrian regime from power.[36] However, the reality

[32] "Syria's Phase of Radicalisation," International Crisis Group, 10 Apr. 2012, http://www.crisisgroup.org/~/media/Files/Middle%20East%20North%20Africa/Iraq%20Syria%20Lebanon/Syria/b033-syrias-phase-of-radicalisation.pdf; Ulrike Putz, "The Burial Brigade of Homs: An Executioner for Syria's Rebels Tells His Story," 29 Mar. 2012, *Der Spiegel International*, http://www.spiegel.de/international/world/profile-of-rebels-in-homs-and-their-executioners-a-824603.html, Sharif Abdel Kouddous, "How the Syrian Revolution Became Militarized," 23 Aug. 2012, *The Nation*, http://www.thenation.com/article/169533/how-syrian-revolution-became-militarized#; "Q&A: Nir Rosen on Syria's Armed Opposition," 13 Feb. 2012, http://www.aljazeera.com/indepth/features/2012/02/201221315020166516.html

[33] "Q&A: Nir Rosen on Syria's Armed Opposition."

[34] "Syria's Phase of Radicalisation."

[35] Joseph Holliday, "Syria's Armed Opposition," Institute for the Study of War, Middle East Security Report 3, Mar. 2012, http://www.understandingwar.org/sites/default/files/Syrias_Armed_Opposition.pdf

[36] "Commander of Free Syrian Army: Al Asad to face Gaddahfi's Fate," Trend, 10 Sep. 2011, http://en.trend.az/regions/met/arabicr/1929681.html

of the situation, namely that the FSA is extremely weak in relation to the Syrian regime's army, led the group to side politically with the SNC, which grew increasingly supportive of the FSA's calls to increase the amount of arms and funds from external sources such as Turkey and the Persian Gulf states.[37]

Disputes within the Opposition

The opposition is divided over a number of contentious issues, including organizational transparency, violence and militarism, international intervention, national autonomy and alliances, sectarianism, political strategy, and dialogue with the regime. The cracks in the opposition were present right at the start of the uprising. While there has been some reconciliation on certain points, for the most part the fragmentation of the opposition has only become more pronounced over time, with divisions being especially apparent during a number of key events, the first of which was the "consultative meeting" of the opposition in Doha in September.

The NBC and the SNC: Divided at their Founding

The NBC was essentially formed in a preemptive rejection of the more militaristic and internationally oriented SNC, and thus the groundwork for disagreements was laid in the geneses of these groups. The fault-lines between them were first highlighted at a meeting in Doha in September 2011 where the Arab Center for Research and Policy Studies, a Qatari think tank, hosted a "Consultative Meeting" of the Syrian opposition. The think tank was led by the Palestinian intellectual Azmi Bishara, a close friend of Hazem al-Nahar, who at that time was a member of the NCB. In total, around twenty-five Syrians representing the NCB, the DD, the Istanbul Group (soon to become the SNC), or other smaller dissident groups were present at the conference. The MB was kept up to date on the proceedings.[38]

During the negotiations in Doha, the Arab League launched a Qatar-backed initiative to solve the Syrian crisis. The text of the initiative made

[37] Alexandra Zavis and Rima Marrouch, "Syria Opposition Groups Agree to Coordinate Efforts," *Los Angeles Times*, 1 Dec. 2011, http://articles.latimes.com/2011/dec/01/world/la-fg-syria-accord-20111202

[38] Lund, "Divided They Stand," p. 22.

specific reference to the NCB, and the core idea was that Bashar al-Assad would serve out his term before stepping down in 2014. This angered some of the groups present in Doha, who suspected that Bishara or Qatar wanted them to submit to NCB leadership and abandon their hopes for immediate regime change. The organizers denied this accusation.

The conference was further marred by disputes over the language to be used in describing the objective of the planned alliance. The exiles of the Istanbul Group pushed for hardline rhetoric, such as "overthrowing the regime" and "turning the page on the dictatorial regime," while the NCB preferred a more ambiguous statement with reference to "national democratic change."

Yet despite these differences, the Doha meeting was still able to produce an agreement between the NCB, the DD, and, at the last minute, the MB. But as the participants returned home, the deal failed to materialize due to internal disagreements in both the DD and in the MB. Most importantly, the MB's Aleppo faction resented the deal, preferring to let its allies in the Istanbul Group launch the Syrian National Council first.

Since then, the question of how hardline a stance must be taken has remained the central issue of contention between these two groups. Both agree that the regime must go, but they continue to debate the cost they are willing to pay for regime change. More specifically, they disagree over the militarization of the opposition and the possibility of international intervention.[39]

Many SNC supporters have accused the NCB of working on behalf of the intelligence apparatus, and point to the presence of ex-Baathist elements and others who uphold working relations with regime officials. But while police infiltration may have succeeded at some level, and some member parties are less enamored of the uprising than others, the NCB leadership is undoubtedly committed to its opposition to the Assad regime. Its ranks are filled with activists who have spent time in Syria's prisons, and several of its members have been jailed, tortured, and killed during the current uprising. Even so, some activists have expressed disappointment with what they view as the NCB's overly cautious stance. As one activist from Damascus explained, "The NCB is committed to taking the regime down, but they are too worried about being allowed to operate

[39] Slim, "Meet Syria's Opposition."

in Syria. They don't make as strong statements as they should, because they want be able to stay inside and work with the *tansiqiya*."[40]

The SNC on the other hand faced criticism due to the preponderance in its membership of exiles who had not lived in Syria for years and were out of touch with the Syrian street. Many activists in Syria have stated that the names of many of the SNC's members were unrecognizable to them and thus evoked little by way of loyalty.[41] In the words of one young activist from Damascus, "These leaders of all these groups like the SNC, they're political dinosaurs. Our generation started the revolution. The leaders of these groups were exiled years ago, after the 'Damascus Spring' or even before, and they don't know what is going on inside. The only thing they can offer is money from outside."[42]

In many ways, the SNC's main strength was its ability to gain the attention of the international community, but this has also polarized the opposition. NCB spokesperson Haytham Manna has openly criticized the FSA as acquiescent to Turkish, Gulf, and Western interests:

> For example, what is the place of the Golan Heights in the external discourse? It is zero, because they do not want to upset "anybody." They want to appease [Hillary] Clinton so that she can receive them. There is a broad process of appeasement that is being carried out by the body that was created on the outside [of Syria] so that it may gain recognition. In contrast, these considerations do not exist on the inside.[43]

Some of the opposition groups that were receiving funds from external actors moved to extremist and often exclusionary methods. This proved to be a mixed blessing. On the one hand, it led to the formation of a force able to fight against the regime effectively, often attracting foreign fighters to participate in some sort of religious war. On the other hand, it reduced the momentum of the opposition as a whole as their brand of *takfiri* politics and sectarianism, which often matched or even surpassed that of the regime, served to alienate other groups and caused

[40] Interview in Beirut with Caitlin Ella Wind, June 2012.

[41] Erika Solomon and Ayman Samir, "Syria Opposition's SNC Seeks Backers but Lacks Leaders," Reuters, 17 Feb. 2012, http://uk.reuters.com/article/2012/02/17/uk-syria-opposition-idUKTRE81G0VM20120217

[42] Interview in Beirut with Caitlin Ella Wind, July 2012.

[43] Bassam Haddad, "The Current Impasse in Syria: Interview with Haytham Manna," Jadaliyya, 30 June 2012, http://www.jadaliyya.com/pages/index/6245/the-current-impasse-in-syria_interview-with-haytha

outside actors to hesitate in their support of the armed opposition. This sense of alienation built on that which emerged in the initial phases of the uprising, when the thuggish behavior of the newly militarized opposition began to mirror that of the regime, thereby preventing the opposition as a whole from occupying the moral high ground.

Intervention, Militarization, and Autonomy: Irreconcilable Differences

Throughout the fall of 2011, the differing stances that divided the opposition seemed to crystallize, and the gaps between the two largest political entities of the opposition grew even larger. The NCB and SNC, despite their contrasting stances on dialogue with the regime and their differing alliances, had in fact agreed on a number of issues. The SNC had taken a hardline from the start, whereby it refused any form of dialogue with the regime. Yet, just like the NCB, the SNC was originally opposed to foreign intervention and violence. While there were some pro-intervention voices within the group, most of the SNC leadership had publicly argued against armed struggle and foreign support. In his initial announcement of the SNC's formation, Bourhan Ghalioun had rejected any call for foreign or military interventions. In February he further stated that "We are not asking the world to undertake the revolution on our behalf, be it peacefully or militarily"[44] and that any external intervention should be limited to providing "international protection for civilians."[45]

Initially, the *tansiqiya* also took a less militaristic stance. In a statement issued on the LCC Facebook page in the fall of 2011 they stated:

> While we understand the motivation to take up arms or call for military intervention, we specifically reject this position as we find it unacceptable politically, nationally, and ethically. Militarizing the revolution would minimize popular

[44] "Syria Opposition Launches National Council in Istanbul," Today's Zaman, 2 Oct. 2011, http://www.todayszaman.com/newsDetail_getNewsById.action?load=detay&newsId=258614&link=258614

[45] "Syrian National Council Launches Political Program, Vague on Foreign Intervention," Al-Akhbar English, 21 Nov. 2011, http://english.al-akhbar.com/content/syrian-national-council-launches-political-program-vague-foreign-intervention-0; "Ma'aaradha sooriyaa tashakkal majlisan wataneyan," Al Jazeera, 2011, http://aljazeera.net/news/pages/de5d57b8–74a3–493f-b7fb-2d4a6a3815dd

support and participation in the revolution. Moreover, militarization would undermine the gravity of the humanitarian catastrophe involved in a confrontation with the regime.[46]

The *tansiqiya* were similarly opposed to foreign intervention in Syria.[47] In July 2011, Ghalioun stated his commitment to the three "no's" of the *tansiqiya* in Syria: "The goal is democracy and the 'three no's' are: no to military intervention; no to sectarian strife; and no to the use of arms in any way."[48] At the same time, there was a current within the SNC that drew inspiration from the events of the NATO-supported regime change in Libya,[49] with some members being quite frank about this. As Malik al-Abdeh of the MJD, a DD member group put it: "Everyone expected that when the SNC formed, we'd have a similar dynamic as in Libya ... When the National Transitional Council [in Libya] formed, before you knew it, you had NATO coming in."

Calls for intervention had not been a common refrain among activists during the initial months of the revolution. However, by autumn, and following the capture of Qaddafi in Libya and the growing brutality of the violence in Syria, activists in many besieged cities and towns began calling for foreign intervention and armed resistance out of desperation. The mood in hotspots such as Homs, Deraa, and Idleb grew very militant, and support for the FSA was on the rise.

Soon after its creation, the SNC began to adapt to the militant attitudes of the demonstrators and media activists in order to avoid losing support on the revolutionary street. At first, the SNC's calls for intervention were couched in demands for "international protection" or "help in stopping the killing machine," and curious requests for a "no-fly zone" (despite the fact that the Syrian regime was not using its air force).

[46] "Syrian Local Coordination Committee on Taking Up Arms and Foreign Intervention," Jadaliyya, 31 Aug. 2011, http://www.jadaliyya.com/pages/index/2539/syrian-local-coordinating-committees-on-taking-up-

[47] Joe Sterling, "Syrian Activists Slam Arab League Mission Head," CNN, 28 Dec. 2011, http://articles.cnn.com/2011–12–28/middleeast/worldmeast_syria-opposition-al-dabi_1_ali-kushayb-local-coordinating-committees-syrian-opposition?_s=PM:MIDDLEEAST

[48] Ibtisam Azem, "The Syrian People Will Determine the Fate of Syria: An Interview with Burhan Ghalyoun," Jadaliyya, 26 July 2011, http://www.jadaliyya.com/pages/index/2203/the-syrian-people-will-determine-the-fate-of-syria

[49] "Syrian Activists Form a 'National' Council."

Nevertheless, soon after it had been established, voices from within the SNC—notably the Muslim Brotherhood and US-linked SNC members such as Radwan Ziadeh, who had publicly supported Turkish intervention and/or the establishment of a no-fly zone as early as November 2011—began to call for a more militaristic approach from the international community.[50]

The NCB meanwhile held firmly to its initial opposition to armed insurrection, despite the idea's growing popularity among the Syrian public at large. In a June 2012 interview, Manna stated:

> The replacement of the rationale of revolution with the rationale of war has made us complicit in the practices of the regime. We are now in search of political money. We are now in search of financial resources. We have started to look for the ally that can provide us with the most arms, irrespective of whether they are democratic or not. The question now is who is willing to supply me and what do they have to offer. Whether or not that ally is Saudi Arabia has little bearing on the matter. The nature of this ally's political system and the relationship with its people are no longer of import. These are not the morals of a revolution.[51]

On the first Friday after the SNC press conference on 2 October 2011, the Syria Revolution Facebook page recommended that activists across Syria demonstrate under the slogan "*al-majlis al-watani yumathiluni*: The National Council Represents Me." News footage from protests later that day showed demonstrators across Syria who had incorporated the slogan on their banners. This gave an immense boost to the SNC's credibility and has raised awareness about the group inside Syria, while it has also allowed it to claim that it is endorsed by the revolutionary masses. As it was further bolstered by support from the international community, with SNC members in exile being more inclined to reach out to members outside of Syria, the SNC finally became the most powerful Syrian opposition group. The NCB, while still highly visible and influential, was relegated to second place.[52]

A Failure to Consolidate the Opposition

By late 2011, there was a general feeling of a stalemate. Armed insurgency was on the rise, and tensions were high. Foreign involvement was

50 "Syrian National Council Launches Political Program, Vague on Foreign Intervention."
51 Haddad, "The Current Impasse in Syria."
52 Lund, "Divided They Stand," p. 26.

also increasing, but with opposition unity as a precondition for material support. In October 2011 the SNC's Burhan Ghalioun stated:

> At first, there was a feeling that this was certainly important, but only with time did it become apparent how important it is that the revolution acquires a single address, where you can go to discuss with it. ... We must stop these splits, this talk of a national and an un-national opposition, an internal and an external opposition. That is the only way we can show the world that a new Syria has already been born.

A serious attempt to unite the SNC and the NBC was initiated by the Arab League, with negotiations held in Cairo on 9 November 2011. During the meeting the tensions over the points of contention between the two groups came to a head. Upon arriving in central Cairo for talks with the Arab League's Nabil al-'Arabi, the NCB leaders were mobbed and beaten and had eggs thrown at them by furious SNC supporters who accused them of working on behalf of the regime.[53] Burhan Ghalioun acted quickly by issuing a strong condemnation of the attack, saying that the NCB members had an honorable history of struggle against the regime and that "a loyalty to the SNC which translates into fanaticism and disrespect for other ideas is not a loyalty to the revolution of freedom and dignity."

The media landscape around Syria, coupled with the geographically diffused nature of the SNC, took a heavy toll on the group's ability to broadcast a clear and consistent message. On multiple occasions, an SNC member would be quoted regarding the group's stance on a particular issue by one international outlet, only to be contradicted by another member at a different conference soon afterwards. Yet while these internal SNC contradictions were commented on by reporters covering Syria, there was still very little coverage of the NCB relative to the SNC in international media outlets, which was partly due to the connections held by SNC members with the international community.

In late December 2011, an agreement signed in Cairo between Manna and Ghalioun collapsed, with the two political opposition groups still in disagreement over the use of arms in the revolution. However, the SNC

[53] "Protesters Hurl Eggs at Syria Delegation in Cairo," *Daily News Egypt*, 9 Nov. 2011, http://dailynewsegypt.com/2011/11/09/protesters-hurl-eggs-at-syria-delegation-in-cairo/

was not only challenged by its disagreements with the NCB. It continued to be racked by its own internal divisions, its rivalries with the NCB, and its polarizing and unclear political positions.[54] In March 2012 one scholar wrote that the SNC "has not stepped up to the plate of being a unifier of the different currents inside the wide Syrian opposition movement. It has yet to be representative of these different currents."[55] In the words of NCB spokesperson Haytham Manna:

> At the [NCB] we are very well coordinated. We know what we want. Most of the time, we would be the ones proposing the ideas, while the other side (the SNC) would modify them ... On the other hand, the SNC is a conglomeration of disparate groups. These groups diverge from each other politically. And when they came together they did not do so on the basis of a program. They came together on the basis of the demand for the fall of the regime. Because of this, establishing a program was very difficult for them.[56]

Another point of contention in the conflict between the NCB and the SNC, which continues to present an obstacle to forming a unified opposition, concerns the best way to ensure adequate representation for Syria's diversity of sects, ethnic groups, and tribes. The NCB struggled to gain influence within Syria without the pull of the influential Sunni Muslim Brotherhood. Meanwhile, the ability of the SNC to incorporate minority groups leaves a lot to be desired, and the group has been plagued by suspicions regarding the overrepresentation of Islamists within its membership. One anonymous SNC member admitted being less than reassured by the Muslim Brotherhood's vague proclamation for a "civil state": "I have no idea what a 'civil state' is. Does that mean we will not be a military state? Does it mean not religious? There's no plan and we should be reaching out more to minorities scared by this. I find this situation worrisome and I've been backing off my SNC work."[57]

[54] Solomon and Samir, "Syria Opposition's SNC Seeks Backers"; As'ad AbuKhalil, "Opposition to the Syrian Opposition: Against the Syrian National Council," Jadaliyya, 8 Mar. 2012, http://www.jadaliyya.com/pages/index/4593/opposition-to-the-syrian-opposition_against-the-sy

[55] "Can Syria's Opposition Unite?" Al Jazeera, 4 Mar. 2012, http://www.aljazeera.com/programmes/insidesyria/2012/03/201234954478454 83.html

[56] Serene Assir, "Haytham al-Manna: The Politics Behind the Pact with Ghalioun," al-Akhbar, 2 Jan. 2012, http://english.al-akhbar.com/node/2985

[57] Slim, "Meet Syria's Opposition"; Solomon and Samir, "Syria Opposition's SNC Seeks Backers."

The election of Kurdish activist Abdelbaset Sayda as the new chairman of the SNC in June 2012 did little to assuage these doubts.[58]

At various points the SNC continued to anger the opposition. One of the group's main advantages over the NCB now started to seem more of a weakness, as the group's attempts to appease its myriad of international backers (many of whom disagreed among themselves on their positions toward Syria) led it to take a number of political missteps. For instance, despite its self-ascribed role as a sort of transitional government which would merely facilitate the establishment of a democratic system, the SNC confusingly indicated its commitment to certain policies which would be put in place following a potential regime change. The SNC President Burhan Ghalioun drew the ire of many Syrians during an interview in which he implied that Syria's future leadership would not maintain the same relationship with Hezbollah and Iran, and would not pursue its right to take back the Israeli-occupied Golan Heights, instead preferring to bank on "our special relationship with the Europeans and western powers in helping us in reclaiming the Golan as fast as possible."[59] Such remarks can be viewed as the SNC's first acquiescence to Western interests with regard to Syria.[60]

The SNC's position continually edged toward growing support for arming the opposition. In the same interview, Ghalioun dropped the last of the three "no's" of the LCCs, namely the objection to armed opposition.[61] The SNC tried to portray the FSA as a group that was fighting in self-defense and in order to protect unarmed demonstrators, disregarding the FSA's own declaration of war against the Syrian army. Manna of the NCB opposed enhancing the FSA's role in the struggle against Assad, accusing the armed opposition of not serving the national interest. In an interview with the Lebanese newspaper *Al-Akhbar* he stated:

[58] International Crisis Group Monthly Summary, June 2012.

[59] Kouichi Shirayanagi, "Syrian SNC Official: A Free Syria Will Never Attack Israel," Tunisia Live, 24 Feb. 2012, http://www.tunisia-live.net/2012/02/24/syrian-snc-official-a-free-syria-will-never-attack-israel/; Bassam Haddad, "The Plot Thickens: Ghalyoun's 'Ill-Conceived' Statements in the WSJ Interview," Jadaliyya, 6 Dec. 2011, http://www.jadaliyya.com/pages/index/3398/the-plot-thickens_ghalyouns-%E2%80%9Cill-conceived%E2%80%9D-statem

[60] Ibid.; "Syrian Opposition Leader Interview Transcript," *Wall Street Journal*, 2 Dec. 2011, http://online.wsj.com/article/SB10001424052970203833104577071960384240668.html?KEYWORDS=ghalioun

[61] "Syrian Opposition Leader Interview Transcript."

We know that the Turkish government plays an important role in the political decisions of the Free Syrian Army. We don't believe that an armed group can be on Turkish territory and remain independent of Turkish decisions. The militarization of the Syrian revolution signifies the death of the internal revolution.[62]

These statements provoked a great deal of criticism from many factions of the Syrian opposition, which were increasingly favorable to the militarization of the conflict.

In March 2012 the SNC announced the formation of a military council in support of the FSA and other armed opposition groups in Syria, following the announcement that some countries, including Saudi Arabia,[63] were ready to arm them.[64] The FSA responded negatively, saying it would not cooperate with the new bureau and that the group did not want any political interference in its own military strategy.[65] FSA chief Riad al-Assad said he was uninvolved in the creation of the council.[66]

In the same month, the SNC called on Turkey to create a bureau to facilitate the distribution of arms to the opposition in Syria. Ankara has hesitated, fearing retaliation from the Damascus government in the form of support for the PKK. Turkish international relations expert Soli Ozel thus argues that "Turkey is caught between [a] rock and [a] hard place. It has made a lot of claims about its power and influence. It is being drawn [into] a quagmire and [is] being asked to do things it does not actually want to do. Absolutely, Turkey wants the cover of some

[62] "Opposition Figure Criticizes SNC Ties to Syrian Rebels," Al-Akhbar English, 13 Jan. 2012, http://english.al-akhbar.com/node/3350

[63] "Syria Opposition Chiefs at Odds Over Military Body," Reuters, 1 Mar. 2012, http://www.reuters.com/article/2012/03/01/us-syria-opposition-idUSTRE8200SA20120301

[64] "Syrian National Council Forms Military Body; Rebels Pull Out of Baba Amro," Al-Arabiya News, 2012, http://english.alarabiya.net/articles/2012/03/01/197926.html

[65] "Guide to the Syrian Opposition."

[66] Syriacomment.com, 1 Mar. 2012; "Tazaayed al-daghout 'alaa al-nidham al-sooree," Al Jazeera, 2 Mar. 2012, http://www.aljazeera.net/news/pages/5715bc96–2c06–422a-afd9-ce190d0ecb7f; Dan Bilefsky, "Factional Splits Hinder Drive to Topple Syria Leader," *The New York Times*, 8 Dec. 2011, http://www.nytimes.com/2011/12/09/world/middleeast/factional-splits-hinder-drive-to-topple-syrias-assad.html?pagewanted=all; Neil MacFarquhar, "After a Year, Deep Divisions Hobble Syria's Opposition," *New York Times*, 23 Feb. 2012, http://www.nytimes.com/2012/02/24/world/middleeast/syrian-opposition-is-hobbled-by-deep-divisions.html?pagewanted=2&_r=3&hp

kind of international legitimacy, which it could not get from the U.N. Security Council."[67] Ankara has strongly denied providing arms to the Syrian opposition.[68] This incident strengthened the perception that the SNC was ineffective, even when negotiating with regional and international players, its supposed "strength" in comparison with other opposition groups.

On 23 February 2012 Kofi Annan was appointed as the UN and Arab League's special envoy to Syria, and on 16 March a six-point peace plan was submitted to the UN. A week later, Annan flew to Moscow in an effort to secure Russian support for his efforts to bring about a ceasefire and to open political dialogue. On 27 March, the envoy's office said that the Syrian government had accepted the peace proposal, and would now work toward implementing it.

But a unified institution that represented the opposition was still lacking. Doubts over the SNC's authority inside Syria were brought sharply into focus by a 24 February meeting of the "Friends of Syria," organized by the Arab League in Tunisia.[69] While member countries were able to reach agreement on specific initiatives, such as implementing travel bans on regime members, boycotting Syrian oil, ceasing investments, and reducing diplomatic ties, no accord was reached on how to bring down Assad, and the international community did not throw its full support behind the SNC or its demands.[70] Soon after, these continued failures to obtain material military support through the SNC led to splits within the SNC itself. Prominent veteran dissident Haitham al-Maleh and other important activists broke away from the SNC, citing lack of support for the armed resistance in Syria.[71]

The "Friends of Syria'" called for a conference to be held on 1 April in Istanbul to bring the divided groups of the SNC back together, but

[67] Dorian Jones, "Syrian Opposition Eyes Turkey for Arms Support," Voice of America, 4 Mar. 2012, http://www.voanews.com/english/news/middle-east/Syrian-Opposition-Eyes-Turkey-for-Arms-Support-141476353.html

[68] Ibid.

[69] Solomon and Samir, "Syria Opposition's SNC Seeks Backers."

[70] John Thorne, "'Friends of Syria' Divided Over How to Oust Assad," *The National*, 26 Feb. 2012, http://www.thenational.ae/news/world/friends-of-syria-divided-over-how-to-oust-assad

[71] Viktoria Kleber, "Jostling for Influence: Syria's Opposition in Exile Plagued by Infighting," *Der Spiegel International*, 4 Apr. 2012, http://www.spiegel.de/international/world/syrian-opposition-in-exile-is-split-a-825477.html

this proposal was essentially stillborn. It was preceded by an SNC-dominated preparatory opposition conference in the city on 26–7 March. The pre-conference meeting was intended to respond to concerns about the SNC's lack of representativeness and rumors of excessive MB influence and to restructure and expand the SNC, which was dominated by pro-Western liberal dissidents. The NCB boycotted the pre-meeting, complaining that its purpose was to impose the SNC as the sole opposition framework.

While those who attended the conference agreed to Maleh's call for support for the armed resistance, Maleh himself made a dramatic exit from the reconciliatory meeting.[72] He had taken umbrage when he, as the eldest delegate, was not given the traditional right to speak following the official opening of the conference.

Personal politics and egos were not the only impediment to the conference, however. Disagreements between the Kurdish minority and the Arab majority were still at play as well. Eight Kurdish delegates followed Maleh after their demands that the new constitution instate Kurdish holidays as national holidays fell on deaf ears.[73]

A New Phase

As 2011 came to a close, disillusionment with the opposition was at an all-time high, and it seemed increasingly unlikely that a political solution would be possible in the absence of a representative opposition group that could take part in negotiations. At the same time, there were several indicators that the Syrian uprising appeared to be creeping toward a new phase. More than 200 Syrians were killed in just a few days in the northwestern towns of Idleb and Jabal al-Zawiyeh. On 23 December 2011, two car bombings ripped through two security services branches in Damascus, resulting in at least forty-four deaths and 150 injuries. The Syrian government declared the bombings to be the work of anti-regime terrorists, while some members of the opposition pinned the blame for the attacks on the regime itself.[74]

[72] "Syria's Phase of Radicalisation," p. 10.

[73] Kleber, "Jostling for Influence: Syria's Opposition in Exile Plagued by Infighting."

[74] "A New Phase? Syria Roundup [Updated]," Jadaliyya, 23 Dec. 2011, http://www.jadaliyya.com/pages/index/3700/a-new-phase-syria-roundup_updated-.

The escalation of violence coincided with the regime's signing of the Arab League "observer" protocol, allowing independent monitors to enter "hot spot" areas to observe protests, check Syria's compliance with the Arab League's peace plan to end the violence, withdraw armed forces from the streets, release prisoners, and open dialogue with the opposition. Nevertheless, the intensity of the violence spoke to a new confrontational phase, rather than the more optimistic assessment that the regime was embarking on a final push before implementing the Arab League plan.[75]

As the numbers taking part in the militarized opposition grew through this period of increased violence, so did its abuses. Reports from several human rights organizations and journalists accused the FSA and other armed opposition groups of committing gross human rights violations across Syria. In March 2012, Human Rights Watch released a report condemning actions committed by Syrian rebels in Homs, followed by a report from *Der Spiegel* on the so-called "Homs Burial Brigade" which admitted executing just under 150 men and imprisoning over 700.[76] While FSA members challenged the details of these reports in conversations with other journalists, they admitted that executions and impromptu "trials" were taking place on a regular basis. These soldiers justified such actions on the grounds that they only occurred after thorough investigation. Nadim Houry of Human Rights Watch countered the FSA's judgment on these processes:

> These kinds of executions can in no way be described as fair trials. Not with confessions that may have come under torture, and the judge and prosecutor integrated into the same institution. They would not pass in a country with rule of law, and there is a need to remind the opposition that the Syrian revolution started out being about personal rights and that these rights should apply to everyone—including prisoners of war.[77]

At the same time, it was becoming more apparent that although the FSA had been characterized as one united, armed opposition group, its

[75] Ibid.

[76] "Sooriya: Jamaa'aat al-ma'aarada al-musalaha tarkab antihakaat," Human Rights Watch, 20 Mar. 2012, http://www.hrw.org/ar/news/2012/03/20

[77] Tobias Havmand, "Free Syrian Army Struggles to Survive Amid Charges That It's Executing Opponents," The Daily Beast, 5 Jan. 2012, http://www.thedailybeast.com/articles/2012/05/01/free-syrian-army-struggles-to-survive-amid-charges-that-it-s-executing-opponents.html

actual structure and membership were nebulous. As the International Crisis Group explained, the FSA is "more a wild card than a known entity."[78] While there clearly was a group which constituted the official FSA, small militias and other armed groups had begun to call themselves FSA without having any authentic, official association, and the international media rarely bothered to distinguish between them. The paucity of media coverage from inside Syria exacerbated the confusion around the various militia affiliations, as coverage was often based largely on YouTube videos or statements issued by the groups themselves.

Meanwhile, as the stalemate continued between the SNC and NBC, many within the hard core of street activists appear to have lost all interest in the organized political opposition. Some now put their hope in the FSA or other armed groups, some in grassroots Islamist networks, and some in their local *tansiqiya* or revolutionary councils.

The scale of the violence continued to grow in 2012, with an increasing number of deaths during each month of the year. Hundreds of thousands of Syrians were internally and externally displaced; by the end of the year, over 60,000 Syrians had been killed. Meanwhile, militarized groups had proliferated in all regions of the country—most notably the Syrian Liberation Army,[79] the Syrian Liberation Front,[80] the Syrian Islamic Front,[81] and Jabhat al-Nusra—and they increasingly refused to associate themselves with the FSA.

As with the *tansiqiya*, the ability of the militarized opposition to engage in effective collective action was severely constrained by Syria's geography. The rebels' ability to translate a growing list of military victories into some sort of regime change has been hindered by their inability to take hold of urban areas in any meaningful way. Military control of the cities is crucial to the rebels' military strategy, but militants have yet to capture one of Syria's major cities fully and permanently. Though they now control vast swaths of the countryside, especially in areas at the border, which facilitates bringing in material support and evading gov-

[78] "Syria's Phase of Radicalisation."
[79] Michael Weiss, "Syrian Rebels are Losing Faith in the West," 14 Feb. 2012, http://blogs.telegraph.co.uk/news/michaelweiss/100137341/syrian-rebels-are-losing-faith-in-the-west/
[80] http://www.reuters.com/article/2012/10/11/us-syria-crisis-rebels-idUSBRE89A0Y920121011
[81] http://alhayat.com/Details/464832

ernment forces, Syria has several large-sized cities in which the regime continues to have a military advantage, enabling it to avoid ceding total control to the rebel militias.[82]

Moreover, and though a great deal of the weaponry acquired by the opposition has come from equipment captured from the regime, militias also compete for foreign funding from a variety of donors. The logistical support provided by Turkey to the FSA was far from the only option. Material reinforcement and foreign fighters could be smuggled by way of any one of Syria's highly porous borders with Iraq, Lebanon, or Jordan, from any number of international supporters, both governmental and non-governmental. Furthermore, the fragmented external political opposition was hardly capable of organizing itself, much less the armed groups inside the country, especially as its members courted some international donors while the armed opposition courted others. These combined geographic factors ensured that while the armed opposition was able to undermine the regime's control of the country, the militarized opposition itself was unable to coalesce and cooperate as one entity that could coordinate with a political opposition in order to form a viable alternative to the regime.

In February 2012 an advisor for the Syrian Liberation Army stated:

> The opposition that has money is the Muslim Brotherhood, [Sheik Adnan] Arour, and the Free Syrian Army [FSA] command. Forget about them, they won't help you. The Free Syrian Army in Turkey is a game, a facade to tell the world that that there is a command. I am here to tell you that nobody on the outside says you are militias, everybody knows that Riad al-As'ad is controlled by the Turks, the Syrian National Council represents itself. The revolution inside must unite, and every area should set up an operations command center.[83]

The Syrian Liberation Army (SLA), based in Idlib, is distinguished from the FSA primarily by virtue of its composition and alliances rather than its ideology. While the FSA initially claimed that its membership was mostly made up of defected members from the Syrian national army

[82] "Syria Uprising Map, December 2012," Political Geography Now Blog, 29 Dec. 2012, http://www.polgeonow.com/2012/12/syria-uprising-map-december-2012.html

[83] Rania Abouzeid, "Syrian Rebels Plot Their Next Moves: A TIME Exclusive," *Time Magazine*, 11 Feb. 2012, http://www.time.com/time/printout/0,8816,2106648,00.html

and had a (strained) alliance with the SNC, the SLA was composed almost exclusively of armed civilians from the outset.[84]

For external analysts and the media, on the other hand, it was the rise of the Islamist groups that was of most concern. Some of these groups were more integrated into the mainstream opposition than others. Many major donors (including Salafi networks, Syrian expats, and the governments of Turkey, Qatar, and Saudi Arabia) favor funding Islamist rebels rather than more moderate groups. The Islamist groups, who by nature have a less nationalist bent, are also composed of many foreign fighters who contribute resources and experience drawn from guerilla warfare elsewhere. Jihadis still make up a minority of the Syrian rebel movement, but they are represented beyond their size in terms of military effectiveness and ideological influence. As such, they will inevitably play a role in the battle for Syria's future.[85]

In October 2012, leaders of Islamist brigades—including the Farooq Brigade of Homs and the Sukour al-Sham Brigade of Idlib—formed the Syrian Liberation Front (SLF), one of Syria's biggest insurgent alliances, with around 20,000 members in twenty different groups. The front overshadows the FSA in several regions. The SLF denies any conflict with the FSA, though most of its member groups originally fought under the FSA banner before switching their allegiances. Some groups appear to consider themselves members of both alliances, and several SLF factions still use the FSA title as a general term for the armed resistance. The alliance also encompasses some groups of the Muslim Brotherhood's Commission for Civilian Protection (other CCP groups are in the FSA).

The Ahrar al-Sham Brigades are probably Syria's largest jihadi faction, with at least a few thousand fighters. Ahrar al-Sham frequently uses suicide bombers against government targets, but it has not engaged in the type of spectacular urban attacks that Jabhat al-Nusra specializes in,[86] being more geared toward traditional guerilla warfare.[87]

[84] Weiss, "Syrian Rebels are Losing Faith in the West."
[85] Aron Lund, "Holy Warriors," *Foreign Policy*, 15 Oct. 2012, http://www.foreignpolicy.com/articles/2012/10/15/holy_warriors?page=0,1
[86] Mohammad Sergie, "Jabhat al-Nusra Shows Its Bloody Mark on Aleppo," Syria Deeply, 15 Dec. 2012, http://alpha.syriadeeply.org/2012/12/nusra-leaves-bloody-mark-aleppo/#.UP29uKFord6
[87] Lund, "Holy Warriors."

The most controversial and among the most well organized of these groups is Jabhat al-Nusra (JN), which has an explicit goal of establishing an Islamist state in Syria.[88] Experts have indicated that the group is a spinoff from the Islamic State of Iraq (ISI), an al-Qaeda faction, while many Syrian opposition groups claim that JN is a regime creation.[89] With approximately 5,000 members, JN is by no means the largest group fighting in the conflict, although it has often been described as the most effective. Among the ranks of JN are a huge number of knowledgeable and skillful fighters with a clear plan and experience in a variety of countries, in contrast to the FSA whose hodgepodge mixture of civilians and ex-military men has led to many tactical setbacks and missteps. Besides the variety of Islamist and regional military groups, there has been a proliferation of small gangs and militias more concerned with turf wars and looting than political or religious ideologies.[90]

Relations between Militarized Groups

Relations between the various armed groups are mixed, with JN as a particular focal point of contention. In November 2012, the US decision to put JN on its list of terrorist groups after the formation of the National Coalition drew ire from across various factions of the opposition, though some applauded the move.[91] Overall, the decision appeared to reinforce support for the group, as other jihadist groups feared that their own efforts would be undermined if JN were forced to withdraw from the conflict because of this designation.[92]

[88] Noman Benotman and Roisin Blake, "Jabhat al-Nusra li-ahl al-Sham min Mujahedi al-Sham fi Sahat al-Jihad: A Strategic Briefing," Quilliam Foundation, http://www.quilliamfoundation.org/wp/wp-content/uploads/publications/free/jabhat-al-nusra-a-strategic-briefing.pdf

[89] http://alhayat.com/OpinionsDetails/462328; Lund, "Holy Warriors."

[90] Ghiath Abdul-Ahad, "'The People of Aleppo Needed Someone to Drag them into the Revolution,'" *The Guardian*, 28 Dec. 2012, http://www.guardian.co.uk/world/2012/dec/28/aleppo-revolution-abu-ali-sulaibi; Ghiath Abdul-Ahad, "Syrian Rebels Sidetracked by Scramble for Spoils of War," *The Guardian*, 27 Dec. 2012, http://www.guardian.co.uk/world/2012/dec/27/syrian-rebels-scramble-spoils-war

[91] Hazem Al-Amine, "Jabhat al-Nusra and the Syrian Opposition's Failure," Al-Monitor, 18 Dec. 2012, http://www.al-monitor.com/pulse/politics/2012/12/syria-opposition-fails-with-jabhat-al-nusra-terrorist-label.html

[92] Benotman and Blake, "Jabhat Al-Nusra: A Strategic Briefing," Quilliam Foundation.

Some FSA brigades threaten to work with JN if the West does not provide enough weapons, while many armed groups or FSA brigades are wary of JN's ultimate intentions for Syria. However, despite fundamental differences of opinion on the shape of a Syrian government post-Assad, JN has on occasion worked with other Islamist brigades or the FSA on operations, preferring to pool resources when their aims converge. An example of this is an attack on Assad's forces undertaken by JN and the FSA in Aleppo, after which they agreed to share the loot, splitting it according to the *sharia*-based tradition of *al-Ghana'im* (spoils of war).[93] Interestingly, JN has not yet formed a coalition with other Islamist forces, though virtually all the other Islamist groups have joined the major alliance fronts.[94]

For now, the relations between the various militias are more civil than might be expected, but these occasional periods of cooperation are likely to be short-lived. As the militarized opposition grows and continues to fragment along ideological and tactical lines, further rivalries and infighting can be expected between the various factions. In particular, competition over funding from international donors and over the spoils of war will likely lead these groups into more outright hostilities and conflict in the near future.[95]

A New Coalition

There seemed to be little hope that the SNC could ever pull together an alliance that was sufficiently inclusive of the opposition to garner international recognition and support. After a week of negotiations in Doha at the invitation of the Arab League, a new entity was established: the National Coalition for Syrian Revolutionary and Opposition Forces (NC). The SNC merged into the new body, with the coalition pulling together some of the splinter factions of the SNC and gaining the approval of factions outside the SNC as well. The Damascene Imam Moaz al-Khatib was elected president of the new umbrella group.[96]

[93] Ibid.

[94] Ibid.

[95] Abdul-Ahad, "Syrian Rebels Sidetracked by Scramble for Spoils of War."

[96] "Composition de la 'Coalition nationale des Forces de la Révolution et de l'Opposition syrienne," Un Oeil Sur La Syrie. Le Monde, 12 Nov. 2012, http://syrie.blog.lemonde.fr/2012/11/12/composition-de-la-coalition-nationale-des-forces-de-la-revolution-et-de-lopposition-syrienne/

The NC quickly garnered international support, receiving the approval of six Gulf states immediately, and over the following two weeks recognition from France, Turkey, the United Kingdom, and Spain as the "sole legitimate representative of the Syrian people." On 20 November 2012, opposition forces reversed course and approved the coalition, which they had initially rejected. However, the coalition was not accepted by the Syrian–Kurdish PYD party.[97]

US President Barack Obama also stated his recognition of the coalition, deeming the group "now inclusive enough" to be granted the elevated status of "sole representative" of the Syrian people. However, the United States also officially designated Jabhat al-Nusra as a terrorist organization, causing anger among its allies in the opposition.[98]

With a new coalition in place, Brahimi, the Arab League envoy, met President Assad and opposition members in Damascus in late December 2012 before visiting Moscow to discuss proposals for ending the conflict. He expressed his strong support for the "Geneva plan" based on the formation of a transitional government.

After meeting with Assad, Brahimi met with representatives of the NC, the SNC, the NCB, and the Syrian Democratic forum to get the opposition to nominate their candidates for the transitional government. However, by this time the opposition, specifically the SNC and the NC, held to the stance that the time for politics had passed and that a decisive military victory was possible in Damascus in the near future. Moaz al-Khatib rejected Moscow's invitation for peace talks and demanded that Russia apologize for its support for Assad. He said that the opposition would be willing to meet in an Arab country if a clear agenda were set.[99]

At the time of writing this chapter in January 2014, it is unclear whether the NC will ultimately be able to overcome the internal fragmentation and outside disputes which the SNC suffered from and if it can lead the opposition to some form of productive collective action.

[97] "Month-By-Month Summary of Developments in Syria (Updated)," International Crisis Group, 2013, available at http://www.jadaliyya.com/pages/index/6343/month-by-month-summary-of-developments-in-syria-(un

[98] Ibid.

[99] "Does the Syrian Opposition Want a Political Solution?" Al-Monitor, 17 Dec. 2012, http://www.al-monitor.com/pulse/politics/2012/12/syrian-opposition-not-interested-in-political-solution.html#ixzz2Ij4ApnD1

While some expressed optimism at the NC's prospects, it is abundantly clear that the regional and international calculations, difficulties at encompassing Syria's vastly diverse society, a polarized media landscape, and spatial factors have only altered slightly altered in the period since the SNC was founded. Indeed, in some cases, these problems have only become more pronounced.

Conclusion

To assume that the Syrian regime succeeded in staying in power for so long, and in staying afloat during the past two years or so solely due to its brutality is to ignore the regime's historical policies, the Syrian political landscape, and how it has used what some have called "the pursuit of great quests" to undermine collective action against it. As a result of the mild form of political bargaining before 1986, and its subsequent shift in alliances towards business interests afterwards, the Syrian regime succeeded in accomplishing two simultaneous and seemingly contradictory goals: first, it created a system of leveling egalitarianism based on its distributive policies and political commitments to labor and most minorities, whereby it kept flagrant forms of social distinction at bay and provided a functional safety net for most social sectors (at least until the early to mid-1990s); on the other hand, it succeeded in keeping the regime afloat economically, and building a strong cross-sectarian base of support among the middle classes. The regime's brutality was the final ingredient in this mix, but it was more a deterrent than a continuous and ubiquitous exercise after 1982. While the threat of brutal repression and force always lingered in the background, it was not the sole means for exacting compliance.

The end result was that the regime undermined the ability of both the losers and winners from its alliance-making to engage in collective action, while maintaining a substantial and loyal political, economic, and social base. The irony is that this took place at the expense of the "state" and the long-term stability of the regime, hence the gradual breakdown of the state since 2011.

Furthermore, a number of important structural factors have remained in play before and during the uprising, namely the geography of Syrian cities, which lie diffused from one another along the borders; a profoundly heterogenous society; a polarized and still unfledged media environment; and a regional and international context in which many opposing and competing actors are attempting to manipulate and administrate the uprising to their own benefit. In a similar vein to the way the regime strategy unfolded, the interference of foreign powers, an empowering media landscape, and easy movement across Syria's many borders strengthened the hand of the opposition against the regime. However, these factors also stifled the short-term need to engage in real dialogue within the opposition to organize a meaningful and encompassing coalition. Regime strategies and the Syrian political landscape thus serve to explain both the slow breakdown of the regime and the simultaneous breakdown of the opposition, the full consequences of which have yet to emerge.

15

BEYOND THE CIVIL WAR IN LIBYA

TOWARD A NEW RULING BARGAIN

Dirk Vandewalle

Of all the "Arab Spring" uprisings, Libya's rebellion against the regime of Mu'ammar al-Qaddafi, which started on 17 February 2011, stands as one of the most idiosyncratic and unexpected in the region.[1] Few observers had predicted that the country's citizens would prove able and willing to stand up against a regime whose mechanisms of repression had been an inextricable part of the divide-and-rule policies of the Qaddafi era, honed over forty-two years of arbitrary and highly exclusionary rule. In so doing Libya's citizens broke an implicit ruling bargain that had traded patronage for political quiescence during the Qaddafi period.

[1] Some Libyans and some outside observers somewhat uneasily refer to what happened in Libya as a revolution. Similarly, there is much disagreement over whether what took place in Libya qualifies as a civil war. Without endorsing or denying the validity of the use of these concepts, I use both throughout this chapter as an expedient shortcut.

Observers had long noted the severe deficiencies in the development of social and political institutions during the Qaddafi years, predicting both long-term chaos and enormous difficulties in reconstructing (or perhaps more accurately, constructing for the first time) a modern state in Libya. Yet when this assertion was first put to the test in national elections, voting went forward without major incidents.[2] Regardless of the enormous difficulties involved, and the limited sense of national identity, the 7 July 2012 elections, barely seventeen months after the uprising against the Qaddafi regime had started, took place in an almost euphoric atmosphere.[3] It quickly became clear that Libya—even though its provisional government and the National Transitional Council (NTC) that had guided the country during the civil war faced enormous challenges—would not implode as many had feared. Furthermore, the country's Islamists were routed, and at least temporarily kept at bay by a coalition of non-Islamic parties assembled under the umbrella of Mahmoud Jibril's National Forces Alliance (NFA).[4]

[2] For background on Libya and the problems associated with oil-led development, see Dirk Vandewalle, *Libya since Independence: Oil and State-Building*, Ithaca: Cornell University Press, 1998. For an update of events, including the country's civil war in 2011, see Dirk Vandewalle, *A History of Modern Libya*, 2nd edn, Cambridge: Cambridge University Press, 2012. Consult also Alison Pargeter, *Libya: The Rise and Fall of Qaddafi*, New Haven: Yale University Press, 2012, and Ethan Chorin, *Exit the Colonel: The Hidden History of the Libyan Revolution*, New York: Public Affairs, 2012.

[3] Polling in Libya is a new phenomenon. However, in one of the first polls after the 2011 uprising, Libyans overwhelmingly identified themselves as Muslim, while being "Libyan" came in a very distant third after tribal/regional identification.

[4] Much has been made of this "victory" over Libya's Muslim Brotherhood in the West—perhaps too much. The JDP's performance was hampered by the fact that the Muslim Brotherhood had effectively been eradicated in Libya by Qaddafi. Thus it had fewer organizational resources to start with than other parties. In addition, because of its leader's national standing during the civil war and beyond, Mahmoud Jibril's Alliance enjoyed a much higher level of visibility that translated into ready votes during these first elections. There is little reason to expect, however, that in subsequent elections—as the memories of the NTC and of its leaders start to fade, as the JDP organizes itself, and as it develops a more sophisticated and detailed political program that goes beyond the paternalistic and abrasive language of its leader Muhammad Sawan—the JDP and other Islamic parties in Libya will not have a more substantial formal representation in the country's political life.

There was some initial hope that Libya could become the country that proved to be the exception to the widely accepted notion that all oil exporters in the Middle East and North Africa are invariably highly authoritarian and uniformly deny their population a political voice. If a more democratic system could indeed take hold, then the notion that oil countries tend to be less democratic or non-democratic could be proven wrong—a claim that has often been made in the rentier literature.[5]

For the first year or so after its revolution, developments in Libya presented a number of intellectual challenges that go to the heart of how the academic community and policy circles have studied and described the durability of Middle Eastern and North African political regimes and their underlying ruling bargains. The literature on the resilience of authoritarianism seemed somewhat tarnished, particularly in the wake of the early period following the end of Libya's civil war. The arguments that "rentier state" theorists had made about the immutability of institutions, about the immobility imposed by one-sided social contracts, and about the resultant difficulties in constructing state institutions over relatively short periods of time appeared equally suspect.

Analysts may well have been right in predicting that Libya would face lingering problems of state- and nation-building as a result of its oil-led development and because the state had been neglected as a focus of identity ever since the country was created in 1951. But no one could have envisioned the relative success the country initially experienced, overcoming what once seemed insurmountable social, political, and institutional problems. Indeed, as events unfolded prior to the general elections of July 2012, it looked as if Libya had been relatively well served by the fact that many of the state institutions it needed to rely on

[5] Among the enormous volume of work on the rentier state that makes this claim, see, for example, Jill Crystal, *Oil and Politics in the Gulf: Rulers and Merchants in Kuwait and Qatar*, Cambridge: Cambridge University Press, 1995; Kiren Aziz Chaudhry, *The Price of Wealth: Economies and Institutions in the Middle East*, Ithaca: Cornell University Press, 1997; Gregory Gause, *Oil Monarchies: Domestic and Security Challenges in the Arab Gulf States*, New York: Council on Foreign Relations Press, 1994; Dirk Vandewalle, *Libya since Independence*. While much has been amended with regard to claims of the rentier literature in recent years, the overall link between oil-led development and authoritarianism remains a disputed part of that literature. See in particular Michael Ross, "The Political Economy of the Resource Curse," *World Politics*, 51 (Jan. 1999), pp. 297–322.

had to be built almost *ex nihilo*, so that Libya did not have to experience the difficult removal of the "deep state" that Egypt and Tunisia had passed through.

Two years after the revolution, it is clear that many of these early predictions and much of the initial optimism have been replaced by more realistic (and unfortunately pessimistic) evaluations. The Libyan population's experience of a honeymoon period with a young political system has now come to an end, and many of the revolution's initial achievements may well be reversed as the country seeks to address one of its most fundamental challenges: electing a national committee—consisting of twenty members from each of the country's three regions—that will draft the country's constitution. While much of what had taken place prior to July 2012 seemed to augur well for the future of the country as a political community, it is also clear that several setbacks materialized in the period between the national elections of 2012 and the elections for the Constitutional Drafting Assembly (CDA) in 2013. One notable sign of these setbacks was the fact that popular registration for the CDA elections was considerably lower than the respective figure for the national elections—despite the efforts of the country's High National Election Commission (HNEC)—an outcome due in part to a growing sense of popular apathy toward the General National Congress (GNC), the legislature that had been elected in the July 2012 elections.

Two years after the revolution, many of the problems that go to the heart of how Libya's new political community will be constructed, and what the duties and obligations of both the state and local society will be vis-à-vis each other, remain unresolved as the initial euphoria of the revolution has given way to lingering chaos in the post-revolution period. Until the 2012 elections Libya's leaders were, unsurprisingly, preoccupied with securing the country (an unresolved task that still leaves many of the country's militias as a potent force), organizing the national elections, and constructing or reconstructing a number of state institutions that had been badly neglected during the Qaddafi period but which were needed to address the everyday challenges of keeping the country's administration running.

At the margins of all this activity a somewhat stilted debate remained about the role of the state in the new Libya and the relationship this state should have with its citizens. This debate assumed greater relevance toward the end of 2012 when it became increasingly clear that the

GNC's role had effectively been hollowed out. As a result, increasing calls were made for the convening of a National Dialogue that would gather not only the country's formal political institutions, but also those informal ones—revolutionaries, local and municipal councils, tribal elders, and non-governmental organizations—necessary to move the country forward. Needless to say, there is little understanding in Libya of precisely how the newly emerging domestic political realities will be formalized into a new ruling bargain for a country where such a pact was traditionally determined without consultation by the state during the Qaddafi regime.

In theory the country's constitution, drawn up by the Constitutional Drafting Assembly (which is scheduled to be elected in February 2014), should provide a clear guideline for resolving these lingering uncertainties about a new social contract between Libya's citizens, the country's provinces, and the national government. Oil countries, and particularly Libya with its checkered history of state-building (or better, state avoidance) during the Qaddafi regime, tend to rely on highly skewed ruling bargains, imposed from the top, with citizens as mere bystanders. The Libyan elections were of course precisely about avoiding this emasculation of the popular will: to enable citizens to become active participants in the country's political future—an unprecedented move in modern Libyan history. But, as events since the elections have made clear, oil and the way the old social contract was implemented in Libya have left some debilitating legacies: among them a profound sense of political atomization that was partly reflected in the rate of registration for the CDA elections, the fact that the state continues to be seen as an indispensable provider by the revolutionaries and the population at large, the lack of interpersonal trust, and, most important of all, the use of extensive patronage via oil-fueled revenues that traditionally kept the ruling bargain in place.

The remainder of this chapter focuses on how Libya's new leaders will be able to reshape or in part create *ex nihilo* a new ruling bargain when faced with some of these structural legacies. To what extent can any new ruling bargain change the role of the state as providential provider in light of the relatively low capacity it continues to possess in Libya, and in light of heightened popular expectations? Can the government avoid the kind of long-term patronage that makes governing easier in the short term for oil-exporting countries, but imposes long-term political and economic consequences on the government? Will this "shadow of the past" continue to loom over Libya, or can a future government move beyond these structural impediments?

The Ruling Bargain in Libya

As defined in this chapter, ruling bargains are implicitly or explicitly defined rules and arrangements that delineate the political and economic rights, duties, and obligations governing relations between those in charge of the state and individuals within the state subject to their governance. They are the most visible—but sometimes the least formally institutionalized—of all the institutions that mediate between the state and society. They formally or informally describe and prescribe, in Douglass North's classic definition, the rules of the game between the ruler and the ruled.[6] These rules may be made explicit or left deliberately opaque; they can develop through custom, or they may simply be imposed single-handedly by the ruler. However, regardless of how they emerge, they tend to become rules or norms that, particularly in authoritarian states like Qaddafi's Libya, clearly limit the political voice of a country's citizens while essentially leaving them depoliticized.

In the traditional European context ruling bargains were carefully calibrated, in most circumstances minutely defined, and backed by guarantees and legal review as a result of long periods of strife and compromise during a state-building process that sometimes lasted centuries. They became intricately woven into the fabric of local societies, often becoming part and parcel of a cultural and religious identity. They continue to be defended by both the organized and non-organized groups that benefit from their content.

Historically, ruling bargains in Europe as well as in Latin America have become highly politicized. As a result, they are most often modified through the political process, requiring a high degree of transparency by a number of regulatory and legal institutions that provide predictability to both sides. They are constantly subject to often acrimonious review

[6] Douglass C. North, *Institutions, Institutional Change and Economic Performance*, Cambridge: Cambridge University Press, 1990; and Douglass C. North and Robert P. Thomas, *The Rise of the Western World: A New Economic History*, Cambridge: Cambridge University Press, 1973.

and adjustment, particularly during periods of economic retrenchment and reform when the state and its "social partners" need to recalibrate their previous positions in order to achieve a common goal.

In Libya, as in many other oil exporters in the Middle East and North Africa, ruling bargains are of a substantially different nature. The citizens of these countries were rarely consulted as the ruling bargains emerged, a result of the more problematic process of state-building in the region which allowed for the systematic exclusion, or minimal inclusion, of certain groups of citizens. Libya was an extreme example of this, based in part on Qaddafi's notion of the Jamahiriyya, which essentially denied any role for modern (Western) state institutions as a guideline for the country. This formative process in Libya—both during the monarchy (1951–69) and during the Qaddafi period—stood in dramatic contrast to the dynamic process of creating and maintaining ruling bargains in Western political systems. This distinction is important not only for gauging the strength and shape of ruling bargains in oil-exporting countries, but also for measuring the maneuvering room they now provide for countries like Libya in reforming their political and economic systems.

It could also be argued that the social, economic, and political arrangements that have emerged in countries such as Libya are not "ruling bargains" in the strict sense of the term. They were certainly not bargains in the traditional sense whereby two sides engage in negotiations in order to agree upon mutually acceptable arrangements. Rather than providing a political voice and access for diverse groups within society, they have often led to political silence. As a result, due to the way in which ruling bargains developed in oil-exporting countries, and particularly in Libya, both sides often failed to view the elements within these bargains as obligations that were contractually binding. Indeed, one of their defining characteristics is their informality due to the fact that they were usually viewed as implicit understandings, at least during the early mobilizational years of Qaddafi's rule. Institutionally, the ruling bargain in Qaddafi's Libya was consequently of a low quality: institutions were bureaucratically inefficient, riddled with corruption and patronage, and they often operated in the absence of clear rules of law.[7]

[7] For indicators of high-quality institutions, see Alberto Alesina, "The Political Economy of High and Low Growth," in World Bank, *Annual World Bank Conference on Development Economics 1997*, Washington, DC: World Bank, 1998, pp. 217–36.

In all developing countries, the colonial powers' bureaucratic legacies played a significant role in the way that local institutions developed, and hence the way states constructed themselves and their ruling bargains. Where local populations had been introduced to and incorporated (even at low levels) into bureaucratic mechanisms during the colonial period—and where the hinterland had been incorporated into a unified economy that made extraction possible—the seeds were sown for political, charity, and civil society organizations that would eventually serve as the torchbearers not only for independence movements but also for articulated regulatory, extractive, and coercive organizations that legitimated the state as the meta-institution for the territory. Where the colonial powers had been content to create settler, landlord economies or had few economic incentives to incorporate local populations into economic frameworks, the notions of state and of the possibility for articulated institutions remained unknown. In Libya, the most extreme example of exclusionary politics during the Italian occupation, the notion of statehood would remain suspect and contested both during the monarchy and after the 1969 Qaddafi coup.[8]

Oil also played an equally important role in how the ruling bargain emerged and took shape in Libya. When the rapid inflows of oil revenues shifted the function of the state almost exclusively toward the distributive (and the coercive), it also eroded the need for clearly articulated institutional development. It obliterated the usual bargaining between ruler and ruled that had marked state-building processes elsewhere into unilateral decisions by a ruler bent on perpetuating a stateless society, a Jamahiriyya. The fact that this process was so contracted and provoked so little local reaction attests to the profound de-politicization in oil-exporting countries and to the fact that the emergence of rent in Libya preceded the process of state-building.

One consequence of this was that the embryonic state institutions that emerged in Libya during the monarchy and then during the Qaddafi years became intricate channels for economic largesse and resource distribution. Meanwhile, their regulatory and legal capacities—already weak because of the initial state-building process—remained inefficient and underdeveloped.[9] Wholesale management, through a

[8] See Lisa Anderson, "The State in the Middle East and North Africa," *Comparative Politics*, 20, 3 (Oct. 1987), pp. 1–18.

[9] This is a highly truncated and somewhat arbitrary categorization made for

tightly controlled network of expatriate technocrats and elites close to the regime, was similarly an expression of the inability to regulate—a political and economic shortcut.[10]

An important corollary for the debate on ruling bargains concerns the kind of political community that is created under these conditions, and how this influences the ability for further reform in the post-civil war period in Libya. Although observers have often invoked—somewhat rashly—the "no taxation, therefore no representation" principle as the rationale for the exclusionary nature of politics in the region, there is little doubt that Libyans have endured a long process of political disenfranchisement that essentially consisted of gaining (relative wealth) at the expense of a formal political voice.[11] As long as external rents can be generated, there is little need for individuals to influence public agencies and to help shape public policy to their material advantage. There is little incentive to engage the state in order to determine the contours of the ruling bargain. Government bureaucrats simply turned into a rentier class.

---

the purpose of this chapter, derived from an enormous amount of earlier literature. See Dirk Vandewalle, *Libya since Independence*, for more detailed discussions of the emergence, nature, and differentiation of institutions.

[10] With regard to the management of Libya's economy, I have often described the country during the Qaddafi years as being a "centrally unplanned economy"—that is, the state reserved to itself all economic decisions but without any sense of discrimination as to priorities or the process of creating an integrated planning mechanism, adding to the sense of institutional disaggregation Libya's new rulers must now deal with.

[11] There are two principal objections to this long-standing claim. The first has been succinctly elaborated by John Waterbury, "The State and Economic Transition in the Middle East and North Africa," in Nemat Shafiq (ed.), *Prospects for Middle Eastern and North African Economies: From Boom to Bust and Back?* London: Macmillan Press Ltd, 1998, pp. 159–77, who not only questions the assertion that Middle East and North African economies are under-taxed, but also rebuts the more general assertion that taxation in the Middle East and North Africa has "evoked demands that governments account for their use of tax monies …" He adds furthermore that "there has been no translation of tax burden into pressures for democratization." The second is that popular demands for some sort of representation often derive from entitlements either based physically on earlier distributive largesse by governments during boom times, or based on shared (often international) norms about what constitutes good governance.

Furthermore, the distributive nature of the Libyan economy and the government's spending patterns resulted in extreme forms of social stratification. This stratification was linked to the regime's need to create small coalitions of support among the population. Although data are exceedingly difficult to obtain, one notable social and economic phenomenon in Libya is the absence of a distinct middle class with its own goals, tactics, and methods that could function as the catalyst for political and economic change. It was virtually impossible to discern class preferences and clearly articulated class goals during the Qaddafi era—in part because the combination of welfare politics and weak institutions atomized the population. In a process that will be familiar to institutional economists, the best way to advance in a country like Libya was never to articulate interests in a common setting, but to pursue them individually.

This emphasis on economic distribution also meant that Qaddafi spent inordinate amounts of time in promoting his clients and creating supporting coalitions to stave off other claimants to the country's wealth and power. Much of this maneuvering was concealed by the way in which the country's revenues were shielded from public scrutiny. Decisions concerning economic policies, distribution, and investments were, as a control mechanism, reserved to the purview of small coalitions, rather than assigned to the market. Distributive largesse was augmented by with reliance on informal mechanisms linked to history, religion, or culture.[12] The enormous bifurcation between formal and informal politics—and the cynicism and apathy this provoked—was the most distinct feature of Libyan politics.

Libya's oil wealth thus allowed for the creation of extensive patronage systems that vitiated pressures for political liberalization and fostered the creation of one-sided, top-down ruling bargains. The Qaddafi regime was able to survive for a long period of time in this peculiar set-up by relying on relatively small coalitions. Libya under Qaddafi demonstrated that the state in oil economies can easily prevent the consolidation of those social groups that were a prelude to democracy in the European

[12] The invention and re-invention of tradition as a means to greater legitimacy has not surprisingly become virtually a national industry, particularly in the GCC countries, where rulers heavily sponsor events that are deemed in line with the country's *turath* (heritage), a word that is invoked again and again in public discourse. For the UAE, see Christopher Davidson, *The United Arab Emirates: A Study in Survival*, Boulder, CO: Lynne Rienner, 2005.

context.[13] In Putnam's formulation, these states can prevent the accretion of the social capital that would give impulse to collective action.[14] Although it is not always clear whether these are explicit policies or simply side-effects of rentier development, it would certainly seem as though they were deliberately intended to depoliticize citizens in the Libyan case.

The 2011 revolution and beyond: a new ruling bargain?

Despite the political atomization and apathy of the Qaddafi period, the Libyan revolution clearly demonstrated that the country's citizens were no longer willing to be subjected to the very one-sided ruling bargain that had increasingly created a visible bifurcation between regime elites and the general population, particularly during the regime's latter years when Libya had effectively become a family kleptocracy. Indeed, the resentment of Libyans was so pronounced that they proved willing to sacrifice an estimated 30,000 to 40,000 individuals to escape from what they collectively judged as a ruling bargain that had been imposed upon them and was no longer acceptable.

But what new ruling bargain is emerging in light of the removal of the Qaddafi regime? According to the country's interim rulers, Libya will become a more equal and more transparent country while its leadership will be subject to higher standards of accountability—these are the promises which were expressed in the various campaigns of the political parties and individuals who took part in the 7 July 2012 elections, and they also represent their expectations as the country moves forward with the CDA elections and a (future) referendum on the constitution.

[13] For applications to the Middle East and North Africa region, see Hootan Shambayati, "The Rentier State, Interest Groups, and the Paradox of Autonomy: State and Business in Turkey and Iran," *Comparative Politics* (Apr. 1994) on Iran; Jill Crystal, "Approaches to the Study of Civil Society in the Gulf," in Richard Augustus Norton (ed.), *Civil Society in the Middle East* (Volume 2), New York: Brill 1996, pp. 260–85, on Kuwait and Qatar; John Entelis, "Oil Wealth and the Prospects for Democratization in the Arabian Peninsula: The Case of Saudi Arabia," in Maiem A. Sherbiny and Mark A. Tessler (eds), *Arab Oil: Impact on the Arab Countries and Global Implications*, New York: Praeger, 1976.

[14] Robert Putnam, *Making Democracy Work: Civic Traditions in Modern Italy*, Princeton: Princeton University Press, 1993.

However, ruling bargains and the accompanying patterns of patronage that sustain them in oil-exporting countries are often very tenacious and difficult to remove, even if one political system is replaced with another. The entitlement aspects linked to both are often particularly hard to reform, and patronage patterns often reestablish themselves in post-revolutionary situations, manipulated by new elites who take over economic access points from their previous occupants. Moreover, ruling bargains develop over relatively long periods of time and reflect the compromises those in charge of the state are willing to make in order to implement their vision of a particular political community. Even if these bargains prove minimal in terms of what they provide—as could be argued in the case of Libya—they are deeply ingrained and form sets of entitlements that citizens come to take for granted in lieu of more tangible political representation. As the upheavals of the Arab Spring have made clear, even small adjustments (or announcements of potential adjustments) to these entitlements can be highly dangerous, and governments are loath to tinker with ruling bargains until pushed to the wall. Libya, as the history of its attempts at economic reform demonstrate, even under the highly authoritarian rule of Qaddafi proved no exception to this general rule.[15]

An even more important aspect is that ruling bargains in authoritarian countries like Libya since 1969—as opposed to modern democracies where they developed in a reciprocal fashion that reflected the changing power of the state and groups within society over time—are rarely codified or formalized. Instead, as in Libya during the Qaddafi period, they consist of an implicit understanding of the rules of the game by those subjected to them, backed up by the coercive institutions at the disposal of those in charge of the state. Informal ruling bargains, particularly in oil states where state-building often proceeds precariously and in a lopsided fashion, often substitute for more formalized institutions.

What happens to these implicit bargains when a revolution takes place that promises to replace these informally understood rules with a more normal, more durable state that relies on formalized, explicitly formu-

[15] Libya attempted to reform its economy during at least three distinctive phases: in 1987, in the 1990s, and after 2003, the latter phase being in part guided by Saif al-Islam al-Qaddafi who, in cooperation with the then Prime Minister Shukri Ghanem, brought in Western expertise to help design the necessary reforms for the country's highly inefficient economy.

lated institutions and rules? Although citizens could be expected to want to trade up for more formal rules in order to enjoy greater security and predictability, the knowledge that entitlement arrangements may be altered often muddies the waters. And as there are few rules to go by given the political uncertainty that follows the overthrow of regimes, the instinct to protect one's own (or one's group's) entitlement at the expense of the overall community usually prevails, at least initially.

It is thus worth taking a closer look at entitlements and their role in politically authoritarian and exclusionary political systems like Libya. One of the most striking features of the Middle East and North Africa's oil exporters has been the extraordinary economic largesse bestowed by states upon their citizens. As mentioned previously, this largesse left both state and society, implicitly or explicitly, with a set of expectations embodied in vaguely defined ruling bargains.[16] Of these expectations, job creation for local citizens and subsidies for a variety of goods have often been the most visible tip of an iceberg of entitlements and privileges that necessitated a whole range of public policies pursued by the region's governments.

In Libya in particular, these policies normally included, in addition to employment, the cultivation of a dominant public sector that did not restrict itself to traditional government activities but also infiltrated private commercial activities—the provision of a whole array of welfare programs ranging from education to housing to healthcare, and the creation of a host of economic regulations, such as import bans and extensive licensing systems, which in effect insulated local enterprises and elite coalitions from exposure to world competition. In most cases in the Middle East and North Africa, but particularly in Libya with its fractured sense of identity, private elite concerns (rather than social ones) fueled the construction of an informal ruling bargain.

When thinking about this kind of ruling bargain in Libya during the Qaddafi period, two distinct aspects must be considered. The first is purely economic: the volume and value of actual goods and services delivered to local citizens, ranging from employment, education, subsidies,

[16] Strictly speaking, in the Middle East and North Africa one needs to distinguish between two different groups of oil exporters in the region: (1) the GCC countries and Libya, where oil revenues have provided the overwhelming share of government revenues; and (2) Iraq, Iran, and Algeria, which have more diversified economies.

free healthcare to a whole array of services and economic interventions. But the second dimension is equally important. Ruling bargains advertently and inadvertently created overlapping social groups—primarily labor, security apparatuses, narrow coalitions of supporters, and the general public—that were targeted as an intricate part of a political management strategy carefully maintained by Qaddafi. In effect, Libya's ruling bargain became an intricate but powerful political instrument that was meant to ensure regime survival through economic patronage.

Libya could not escape this dual logic despite the upheavals of Qaddafi's revolution and his emphasis on statelessness. The revolution produced a bifurcated economic and social system, each with its own distinct set of entitlements whose contents depended on how crucial Qaddafi judged each group to be for the survival of his regime. The first group consisted of the general population which was kept politically silent through relatively low levels of distributive politics centered on state employment and subsidies. The second set consisted of the tribal, family, or military elites that were judged to be essential for regime survival—and hence eligible for far greater hand-outs. The peculiar shape of Libya's bifurcated ruling bargain determined the dynamics of the Qaddafi regime's response to the economic and political difficulties it faced from the 1980s onwards and until the country was eventually reintegrated into the international community in 2003.

As was the case for other regional oil-exporting countries, the 1980s and 1990s were a period in which Libya was forced to make difficult adjustments to a number of local, regional, and international economic realities that reshaped the role of the Qaddafi regime and Libya's ruling bargain, which needed to adapt to new economic circumstances.

Why then did Libya avoid, delay, or abrogate these necessary reforms in favor of incremental adjustments or consumer *infitah*s (economic liberalization)—even when Qaddafi understood the economic difficulties Libya faced, and, at least rhetorically, was willing to implement economic changes? This conundrum—where a seemingly powerful state that regulated the minutiae of its citizens' lives could not muster the willingness, strength, or capability to implement and sustain successful economic reforms—hints at the broader social and political structures within which Libya's political economy was embedded, as well as the future difficulties that the country will face.[17] Libya's ruling bargain was

[17] A conundrum Nazih Ayubi brilliantly analyzed in his *Over-stating the Arab*

simply the most visible expression of such structures: they clearly showed the compromises Libya's ruler felt he needed to make (or not make), and the dense networks of coalitions he created in pursuit of power and survival. Economic reform and change in Libya were inextricably linked to recalibrating political power between ruled and the ruler (that is to changing existing ruling bargains that had been imposed by the ruler).

The broader question in the current post-revolution context is whether this combination of a fierce state (that is, a coercively powerful state) with a low-quality social contract, which has proven incapable of economic reform even when in relatively dire financial straits, is a harbinger of things to come in Libya. By the spring of 2014 the euphoria of the 2012 national elections had dissipated. In their attempt to create new state institutions that would have greater accountability and greater regulatory power, Libyan policy-makers faced the fact that the country's newly created political institutions—and particularly the GNC—had become valued more for what they could deliver in patronage than as viable institutions where citizens' interests were debated and accommodated. The attempt to create a National Dialogue in 2013 was a clear indication that the country's formal political institutions lacked the capacity to move the country forward, and that the incorporation of a number of informal institutions was necessary to continue the political process.

Elections in Libya

Profound upheavals like the Libyan uprising and the ensuing civil war change the contours of whatever ruling bargain previously existed. The determination to hold national elections and to proceed on the basis of a roadmap that will eventually lead to a constitution and a new, popularly elected parliament already indicate that the interaction between state and society in Libya has inexorably changed.

During the national elections in 2012, Libyan citizens were asked to participate in free, multi-party national elections that would provide

---

State: Politics and Society in the Middle East, London: I.B. Tauris, 1996, where he distinguished between fierce states—which rely overwhelmingly on coercion—and strong states which have clearly delineated institutions which allow them to take on a number of state tasks.

them with a political voice they had never possessed before.[18] The elections were by many standards idiosyncratic. Much of the attention focused on whether the fortunes of the region's Islamist parties would be extended. The conditions in Libya for organizing elections—particularly on such short notice—were far from favorable. The lingering chaos in the country, the truncated time in which to organize the enormous logistical machinery of the elections, the lack of a political tradition, and the absence of any organized political party structure all weighed on the minds of the participants involved in organizing the elections as the country moved forward along the lines of the National Transitional Council's (NTC) original roadmap, created during the civil war.

In light of these handicaps, many observers expected Libya's first national elections to be disorganized and dominated—as in neighboring countries—by the Islamist parties. In the end, both predictions were wrong: the elections were exceptionally well run and brought Mahmoud Jibril's secular National Forces Alliance to power. Jibril had previously served as the head of the National Planning Council during the final years of the Qaddafi regime in 2007–11 before becoming prime minster of the transitional government established during the civil war—a position he later abandoned in favor of Abdurrahim al-Keeb.

When the elections eventually took place on 7 July,[19] the atmosphere can only be described as electrifying. Despite the protracted period of preparation for the elections—barely seventeen months had passed between the start of the uprising on 17 February 2011 and the day of voting—much thought and effort had been expended in preparing the country for the actual event. Following a constitutional declaration on 3 August 2011, the NTC had adopted Law No. 3 on 7 February 2012,

[18] Political parties were disbanded in 1952, shortly after the Kingdom of Libya was created. Although there were elections (without parties) for the country's parliament in subsequent years, the July 2012 elections can be considered the country's first multi-party elections in six decades since 1952. And taking into account that Libya in 1952 hardly resembled a political community, the July 2012 elections can for all practical purposes be called the first truly competitive multi-party elections the country has ever witnessed since it was created in the wake of the Second World War.

[19] They had initially been scheduled for 19 June, but were briefly postponed due mostly to logistical difficulties, the extra time needed to register and vet candidates, and the need to give the political parties some additional time to present their programs to the voters.

which established the Higher National Election Commission (HNEC) that guided the procedures for the elections. An electoral law (Law No. 4) detailing the electoral system, voter and candidate eligibility, and the further minutiae of the country's elections had been adopted ten days earlier, on 28 January. The infrastructure to enable the elections to take place had been created in the months leading up to July with help from the United Nations and technical assistance from the International Foundation for Electoral Systems (IFES), along with other institutions.

The elections were carefully supervised by a large number of national and international observers, assessment teams, and invited guests: the Libyan Association for Election Observation, the European Union, the Arab League, the Carter Center, the African Union, Shahed, Rasid, Gender Concern International, and a large number of local civil society participants, with around 27,000 observers in total. In the aftermath of the elections several of these groups issued their own reports, in some cases supported by press conferences. And while each published report contained suggestions for future improvements, the overall conclusion was that the Libyan elections had been well prepared, were transparent, and had not exhibited any noticeable forms of fraud or intimidation.

This was a major accomplishment for a country that had only just shrugged off a long-standing dictatorship whose longevity could largely be attributed to the destruction of the same interpersonal and group dynamics that were now needed to make the election a success. Of Libya's 3.5 million possible voters, 2.866 million registered to vote (82 percent of those qualified). The actual number of voters was between 1.7 and 1.8 million, representing a turnout of around 62 percent. And while there had been a few incidents of violence and the destruction of voting materials in the days leading up to the elections, the overall process proceeded without major incidents on the day itself.

The purpose of the elections was to create a National Congress of 200 individuals—eighty elected on the basis of political party affiliation, and the remaining 120 elected on an individual basis. This mixture of proportional and majoritarian representation was deliberately designed to ensure that no single political group would be able to dominate the legislative process. The selection for the eighty political party seats also included a provision that was meant to ensure that women would be adequately represented. In the event, female candidates won a total of thirty-three seats, 17 percent of the total.

Mahmoud Jibril's National Alliance (a coalition of over forty smaller parties) emerged as the dominant player, with thirty-nine of the seats assigned for political parties, while the second largest party, the Party for Justice and Construction (the Muslim Brotherhood organization), obtained nineteen seats. Neither the National Front (headed by long-term Qaddafi opponent Dr Mohamed Mugharief) nor the Nation Party (an Islamist party whose members include Abdul Hakim Belhaj, a prominent Islamist) managed to gain a national following. Belhaj himself failed to get elected. As it seems likely that whoever emerges victorious may need to create a coalition to rule, however, the individual candidates cannot be neglected—especially Dr Mugharief, whose long-standing opposition to Qaddafi has given him an important personal stature, and who was eventually appointed as president of the National Congress.

The Libyan elections of July 2012 made a number of issues clear. First, Libya had been able to take an important step toward the construction of a modern state, despite the country's turbulent political history since 1969. The elections may not have been perfect, but they were symbolically important in pushing the country as a political community away from the shadows of the Qaddafi regime. They served as an important confidence-building measure, one that lent, at least temporarily, a degree of legitimacy to the country's emerging political institutions.

Second, the elections demonstrated the extent to which the Libyan political system remained in its infancy. The platforms of the parties involved in the elections were rarely articulated, with the elections themselves often revolving around individuals rather than differing political views. At a local level, there was often only a rudimentary understanding of what exactly the country's political process and procedures entailed.

Third, the national elections, as subsequent developments were to prove, were only the beginning of a very long, complex, and drawn-out process that involves writing a constitution and creating a new government—and, in doing so, creating a new ruling bargain. For the reasons described in this chapter, which in turn date back to the creation of Libya in 1951, this is bound to be a contentious process that will once again bring into focus those issues that have traditionally divided the country. Violent incidents in eastern Libya, centered on the long-standing issue of the relative power of Cyrenaica versus Tripolitania, in the weeks leading up to and immediately preceding the national elections indicated that national cohesion and consensus remained important issues to be dealt with, and that different sides (Tripolitania versus Cyrenaica in particular) and different actors (the revolutionaries versus the established political order) have different opinions on how the new ruling bargain should be re-constructed.

This has become particularly clear in the country's political life since the national elections. If the period between the end of Libya's civil war and the national elections of 2012 marked a moment of enthusiasm, events since then have clearly revealed the lingering fragilities of the country's political system. The national mood had noticeably soured immediately prior to the CDA elections in February 2013. The General National Council, created by the July 2012 elections, had become a hollowed-out institution, valued more for what it could deliver for constituencies than as a true national political institution. And while the preparations for the CDA elections proceeded, it seemed as if a noticeable bifurcation was starting to take place in Libya's newly formulated politics: the country's national political institutions continued to be shaped and institutionalized, but their impact and relevance to the political life of the country seemed to have diminished. Whether the National Dialogue can serve as a bridge and reinvigorate that political life remains an open question as the country starts the process of writing its constitution, which will set out the rules of Libya's new ruling bargain. How Libya will design its new constitution, and create the institutional mechanisms to include citizens and build a national consensus to entice different groups to "buy into" this national project and a new ruling bargain, remains the major challenge ahead. Events since the 2012 national elections indicate the difficulties that the country will face when the CDA embarks upon this process.

Conclusion: State-Building, Revolution, and Ruling Bargains

The construction of a new ruling bargain in Libya in the wake of the country's civil war has started in earnest. The 2012 national elections were the first tangible sign of a consultation process that hints at a new understanding of how the state and the country's citizens will interact. As a result of its history, its emergence as an oil economy, and the idiosyncratic rule of Muammar al-Qaddafi, Libya emerged as a country where neither state institutions nor the country's ruling bargain were clearly articulated. States, and the ruling bargains they create and nurture, develop in response to a number of conditions and challenges that vary over time: physical resources, the initial political, intellectual, and social riches states possess or lack, the vision of their leaders, the slow accretion of rules, regulations, and reputations that start to permeate the daily lives of the state and society alike, and, finally, the real or perceived threats posed by outside actors.

History has not been kind in this regard to Libya. Its emergence at the behest of the great powers after the Second World War immediately challenged its sense of national identity. Its natural resource base led to a concentration of economic power, but the state's social and economic regulatory mechanisms remained weak. In the Qaddafi years a set of bureaucratic distributive mechanisms emerged that were culturally and institutionally untested, and which developed in response to the exigencies of an imposed ruling bargain rather than to actual bureaucratic needs. Libya was thus an anomaly: it possessed a ruling bargain that regulated how citizens behaved, but it lacked the institutional flexibility or capacity to implement political or economic reform.

In the wake of the country's civil war, and particularly in light of events since the 2012 national elections, the importance of creating and implementing the underlying conditions that can lead to political reform or to the creation of new institutional arrangements should not be underestimated.[20] Current research on reform and the changing or adjusting of ruling bargains often assumes the existence of some type of "meta-institution" (a coherent state) which can be relied upon to nurture and promote social coalitions and ruling bargains that are able to prevent coordination failures over long periods of time. But this assumption does not yet hold in Libya: the state remains fragmented, has little capacity, and does not possess a monopoly over the means of violence.

Ruling bargains are part and parcel of the strategies that states use to promote growth, inclusiveness, and reform. Yet the question of whether or not Libya will be able to pursue such strategies remains somewhat unclear. As Libya's experience has so far demonstrated, creating a new ruling bargain with the aid of more finely tuned regulatory and legal institutions opens the process to public discussion and debate—something that has proven very destabilizing in a young and inexperienced

[20] Dani Rodrik, "Governing the Global Economy: Does One Architectural Style Fit All?" Harvard University, unpublished paper, June 1999, p. 4.

political system, where the rules of accommodation and compromise have not yet been honed.

As Libya demonstrates, the notion that countries can simply create or change existing ruling bargains underestimates the complexities of the process and the wide range of technical, social, and political obstacles that must be overcome. In Libya, this process has been made all the more difficult due to the harm done by the relative autonomy that the Qaddafi regime was able to purchase during its own "institutionalization phase." This in turn makes the organizational strength of the narrow social coalitions that are distinctly tied to the truncated evolution of state-building in the country particularly surprising. It is against this background that the ongoing efforts to craft a new political formula and a new ruling bargain in Libya must be judged. In light of the country's history, it should come as no surprise that the process so far been rocky and uneven. The more unexpected development is that, despite this history and despite all that has gone wrong since the end of the revolution, the country has not veered off into even greater turmoil.

INDEX

INDEX

INDEX